CONTROVERSY IN AMERICAN EDUCATION

CONTROVERSY IN AMERICAN EDUCATION

An Anthology of Crucial Issues

HAROLD FULL

Queens College
of The City University of New York

THE MACMILLAN COMPANY

COLLIER-MACMILLAN LIMITED
London

© Copyright, HAROLD FULL, 1967

Sixth Printing, 1969

Library of Congress catalog card number: 66–27010

THE MACMILLAN COMPANY
COLLIER-MACMILLAN CANADA, LTD., TORONTO, ONTARIO
PRINTED IN THE UNITED STATES OF AMERICA

To
T. N. W.
to whom much is owed,
and much more is due

PREFACE

Controversy is a part of the American educational tradition, a tradition that American education shares with the total democratic society. As it relates to education, controversy has played an influential role in the growth and development of education from its meager beginnings in Colonial times to the vast systems of public and private institutions that today encompass prenursery schooling through postdoctoral university programs. The role of controversy in education, however, has changed markedly in that long history. Earlier struggles, such as Horace Mann's movement for a free, public, nonsectarian, common school, centered on a few issues; these issues were debated over long periods of time.

Today's controversy in education has no focus; conflicting and contradictory opinions are voiced on every aspect of education in an ever-changing pattern of emphases and degrees. One is easily tempted to regard controversy as a modern-day phenomenon. A more accurate observation, however, is that current controversy is in some degree an intensification of yesterday's conflicts, but in larger measure is an outgrowth of the conflicts and challenges unique to a highly complex, technological society.

The readings in this anthology represent a selected sampling of the dissension, debates, and disputes that characterize controversy in American education today. The readings are designed specifically for those—students, teachers, administrators, laymen—who want to engage in the challenging intellectual task of examining objectively their own thoughts and feelings, of expanding their knowledge of current conflicts, and of deepening their understanding of education and society and of the intimate relationship between the two. Yet it is hoped that even those who peruse these readings simply to find views to confirm their own beliefs will discover something of the complex nature of current controversy and will be stimulated to seek a more informed position. Controversy itself is born when conflict arises, when challenges confront us, when doubt is expressed. An examination of controversy in American education cannot proceed productively unless inquiry begins not with a statement but with a question.

One of the modern-day views that seriously interferes with intelligent discussion of crucial issues in education is the commonly heard expression, "There are two sides to every question." Presumably, the intent of this statement is to force the listener to be "objective," to examine a view opposed to his own. Unfortunately, though undertaken with this intent, the ultimate effect of this statement is often the stifling of further inquiry. One is thus exposed to only the extreme positions on any issue and is prevented from observing the wide range of alternatives between them. As John Dewey cautioned in his 1938 Kappa Delta Pi address, many of the fundamental mistakes made in education stem from seeing problems in an *either-or* context that recognizes no intermediate possibilities.[1]

In keeping with this point of view, no attempt has been made to select articles *for* and articles *against* a particular issue in order to achieve a "balanced" presentation. If the issues selected are indeed crucial ones, then the variety and diversity of current views represent a broad range of alternate positions, some varying subtly, yet importantly, from others, some representing a wider divergency of opinion. Obviously, because of the limitations of space, the readings contained herein cannot present all of the varying views on all issues. The total scope of opinions, however, gives a representative sampling of the issues and an adequate presentation of the authors' points of view so that the reader can appreciate the authentic flavor of current controversies in education. It is obvious, too, that all issues included are not of equal importance, though it should not be assumed that the amount of space given to any issue is an accurate reflection of its importance. In some instances, it was necessary to select several readings about one issue so that a reasonably sufficient sampling of views could be presented; in other cases, a single article gives a thorough discussion of basic considerations and suggested alternatives.

This anthology is organized in five parts, each preceded by an essay in which the editor discusses the nature of the controversy concerned to assist the reader in examining more carefully the issues and problems encountered throughout the remainder of the volume.

In Part One the readings are focused on a brief, yet significant, background survey concerning the complex nature of change and conflict in contemporary society. The editor regards this knowledge as essential to any intelligent insight into the issues and problems of education and the schools. All too often the study of education—whether it be history, curriculum, philosophy, and so on—proceeds in almost total disregard of the current political, economic, social, or scientific mainstreams, in spite of repetition of the belief that the schools are a part of a larger society that affects them and that they in turn affect. It is especially pertinent to the study of controversy to have some conception of the nature of the society in which we live, because many of the controversies in education are reflections of the larger conflicts in society itself.

Part Two deals with what some might regard as the heart of current educational controversy: the manifold demands on the schools, and the schools' attempts— sometimes feeble, sometimes effective—to meet these demands. In large measure these demands upon the schools come from the consumers of education, children and youth. Perhaps no greater challenge has ever been faced by American education than the current one to provide a vital educational program of quality and

---

[1] John Dewey, *Experience and Education* (New York: The Macmillan Company, 1938).

excellence that will engage the interest and intellect of *all* youth—the haves and have-nots, the advantaged and the disadvantaged, the urban and the rural, the difficult and those desirably motivated.

Part Three enlists the talents of some of our most respected writers, who exhibit a sensitivity to the challenges that youth proclaims.

The readings in Part Four are organized around two mutually reinforcing themes: (1) the problems concerning the sources and the changing nature of educational authority; and (2) the problems concerning the profession—its organization, its qualifications, its autonomy. Part Four concludes with two essays that deal with an issue, "Is education a discipline?" This issue is destined, perhaps, to become the most controversial topic in education during the next two decades, engaging, as it will, not only those in professional education, but those from every established discipline.

Some of the controversial opinions about education stem from comparisons of the American system of public schools with efforts being made by European countries. Part Five is intended as a brief introduction to some of the current developments and controversies in European schools, with particular emphasis on England, France, and the Soviet Union. This section should be regarded as an overview, and one, it is hoped, that will encourage students to delve more deeply into problems of comparative education.

The editor is deeply grateful for the generous approval of the selected authors and publications for permission to reprint their material in this anthology. Since these works are organized in a form different from their original presentation, the authors' divergent views gain new significance. As their opinions contribute to a more meaningful understanding of the essential character of controversy in American education, new dimensions are seen, not in isolation, but in relation to the thinking of other authors. These new dimensions, added to the reader's own experience and background, should lead him to a deeper analysis of the issues posed and should prevent a premature crystallization of thought and attitude.

The editor would be less than grateful if he did not express his deep appreciation to Miss Maureen Nasse and Mrs. Ruth Brodie for their valuable secretarial help in compiling this book of readings.

H. F.

SUGGESTIONS TO
INSTRUCTORS

To engage students in a vital and meaningful understanding of the crucial problems of contemporary American education and to help them participate in the educationally valuable experience of discussing controversial issues are two purposes for which this anthology was designed. In achieving these important general objectives, as well as specific aims tailored to individual classroom situations, many kinds of flexible arrangements for using this book are possible.

The readings meet the needs of both undergraduate and graduate levels of instruction and of both elementary and secondary specialization. The kinds of courses for which the anthology can be adapted are also varied. Although ideally suited to the basic foundations course characteristic of many college undergraduate or graduate programs, the readings can provide an important focus for courses in the history of education, educational sociology, educational administration, curriculum and methods (both general and special), and philosophy of education, and for courses whose organizational structure cuts across conventional areas, such as current educational problems and issues, history of ideas in education, and so on. Within each of these particular kinds of courses, the book lends itself to a variety of approaches. The ideas here presented are not intended to prescribe or limit the uses of this book, but to stimulate each instructor to create methods or activities that meet the specific requirements of his course. The suggestions reflect the editor's experience in teaching a basic foundations course at Queens College for the past ten years.

1. There are important philosophical questions in education which should direct and guide the student's reading and thinking, regardless of the specific issue under discussion. These questions are implicit in all the readings, yet need to be referred to from time to time so that the student gains an understanding of the assumptions on which each author's article is based. What does it mean to be "educated" in today's world? To what valid objectives should education be directed? What are the most desirable conditions for this education to take place? What is teaching? What is learning? What is knowledge? What knowledge is of the most worth? Who should be educated? For how long? Under what conditions? What is the role of the school in a democratic society? How does the

school supplement, complement, or coincide with other social agencies? What is the source of curriculum content? Since everything cannot be taught, how is intelligent selection to be made? What kind of organization is necessary for carrying out objectives agreed upon? What is subject matter?

This list of questions is not intended to be exhaustive, but it suggests the order of questions and concerns that are inherent in all of the material in this volume.

2. A specific requirement for any article, to be completed as an individual written or oral assignment or to be used as a guide to the student's reading for follow-up class discussion, can be focused on these questions: What is the author's major thesis? What examples does he give to support this thesis? What is the relevance of his views to other problems—in education, in other fields, in society? What questions would you raise on the author's point of view? In what ways does his position relate to other authors you have read? Did the author force you to examine your previously held ideas, values, beliefs?

3. Have students prepare a short questionnaire for recording the reactions of parents, neighbors, students, and teachers regarding the important aspects of any of the controversial questions raised by the articles. This assignment could also be made in the form of a personal interview.

4. A valuable supplementary resource that is not used widely is that of speeches recorded on tape. Most educational organizations and other groups record important speeches from their national conventions on tapes that are available for rent or purchase. College and public libraries and audiovisual departments increasingly spend more money for such material. These tapes provide an opportunity for a new kind of individual or group assignment. Listening sessions can be set up for individuals or small groups in the library or audio room.

5. Germane to the subject matter of this book is an assignment tracing the historical development of one of the issues presented. Such an assignment is well adapted for a semester project or a term paper. Take, for instance, the general topic of religion and the schools. Throughout the history of the United States many problems and issues have centered around this theme, although never in the same manner. Every issue grew out of the political, social, and economic changes and conditions at the time and can be understood only in relation to the larger events. In fact, a large theme such as this has such a wealth of material that it could be undertaken by several students, each developing a particular phase of the historical background.

6. The instructor may wish, however, to develop an approach almost the opposite of the historical—to focus on the contemporary. About each issue in this volume, the student will be able to research in current professional journals or scholarly periodicals in order to update the information presented herein. In our ever-changing world, new aspects, new knowledge, new developments spur authors into print with new ideas and reformulations of the old. One such issue that is almost certain to receive more attention in the future than it has in the past is the role of the Federal Government in education. One facet of the problem is

the ever-increasing volume of funds for education; another is the authority of the United States Office of Education.

7. The format of this book groups articles around five vital centers where conflicts and disputes center—the society, the school, the youth, the profession, and the schools of Europe. Another method of organizing the material would have been around the issues themselves. This approach was rejected in favor of the former for two primary reasons. In the first place, an organization around issues forces the editor to select either the superficial approach of using only the *pro's* and *con's* of the specific issue or the depth approach showing many alternative points of view, but limiting the number of issues to be dealt with.

Secondly, the editor feels that the present organization provides the instructor with greater opportunities to help the student assume more responsibility for his own learning. In the present format the student is forced not only to identify the issues, but also to become more skillful in seeing points of view that may vary only subtly from others. Further, the instructor has the opportunity of making assignments from the selected references, or from his own sources, to help the student obtain greater insight into and a fuller understanding of the complex nature of each issue.

8. Using the material in this book as a starting point, the instructor can tailor individual assignments for investigation and research to the student's subject specialization. What changes and new developments in his specialization have led to conflicts and disputes that give rise to controversial issues? This question gives the student an opportunity to apply knowledge gained in one area to a different situation and to become more skillful in searching for crucial issues. Such an investigation can be made at any level—early childhood education, elementary, or secondary education, with the secondary level further subdivided by subject fields.

9. Panel discussions are invaluable in helping the student to become more directly involved in the issues under study. Care must be taken, however, to see that the members of the panel understand that a panel discussion is not a debate, not an argument, nor a formal presentation of prepared material. Preparation is indeed required, but the panel itself should be considered a forum for the sharing of ideas concerning, in this instance, a controversial issue. Whether the panel members are selected by the instructor or chosen by the students themselves, they need guidance from the instructor in their organization and presentation. With adequate preparation, no other method is so effective in helping students to become engaged in the process of identifying, examining, and evaluating controversial ideas.

10. This list of suggestions, together with the instructor's own ideas for presentation and discussion, are all valuable means for evaluating the student's progress. Yet within the context of these suggestions, the formal examination plays an important role. Of the various types of examinations available, it seems almost a necessity to use the essay form as the most appropriate for the subject matter of controversy. Such examinations, however, are extremely time-consuming to evaluate. The editor has found that a variation of the essay form, which he calls an

"essay-type" examination, can be at least as reliable, and in some respects more accurate, than the regular essay form. An "essay-type" requires the student to list the major ideas or points he would use to develop his answer, without actually formulating his thoughts into a finished essay. Such a procedure provides the student with more time to think about the problem and forces him to be more precise in organizing and setting down his ideas.

11. Two additional instructional aids are found at the conclusion of the introductions to each of the five parts of this volume. One aid is a list of questions for further study that focus on the specific material in each section. The second is a bibliography of carefully screened, selected references, which provide the instructor and the student with an important guide for further study of the issues under discussion.

CONTENTS

PART III

PART IV

PART V

CONTROVERSY IN AMERICAN EDUCATION

THE NATURE OF
CONTROVERSY

Controversy, whether in education or in other areas of social life, has its basis in the contradictory yet interrelated needs, ideas, beliefs, and values of men. Controversy is the intellectual expression of the conflicts, anxieties, and hostilities in society and serves to ease these tensions by permitting the peaceful processes of discussion and debate to minimize the danger of open strife and rebellion. Though some form of conflict is a precondition for controversy, controversy itself can channel these continuing conflicts in desirable directions by creating an intellectual climate that, by moving beyond the immediate dispute, can permit opportunities to develop for reasoned evaluation or resolution. Such creative interaction can prepare the society for intelligent change and progress.[1]

Although conflict and controversy alone cannot account for all the myriad changes that take place in a society, they can, and do, set the stage for changes to occur. The United States as the most open, most mobile, most dynamic society in the world is also a society that is characterized by the greatest frequency of conflicts and controversies. The openness of a society is conducive to divergent ideas and beliefs. It creates an atmosphere for the acceptance of change. The society that resists change and controversy fails to realize the greater danger that confronts it, a danger arising from its inadaptability and static nature. In a society dominated by revolutionary changes that are taking place at an accelerating pace, characteristic of the United States today, it seems essential to develop an intelligent understanding of the nature of controversy and its role in a contemporary democratic society.

Controversy is embedded in the tradition of American democracy. The freedoms embodied in the Constitution were not given to Americans; they were the result of a long series of struggles and conflicts in which

[1] Some ideas in this essay have been freely adapted from Lewis A. Coser, *The Functions of Social Conflict* (Glencoe, Ill.: The Free Press, 1956) and Georg Simmel, *Conflict and the Web of Group Associations* (Glencoe, Ill.: The Free Press, 1955).

1

controversy played an important role. Controversy helped to resolve the enormous problems facing a growing nation. In the settling of forty million new immigrants, in the giant growth of industry, in the tremendous expansion Westward, in the zealous movements for social and political reform, and in the unique development of a system of free public schools open to all, the continuous give and take of conflicting points of view opened the way for the development of levels of understanding that was more inclusive than the ideas or practices of the contending parties. Through this process new questions were raised and new alternatives were seen. Current pressing problems, some new, some reformulations of the old, are being tested in the fires of controversy, and, if intelligently directed, new concepts or new modes of behavior can emerge to provide the society with enough elasticity to meet the radical changes underway.

In examining past and present controversies, it seems that at least six basic phases can be identified. The term *phases of controversy* (*stages of controversy* would also be acceptable), rather than kinds or types of controversy, was deliberately selected to indicate the dynamic nature of controversy. *Phases* suggests the movement that takes place in any discussion that involves conflicting points of view. Even when a controversy becomes hardened into intransigent positions attracting few new participants or new ideas, it becomes static only temporarily and can flare up again in new dress to meet current fashion. Once this quality of controversy is recognized, it should be understood that the following identified phases are not intended to make distinctions so sharp that rigid boundaries between them are established. Nor do controversies proceed precisely in the manner outlined. They can, and do, begin at any one of the phases, or at several phases simultaneously. Being aware of these qualifications, the reader should find these classifications useful in stimulating him to closer examination of the conflicting points of view presented in the articles in this anthology and helpful in identifying the dominant phases in current disputes.

Phase One. This phase is represented by oversimplification. Very complicated problems are reduced to a single cause. Statements such as this are typical, "The way to prevent juvenile delinquency is to impose a curfew." Little effort is made to identify the issue under discussion or to evaluate it within the conditions that currently prevail. This leads to great fragmentation. What is seen are single units, individual parts, without any relationship to each other or to the whole.

Phase Two. This stage is identified by a polarization of thought. Arguments are put in the form of extremes; beliefs are formulated in an *either-or* context. The participants are so profoundly discontented that they are able to identify only the black and white contrasts between extreme opposites. Charges that cannot be substantiated are often made. This phase is further characterized by the introduction of irrelevant information, and frequently proponents of opposing views are derided and belittled by personal attacks. To bolster their views, the disputants will take refuge in the past, seeking to find "answers" for the contemporary problem or to discover authority figures whom they can romanticize and whose views can be made to conform to their opinions.

Phase Three. As controversy proceeds, the discussion is sometimes directed against a secondary object instead of the original cause of the conflict. The danger here is two-fold: it is possible to hurt or offend the secondary object, and it is possible, unless care is taken, to mistake the secondary object as the source of the problem. This practice makes repeated use of stereotype and exaggerated generalization as techniques for suppressing discussion of fundamental issues. For example, appeals were made by some politicians who were opposed to the recent Federal medical care program for the aged on the grounds that this was "socialized medicine," knowing that with many people this phrase would carry a negative connotation and knowing also that these people would be directed away from examining the basic need for medical care for the aged. These techniques used against objects, however, are harmless compared with their destructive quality when employed against individuals or groups. A moment's reflection can recall numerous instances in which group stereotype has done immeasurable harm to the group and to individuals within the group and that in turn has effectively prevented further examination of the real problem.

Phase Four. This phase concerns controversy among individuals within the same group. It can best be characterized by attempts among members of a group to gain conformity. This phase does not occur in all controversies.

Through discussions of controversial matters groups become established and are maintained. Controversy, in this instance, helps a group affirm its identity as a group. Conformity to the views of the group under these conditions has a positive value; it serves to maintain the unity of the group. If groups are engaged in continued controversy with those outside the group, however, they can in time become intolerant of individuals within the group who deviate from the common ideas, values, or beliefs shared by most of the other members. These conflicting positions are regarded as a threat both to the unity of the group and to its identity. The bitter controversy within the Republican Party during the 1964 presidential election campaign illustrates such intra-group conflicts and controversies.

Should the in-group hostility continue long enough, the group, believing, rightly or wrongly, that its identity is threatened, can restrict or limit its membership only to those who conform to the will of the majority. The group then tends to assume a sect-like character, and, in order to maintain cohesion, searches for disputes from an outside threat although none is actually present. Many extremist groups in the United States bear resemblance to this description.

Phase Five. This phase can be identified as a search for common ground. Participants in the controversy explore ways and means to resolve the conflict. They seek alternatives that may exist between the most extreme positions represented; they seek views or ideas that parallel and could displace other values or beliefs. Although their ultimate goals or beliefs remain widely separated, ground for compromise or for resolution of the controversy is sought on lesser values or interests which the participants may share. In fact, what is sought is some resolution of the controversy in terms that make possible the continuation of differences and even fundamental disagreements.

Charles Frankel puts it this way: "The failure to see that men can work well together without the same ultimate goals leads to a failure to take account of the most distinctive technique of a liberal society for maintaining voluntary cooperation—the technique of compromise. For compromise does not only take place when men are bound by a common creed. It takes place at least as often for a much simpler reason—that men have other values besides those that are in dispute. As a result, they do not choose to risk everything on a single issue." [2]

Phase Six. As controversy continues one can expect to discern a shifting of emphasis among participants. Positions change as new, more objective, ground is broken. New kinds of questions are asked; new alternatives sought. Entirely different views of the world and new images of man may be introduced. From these varying views, new perspectives are gained from which to view old disputes in a new context and from which to discern new problems. The participants and those on the sidelines are educated to new ideas that without controversy may have taken longer to hear about or to understand.

It is evident from the description of this phase that it represents the most productive plane for a controversy to be waged on. Unfortunately, not all, perhaps only a few, controversies ever reach this stage. Often the participants are trapped, or trap themselves, at one of the beginning phases and fail to realize the potential of the issue under discussion or their own potential for intellectual growth. Yet the opposite is also true. Some controversies begin at this phase and descend to the level of oversimplification or polarization

---

[2] Charles Frankel, *The Case For Modern Man* (New York: Harper and Brothers, 1956), p. 82.

of thought where stereotypes are substituted for reason and logic. John Dewey's philosophy of education is a case in point. His theory of experience based on intellectual and moral standards for a scientific age offered a new vision of what education was all about, of what must be worthy of the name *education*. Soon, however, those who took up his banner, being either uninformed or misinformed, substituted catch phrases or slogans—"progressive" education versus "traditional" education—for the fundamental issue. They became more noted for what they opposed than what they stood for.

Implicit in the six phases just described is a hierarchy of stages through which controversy may move, proceeding from the least informed to the most informed. Also implicit in these descriptions are various levels at which controversy may be enjoined. *Levels*, in this sense, implies the ability to see the issue under discussion from its simplest formulation to its most complex proportions or to see its immediate and practical as well as its theoretical dimensions. The more levels one is able to identify, the greater is his understanding and the deeper his insight into the controversy.

An illustration of the levels of controversy is the great controversy surrounding the famous Scopes trial in Tennessee in 1925 concerning the teaching of Darwin's theory of evolution in the public schools. What began originally as a controversy between science and religion was later sharpened into a clash among the various shades of opinion held by the religious modernists and the religious fundamentalists. Still later the controversy was focused on the larger issues surrounding the relation of church and state in the control of education. Embedded within these central concerns was a range of opinion grouped around other conflicting themes—God versus atheism, rural versus urban, old versus new, conservative versus liberal, censorship versus freedom. Because much of the discussion represented extreme positions, attention was diverted from some of the major, overriding issues implicit in a thorough understanding of the controversy— What is science? What is religion? Should the will of a minority be forced upon the majority?

The negative and positive features of controversy are revealed from further examination of the six phases presented. At first glance the negative aspects do seem to loom large. Frequently in controversy thought is polarized, issues are oversimplified, objects and groups are stereotyped, and pressures are exerted to conform. In assessing the negative results of controversy, some see these factors as paramount, leading them to the conclusion that controversy should be avoided.

This view seems rather widespread in the field of education, where some teachers and administrators in the public schools and some of those engaged in teacher education in the colleges become overly sensitive, hence defensive, when conflicting opinions are aired concerning the important educational issues of our time. Part of this defensive posture might be accounted for by their lack of historical perspective. By being involved in the wealth of current educational controversy, some educators are led to believe that contemporary conflicts are the first, or at least the greatest, the schools have ever faced; they fail to realize that the disputes of the past were many and long and bitter.

Secondly, it is not uncommon that little distinction is made among the sources of controversy. Criticism of the schools comes from those who are dedicated in their support of public education, as well as from a minority who seek to subvert the goal of education for all American youth. Some educators' lack of discrimination in evaluating sources of criticism reflects unfortunately in their opposing arguments, which are often a strong defense of both the weaknesses and the strengths of public education. Quite naturally, this defensive stance gives the impression of weakness or implies that an apology is in order for the unsettled state of affairs in education today. Such reactions prevent professionals in education from rendering informed leadership to the public and limit their responsibility to develop with youth a mature, reasoned, and sophisticated approach to controversy.

The positive dimensions of controversy seem to outweigh those of the negative. Not all controversies are brought out into the open; some are suppressed by individuals or the group. The motivation for expressing a difference of opinion must be strong enough to overcome any doubts that a person or group may have about expressing the opinion. In this sense, then, conflicting points of view can have a counterbalancing effect on the pressures of conformity in society. The motivation for expressing differing views provides democracy with a vital spirit for self-renewal.

The act of entering into controversy serves to establish relations where none existed before and to provide the possibility that other relations are likely to follow. Once these new relationships are created the climate is ripe for additional interaction. Further, through the course of controversy, new situations develop that call for new rules, new norms, new ideas, new values to be created while old rules, norms, ideas, and values are being revised, reformulated, or replaced. Thus, the very nature of controversy safeguards the society from becoming static and helps the participants to derive inner satisfaction. And by reducing hostilities or by diminishing tensions controversy allows the participants to view their problems more objectively.

Controversy assists in maintaining a balance in society. The pluralistic structure of American society provides stability for its social system through the interdependence of conflicting groups whose crisscrossing controversies provide opportunities for individuals and groups to test their relative strength and to reassess their relative power. By intelligent discussion of controversial issues individuals and groups are allowed to shift and choose among various values and beliefs. This process brings about new forms of flexible social arrangements that create avenues for channeling positive and desirable social action. Thus, controversy is a vital form of social interaction. Through this form of social interaction the area is widened for man to act by free choice and not by coercion. The free give and take of conflicting ideas, values, and beliefs forces man to go beyond the parochial point of view, to expand his horizons. This process maintains the vitality of the democratic open society and provides the means by which the society can continue to be open.

Conformity, in its various guises, is the enemy of the very openness of society that controversy helps to sustain. By the throttling of discussion, conformity closes many avenues of social communication and reduces opportunities for individuals to think, to criticize, to evaluate for themselves. Further, in narrowing the choices available to the individual, or the opportunities for making choices, his personal and social responsibilities are severely restricted. Conformity encourages the receptive mind; controversy develops the inquiring mind. The unsettling pace of modern change breeds doubt and an uneasiness of the mind on which conformity, by providing a false sense of security, thrives. Thus, man is robbed of his vision of an endless future with unlimited possibilities, and his awareness of belonging to a larger community of mankind is dulled.

There are moments in the life of almost every man when he feels a yearning to escape into the past to a more simple age, when society and its problems were less complex, or to escape to some future utopia, where common agreement and consent will banish problems and conflicts and bring continual happiness, comfort, and security. There are other moments when man feels resentful that problems he did not create are imposed upon him. Yet in these resentful moments, as in the moments of escape, he knows that he cannot evade the exceptional moment in which he is living, with all its problems, crises, and controversies, nor can he ignore them. He knows that he must live in their full gravity under all conditions and with all consequences.

SELECTED REFERENCES

Berlyne, D. E. *Conflict, Arousal, and Curiosity*. New York: McGraw-Hill, 1960.
Coser, Lewis A. *Sociological Theory: A Book of Readings* (2nd ed.). New York: The Macmillan Company, 1964.

Coser, Lewis A. *The Functions of Social Conflict.* Glencoe, Ill.: The Free Press, 1956.

Falk, W. D. "Symposium: Reasons," *The Journal of Philosophy* (November 1963), pp. 702–718.

Henderson, Donald. "Minority Response and the Conflict Problem," *Phylon* (Spring 1964), pp. 18–26.

Horowitz, Irving L. "Concensus, Conflict, and Cooperation: A Sociological Inventory," *Social Forces* (December 1962), pp. 177–188.

Simmel, Georg. *Conflict and the Web of Group Associations.* Glencoe, Ill.: The Free Press, 1955.

PART I
THE SOCIETY
Challenges and Conflicts

The thrust of increasingly powerful rockets sending astronauts and highly technical instruments into space dramatizes the amazing sophistication of man's scientific intelligence and his technological knowledge. These triumphs of science, however, represent but one manifestation of the incredible growth of man's ability to control nature and his environment. What has happened has been a revolution in human affairs.

Important areas in the vast change going on continually in American society include the increasing specialization of labor; the continued growth of great centers of population; the ever-increasing mobility of occupations, with a corresponding mobility of population; the development of new areas, such as cybernetics, to identify the processes of communication and control in men and machines; the growth of special interest groups and of government; the continued expansion of the concept of human rights; the fundamental transformation of an economy in which the production of services is greater than the production of goods; the reversal in the classical conception of work and leisure, with the less educated having more time for leisure than those with more skill or knowledge; and the tremendous advances in biology and chemistry, with corresponding advances in allied fields such as medicine. These, and an almost endless list of others, represent an extraordinary explosion of knowledge in just the past twenty years that has affected practically every sphere of human endeavor.

The depth of most of these changes is difficult to comprehend. The focus is likely to be on the dramatic forms of change represented by the incredible ventures into space without a realization of the extent of change that is constantly going on in the normal ways of living. Difficult as it is to grasp the

9

significance of change, there is yet another important dimension to take into account—the rapidity of change. In times past the rate of change was slow enough to permit a comfortable margin of acceptance over a long period of time. This luxury does not exist today. Current changes are hardly understood by the average individual before vast new transitions are in order. This accelerating pace of change in our society has permeated the culture to such an extent that the basic values and beliefs characteristic of Western civilization are being challenged, revised, and reformulated. The quantitative effect of change is responsible for a qualitatively different society.

This radical transformation of the world in which we live, with the resultant conflicts, tensions, and anxieties, leaves man with few opportunities to reflect on what is happening, where he is going, or where all these changes are taking him. His responses are many and varied, informed and uninformed. Some of the changes have been accepted and are already affecting the lives of most members of society at all levels; others, representing vastly different ideas or ways of performing, are not widely understood and not generally accepted. Some changes develop as alternative ways of production or ideas and beliefs that parallel existing ideas or processes; others are more subtle, more fragmentary, involving only separate specialities that do not immediately affect the whole society.

Some react to change by withdrawing and seeking security in the past where, it is thought, answers to most of the current problems exist. It is as though, Katherine Kuh says, "as our world becomes larger our sights tend to shrink, in repudiation, perhaps, of a *vastly expanded* universe." [1] Others, overwhelmed by the change going on about them, try to ignore these events as if by their neglect the changes will disappear. A more arrogant variation of the same attitude is that expressed by a shrug of the shoulders and a "so what?" when one is reminded of the change in the world in which he lives.

Those who have anything to do with education in America today have a solemn responsibility to reflect on the revolutionary changes going on about them and to help prepare the children and youth to meet an ever-changing future. Instead of becoming engulfed by what is happening around him, each individual must be helped to see that man's intelligence can govern the changes taking place, can shape their direction, and can create enlightened attitudes toward desirable changes that are necessary for the growth of a dynamic society.

The importance in studying change is the certainty that changes will increase in the future. It is especially pertinent in the study of controversy in education that one have some conception of the nature of the society in

[1] Katherine Kuh, "Art's Voyage of Discovery," *Saturday Review* (August 29, 1964), p. 150.

which he lives, because many of the conflicts of the larger society are reflected in those that affect education. It is in this belief that this section of the readings is presented.

The great transition man is currently making is perceptively viewed by Kenneth Boulding as being the stage of post-civilization. By comparing the extent of change present in past revolutions, Boulding makes it clear that the current transition greatly exceeds those that have gone before. It is a transition that not only affects science, technology, and forms of energy, but one that shapes social institutions, beliefs, and ideologies, not only in Western society, but in cultures around the world. Yet he sees four new horsemen of the apocalypse, who can drastically alter either the transition or its direction —war, population, technology, ennui. Although not dismissing their relevance, Emmanuel Mesthene, Executive Director of the Harvard University Program on Science and Technology, sees these four "traps" to man's progress as a "failure of nerve," a lack of faith in man's intelligence to do almost anything he wants to do. The risk is great, but so is the reward—the wisdom for mastery over our technology instead of becoming its slave.

While Boulding and Mesthene are exploring larger dimensions of science and society, Donald Michael focuses on a particular aspect of the technological world, that of cybernation. This term was invented to refer to devices used in both automation and computers. He accepts some of the caution of Boulding and some of the optimism of Mesthene in revealing the problems of society and of education in the control of cybernation. In examining the effects of science in our society, these three authors have not dealt with the influence of these developments on values of individuals in the society. Two other writers discuss this phase.

Philip Phenix sees the traditional values that have achieved a kind of permanence in American society as being ones that will have additional relevance for our transforming culture. Hudson Hoagland sees the problems of values and science in different terms. Although man has used science to achieve unbelievable results in what Hoagland refers to as the "psychosocial" revolution, he has not used science to any significant extent to test and direct his value system for the common good. Hoagland believes that science has learned enough about human nature to direct a cultural evolution in a nuclear age.

QUESTIONS FOR DISCUSSION AND FURTHER STUDY

1. Many thoughtful authors have observed that the future for the present generation of children and youth and those that follow is difficult, if not impossible,

to predict. In the past there has always existed enough knowledge concerning trends and direction of society to make it possible to predict fairly accurately the kind of future most youth would face—what kinds of work would be available, what kind of education would be most valuable, what kinds of rights, responsibilities, leisure could be expected.

Today, however, youth face an unknown future. If this statement is to be taken seriously, as leaders in many fields insist, what does it imply for education? How can the schools educate for the unknown when most of their past efforts have been directed to teaching the known? What radical changes must occur? After reading the articles in Part Two concerning the responses the schools are currently making to the challenges of today's world, which of the authors seem to have come to grips with this crucial problem? Are new conceptions needed for the role of the school in the total education of youth?

2. In this introduction various attitudes toward change in society were sketched briefly. What additional reactions can be identified? Is it important in today's world to develop positive attitudes and intelligent understandings concerning the nature of change in society? If so, in what manner can the schools prepare youth to accept change? Further, can the schools serve as a vital force in directing change?

3. In addition to the views of Phenix and Hoagland concerning values in an age of science presented in this section, two essays listed in the selected references discuss this theme from the standpoint of scientists. The opinions are those of René Dubos of the Rockefeller Institute and Ludwig von Bertalanffy, Professor of Zoology and Psychology at the University of Alberta, Canada. In what respects do these views complement or contrast with those of Hoagland or Phenix? Which author seems to reflect the spirit of "The Great Transition" by Kenneth Boulding? In addition to reading these and other pertinent materials, what other kinds of experiences can be suggested for further study of the values-science discussion?

4. In Donald Michael's book, *The Next Generation*, listed in the selected references, a valuable appendix contains some provocative questions and pertinent actions for orienting youth-development programs that will meet the radical changes youth must face in the future. These are well worth examining if only to see the difficult process that must be undertaken to plan intelligently for the foreseeable future. Michael's suggestions are less important than the impetus they provide to stimulate your own thinking.

SELECTED REFERENCES

Aron, Raymond, George Keenan, Robert Oppenheimer, *et al. World Technology and Human Destiny.* Ann Arbor: University of Michigan Press, 1963.

Asbell, Bernard. *The New Improved American.* New York: McGraw-Hill, 1965.

Bertalanffy, Ludwig von. "The World of Science and the World of Value," *Teachers College Record* (March 1964), pp. 496–507.

Boulding, Kenneth E. *The Meaning of the Twentieth Century: The Great Transition.* New York: Harper and Row, 1964.

Drucker, Peter F. "American Directions: A Forecast," *Harper's Magazine* (February 1965), pp. 39–45.

Dubos, René. "Escape from the Land of the Lotus Eaters," *Teachers College Record* (May 1963), pp. 660–670.

Frankel, Charles. *The Case for Modern Man.* New York: Harper and Brothers, 1956.

Heilbroner, Robert L. *The Future As History.* New York: Grove Press, 1961.

Holton, Gerald (ed.). "Science and Technology in Contemporary Society," *Daedalus* (Spring 1962).

Jones, Howard Mumford. "History and the Contemporary," *Teachers College Record* (May 1963), pp. 625–636.

Krutch, Joseph Wood. "Can We Survive the Fun Explosion?" *Saturday Review* (January 16, 1965), pp. 14–16.

La Piere, R. T. *Social Change.* New York: McGraw–Hill, 1965.

Maruyana, Magorah. "Cybernetics," *NEA Journal* (December 1964), pp. 51–54.

Mead, Margaret. "The Future as a Basis for Establishing a Shared Culture," *Daedalus* (Winter 1965), pp. 135–155.

Melman, Seymour. *The Depleted Society.* New York: Holt, Rinehart, and Winston, 1965.

Michael, Donald N. *The Next Generation: The Prospects Ahead for the Youth of Today and Tomorrow.* New York: Random House, 1965.

———. *Cybernation: The Silent Conquest.* Santa Barbara, Calif.: Center for the Study of Democratic Institutions, 1962.

Philipson, Morris (ed.). *Automation: Implications for the Future.* New York: Vintage Books, 1962.

Piel, Gerard. *Science in the Cause of Man.* New York: Alfred A. Knopf, 1961.

Shinn, Roger T. *Tangled World.* New York: Charles Scribner's Sons, 1965.

THE GREAT TRANSITION

KENNETH E. BOULDING

The twentieth century marks the middle period of a great transition in the state of the human race. It may properly be called the second great transition in the history of mankind.

The first transition was that from precivilized to civilized society which began to take place about five (or ten) thousand years ago.[1] This is a transition that is still going on in some parts of the world, although it can be regarded as almost complete. Precivilized society can now be found only in small and rapidly diminishing pockets in remote areas. It is doubtful whether more than 5 per cent of the world's population could now be classified as living in a genuinely precivilized society.

Even as the first great transition is approaching completion, however, a second great transition is treading on its heels. It may be called the transition from civilized to postcivilized society. We are so accustomed to giving the word civilization a favorable overtone that the words postcivilized or postcivilization may strike us as implying something unfavorable. If, therefore, the word technological or the term developed society is preferred I would have no objection. The word postcivilized, however, does bring out the fact that civilization is an intermediate state of man dividing the million or so years of precivilized society from an equally long or longer period which we may expect to extend into the future postcivilization. It is furthermore a rather disagreeable state for most people living in it, and its disappearance need occasion few tears.

The origins of the first great transition from precivilized society are lost in the mists of prehistory except in so far as they can be reconstructed with the aid of archeology. The more we know the further these origins seem to recede in time, and it now seems clear that the beginning of agriculture and the domestication of animals can be traced back at least ten thousand years. Agriculture is a precondition of the development of civilization because it is not until man settles down and begins to cultivate crops and domesticate livestock that he is able to develop a surplus of food from the food producer above and beyond what the food producer

FROM "The Great Transition" in *The Meaning of the 20th Century* by Kenneth Boulding. Copyright © 1964 by Kenneth Ewart Boulding. Reprinted by permission of Harper and Row, Publishers, and George Allen & Unwin, Ltd.

[1] The first transition falls into two parts, the transition from the paleolithic to the neolithic, following the invention of agriculture, and the subsequent transition from the neolithic village to urban civilization. I prefer to think of these two parts as parts of a single process, but some may prefer to regard them as two separate transitions, in which case the modern transition would be the "third."

---

and his family require themselves for their own maintenance. In hunting, fishing and pastoral societies it seems to have been hard for the food producer to produce much more than the immediate requirements of himself and his family. In these circumstances it is clear that no urban culture can possibly exist. If persons who do not produce food are to be fed, there must be surplus food available from the food producer. Some precivilized societies seem to have enjoyed such a surplus, but it was always precarious and temporary. There must be a continuous and reasonably stable excess of food production above the requirements of the food producer if civilization is to be established.

The mere existence of surplus food, while it is a prerequisite for the existence of civilization, does not necessarily produce it, for surplus may be "wasted" in leisure or unproductive activities. In order for towns and cities to exist there must be some machinery whereby the food surplus of the food producer is extracted from him and collected in one place so that the kings, priests, soldiers, builders, and artisans of civilization can subsist. I am assuming here that the prime mark of civilization is the city. This is indeed what the derivation of the word civilization suggests. In its earliest form the city seems to have been a product of some system of coercion. Agriculture provides the opportunity, but in the early stages at least it seems to take some form of coercion to take advantage of it. The earliest forms of coercion may well have been spiritual, for there is some evidence that the earliest cities were organized as theocracies. A priesthood arises which claims a monopoly on the supposedly supernatural forces which govern the affairs of man and the fertility of crops and livestock. The priest then is able to extract food from the food producer by threatening to deprive him of the assistance of these supernatural forces. The coercive system of the priest, however, is based to a large extent on bluff, for the priest does not really control the forces that make the crops grow. When the priest ceases to inspire belief in his imaginary powers the spiritual coercive system usually seems to be replaced by a more physical coercive system in the shape of a king and army. In isolation this is a fairly stable system because when the king has sufficient means of violence at his disposal he can threaten the food producer enough to make him give up his surplus. With this food surplus the king can feed his army and so reinforce the threat if necessary. With what is left over from feeding the army, the king can feed architects, builders, priests, philosophers, and other adornments of civilization. In this stage an alliance is frequently made between the king and the priest, and physical and spiritual threats reinforce each other. The economic basis on which classical civilization has been built, however, has universally been meager. Whether it was Sumeria, Egypt, Greece, Rome, Ancient China, the Incas, or the Mayans, all these were societies based on a food surplus from the food producer that rarely exceeded 20 or 25 per cent of the total product. In these circumstances three quarters to four fifths of the population must be in agriculture or other food production, and these people barely produce enough to feed the remaining quarter or fifth of the population in the towns and in the army. Almost all the cities of classical civilization were within a few weeks of starvation at any time, and a relatively small worsening in general conditions, in the means of transportation or in conditions of peace and war, was frequently enough to undermine the precarious foundation of civilized life. I have never seen any figure for the expectation of life of the city itself under conditions of classical civilization, but I would be surprised if this turned out to be more than about three hundred years.

The origins of the second great transition are perhaps not so obscure as the origins of the first, but there are many puzzling and unresolved questions connected with them. All through the history of civilization, indeed, one can detect a slowly rising stream of knowledge and organization that has a different quality from that of the civilized society around it. The astronomy of Babylonia, the geometry of the Greeks, and the algebra of the Arabs represent as it were foretastes of the great flood of knowledge and technological change to come. Some of the ancient empires, even the Roman Empire, seem to have been technologically stagnant and scientifically backward. If one is looking for the beginning of a continuous process of scientific and technological development, this might be traced to the monastic movement in the West of the sixth century A.D., especially the Benedictines. Here for almost the first time in history we had intellectuals who worked with their hands, and who belonged to a religion which regarded the physical world as in some sense sacred and capable of enshrining goodness. It is not surprising therefore that an interest in the economizing of labor and in extending its productive powers began in the monasteries, however slowly. From the sixth century on we can trace a slowly expanding technology. The water wheel comes in the sixth century, the stirrup in the eighth, the horse collar and the rudder in the ninth, the windmill in the twelfth, and so on. For Europe the invention of printing in the fifteenth century represents an irreversible take-off, because from this point on the dissemination of information increased with great rapidity. The seventeenth century saw the beginning of science, the eighteenth century an acceleration of technological change so great that it has been called, perhaps rather misleadingly, the Industrial Revolution. The nineteenth century saw the development of science as an ongoing social organization, and the twentieth century has seen research and development heavily institutionalized with an enormous increase in the rate of change both of knowledge and of technology as a result. It must be emphasized that the rate of change still seems to be accelerating. We may not even have reached the middle of whatever process we are passing through, and there are certainly no signs that the rate of change is slowing down. It seems clear for instance that we are now on the edge of a biological revolution which may have results for mankind just as dramatic as the nuclear revolution of a generation ago.

A few symptoms will indicate the magnitude of the change through which we are now passing. Consider for instance the position of agriculture in the most developed societies today. In all societies of classical civilization, as we have seen, at least 75 per cent of the population, and often a larger percentage, were engaged in agriculture and would merely produce enough to support themselves and the remaining urban 25 per cent. Even in the United States at the time of the American Revolution, it has been estimated that about 90 per cent of the people were in agriculture. Today in the United States only about 10 per cent of the population are so engaged, and if present trends continue it will not be long before we can produce all the food that we need with 5 per cent, or even less, of the population. This is because with modern techniques, a single farmer and his family can produce enough food to feed ten, twenty, or even thirty families. This releases more than 90 per cent of the population to work on other things, and to produce automobiles, houses, clothing, all the luxuries and conveniences of life as well as missiles and nuclear weapons.

Another indication of the magnitude of the present transition is the fact that, as far as many statistical series related to activities of mankind are concerned, the date that divides human history into two equal parts is well within living memory. For the volume and number of chemical publications, for instance, this date is now (*i.e.* 1964) about 1950. For many statistical series of quantities of metal or other materials extracted, this date is about 1910. That is, man took about as much out of mines before 1910 as he did after 1910. Another startling fact is that about 25 per cent of the human beings who have ever lived are now alive, and what is even more astonishing, something like 90 per cent of all the scientists who have ever lived are now alive. My eight-year-old son asked me the other day, "Daddy, were you born in the olden days?" It is the sort of question that makes a parent feel suddenly middle-aged. There is perhaps more truth in his remark than he knew. In a very real sense the changes in the state of mankind since the date of my birth have been greater than the changes that took place in many thousands of years before this date.

Another indication of the magnitude of the transition is the extraordinary ability of modern societies to recover from disaster. In 1945, for instance, many of the cities of Germany and Japan lay in almost total ruin. Today it is hard to tell that they were ever destroyed, for they have been completely rebuilt in a space of less than twenty years. It took Western Europe almost three hundred years to recover from the fall of the Roman Empire, and took Germany decades to recover from the Thirty Years War (1618–1648). It is perhaps an optimistic feature of the present time that as well as great powers of destruction, we also have greatly increased powers of recuperation and recovery.

The great transition is not only something that takes place in science, technology, the physical machinery of society, and in the utilization of physical energy. It is also a transition in social institutions. Changes in technology produce change in social institutions, and changes in institutions produce change in technology. In the enormously complex world of social interrelations we cannot say in any simple way that one change produces the other, only that they are enormously interrelated and both aspects of human life change together. For instance, it has been argued that the invention of the rudder and the improvement in the arts of navigation and shipbuilding which took place in Europe in the fifteenth century led inevitably to the discovery of America by Europeans. As a schoolboy is reported to have said, "How could Columbus miss it?" Once it was possible to navigate a course of three thousand miles in a straight line, the discovery of America by the Europeans was virtually inevitable, and of course this discovery enormously expanded the horizon and the opportunities of these European societies.

On the other hand, the societies which pioneered in the discovery of America did not ultimately profit very much from it. Spain and Portugal obtained a great empire and a sizable inflation but stagnated as a result, because of the failure of their social institutions to adapt.

It has likewise been argued that the discovery of the horse collar eventually led to the abolition of slavery, at least in its more extreme forms, because of the fact that with a horse collar the horse became a much more efficient source of mere animal power than a human, and the slave as a simple source of power could not compete with him. A horse collar seems to be such an obvious invention that one can hardly believe that it took until the ninth century for mankind to think of it. However, it seems to be clear that the Romans did not use it, and that the Roman horse pulled on rope that was something like a noose around its neck, which greatly reduced its efficiency. The horse collar, coupled with the development of the three-field system, led to a substantial improvement in the techniques of agriculture in Europe in the ninth, tenth, and eleventh centuries which was the foundation on which the cultural and architectural achievements of the later Middle Ages were built. Here again, however, the social institutions of its feudal and authoritarian societies led to a freezing of the technological situation, and further advance in agriculture did not come until the institutions of the Middle Ages had largely disintegrated or at least were weakened through the inflation which followed on the inflow of the Spanish gold from the New World. The rise of Protestantism and the breakup of the old transitional society produced a situation in Holland and in England in which innovation was once more possible, and the agricultural revolution of the seventeenth and early eighteenth centuries grew out of the developing of root crops, the use of intertilled crops on previously fallow ground, and the sowing of artificial grasses. This improvement in agriculture, at least in England and the Low Countries in the early eighteenth century, laid the foundation for a growing food surplus for the industrial cities to come.

The social invention of parliamentary democracy permitted societies to develop with much greater diversity and wider distribution of power than in the earlier absolute monarchies, and the rise of modern science is quite closely associated with the development of democratic and pluralistic institutions of this kind. It could not arise, for instance, in imperial China or feudal Japan. It is no accident that an acceleration in the growth of science took place in Western Europe following the French Revolution. It is clear that we must look at pure science, technological change, and social invention as parts of a single pattern of development in which each element supports the other. It may be argued indeed that social institutions play more of a negative than a positive role, in that they can inhibit scientific and technological change but cannot initiate it. Even this proposition, however, must now be called in question. Organized research and development is essentially a social invention which has resulted in an enormous increase in the pace of technological change.

As another example of the interrelation of technical and political change it can be argued, for instance, that it is the progress of technology, especially under the stimulus of organized research and development, that has effectively abolished imperialism. Ancient civilization, as we have seen, rested firmly on a basis of coercion. The food producer had to be coerced into giving up the surplus to king or priest because there was nothing much that either of them produced that could be exchanged for it. The ancient city is to a large extent an instrument of exploitation and must be regarded as parasitic on the food producer. In the modern world things are different. Since the development of industrial society, exchange has replaced coercion as the principal means of social organization even though coercion and the threat of violence still retain a great importance in the relations of national states. But with the coming of science and technology, it is fair to say that we can get ten dollars out of nature for every dollar that we can squeeze out of man. Under these circumstances imperial adventure or political coercion is simply an investment with a much lower rate of return than investment in applied science and technological progress at home. We see this very clearly, for instance, in the case of Portugal, which now has probably the largest *per capita* empire and the lowest *per capita* income in Europe. By contrast, the Scandinavian countries and Switzerland, which have refrained from imperial adventures, have probably done better economically than their more imperial counterparts. The progressive abandonment of empire by the British, the French, the Dutch, and the Belgians reflects not so much a power shift on the part of these countries as their recognition that in terms of the values of a modern society, empire simply does not pay.

Social inventions often take place so softly and imperceptibly that they are hardly noticed, and the history of social invention as a result still largely remains to be written. Who for instance invented the handshake? How did we change from a society in which almost every man went armed to a society in which we have achieved almost complete personal disarmament, and in which human relations are governed by conventions of politeness, by disarming methods of communication, and by largely nonviolent techniques of conflict? Most of all, how do changes take place in child rearing? These perhaps are the most fundamental social inventions of all, for the personality structure of one generation depends mainly on the way children were brought up in the previous generation.

As part of the ongoing process of social invention the great transition involves changes in moral, religious, and aesthetic aspects of life just as much as it involves changes in our knowledge and use of the physical world. It involves, for instance, change in the nature of the family and in the patterns of child rearing. Civilized society on the whole is characterized by the extended family, and by strong loyalty to kinfolk and by methods of child rearing which generally involve a rough transition from an extremely permissive and protective early childhood to an authoritarian and unpleasant regime in later childhood. As we move to post-civilized society, we find an extension of loyalty from the kinship to larger areas such as the national state, or even to the world as a whole. The family structure and living arrangement tend to shift from the extended family group and large household to the small nuclear family of parents and children, and we find that the child-rearing practices which may be well adapted to a society in which the threat systems are important and aggression pays off, have become poorly adapted to a society in which the subtler arts of personal manipulation replace the more violent forms of aggression. We therefore find a shift in the methods of child rearing from those which produce the authoritarian personalities which are characteristic of civilized societies to those which produce more flexible, adaptable, and manipulative persons.

Drastic changes in the nature and behavior of the family are also implied by the health revolution which is also a part of the transition. In civilized society, mortality is high and there is a necessity therefore for a high birth rate. Civilized society can be in equilibrium with birth and death rates between thirty and forty per thousand and a corresponding expectation of life between thirty-three and twenty-five. It is a matter of simple arithmetic that in an equilibrium population in which birth rate and death rate are equal, the level of the birth and death rates is the simple reciprocal of the average age at death. In the advanced societies today the average age at death is about seventy, and for such a population to be in equilibrium the birth and death rate must be about fourteen. To put the matter in somewhat different terms, if all children live to maturity and if the whole population marries, then the average number of children in one family cannot exceed two, if population is to be stable. This also implies no more than an average of two births per family. This involves an enormous shift in attitude toward children and even perhaps toward sex. Yet this is an essential part of the transition. If this part of the transition is not made, all the rest cannot be made either, except as a temporary and unstable condition.

The great transition likewise involves a profound change in the nature of religion and ideology. In a society in which religion is associated with animistic views of the universe and with a belief in magic, the behavior changes which are necessary to the great transition can hardly take place. If man believes that natural objects like stones, wind, water, and crops are moved by essentially arbitrary wills, either he will despair of manipulating nature to his own advantage or he will attempt to do this in the same way that he would attempt to manipulate his fellow man— that is, by attempts at verbal or symbolic communication, in the form of incantation and ritual. It is not until animism is replaced by an attitude which regards will as essentially and solely a property of the minds and souls of men, rather than of inanimate natural objects, that a scientific and technological attitude toward the material world becomes possible. It is no accident therefore that the scientific transition originated in Western Europe, where the prevailing religion was an ethical monotheism, which either tended to concentrate the whole animistic enterprise in a single sacramental act of the Mass, as in Catholic Christianity, or which denied even this apparent remnant of animism by stressing that the operation of the will of God takes place principally in the souls of men, as in Protestant Christianity.

We may even attribute the success of atheistic communism in promoting economic development and the movement toward postcivilized society not so much to its specific dogmas as to the fact that it is an instrument for undermining primitive animism and for replacing a belief in the arbitrary and willful nature of the material world by a belief in its stability and orderliness. Whether this view can ultimately satisfy the spiritual needs of man is another question altogether. It is clear that the scientific and technological transition is consistent with many different views about the ultimate nature of the universe, provided that they all involve a faith in the orderliness of the natural world, faith in man's ability to perceive this order and manipulate it for his own benefit, and faith in processes of learning which involve direct experience rather than mere acceptance of the received tradition from the elders.

The various civilizations which resulted from the first great transition, even though they had much in common, nevertheless exhibited great differences. One needs merely to think of Ancient Egypt, Babylonia, Greece, Rome, medieval Europe, and China. Similarly it seems probable that the second great transition will not immediately at least result in a uniform world culture but will result in a considerable variety of cultural patterns, each of them however exhibiting very similar technologies and levels of income. But it is probable that postcivilized society, simply because of the fact that its techniques are much less bound either to geography or to past culture than are the techniques of civilized society, will turn out to be much more uniform than the civilized societies have been. We see this, for instance, in the airports of the world. Air travel is a distinct mark of postcivilized society, and airports are much the same whether we find them in Bangkok or in Chicago. Similarly, steel mills are much the same in Volta Redonda in Brazil, in Birmingham, Alabama, or in India. In so far as civilization was based on agriculture, the physical basis made for wide differences. The agriculture of the Nile delta is very different from the agriculture of wheat fields of the steppes and prairies, which again is different from that of the rice paddies of Asia. We should therefore expect that civilizations based on agriculture would exhibit markedly different technological as well as cultural forms. Professor Wittfogel[2] has suggested indeed that the political and social institutions of civilized society are closely related to the type of agriculture from which it draws its food supply, and in particular an agriculture which requires extensive public works and irrigation like that of Ancient Egypt and China is much more likely to develop hierarchical and authoritarian societies than an agriculture based on small peasant holdings in humid lands where no public organization of any great magnitude or large public works are needed in order to grow food. Even in postcivilized societies, of course, rice paddies are different from wheat fields and produce a different kind of culture. Nevertheless the tractor is much the same everywhere, just as the automobile and factories are much the same everywhere, and this imposes a uniformity at least on the technological culture of the world which it never possessed before.

Furthermore the rapid and easy transportation which postcivilization permits makes it much more difficult to maintain culture traits in isolation. Civilizations

[2] Karl A. Wittfogel, Oriental Despotism (New Haven: Yale University Press, 1957).

could flourish at the same time on the earth which had little or no contact one with another. The Mayan civilization certainly had no contact with Rome, and Rome had very little contact with China. The transition to civilization indeed may have been accomplished in at least three independent locations or perhaps even more, though these origins are so obscure that we cannot be sure of this. Now, however, it is as easy to go halfway around the world as it used to be to go to a neighboring town, and under these circumstances an enormous process of cultural mixture is taking place which can hardly help producing much greater uniformity even in a few hundred years. It is doubtful whether a single world language will emerge in the near future, but certainly in styles of clothing, housing, mass entertainment, and transportation it is becoming increasingly hard to distinguish one part of the world from another.

An important difference which is likely to be maintained for a considerable time is that between societies which are making the transition under democratic and capitalistic institutions and those which are making the transition under institutions of totalitarian socialism. It certainly seems possible to make the technological transition under both sets of institutions. Nevertheless the societies which will emerge as a result might be quite different not only in the political and social institutions but in the value systems and the nature and quality of human life which they support. In the short run this raises many problems and unquestionably increases the danger of war and the probability that the transition will not be made. In the long perspective of history, however, this may turn out to have been a fortunate accident, if indeed it is an accident. It might well be that one of the greatest problems of postcivilized society will be how to preserve enough differentiation of human culture and how to prevent the universal spread of a drab uniformity. Cultural change and development at all times has frequently come about as a result of the interaction of cultures which previously have developed in isolation. This is a phenomenon somewhat analogous to the development of hybrid varieties in plants and animals. If we are to have hybrid cultures, however, just as if we are to have hybrid animals, there must be pure stocks maintained to interbreed. The strength of the mule and the fertility of hybrid corn would be impossible if the pure stocks from which these hybrids are derived are not maintained. Similarly in the case of cultures if we are to have vigorous hybrid cultures, the pure cultures from which these are derived must be maintained, and in a world of easy travel and rapid communication the maintenance of the pure cultures may be difficult. It may therefore be possible that things which now we regard as unfortunate sources of conflict and separation may turn out to be blessings in disguise. If socialist culture and free-market culture can develop side by side without fatal conflict, their constant interaction may be beneficial to both parties. Similarly even the development of religious sects and subcultures which are isolated from the world by what may seem a nonrational ideology may turn out to be extremely useful devices for preserving the diversity of mankind.

Perhaps the most difficult of all these problems involving diversity and uniformity is the problem of the future of different races. The different races of mankind have a sufficient sexual attraction for each other so that in the absence of any geographical or cultural obstacles to genetic mixture it is highly probable that in the course of a few thousand years the human race would become racially uniform, and the existing differences between races will be largely eliminated. From some points of view this may be very desirable, and it will certainly eliminate certain problems of interhuman conflict, most of which however are defined culturally rather than biologically. We know so little about human genetics, however, especially on the positive side of the forces which lead to genetic excellence, that it is impossible now to prophesy what may be regarded as eugenic in the future. The eugenic movement of the nineteenth century was based on inadequate knowledge of human genetics and hence could not get very far. If we develop as we may well do more accurate knowledge of the genetic factors which made for human excellence both of mind and body, the consequences for ethics, for almost all social relations, and for political behavior might be immense. But this is a bridge which we have not yet come to, and it may be well to postpone worrying about it until we do. In the meantime knowledge of human genetics, apart from a few factors making for certain defects, is not developed enough so that from it we can justify either racial purity or racial admixture. It might well be indeed that we will end by classifying mankind genetically along quite different lines from the way in which the races are now classified by strictly superficial characteristics, and we may then be able to warn against dangerous genetic combinations, as we do already with the Rh factor, and perhaps even encourage desirable combinations. Much of this, however, is in the future, though at the rate at which the biological sciences are now developing it may not be in the very distant future.

The great question as to whether the transition from civilization to postcivilization is a "good" change is one that cannot be answered completely until we know the nature and quality of different postcivilized societies. We might well argue in contemplating the first great transition from precivilized to civilized societies that in many cases this was a transition from a better state of man to a worse. As we contemplate the innumerable wars of civilized societies, as we contemplate the hideous religion of human sacrifice and the bloody backs of innumerable slaves on which the great monuments of civilization have been built, it is sometimes hard to refrain from a certain romantic nostalgia for the "noble savage." Indeed, the *philosophes* of the eighteenth century indulged in this feeling at great length. Anthropologists have somewhat dispelled the romantic view of precivilized society, which was in many cases not only poor but cruel and disagreeable beyond even the excesses of civilization. Nevertheless it will not be difficult to contrast the best of precivilized societies and the worst of civilized societies and come out much in favor of the precivilized. Similarly a type of postcivilized society is possible as portrayed, for instance, in the anti-Utopias of George Orwell and Aldous Huxley in the middle of the twentieth century, in which the quality of human life and the dignity of man seem to be much inferior to that in the best of civilized societies.

There is clearly here a problem to be solved. We do not make men automatically good and virtuous by making them rich and powerful; indeed the truth frequently seems to be the opposite. Nevertheless we must not fall into the other trap of equating innocence with ignorance or of thinking that impotence is the same thing as virtue. An increase in power increases the potential both for good and for evil. A postcivilized society of unshakable tyranny, resting upon all the knowledge which we are going to gain in social sciences, and of unspeakable corruption resting on man's enormous power over nature, especially biological nature, is by no means inconceivable. On the other hand the techniques of postcivilization also offer us the possibility of a society in which the major sources of human misery have been eliminated, a society in which there will be no war, poverty, or disease, and in which a large majority of human beings will be able to live out their lives in relative freedom from most of the ills which now oppress a major part of mankind. This is a prize worth driving for even at the risk of tyranny and corruption. There is no real virtue in impotence, and the virtue to strive for is surely the combination of power with goodness.

In any case there is probably no way back. The growth of knowledge is one of the most irreversible forces known to mankind. It takes a catastrophe of very large dimensions to diminish the total stock of knowledge in the possession of man. Even in the rise and fall of great civilizations surprisingly little has been permanently lost, and much that was lost for a short time was easily regained. Hence there is no hope for ignorance or for a morality based on it. Once we have tasted the fruit of the tree of knowledge, as the Biblical story illustrates so well, Eden is closed to us. We cannot go back to the childhood of our race any more than we can go back to our own childhood without disaster. Eden has been lost to us forever and an angel with a flaming sword stands guard at its gates. Therefore either we must wander hopelessly in the world or we must press forward to Zion. We must learn to master ourselves as we are learning to master nature. There is no reason in the nature of things which says that ethical development is impossible, and indeed one would expect that the process of development, whether economic, political, or social, will go hand in hand with a similar process of ethical development which will enable us to use wisely the power that we have gained. This ethical development may take forms which will seem strange to us now, but just as we can trace development in the values and ethical standards of mankind as his economic and physical powers increased from precivilized society, so it is reasonable that new ethical standards will arise appropriate to the new technology of postcivilization.

We must emphasize that there is no inevitability and no determinism in making this great transition. There are a number of traps which lies along the way and which may either prevent man and his planet earth from making the transition altogether or delay it for many generations or even thousands of years. The first most obvious and immediate trap is the war trap. It is now theoretically possible for man to build a device which will eliminate all life from the earth. Even if this extreme event is highly improbable, less extreme disasters are at least within a range of probability that makes them a matter of serious concern. A major nuclear war would unquestionably set back the transition to a postcivilized world by many generations, and it might indeed eliminate the possibility of making this transition altogether. The effect of such war on the whole ecological system of the planet is so unpredictable that we cannot tell how large a disaster it will be, although we know it will be very large. It is possible that such a disaster will be irretrievable. It is also possible that even if we had a retrievable disaster we might not learn enough from it to retrieve ourselves. It is clear that what is desperately needed at the present time is to diminish the probability of such a disaster to the vanishing point.

Another possible trap which might delay the attainment of the transition for a long time is the population trap. This is perhaps the main reason for believing that the impact of a few postcivilized techniques on existing civilized societies might easily be disastrous in the next hundred years or so. One of the first impacts of postcivilized medicine and medical knowledge on civilized society is a large and immediate reduction in the death rate, especially in infant mortality. This is seldom if ever accompanied by a similar decrease in birth rate, and hence the first impact of postcivilized techniques on a previously stable civilized society is a tremendous upsurge in the rate of population increase. This increase may be so large that the society is incapable of adapting itself to it, and incapable in particular of devoting sufficient resources to the education of its unusually large cohorts of young people. We therefore have the tragic situation that the alleviation of much human misery and suffering in the short run may result in enormous insoluble problems in a longer period.

A third possible trap is the technological trap itself: that we may not be able to develop a genuinely stable high-level technology which is independent of exhaustible resources. Technology at the present time, even the highest technology, is largely dependent for its sources of energy and materials on accumulations in the earth which date from its geological past. In a few centuries, or at most a few thousand years, these are likely to be exhausted, and either man will fall back on a more primitive technology or he will have to advance to knowledge well beyond what he has now. Fortunately there are signs that this transition to a stable high-level technology may be accomplished, but we certainly cannot claim that it has been accomplished up to date.

A fourth possible trap may lie in the very nature of man itself. If the dangers and difficulties which now beset man are eliminated in postcivilized society and if he has no longer anything to fear but death itself, will not his creativity be diminished and may he not dissipate his energies in a vast ennui and boredom? This is a question which cannot be answered. But it lurks uneasily at the back of all optimistic statements about the long-run future of man.

LEARNING TO LIVE
WITH SCIENCE

EMMANUEL G. MESTHENE

It was Gilbert Murray who first used the celebrated phrase "the failure of nerve." Writing about ancient Greek religions, Murray characterized as a failure of nerve the change of temper that occurred in Hellenistic civilization around the turn of the era. The Greeks of the fifth and fourth centuries B.C. believed in the ultimate intelligibility of the universe. There was nothing in the nature of existence or of man that was inherently unknowable. They accordingly believed also in the power of the human intelligence to know all there was to know about the world, and to guide man's career in it.

The wars, increased commerce, and infiltration of Oriental cultures that marked the subsequent period brought with them vicissitude and uncertainty that shook this classic faith in the intelligibility of the world and in the capacity of men to know and to do. There was henceforth to be a realm of knowledge available only to God, not achievable by human reason. Men, in other words, more and more turned to God to do for them what they no longer felt confident to do for themselves. That was the failure of nerve.

I think things are changing. I doubt that there are many men today who would question that life will be produced in the laboratory, that psychologists and their personality drugs will soon reveal what really makes men tick, that scientific prediction is a far more promising guide to the future than divination, and that the heavens cannot long remain mysterious in the face of our ability to hit the moon today and the stars tomorrow. In a recent article, Daniel Bell characterized this new-found faith as follows: "Today we feel that there are no inherent secrets in the universe . . . and this is one of the significant changes in the modern moral temper." I would say, indeed, that this is a major implication of our new world of science and technology. We are witnessing a widespread recovery of nerve.

Paradoxically, this taking on of new courage is tending at the same time to produce an opposite reaction, vague but disturbingly widespread. At the same time that we admire the new machines we build—the ones that play chess, and translate Russian, and catch and correct their own mistakes, and tend each other— we also begin to fear them. We fear them in two ways—one that we talk about, and one that we joke about.

FROM the *Saturday Review*, XLVIII, 29 (July 17, 1965), pp. 14–17. Reprinted by permission.

We talk quite openly about our fear that machines may take away jobs, deprive people of work. But we dare only to joke about our fear that machines will replace people, not only as workers, but as people. Already they do arithmetic better than any of us. How much longer can it be before they make people obsolete? This fear is part of our technological world, but I see it only as derivative. I think it has its roots in a deeper, moral implication.

Some who have seen farthest and most clearly in recent decades have warned of a growing imbalance between man's capabilities in the physical and in the social realms. John Dewey, for example, said: "We have displayed enough intelligence in the physical field to create the new and powerful instrument of science and technology. We have not as yet had enough intelligence to use this instrument deliberately and systematically to control its social operations and consequences." Dewey said this more than thirty years ago, before television, before atomic power, before electronic computers, before space satellites. He had been saying it, moreover, for at least thirty years before that. He saw early the problems that would arise when man learned to do anything he wanted before he learned what he wanted.

I think the time Dewey warned about is here. My more thoughtful scientific friends tell me that we now have, or know how to acquire, the technical capability to do very nearly anything we want. Can we transplant human hearts, control personality, order the weather that suits us, travel to Mars or to Venus? Of course we can, if not now or in five to ten years, then certainly in twenty-five, or in fifty or a hundred. If each of us examined the extent of his own restored faith in the essential intelligibility of the world, we might find that we have recovered our nerve to the point that we are becoming almost nervy. (I think, incidentally, that this recovery of nerve largely explains the current crisis of the churches. After twenty centuries of doing man's work, they are now having to learn how to do God's. The Ecumenical Council is evidence that the long but false war between religion and science is ended, and that we are once more facing Augustine's problem, to distinguish what is God's and what is man's.)

If the answer to the question "What can we do?" is "Anything," then the emphasis shifts far more heavily than before onto the question "What should we do?" The commitment to universal intelligibility entails moral responsibility. Abandonment of the belief in intelligibility 2,000 years ago was justly described as a failure of nerve because it was the prelude to moral surrender. Men gave up the effort to be wise because they found it too hard. Renewed belief in intelligibility 2,000 years later means that men must take up again the hard work of becoming wise. And it is much harder work now, because we have so much more power than the Greeks. On the other hand, the benefits of wisdom are potentially greater, too, because we have the means at hand to *make* the good life, right here and now, rather than just to go on contemplating it in Plato's heaven.

The question "What should we do?" is thus no idle one but challenges each one of us. That, I think, is the principal moral implication of our new world. It is what all the shouting is about in the mounting concern about the relations of science and public policy, and about the impact of technology on society. Our almost total mastery of the physical world entails a challenge to the public intelligence of a degree heretofore unknown in history.

But how do we come to grips with the challenge? How do we pull together and learn to use the knowledge we already have, and in using it learn the other things we need to know? What do the implications of our great contemporary scientific and technical spurt forward add up to? I do not have the answers, but I should like to propose some hypotheses.

My first hypothesis is that the time will come when machines will put most people permanently out of work. What will happen to people when there is no longer work for them to do? Consider the foreman in a steel plant. He brings thirty years' experience to one of the half-dozen really crucial jobs in the mill. At the critical point in the process, it is his trained eye that tells him the molten metal is ready to pour, and it is his well-developed sense of timing and steady hand that tip the cauldron synchronously with the processes that precede and follow. For this he is well paid, and can provide for his family perhaps better than the average. For this, too, he is looked up to by his fellows. They seek him out as a friend. He has prestige at his work, status in the town, and the respect of his children. He belongs. He contributes. He is needed.

Then you move in a machine that takes his job away, and does it better. What happens to this man? What happens to his many juniors at the mill whose aspiration was to an achievement like his? One of the pervasive characteristics of our civilization has been the identification of life's meaning with life's work. The evidence is strong in the problem of the aged: how do they fight the conviction that their life is done, that the world could do very well, perhaps better, without them? Are we heading toward a time when society will be burdened with a problem of the aged beginning in most cases at age twenty, because there will no longer be work to enter upon, let alone retire from, at the age of sixty-five?

Among the suggestions for banishing this specter are two that do not impress me much. The first is essentially a cry of anguish. Stop automation! Stop making more and more complicated machines! What business have we going to the moon, or tampering with life and heredity? Life is difficult enough without going out of our way to make it more so.

All the odds are against the success of that kind of solution. The technologies of the atom bomb, the automobile, the industrial revolution, gunpowder, all provoked social dislocations accompanied by similar demands that they be stopped. But there is clearly no stopping. Aristotle said a long time ago that "man by nature desires to know." He will probe and learn all that his curiosity leads him to and his brain makes possible, until he is dead. The cry of "stop" is the fear reaction I talked about earlier. It come from those who have not yet recovered their nerve.

A second suggestion, specifically aimed at the prospect of loss of work, is that we find better ways to employ leisure. There is a whole literature growing up on this theme, and I think it should be encouraged. Other things being equal, and given my own biases, it is better to read a good book than to watch television, or to play a Beethoven quartet than listen to the Beatles. But leisure activity, no matter how uplifting and educational, is not a substitute for work. The very concept loses meaning in the absence of the correlative concept of "work." No, I do not think that is the happiest solution.

But then that may not be the problem either. My second hypothesis is that my first hypothesis is wrong. Machines might not in fact put a significant number of people out of work permanently. It might just be that machines will simply take over the kinds of work that people have done up to now, and that people will then be freed, not to become problems to themselves and to society, but to do entirely new kinds of work that have hardly been thought about seriously because there has not yet been a serious possibility that they could be done.

It is often said, for example, that as work in agriculture and industry is progressively mechanized, job opportunities in the service sector of the economy will increase and absorb released manpower. I assume that production processes will not be mechanized except as machines prove more efficient than human labor. There should then follow a significant increment in wealth, which, adequately distributed, could buy more of the services already available, from baby-sitting to education and government and from better waiters to art and religion. The structure of the work force might thus be altered significantly.

Even more exciting is the possibility that the nature of service itself might be altered. I suggest a trivial, perhaps ridiculous example. Doubled police forces and quadrupled sanitation forces could give us, for the first time, really safe and really clean cities. Put 20,000 people into the streets every day to catch the cigarette butts before they even hit the ground, and you might have a clean city.

Inherently, there is nothing ridiculous about a clean city. If the suggestion makes one smile, it is rather because such use of people, by today's standards, is ridiculously uneconomical. People are more efficiently employed to produce the goods we consume. But if machines will be doing most of that, then maybe people can be employed to produce the services, such as street-cleaning or teaching, that we would like to have more of if we could.

Consider another example. One of the genuinely new and exciting ideas of the Kennedy Administration, I think, was the Peace Corps, the idea that young Americans in large numbers could, by example, help less favored peoples to help themselves. Imagine a Peace Corps 50,000,000 strong in Africa, released by machines to pour the kind of sweat that machines will never pour. This is the kind of service that can anticipate, peacefully and constructively, the ugly danger that the have-nots of the world will resort to uncontrollable violence as the gap between their expectations and reality widens. It is also the kind of service that might provide to individuals a satisfaction and a goal to life undreamed of by today's assembly-line worker in Detroit, however fully employed. From such a perspective, the new machines and the new technologies may spell, not the end of the world, but the beginning of a new one. We might begin to see, for the first time, what God meant when he said that the meek shall inherit the earth.

There has been a long tradition that divides work into creative and intellectual for the few, and routine and mechanical for the many. There has grown up around that distinction (although we are told that that was not yet true in the time of the Greeks) a moral judgment: that the first kind of work was for superior people, the second for inferior people. There then occurred, I think, one of those curious inversions of history whereby an effect is later seen as cause. The reason the majority of people did routine and mechanical work, we were told, was that that was the only kind of work they were fit to do, because they were inferior.

It seems to me much more plausible, however, that the reason the majority of people have done routine and mechanical work is that there has been a very great deal of routine and mechanical work to do. I am not denying that some people are more gifted than other people. But it seems to me that we have not yet been motivated to inquire sufficiently into how many people of what kinds can do what, because there has up to now been so much routine and mechanical work to do that most people have necessarily been impressed into doing it.

I suggest also that it is this same imperative of a great deal of routine and mechanical work to do that has led to the ivory-tower syndrome on the part of creative, intellectual workers. I doubt that artists and scientists have typically detached themselves from the world because they liked it that way. The cry for application of knowledge, at least since Francis Bacon, and the essential need of the artist to communicate preclude that view. I suspect, rather, that there may be another reversal of cause and effect here: that the ivory tower may be symptomatic of a world by necessity too preoccupied with the routine and mechanical to generate a real demand for the product of the artist and the scholar. It is no accident that art and philosophy were the exclusive province of the freemen, not the slaves, in Greece, or that science, even in our own age, has for most of its history been indulged in by the gifted amateur who was rich in fact or by philanthropy.

And now machines will do the routine and mechanical work of the world. Very large numbers of human resources will be released and available for services to mankind beyond those required for subsistence. The need to discover the nature of this new kind of work, to plan it and to do it, just might overcome the traditional gap between the creative and the routine. The many will be challenged, as they have not been before, to rise to their maximum potentialities. The few—the scholars and the artists—may find that there is a new demand for them in the world, to muster, to shape, and to guide this new force. The two historical judgments that I have criticized as inverted, in other words, might become true from now on in: work could finally become the measure of man, and efficacy the measure of ideas.

What will be the nature of this new work? What goals will it serve? How will it be done? What talents will be needed for it? I do not know the answers to these questions, either. Each, I think, provides an opportunity for imaginative inquiry still to be done. I have undertaken only to state a hypothesis, or, more accurately, to indicate a hunch that precedes hypothesis. My hunch is that man may have finally expiated his original sin, and might now aspire to bliss. I think also that my hunch may hang together historically. Original sin was invented after, and to account for, the failure of nerve. With the recovery of nerve, we do not need the concept any more, and the advance of technology frees us from the drudgery it has imposed.

But freedom from drudgery, as I have suggested, entails a commitment to wisdom. Consider, as one example, the staggering implications for education. Education (in foot-high letters on public billboards) has become a panacean word. But education for what? For whom? What kind of education? And when? There is very little small print on the billboards to answer those questions.

The response of education to the new world of science and technology up to now has taken the form of five principal proposals or goals: 1) more education for more people, 2) educational booster shots in some form of continuing adult education, 3) increased production of scientists and engineers, 4) expanded vocational training, and 5) mid-career refresher training or retraining for a different specialty.

It is hard to quarrel with more education, or with continuing education. With respect to the other three goals, however, one can raise the question "For how long?" To be sure, we need more scientists and engineers than we have now, but we already hear warnings that the demand will level off, and it is perhaps not too early to start thinking about a massive effort in the social sciences and the humanities.

Similarly with vocational education. Training in a trade is desirable and useful. But in which trade? Certainly not in those doomed to extinction in the next ten to twenty years. The informal experience of the young people who have recently been crusading in Mississippi and Alabama might prove a much more relevant vocational education for the future that lies ahead of us.

Today's best educational judgments, in other words, might turn into tomorrow's worst mistakes, because they depend on forecasting successfully the shape of what is coming. Of course, the judgments must still be made today, despite the risk, despite the increased uncertainties of a world that changes shape rapidly and radically. This is a measure of the difficulty of the modern educator's task. Yet in this very change may lie a relative certainty, with a particular further implication for the job of education. I add a word about that.

There were two ancient Greek philosophers, long before even Socrates haunted the streets of Athens, who had diametrically opposed views about reality. There was Parmenides, who argued that all change is illusory, transitory, imperfect, unreal. And later there was Heraclitus, who saw reality as a flowing river, apparently the same but never the same, to whom all was constant flux and change, and who dismissed the permanent as unreal, as evidence of human imperfection, as a distortion of reality.

I go back to those ancient thinkers, because each gave his name to a major and persistent theme in Western intellectual history. Parmenides, the apostle of the eternal, has had his emulators in Christian theology, in romantic idealism, and in twentieth-century mathematics and logic. The followers of Heraclitus, who saw the world as flux, include the medieval nominalists, the nineteenth-century evolutionary philosophers, and today's existentialists.

Are we Parmenidians or Heracliteans? In our social attitudes, we certainly lean to Parmenides. In our concept of work, the real is the career that holds together, makes sense, and lasts a lifetime. If a man changes jobs too often, we consider him a drifter, or, if we like him, we say he has not yet found his proper work. We see the change as unnatural, unreal, unwanted, and feel much more comfortable with the permanent, the stable.

Similarly with our social institutions. Democracy, capitalism, socialism, the organized faiths—these are the real, the cherished, and any change is transitional, accidental, to be avoided, or dealt with as quickly as possible, to return to the stable, the familiar, the true.

The evidence is becoming compelling that we are going to have to change these attitudes and comfortable habits. Careers are increasingly becoming shorter-lived than people. The complexities of national existence lead to an increasing and inevitable mixing-up of the public and the private. State's rights, that honored mark of eighteenth-century federalism, has become a slogan of those who would have us return to the eighteenth century. The profit motive is being introduced into the Soviet economy, and the world's religions are beginning to talk to each other. All our familiar institutions, in other words, are changing so rapidly and so constantly that the change is becoming more familiar now than the institutions that are changing. The change is the new reality. We are entering an era that might aptly be called Social Heracliteanism.

The challenge to education is indeed staggering. Teachers who have been brought up to cherish the stable must take the children of parents who have been brought up to cherish the stable, and try to teach them that the stable, the un-changing, is unreal, constraining, a false goal, and that they will survive in an age of change to the degree that they become familiar with change, feel comfortable with it, understand it, master and control it.

When that task is done, the recovery of nerve will be complete, because our new technical mastery will have been supplemented by the wisdom necessary to harness it to human ends. John Dewey's dream will have been realized. We will be the masters of our techniques instead of their slaves, and we might just become the first civilization since 500 B.C. to be able to look the Greeks in the face with pride, instead of just with wonder. I do not like to think of the alternative, which is that the people of a century from now will say of us: "Look at the trouble and woe they had with their technology, and look what ours has done for us."

THE CONTROL
OF CYBERNATION

DONALD N. MICHAEL

Time is crucial in any plan to cope with cybernation. Ways of ameliorating its adverse effects require thinking farther ahead than we ever do. In a society in the process of becoming cybernated, education and training for work as well as education and training for leisure must begin early in life. Shifts in behavior, attitudes, and aspirations take a long time to mature. It will be extraordinarily difficult to produce appropriate "culture-bearers," both parents and teachers, in sufficient numbers, distribution, and quality in the relatively brief time available. It is hard to see, for example, how Congress, composed in good part of older men acting from traditional perspectives and operating by seniority, could recognize soon enough and then legislate well enough to produce the fundamental shifts needed to meet the complexities of cybernation. It is hard to see how our style of pragmatic making-do and frantic crash programs can radically change in the next few years. This is especially hard to visualize when the whole cybernation situation is such that we find it impossible to determine the consequences of cybernation even in the medium long run. The differences expressed in the public statements of business and labor demonstrate that any reconciliation of interests will be a very long-range effort indeed. "Drastic" actions to forestall or eliminate the ill-effects of cybernation will not be taken in time unless we change our operating style drastically.

EDUCATION: OCCUPATIONS AND ATTITUDES

Among the many factors contributing to the stability of a social system are two intimately intertwined ones: the types of tasks that are performed; and the nature of the relationship between the attitudes of the members of the society toward these tasks and their opinions about the proper goals of the individual members of the society and the right ways of reaching them.

The long-range stability of the social system depends on a population of young people properly educated to enter the adult world of tasks and attitudes. Once, the pace of change was slow enough to permit a comfortable margin of compatibility between the adult world and the one children were trained to expect. This

Reprinted by permission FROM *Cybernation: The Silent Conquest* by Donald N. Michael. Santa Barbara, Calif.: Center for the Study of Democratic Institutions, 1962, pp. 40–46.

compatibility no longer exists. Now we have to ask: What should be the education of a population more and more enveloped in cybernation? What are the appropriate attitudes toward and training for participation in government, the use of leisure, standards of consumption, particular occupations?

Education must cope with the transitional period when the disruption among different socio-economic and occupational groups will be the greatest; and the later, relatively stable period, if it ever comes to exist, when most people would have adequate income and shorter working hours. The problem involves looking ahead five, ten, twenty years to see what are likely to be the occupational and social needs and attitudes of those future periods; planning the intellectual and social education of each age group in the numbers needed; motivating young people to seek certain types of jobs and to adopt the desirable and necessary attitudes; providing enough suitable teachers; being able to alter all of these as the actualities in society and technology indicate; and directing the pattern of cybernation so that it fits with the expected kinds and distribution of abilities and attitudes produced by home and school.

To what extent education and technology can be coordinated is not at all clear, if only because we do not know, even for today's world, the criteria for judging the consonance or dissonance in our educational, attitudinal, and occupational systems. We think that parts of the social system are badly out of phase with other parts and that, as a whole, the system is progressively less capable of coping with the problems it produces. But there is little consensus on the "causes" and even less on what can be done about them. All we have at present is the hope that most people can be educated for significant participation in such a world as we have foreseen here—we have no evidence that it can be done.

If we do not find the answers to these questions soon, we will have a population in the next ten to twenty years more and more out of touch with national and international realities, ever more the victims of insecurity on the one hand and ennui on the other, and more and more mismatched to the occupational needs of the day. If we fail to find the answers, we can bumble along, very probably heading into disaster, or we can restrict the extension of cybernation, permitting it only where necessary for the national interest. But judging the national interest and distinguishing it from private interests would confront us with most of the problems that have been outlined in this paper.

Perhaps time has already run out. Even if our style somehow should shift to long-range planning, it would not eliminate the inadequate training and inadequate values of much of our present adolescent and pre-adolescent population, as well as of those adults who will be displaced or remain unhired as a result of cybernation in the next decade. Only a partial solution exists in this case: Begin now a program of economic and social first aid for these people.

A MORATORIUM ON CYBERNATION?

Can we control the effects of cybernation by making it illegal or unprofitable to develop cybernation technology? No, not without virtually stopping the development of almost all of new technology and a good part of the general development of scientific knowledge. The accumulation of knowledge in many areas of science depends on computers. To refine computers and make them more versatile requires research in almost every scientific area. It also requires the development of a technology, usually automated, to produce the articles needed to build new computers. As long as we choose to compete with other parts of the world, we shall have to develop new products and new means for producing them better. Cybernation is the only way to do it on a significant scale. As long as we choose to live in a world guided by science and its technology we have no choice but to encourage the development of cybernation. If we insist on this framework, the answers to coping with its effects must be found elsewhere than in a moratorium on its development.

CONTROL: PUBLIC OR PRIVATE?

There has always been tension between big industry, with its concern for profit and market control, and government, with its concern for the national interest. The tension has increased as big business has become so large as to be quasi-governmental in its influence and as government has had to turn to and even subsidize parts of business in order to meet parts of the national interest within a free-enterprise framework. Under these circumstances we can expect strong differences between government and business as to when and where it is socially legitimate to introduce automation.

Sufficient governmental control over who can cybernate, when, and where would not come easily. In the first place, decisions about control would have to be based on the intentions of local business and industry as well as on the national picture. For example, the effects on Congressional seating of shifts in populations as a result of cybernation-based industrial relocation would presumably enter the calculations. Longer-run consequences would have to be balanced against short-run profits or social dislocations. Implications for our military posture and for international trade would be significant. Moreover, it would be difficult for the government to make a case for control of private organizations on the basis of ambiguous estimates of the effects of automation on hiring policy. In any particular case, it becomes clear only well after the fact of cybernation whether increases or changes in production resulted in a corresponding increase in man-hours of work sufficient to compensate the economy for the jobs lost or the people unhired.

Finally, it must be kept in mind that the power of some of the largest unions is seriously threatened by automation. In a relatively short time they may not have the leverage they now have. Thus, a crucial counterbalance to the pressures from business may be absent when it is most needed. It is possible that the crisis that will arouse the government to exert control will not be evident until the blue-collar work force has been so eroded as to have weakened the unions irreparably.

Yet some sort of control is going to be necessary. There are, of course, the federal regulatory agencies. However, they have never been distinguished for applying their powers with the vigor sometimes allowed by their mandates, and there is no reason to suppose that their traditional weaknesses would suddenly disappear and that an agency created to cope with cybernation would be effective. Nor is there any reason to believe that an agency with the very wide-ranging powers that it would need would be approved before the crisis that it was supposed to avert was upon us.

In theory, control could be exercised by private enterprise. But in the unlikely case that competitors could see their mutual interests clearly enough to join forces, the very act of cooperative control would be incompatible with our anti-trust laws. Whether the government or some alter-government comprised of business, labor, and industry were to do the controlling, either group would have to undertake a degree of national planning and control thoroughly incompatible with the way in which we look upon the management of our economic and social system today.

AFTER THE TAKE-OVER

In twenty years, other things being equal, most of the routine blue-collar and white-collar tasks that can be done by cybernation will be. Our schools will probably be turning out a larger proportion of the population better educated than they are today, but most of our citizens will be unable to understand the cybernated world in which they live. Perhaps they will understand the rudiments of calculus, biology, nuclear physics, and the humanities. But the research realm of scientists, the problems of government, and the interplay between them will be beyond the ken even of our college graduates. Besides, most people will have had to recognize that, when it comes to logic, the machines by and large can think better than they, for in that time reasonably good thinking computers should be operating on a large scale.

There will be a small, almost separate, society of people in rapport with the advanced computers. These cyberneticians will have established a relationship with their machines that cannot be shared with the average man any more than the average man today can understand the problems of molecular biology, nuclear physics, or neuropsychiatry. Indeed, many scholars will not have the capacity to share their knowledge or feeling about this new man-machine relationship. Those with the talent for the work probably will have to develop it from childhood and will be trained as intensively as the classical ballerina.

Some of the remaining population will be productively engaged in human-to-human or human-to-machine activities requiring judgment and a high level of intelligence and training. But the rest, whose innate intelligence or training is not of the highest, what will they do? We can foresee a nation with a large portion of its people doing, directly or indirectly, the endless public tasks that the welfare state needs and that the government will not allow to be cybernated because of the serious unemployment that would result. These people will work short hours, with much time for the pursuit of leisure activities.

Even with a college education, what will they do all their long lives, day after day, four-day week-end after week-end, vacation after vacation, in a more and more crowded world? (There is a population explosion to face in another ten to thirty years.) What will they believe in and aspire to as they work their shorter hours and, on the outside, pursue their "self-fulfilling" activities, whatever they may be? No one has ever seriously envisioned what characteristics these activities might have in order to be able to engross most men and women most of their adult lives. What will be the relationship of these people to government, to the "upper intellectuals," to the rest of the world, to themselves?

Obviously, attitudes toward work, play, and social responsibility will have changed greatly. Somehow we shall have had to cope emotionally with the vast gap in living standards that will then typify the difference between us and the have-not nations. We shall presumably have found some way to give meaning to the consumption of mass leisure. It would seem that a life oriented to private recreation might carry with it an attitude of relative indifference to public responsibility. This indifference, plus the centralization of authority, would seem to imply a governing élite and a popular acceptance of such an élite.

If this world is to exist as a coherent society, it will have to have its own "logic," so that it will make sense to its inhabitants. Today, for most of our population, our society makes sense, even though some other eyes hardly see us as logical in the formal sense of the word and the eyes of some of our own people look on us as a more or less pointless society. We make and solve our problems chiefly by other than mathematical-logical standards, and so must the cybernated generations. What these standards might be, we do not know. But if they are inadequate, the frustration and pointlessness that they produce may well evoke, in turn, a war of desperation—ostensibly against some external enemy but, in fact, a war to make the world safe for human beings by destroying most of society's sophisticated technological base. One thing is clear: if the new "logic" is to resolve the problems raised here, it will have to generate beliefs, behavior, and goals far different from those which we have held until now and which are driving us more and more inexorably into a contradictory world run by (and for?) ever more intelligent, ever more versatile slaves.

VALUES IN THE EMERGING AMERICAN CIVILIZATION

PHILIP H. PHENIX

My task is to delineate the value system upon which our educational efforts of a decade or two hence may be built—to characterize some of the dominant

FROM *Teachers College Record*, 61:355–366 (April 1960), Teachers College, Columbia University, N. Y. Reprinted by permission.

commitments and purposes which we may reasonably expect will guide Americans of 1970 or 1980 as they seek to perpetuate and improve their civilization.

A well-nigh impossible task this is, not only because the prevailing values embrace all aspects of a culture but also because the pace of contemporary cultural transformations is so breath-taking and because the most serious unresolved conflicts of our plural civilization revolve about differences in values. Yet, speculative and tentative though the effort must necessarily be, it should be made, for values are the soul of civilization. Apart from the values by which we make our choices, things and activities are empty of meaning. In particular, since teaching and learning necessarily presuppose guiding commitments, we cannot think about the future of American education without some forecast of values in our emerging civilization.

What do we mean by the word "value"? Two distinct meanings are in common use by laymen and scholars alike. According to the first, a value is anything which a person or persons actually approve, desire, affirm, or exert themselves to obtain, preserve, or assist. According to the second meaning, a value is anything which *ought to be* approved, desired, and so forth, whether or not any given person or persons in fact do adopt these positive attitudes toward it. Values in the first sense are human preferences which can be systematically described by the regular tools of empirical inquiry such as those employed in sociology, anthropology, and psychology. Values in the second sense are not facts at all, but ideals, standards, or norms by which actual human preferences are to be appraised; they are not obtainable by empirical inquiry but by revelation, rational intuition, personal decision, or social convention usually contained in the traditions of the civilization.

What Americans actually *do* crave in 1960, or *will* desire in 1970 or 1980 obviously is and will be far different from what they *ought to want*. A popular demand for amusement and tranquillizers may make these things more valuable in the first sense than disciplined skill and sympathy for those who suffer, but in the second sense the order of preference may be just the reverse. Agreement between the desired and the desirable would be found only in a society of saints, and we cannot yet claim to have achieved that condition.

Necessary though this distinction is, I do not think we must simply choose between the two meanings of value. Instead, they must be maintained in constant reciprocal tension. Acknowledgment of desire without ethical criticism by a standard of obligation simply confirms the *status quo*. On the other hand, affirmation of ideals without regard to actual human wants or interests makes these standards irrelevant and ineffective.

The two contrasting conceptions of value are particularly evident in educational practice. Value in the sense of what people actually want underlies education emphasizing the felt needs and interests of the learner. Value in the sense of what people ought to want underlies education emphasizing discipline, standards, and tradition. I am convinced that we need not choose the one or the other, but that the educator's task is to secure continuity between the interests of the learner and standards of excellence which transcend the immediate desires of the immature. This goal can be realized only if there is a basic harmony between informed desire and the truly excellent; that is to say, only if human longings provide clues to and directions toward ideal values and if ideals are confirmed and verified in the fulfillment of enduring human wants.

The distinction between values as actual desires and as desirable goals has important bearings on the question of changes in values. Actual wants are modified along with the conditions of society and culture. Many of the things people value today, such as automobiles and the thirty-hour week, were not values for earlier generations simply because these objects of desire did not then exist as genuine possibilities. Over the next ten to twenty years our rapidly changing technical civilization is bound to introduce many new things which will be desired, thus significantly modifying the actual value system of American society.

On the other hand, normative values—ideal standards—are independent of or less dependent on particular cultural changes. According to some thinkers, there are certain "ultimate" values which are absolute and unchanging. Thus, they would say, the values we should live by and educate for will be the same in 1970 or 1980 as they are today and as they have always been from the beginning. When it comes to basic values, they believe there is no such thing as modernity and no risk in prediction, for right and truth are eternal.

I hold the view that there are certain values of wide generality and persistent relevance, but that these values require expression in the concrete and varying terms of human personality and society. Thus, the values of 1970–1980 at a profound level will be the same as those of today or of a century or a millennium ago, but they will necessarily exercise their power in human life in the new shapes of things in years to come, and to that extent will be different values.

I foresee and welcome the increasing unification of the descriptive and normative concepts of value. We are going to be increasingly dissatisfied with values which are presented either as detached eternal principles or as the shifting interests and conventions of particular cultures. The realization is going to grow that the proper ideals of civilization must find their justification in the facts of human nature. The humanly valuable is that which sustains the most complete actualizing of the potentialities resident in human nature. Thus I predict that the educationally significant values of future decades will be established increasingly on a humanistic and scientific foundation and that the old polarity of absolutism and relativism in values will disappear.

I believe that empirical investigators of man and society—social scientists and psychologists—will more and more become concerned with the ethical consequences of their inquiries; that is, with the salient facts about human nature, its potentialities, and the necessary conditions for their fulfillment which these studies reveal. I believe further that these scientific investigations will increasingly be confirmed, corrected, and supplemented by the traditionally humanistic studies, so that there will emerge at length a unified and coherent idea of man and his possibilities which will become the basis for a secure knowledge of human values. As the years pass I foresee the disappearance of the boundary between those who investigate facts—the scientists—and those who purvey ideals—the prophets, mystics, and moral philosophers. I envision, not long hence, a time when aspirations will be disciplined by a knowledge of the humanly actual and possible and when scientific inquiry will be devoted to the discovery and realization of the *summum bonum.*

What can now be said, in a tentative way, about the realistic ideals which should guide us Americans a decade or two hence? What do humanistic and scientific inquiries to date suggest as values appropriate to the era into which our civilization is now moving? Here I can only suggest in broad outline the values I see emerging, with only passing reference to the evidence for their rootage in the facts of human nature.

The basic values are human personality and its social concomitant, democracy. The emerging American civilization for which we should struggle is founded upon the twin ideals of freedom and responsibility; that is to say, of maximum personal realization within the context of social justice. Furthermore, because personality is social in its very essence, personal fulfillment and social equity are complementary aspects of one personal-social value.

PIVOTAL VALUES

These are still high abstractions. They need now to be more precisely analyzed. To this end, I suggest that human realization encompasses four pivotal values; namely, intelligence, creativity, conscience, and reverence. These are the pillars of selfhood and democracy. These are the value-foundations for American education of 1970–1980 and beyond.

INTELLIGENCE

First, then, intelligence. Human beings are of the species *homo sapiens.* It is by virtue of intelligence that man is distinguished from the lower animals. Reason is the sovereign tool by which all the achievements of culture are possible. The capacity to make, to decide, and to worship—all the other values which we shall discuss—depend upon rational insight. We must awaken to the realization that primary concern for intelligence does not mean an exclusive aristocratic intellectualism. Democracy presupposes full development of reason in all members of society. No other ideal of human organization places so high a premium on intelligence. When a so-called democracy in the uncritical pursuit of equality develops anti-intellectual mediocrity and commonplaceness, that society is on the road to degradation and ultimately to subversion by clever and unscrupulous tyrants.

We shall need to value highly the ability to think clearly and cogently, to discriminate meanings with precision, to argue validly and to detect the fallacies in invalid arguments, to know good evidence from bad, and to use sources of knowledge responsibly. Scientific methods must become widely understood and the spirit of critical inquiry must suffuse our common life. At the same time, we will come to see that not all competent thinking proceeds according to the canons of deductive logic or of experimental investigation in the natural sciences. The specific and unique methods of thought in the social and psychological sciences, in historical study, in philosophy, literature, and the other arts will be recognized and appropriately applied.

There must arise a new dedication to the ancient ideal of truth, to the fullest possible correspondence between word and fact, between symbol and act. More and more the fabric of civilization will be woven of verbal symbols, and correspondingly important will be the preservation of integrity in the employment of these instruments. Our present-day carelessness with language and our commonly practiced hypocrisy and deceit must promptly be seen in their true light as exceedingly virulent poisons to civilized existence, and a renewed respect for words and their responsible employment must speedily develop.

Of particular urgency is the establishment of the intellectual integrity of the mass media of communication. As never before in human history, time and distance have been annihilated by instruments for the transmission of symbols, and the whole life of mankind has been made available to each person, wherever or whoever he is, by these common agencies of information. The simple and settled symbolic environments of the past have been replaced by a complex and rapidly shifting envelope of sight and sound compacted of elements from far and near. For this unprecedented and surprising development our traditional patterns of judgment and control do not suffice. What has commonly been regarded as an interesting "fringe benefit" of modern technology, to be employed for the more efficient conduct of old business or for amusement, must henceforth be recognized as what it is: the most potent and most pervasive culture-forming and character-forming influence in modern society.

From this recognition will spring tomorrow's demand for a keener sense of responsibility for truth in what is published and broadcast. The concept of freedom of speech through the mass media must be re-examined to ascertain the limits beyond which freedom in this public domain becomes dangerous license and a means to the most profound·enslavement of others. At the same time, a premium must be placed on the cultivation of critical judgment in all citizens, so that they may better sift truth from falsehood and exercise selectivity in what they attend to and accept.

CREATIVITY

After intelligence, the next pivotal value is creativity. Human beings are not only thinkers and knowers but also makers. No person can achieve his full measure of manhood unless he engages in acts of creation. Such creativity is thus in essence an esthetic experience. Modern civilization, with its concern for power and sheer quantity of production, has tended to neglect the qualitative dimensions of experience. Obsession with mechanism has dulled our sensitivity to significant forms. Meaning has been sacrificed to efficiency, and life has thereby been impoverished. The feeling of depth in appreciation of delightful things has been replaced by the superficial and partial understanding necessary for technical mastery and manipulation.

These dehumanizing tendencies in contemporary culture should give way before a growing awareness of the importance of the esthetic—of beauty and elegance, of good taste and cultivated style. Especially as we move into an age in which machines will take over from human beings most of the chores which have hitherto kept us from the free choice of qualitative enjoyment, the need to recognize the importance of the creative arts in the enhancement of human life will become evident. Esthetic resources will no longer be chiefly for serious pursuit by a professional elite or for the amusement of the idle rich or of the "beats." They must be ingredients in the common life, raising it above the commonplace to new levels of immediate significance and satisfaction.

One of the features of modern American culture which most clearly betrays our present lack of concern for quality of experience is the disintegration of manners. In the name of equality, modernity, and democracy traditional patterns of social conduct have been abandoned and customary modes of showing respect and consideration have become matters of individual choice rather than of social constraint.

I forecast a revived interest in manners. We shall once again realize that customary acts of deference and traditional styles of deportment are not necessarily undemocratic, but are in fact essential to democratic culture. Manners may be hypocritical and humiliating to others or they may be sincere and exalting. An urgent task for the future of America is the formation of a code of expected behavior which will vividly express that respect for each person's dignity which is the wellspring of democratic order. Such a code will be based upon a due regard for significant functional differences. We must not commit the blunder of confusing equality of personal right and dignity with identity of social function.

This renewed emphasis on the ennobling formalities of life will provide sorely needed social symbols for the celebration of our common life. We are today ceremonially impoverished. For the future we require an array of vivid and familiar acts with which to express overtly the convictions by which we live as a people.

In quite a different way, the value of creativity will be acknowledged in a fresh assessment of the significance of work. Because man is by nature a maker, he must fulfill his being through productive labor. Because he is by nature social, he must serve others in exchange for their efforts on his behalf. In past eras of human history the attitude toward work has been at best ambiguous. For many if not most people it has been regarded, often not without justification, as a burden or a curse rather than as a creative opportunity. As we consider the future of our civilization, it is then not unnatural to expect that many will value highly the progressive emancipation from labor which advancing machine production makes possible. I believe such a simple extrapolation from the past is quite mistaken, and that values for the new age must not include escape from work but a restoration of the ideal of work as creative vocation.

Modern man is haunted by a feeling of emptiness, despite the ceaseless busyness of his existence. His days are filled with activity, he travels quickly and produces things efficiently, but he is gnawed by a sense of meaningless and futility. Why? In large part because he does not find in his daily occupation sufficient opportunity to realize significant purposes which are truly his own. He regards himself as an interchangeable part in an impersonal social mechanism.

Therefore, high on the agenda for tomorrow's Americans should be the rediscovery of authentic vocation. The next generation must be enabled to experience widely what the creative minority have always known: the joy and salvation in significant work. This will require a reduction in the value assigned to mere speed and efficiency of production. Modern concepts of narrow specialization will have to be revised in favor of broader individual grasp of the total productive process. Prevailing patterns of centralized industrial organization and hierarchical control will need to be altered to permit a higher degree of individual participation and responsibility.

Complementing the value of true vocation there should be a reconstruction of the ideal of play. The long-term purposes of work require supplementing by the immediacies of recreation. Human creativity has a rhythmic character. It does not retain its zest and freshness under the demands of unremitting work. Its fruition depends upon the periodic alternation of short- and long-range activities. Yet, properly conceived, play is not merely surcease from work. It should not be regarded simply as temporary release and relief from the burdens of the job. Its value lies in the contrast in type of creative engagement it affords.

Perhaps the onset of the do-it-yourself age gives some hint as to the quality of play we shall increasingly learn to prize. Surely the spirit of man the maker cannot long find satisfaction in cheap amusements and in watching other people play. Nor will the multiplication of manufactured gadgets for young or old answer the deeply felt need to exercise the capacity for free, imaginative experiment and construction. We are waking up to the obvious truth that the joy of play is in the playing, not in merely observing what others do or in possessing what others have made.

Creative play for the future, I submit, will be marked by simplicity—perhaps even by a touch of the ascetic. As life in so many respects necessarily becomes more complicated, we shall yearn for some experience of plainness. As the marvels of technology multiply about us, we shall long for some unprefabricated crudeness to which we can individually and personally lend form and refinement. As pain and hardship are progressively lifted from us, we shall seek in play some chance to prove our physical courage and power to endure.

Finally, play is necessary to democracy, for it is one of the clearest expressions of freedom. Men who do not know how to play are slaves, not free men. Furthermore, any form of play which is dictated by society is not truly play, because it is not free. Recreational activity in accord with the democratic ideal grows from individual choice or consent. It is a measure and mark of an open society in which the unique qualities of each person are recognized and encouraged.

CONSCIENCE

I turn now to the third great value. To intelligence and creativity we must add the value of conscience, or moral purpose. To make moral choices is fundamental to human nature. To be free is to be able to choose. Freedom is perfected as choice follows the principles required by the facts of human nature and potentiality. For convenience, let us consider some of the crucial elements in the moral conscience by reference to man's relationships first to nature, then to himself, and finally to other people in his environment.

One of the most critical re-evaluations Americans are going to be forced to make, and that not long hence, concerns our employment of natural resources. The technical revolution of modern times has put in our hands unprecedented powers of exploiting nature. Man has become the major force in geologic change. He has gained mastery of material things, tamed the wild energies of the cosmos, and turned erstwhile natural enemies into servants of his will.

At length the realization is dawning that nature's bounty has limits and that man has responsibilities for the wise administration of his natural estate. Even though the continued growth of cities will continue to take our people away from the soil and from a life which automatically breeds respect for the earth as the source of all material well-being, I am confident that a more vivid awareness of our dependence on nature is inevitable. We shall not much longer be able to take abundant material resources for granted. We shall need to deal quickly and decisively with the population explosion. The voluntary limitation of family size must be widely encouraged. Respect for individual dignity and worth dictates that procreation be regulated by due concern for the optimum balance between population and resources. Here is an issue in which the practical consequences of a belief in the basic value of human personality are vividly apparent.

Parallel to this heightened valuation of nature must be increased respect for the human organism and greater concern for its healthful functioning. We have mistakenly tended to regard the ingestion of materials into the body, whether in the solid, liquid, or vaporous state, as not morally significant. As more is learned about the consequences of overeating, drinking, and inhaling various substances, the value of choosing the wholesome and avoiding the noxious ones will become clearer. I hope and expect that in the 1970's we shall be well on our way toward an assessment of diet, alcohol consumption, tobacco use, and drug employment which will be founded upon well-tested knowledge of human physiology and psychology rather than upon the pronouncements of faddists and reformers or upon aversive reactions to moralistic zealots. Eating, drinking, and smoking are matters of moral conscience, not merely of personal taste and inclination. A high value for our civilization should be the cultivation of healthful habits and social endorsement of the same without any imputation of dreariness or intolerance on account of such advocacy.

Most of the claims of conscience involve social relationships. Perhaps the most significant of these concern sex and family life. In no domain is the formulation of an ideal by simple extrapolation of present tendencies more misleading than in the ethics of sex. Since Freud, and more recently Kinsey, the idea has become commonplace that fairly uninhibited sexual activity best meets the needs of human nature. I do not think the most searching analysis of the psychology of sex supports this evaluation. I anticipate a growing, informed conviction as to the importance and healthfulness of appropriate discipline of sexual drives. I believe attention will move away from the view of sex as a natural animal appetite which should be regularly gratified to one in which the spiritual and personalistic dimensions of sex are regarded as paramount, so that direction and control of the biological impulse become the crucial considerations.

Democracy in sexual relations will not, as some incorrectly assume, mean license and promiscuity. On the contrary, it will mean the use of sex as a way of serving and honoring another person—as the expression of self-giving devotion to one with whom a unique, enduring, and profound relationship of mutual fidelity and support has been established. Thus, the monogamous family with marriage for life will remain as a fundamental of the democratic ideal.

We shall also need to reconsider some current assumptions about the equality of the sexes. While the trend toward equality of occupational opportunity for men and women probably will not and most likely should not be reversed, a greater value should be placed on the differences between males and females. Democracy does not presuppose identity and interchangeability of persons, as in a collectivist society, but rather the orchestration of differences into a rich and harmonious social commonwealth. We need to examine much more thoroughly the ways in in which the special qualities inherent in maleness and femaleness may be employed for the enhancement of life.

We should grow in our appreciation of other differences too. Conscience does not require equality in all things, but equity in accommodating qualitative variation. Each person should have an opportunity to develop to the full his special talents. None should be constrained to conform to others, and condemned to mediocrity, on the strength of a simple (and quite undemocratic) egalitarian dogma.

Still, this affirmation of individual differences in no way negates the traditional and enduring American opposition to social classes. The classless society is an authentic part of our democratic ideal. We acknowledge differences, and we grant the technical usefulness of classifying people by such indices as age, sex, income, place of residence, and occupation. But we know, or ought to know, that such groupings are abstractions, valid only for limited statistical purposes, and that they do not represent real lines of division between actual people. Such designations as "middle income," "Southern," and "manual worker," for example, do not mark people off into separate subspecies of the species *homo sapiens*, justifying total treatment as a class, including aspects of life other than the special characteristics defining each group. We must hold high the importance of treating each person on his own merits, recognizing his unique array of characteristics, each of which puts him in a classification with others similar in that one respect. Every person is abstractly classifiable in an infinite number of ways, but no one should ever be identified concretely and personally, and dealt with totally, as a member of any class or group.

A particular vivid illustration of the ideal of classlessness is found in the principle of racial equality. In few if any other matters of social concern is moral conscience more surely guided by the empirical study of human nature than in race relations. Such study reveals with great clarity how superficial are the characteristics by which one so-called "race" is distinguished from another, how fundamentally alike we all are under the skin, and to what a major extent alleged inborn racial traits are in fact produced by alterable social conditions. While the scientific study of human nature does not automatically prove the value of human personality or the desirability of brotherly attitudes, it at least exposes the falsehoods upon which most racial prejudice rests, demonstrates the baneful social and psychological consequences of racial discrimination, shows the compatibility of non-discriminatory policies with the known facts of human inheritance and development, and helps to supply the means for eliminating the sources and effects of racial bias.

The already growing realization of racial equality in all of the major spheres of social life—economic, residential, legal, political, educational, vocational, and religious—must continue as a key imperative for the moral conscience of America.

With respect to economic values generally, I believe that material accumulation is likely to diminish as a dominant goal for many Americans. It should become apparent that wealth can be burdensome as well as satisfying and that material goods do not in themselves produce felicity. Human beings thrive not on surfeit but on modest sufficiency. Nevertheless, private ownership and control of property, within limits, must continue as a basic democratic value. The sphere of social control of property rights, through taxation and government ownership or regulation, cannot without severe damage be indefinitely extended. We need to reaffirm limited private ownership, not merely as a means of guarding individual security and insuring personal incentive but also as a visible symbol of the freedom of the human person and of his integrity and inviolability.

At the same time, and on the same principles, we shall insist upon the right to the means of healthful subsistence of persons who, because of their age or through misfortune or incapacity of any kind, are unable to earn a livelihood. We should also so organize our economic life that material rewards beyond the subsistence level are in proportion to social contribution.

Under our conditions of increasing economic complexity and interdependence we shall of necessity place increasingly high value on the ability to manage economic resources knowledgeably and equitably. We shall depend very heavily upon those who both understand the intricacies of the economic machine and are dedicated to the ideals of distributive justice. But we cannot rely upon managers or bureaucrats alone, however wise and just. The security and prosperity of our material existence rest ultimately upon the assumption by each citizen of moral responsibility to do his work with diligence and, when required, to render a scrupulously honest accounting of his financial stewardship.

Moving now from economic to political morality, it should certainly be evident that the awesome problems of our corporate life necessitate an upward revision in the importance assigned to political life and leadership. Politics must cease to be regarded as the characteristic domain of scoundrels and opportunists. The ideal of statesmanship as a high (if not the highest) calling must be reinstated. Furthermore, we must dispel the pseudo-democratic notion that all men are equally competent to govern, and abandon our perilous practice of electing to positions of high leadership commonplace men and women with whom we feel at ease but who do not inspire our profound admiration and respect. Representative government ought to mean that our elected officials represent us not as we on the average are, but as we aspire to be, and this requires calling to public service men and women of the most extraordinary ability and character.

It is one of the truly astonishing facts of modern history that American constitutional government, though devised for a newly formed, sparsely settled agricultural society, still persists in its essential features nearly two centuries later as an effective instrument for the control of our present populous industrial commonwealth. We hold now as firmly as ever to such basic American democratic principles as majority rule, minority rights, and the separation of powers. What remains is the concrete application of our political ideals under the altered conditions of the new age.

Two current problems are particularly urgent. First, in a world where decisive governmental action must sometimes be taken quickly, there may not always be time for the relatively slow deliberative processes of representative assemblies to operate. It is likely that we shall need to give higher value in the future to freedom and flexibility of executive action, still reserving to the legislative and judicial bodies—ultimately to the people as a whole—the right and duty to review, revise, and recall. Such an enhancement of executive prerogatives goes hand in hand with the aforementioned insistence on the selection of superior persons for positions of leadership.

The second problem is related to the first but opposite in emphasis. Our enormous size and power tend to create in the average citizen a sense of political impotence and hence indifference. We need to recapture in the megapolitan age the high value of individual civic responsibility that characterized the citizens when all government was done in the town meeting. This can be achieved only if we as a people resist the trend toward indefinite centralization of government in all fields and reserve to states and local communities well-defined and significant powers and responsibilities. To the same end, it will also be important to preserve the local stake in federal government through the vigorous pursuit of the honored activity of party politics.

A final aspect of social conscience is concerned with world responsibility. I need not elaborate the obvious importance of world-mindedness. National and local provincialism is becoming increasingly difficult and dangerous in our inter-dependent world. Travel abroad is just now coming within the reach of most Americans. Overseas military service, business in other countries, governmental foreign service, and student travel are combining with ordinary tourism, world news coverage, visits from citizens of other lands, and numerous intercultural exchanges to make Americans vividly conscious of other places and peoples.

This world-knowledge and these world-associations add richness to our experience but also impose heavy demands and create fresh conflicts. Our moral horizons must now embrace all peoples. We shall now have to value the security and welfare not only of our own nation but of mankind everywhere. The value assigned to national self-preservation, with its concomitant exaltation of armed might, must be exceeded by devotion to human welfare everywhere and by the untiring determination to create a family of nations living in peace and cooperation.

The preservation of world order is, in fact, the primal imperative for modern man. With the present destructive powers at the disposal of all major nations, civilization and all of its values will be destroyed unless general armed conflict can be avoided. In the event of war, none of the values previously discussed would have any practical worth, for there would exist no tolerable physical basis within which they could be realized. From this fact the fundamental value of measures which will secure reasonable global stability is readily evident.

One of the ways in which world peace is today being promoted is through the study of other cultural traditions. While I do not doubt the contemporary worth of this undertaking, I venture the somewhat unorthodox prediction that large-scale cross-cultural explorations will become less and less useful, because a world culture will emerge and at length envelop and absorb all prior cultures. At the risk of being charged with hopeless provincialism, I further predict that this world culture will be largely characterized by the scientific outlook and modern democratic ideals. This speculation rests on the conviction that science and democracy are substantially more in accord with the facts and potentialities of human nature than most nonscientific and nondemocratic cultural systems. This viewpoint suggests that the values suitable for America's future may also be in their major outlines values for the coming world civilization, and thus for all mankind. Americans should not be ashamed to have a mission in the world, provided it is performed in humility and in full obedience to the principles of critical inquiry and democratic persuasion.

REVERENCE

The last of the four fundamental values is reverence. Intelligence, creativity, and conscience are undergirded and completed by reverence. This is the office of religion, broadly conceived. By religion I mean concern with and devotion to the ultimate, which may be understood and symbolized in many ways, as in the great historical religions (and outside of them also). The ultimate refers to the sources and ends of our being, to the matters of supreme worth—of life-and-death import —and to our attitude toward experience in its depth and totality. As I see it, human nature is inescapably faced with religious questions. Reason forever drives beyond finite understanding, the human powers of creation unceasingly seek to plumb new depths of being, and conscience remains unsatisfied with its proximate forms of justice. Reverence is the perception of the inexhaustible wellsprings of truth, beauty, and goodness, and devotion to the ever fuller realization of these values.

Reverence is the saving grace and the generative power of civilization. It saves us from the arrogant presumption that we ever possess perfect knowledge, unsurpassable loveliness, or absolute righteousness. Its infinite ideal lures us ever on to the higher levels of civilized achievement. Reverence is also the final guardian of democracy, because it refutes the absolute claim of any person or group of persons. It submits every person and system to the judgment of superior and yet unrealized possibilities.

That the trend of our times is toward increased religious interest is generally agreed. How much of this is a retreat from the anxieties and stern demands of the present age into the ready-made answers of traditional faiths it is difficult to estimate. I suspect that much of the alleged religious revival of our times does not spring from reverence. Nevertheless, I do believe that modern men are groping toward reverence. They desperately want to experience a devotion to something more than their own small and pitiable lives and their own frail and fallible institutions. I believe that in the 1960's, 1970's and 1980's, as in all epochs of human history, reverence will be the consummatory human value, and that all the ideals of our civilization will find their proper ground and goal in the vision of holiness.

SCIENCE AND THE
NEW HUMANISM

HUDSON HOAGLAND

Man's unique characteristic among animals is his ability to direct and control his own evolution, and science is his most powerful tool for doing this. We are a product of two kinds of evolution, biological and cultural. We are here as a result of the same processes of natural selection that have produced all the other plants and animals. Over 2000 million years ago certain carbon compounds, among many believed to have formed spontaneously, possessed the unusual ability to utilize energy from the environment to reproduce themselves.

FROM *Science* (January 10, 1964), 143:111–114. Copyright 1964 by the American Association for the Advancement of Science. Reprinted by permission.

Examples of such reproducing molecules known today are polymers of the nucleic acids. We know that self-replicating DNA and RNA molecules comprising the genes and viruses have carried information in the form of a chemical code from one generation to the next to instruct each species how to propagate and project itself over vast stretches of time. Organic or biological evolution has operated on phenotypes by natural selection, eliminating those forms that were not adapted to conditions of their particular time and place. Thus, by a very wasteful system of elimination, we now have the rich variety of successful plants and animals, including ourselves, we see about us.

A second kind of evolution is psychosocial or cultural evolution. This is unique to man. Its history is very recent; it started roughly a million years ago with our hominid tool-making ancestors. It accelerated markedly in the last 100,000 years with the emergence of *Homo sapiens*. Our ape-like ancestors managed to make crude weapons and tools. This gave them an advantage over other animals in spite of their lack of fighting teeth, of claws or horns, of tough hide and speed of locomotion. Our ancestors became dominant through the rapid evolution of a remarkable cerebral cortex which has doubled in size in the last million years. This rapid development may have been a result of the advantages that accrued to these animals by natural selection when they applied their brains to solving problems. Success had a feedback action aiding selection for survival of the more competent individuals, who could make superior tools and weapons and communicate with each other effectively. With advancing cortical development came the use of words as symbols for ideas. Thus, man with his unique ability to speak and later to write could pass on newly acquired information from father to son and from leader to follower. In this way a new dimension of evolution was added. Agriculture was invented roughly 10,000 years ago, and city-states, 5000 years ago. The whole history of invention, including that of social institutions, is the core of this special evolution. In the last 300 years the ever-accelerating developments through science are a continuation of this psychosocial evolution, which, in terms of progress, is thousands of times faster than biological evolution resulting from genetic mutations.

MUTATIONS AND NEW IDEAS

There is a suggestive analogy between biological evolution through mutations of genes, on the one hand, and social evolution through novel ideas, on the other. For example, a creative scientist is one who has many ideas and who is free to test and develop them. Many of these he discards as worthless, but some withstand the rigor of experimental testing and may constitute valuable advances. Several writers have pointed out that new ideas—that is, new insights—are analogous to new mutations of genes.

Henry A. Murray has coined the term *idene* in relation to social evolution as an analog to *gene* in biological evolution. We know that most genetic mutations are lethal and harmful; a very few constitute the basis of biological progress by appearing at a time when the environment happens to confer an advantage on the organism possessing that mutation. There is environmental selectivity to favor not only the rare gene mutation responsible for biological progress, but also social environmental selectivity to favor new ideas contributing to social progress. Like mutant genes, an idea may be before its time—that is, the social climate may not be right for its acceptance.

Many ideas are harmful and may even be lethal to the individual and to a society, especially when they become institutionalized. Here one might mention as examples the institutions of slavery, of ritual human sacrifice, of racism, of Nazism and other rigid authoritarian political systems, including various forms of chauvinistic nationalism. Just as mutant genes may be lethal for a species and lead to its extinction, so ideas in the minds of men may produce a catastrophe such as a nuclear war, which could in time, if the arms race continues, be lethal to the human species. The nation-state is a relatively recent social invention, and its primary function has been to give security to its nationals. It became obsolete in 1945 with the advent of nuclear weapons, although few people are aware that this has happened. If its sovereignty continues to be uncontrolled by enforceable supranational law, it may, in our post-1945 environment containing nuclear weapons, produce its own destruction, along with widespread genocide.

Thus, ideas and the institutions they generate may be considered related to social evolution as genes and their phenotypes are related to biological evolution, and selective processes operate upon both. Societies are built by ideas, and, within limits, the more new ideas there are competing with each other for social acceptance, the more effective social evolution is likely to be. Freedom of individuals to express and develop many ideas is necessary for progress in social evolution, just as many mutations must be screened by natural selection for the development of an improved or a new species of plant or animal. In the case of social evolution the impact of ideas is measurable in years or at least in centuries, while in biological evolution the time scale for mutant genes to establish new forms is measurable in millions of years.

While novelty in the form of mutations and ideas is necessary, respectively, for biological and social progress, the environmentally tested genes and ideas must have stability and continuity to maintain stable species and stable societies to resist the effects of lethal genes and idenes. In other words, conservation as well as plasticity and novelty is necessary for progress. The application of the behavioral and social sciences to testing the values men live by has, I believe, marked potentialities for the advancement of cultural evolution.

THE ETHICS OF SCIENCE

Quite aside from the justification of science in terms of its contributions to technology and medicine, we hold a basic assumption that science is concerned with discovering truth, and that truth is intrinsically good. The idea that truth makes men free is an article of faith of Western culture.

Philipp Frank has pointed out that there is widespread belief that the rising contempt for tolerance and peace throughout the world is somehow related to the rising influence of scientific thought, and the declining influence of ethics, religion, and art as a guidance of human actions. He argues, however, that there is hardly a doubt that the causes of war can be traced back frequently to religious or quasi-religious political creeds and rarely, if ever, to the doctrines of science. The humanities, including religion and ethics, have been for centuries the basis of education, and the result has been, conservatively speaking, no decline in the ferocity of men.

On the other hand, the scientists have never had a chance to shape the minds of several generations. Therefore, Frank feels it would be more just to attribute the failure of our institutions to produce a peace-loving generation to the failure of ethical and religious leaders, than to construe it as a responsibility of the scientists. As a matter of fact, scientists have an interesting operational ethic of their own which, if more widely understood and developed, could, I believe, have far-reaching repercussions for the common good.

What is the nature of this ethic? Anatol Rapoport has pointed out that the ethical principles inherent in scientific practice are the conviction that there exist objective truth and rules for discovering it; moreover, that on the basis of objective truth unanimity is both possible and desirable. But this unanimity must be achieved by independent arrival at convictions, not through coercion, personal argument, or appeal to authority. He considers that this conviction represents a respectable chunk of any ethical system, and that it could well be spread more extensively. Science, like all other systems of thought, seeks answers to questions which men hold to be of importance. But, whereas in other outlooks answers are accepted that harmonize with particular world views and mythologies peculiar to different special cultural groups, science seeks answers which are reducible to everyone's experience. It thus taps the communality of human experience at its roots and is shared by all participants, irrespective of creed, color, class, or nationality.

Every system of knowledge, including scientific knowledge, rests on some system of fiction. But scientific knowledge, by definition, alone can survive the shattering of its fictions, and when they are shattered it becomes, paradoxically, more organized rather than disorganized and demoralized. Thus, nearly all of our scientific theories have changed in the last 100 years—in physics, chemistry, biology, medicine, and psychology. The fictions—that is, the hypotheses and theories—of science are not sacrosanct.

The concept of the dignity and brotherhood of man which is common to many ethical systems is a condition necessary to the pursuit of truth. Science leaves no room for the rationalization of quasi-ethical totalitarian ideologies and racial hatreds. These are maintained by coercion and by exclusion of experience and are supported by sacrosanct fictions which are shattered once scientific inquiry is turned upon them.

Another commentator on these matters is Jacob Bronowski, who shows that, contrary to popular belief, the activities of science and the people who practice it are far from ethically neutral. He points out that we can only practice science if we value the truth. When we practice science we look for new facts by grouping the facts we have into concepts and organizing hypotheses to account for them, and we judge the concepts and hypotheses by determining whether they turn out to be true in the sense of conforming to the facts and whether they lead on to the discovery of new facts. This procedure is meaningless unless we are deeply concerned with the elimination of the false. This activity presupposes that truth is an end in itself. But truth as developed by scientific activity can also become a source of social values. It can do so, however, only when a whole society, or a large part of it, accepts the assumption that no belief will survive, regardless of its attraction in terms of wishful thinking, if it conflicts with factual truth. This means the setting up of the discovering of truth as a major social end, not only for the individual but for society as a whole. No society, of course, has ever been really dedicated to this end. But there are varying degrees of such concern. In a scientifically oriented society the quest for truth is the important thing, even though we know that ultimate, final truth with a capital T is not to be found.

Bronowski considers that a society that believes that it has found ultimate, final truth—for example, in some political ideology or religion—is an authoritarian society and simply imposes its view of the truth by force if it has the power to do so. Such a society resists all change, for what is there to change for? He points out that this is in contrast to a scientifically oriented society in which progress is a result of the search for truth, since the very search itself demands that the society shall evolve.

The individual who seeks the truth must be independent and free from coercion, and the society that values the truth must safeguard his independence. In a scientifically oriented society, excellence, independence, and originality are esteemed assets and must be protected by respect for the right of dissent. Bronowski considers that the high spots in our Western civilization have been great moments of dissent—the Declaration of Independence, the writings of Milton, the sermons of John Wesley. In science the open challenges of men like Copernicus, Galileo, Newton, Darwin, and Einstein have brought fresh insights and surges of social progress in their wakes. Dissent is thus an instrument of social evolution. All scientists must be heretics and dissenters against accepted views in science if science itself is to advance. Freedom is thus essential to a scientific society, one in evolution. It is merely a nuisance to be discouraged in a static, authoritarian society.

The international society of scientists has stability, binding together Englishmen, Germans, Japanese, Indians, Americans, and Russians in unity of spirit. Bronowski asks if the foregoing considerations lend support to the myth that science is inhuman and impersonal and that the activity of science generates no values to unite those engaged in it.

We have considered the role of science in advancing psychosocial evolution and the ethical principles involved in the practice of science. Unfortunately the general "fallout" from these ethical practices for the common good, so far has not been great. Scientists often are as unwise in their human relations as anyone else, and there often is little carry-over of their pursuit of truth in the field and laboratory to everyday affairs. Many compartmentalize their thinking. Their interpersonal relations, religion, politics, and science are walled off from each other. Thus, for example, excellent scientific work is done in Communist countries by men dominated by authoritarian Marxist dogma. This work, however, must be done in fields that do not conflict with politics. But the prestige of science and the emphasis on scientific education in the Soviet Union have had, in my opinion, an eroding action on the dogmatism of communism, as it must have in time on all dogmatism. Whatever the reasons, since Stalin's death the virus of communism has become considerably attenuated in the U.S.S.R., and this is the main source of the present contention between the Soviet Union and Communist China.

MECHANISMS, FREEDOM, AND PURPOSE

Many are antagonistic to the humanistic claims of science. They regard science from a 19th-century view as materialistic and mechanistic and devoid of cultural significance. They assume that, by its nature, science precludes concepts of freedom and purpose so fundamental to our value system. Because of this widespread view of science, I would like to comment on some changes in concepts of mechanisms, purpose, and freedom that have come about in recent years.

It is true that a scientist operates under the tacit assumption that there is order underlying all phenomena that he studies. Otherwise his work would be pointless. He hopes to find the nature of this order. He also assumes that all forms of order are determined—that is to say, are caused—and his job is to discover these determinants or causes. If he is studying behavior of either animate or inanimate systems, he seeks the mechanisms of the behavior. I know of no scientist today who works outside of a deterministic framework. Thus, the student of human behavior may be interested in neurophysiological mechanisms and how they produce behavior; or he may be a psychiatrist not interested in the brain but concerned with psychological mechanisms. He wants to know what events occurred in the life of his patient, especially in his childhood, to produce his patterns of neurotic behavior, and he speaks of psychodynamic mechanisms. The social scientist is also concerned with mechanisms. He may be interested in the failure of established mechanisms to control our balance of payments, or in the effects of tariffs on international exchange, or in the mechanisms involved in currency inflation. As a historian he may be interested in the causes of the decline and fall of the Roman Empire. In this broad sense science is primarily concerned with understanding mechanisms.

Ideas about the nature of purpose and of mechanism have changed from those of the 19th century. The principle of negative feedback, whereby energy or information (and I use them here interchangeably) released from part of a system returns to regulate and control further release of energy or information by the system, is the basic principle involved in cybernetic mechanisms. Examples of these mechanisms are automatic engine governors, the thermostat that regulates the heating of one's house, the guided missile that bounces its own radar waves back from the target and uses this feedback to regulate its steering and the power to make it home on its target. Computers involve a remarkable complex of feed-back processes, including the utilization of information storage and its appropriate retrieval, which corresponds to memory and recall in man. Purpose can be defined operationally in terms of mechanisms controlled by negative feedback. Purpose so defined is built into the guided missile, the computer, and the thermostat, enabling these mechanisms to accomplish ends of various degrees of complexity. Problem-solving computers can play a good game of chess, translate one language into another, and increase their capacity to discriminate as a result of past experience—that is, computers can learn. Objection may well be raised to calling such mechanisms purposive, since their purpose has been built into them by man. But man himself and his behavior are an emergent product of purely fortuitous mutations and evolution by natural selection acting upon them. Nonpurposive natural selection has produced purposive human behavior, which in turn has produced purposive behavior of the computers.

While feedback devices of control have developed rapidly in engineering in the past 20 years as a product of social evolution, biological evolution by natural selection brought these mechanisms to a high order of perfection some hundreds of millions of years ago, and the engineers have been copying, in principle, some of these processes. Cybernetic mechanisms are dominant ones of nerve nets and central nerve ganglia or brains.

All coordinated behavior, conscious or unconscious, uses such mechanisms; without them organized purposive behavior would be impossible. By definition these mechanisms controlled by their own feedback are purposive mechanisms. Thus, the behavior of the organism as a whole in adjusting to its external environment is controlled by information fed back to it in response to its own behavior. In the case of ourselves, words are spoken and acts are performed that produce responses from our environment, and from our fellows as part of the environment. Acts that they then perform in response to ours serve to further modify our behavior. Feedback to the organism of information from its external environment determines learning and conditioning by way of rewards and punishments, as reinforcing and aversive conditions.

To some students of behavior, free will is an epiphenomenon—an illusion—since all behavior may be regarded as the resultant of our phylogenetic development and the individual's day-to-day experiences. However, the fact is that we can never hope to know in detail the meaning to an individual of his plethora of past experiences, nor can we know the details of his genetic makeup and its impact on his brain function; for all practical purposes much of his behavior must remain relatively undetermined, both to himself and to others. Thus, man may be considered to have free will.

While matter and energy have become conceptually fused and the old materialism based upon naive concepts of physics is no longer tenable, the question of whether or not one has freedom to choose is not resolved by anything inherent in the newer physics. Heisenberg's principle of indeterminacy, which has been used by some as an escape from the deterministic dilemma, is not a valid way out. In my opinion arguments about physical indeterminacy have not contributed to a resolution of this problem. However, the concept of logical indeterminancy, recently called to my attention by a paper of Donald M. Mackay's, may possibly offer an escape from the ancient dilemma. The concept may be illustrated as follows. Let us assume that I am an omnipotent physiologist with a complete knowledge of the physiology, chemistry, and molecular activities of your brain at any given moment. With this knowledge I can then predict precisely what you will do as a result of the operation of your brain's mechanisms, since your behavior, including your conscious and verbal behavior, is completely correlated with your neural functioning. But this only applies if I do not tell you my prediction. Suppose that I tell you what you will do as a result of my complete knowledge of the state of your brain. In doing this I shall have changed the physiology of your brain by furnishing it with this information. This makes it possible for you then to behave in a way quite different from my prediction. This independence from prediction is precisely what most people mean by free choice. If I were to try to allow before-hand for the effects of telling you my prediction, I would be doomed to an endless regression—logically, as Mackay points out, chasing my own tail in an effort to allow for the effects of allowing for the effects of allowing for the effects, indefinitely.

CONCLUSION

In all human relations, accountability is a necessity. Empirically I cannot see how a modern society emancipated from magic, superstition, and animism can function unless the individuals believe that they are free and responsible for their actions, and unless society can hold them responsible. Certainly our deepest convictions tell us we are free to make choices. The creation and advancement of civilizations appear to require this assumption.

Our highly developed ability to think and relate past and future events, to make tools, and to speak and write, has made us the dominant animal, but, unlike animals well-armed by biological evolution and equipped with instincts to control their lethal fangs, claws, horns, and tusks, our only control of our aggressions in the nuclear age is our ability to think intelligently, to foresee the consequences of our acts, and to control our acts in terms of reason and our ethical principles. Ethical thinking is hard to change, but history teaches us that it does change. There are a number of human institutions and practices that have been abolished that were supported in the past by the thoughts and ethics of the very best men of their times. These include slavery, infanticide, burning of witches, gladiatorial circuses, and human religious sacrifices. War must also be abolished in this nuclear age or it will abolish us.

Man has not used science to any significant extent to test and direct his value systems for the common good. Our beliefs, for the most part, are based on myths and parochial traditions we learned hit-or-miss from parents and other prestigious persons before we were 7 years old. As Brock Chisholm has pointed out, these emotionally charged beliefs and value systems are the results of accidents of birth in time, place, race, class, and nation. Intense and often irrational group loyalties leave no room in conscience for considerations of the great human problems of our time. Racial discrimination, chauvinistic nationalism, and objection to population control by methods of contraception represent value systems based on archaic and parochial notions at variance with what science has learned about the nature of human conduct necessary to advance cultural evolution in the nuclear age.

As George Gaylord Simpson has pointed out, biological evolution is not in itself a moral process. The word *moral* is simply irrelevant in this connection. But evolution has produced a moral and ethical animal. Man is not the "darling of the gods," as he thought he was before Darwin. He is responsible to himself and for himself, and he is unique among animals in being able to direct and control his own evolution.

PART II

THE SCHOOL

Pressures and Responses

If ever there were a time for the school to perform a vital, dynamic role in society, the time is now. It is the one social institution, outside the family, that comes into any significant relationship with practically the entire population, and its effect for good or ill is found not only in the present generation, but in succeeding ones. The school is under tremendous pressures from an ever-changing society to become a more meaningful influence in the lives of today's youth. World events force the school to ask what kind of knowledge, understanding, and awareness it can develop of the newly emerging nations; of the growing imbalance among the developed and underdeveloped nations; of the problems centered around the world's exploding population, a problem unique in its dimension in the history of mankind; of the sophistication and phenomenal growth of man's knowledge; of the revolutionary technology that has spurred man's never-ending exploration from the depths of the oceans to the infinite reaches of space; and of the problems of nuclear energy, which can bring on a new era in man's control of his environment, or his destruction.

What kind of knowledge and understanding can the school hope to develop in those it is charged to induct into the highly complex technological society that the United States represents today? What understanding and guidance can it bring of the anticipated upheavals in the work force brought about by the increasingly widespread use of the techniques of cybernation, of the continued expansion of huge corporations and centralized Federal Government, of the vital health problems arising from the wholesale pollution of the air and water and the wasteful destruction of plant and animal life? Can the school help youth to understand the nature of the

59

urban trends toward megalopolis (by 1980, it is estimated, 75 per cent of the population of the United States will be living in great population centers, and unless care is taken, the present huge areas of urban blight and the growth of the ghettoes will be expanded and accelerated)? Or to understand that many of these problems transcend the presently organized units of government at the state and local levels and must be attacked by long-range regional planning on a scale not yet envisioned. Can the school, then, prepare youth, who as adults must be flexible enough to deal effectively with the problems of continuing change that they must face as part of their everyday lives?

Pressured by the problems of society, only a few of which have been mentioned, and by the problems of youth growing up in that society, to be identified in Part Three, the schools are caught in a classic struggle to free themselves from the inertia of the past and to strike boldly for a more dynamic conception of their role in society. To complicate an already difficult situation, the schools are faced with counteracting demands and dualistic conflicts inside and outside their ranks. At a time of increased demand for extension of the system of mass education there is also a renewed emphasis on more individual instruction; a demand for more discipline as well as emphasis on greater freedom; a demand for earlier specialization as well as emphasis on general education; a demand for conformity and uniformity as well as growing stress on creativity, individuality, and diversity; a demand for more effective vocational preparation as well as emphasis on a liberal arts background; a demand for greater emphasis on mathematics and science as well as an insistence on a balanced curriculum.

Such concerns give at least an indication of the demands and pressures which, even though admittedly unrealistic, are forced upon the school. Realistically viewed, no one social institution can possibly cope with all these myriad changes and pressures, but, just as realistically, an alternative cannot be found in inaction or apathy. What are the chances that the schools of today will respond in a positive manner to the bold thinking and bold planning that seems to be called for? If we are to gauge our response from a look at the historical development of the school in our society, the answer would not be at all reassuring.

It seems as though the school has always been haunted by the question, "Where do we go from here?" a question asked more often with a note of despair than of hope. In its past history, the school has shared with other social institutions a resistance to change, yet it is the one social agency whose basic purpose has been to effect change in the lives of those who come under its direction. Either by its resistance to change or by the ignoring of it, the school seldom really solved or resolved its problems. When changes were made, they were additive by nature—the schools retained everything they were presently engaged in and added a few new ideas, usually in the form of new courses. Admittedly this was the safest way to proceed; it pleased everybody, but stimulated nobody. In this manner the schools subdued real forms of controversy and disputes that may have enlivened or enriched their active role in society.

There were, of course, the Horace Manns, the Henry Barnards, the John Deweys, who formulated, each in his own way, visions of the school that were bold and dynamic, and stirred, at least for the moment, fundamental questions about the nature of the school in society. Instead of using the discussions that ensued for the dissemination of new knowledge or for the examination of new alternatives, however, proponents and adversaries all too quickly adopted clichés and stereotyped versions of the original ideas. In the case of Dewey, for instance, the ideas were soon translated into catch phrases such as "learning by doing," "teach the child not subject matter," with his challenge to education being interpreted as a clash between "progressivism" and "traditionalism." The real question, as Dewey pointed out, was "of what anything whatever must be to be worthy of the name *education.*"[1]

If the schools are to achieve positive direction and play a significant role in society today and tomorrow, they must begin again with the challenge Dewey issued—what is it that is worthy of the name *education.* This is no rigid standard that he proposed, but one that is flexible enough to meet changing conditions and situations. His ideas regarding the worthiness of education may or may not be the ones that hold greatest relevance today. That search, though increasingly difficult, must go on in every age. The schools are challenged today to prepare students for an unknown future, yet even in a future that is not known, it is still possible to sense likely developments, to anticipate, to plan, to look for alternatives, and to continue an intelligent discussion of conflicting views. Since no one "right" answer is possible, it holds that those who have responsibility for the schools should refrain from actions based on narrow assumptions, or from using crises for expedient changes.

The next twenty to thirty years in education will be filled with critical needs that must be met. Decisions regarding what must be done will be radical ones affecting all facets of the school—curriculum, organization, instruction, school design, and so on—and even the conception of formal education itself. There is every indication that all education in schools and colleges will be so different in degree as to have a profound difference in kind. Such challenges will demand the intellectual endeavors of scholars in every field.

[1] John Dewey, *Experience and Education* (New York: The Macmillan Company, 1937), p. 90.

In contemplating the current controversies in education, one must look backward into the past for a vantage point from which to see old problems and conflicts in new perspective, to look to the present to define clearly today's issues and how they relate to previous conflicts, and to look forward to the future to anticipate newly emerging issues and how they will affect and be affected by current problems.

The selected articles in Part Two present conflicting views concerning the schools' responses to the pressures from within the profession and those from the larger society. Not every view is represented; it could not be. An important element in the selection was the choice of those views that are not widely held or those that have not gained wide circulation, to be used as a stimulus to provoke lively discussion.

The first three articles although dealing with different levels of education —secondary, elementary, nursery—have a common point of reference. Each author cautions against the uncritical acceptance of current innovations in the curriculum. Lack of thorough discussion in which conflicting opinions could be aired and examined has caused either a glossing over of the weaknesses that threaten the continued development of the new program or has permitted labels and clichés to hide the fact that no significant changes have taken place.

Theodore Sizer, Dean of the Harvard Graduate School of Education, examines the "classroom revolution" in the secondary schools based on the structure-of-the-discipline approach popularized by Jerome Bruner in *The Process of Education*.[2] A different approach, whose basic premise is opposed to the underlying assumption on which the Sizer article is based, is that of the nongraded school. Here the beginning question is not "Is the child ready for school?" but "What is the child ready for?" John Goodlad relates his experiences in freeing children from the grade-level box at the University of California's Elementary School. He attacks the graded system so prevalent in American education for its conformity to predetermined standards, yet he is objective enough in his appraisal to recognize that the nongraded school may be only one step in a desirable direction. The third idea to gain uncritical acceptance is in some respects an anachronism. Dr. Maria Montessori's nursery school concept of freedom within a controlled environment, popular forty years ago in the United States and even earlier in Italy, is currently enjoying a revival here. Ignoring newer psychological research in child growth and development, her enthusiasts maintain that hers is not only the best method, but the only way to educate preschool children.

Since education is an integral, indispensable part of the scientific enterprise, Professor Jacobson of Teachers College, Columbia University, argues

[2] Jerome Bruner, *The Process of Education* (Cambridge, Mass.: Harvard University Press, 1960).

for greater support for an effective program of science both for future scientists, who are needed to maintain the profession, and for laymen, who need a clearer understanding of modern science and from whom support for scientific endeavors must be obtained. The plea for balance in the high school by Professor Klausmeier, University of Wisconsin, is for more attention to the vocational and nonverbal aspects of the curriculum. He is reacting against the preoccupation with cognitive learning in the schools, which, by itself, provides different kinds of students little opportunity to explore their own reality. Professor Klausmeier's position needs to be contrasted with the Sizer article, which begins this section, and the Tyler essay, which follows. Much has been written about the "knowledge explosion," although curriculum experts disagree over the extent of its application to secondary education. The crucial problem the explosion presents is that of intelligent selection. Since everything obviously cannot be taught, what criteria should be used for intelligent selection? Dr. Ralph Tyler discusses these questions and others.

The junior high school entered the organizational structure of American education in 1910 to meet the psychological, social, and intellectual needs of the age group that became known as early adolescents. This school, varying from two to three years, was intended to bridge the gap between the earlier elementary school and the high school. Research in growth and development since that time has revealed that early adolescence for many begins earlier than was previously thought. This knowledge is the basic rationale for a new type of school organization, known as the *middle school*, which embraces the grade levels from five through eight. Conflicting opinions on the middle school are presented by Professors Alexander and Williams.

The area of the high school curriculum to come under close scrutiny most recently is vocational education. Since the Smith-Hughes Act of 1916, vocational education has been strictly regulated, a control that many educators currently feel hampers the development of new approaches for changing manpower needs. They feel that vocational education has been too narrowly conceived and has been restricted to the segment of youth who often do poorly in academic work. The Educational Policies Commission has pointed out that "concern with career need not be illiberal or narrow . . . [and] liberal education need not be antivocational."[3] Fred T. Wilhelms' article reflects this new criticism of vocational education by those who basically support its inclusion in the curriculum. Robert Hutchins' point of view clashes both with that of the Educational Policies Commission and with Wilhelms. The article by Klausmeier previously referred to stresses the psychological value of vocational education.

[3] *Manpower and Education* (Washington, D. C.: Educational Policies Commission (NEA), 1956), p. 68.

The issues surrounding academic freedom have been of continuing concern in the historical development of American education, and constant vigilance seems necessary to protect its exercise in the classroom. Four of the articles included explore some of its many dimensions from differing perspectives. Walter Lippmann, distinguished American journalist, examines the idea of freedom as it relates to the press, but his comments have a much wider application for society at large as well as for education. Mr. Lippmann's remarks were originally made to the International Press Institute's Conference in London. Mrs. Olson, Director of Publications and Public Relations for the National Conference of Teachers of English, agrees essentially with Lippmann in the belief that the fabric of freedom is seamless. Her specific concern is with censorship in the schools, which she vigorously attacks as dangerous, primarily because it easily becomes a habit of mind that jeopardizes the democratic community. Richard Hart sees the issue of freedom in the schools posed by the question, "Is it really possible to be neutral in our schools?" He examines the question using educational decisions that the schools must make in everyday concerns. In the final article dealing with academic freedom, William Griffen supports the view that frank discussions concerning life's values should be more frequent in the school, even when the views expressed conflict with community opinion.

Perhaps no other term is used by the schools more frequently, and understood less, than that of "creativity." The schools are not wholly at fault. Countless books, articles, and research studies have presented a welter of conflicting ideas, opinions, and claims regarding the nature of creativity and the distinguishing characteristics of the creative child or youth. It would be impossible to present in this section even a fair sampling of the controversy that is aroused by the use of the term. The editor feels that the article by Dr. Richard Mueller of Northern Illinois University can serve as a good springboard for further study of a vitally important, if misunderstood, goal in the learning process. The study could begin with the Summer 1965 issue of *Daedalus* listed in the selected references. It is not too great an assumption to make that a large measure of creativity is stifled in the school by the many forms of competition exhibited, each fraught with anxiety, dissatisfaction, and segregation. "There is no opportunity to call a moratorium on the struggle in order to enjoy learning and follow the dictates of curiosity," states Professor Carl Weinberg of the University of California in his provocative paper assessing "The Price of Competition." Challenging the rule of the competitive principle, Weinberg joins the ranks of those who see cognitive mastery as a means of personal liberation, a mastery that each student attains not by the imposition of external standards, but by internal criteria. Since mass media in the United States are commercial enterprises, too many educators at all levels dismiss them as not being worthy of serious thought and attention. Yet their students look, listen, and read, and are being educated, for good or ill, by the mass media. Charles S. Steinberg believes that the "mass media can serve as sources of emancipation and liberation from both extremism and ignorance." The reader may feel that his statement is extreme, but should be stimulated to examine more carefully the desirable potential of these powerful instruments.

QUESTIONS FOR DISCUSSION AND FURTHER STUDY

1. A crucial problem identified in the introduction is the selection of content to be included in the curriculum. Before any intelligent selection can be made, however, reliable criteria must be established to guide that selection. What intelligent criteria can be set up for the selection of content in the elementary school? for French, mathematics, social studies, English, and so on, in the secondary school?

2. Increasingly critical attention is being directed at vocational education programs. College students, most of whom have had little familiarity with this phase of secondary education because they are the products of college preparatory programs, should seek opportunities to become more informed and concerned about what is taking place. Observations in vocational education programs; talking with those enrolled about their problems, ambitions, and goals; and some of the selected references will develop a greater understanding. What is vocational education? What is liberal education? Are these terms mutually exclusive? What new meaning would be gained by substituting the word *career* for *vocational*? Do these labels help develop a clear understanding of the essential nature of *education*?

3. At a recent educational conference a speaker stated that elementary school children of today were being educated for a world that would be obsolescent by the time they were forty years old, just at the time when they would be taking leadership in society. That statement raises sobering questions about the kind of education they should receive. How would the various authors writing about curriculum change in this section react to this statement? Which of their proposals would seem to prepare students to meet their responsibilities in A.D. 2000 realistically?

4. Which of the issues discussed in this section did you find most important? Which authors stimulated the greatest number of new questions, ideas, thoughts? What suggestions can you offer for the inclusion of additional issues?

SELECTED REFERENCES

Aschner, Mary Jane, and Charles Bish (eds.). *Productive Thinking in Education.* Washington, D. C.: National Education Association, 1965.

Bellack, Arno A. "What Knowledge Is the Most Worth?" *High School Journal* (February 1965), pp. 318–332.

Bossing, Nelson L., and Roscoe V. Cramer. *The Junior High School*. Boston: Houghton Mifflin Company, 1965.

Brown, B. Frank. *The Nongraded High School*. Englewood Cliffs, N. J.: Prentice-Hall, Inc., 1963.

Chase, Edward T. "Learning to Be Unemployable," *Harper's* (April 1963), pp. 33–40.

"Creativity and Learning," *Daedalus* (Summer 1965).

de Grazia, Alfred, and David A. Sohn (eds.). *Programs, Teachers, and Machines*. New York: Bantam Books, 1964.

———. *Revolution in Teaching: New Theory, Technology, and Curricula*. New York: Bantam Books, 1964.

Ford, G. W., and Lawrence Pugno. *The Structure of Knowledge and the Curriculum*. Chicago: Rand McNally, 1964.

Glatthorn, Allan A., and Carl J. Manone. "The 9–10 School: A Novelty or a Better Answer?" *Educational Leadership* (January 1966), pp. 285–289.

Kerber, August, and Barbara Bommarito (eds.). *The Schools and the Urban Crisis*. New York: Holt, Rinehart, and Winston, 1965.

Kimball, Solon T., and James E. McClellan, Jr. *Education in the New America*. New York: Random House, 1962.

Klopf, Gordon J., and Israel A. Laster (eds.). *Integrating the Urban School*. New York: Bureau of Publications, Teachers College, Columbia University, 1963.

Kohler, Mary Conway, and André Fontaine. "We Waste a Million Kids a Year," *Saturday Evening Post* (March 10, 1962), pp. 15–22; (March 17, 1962), pp. 50–54, 68; (March 24, 1962), pp. 58, 61–62.

Loretan, Joseph O. "The Decline and Fall of Intelligence Testing," *Teachers College Record* (October 1965), pp. 10–17.

McMurrin, Sterling M. "Academic Freedom in the Schools," *Teachers College Record* (May 1964), pp. 658–663.

McNeal, Archie L. "Intellectual Freedom and Censorship," *Teachers College Record* (April 1965), pp. 574–578.

National Society for the Study of Education. *Individualizing Instruction*. 61st Yearbook, Part I. Chicago: University of Chicago Press, 1962.

———. *The Impact and Improvement of School Testing Programs*. 62nd Yearbook, Part II. Chicago: University of Chicago Press, 1963.

———. *Vocational Education*. 64th Yearbook, Part I. Chicago: University of Chicago Press, 1965.

Portnoy, Julius. "Creators, Censors, Censorship," *Teachers College Record* (April 1965), pp. 579–587.

Resnick, Lauren B. "Programmed Instruction and the Teaching of Complex Intellectual Skills: Problems and Prospects," *Harvard Educational Review* (Fall 1963), pp. 439–471.

Reisman, David. *Constraint and Variety in American Education.* Lincoln: University of Nebraska Press, 1956.

Rieber, Alfred. "Teaching About Communism in the U.S. High Schools," *Teachers College Record* (April 1964), pp. 603–608.

Shaplin, Judson T., and Henry F. Olds, Jr. (eds.). *Team Teaching.* New York: Harper and Row, 1964.

Sharp, Evelyn. "Progress Report on the Mathematics Revolution," *Saturday Review* (March 20, 1965), pp. 62–63, 74–75.

Smith Robert. "Educating Youth in a Revolutionary Society," *Educational Leadership* (January 1966), pp. 279–284.

"Symposium: Technology's Challenge to Education," *Saturday Review* (December 12, 1964), pp. 21–25, 77–79.

Tanner, Daniel. *Schools for Youth: Change and Challenge in Secondary Education.* New York: The Macmillan Company, 1965.

Weingartner, Charles. "English for What?" *Teachers College Record* (December 1965), pp. 201–206.

Westby-Gibson, Dorothy. *Social Perspectives on Education: The Society, the Student, the School.* New York: John Wiley and Sons, 1965.

Williams, Lloyd P. "The Struggle for Balance—Vocational Education in the Western World," *Phi Delta Kappan* (April 1965), pp. 335–359.

Wolfbein, Seymour L. "Automation, Education, and Individual Liberty," *Teachers College Record* (October 1964), pp. 27–32.

CLASSROOM REVOLUTION
Reform Movement or Panacea?

THEODORE R. SIZER

The current effort to reform the curricula of the schools is the most exciting sector of activity in the educational world. Unfortunately, however—and perhaps inevitably—curriculum development now runs the risk of becoming a panacea. The approaches used by the first innovators are being accepted by the unwary as gospel. Because this is unworthy of the movement, it behooves us to stand back and look at what we are doing to try to see what yet needs to be done.

The reforms, which started with the work of the Physical Science Study Committee in the 1950s and now includes a vast array of projects in all parts of the country, made the educational community look carefully at what children are taught and ask why they were taught as they were. The new curricula raised standards by requiring students to master more material in a shorter period of time. It raised the expectations for high school students and its success is now seen in raising standards in undergraduate colleges.

The movement also brought with it a revival of concern for educational method. To some—who have assumed that traditional educationists were excessively concerned with "methods of teaching"—this may come as a surprise. But the fact is that educational "method," in the sense that John Dewey meant it, has, in the past, been poorly developed. The assumption that a subject—for example, physics—had an inherent logic of its own that could be developed by the students themselves represented a major step in educational thinking. The reform movement has thus carried forward the very thing that Dewey suggested fully fifty years ago in his book *Democracy and Education*—a sad commentary on the rate of educational change.

The movement also brought back into the school world the "academic" professors who had been largely apart from it since the turn of the century. While this did little to narrow the chasm between schools of education and schools of arts and sciences, it clearly reduced the distance between school teachers and academic professors—a thoroughly worthwhile development. Finally, by creating

FROM the *Saturday Review*, XLVIII, 25 (June 19, 1965), pp. 52–54, 72. Reprinted by permission.

curricula systematically aimed at a national market, the reformers tried for the first time to improve American school standards as a whole.

These are some of the contributions of the curriculum reformers, and major ones they are indeed. But with them have come difficulties. Some of these difficulties stem from the limitations of the approaches used so far, while others seem to have resulted from factors that were overlooked or given low priority.

The major weakness of the reform movement today is its tacit acceptance of the way the schools are presently organized. Virtually all of the curriculum reformers —the Physical Science Study Committee, the School Mathematics Study Group, and the rest—have assumed that their subjects will be taught for a certain number of hours per week in classes of a certain size; that there will be little interrelationship between subjects; that each class will be taught mainly by a single teacher; and that this teacher should be made as much like other teachers of the same subject as possible. These are serious considerations, and it is unfair to say that the reform leaders were unaware of them. For understandable practical reasons many reformers preferred to overlook them and to concentrate first on the reform of the curriculum itself. Unfortunately, however, the next step has not yet followed. The limited approaches adopted at the beginning are accepted by many as the only or the best approaches. As a result, the ferment so badly needed to reorganize the conduct of instruction is missing. In this respect, we still are where we were in the middle Fifties, and it will take a new effort to break the grip of the *status quo*. Good though they be, if the new curricula come subject by subject into the schools the fragmentation of the curriculum as a whole remains. Thus the movement forward is hindered by the limited objectives of the particular subjects involved.

We need to look at the curriculum as a whole as well as subject by subject, and we must do both simultaneously. The strategy for a broad-gauged attack must necessarily be more complex than that for dealing with individual subjects. Just as the reformers started by looking at the inherent logic of each subject and at the ends for which the student studied it, so we must look at the underlying rationale for formal schooling and the particular ends for which a particular school is preparing. We must have the same kind of rigorous discussion among scholars over these issues as the early subject revisions had. We must involve a wide range of subjects and academic disciplines: sociology and psychology as they bear on the process of learning and the interaction of students and teachers; the wide range of academic subjects to be taught in the schools, each forced to look not only within itself, but also for its points of contact and overlap with related subjects; school administration and political science as they deal with both the past and present realities of American schools and with the means of consent for reforms.

Let me suggest some ideas presently being considered by a group of my colleagues at Harvard and elsewhere. A group of scholars and educationists should begin with the rigorous intellectual discussion that must precede a radical rearrangement of the school since a wide variety of models must be developed for schools in different kinds of neighborhoods. As an example, let us begin with an urban comprehensive high school as a prototype of one most in need of serious revision. After identifying a series of explicit goals, means for reaching these goals would be laid out, starting not with traditional academic disciplines but rather with a careful discussion of the kinds of behaviors that seem desirable for children to develop. As these behaviors appear to pattern out, careful discussion of ways and means of teaching them might be developed subject by subject. Which subjects should be taught, and at what levels? How should they be presented? What should the sequence be? How should they be interrelated? How often should children be taught in groups, and how often should they work on their own? When is a subject taught better in blocks of fifty minutes five times a week, and when in blocks of three hours once a week? What is the most efficient way of organizing teachers to meet the ends identified and how can we make it possible for teachers to plan together for instruction? What kind of informal curricula should be developed, with the ends of the school identified as they are? How might a school clearly be related to surrounding institutions, local libraries, museums, as well as employers and colleges? How can the school best adapt to the kinds of social patterns within the community in which it sits?

While the answers to these questions will vary sharply from school to school, identification of the necessary kinds of questions has important general value for all schools. In my judgment, many schools are inadequate not because the answers that educationists have developed for them are poor, but rather because educationists have not known which questions to ask. We have concerned ourselves too much with the less important issues, and we have neglected some of the major considerations. An intensive study of these questions by a diverse group could create a model list that could be used as a point of departure for many schools.

The next step would be for this group to take over a portion of an appropriate school, and to carry forward in a modest way a series of experiments to test the hypotheses that have been developed. Rather than taking a large group of children and garnering a small portion of their time for experiment, this group would rather take a small group of children and assume complete responsibility for their entire instruction. Complete freedom would be needed to carry forward the work, and evaluative arrangements established as early as possible. Quite clearly "research" would be impossible at this stage, and a period of seat-of-the-pants development would be needed before any kind of respectable testing might evolve. Further, as in so many aspects of schooling, tight research may never really be possible considering the state of our knowledge of human learning. Nonetheless, an attempt at evaluation should go forward.

As patterns evolve, the experiment could be widened to include a larger portion of the school under study, and—equally important—parts of schools that enroll different kinds of children and teachers. Comparison of urban, rural, and suburban schools, for example, might productively shed light on all three. The differences, as well as the similarities, among them might be clarified. As a varied group of schools developed into successful prototypes, a systematic effort at spreading ideas that appeared to work should be developed, using the schools themselves as examples. For instance, teachers might be trained within these schools, and institutes could be organized for experienced teachers and administrators who could be brought in for short periods of time. This kind of demonstration is more likely to be effective than any amount of printed reports alone. The kind of issue about which we are concerned here is difficult to record on paper. This is not to deny the value of efforts to report and to recount the kind of developments and questions asked for general use. It is just that such written reporting is only a partial solution.

The curriculum development movement, then, in its attempts to improve the schools subject by subject has performed a useful service. The time has come now for such inquiry to go forward on a broad front. Scholars in the various subjects should cooperate so that children are not faced with a collection of largely unrelated subjects taught in the inefficient manner of the present. Rather they should be given a closely related pattern of well-taught and, when appropriate, sequential materials which, taken together, make up a significant whole. We must recognize these larger issues, or the anarchic pattern in which we seem to be struck will persist.

A second problem raised by the curriculum development movement is that of the teacher's autonomy. The "packaged curriculum" often gives the individual teacher little room to maneuver; indeed, the package may be designed so that it is as nearly as possible "teacher proof." Such a plan, given the degree of training and efficiency of many teachers today, may be deliberate and desirable. But as the curriculum becomes increasingly inflexible, so too does the frustration of the ablest teachers, the ones whom we most want in the schools. What to do?

Most important, there should be a concerted effort to develop a wide variety of curriculum materials from which teachers might select. There must be as many patterns as are economically and intellectually feasible, and teacher training institutions should emphasize training the most able teachers fully to know about these various options and to deal with them. The crucial man in the secondary school—and, if specialization in the best sense extends to elementary schools, there as well—is the department chairman, and teacher training institutions must look much more carefully than heretofore at his training and his role. Ironically, the autonomy of the individual teacher is best protected by developing a corps of first-rate senior school men who as leaders can both tie the hands of the inept and free the bonds of the master. The principal himself should be a man of this order, and he should be freed from the kind of bureaucratic restraints that so many school administrators seem to suffer. The best chance to move education forward is to strengthen the top leadership of individual schools, and by the same token the autonomy necessary to hold a superior person in the classroom is best developed by such a corps. For those concerned with curriculum development, the message here is clear. We must conscientiously develop a diversity of curricula and try to create diversity within each single curriculum as well, thus creating options from which a group of concerned teachers under well-trained leaders can select. We must not let the improved curricula (which include the restraints that improvement appears often to require) drive out of the classrooms the very teachers we need. Instead, we must bring teachers closely into the process of selecting material for their own children—and, in so doing, into the continuing process of curriculum development itself.

A third danger in the curriculum development movement is that the process may at first seem to be a deceptively easy one, requiring only a relatively short time to complete. The pattern, as it is now too often interpreted, goes like this: a group of college professors, joined by a group of school teachers, spends a sequence of summers and perhaps an academic year in working up new materials such as books, course guides, film, and laboratory equipment. This material is developed in short, intense sessions, tried out by the teachers, refined, and put into "final" form. At the end of this period, all go home, the curriculum is often taken over by a publisher, and the revision is left to him.

This pattern is obviously unwise, as all of the sensitive leaders of the movement would point out, but the fact remains that the reform movement seems to be caught in this foolish process. Curriculum *development* is just that—the curriculum is developed and redeveloped in an endless process. There is no such thing as a finished curriculum any more than there is any such thing as an academic discipline that stands still. There is continuous reworking; curriculum development requires a permanent establishment.

It is here that the weakness of schools of education is so apparent. Yet where else should this kind of permanent establishment be than in a professional school whose ostensible purpose is the improvement of education? Somehow means must be found to bridge the chasm that still seems to exist between many academic scholars and professors of education. Discussion of this problem is all too familiar by now, but there is yet too much arrogance on both sides. There is no more room for such silliness, no more room for the high-handed superiority of the "subject matter specialist" (ugly phrase!) or the defensive idiocy of many educationists. In my view, a school of education is simply a holding company for the work of all those people in the university and in the schools whose concern is the improvement of education. Thus the curriculum reform projects should happily find a home therein. Since curriculum development is a long-range, continuing process, many of the key men involved must be those whose careers are largely devoted to it. The task is too difficult to leave completely to the hit-and-run professor or to the part-time worker. We must develop a new generation of professors of education with the kind of expertise required. At the same time, we must recruit into schools of education many men from the academic disciplines who up to now were in arts faculties but whose real interest seems to be in the work of the curriculum. They can serve as continual catalysts for all in the universities and the schools who from time to time work on the problems of educating children.

A fourth problem that seems to bedevil us is what I like to call the "gee whiz disease." There is nothing more exciting than seeing a young child or adolescent suddenly reaching an understanding which he has never had before. Light seems suddenly to break through when the child sees order in something which had been previously disordered, and one new to teaching is deeply excited by this phenomenon of intuition. Now I am all for our new teacher or new curriculum developer to be excited, but I also expect both to go beyond that first stage. Too often both stay right there, and justify what they do simply in terms of the children's *apparent* procession of successful intuitive leaps. While such points of learning are the heart of education, what is significant is their sequence. Too often curriculum development has been so overwhelmed by this phenomenon that the "development" seems to consist simply of a series of experiments designed to give the instructor his "gee-whiz" kick. The kids like this, and the teachers too, but there are more profound questions that we all should be asking.

What really is happening to the children who apparently respond to a particular experiment? Are they learning precisely what the curriculum developer has in mind? Or are they merely reacting to a gadget or a gimmick which is somewhat unusual compared to their traditional classroom experience? What is the underlying logic of a sequence of experiences, and how rigorous is the evaluation of this sequence? We cannot build a curriculum on top of a series of relatively unconnected experiments which lead to a supposed learning. The "gee-whiz" reaction simply is not enough.

In a sense, what I am asking for here—surprising though it may sound—is more scholarly rigor in the whole process of curriculum development. Ironically, many scholars involved in the process have been remiss in the extent of their self-criticism. All too rarely have psychologists and sociologists been included. All too rarely has some kind of systematic curriculum evaluation been built in. All too often have experiments been carried on with highly motivated children in highly ideal surroundings, and the merit of the curricula has been proclaimed on the basis of the successful reactions of a very small sample. This kind of sloppy work in curriculum development is tolerated by many scholars who would not tolerate it in their own disciplines. While rigor needs to be brought into this whole process, I am not suggesting that the state of the art allows us to button up every point. I am merely saying that we need intellectual honesty and humility as well as enthusiasm. We cannot be carried away by the inherent excitement of the process of education and the process of teaching. Curriculum developers and the children they teach deserve better.

A final concern is that our efforts now embrace all the subjects of the curriculum and, indeed, even the extra-curriculum. Curriculum development up to now has largely been in mathematics and the physical and social sciences. Lying before us are the vast areas of the humanities, and the attack on their reform must be cast in a very different way than the attack on the sciences. The state of the various disciplines which make up the humanities is far more chaotic than was, let us say, physics in the 1950s. Further, there are important areas of the curriculum which need radical revision, areas such as those now gathered under the somewhat unhappy title "vocational education," and other subjects such as health education and civic education. We must look at the entire curriculum of a school. We must, however, still look intensively at the nature of individual disciplines, at the nature of the humanities, and sort out the particular problems in those fields as well as seeing how they link with others. What, for example, is "English"? Is it rhetoric? Grammar? The appreciation of literature? The reading of business letters? The study of logic? The study of social issues? The debate of social issues? The wrestling with one's own soul and the playing out of one's deepest thoughts in speech and upon paper? Social history? The study of great authors and great men? Unfortunately, English, as taught in schools, tends to be all of these and none of these. Radical review is necessary. And what I have said about English applies as well to music and history and the visual arts.

Vocational education presents a new set of problems, and in any discussion of this area we must work very closely with the economists. It is not enough to lay out courses of study; we must attempt to identify curricula appropriate to the nation's as well as the individual's needs. Among other things, this means identifying national and regional labor patterns and determining the speed with which jobs seem to be changing and new skills are in demand. It also means fundamental study of the idea of "general" education for certain kinds of vocations. No area of the curriculum is so clearly inefficient, and in no area of the curriculum will radical reform be as difficult to carry out. Intransigent interests here are deep.

And finally, the extra-curriculum. In our study of the school as a whole, we must look at problems in character development and at the relationship of children with one another and with the adult world. Many of these issues are not effectively taught in any formal sense. They are probably best taught by example, by the way a school is organized and how it administers its own kind of justice. A great deal of work needs to be done in these areas, work of an unsentimental and rigorous kind. We greatly underestimate what James Coleman has called the "adolescent society," and we must learn to capitalize on it within our schools. We fool ourselves by thinking that what teachers teach is all—or even most—of what children really learn.

In sum, while the curriculum development movement represents a great step forward in American education, it is at a stage now where it runs the risk of becoming uncritical. This would be unworthy of its excellent beginnings. The leaders must recognize that there are new steps to be taken, and they should take them with the kind of vigor which marked their start in the middle of the last decade.

NONGRADED SCHOOLS
Meeting Children Where They Are

JOHN I. GOODLAD

The University Elementary School of the University of California, Los Angeles, is a nongraded school. Children normally enter before the age of four and move upward through their twelfth year without encountering the grade levels so characteristic of our educational system. They are not promoted from grade to grade; nor do they repeat grades. There are no grades.

This school stands with a small but growing company of schools now abandoning the grade labels—grades one, four, seven, or eleven—in favor of what educators call a continuous progress plan. These nongraded schools are not alike, any more than graded schools are alike. The educators responsible for them are not agreed on what nongrading is or could be. But they all have one feature in common: the grade labels have been removed from a substantial portion of the school. University Elementary School at UCLA is a completely gradeless school.

There is no magic in the removal of grade labels. If this is all that takes place, we have the same old school under a new name and a fraud has been perpetrated. There are fads in education as in everything else. Not to be caught up nowadays in nongrading, team teaching, programmed instruction, or educational television is to be regarded in some educational circles as to be woefully out of touch. Consequently, there are those administrators who have merely removed the labels and then declared a nongraded school to be in existence. Others have replaced three or four grade levels with twelve or more rigidly arbitrary achievement levels. Fortunately, some schools are being redesigned in a much more fundamental way.

Until recently, nongrading was thought of as an organizational device for permitting youngsters to move through a common body of material at somewhat differing rates of speed, according to their individual readiness to proceed. Most thinking and most nongraded schools are geared to this conception. But differentiated progress through what are still essentially graded assignments represents, at best, only insignificant tampering with a concept of education that has been seriously questioned by educational reformers from Rousseau to Bruno Bettelheim and A. S. Neill.

Nongrading, as used and defined in the balance of this paper, is both a concept and a plan within a larger view of education embracing a few simple but

FROM the *Saturday Review*, XLVIII, 12 (March 20, 1965), pp. 57–59, 72–74. Reprinted by permission.

nonetheless compelling principles of child development, learning, school function, and pedagogical practice.

First, children are different, much more different than we have up to now recognized. We have been shamefully remiss in taking these differences into account in our planning and teaching.

Second, in seeking to provide intelligently for these differences, educational diagnosis of and prescription for the individual is essential. Mass techniques and common expectations for all are inimical to these highly sensitive human processes.

Third, there must be alternatives from which to fill the prescriptions. A monolithic school structure providing only pass or fail as the alternatives in regulating pupil progress simply does not square with the range of alternatives necessary to coping imaginatively with human variability.

Fourth, the proper question to ask in starting a child off on his school career is not, "Is this child ready for school?" but, "What is this child ready for?" This is the most pregnant idea and is, indeed, at the heart of nongrading.

Fifth, criterion standards replace normative standards as the measure of pupil progress. Normative standards are sloppy standards based on group performance. They tend to result in unjustified rewards for high but inadequate performance on the part of the able and relentless, punishing failure for the slow and deprived. It has been estimated that 25 per cent of children in school receive 75 per cent of the failing grades based on normative standards. These children ultimately come to regard themselves as failures—not just in school but in life itself. Most of this loss to mankind could have been prevented by asking and carefully answering the question, "What is this child ready for?"

Criterion standards arrange a sequence of difficulty or a meaningful progression in work assignments. Instead of pronouncing the child to be at the fourth-grade level, which tells us very little and most of that misleading, these standards seek to provide a profile of where the child is now functioning with respect to the skills and concepts comprising the sequence of learning. These are really tougher standards, each child pitting himself against the rigor of the material rather than the uncertainties of group competence and variability. Unfortunately, we are still at a relatively primitive stage in the development of these criterion measures but rapid progress is being made in projects designed to change the curricula of America's schools.

Sixth, sound learning is cumulative. That is, the child's progression should not suffer from what psychologists call retroactive and proactive interference. A percentage problem for the child has no conception of parts and wholes, let alone the number base on which per cent depends, contaminates his present mathematical knowledge and interferes with what follows. Such is the unhappy, cumulative product of several "bare passes" in a graded system.

The graded school was brought into being at a time when we knew little about individual differences in learning. The assumption then, in the middle of the nineteenth century, was that the content of instruction could be divided into roughly equal packages and mastered, a year at a time, by children of the same age. Soon, there came to be graded content, graded textbooks, graded children, graded teachers, and graded expectations for schooling. Graded tests and graded norms came later. The entire graded machinery was efficient in classifying the hordes of children pouring into our schools in increasing numbers throughout the balance of the nineteenth century and into the twentieth.

But the children didn't fit. Some simply could not master the work of a grade in a year; others romped through it. Good teaching raised the level throughout; poor teaching lowered it. A formidable gap between the swift and the slow remained.

Nonpromotion (grade failure) and double promotion (grade skipping) were used—and still are used—to narrow the gap within any one grade. Neither has proved effective. The nonpromoted child, repeating the grade, rarely is stimulated anew. Studies reveal that nonpromoted children generally do worse than children of like ability and past performance who are promoted to the next grade. In fact, some nonpromoted children fail to equal their own performance of the previous year on the second time around.

The answer, however, is not simply to promote the slow-learning child. Inadequate or faulty comprehension, if not checked, leads to an accumulation and compounding of inadequacy. Promotion and nonpromotion are the ineffective adjustment mechanisms of the graded system. The answer appears to be to transform or replace the system.

The nongraded school is one replacement for the graded system. It is not simply a corrective mechanism. The component parts of grading and nongrading are not interchangeable. The two systems are built on differing assumptions, arouse differing expectations, and demand differing teacher behavior. They require differing language for their description and interpretation but, unfortunately, a language of nongrading has not yet developed. We are forced to think and talk about nongrading using the terms characteristic of grading and, as a consequence, we never quite escape gradedness.

Let us not abandon the graded school out of hand. Let us, instead, create alternatives. There can be no meaningful comparisons of what we now have without alternatives. Let us not create alternatives capriciously, however. Let us instead build alternatives which can be argued vigorously from supporting data.

The facts of individual differences among learners support the nongraded alternative. The usual fourth grade class contains children achieving at second, third, fourth, fifth, and sixth grades in some aspects of their school work—and even occasionally above and below these levels. The average spread in achievement is four years. In a fifth grade class it is five; in a sixth, six years in tested achievement, and so on. These are not fourth or fifth or sixth grades except in name. They are composites of many grades, each graded class overlapping graded classes above and below. In a field such as reading, the picture is even more startling. Children in a fifth grade class commonly range in reading from the second or third to the ninth or tenth.

The commonsense protest here is that, given ideal school conditions, these slow pupils could be pulled up substantially. True, but given equally ideal conditions for the able, they too would move up beyond these performances.

A commonsense solution to managing this vast range of attainments, frequently posed by lay critics of the schools, is to group those of like achievement in a single class. (The term used often but incorrectly for this achievement grouping is ability grouping.) But some additional evidence gives us pause. The variability in attainments within one child sometimes parallels the variability in an entire class. A child, like a class, is not a second, fourth, or sixth grader. Johnny can be in the fifth grade for arithmetic computation, the sixth for arithmetic reasoning, the seventh for spelling, the eighth for word meaning, the ninth for paragraph meaning, and the tenth for language—and yet be officially registered in the sixth grade. In the same class is Jean, whose scores range from low third to high seventh; Bill, from high second to high fifth; and Pat, from fourth to tenth. (These figures, incidentally, are taken from actual class roles.) Children are downright ornery. They refuse to grow up all of a piece.

Under a plan of grouping for likeness in achievement, Johnny, Jean, Bill, and Pat would join a new group for each subject and rarely would be together in the same groups. Their class groups, to be closely homogeneous (that is, comparable in attainment), would be composed of children from throughout the building, brought together because of their assumed readiness for identical learnings. A monstrous scheduling problem is involved. This can readily be managed through modern computer techniques.

The main problem is not logistics. Three other matters come in for attention: the composition of the class groups brought together in this fashion, the degree of homogeneity actually produced, and the accomplishments of students in such groups.

Strange partners often come together. Is a class made up of pupils ranging from seven to twelve years of age but alike in reading attainment a teachable reading group? Are the same materials for all likely to be appropriate? The answer to both questions, of course, is no. A new and at least equally perplexing problem of dealing with individual differences has been created. This is a caricature, admittedly, but it serves to sharpen the fact that grouping children for likeness in one trait creates groups of vast differences in most other traits.

Still another problem arises from the fact that students grouped for likeness on a trait are not alike on sub-elements of that trait. When two things look alike, this usually means that the viewer is not looking deeply or carefully enough. Children grouped for likeness in reading achievement, for example, usually have comparable test scores representing a combination of paragraph meaning and word recognition. But when one examines these children for six or eight separate factors involved in reading, he discovers that these "homogeneously" grouped youngsters are really very different on each of them. The grouping pattern performs a disservice because it lulls the teachers into proceeding as though the group were one when in reality it is markedly diverse in the components which must be provided for in the productive teaching of reading. Patterns of school organization should reveal, not hide, human variability.

Presumably, students of like ability are brought together to enhance their learning. The evidence is not convincing. Studies in England, Sweden, and the United States show no significant advantages in achievement for homogeneous groups over mixed or heterogeneous groups. The findings in any given study are either inconclusive or, if statistically significant, are offset by another study concluding the exact opposite. Grouping of any kind is productive only when designed to serve a specific purpose and when accompanied by special provisions of an intimate and highly individualized sort.

The potentiality of complex grouping patterns fades and the crucial significance of individualizing instruction looms large. Needed is a system of such flexibility and responsiveness that it is scarcely a system at all. Such a system must reveal individuality, not disguise or obscure it. Once revealed, human variability most assuredly will demand alternatives. The nongraded school is but a part, albeit a significant one, of the total educational system needed for the identification and proper nurturing of precious, individual, human talent.

It will be more helpful now to talk specifically about one nongraded school than to talk in general about the alternatives in content, grouping, pedagogy, and and expectations for children available through nongrading. In 1960, UCLA's University Elementary School consisted of seventeen graded rooms: three nursery school, two kindergarten, and two each subsequent grade through the sixth. Each was largely self-contained; that is, teachers worked alone in providing the daily diet of reading, arithmetic, language arts, social studies, and science but called upon help as desired for art, music, health, and physical education.

Today, five years later, University Elementary School consists of nine nongraded clusters of children and teachers, each cluster ranging in size from as few as twenty-five to as many as seventy-five children. Each child is assigned to one of these clusters and, subsequently, to sub-clusters within these larger ones, on the basis of diagnosis and prescription. Instead of the alternatives being pass or fail, the alternatives are several in number, no one of which is grade repetition or skipping. The clusters were different in number and organization last year; they will be different again next year. The school evolves as the staff clarifies beliefs and subjects them to test.

Most clusters are staffed by teams of full-time and part-time teachers. This team teaching has facilitated the inclusion of part-time personnel, some of them students in the university, in a way that was not possible five years ago. Although the budget is only slightly larger, because of normal salary increases, 50 per cent more people are on the payroll. Not all teachers are in teams. Some maintain about the same pattern of self-sufficiency that existed throughout the school five years ago. Teachers, too, are individuals and deserve alternatives.

Team teaching is not essential to nongrading. There are nongraded schools with self-contained classrooms and team-taught schools with grade levels. But team teaching as a way of clustering children and teachers fits nicely with nongrading as a way of guiding students upward through the school. They are compatible, flexible patterns of school and classroom organization which provide a useful array of alternatives for dealing with pupil variability. Since University Elementary School developed both at about the same time, the two are almost indistinguishably interwoven in practice and, consequently, in this description.

Let no one think that change comes naturally to a laboratory school, especially if its primary function has been demonstration. Such a school is in the public eye. To change what has long been demonstrated and from what have come success and recognition is to suggest that the practices being replaced were never good when, in reality, they may have been first-rate for their time. Further, time for planning change is hard to come by. In a laboratory school, the work load of teaching children, advising future teachers, assisting many university faculty members in the conduct of their research, demonstrating various procedures, and interpreting programs to endless streams of visitors is almost unbelievably demanding. To effect basic changes while keeping the ship afloat is an unsettling experience.

The route from yesterday to today was often a tortuous one. It included changing the function of this laboratory school from demonstration to inquiry, innovation, experimentation, and research in schooling. It began with two aspects of teacher dissatisfaction which were traced to a common source. First, class membership remained rather constant from year to year, as is typical in a graded school. Consequently, children were always the oldest or youngest and rather consistently followers or leaders. They had little opportunity to shift roles and explore new relationships. Second, certain learning ills persisted for some children into the upper elementary years. The problem was less pronounced than in most schools but it was particularly frustrating for these teachers because the school was highly regarded for its instruction, and rightfully so. Teachers did everything possible within the graded organization characteristic of schools generally but often were unable to overcome what appeared to be unfortunate but irrevocable pupil placements. The placement adjustment for inadequate learning appeared to be retention and grade repetition, a solution which these teachers regarded as disagreeable and noncorrective.

They were boxed in by the graded system, a system that they had often stretched to the near-breaking point but had always retained. It is unwise to break away from long-established practice when no reasonably clear alternative is in sight. The search for an acceptable alternative led to better understanding of what was hidden by the graded structure, the fact that the seventeen classrooms were graded in name but not in the attainment of pupils. The graded structure now looked less sacred and inviolable than it had before. Some teachers who had read or otherwise learned about nongrading wanted to abolish the graded system then and there. This decision was not to come for another year.

By collapsing the next three years, we come to the present. The school is now viewed as having three broad levels of function and expectations, each successive level overlapping the previous one both in function and expectations and in the age of children assigned to it.

The early childhood level enrolls children from under four to over six. The primary function is to develop a sturdy, wholesome self-concept. Children are expected to interact productively and satisfyingly with the children, adults, and things of their daily environment. Teachers are there to assist them in working at these relationships. Concern for this wholesome self-concept carries over into the lower elementary level where diagnosis and prescription for needs in this area continue. But now the central function becomes progressive development in the fundamental skills of self-directed learning, especially reading. The age spread is now from about six to eight or nine, but age is not a primary factor in placement. The upper elementary level of function normally embraces children from eight or nine to eleven or twelve years of age. Again, attention to wholesome self-development continues, particularly as it relates to inadequate learning skills demanding special attention. The central goal now, however, is to develop the ability to understand and use man's approaches to studying social and natural phenomena. Hopefully, children will leave the school with a desire to continue learning as well as considerable self-directing proficiency in the process.

These three levels of function are not organizational units of the school, although at one point in the school's recent evolution they were. The nine broad clusters of children are not evenly distributed among them. One cluster, for example, enrolling sixty-five children from age seven to age eleven, obviously cuts across both lower and upper elementary levels, reaching toward the bottom of the former, and well up in the latter. The three-levels concept of function underlying University Elementary School simply emphasizes that the function of elementary education is not unitary throughout but, rather, shifts in emphasis from the early childhood to the early adolescent years.

Each cluster of children, whether large or small, whether team-taught or self-contained, has a wide spread in age. For example, a cluster entirely within the lower elementary level might contain children of age six, seven, and eight. Another conceived to be entirely within this same lower elementary level of function might contain children from seven to nine. One cutting across lower and upper elementary conceptions of function might spread from age seven to twelve.

This system of school organization virtually forces teachers to recognize and provide for individual differences. Several ages together serve as a blinking light reminding teachers that the students are not all alike. A single age group could lull them into forgetting the wide range of differences actually residing in it. With a little care, a mixed age group can be put together so that the overall individual differences are little or no greater than in a single age group. But experience suggests that the revelation of one kind of difference—namely, in age—creates pressure to deal with differences generally.

The learning environment in a cluster of children provides a wide range of activities appropriate to the functions involved. A cluster of forty children from age four through six, for example, shares two rooms that formerly were separate classrooms but that have now been merged by knocking out part of an intervening wall. It is not unusual for them to share other indoor spaces with neighboring clusters and the simultaneous sharing of outdoor spaces is standard practice. The skilled observer would see a certain rhythm to the daily activities. At a given moment, a sub-group is talking about a walk from which the children have just returned; another is busily engaged in a variety of jumping and balancing activities; another is sitting at a table with reading materials; and little clusters of two and three are deeply involved in still other tasks. What one child is doing now, another will be doing an hour from now. The range and variety are in part possible because, in expanding total cluster size, additional personnel also are added.

Each of the tasks mentioned above is believed to be prelude to or part of reading. Each child is working at a point thought to be appropriate for him and, most of the time, selected by him. Progression through such tasks is far from ordered, partly because some of them are parallel rather than sequential and partly because research has not yet defined the most productive sequences. Further, a productive sequence for one child usually only partly overlaps a productive sequence for another. Individual diagnosis and prescription are essential. The child is not incapable of self-diagnosis and prescription, especially if the range of alternatives is broad, visible, and attractive and he is helped to see what these alternatives are designed to accomplish.

Progress through any sequence is only very loosely related to age. The number of years a human being has lived is a poor yardstick for determining what he is ready to learn. Each of the subgroups above contained fours, fives, and sixes, for whom the task at hand was appropriate. The sub-groups assembled for the next tasks of the day also would contain this age distribution but the children comprising the group would not be entirely the same. Here we see sharply revealed a key difference between grading and nongrading. The graded school is geared rather closely to age and to arbitrary provision of what children of that age (and grade) are to learn. The nongraded school is geared to readiness to learn, which, in turn, is determined from continuing diagnosis.

Another key difference is flexibility in expectations for children. The graded school presents a series of graded expectations. Contrary to much popular opinion, these are not rigorous expectations for all. But they are unfair. As pointed out earlier, they punish the weak and fail to challenge the strong.

University Elementary School provides a broad range of expectations—broad enough to reach from the floor to the ceiling of individual attainment—within each level of function. A child is not expected to reach a set level of reading by the age of six. Nor is he retained in an early childhood cluster of children until he does. But he will have engaged in activities considered basic to reading (many of which, unfortunately, are not seen as such by the layman) as well as in many other kinds of learnings. On moving to join older clusters of children, where these children will now be the youngest rather than the oldest, some will be among the most proficient readers in the new environment, some among the slowest. New groupings for reading will occur to take these individual differences into account. Staff and resources are now geared to make special provision for reading, with a range of expectations far in excess of those normally assumed under the label, "grade."

A child in University Elementary School seldom remains less than a year or more than three years with a cluster of children and teachers, depending on the size of that cluster, the age spread in it, and the diagnosis of that child. In principle, a child is moved whenever placement in another cluster appears to be desirable. In practice, however, every effort is made to keep a child in a cluster of children for at least a year, on the assumption that this continuity contributes to his sense of identity in a world of increasing anonymity. A child in a cluster for three years will have seen children come and go each year, will have had a long-term continuing relationship with some of these children and with several teachers, and will have enjoyed the experience of being at first one of the youngest and then one of the oldest members of the group.

Placement for each subsequent year grows out of a series of meetings taking place in the spring of each year. There are total faculty meetings in which general policies are reiterated and refined. There are single cluster meetings in which teachers who have been closely associated with these children, sometimes for as long as three years, pool data and observations concerning each child. There are cross-cluster conferences in which children likely to be assigned to one of several possible alternative clusters are discussed in relation to the teachers and to the expectations of each cluster. The data come from many sources but particularly from children's present teachers, parents, the school principal, and the children themselves.

At no time is there a squaring of each child's performance with a predetermined set of common expectancies for all four-year-olds or all nine-year-olds. Criteria are derived from the functions of the level of schooling; adequacy from a study of the child's performance over a long period of time. These are decisions for teachers to make, teachers who are close to the data. The principal participates as a member of the team, not as a final arbiter "passing on" each decision.

When the decision is to move a child from his present placement to a new one, the question is, "Which alternative?" In a carefully organized nongraded school, there should be a minimum of three alternatives from which to choose. Each of these alternatives will differ in several strategic ways, the most significant of which are the differences among the teachers. It is the responsibility of the total staff, with the principal's guidance, to determine just how these alternatives will differ: in anticipated learning activities, in the teachers to be in charge, in group size, and in actual group membership. All of these can be and should be manipulated in seeking to set up productive clusters of teachers and children for each subsequent year. Consequently, at University Elementary School, final placements of children are held up until the composition of each tentative cluster has been carefully examined. Frequently, on the basis of this examination, clusters initially proposed are modified through reassigning children.

Teachers find this process to be excruciatingly difficult at first. They must consider much more than the relatively simple alternatives: to promote or not to

84   THE SCHOOL: PRESSURES AND RESPONSES

promote. They need to know a great deal about the children with whom they have been working—parental expectations and their effects, peer group associations, feelings of success and failure, ability to tolerate restrictions or permissiveness, and so on—and about their colleagues. They are uncertain about the criteria to use, largely because, as a total staff or as sub-groups of that staff, they have not previously discussed the matter. And, to their surprise and frustration, they usually discover that they possess far too little useful information about the children with whom they have been working. In brief, they are confronted with a new and highly challenging professional task and, understandably, can be somewhat unnerved by it.

Supported and encouraged, however, most teachers learn the behavior required and practice it with growing satisfaction. At University Elementary School, the second round of spring meetings was a marked improvement over the first. Teachers came armed with data and hammered out the criteria in the process of making pupil placements. The third round was strikingly professional. But now a new kind of frustration emerged. The teachers wanted data going beyond their own observations, sensitive test data in all areas of child development—data derived from criterion measures, not normative data derived from graded standards. Such data are conspicuously absent in education. To create a demand for them is to speed their coming. Nongraded schools, of the type conceived here, create this demand.

Needed in a nongraded school is a person knowledgeable in both education and the informative sciences. He might well be the guidance counselor. His job is to set up a system for the collection, organization, storage, and retrieval of data designed to assist teachers in their vital decisions of diagnosis and prescription. He must join the teachers in these processes, learning more about them, bringing data to bear, and refining the information processing system as needed. The necessity for collecting masses of data, for maintaining them over long periods of time, for assembling them in many different ways, and for quick retrieval suggests the potentiality of a computer serving several schools or school systems simultaneously. Computers are now being used experimentally for similar purposes in research projects scattered across the country.

Complex? Yes, at first, simply because these are not familiar modes of thought to most people. It is not easy to escape more than a century of gradedness. The early phases of comprehending nongradedness are something like a first experience with English money. One is forever trying to translate pence, shillings, and pounds into cents, quarters, and dollars (and those half-crowns are maddening!). Or, perhaps better, it is comparable to the way most of us struggle initially and awkwardly with a foreign language. We seek to translate French literally into English rather than to think and to communicate in French. What a revelation it is when the intervening translation disappears and we find ourselves thinking, reading, and speaking French!

Similarly, before the potentialities of this redefined and redesigned school open up we must come to think in nongraded terms. To translate nongrading into graded nomenclature is to stay within the limited possibilities of yesterday's schools. Until fully functioning nongraded models have been carefully developed, meaningful discourse about and comparisons of nongrading and grading will be impossible. But even with models of both standing side by side, experimental comparison will be difficult and, for persons holding differing conceptions of education, probably impossible. For grading and nongrading are fundamentally differing expressions of schooling, based on fundamentally differing conceptions of what schools are for and of how learners should progress in them. Ask not if this child is ready for school but what this child is ready for.

University Elementary School is still becoming. The promise of the future far outstrips the accomplishments of the past. Three years have elapsed since the faculty committed itself to nongrading and jokingly promised to fine its members for each use of the word, "graded." The school is not yet fully nongraded; it never will be. For, as quickly as one goal is attained, others come into view. As former Chancellor Lawrence Kimpton once said about the University of Chicago over which he presided, "This probably isn't a very good place for the pursuit of happiness, but it's a wonderful place to find happiness in pursuit."

THE RETURN OF
MONTESSORI

EDWARD WAKIN

At the turn of the century, a remarkable Italian woman physician turned her considerable talents to education, proclaimed the "Century of the Child," and launched a child-centered program of education. When Dr. Maria Montessori died in 1952 at the age of eighty-one, she had long been recognized as the founder of an international movement whose congresses attracted official representatives from Belgium, Chile, Czechoslovakia, Egypt, France, Greece, the USSR and the United States.

Some forty years after the movement's dramatic rise and sudden fall in the United States, it reappeared in an unusual do-it-yourself resurrection wrought by parents concerned about the education of their preschool children. The movement born in Italian slums in the beginning of the "Century of the Child" reappeared in the post-World War II period of the anxious American middle-class parent.

The opening of the "pure Montessori" Whitby School in suburban Greenwich,

FROM the *Saturday Review*, XLVIII, 25 (November 21, 1964), pp. 61–63. Reprinted by permission.

Connecticut, in 1958, set off widespread fanfare about a school where preschoolers were already learning the three R's. The reactions were predictable: Montessori schools were glamorized, publicized, overexposed, overestimated, and, at least partially, misunderstood.

Parents took matters into their own hands, organizing Montessori schools for children three to five years of age. Since 1958, over one hundred Montessori schools have been opened all over the country. According to the American Montessori Society, about thirty were opened this fall and another forty are in the planning stage.

Until now, the Montessori message in America has been carried by a former associate of Dr. Montessori, E. M. Standing, and a dedicated disciple, Nancy McCormick Rambusch, who set the revival in motion by opening the Whitby School. With the publication of three basic but formerly out-of-print books written by Dr. Montessori, first-hand source material on her educational movement has finally become available.

The books are a noteworthy contribution to the literature of educational theory and practice and a necessary trilogy for anyone interested in the Montessori movement. The most important of the three, from the viewpoint of the current revival, is *The Montessori Method*, which focuses on the education of children from three to six. The other two concern education from seven to eleven: *Spontaneous Activity in Education*, which is theoretical, philosophic and persuasive in content, and *The Montessori Elementary Material*, which is practically a teaching manual.

For the educator, these books are bound to provide historical perspective and insights into the art of teaching; for the Montessori devotee, they will sit on the bookshelf next to the Bible. For the conscientious parent, there is much advice, understanding and analysis of the child as human being and as pupil, though more contemporary accounts may serve better as a parental guidebook.

What emerges from this trilogy is a picture of a sensitive, even profound, innovator who has a grand sweep and manner. Considering their vintage, the books are an impressive summing-up in which Dr. Montessori moves from inspirational pleas for understanding the child to such practical matters as the role of the classroom desk.

The basic Montessori concepts are by now well known. The teaching must pay attention to the child, rather than vice versa. The child proceeds at his own pace in an environment controlled to provide the means of learning. Imaginative teaching materials are the heart of the process. Each of them is self-correcting, thus enabling the child to proceed at his own pace and see his own mistakes. Many of these materials in one form or other are already evident in American nursery schools and in educational toys. Particularly exciting is the engagement of the child's muscles and tactile senses in the learning process, as in the use of sandpaper letters so the child can "feel" them.

The inside of a Montessori classroom gives an overall impression of "controlled chaos," each child quietly working at his private encounter with a learning situation he has chosen. At the Whitby School, a class of pre-schoolers was typical of what is found in the Montessori classroom. A boy sat at his desk endlessly tracing circles within the boundaries of a metal inset and filling in the circles with parallel lines. He was learning to handle a pencil as he became familiar with geometric shapes. A girl sat on her personal rug fitting the countries of Europe into a metal jigsaw puzzle; another fitted pegs of various sizes into holes of matching sizes. They were using the self-correcting learning materials. Others formed words with colored letters, used red and blue rods to grasp addition and subtraction, beads for counting, boxes with compartments numbered zero to nine that contained corresponding numbers of sticks. The teacher moved among them unnoticed, guiding and encouraging them individually, but not intruding or interfering. She was on the alert, waiting for each child to be ready for the next step in a graduated system of learning.

While Dr. Montessori's advice to the teacher is no longer as revolutionary as it was, it is still worth recalling: "To be thus helpful it is necessary rigorously to avoid the arrest of spontaneous movements and the imposition of arbitrary tasks. It is of course understood that here we do not speak of useless or dangerous acts, for these must be suppressed, destroyed." Dr. Montessori wanted self-discipline in the child, controlled—and only seeming—chaos in the classroom, and attention to individual needs on the part of the teacher.

The main contribution of the current Montessori revival is already taken for granted: the preschool child is ready to learn. The revival was an important reminder of this fact for both parents and educators. But awareness of this fact of child life has been growing independently of Dr. Montessori's followers for some years, particularly in the work of psychologist Jerome Bruner at Harvard. At Rutgers, psychologist O. K. Moore has shown that even two-year-olds can learn to read, while mathematicians, scientists and economists have been lowering the age threshold for learning their specialties. A Montessori devotee would call this a return to principles perceived by the founder of their movement; the child is no longer underestimated.

As these three books demonstrate, there are two aspects to the Montessori movement: its mystique and its methods. The methods are no longer revolutionary, though they are still eminently suggestive and, judging from the Montessori results with preschoolers, successful. But, as various educators have noted, updating of Montessori is needed to bring into the picture the scientific and pedagogical developments which have taken place since Dr. Montessori formulated her philosophy. Nor does it seem plausible to accept the attitude of Montessori purists that her method is not only the best way, but the only way, of educating preschool children.

In this country, Montessori schools have had numerous built-in advantages. Their pupils are culturally advantaged rather than deprived, the classes small and richly endowed with learning materials, the teachers dedicated and attentive. Even without the Montessori philosophy, a nursery school with such advantages would produce results. What is still lacking are systematic studies on the superiority of the Montessori classroom, all things being equal. The Montessorians promise to produce such data.

The Montessori mystique is another matter, and it comes through dramatically in the writings of Dr. Montessori. *The Montessori Method* and *Spontaneous Activity in Education* constitute a personal, carefully reasoned, and inspired exposition by the movement's founder. It is the same mystique that fills those Montessori classrooms which this writer has observed. No parent would hesitate to surrender his child to such tender and attentive hands. Anyone who has confronted his own child or other children in a Montessori classroom is bound to respond with sympathy and appreciation.

These writings of Maria Montessori ring with the spirit of reform that was emerging in the early part of the century. Sometimes they reflect their vintage in the conditions described and the indignation expressed. Her idealism and optimism are summed up in *The Montessori Method* when she speaks out for liberty (within bounds): "Even as life in the social environment triumphs against every cause of poverty and death, and proceeds to new conquests, so the instinct of liberty conquers all obstacles, going from victory to victory." She is emphatic in arguing for liberation of the "inner force" in man and for removal of the "real punishment of the normal man," which she describes as "loss of the consciousness of that individual power and greatness which are the sources of his inner life."

Dr. Montessori's followers can undermine her contribution by overselling her ideas and presenting them as a panacea, instead of a provocative approach that can fit into current educational reforms. The Montessori movement may have lost its first battle in America because of unfair and one-sided criticism by John Dewey's progressive disciples, but it cannot win its current battle on enthusiasm alone, particularly if it is not brought into the mainstream of American education.

Its prospects are not helped by the internal dissension within the Montessori movement, but this was inevitable since it is a do-it-yourself movement carried forward by zealots and enthusiasts. The range of disagreement oscillates between ultra-orthodox Montessorians who are accused of being cultists and moderate Montessorians who are accused of deviationism. But this is an intramural battle more important to Montessorians than to educators in general.

Today, the educational climate is conducive to Montessori, particularly with the emphasis on the culturally deprived slum child. This is where Montessori will face its suitable test, not in suburbia where advantages are heaped upon the advantaged and where it is difficult to separate what the home does from what the school does. One such test, with Chicago slum children, already has had promising results.

Meanwhile, the American Montessori Society and Mrs. Rambusch in particular, emphasize that the movement is non-denominational, though its origins both in this country and Italy were strongly Catholic. A recent survey conducted by the Society of thirty-eight Montessori schools in the United States found that only fourteen were denominational (thirteen Catholic, and one Presbyterian). The rest were non-denominational. As with the movement as a whole, the survey showed that almost all the children were preschoolers between three and five and that the schools had been organized by parents.

The mail arriving steadily at the Society's headquarters, which soars periodically with each new article or TV program, testifies to the reservoir of interest and dissatisfaction tapped by the Montessori movement. But Montessori needs to emerge from its revivalist spirit if it is to convince educators and officials. If professionalization is abused in American education, do-it-yourself is no answer.

The appearance of these three basic Montessori books is a useful step in the direction of examining and studying the Montessori possibilities. As Martin Mayer remarks in his introduction to *The Montessori Method*, "Nobody who reads Montessori ever looks at education in quite the same way again, and the change is always for the better." This is not faint praise; few books in the laboring mountains of educational literature do as much.

REFERENCES

The three basic books by Dr. Maria Montessori referred to in this article are:

The Montessori Method. Cambridge, Mass.: Robert Bentley, Inc., 1964.
Spontaneous Activity in Education. Cambridge, Mass.: Robert Bentley, Inc., 1964.
The Montessori Elementary Material. Cambridge, Mass.: Robert Bentley, Inc., 1964.

SCIENCE EDUCATION UNDER CHALLENGE

WILLARD J. JACOBSON

Education is an integral, indispensable part of the scientific enterprise. In science, education is not a peripheral matter, for without education the individual scientist withers into obsolescence, and science as an institution is ineffectual and deprived of its supply of new blood and ideas. All is not well in science education, and to recognize that education is central in the scientific enterprise is essential if we are to have a dynamic science and effective science education. Some examples may illustrate the importance of considering education as an integral part of the scientific enterprise.

FROM *Teachers College Record*, 65:627–634 (April 1964), Teachers College, Columbia University, N. Y. Reprinted by permission.

To cope with the very serious nutritional problems in Central America, the nations in that region cooperated in 1949 in founding the Institute of Nutrition of Central America and Panama (INCAP). In a series of brilliant investigations, the scientists who were assembled and trained for research at INCAP identified the protein-deficiency disease *kwashiorkor* as one of the major public health problems in Central America and, using indigenous foodstuffs, developed diets that contained the needed amino acids which could be used to prevent it. But still, among the Indian and Ladino populations, it has been found that "Every year about 170 in every 1,000 in the age group from one to five years die." [1] We know how to prevent these deaths, but the children still die. Obviously, education is of central importance in dealing with this problem; our knowledge is useless unless it becomes a widely understood and well traveled route to health. Many other examples could be given of the importance of recognizing education as a part of the scientific enterprise if science is to be humanly effective.

Similarly, the scientist or engineer who does not educate himself and others is threatened with obsolescence. This seems obvious, but its implications for individual scientists are sometimes difficult to face. For example, there are engineers associated with our space program who, in the last ten years, have been, successively, piston-engine engineers, turbo-engine engineers, jet-engine engineers, rocket-engine engineers, and nuclear-engine engineers. Many other illustrations, though hardly more striking ones, could be drawn from many areas of science and engineering. These men and women must continually educate themselves. Those who embark on a life in the scientific enterprise commit themselves to a life of educating and being educated.

URGENCY OF YOUTH

In addition to educating themselves, members of the scientific enterprise must teach those who are to carry it on. In sciences such as physics, much of the most important work is done by young men and women in their twenties. It may be that the mental energy required to reach and push forward the frontiers in these fields is so great that it can best be done at an early age. Certainly then, all who are engaged in science have a stake in making it possible for these young men and women to make their contributions early in life.

Nations, too, have a concern that their citizens and future citizens have the science education necessary to operate their institutions, carry on needed teaching and research, and keep the society moving forward. The United States with about 30 per cent of its population enrolled full time in some kind of educational institution, with 42 per cent of the college and university age group enrolled in some form of higher education, and with 70,000 graduates in science and engineering, still has a growing shortage of highly qualified scientists, engineers, physicians, and teachers. It is little wonder that some European nations, with perhaps five per cent of their

---

[1] H. Scrimshaw, "Malnutrition in Central America," in Anne Burgess and R. Dean, *Malnutrition and Food Habits* (London: Tavistock Publishers, 1962).

college and university age group enrolled in higher education, are building universities as fast as they can. It is easy to understand why newly developing nations may allocate 30 to 40 per cent of their national budgets for education, much of it for scientific and technical training.

To view education as an integral, indispensable part of the scientific enterprise is to take a realistic view of the nature of science as an institution and to make a plea that all scientists take some responsibility for the educational dimension of their profession. An increased sense of responsibility for education in the sciences has been an important factor in recent developments in science education.

The last seven years have seen rapid progress in science education, and education has received increasing recognition as a part of the scientific enterprise. In the past, the improvement of the content of science courses and the development of science education materials was the task of lonely science educators, almost destitute of financial resources, helped at times by dedicated teachers willing to sacrifice vacation periods and the hours after midnight. Now they have been joined by some of their colleagues from the laboratories who, recognizing the central importance of education, have been willing to devote time and energy to such jobs as identifying and making available the kinds of resources that are necessary for the development of first-rate materials in science education.

RECENT DEVELOPMENTS

Three of the important, little-recognized by-products of the recent efforts in science education are:

(a) a wider recognition of the importance and complexities of the issues in science education;

(b) a commitment on the part of many to move beyond hasty exhortation and dogmatic platitudes to "dirty their hands" with the problems; and

(c) the recruitment to science education of new and able workers who will keep the vineyard fertile and productive.

In the long run, these by-products may rival in importance the more tangible results like curricula and syllabi, which, like all teaching materials in the sciences, quickly become dated.

Less attention and practically no resources have been devoted to research in science education. In fact, it appears that there has been a decline in the amount of research in science education. This is probably due to the amount of attention and energy devoted to improving course content and to the development of instructional materials. There has also been, however, a lack of recognition among some scientists of the importance of research in science education. "Pure" research in the most abstruse fields is quickly defended from well prepared positions. Important investigations into the learning process in science are usually not supported with equal zeal. There has not even been a satisfactory research program developed to gather and evaluate data concerning the extent of the use and effectiveness of the new science courses. The problems of science education will not conveniently disappear, and if they are to be intelligently resolved, they must be dealt with through careful and systematic investigation.

As in almost all areas of human concern, the tasks in science education are never really finished. There may be a shift in arenas and a change in the players, but the game goes on. For example, we have not succeeded in developing adequate science programs for Everyman, although almost everyone agrees that this is urgently needed. If our future is to be inextricably intertwined with developments in science and technology—and this clearly seems to be the case—then every young person has a right to the intellectual equipment that will help him to understand and perhaps to take part in these developments. If the next half century is to be an era of unrivalled intellectual excitement and a period of exploration unmatched in human history, then every youngster should have the opportunity to share in the intellectual quests and the adventures of exploration that are part of his age. It is doubtful that many of our children and young people will have these opportunities unless new and better programs of science education for Everyman are wisely and vigorously created.

At present, our programs of science for everyone are apparently so inadequate that some critics of science education are suggesting extremely radical measures. The historian of science, Derek de Solla Price, has offered as his principal suggestion, "... that we might well cut from the school syllabus some half or three-quarters of the science program, including all laboratory instruction, and devote the time and energy thus saved to teaching by historians (and other humanists) about science and the way it works as a human activity." [2] William Mathewson has suggested that the emphasis in general education courses in science should be shifted to a study of scientists rather than of science: "If the layman is to learn to work with scientists, to judge statements made by scientists, to communicate his own values and purposes to scientists, he must gain as true a picture as possible of what a scientist really is." [3]

PLURAL ROADS TO TRUTH

Science programs for Everyman must, of course, serve a variety of purposes, and a fruitful hypothesis for further exploration may be that such programs must incorporate a variety of approaches to the study of science. Part of the effort probably should, as Price suggests, involve a "talking about science" and the study of science as a human activity. There might also be, as Mathewson suggests, an approach that emphasizes the study of scientists and their works, although care must be taken not to give the impression that scientists are so different from other human beings that they must be set apart. Also, there should certainly be a study of those areas of science, such as nutrition and physiology, that have a direct bearing upon our health and well-being. In addition, it is still possible for children

---

[2] " Two Cultures—And One Historian of Science," *Teachers College Record* (1963), 64:533.
[3] " Science for the Citizen: An Educational Problem," *Science* (1962), 138:1378.

and young people to engage directly in scientific investigations, and actual experiences in carrying out investigations should be an important part of any science program. Most of the projects for the improvement of science programs in the elementary and junior high schools entail vigorous attempts to find more and better ways to involve children in these kinds of inquiries. Many would also argue that students should have some experience in dealing with the controversies related to science and technology that must be dealt with in a democracy in some way or other by its citizens. Then, certainly, students should have opportunities to study and consider those profound questions about ourselves and our world which have always been asked by children and wise men.

One of the laudable movements in science education is the drive to develop scientific literacy. Alan Waterman, the former director of the National Science Foundation, has highlighted the importance of this goal. "We have an obligation not only to train the scientists that our society requires but to make sure that the entire school population is at least literate in science and has some appreciation of the forces that are shaping our world." [4] But literacy involves more than learning how to understand the words that scientists use. The parents of children suffering from kwashiorkor would not be scientifically literate if they simply read about the disease and its prevention but failed to perceive the application to themselves and the way they feed their children. Scientific literacy involving *using* science as well as *understanding* it. This broader definition of scientific literacy raises the sights of science education and suggests a more significant role for science education in the life of Everyman.

SCIENCE AS MODERNITY

It is a truism that education should be related to the major activities and problems of the time. One of the major criticisms of some of the new science courses is that although our society is so dependent upon its highly developed technology for its prosperity and survival, the study of technology and the basic scientific principles on which it operates has been neglected and in some cases deliberately excluded. Our generation will probably be known as the one that finally loosened the gravitational chains that have tied us to the planet Earth. This has been made possible by the sophisticated use of principles of science. Should not our science programs help children and young people to gain a better and more profound understanding of these scientific principles in the context of their use?

One of the useful ways to teach science as relevant to our time is to start with contemporary technology. We can, in all likelihood, do a better job of teaching Newton's Laws of Motion by beginning with motions in space than we can by starting with the conventional idealized situations that are less related to the events discussed in our daily newspaper. If we can make our science courses consistent with our times, they will certainly be more exciting and probably more useful.

[4] "Science and Society: Integration Through Education," *Teachers College Record* (1962), 64:158.

Without this deliberate emphasis on modernity, there is a danger that we may "twiddle while the world turns." For example, one of the major social problems of our day relates to race relations. We teach a certain amount of genetics in our secondary school science courses. Some of this material could be used to gain a better comprehension of human populations. Secondary school students could profitably probe such books as Dobzhansky's *Evolution, Genetics, and Man* and Scheinfeld's *You and Heredity*, and science teachers could properly prepare themselves through a study of works like Boyd's *Genetics and the Races of Man*. Science courses that are at appropriate times related to the major issues of our day may give students both a better understanding of science and a sharper sense of its human relevance.

If we are to use a variety of approaches to science education, if we are to deal with the science that is important for our times in a profound rather than a superficial way, and if we also are to give our children and young people some contact with what is important in some of the sciences that are not now adequately represented in our schools, then we shall have to plan our over-all programs as carefully as our particular courses. In many of our schools, there is some provision for science from kindergarten through the twelfth grade. A K-12 science program provides science educators with all the time they reasonably can expect, but thoughtful planning is needed if we are to do what needs to be done in science.

PROGRAMS AND TEACHERS

In the future, science programs will probably be planned in terms of approaches to science as well as the subject matter to be covered. It may be that in a particular year of science, it will be desirable to deal with some field in which an historical approach is used, another in which a laboratory investigation is emphasized, and a third in which a field study is the major mode of attack. In each of these cases, the studies would be carried out in sufficient depth so that children and young people may gain an appreciation of the *methods* used as well as of the major *ideas* involved.

The development of a truly effective K-12 science program is one of the most important challenges facing science educators. It will be a complex undertaking in which there must be a concern for the wide range of the subject matter of the sciences, the variety of methods of investigation, the differing capabilities and potentialities of our youngsters, and the differences among the communities in which we teach. Attempts have been made to develop K-12 science programs in which all such factors are taken into account. All these attempts, however, need much further testing and refinement in the crucible of day-to-day school practice.

The new science courses and programs have, of course, one thing in common: They require greater insight and competence on the part of the teacher. Guidelines have been developed, outlining the kinds of educational experiences that are believed to be essential for the effective teaching of science.[5] But very little has been done systematically to improve teacher education in science. A Council on the Education of Science Teachers, recently organized by the National Science Teachers Association and the Association for the Education of Teachers in Science, may be able to initiate needed developments on this score.

It would be desirable if the science courses which are a part of teacher-education programs were related in both approach and content to the kind of science that the teacher will teach. Too often, college science is of little help to a first grade teacher as she works with a group of inquisitive youngsters. The science courses that future science teachers now take are often designed to meet the needs of the future specialist, whether physician or physicist, but are of less value for the science teacher. There is a serious need for a fresh look at the science programs offered our future teachers.

The future teacher of science also has professional concerns about teaching science. He needs to learn how to use instructional equipment which often differs from the apparatus used in science laboratories, to have some experience in working with youngsters in science, to give some thought to the goals of science instruction in our society, to become aware of some of the research and theory that is basic in his field, and to prepare himself to grow in his profession. There has been no recent large-scale attack on the serious problems involved in teacher education in science. The day is late.

MANPOWER ISSUES

With all the stress that has been accorded to science education these last few years, it is distressing that we have not achieved greater success in attracting more able young men and women to science and science-related professions. The percentage of college students choosing science careers has remained about the same, and the number electing engineering has actually declined. Medical schools report an ominous drop in applications for admission that makes it impossible for them to be as selective as they once were. The manpower situation in science teaching continues to be dark. These continuing shortages must be viewed in the light of a greatly increased national need for scientists, engineers, and science teachers.

Many reasons may account for this failure to attract more young men and women to science. We have apparently failed to stir the imaginations of young people to see science as an exciting adventure and as an invitation to exploration. There is some evidence that children and early adolescents view science with considerable idealism. Perhaps they are disillusioned by the humdrum "science" they encounter in too many schools where the cult of the difficult repels those who seek an interesting field and recruits for science only those who would become scientists anyway.

[5] *Guidelines for Preparation Programs of Teachers of Secondary School Science and Mathematics* (1961), and *Guidelines for Science and Mathematics in the Preparation Program of Elementary School Teachers* (Washington, D. C.: American Association for the Advancement of Science).

Some way must be found to keep the doors to science open to youngsters from families where careers in science and engineering have not been considered a possibility, to students who have missed essential mathematics because of illness or because their families moved several times during the critical high school years or because of faulty teaching or guidance, and to students who decide relatively late in their schooling that they might like to pursue a career in science. Most importantly, the science that the students encounter in schools must not have been disinfected of all its excitement. Its magnetic, stimulating appeal to the imaginative and the adventuresome must not be clouded by inept planning and dull teaching.

Perhaps the most fruitful point of view for moving ahead in science education is to consider it as an integral part of science. Unless those who are active in the various fields of science contribute to the development of effective programs in the schools, there is a danger that we shall be teaching tomorrow's adults yesterday's science. Unless those who are responsibly familiar with learners and the learning process also contribute to the development of science education, then courses and materials may be ill-suited to our varied goals and incomprehensible to our youngsters. The burden of quality here must be widely shared.

RESEARCH FOR EXCELLENCE

The recognition of the importance of research in science education is urgently necessary. We need far more knowledge of the processes and outcomes of science education; and with the spirit of inquiry the very hallmark of science, teachers can best exemplify this aspect of the enterprise by an active, visible, and meaningful involvement in relevant research, including the systematic evaluation and revision of their own procedures and materials. In the secondary schools, students can also be involved in the design and execution of research in science education and in this way have some first-hand experience with the excitement and the labor of investigation. It is unfortunate that some scientists seem to have implied that research in science education is hardly a respectable undertaking. If science education is an integral part of science, they might do better by helping to improve the quality of the research.

The development of ways of working with children to help them investigate the world of science is receiving a great deal of attention and energy on the part of scientists and science educators, and it is certainly a promising way for advancing the cogency and importance of science education. It is possible, for instance, for elementary and secondary school students to engage in the study of scientific problems to which the answers are not yet known. There are many such issues in earth science, ecology, natural history, climatology, animal behavior, etc. The problems may or may not be of great intrinsic consequence, but they provide the vehicle by which children and young people can begin to learn the methods of inquiry that are used in some of the sciences to roll back the horizons of knowledge.

Science instruction should be organized so that it is more consistent with the scientific enterprise. For example, science is a social enterprise utterly dependent upon communication between scientists and to an increasing extent between scientists and the larger public. This communication takes place through publications, private correspondence, conferences, and seminars. Should not participation in such activities be a part of science instruction? Science fairs have some merits, but there are few fairs held within the actual scientific enterprise. It would seem more desirable for students to take part in conferences and seminars where they can report their own work and discuss the work of others. The student science conferences now being co-sponsored by the National Science Teachers Association and the National Aeronautics and Space Administration are steps in the right direction. Scientists and science educators could share the burden of leadership in providing more opportunities, organize reports, and meet to interpret and discuss their work.

The challenge is to build a science education that will give our children and young people a chance to deal with tomorrow; and deal with it they must, although its problems may be both novel and frightening. Important beginnings have been made in the last few years, but science education is not yet fully recognized as an essential part of the very fabric of science. Perhaps the most important step to be taken for the improvement of science education is to acknowledge it as an integral part of science and to make it more consistent with science as a structure of human thought.

BALANCE IN HIGH SCHOOL EDUCATION

HERBERT J. KLAUSMEIER

According to Lawrence A. Cremin,[1] educational leaders in the early 1900's were successful in overcoming the narrowness and formalism of a curriculum that had prevented American high school education from being of value to many youth. During the early twentieth century many new subjects, especially vocational, were added to the high school curriculum; a much higher percent of all students attended high school; and teaching methods became less formal, less repressive. The high school seemed to be progressing successfully to meet social needs. By

FROM *Teachers College Record*, 67:18–25 (October 1965), Teachers College, Columbia University, N. Y. Reprinted by permission.

[1] L. A. Cremin, *The Transformation of the School: Progressivism in American Education* (New York: Alfred A. Knopf, 1961).

the late 1940's, however, it was apparent that education was no longer keeping up with the transformation of American society.

The effects of World War II upon education cannot yet be clearly established; but, in the 1950's high school education was regressing to the narrowly conceived subject orientation of the late nineteenth century. Some lay persons and professors emphasized only one function of the high school for all students, namely, developing the ability to think. In order to develop that ability, it was said, learning should be hard and painful, and all high school students should take the same subjects: English, foreign languages, mathematics, science, and social studies, especially history. A highly vocal group urging that these subjects dominate the high school curriculum for all students is the Council for Basic Education.[2]

James B. Conant, unlike the Council for Basic Education, has vigorously defended the continuation and strengthening of the American comprehensive high school, including its role in vocational education. However, he proposes a very narrow curriculum in the five "academic" subjects for academically talented students.[3] Although he would have academically talented students take 20 units in mathematics, science, English, social studies, and foreign languages prior to any electives in art, music, or vocational subjects, he insists that the majority of high school students should learn a marketable skill through a program of vocational education. For girls he suggests such courses as home economics, typing, stenography, or the use of clerical machines; for boys, vocational courses such as auto mechanics or machine-shop.

OBJECTIONS TO VERBAL CONCENTRATION

That many high school students during and immediately after World War II took too little work in the academic subjects is not debated. The critical point is that a desirable balance in education cannot be achieved by eliminating the non-verbal, fine arts and vocational subjects from the curriculum, as is now happening in many schools. Quality education cannot be exclusively verbal. Thinking critically about many significant problems requires some use of non-verbal symbols, often some actual psychomotor activity. To recommend only the five academic subjects for all high school students, including the academically talented, suggests ignorance of the diversity of human abilities and interests, lack of respect for the contribution of the non-verbal arts and work to the individual and society, and distrust of the democratic principle of freedom to choose from among various alternatives. One student may eventually achieve self-realization and make a maximum contribution to society as a scientist, another as an artist, another as a secretary, another as an auto mechanic, another as a homemaker. A balanced education, not an identical group of subjects, must be available in the secondary school for all these students and many others.

[2] J. D. Koerner (ed.), The Case for Basic Education (Boston: Little, Brown, 1959).
[3] J. B. Conant, The American High School Today (New York: McGraw-Hill Book Company, 1959).

VOCATIONAL EDUCATION REAPPRAISED

Since 1960, several conditions have resulted in a reappraisal of vocational education in the high school. Unemployment of young people, age 18 to 24, is as alarmingly high as the unemployment of older persons that is attributed to automation. Many college students quit prior to graduation for lack of money. The home is increasingly unable to provide vocational education. Personality deterioration may be related to the false value that through education one can avoid work. Chase has recently stated the case for vocational education[4]:

Unless interest in vocational education is awakened on a massive national scale, the United States will lose a crucial lap in 'the race between education and catastrophe'—in H. G. Wells' annually more apt definition of history.

... Today rational education must include training for the 80 per cent of all young Americans who enter the labor market without college degrees. To ignore their vocational training is a reverse twist on the Eskimos' fabled custom of pushing their unproductive senior citizens onto the ice pack. That practice at least has a certain economic logic. Our system is managing to be at once inhumane and economically suicidal.

Recent information about our population and jobs dramatizes the need for vocational education. Out of every 10 youngsters now in grade school, three will not finish high school. Seven will be graduated from high school. Three will go to work, some as wives and mothers. Four will continue into higher education but only two will finish college.

Twenty-six million young workers will have started work between 1960 and 1970. The most rapidly expanding occupations for the decade are, in this order: professional and technical, clerical and sales, service, skilled workers and proprietors, managers about equally, and semi-skilled last.[5]

The changing picture of both jobs and labor force suggests a need for the reappraisal of the entire field of vocational education, similar to what is occurring in the academic subject areas. Although this is the case, the comprehensive high school should now have a strong program in business education and in distributive education. Technicians, machine operators, mechanics and others in jobs related to the production, operation, and maintenance of machines will be needed in increasing numbers. Schools should be equipped immediately to teach general shop skills, psychomotor skills, knowledge, and attitudes which have transfer value for the jobs enumerated. The future of home economics and agriculture is uncertain, inasmuch as life in the home and on the farm is changing so rapidly. Fewer persons will work on the farms; more women will work outside the home. There is clearly a greater need for other types of vocational education.

In spite of the need for appraisal, we cannot afford to eliminate vocational education from the comprehensive high school. On the contrary, it should be possible for any student, including the academically talented, to pursue a major of

---

[4] E. T. Chase, "Learning to Be Unemployable," *Harper's* (April 1963), pp. 33–40.
[5] P. G. Haines (ed.), "A Time for Professional Statesmanship," *Delta Pi Epsilon Journal* (1963), 5:33.

three units in a vocational field. The larger high school might profitably have at least four general vocational programs, two particularly appropriate for girls and two for boys. Not every student should be required to take even one semester in a vocational subject, but a major of three units should not be denied to any student who desires to elect it. It is possible, of course, that many academically talented students will elect courses in the non-verbal fine arts rather than in a vocational field.

MANUAL LABOR BY UNDERGRADUATES

Vocational education is not solely for students who do not attend college. Many college students require vocational education because their families cannot support them. Lins studied students' expenses and sources of income on the Madison campus of the University of Wisconsin for the academic year 1960–61.[6] Information from his study is presented only for the *unmarried, undergraduate students who were residents of Wisconsin and not living at home*. The average cost of university attendance was $1,485 for these students, and their average total income was $1,619. Men received 31.7 per cent and women received 57.3 per cent of their income from family contributions. The average income from various sources was scholarships $82, work during the year $154, summer work $398, savings $169, loan $74, family contribution $660, and other including ROTC and military reserves $82.

About 46 per cent of the men and 42 per cent of the women worked. Of the working freshmen 50 per cent or more worked 8.5 or more hours per week; of the working seniors 50 per cent worked 12.5 or more hours per week. The average pay per hour was $.99 for freshmen and $1.38 for seniors. Ninety per cent of the working freshmen earned between $.59 and $1.22 and ninety per cent of the seniors earned between $.90 and $3.29 per hour. The minimum pay by the University for student hourly help was $.96 per hour.

Thirty-five per cent of the parents of males and 22 per cent of the parents of females earned less than $6,000 during 1960. About one-third of the mothers were working in occupations other than in the home. Twenty per cent of these students received no family support. Slightly above 16 per cent were in debt. Of all sophomores, juniors, and seniors who had been out of school for one semester or more since entrance, about two-thirds gave finances as the first or second reason for drop-out.

The Director of Student Employment at the University of Wisconsin states that the principal employment of males during the academic year, on and off campus, is in kitchens and dining facilities, laboratories, and libraries doing odd jobs, mostly *unskilled manual labor*. Males could be employed in clerical and to a lesser extent distributive occupations, if they had the skills. The principal employment of females is in clerical jobs, dining and kitchen facilities, and library and laboratories. The supply of typists who can type at moderate speeds nearly meets the demand

---

[6] L. J. Lins, *Student Expenses and Sources of Income 1960–1961: University of Wisconsin, Madison Campus* (Madison: University of Wisconsin, Office of Institutional Studies, 1961).

in University jobs; the supply of stenographers who can take shorthand at moderate speeds is far short of the demand. The supply of all jobs is, on and off campus, less than the demand.

The urban family experiences unsurmountable difficulty in providing household chores, much less work experience and vocational education, for children. Parents find it nearly impossible to locate work activities, in or outside the home, with or without pay, that is suited to the interests and abilities of adolescent boys, age 13 to 18. High school girls who baby sit, clean house, and prepare meals get little or no satisfaction from these activities, when repeated year after year. Manual labor tasks, distasteful to adults or for which the hourly rate is exceedingly low, are about the only ones available to high school students, and to able college students, as was shown previously. Even these jobs for youth are disappearing as chronic unemployment of unskilled and semi-skilled adults increases.

Education about work and careers also is meager in the modern home. The son usually does not see his father at work, much less learn the job from him. The same is true of the girl whose mother works. Most parents are only semi-literate about economic affairs, apparently preferring to permit others to manipulate much of their economic life. So poor is the total program of vocational education in the home and school that many unmarried female college graduates with majors in one of the liberal arts or sciences enroll in a business college in order to prepare themselves for a job. Also many industries employ some of the liberal arts graduates for less money than they pay equally young skilled workers—high school graduates with four years of work experience.

PERSONALITY, CULTURE, AND WORK

Work is closely related to individual personality and to culture. Man has progressed from prehistoric times to his present state only as he has been able, through work, to change the environment so that his many abilities might emerge and develop. His evolution is not so much a process of adjusting to the environment as adjusting the environment to suit his needs and emergent abilities.

Smith points out that most capitalist and socialist writers have treated work behavior narrowly either as a means of production, as a source of wealth, or as a limited aspect of technology; but not as a critical aspect of human behavior and adjustment.[7] He then develops a comprehensive theory to explain work as the primary determinant of the human condition. In this comprehensive theory, he relates how work in man has contributed to his evolution, how its feedback effects define the personality of each individual, how it has provided the dynamic human motivation toward social and economic development, and how its behavior mechanisms are regulated.

From a biosocial account of work, Smith theorizes how the feedback effects of occupation determine the specific properties of individual adjustment, mental

[7] K. U. Smith, *Behavior Organization and Work* (Madison, Wis.: College Printing and Typographical Co., 1962).

health, motivation, social integration, aging, and individual behavior resources. In referring to work and personality he says:

Throughout the ages of man's civilized existence, the events of work have borne an interacting relation to what is called personality. This relation at times has been decisive not only in structuring the human condition of existence and aspiration, but in specifically determining the social circumstances of individuality. In ancient periods, occupation determined class, caste, and the dominant personality association of each. . . . As the structure of institutional organization in industry has become more complex, the pattern of individual social behavior within the organized work systems has become more stylized and group-structured, leading to greater emphasis than heretofore on both the assessment and control of the over-all pattern of social-emotional behavior.

This approach to work behavior bears analysis, not only in America but throughout the world. Until recently, a minority in most nations of the Western world has argued successfully for liberal education of a wealthy elite ruling class, educated to accrue wealth, to rule, to lead, and on the other hand, low-cost, technical education or no education for the masses of working people. Until recently, America has successfully pursued a different course through its comprehensive high school, which has included vocational education as a primary objective.

VALUES OF NON-VERBAL ARTS

Instrumental music, the visual arts, and dance are relatively non-verbal in comparison with English, mathematics, science, social studies, and foreign languages. Vocal music and dramatics are also non-verbal in many respects. The content of these non-verbal arts may not be selected intelligently and the courses may not be taught well in many high schools at the present time. Though this is the case, it is almost unbelievable that liberally educated persons are recommending, explicitly or implicitly, that academically talented high school students should not take work for credit in these arts. The truly educated person appreciates the cultural heritage more fully through understanding at least one of the non-verbal arts. He has liberated himself from ignorance about a most important area of human activity and has also learned to control his own instrumental acts in an individually and socially constructive manner. A kind of blindness concerning the purpose of man and civilized society has led some to treat the non-verbal fine arts as non-essential to liberal education.

Taking a course in painting or instrumental music for credit can be defended as readily as taking a course in a modern foreign language if the primary purposes of the foreign language are to learn to understand and speak the language, to read and write it, and to understand the culture of other people who speak the language. Learning to express oneself with a musical instrument is a more complex psycho-motor skill; but understanding music notation and composition is as worth while an intellectual operation as is understanding the grammar of the language. Great musical compositions are understood by people from many lands and are part of the culture of many nations. Music and visual arts are surely more nearly universal than is any verbal language.

The greatest value to be derived from acquiring competence in one of the arts is the ability to express one's feelings and ideas in a medium other than words. The need to achieve is very strong in our society. Many students are frustrated in connection with their perceived lack of competence in one or another academic subject or in other daily affairs. Gaining mastery over self, over the musical instrument or art medium, and over the self-medium relationship should not be underestimated as a means of achieving self-realization.

To propose that instruction in the arts should be at the expense of the parents is to deny most high school students the instruction. To propose that this work can be taken solely in the summer or as extracurricular activity is to indicate that one's value system is negatively oriented toward the arts. The many liberal arts colleges, public and private universities, and state colleges which offer majors in music and art are tangible evidence that these subject fields have a substantial content and should not be dismissed as frills, unworthy of credit in the high school.

Unless there is some threat to national security of which the writer is unaware, the taking of twenty units of work in the five academic subjects prior to any work in the fine arts cannot be justified. On the contrary, every academically talented student should be permitted to take a full major of three units or years of work in one of the non-verbal arts, or three years in a combination of them. Every high school should offer at least three years of work in music and three years in the visual arts. There also should be course work, to be counted toward high school graduation, in dance and in dramatics. It is possible, of course, that the content and methods of instruction in the non-verbal arts need thorough revision.

RECOMMENDATIONS FOR BALANCE

Although vast changes should be made in secondary schooling in the next decades, let us assume that the majority of high school students will spend from three to five years completing what are now normally Grades 9 through 12 in a comprehensive high school. The balance to be achieved in high school is among the three main objectives: general education, incorporated in the required program for all students; vocational education, including the acquisition of a marketable skill or the beginning of it; and education to prepare for college attendance.

The general education requirement for all students might be 9 years or units: 3 in English, 2 in social studies, 1 each in mathematics, science, and a fine art, and 1 additional unit in one of the first four subject fields. The student who does not plan to go to college might take the remaining 7 of 16 units in any combination of subjects but should probably take at least three in a vocational area.

The academically talented students need a different, but flexible program. It is the academically talented who are now being put on a diet of only academic subjects. Further, even the oldest, brightest students are forced to stay in high school for four years, instead of being permitted to graduate after three or three and one-half years, in order to complete 18 to 20 units in the five academic subjects. The six recommendations which follow are intended to provide for balance in the program for academically talented high school students.[8]

1. Every student identified as academically talented in English, foreign languages, mathematics, science, or social studies toward the end of Grade 6 or the beginning of Grade 7 or 8 should be given the opportunity to take condensed work in each subject in which he is superior and should receive full credit toward high school graduation for any work of high school caliber completed by the end of Grade 8, up to a total of four units. The student superior in all subjects should complete any four of the following subjects, normally ninth-grade subjects, by the end of Grade 8; general science, algebra, civics or some other social studies, Grade 9 English, and Grade 9 foreign language. The student superior in one, two, or three fields should complete one, two, or three units in the respective subjects by the end of Grade 8.

2. The academically talented student should be permitted to take five courses, in addition to physical education, during each year, Grades 9–12, and should be required to take at least four courses.

3. The academically talented student who completes 6 to 9 units required for high school graduation by the end of Grade 9 should have the following options available in the senior high school (Grades 10–12):

a. Attend senior high school for three years and take one or more courses designed specifically for admission to college with advanced standing.

b. Attend senior high school for three years and take for college credit one or more courses at an easily accessible local university or college during the senior year.

c. Attend senior high school for two or two and one-half years, be graduated, and then enter an easily accessible local university or college full time.

d. Attend senior high school for two or two and one-half years, be graduated, and then enter any university or college of the student's choice full time.

e. Attend senior high school for three school years but take no course designed specifically for college admission with advanced standing (no acceleration involved).

f. Attend senior high school for three years but have released time for part time employment in the senior year (no acceleration involved).

4. Each student identified as academically talented as early as Grade 10 should be required to complete at least 12 units in the academic subjects and at least a total of 17 units in all subjects for high school graduation, excluding physical education. The 12 units required in the academic subjects should be distributed as follows: 3 in English, 2 in mathematics, 2 in foreign language, 2 in science, 2 in social studies, and 1 additional unit in any of the five subject fields. Each academically talented student should thus be required to complete a minor of 2 units in four

[8] H. J. Klausmeier, *Desirable Education for High School Students of Superior Learning Abilities* (Madison: Wisconsin Improvement Program, 1962), pp. 38–43.

academic subjects and a major of 3 or 4 units in one, or a major of 3 units in two subjects and a minor in each of the other three. The 5 additional elective units might be totally in the non-verbal arts and/or vocational subjects or they might be distributed among the academic subjects, the non-verbal arts, and vocational subjects as outlined in the next recommendation.

5. The academically talented student should be required to take one unit in the non-verbal arts and/or vocational subjects for each unit above fourteen taken in the academic subjects. Thus, the student graduating with 18 units should be permitted to take a maximum of 16 units in the academic subjects and should be required to take a minimum of 2 units in the non-verbal arts and/or vocational subjects; the student graduating with 20 units should be permitted to take a maximum of 17 units in the academic subjects and should be required to take a minimum of 3 units in the fine arts and/or vocational subjects.

6. The academically talented student should complete 4 units in at least three subject fields before completing 5 units in any field, and should not be permitted to complete more than 6 units in any subject field during Grades 8–12. The student completing 22 units, 18 in the academic subjects and 4 in the fine arts and vocational subjects, could take 3 units in each of two academic subjects and 4 in each of the other three for a total of 18; or he might take 2 units in each of two subjects, 4 units in each of two others, and 6 in the fifth for a total of 18 units in the academic subjects. The 4 units in the fine arts and/or vocational subjects likewise could be distributed or all in one subject.

If college-bound students are permitted to acquire a saleable skill at a beginning level or to pursue a non-verbal art, there is some hope that vocational education and the non-verbal arts will survive in the comprehensive high school for the non-college bound students. We should not expect the fine arts or any vocational subject to survive when the many students who think they will go to college, the high school counselors, principals, and teachers in the academic subjects shun them as unworthy of serious study, unworthy of credit toward graduation. Unless the non-verbal arts, as well as vocational education, receive proper attention in arranging a balanced education for each student, our system will not only be inhumane and economically suicidal, as Chase has pointed out, it will also be culturally sterile.

THE KNOWLEDGE EXPLOSION
Implications for Secondary Education

RALPH W. TYLER

We speak of the knowledge explosion because of the exponential rate at which new facts are being discovered in the sciences. Scientific information is doubling in every 10 to 15 years so that its mere storage is a very serious problem. Great libraries are crowded beyond belief, and electronic methods for locating articles, books and papers are being experimented with in an effort to keep all this new knowledge available for man's use. The National Science Foundation and the Department of Defense, among other government agencies, have made grants and contracts to several institutions to experiment with more effective ways for searching for information. Scientists, scholars and reference librarians are overwhelmed by the mass of printed material passing over their desks. Because more and more research investigations are undertaken, new facts are being reported at an ever increasing rate.

This obviously has implications for the school curriculum. Are our high school courses up-to-date or do they represent science and scholarship which has been outmoded? Can we cover all we need to cover? Textbooks cannot be expanded indefinitely. Learning takes time. For young people to gain an understanding of ideas, of principles and of facts, requires an active effort on their part in expressing these ideas, principles and facts in their own words, in using them to explain phenomena and to guide actions. Effective learning is not passively recalling what is presented. It is an active endeavor on the part of the learner, and what becomes part of him is what he has actively formulated, responded to or used in some way that is relevant.

Knowledge can be used in several ways. Some knowledge helps in developing understanding so that we now can explain things that we could not explain before. Some is useful for guiding action, such as knowledge of technology that tells how to do things. Some knowledge is useful in developing our feelings so that we are aided in getting new satisfactions and meanings out of various kinds of esthetic experiences. All of these uses of knowledge require active participation on the part of the learner. When more material is presented to students than they have time to treat in this way, they attempt to memorize it by rote and to parrot back statements

FROM *The Educational Forum*, 29:145–153 (January 1965). Copyright: Kappa Delta Pi, An Honor Society in Education. Reprinted by permission.

from their textbooks. This is not the kind of learning required for knowledge to be a part of their thinking, feeling and acting.

Not only are the numbers of facts increasing at a rapid rate, but new discoveries change the meanings and implications of many of the facts which were previously known. Hence, memorizing huge numbers of facts today will not provide adequate understanding for tomorrow. Students who are crammed full in this way will find several years hence that they have a mixture of information and misinformation rather than an adequate background to understand our changing world and to use its material, intellectual, and esthetic resources effectively.

SCHOOL LEARNINGS

What can the high schools do when knowledge is expanding so rapidly? I should like to suggest six approaches or steps which can be taken to aid in solving this difficult problem. A first step is to concentrate the major efforts of the high school on important tasks which it can do best. This is not new. High schools have been giving some attention to this since the end of World War II, seeking to identify educational tasks so as to emphasize those particularly appropriate for the school in contrast to those that are best carried on by other educative agencies. In this changing world, every generation requires additional educational services because there is an increasing range of things to be learned. It is only natural, since our public schools are supported by public funds, for the schools to be asked to assume responsibility for all new learning jobs. But when schools attempt this they are overwhelmed by more tasks than they can do well. They find themselves spending time in teaching things that could be taught effectively elsewhere. In the case of particular tasks, like swimming or driver education, there may be conditions in some communities that justify school attention, but the general principle remains the same—that there are some things that the school and the school alone is likely to do effectively. Those are the things that require first, a well-educated faculty, people who know far more than the usual parent and community member who has not had this opportunity for education; second, what is to be learned necessitates well-organized experiences over time. The basic concepts and modes of inquiry in science, English, history or mathematics cannot usually be picked up in a few hours here and a few hours there. Such learning must be carefully organized over time, so the student is building a structure systematically in order to reach a relatively high level of understanding.

Third, the school is particularly needed to provide learning opportunities in cases in which the essential factors are not obvious to the observer and the principles, concepts, and meanings must be specially brought to the attention of the learner. Thus, the scientific concepts and principles which explain the growth and development of plants are not obvious to the observer of plants or even to an uneducated farm hand. The school can more effectively provide for this learning than can the job.

Fourth, it is particularly appropriate for the school to provide learning experiences that cannot be provided directly in the ordinary activities of daily life. Geography and history are excellent illustrations of fields where daily life experience alone is not likely to provide sufficient insight into historic matters and affairs relating to places far removed.

Fifth, a kind of learning particularly appropriate for the school is that which requires more "purified" experience than is commonly available in life outside the school. Students may learn something of art, music, literature, or human relations from the examples commonly found in the community, but when these fall short of the best, the students have no chance to set high standards for themselves. The school can provide examples for study and enjoyment which represent the best available.

Finally, another kind of learning particularly appropriate to the school is that in which re-examination and interpretation of experience are essential. Our basic ethical values are commonly involved in the daily experiences of youth. Questions of justice, fairness, goodness arise again and again on the playground, in the market place, and elsewhere. It is not likely, however, that mere contact with these ideas will be enough to help youth develop for themselves values that are clearly understood and effectively utilized. The school can provide opportunity from time to time to recall these experiences, to examine them and to interpret them, and thus to clarify the meanings of values as well as to help students to appreciate them more adequately.

These six kinds of learning which are peculiarly appropriate to the school ought to be strongly emphasized in the school program in contrast to other learnings which can be provided by other agencies. This selection will reduce the educational tasks of the school somewhat, but the fields remaining are vast and growing rapidly, so that this step alone is not enough to solve the problem.

UPDATING CURRICULUM

A second step is to see that the curriculum in each field is periodically, if not continuously, updated as to its objectives, its content and emphasis, and its learning experiences. A national effort to update the curriculum in science and mathematics was begun in 1959 when the National Science Foundation made an initial grant to the Physical Science Study Committee which is headed by Jerold Zacharias at MIT. This committee brought together very able physicists, teachers, school administrators, professors of education, and students of human learning to work intensively to build a new high school course in physics. The committee examined the textbooks, courses of study, and curriculum guides in physics and found that there had been no real change in the basic physics course since 1910. These materials did not represent modern physics. They reported that the content was outmoded, the notions of what physics is had been changed, and the objectives were not those that are now believed most important ones by leading physicists and teachers. A new course was needed. Then the Physical Science Study Group began its pioneering effort to build a new high school physics course which is now being tried in hundreds of schools. This task has taken a great deal of time and money. It could not be done by every school system nor by every state, because neither individual schools nor many states can obtain the services of highly competent scientists, a group of able teachers and other specialists who have been thinking about curriculum problems and working with new materials. Hence, updating the school curriculum is now recognized increasingly as a matter of national concern.

The National Science Foundation has supported or is supporting a number of other curriculum projects in the sciences and in mathematics and has granted more than 30 million dollars to the work. One of the significant policies of the Foundation is that in any field there will be at least two approaches to the new curriculum, because no one group is likely to have all the knowledge and all the good ideas which need to be tried. In line with this policy, a grant has recently been made to a new group in the field of physics to develop a modern physics program in the high school, not to update PSSC but to provide some new approaches, because other good physicists saw new ways of trying to make physics more meaningful and understandable. There are presently two projects in high school chemistry, three approaches to high school biology, and several in mathematics.

In addition to new courses in the natural sciences, there are national projects in the social sciences. These include geography, anthropology, sociology, economics, political science, and social psychology. Furthermore, the U.S. Office of Education is now authorized to support work in English, foreign languages, and the social studies. The new vocational education act of 1963 provides that ten per cent of the funds made available are to be used in experimentation, including experimentation with new curricula.

What is required in order to do an adequate job in updating a curriculum is to bring together scholars, scientists, teachers, experts in learning, administrators, and other persons familiar with school conditions who will work on the several major parts of the task. They will seek to clarify the kinds of contribution that each field can make to the education of young people that will help them to understand the world and their own lives, to act effectively, and to get more meaning and satisfaction from their experiences. In the light of the proposed objectives, relevant content is then selected, learning experiences and materials are designed and then tried out. Revisions are made as a result of the tryouts. This is a long term effort, but nothing less will do.

LIFE-LONG LEARNING

A third step in dealing with the rapid explosion of knowledge is to emphasize throughout the curriculum the concept of education as a process of continued life-long learning. It is not possible for us to master in three years, twelve years, sixteen years, or in any specific time, all that we need to learn. Hence, the secondary school should help students develop the interests, abilities and habits required for carrying on life-long learning. They include, first, developing interest in study and learning so that students find out the satisfaction and joy of getting new ideas, of learning new things, and of keeping up with developments in a field. Second, students must acquire the abilities required to study and learn in each field. In some cases these are abilities needed to get things from books, periodicals, and reference material. In some cases, as in the sciences, the ability to make observations and to use laboratories appropriately are required. In most fields the ability to study demands skill in identifying and formulating the right questions to ask, the ability to organize observations and to identify relationships. In some fields studying is trying out things, as in the plastic arts or the vocational and industrial arts.

Furthermore, the school can help students acquire the habit of seeking new knowledge and understanding. For habits to be formed, the students need consistent and continuing practice in study and inquiry. Each high school course will provide opportunities for investigation and study rather than a series of recitations from the textbook. In science, for example, questions are being raised, and students are going to the laboratory, to books, and to the field for information on which to formulate and test ideas. To take another illustration, the course in literature becomes a quest for meanings and satisfactions in books. In all courses, stressing the process of study and the use of inquiry in the daily lives of students helps them to become life-long learners.

ORGANIZE MATERIAL

A fourth step which helps to make significant education possible, in spite of the great mass of material accumulating in each field, is to select and organize the content in a way that can be understood by the student and used by him effectively. Knowledge is not a vast collection of isolated items. Each field of knowledge has developed as an organized structure, that is, the field is not just a miscellaneous collection of facts. To understand biology, for example, is not to remember thousands of specific unrelated facts but to have in mind certain concepts and principles with related facts that help to explain and give meaning to biological phenomena. To learn a foreign language, to use another example, it is not necessary to memorize the entire vocabulary or to read all the latest books in the language. Each language has a structure, a language pattern, which when understood, enables the student to use the language effectively and to continue to broaden and deepen his skill and understanding. Because of the structure developed by the scholars in each subject it is possible to organize learning experiences for more efficient learning. Hence, although knowledge may double in ten or fifteen years it is not actually true that the requirements for understanding double in that period.

The curriculum work of the Physical Science Study Group is a good illustration of the economy of learning with an organized body of knowledge. This high school physics course utilizes only a relatively small number of concepts, such as energy, time and motion. Actually only thirty-four concepts are stressed, and around these concepts the whole high school physics course is built. If the youngster understands these basic notions, and the facts related to them, he is able to explain most physical phenomena with which he has experience.

The new courses in mathematics are also constructed around a few basic notions on which the logical operations of that field are carried on. In the field of language there are a small number of fundamental ideas that are very essential to the elaboration of language skills and understanding.

The structure of a subject usually includes some other elements in addition to concepts. In science, for example, there are principles, that is relationships among observed facts. Each principle serves to summarize or generalize a large number of specific items. Hence, to understand a principle is to comprehend a great deal of material. There is a danger that students will treat principles as empty forms and try to memorize them without comprehending the specific matters to which they relate. This can be obviated by having the student formulate the principle in his own words as he attempts to generalize the relationships he finds from the concrete cases which he encounters, and by asking him to give illustrations of the principle whenever he states it. Implicit in the structure of every subject are the kinds of questions it seeks to answer, and the kinds of methods it uses in carrying on its inquiry. These are matters which the student should understand and that will help him to find his way about in the great mass of current knowledge. To summarize, content can be organized for teaching and learning so as to aid the student in understanding its structure. In every course, the student should be able to answer the following:

1. What kinds of questions does this subject seek to answer?
2. What kinds of methods does it use to study these questions?
3. What concepts are basic in this subject to give order and meaning to its specific data?
4. What generalizations are being obtained and what are illustrations of the specific items to which these generalizations apply?
5. How can this subject be used in my daily life?

If he can answer those five questions, we have helped to organize the subject for learning. It is amazing how much can be understood, remembered, and used by the students when materials are selected and dealt with in this way.

BETTER SEQUENCES

A fifth step for dealing with the knowledge explosion is to work out better sequences of learning in the several fields. We do not have yet good sequences of learning in all subjects. Attention has been given to sequential development in foreign languages, but the high school social studies program is typically not one in which the second year builds upon the first and carries the ideas, skills, and values introduced in the first year to a much deeper and broader level in the second. The third year does not build very comprehensively upon the second nor the fourth year upon the third. In English, science, and the arts the curriculum lacks sequential development. Even mathematics is not well developed sequentially when algebra in the first year is followed by geometry in the second and trigonometry in the third. When a comprehensive sequence is developed, the students can attain a much higher level of competence than when sequential treatment is neglected and each course starts at the beginning.

CONDITIONS OF LEARNING

Finally, a sixth step is to give much more careful attention to efficient learning. Although there are many specific factors about learning which are not precisely understood, research and experience have provided knowledge of several conditions which influence the effectiveness of learning. If these conditions were more adequately met, the efficiency of education could be markedly increased.

I mean such well understood conditions for learning as that the learner must carry on the behavior he is to learn. In the final analysis, it is not what the teacher does, but what the learner does, which determines learning. If the learner is to acquire a skill, he must perform the operations involved in the skill until it has become part of his continuing repertoire of behavior. If he is to gain understanding, he must carry on the intellectual behavior involved, such as explaining relationships, comparing and contrasting concepts, predicting consequences. If he is to develop attitudes, he must have experience in perceiving the phenomena from the relevant points of view. Furthermore, learning not only requires the learner to carry on the behavior he is to learn, but he must also find it rewarding. Unless he obtains satisfaction from the behavior, it will not become a continuing part of his repertoire of behavior.

These two basic conditions for learning provide the primary guides to devising educational programs. Whatever the forms of teaching and learning used, they must enable the student to carry on the behavior he is to learn, and they must enable him to obtain satisfaction from carrying on the behavior successfully. Keeping these two conditions in mind helps greatly in planning what is to be done, but there are several other conditions required for learning to be effective which can be used in planning. One of these is the motivation of the student. Since he learns what he is thinking, feeling or doing, learning is not possible except as the learner is involved in it. This must be considered in planning the educational program. What present motivations can be built on? What new motivations can be developed which will involve the students more deeply in the program?

A fourth condition is that the student finds his previous ways of reacting unsatisfactory so that he is stimulated to try new ways. As long as he does not recognize that earlier modes of behavior in this field are inappropriate, he will keep on doing what he has been doing before and will not really learn anything new. For example, persons trying to learn new skills often do not recognize that the new skill is based on a point of view quite different from the one they have been holding. When motivated to learn the new skill, they put more effort in trying to perform the operations with the old point of view, which is in conflict with the new. It is necessary for the teacher to help the student discover that his earlier point of view is not a satisfactory one on which to develop the new skills.

A fifth condition is for the student to have some guidance in trying to carry on the new behavior he is to learn. If he simply tries new behavior by trial and error, learning is very slow and he is often discouraged and gives up. Learners very commonly look to the teacher as a guide. If the teacher demonstrates what the learner is to do, this is very helpful. Unfortunately, many teachers lecture about the subject rather than showing how the subject is attacked. In such cases, the trainees think they are to memorize what the teacher says, rather than to question, seek to explain, apply in practice, or carry on other desired behavior.

A sixth condition is for the student to have appropriate materials to work on. If he is to learn to solve problems, he has to have problems to be solved; if he is to gain skills, he must have tasks which give him the opportunity to practice these skills; if he is to develop attitudes, he must have opportunities to see the phenomena in new perspective and to be able to respond to the situation with new feeling tones. When students have only texts and lectures, they do not have enough material to attain the objectives sought.

A seventh condition is obviously a corollary of the sixth. The student must have *time* to carry on the behavior, to keep practicing it. Often educational programs assume that if time is provided for the presentation of material, adequate time has been allocated for learning. Actually, the time the student spends in practicing the behavior to be learned is the most critical in determining whether he really learns. The time set for this is usually insufficient.

These seven are not all the conditions which are known to have a marked influence on the effectiveness of learning, but they are among the most important ones. Careful efforts to provide and maintain these conditions would increase greatly the effectiveness of our educational programs at a time when the total educational job is so great that every means to improve learning should be utilized.

SUMMARY

Knowledge is being acquired at an exponential rate. This increases greatly the educational task of the secondary school. Today, the high school graduate is expected to be as well educated as was a college graduate 50 to 60 years ago. This is a great responsibility, but not an impossible one. There are steps we can take that will help us to increase our effectiveness in dealing with rapidly expanding knowledge. First, we can review our educational program to see that we do not undertake in our schools tasks that can be done elsewhere, and that we concentrate our attention upon the things that are most important and that require the conditions of the school for effective learning. Second, we can encourage and participate in the efforts to update the curriculum in each of the major fields. Third, we can stress in each course the concept of education as study and inquiry rather than memorizing answers to questions. Fourth, we can see that the courses are developed in such a way that they are well organized in psychological terms for the student to understand and to use the resources they provide. Fifth, we can work out better sequences of courses from the elementary school through the high school so as to reach an increasingly higher level of learning. Finally, we can give more attention to providing the conditions for learning that will markedly increase its effectiveness. By doing these things, we can deal constructively with the knowledge explosion so that in another generation high school graduates will be actively using the current additions to knowledge rather than being overwhelmed by them.

SCHOOLS FOR THE MIDDLE SCHOOL YEARS

WILLIAM M. ALEXANDER and EMMETT L. WILLIAMS

What school organization is best for pupils in that stage of development between childhood and adolescence? Some fifty years ago, the answer was to be a new *unior high* school for grades 7, 8 and 9. This pattern spread relatively rapidly, and a six-year (or six plus kindergarten) elementary followed by a three-year junior and three-year senior high has become the prevailing school organization in the United States.

Yet while these past decades of experience with this pattern have produced many significant and lasting features, there seems today increasing disenchantment with the schools for the middle school years. Some question whether the junior high school is a bridge between elementary and high school or a vestibule to the latter; others are urging change upon the typical graded, self-contained classroom of the elementary school, especially in its upper grades.

THE 6-3-3 PLAN?

Certainly there is not an adequate basis in research for strict adherence to the status quo. Research on school organization does not demonstrate the clear superiority of any one organizational arrangement over all others. Anderson's review [1] of research on organization in relation to staff utilization and deployment led him to conclude that "... recent research upon which policies of staff utilization and deployment must be based, at least temporarily, is woefully inadequate." What can be concluded from a review of the literature is that existing arrangements

[1] Robert H. Anderson, "Organizational Character of Education: Staff Utilization and Deployment," *Review of Educational Research* (October 1964) 34:455–69.

do not seem to satisfy some criteria for a school organization and a program consistent with psychological and physiological needs of pupils and relevant to modern societal demands.

For example, there is little research evidence to support, and some reason to question, the assumption that a junior high, separate and distinct from both elementary and senior high school, is a necessity because of the unique characteristics of the age group. On the contrary side, Margaret Mead[2] argues that the grades included in junior high "were postulated on age, and not on size, strength, or stage of puberty." As a result she observes that:

They have resulted inadvertently in classifying together boys and girls when they vary most, within each sex, and between the sexes, and are least suited to a segregated social existence. Also, they have divorced them from the reassurances of association with the children like their own recent past selves and older adolescents like whom they will some day become. When a type of school that was designed to cushion the shock of change in scholastic demands has become the focus of the social pressures which were once exerted in senior high school, problems have been multiplied.

From his viewpoint as a psychiatrist, Berman[3] sees the change from elementary to junior high school as quite poorly timed for children. He declares that "in the midst of deciding who they are, they shouldn't have to waste any energy finding out where they are." His opinion is that "during the highly volatile years of eleven through thirteen or fourteen, youngsters should have a familiar, secure background in which to operate."

Dacus'[4] study of pupils in grades five through ten raises interesting questions. On the criterion measures of social, emotional, and physical maturity, and opposite-sex choices, the *least* differences were found between pupils in grades six and seven, and pupils in grades nine and ten. Yet it is between these grades that our present 6-3-3 plan divides children.

The junior high school is most often defended on the grounds of the *bridge* function. It is supposed to serve as a bridge between the relatively untroubled, relaxed world of childhood and the more rigorous, stressful, disciplined world of high school. Johnson[5] declares: "In a world in which adults expound one set of values and espouse another, in which schooling is prolonged and economic dependence is protracted, and in which social life is largely outside the family, the value of a haven the junior high attempts to be is readily recognized" but notes that not all junior high schools have succeeded in this regard. He criticized the junior high for its tendency to imitate the senior high.

---

[2] Margaret Mead, "Early Adolescence in the United States," *Bulletin of the National Association of Secondary School Principals* (April 1965), 49:5–10.
[3] Sidney Berman, "As a Psychiatrist Sees Pressures on Middle Class Teenagers," *NEA Journal* (February 1965), 54:17–24.
[4] Wilfred P. Dacus, "A Study of the Grade Organizational Structure of the Junior High School As Measured by Social Maturity, Emotional Maturity, Physical Maturity, and Opposite-Sex Choices," *Dissertation Abstracts* (University of Houston, 1963), 24:1461–62.
[5] Mauritz Johnson, Jr., "School in the Middle—Junior High: Education's Problem Child," *Saturday Review* (July 21, 1962), 45:40–42, 56.

Hull[6] claims that junior high "is a poor investment," and that "it puts the unstable child at a most vulnerable period in his life in a situation more appropriate for older youth." On the other hand, it is commonly observed that today's children grow up faster in many ways. Havighurst[7] states that ". . . the adolescent today is more *precocious* and more *complex*. . . . He has many experiences *earlier* than his parents had these experiences." But does the present "bridge" school serve the intellectual needs of such children? Lounsbury and Marani[8] concluded from "shadow studies" in grade 8 classrooms across the country that the learning environment "was often unstimulating; there was lack of diversity in the program of required subjects; and there was little provision for individual differences among pupils."

PROPOSED: A MODEL MIDDLE SCHOOL

Along with the scholars and researchers cited, the present authors seriously question whether the currently dominant organizational arrangements for educating older children, preadolescents, and early adolescents provide optimum possibilities. New middle school organizations and programs[9] now being developed in various communities across the United States indicate considerable interest in experimentation with patterns differing from those now characteristic of the upper elementary and junior high school years. For consideration by others interested in developing alternative models, we offer the following as one set of possibilities for a model middle school.

GUIDELINES

A real middle school should be designed to serve the needs of older children, preadolescents, and early adolescents. Pupils would enter the middle school at the approximate age of ten years and would progress to the upper or high school at the approximate age of fourteen. Today's children in this age bracket need freedom of movement, opportunities for independence, a voice in the running of their own affairs, the intellectual stimulation of working with different groups and with different teacher specialists.

They are eager and ready for experiences quite different from those available in the typical elementary school. On the other hand, a congenial school environment for these children should be free of the rigidity of total departmentalization, the pressures of interschool competitions, and the tensions of older adolescent social functions that loom so large in typical junior high schools. The middle school would be planned to serve a truly transitional function from childhood to adolescence. Its organizational arrangements should foster growth from childhood dependence toward a high degree of self-sufficiency.

[6] J. H. Hull, "The Junior High School Is a Poor Investment," *Nation's Schools* (April 1960), 65:78–81.
[7] Robert J. Havighurst, "Lost Innocence—Modern Junior High Youth," *Bulletin of the National Association of Secondary School Principals* (April 1965), 49:1–4.
[8] John Lounsbury and Jean Marani, *The Junior High School We Saw: One Day in the Eighth Grade* (Washington, D. C.: Association for Supervision and Curriculum Development, 1964).
[9] Judith Murphy, *Middle Schools* (New York: Educational Facilities Laboratories, 1965).

A middle school organization should make a reality of the long-held ideal of individualized instruction. Every pupil would be assigned a teacher-counselor who coordinates the learner's total program throughout the middle school years in conjunction with other teachers and specialists who know him. An adequate program of diagnostic services would permit teachers to plan individual deviations from standard programs.

Pupils would be scheduled to work in special instructional centers where they may either catch up on needed skills or branch out into further exploration. Programmed instructional materials and other individually paced approaches would be utilized, and self-directed learning emphasized. Non-graded arrangements could permit students to progress at different rates and to different depths.

A middle school program should give high priority to the intellectual components of the curriculum. There should be a planned sequence of concepts and skills for the general education areas of the curriculum. This does not imply emphasis on mastery of content of a narrow range of academic subjects, but rather that every effort would be made to create a climate in which learning is exciting and rewarding. What is required is not attainment of uniform standards but that every learner be challenged to perform well at whatever level he is capable of attaining.

In such an environment, intellectual pursuits would be as respected as the social and athletic components of the program, and children would be helped to see that learning can be its own reward uncluttered by any extrinsic system of grades as reward or punishment. Every pupil would be scheduled in a series of planned opportunities for developing both creative and disciplined thinking.

A middle school program should place primary emphasis on skills of continued learning. Direct instruction in use of various modes of inquiry and the discovery method helps children to experience joy in learning. In all studies, continued attention would be given to the learning process itself. Teachers would guide pupils in the use of sources, teach them to formulate questions, gather information and materials, and test hypotheses. Pupils would be given increasing opportunities to assume responsibility for portions of their own learning through use of independent study plans.

A middle school should provide a rich program of exploratory experiences. The child of middle school age needs many opportunities to explore new interests. Special interest centers, competently supervised and operated on a flexible time basis, should provide individualized instruction in each curriculum area and also in such varied activities as reading, acting, photography, ceramics, typing, personal grooming, and many others. Boy Scout merit badge and Girl Scout proficiency badge work, and other youth programs could be incorporated into the school program under the coordination of the teacher-counselor. A portion of every pupil's schedule would include exploratory experiences.

A program of health and physical education should be designed especially for boys and girls of the middle school years. Direct instruction in essential knowledge of personal hygiene would be combined with regular participation in fitness activities, heterosexual group games, and carry-over sports activities. Adequate facilities and specialized supervision should be provided for a total range of physical and health needs including corrective and remedial programs.

An emphasis on values should underline all aspects of a middle school program. A middle school should offer unique advantages for helping children to formulate personal values and standards, and to analyze and question social attitudes and group behaviors. Children of this age are approaching or undergoing physical and psychological changes which they are striving to understand. They are beginning to establish new roles for themselves which sometimes conflict with adult expectations. They are increasingly aware of discrepancies between stated ideals and observed actions. Intellectually honest and emotionally calm exploration of these value areas with competent adult guidance would be a part of each pupil's regularly scheduled program.

The organization of a middle school would facilitate most effective use of the special competencies and interests of the teaching staff. Cooperative arrangements for teaching and guidance, special instructional center personnel, technicians and other aides, and ample supervisory staff would be utilized to enable each person to make his maximum contribution to the total program. Ample instructional planning time and in-service training opportunities would be provided for each teacher. The staff should be employed on a twelve-months contract with provisions for periodic study-leave.

THE CURRICULUM PLAN

The curriculum plan of a real middle school would consist of planned programs in three phases: Learning Skills; General Studies; and Personal Development. Every pupil would be scheduled into each of the three phases each year in school. The time requirements and the nature of the work in each phase would vary for individual pupil programs, but the general plan is seen as follows:

1. *Learning Skills Phase.* Continues and expands basic communicational and computational skills development begun at the primary school level, with increasing emphasis on use of library tools and skills of independent study. Skills for emphasis are identified and included along with content goals in each unit of work in all General Studies areas. A remedial program of skills development is conducted in special laboratory centers.

2. *General Studies Phase.* Includes those learning experiences which give the learner a heightened awareness of his cultural heritage and those other common learnings essential to civic and economic literacy. Content would be focused on major concepts and unifying themes drawn from the areas of literature, social studies, mathematics, science, and fine arts. Some of the instruction in this phase might be in groups of up to 100 pupils.

3. *Personal Development Phase.* Includes those experiences which fulfill personal and remedial needs, permit exploration of personal interests, and promote physical and social growth; health and physical education geared to the 10–14 year-old; individually planned experiences in foreign languages, typing, technical training,

music, art, dramatics, journalism; student-managed enterprises; community work projects; advanced work in science, mathematics, and other areas of individual special competence and interest.

ORGANIZATION FOR INSTRUCTION

The organization for instruction would be designed to facilitate an optimum curriculum and continuous progress for every pupil. Pupils in the middle school would not be expected to progress at the same rate or to the same depth. Neither would a student be expected to be at the same graded level in all of his studies. Planning and evaluation of an individual's progress through the curriculum should be a cooperative process based on diagnostic and evaluative data and involving his homeroom teacher, other teachers who work with him, and other special personnel, with the pupil himself involved at appropriate levels. Most children would remain in the middle school for a period of four years; however, some might be ready to move into the upper or high school after three years, and some might need to remain in the middle school for a fifth year.

The basic instructional unit of a middle school should be the individual. The significant organizational arrangements can be described by analyzing the various groups and centers through which an individual student would be scheduled.

1. *Homeroom Unit.* Each pupil would be a member of a homeroom group of about 25 pupils who are in the same year in school but are heterogeneously grouped on other criteria. A homeroom teacher-counselor, competent to give basic instruction in the General Studies area, and skilled in planning individual programs, would be assigned to each Homeroom Unit. The teacher-counselor would work out an individual program with each pupil, mandated by diagnostic and performance data and on the judgments of other teachers who also work with the pupil. The amount of time spent with the Homeroom Unit would vary with individuals, and typically decrease as a pupil moves from the first through later years in the school.

2. *Wing Unit.* A Wing Unit would combine four homeroom units and their teachers for cooperative planning and instruction in the General Studies area. The pupils in the Wing Unit would be in the same year in school but otherwise heterogeneously grouped. Four homeroom teachers, each representing a special competence in one of the General Studies areas of language arts, social studies, science, or mathematics would meet regularly to cooperatively plan the instruction for the 100 pupils in the Wing Unit. The teachers in the Wing Unit would function as a curriculum planning committee and as a teaching team. The team may arrange for some of the instruction to be in large groups containing all of the 100 students, and some of the work to be in small groups for interactive discussions, or instruction in basic skills.

3. *Vertical Unit.* The Vertical Unit, consisting of approximately 400 pupils and 16 teachers, would provide an environment that is at once stimulating and secure, stable and flexible. The Vertical Unit (a "school within a school") gives the

pupil a wider community in which to live, explore, and develop new social understandings. At the same time, this unit is small enough to promote a sense of identity and belongingness. All four year levels of the school would be represented in the Vertical Unit, and provisions for vertical acceleration through any area of the curriculum would promote greater individualization and program flexibility. Younger students would have opportunities to work and plan with and learn from more mature ones, and the older student would have special opportunity to provide leadership within the Vertical Unit.

4. *Special Learning Centers.* The use of Special Learning Centers to serve the exploratory interests and the special and remedial needs of the middle school pupils would be a distinctive feature of the organization. Pupils would be scheduled for work in these centers on an individual basis for both short-term and long-term instruction in the Personal Development and Learning Skills portions of the curriculum. The centers should be adequately equipped and manned by special personnel competent to direct group study and individual projects. Special Learning Centers would include: library, reading laboratory, home arts, typing and writing laboratory, foreign language laboratory, arts and hobby center, music room, and physical education-recreation center. Centers would be operated on a flexible schedule and would be open to pupils after school and on Saturday.

The key to the implementation of a successful middle school program is a staff of adults of uncommon talents and abilities. The teachers must be as knowledgeable as possible in their chosen academic fields and must have training in the guidance and counseling of children of middle school age. A program of selection, recruitment, and training would be necessary to develop a staff with these special qualifications.

Obviously such a school would be expensive—perhaps costing up to half as much more per pupil than average schools for children of the middle school years. But the loss of human potential in current educational organizations and programs for this age group may be far more costly.

If these ideas merit investigation, increased costs for their careful testing could surely be justified.

VOCATIONAL EDUCATION
What Are the Big Questions?

FRED T. WILHELMS

NASSP's members have let it be known in no uncertain terms that they are deeply puzzled and concerned—"worried" might not be too strong a word—about vocational education.

And well they might be! For this is vocational education's time of decision, and there are grave doubts as to what the decisions should be. Events are crowding in at a dizzying rate, and new forces and conditions are hard to understand.

One solid fact stands out: The Vocational Education Act of 1963 not only poured in unprecedented amounts of money, but also ripped the old rigidities wide open. Right now we are exceptionally free to dream up creative ideas and to do whatever our best professional judgment says we ought to do. But, functionally, that freedom may be short-lived. Everybody knows that the "old" vocational education had got too rigid, too narrow, too stereotyped—that just more of the same will not be good enough. We have a little time now to break the mold and dream and dare. After that, bureaucracies being what they are, we can expect the hardening of a new set. The time is now!

This situation is complicated by another fact: At least at the federal level, as Jimmy Durante says, "Everybody wants to get into the act." Several agencies are mounting programs that may take large sectors of vocational preparation out of the regular schools and into a variety of other centers. That may be good and necessary, and perhaps we should welcome all the allies we can get. On the other hand, it may be a wedge to split our educational system, with one set of institutions for the upper group, another for the lower. We moved toward such a dual system once before, in the thirties, and probably it was only the war that halted the trend. Do we wish to go that way again? The question is fundamental, and well-intentioned impulse and drift are no substitute for thought and planning.

There is still another fact, this one cold and grim: We have more youth unemployed than we had during the great depression—over a million out of school, out of work. Joblessness runs about five times as high among men under 21 as among mature married men, and the situation may well get worse. The record is better for high school graduates than for dropouts (though the graduates are having their troubles, too), and it is spectacularly different for those who have had

Reprinted by permission FROM the *Bulletin of the National Association of Secondary School Principals* (May 1965). Copyright: Washington, D. C.

competent job training. We are driven to the conclusion that vocational preparation for all is a *must*. It may be deferred to junior college for some, or even to the graduate school; it may have to reach down into the junior high school for others. But somehow, somewhere, the job has got to be done.

Beyond these facts we move into speculation. Given the universal need for vocational preparation, the salient question remains: In these times, *what sort of vocational education really makes sense?*

"Automation" is one factor that beclouds the question. It hangs over us, a vast and shadowy imponderable. Even those who know most about it argue almost diametrically opposite predictions. Yet even the more moderate prognoses establish two points:

1. Ahead of us lies a time of swift change. Even within a given job, skills will shift very fast. And it is commonly predicted that the very nature of the job will change three times in the career of a youngster now entering the world of work.

2. A radically increasing proportion of jobs will put a premium on general intellectual alertness, on ability to read and compute and analyze and solve problems, and on ability to communicate with others and work cooperatively with them.

Now both of these assumptions look like stern warnings against overly specific skills training, against letting a youngster "get stuck with" a preformed package of know-how without a built-in adapter system. Maybe, as Peter Drucker has said, the worst thing you can do for a young man is to train him too well for his first job. Some educators believe this so strongly that they almost say, "The best vocational education is a good general education"—with perhaps, some little tincture of vocational work. Many more will insist that general education be very carefully guarded, and that vocational education be kept as small as practicable. Others—including many in vocational departments—grant the basic point, but argue that well-handled vocational programs can themselves include a high element of the "general and liberal."

Whatever the solution, it is clear that vocational education for the future has to make provision for swift change and for a larger mental ingredient in most people's work. Yet, as of now, it also seems clear that the possession of specific, saleable competencies is the surest guarantee that a youngster can get his toe in the economic door. And the way things are going, getting—or not getting—that first job may be the most crucial event in a young person's life. There is no guarantee that all who leave our schools this year will *ever* hold a job. It is as tough as that. Therefore the tension among curriculum planners, pulled one way by the short-range need for skills and the other way by long-range need for breadth and flexibility, is acute.

And then there is the question of form of school organization. Vocational education is relatively expensive. If we are settling down to broaden and intensify it, we are going to run into a blizzard of costs for facilities and equipment and staff, over a wide range of fields. Some educators are sure that the costs can be justified and the programs can be most effective only in the setting of the special schools.

Federal legislation provides for area vocational schools, and they are being built. There is much in the air to encourage the establishment of special institutions to handle the increased vocational load.

Yet, at the very same time, some cities are turning their backs on systems of special schools and beating their way back to comprehensive schools. Many educators hear "an alarm bell in the night" when they contemplate the danger that the development of special vocational schools may finally shatter what Conant has called the one truly distinctive feature of American secondary education—the comprehensive high school. Even if these educators grant the economy and educational efficiency of specialization, they look ahead with fear to grave social consequences.

Situations differ, and there may be no one universally good form of organization. But, at the very least, this question deserves concerned thought and a sober assessment of the consequences of impulsive improvising.

Maybe one big problem is that we insist on thinking of "vocational education" as if it were all one piece. In a sense, what we are used to calling vocational education has been one piece—and that is part of the problem we are up against. It has left out too much. Sticking closely within the prescriptions of a few federal programs, it has generally covered only a narrow range of jobs. More important, it has suited only a narrow range of *people*. Distributive education, secretarial training, trades and industries programs—these have all been adapted to roughly a middle and lower-middle "stripe" of our student body.

To think intelligently about modern vocational preparation we must consider an added "stripe" on each side of that center. Above it lies that burgeoning occupational area we encompass in the term "technical." It is growing rapidly, as the need for educated technicians grows in many areas, from engineering to medicine to social work. It demands students of at least high-average potential. Most of the special education involved may fit best in the junior college, but that does not mean that the secondary schools have no role. At a minimum, they bear responsibility for an alert guidance system to help able youngsters into the technical fields—and they are fields that include highly desirable jobs. Apparently many schools have not met even this minimum of providing guidance, being preoccupied with the two poles of old-style "vocational" education for one end of the distribution and "professional" preparation for the other. Beyond guidance, the secondary schools could do a great deal of "get-ready" work with technical students—and even, in some areas, place some of them directly in a job.

The third "stripe" of people and jobs lies below those of the traditional vocational programs. Think of the boys and girls we have let into our machine shops and secretarial courses only because we had no suitable place for them. Often they have cluttered up the traditional vocational program and made it ineffective. Often their presence has made courses presumably preparing people for rather high-level jobs look like mere dumping grounds. The students who really belonged in those courses looked upon them with contempt. And little if any good was accomplished, because the low-ability, low-drive students who got into those courses had practically no chance anyway of getting and holding jobs in those demanding areas.

We need to figure out a whole new range of programs genuinely suited to this lowest group. The preparation will have to be simple, as the jobs which they will hold will be simple. These are the people whose future is most at hazard in an increasingly technical world. They need all the help we can give them. And we can help them best by being toughly realistic. We shall need to use every bit of ingenuity at our command to get them incorporated into the economic world at all. But—in a growing range of service jobs—society does need what they can do, if we are visonary enough to develop it.

Perhaps, if we look at vocational preparation in this "three-stripe" image (if you care to complete the picture you can add a fourth at the top, for those whose professional education will be deferred into senior college and graduate school), some of our perplexities will clear up a little. Then we can think clearly about the sharing of load among technical institutes and junior colleges, specialized or area schools for expensive and esoteric programs, comprehensive programs in the more popular, less costly areas, and work-study programs of many sorts, including sheltered workshops for the least adequate students.

But this sounds as if I am beginning to say what the answers are—and that proves it must be time to stop. I do not know what the answers are, either. I only know that there are some very fundamental questions, and I am not sure they are being pondered adequately, in any concentrated way. In the next three or four years, willy-nilly, these questions are going to be responded to—whether or not adequate thought has gone into them—in ways that may set a pattern for another generation. I hope that before that crystallization hardens into a new set, the profession and the public will mobilize serious study and planning.

ARE WE EDUCATING OUR CHILDREN FOR THE WRONG FUTURE?

ROBERT MAYNARD HUTCHINS

The world is new and is getting newer every minute. Anything may happen, and what is most likely to happen may be what we least expect.

FROM the Saturday Review, XLVIII, 37 (September 11, 1965), pp. 66–67, 83. Reprinted by permission.

Almost every "fact" I was taught from the first grade through law school is no longer a fact. Almost every tendency that was proclaimed has failed to materialize. The "facts" and tendencies of today are those that nobody foresaw fifty years ago. I clearly remember the table of immutable elements and atomic weights that hung on the wall of the chemistry laboratory in 1916. I also recall my history professor's description at that date of the bright future of British rule in South Africa.

I am especially embarrassed by the facts and tendencies I proclaimed myself. I can only hope the students in the Yale Law School have forgotten what I taught them. The courts have overruled and the legislatures repealed most of what I knew.

Education, in the nature of the case, has to be concerned with the future. But if we ask ourselves what we positively know of the future, about all we can say is that it will not be like the present. The whole world is committed to the highest possible rate of technological change. The daily accomplishments of science are such as to convince us that we are eventually going to know how everything works. Then we shall be able to do anything, and anything can happen.

The first question about education we have to try to answer is: How can it prepare for a future so uncertain and contingent that the main outlines of it are, as Disraeli used to say, "shrouded in the dark shadows of dubiety"?

The second question results from the one big, central, fundamental change we can foresee, and that is in man's relation to his work and in society's concern with production. This point requires some elaboration.

Ever since Adam and Eve were driven from Paradise and told to get to work, subsistence has been the primary preoccupation of men everywhere. Production has been regarded as so important that men were rewarded only if they produced. They were paid to work. If they did not work, they did not eat. Work and production were the means of individual and national strength, support, and salvation.

As recently as 1940 Wendell Wilkie was stumping the country with the slogan, "Only the productive can be strong." Today we have billions of bushels of food we cannot get rid of. We could produce billions more if we wanted to. Every major industry could turn out infinitely more than is now being manufactured. The excess productive capacity of the United States is estimated at somewhere between $30 billion and $60 billion a year. It does not make much difference which figure you choose: it will be higher shortly.

There is a great deal of work to be done, but the question is whether and how soon we are going to get around to doing it. One-third of the population of this country lives below the poverty line. Urban slums are a disgrace, and now we are adding suburban slums to them. We need all kinds of things, notably schools, colleges, universities, hospitals, and libraries.

But we have been brought up to believe that the only desirable expenditures in the public sector are those for military purposes.

The budget for the space program, which is supported on military grounds, is

$5.4 billion a year. This is $2 billion more than the total annual cost of all the colleges and universities in the United States.

President Johnson has had to call the effort to alleviate poverty a "war" in order to get anybody interested in it. But we have less than $1 billion appropriated now for the great war against poverty, as against $50 billion we are ready to put annually into defense.

There is a great deal of work to be done outside this country. Although we are willing to help other peoples in the name of military security, we are reluctant to assist them merely because they are human beings in need. This despite the fact that the most explosive situation in the world today arises because of the division between the have and the have-not countries.

Since the war, the rich nations have got richer and the poor poorer. The poor ones are mostly primary producers. They sell raw materials and buy manufactured goods. The prices of manufactured goods have risen, and those of raw materials have declined. The resulting loss to the developing countries exceeds the total of all the aid they have received.

If we are not moved by humanitarian considerations, we might at least remember that we have some interest in holding the world together. The Marshall Plan on behalf of Western Europe was, to state it in its lowest terms, a great and successful example of enlightened self-interest at work.

The war against poverty should be conducted on a global scale. The question is, again, the rate at which it can be carried on. Trained men and good ideas are indispensable if money and goods are to accomplish anything. They are available in Europe. They are in short supply in the developing countries. So, even if we were prepared as we should be to put our superfluity at the disposal of these countries, we would find them incapable of absorbing assistance fast enough to make any telling impression on the flood of our production.

Suppose we spent each year ten times as much fighting poverty as we now propose, or on the order of $10 billion. Suppose we spent three times as much on higher education, another $10 billion. Suppose we tripled our expenditure on foreign aid, another $10 billion. We would then have absorbed $30 billion of our excess capacity. By the time we got around to making these expenditures our excess capacity would have risen by at least $30 billion.

This is not the whole story. It is now official government policy to produce a "bigger bang for a buck." The effects are already visible in those parts of the country, like California, in which a large proportion of the population is dependent on the arms industry.

For every billion knocked off the arms bill, we shall have to spend a billion somewhere else if we are to have any hope of maintaining employment.

The Administration's plan for bridging the widening gap between production and consumption is to cut taxes. The expectation is that this will stimulate demand, mop up surplus production, and lead to some reduction in unemployment.

But what if increasing production does not mean increasing employment? While production has been rising, unemployment has been holding steady.

Although we are to have a tax cut of $11 billion, nobody expects unemployment to go below 4 per cent. This is the new definition of an "acceptable" rate. It is twice the rate considered acceptable in Western Europe.

Meanwhile, in the advanced industrial countries of the West, the link between production and employment is being broken, Dr. Solomon Fabricant, the cautious director of research for the National Bureau of Economic Research, says: "Our immediate historical evidence indicates that there have been changes in basic materials and energy sources and tools and machines and in the relationship of the worker to his job. Eventually this will add up to a new industrial revolution."

What these somewhat opaque words mean is that automation and cybernetics are changing the world. They substitute the machine not only for muscles but also for minds. This is new, and no reassuring historical example, like the effect of the invention of the automobile on employment, is relevant.

W. Willard Wirtz, the Secretary of Labor, has said that machines can now do, on the average, whatever a high school graduate can do. If they can do that now, why should we expect them to stop there? They will go on until they can do whatever a college graduate can do, and perhaps more.

The effects on unskilled, or muscle, labor are obvious. The disappearance of the muscular miner reflects a universal tendency. The importation of seasonal Mexican farm labor into California was discontinued because Americans wanted, or were said to want, the 60,000 jobs at stake. Now it seems unlikely that there will be any jobs. Machines are being developed to do the work.

The skilled worker is going, too. The managing director of Bahlsen's, the great automatic bakery in Western Germany, says, "Here the skill of the baker dies." The skilled baker is likely to be dangerous, because he may think (quite wrongly) that he can improve the product by interfering with the machine.

The *Wall Street Journal* has described the effects of automation on the skilled white-collar worker. White-collar employment in the financial concerns of Manhattan, for example, was lower in 1963 than in 1962. Employment in brokerage houses declined while the volume of trading increased. The New York Life Insurance Company tripled its business in ten years; but the number of its employees rose by only 300, or less than 10 per cent.

These effects are now being felt by what is called "middle management." This is composed of highly skilled, white-collar people, mostly college graduates. Although they do not make important decisions on policy, they supply much of the information required for those decisions. They watch the flow of goods and money and see to it that both are in the right place at the right time. Computers can do better. They are quicker, more reliable, and, in the long run, cheaper. As they are improved and become still cheaper, they will drive the middle managers from the field.

The service trades seem a weak reed to lean on. Self-service and automatic vending machines are invading every department of retailing. The solemn and conservative magazine *U.S. News & World Report* says, "Food shopping at the supermarket will be automated. There'll be only one sample of every item on display, along with a punch card. Simply take a card for each item you want to buy, take the cards to the checkout counter. There, a machine will tally the cost. While you pay the clerk, all your purchases will be assembled, packed in a box or bag, and delivered to you as you leave the store."

Quoting "a top official of the General Electric Company," the article goes on to portray the automation of the home through computers that will make up your grocery list, remind you of appointments and anniversaries, take care of your finances, pay your bills, write your checks, figure out your income tax, and answer your telephone. Reproduction will be the only function performed by human labor.

The only possible conclusion is that the happy marriage between production and employment is being dissolved. The political, economic, social, cultural, and educational consequences cannot be overestimated.

What are we going to do with ourselves? Gerard Piel, publisher of *Scientific American*, has pointed out in a pamphlet written for the Center for the Study of Democratic Institutions that if we had continued with the sixty-hour week we would now have 27,000,000 unemployed. By reducing the hours of labor, we have spread work and leisure. Any proposal for the future must proceed along the same line. But I must emphasize that at the end of the line we shall find ourselves largely without work as we have understood work in the past.

Yet education has never been as job-oriented as it is today. This is a melancholy instance of the general truth that a doctrine seldom gains acceptance until it is obsolete.

The doctrine never was any good. In any country that has a highly mobile population and a rapidly changing technology, the more specifically education is directed to jobs, the more ineffective it is bound to be. Today such education is patently absurd. Everybody is aware that the official rate of unemployment among young people is double that among adults. The actual rate is undoubtedly higher, because many young people have thought it useless to apply for work. The general reaction to this situation borders on fantasy: it is to propose widespread extension of vocational training. In short, the cure for the disease of no jobs is training for them.

The archaic quality of such aspirations is sufficiently demonstrated by the case of key punch operators. They have now been superseded by machines and have been declared surplus by the California Employment Service. Today five vocational schools in Los Angeles advertise that they train key punch operators.

The matter goes deeper. A dozen years ago, a British group known as the Archbishop of Canterbury's Fifth Committee delivered itself of a statement that sums up the basic issue. It said, "A nation which regards education primarily as a means of converting its members into more efficient instruments of production is likely not only to jeopardize its moral standards and educational ideals, but to discover that by such methods it cannot attain even the limited success at which it aims."

Our educational ideals these days are expressed in the phrase "marketable skills." But entirely apart from the inability of the educational system to keep up with the market and forecast what skills it will buy, and entirely apart from the inefficiency of vocational training in school as compared with that on the job, the idea of producing marketable skills is ignoble and degrading for an educational system. It is an ideal that seduces the system into doing what it cannot and should not do and that forces it to neglect what it can and should do.

What education can and should do is help people become human. The object of education is not manpower, but manhood. This object we are now able to attain. We can now make the transition from a working to a learning society.

We started with two questions: how to educate for an undecipherable future, and how to prepare for a world in which work has lost its significance. The answer to both questions turns out to be the same. The man who is truly educated, rather than narrowly trained, is ready for anything. He has developed his human powers and is able to use them and his understanding of the world to meet any new problem he has to face. He is prepared by his education to go on learning.

Hence he is prepared for the human use of his free time. This is, in fact, the purpose of education in childhood and youth. It is to inspire the desire for life-long learning and to supply the training that will make it possible.

The democratic society is the learning society *par excellence*. The Constitution of the United States is intelligible only as a charter of learning. In the spirit of the Preamble, we are to learn together to govern ourselves. The law, the professions, the voluntary associations to which we belong, the political campaigns through which we suffer—all the institutions in our society should be regarded as teachers. Through them, as well as through the educational system, we can learn how to become human and how to organize a human society.

The special function of our educational institutions is to supply the intellectual tools, the intellectual discipline, and the intellectual framework necessary to understand the new problems we shall face. Support for this position comes from an unexpected but highly practical source, the Chief of Police of Chicago. He remarked the other day that he wanted a "completely professionalized" force.

Then he went on to say, "But the professionalism must be based on a foundation of liberal arts. It's necessary to get a complete man who has an understanding of his society and its people—a sense of perspective that can only come from a knowledge of history and philosophy." One might almost say that now the most practical education is a theoretical one: the man with the theoretical framework will comprehend the new situation, whereas the man without it has no recourse but to muddle through.

For the educational system the transition from a working to a learning society means a drastic reorientation of schools, colleges, and universities away from jobs and toward intellectual power. It also means that the present miscellaneous, superficial, and inadequate programs offered under the head of adult education must be replaced by continuous opportunities for learning open to all inhabitants of the country all their lives. The obligation of our educational system to provide these opportunities is just as serious as their obligation to the young.

If we can readjust our prejudices, we can get started toward a learning society. I do not underestimate the difficulties of making the readjustment. We can understand why Lord Keynes, the famous British economist, looking forward to a workless West, said he viewed the prospect with a "certain dread." We were brought up on Horatio Alger and the doctrine of salvation by work. Our last formal declaration of public policy on this subject was the so-called Full Employment Act of 1946.

Horatio Alger will soon be as out of date as *The Arabian Nights*. If work is our salvation, we are lost indeed, and we are on the way from full employment to full unemployment. But if we will only recognize it, the great opportunity that men have always yearned for is ours at last.

Other nations have had affluence and leisure, or their ruling classes have had them. They have been destroyed, usually from within, and usually from causes associated with affluence and leisure. The experience of Athens was unique, and it was too limited and too brief to be reassuring.

Now one can seriously raise the question whether the American democracy will turn out, like the Athenian, to be a temporary flowering from an almost accidental combination of favorable circumstances. One can seriously ask whether in a country like this, in a world like this, democracy is any longer possible. I believe it is. But I believe it is only if we can achieve the learning society.

ON THE IMPORTANCE
OF BEING FREE

WALTER LIPPMANN

We all know that the opportunity to speak and to print with even a modicum of freedom is by itself a satisfying and enjoyable thing to do. But the fundamental principle of a free press cannot be merely that men have a right to express themselves. No journalist can be satisfied to print a newspaper that has no readers. Journalism must be something more than singing in the shower bath or uttering soliloquies, however magnificent, to the desert air. For while philosophers may argue whether a painting exists if no human eye beholds it, there can be no argument that journalists write in order to be read, and that they are like Nietzsche who exclaimed that he had to have ears.

Thus, journalism is not a soliloquy without an audience. Moreover, and this has

FROM *Encounter*, 25:88–90 (August 1965). Reprinted by permission.

some practical bearing in the world as it is today, free journalism is not a monologue delivered to a captive audience which must at least pretend to be listening. As a matter of fact, since journalists and editors and publishers are men, and therefore human, and therefore liable to error and prejudice and to stupidity, a free press exists only where newspaper readers have access to other newspapers which are competitors and rivals, so that editorial comment and news reports can regularly and promptly be compared, verified, and validated. A press monopoly is incompatible with a free press, and one can proceed with this principle, if there is a monopoly of the means of communication—of radio, television, magazines, books, public meetings—it follows that this society is by definition and in fact deprived of freedom.

A free press is not a privilege but an organic necessity in a great society. I use the term "great society" in its original sense, as it was used in passing by Adam Smith himself and made current in this century by Graham Wallas, who taught in this city at the London School of Economics. As Wallas used the term, a great society is not necessarily the good society which President Johnson, for example, hopes to make it. A great society is simply a big and complicated urban society.

In such a great society the environment in which individuals act and react is not the visible world of their homes and their neighbourhoods and their communities. It is an invisible environment which has to be reported to them. For this reason, a great society cannot be governed, its inhabitants cannot conduct the business of their lives, unless they have access to the services of information and of argument and of criticism which are provided by a free press.

Without criticism and reliable and intelligible reporting, the government cannot govern. For there is no adequate way in which it can keep itself informed about what the people of the country are thinking and doing and wanting. The most elaborate government intelligence service is an insufficient provider of the knowledge which the government must have in order to legislate well and to administer public affairs.

Where there is a turbulent, pluralistic electorate, the rulers, the official bureaucracy, and the legislature will be in the dark, they will not know where they are and what they are doing, if they are deprived of the competitive reporting and the competing editorial commentaries and also the forum in which the spokesman of the various shades of opinion can say their say. This is what a free press is supposed to provide.

In a great society, controversial laws cannot be enforced successfully, innovating policy cannot be administered, unless and until the government can find among the people of the country a reasonably high degree of consent. No government is able for long, except under the extreme, abnormal pressures of war, to impose its rule and its opinions and its policies without public consent.

In my country we use a rough rule of thumb. It is that for controversial measures, the government should aim to rally a consensus, which in practical terms means a majority big enough to include from 60 to 75 per cent of the voters. Only then will those who observe the law willingly and support the policy actively be numerous enough to persuade and induce the recalcitrant and dissident minority, leaving only a marginal minimum where legal coercion is needed.

To create such a consensus requires a considerable period of public education and debate. The consensus must not be confused with the plebiscites conducted by tyrannical governments where the government majority is 99.9 per cent of the voters. In a society where there is such a superficial appearance of unanimity and conformity, there will always be at least a minority, it may even be a majority, who, though silenced, remain unconverted and unconvinced. The government of the tyrannical state will be forced to rely on secret agents who, because they operate in the dark, can never be wholly relied upon, being subject to intrigue and corruption and other hidden influences. Thus, there is raised up between the people and the government an impenetrable curtain through which there is no dependable communication.

It is evident that the interests of a great society extend far beyond the business of governing it. An essential characteristic of a great society is that it is not monolithic and cannot be planned or directed centrally. It is too complex for that. It has too many functions. Its needs are too varied, and there are no men who have the minds, even if they are assisted by computers, capable of grasping all the data and all the variables which are needed for the central planning and direction of a great society.

Inevitably, therefore, by the very nature of things, a great society is a pluralist society, with local and regional interests and activities and organisations. They are bound to have a certain autonomy, and some degree of self-determination, and in some significant sense they are bound to have freedom of initiative and of enterprise.

In order for such a pluralist society to work, there must be available a great mass of data: the current state of the markets for labour, for goods, for services, for money—what is and was for sale and at what price—what can be seen in the theatre, what is coming on radio and television, what games are being played and how they were played and who won them, what is visible in the art shows, where one can go to church and what was preached there, and what is in the lecture halls, in the shops and department stores, where one can travel and enjoy life, who has been born, who has been married, and who has died. The list is as endless as the activities of a great society. Experience shows, too, that the naked data are not enough. The naked data are unintelligible and so have to be interpreted and cross-interpreted by political analysts, financial analysts, drama critics, book reviewers, and the like. There has to be criticism of plays and books and concerts and television and magazines and newspapers themselves. There has to be advocacy and there has to be rebuttal.

I must now talk about some of the key problems which present themselves when the freedom of the press has been established by law and when sufficient private financial resources have become available to support the publication of separate and competing newspapers. These are the preliminary problems. They consist of getting rid of the censor and the domination of the advertiser and of financial groups. Then come the problems of maturity. They become crucial when the preliminary problems have in some substantial measure been solved.

I have in mind, to begin with, the conflict between, on the one hand, the public's right to know, or it may be the public's curiosity to know, and, on the other hand, the right and the need of the government to be able to deliberate confidentially before announcing a conclusion, and in certain circumstances, especially in its foreign relations, the government's right to a measure of secrecy and dispatch.

This conflict is, I am inclined to believe, perennial in the sense that there is no abstract principle which resolves it. The right of the press to know and the right of the responsible authority to withhold must coexist. In my country, we have a continual tension between public officials and reporters about the disclosure of coming events, what is going to be announced, what policy is going to be adopted, who is going to be appointed, what will be said to a foreign government. There is also a conflict about what has happened and why it happened and who was responsible for its happening.

The tension is between vigilant, ingenious, and suspicious reporters who haunt and pursue officials, causing these officials never to be allowed to forget that they are withholding information at their peril, at the risk of being scalped in the newspapers. It is not a neat or an elegant relationship, but a *modus vivendi* which works tolerably well, at least in time of peace.

An important aspect of this problem is in the field of crime and punishment. Here the press is often in conflict with those whose business it is to catch the guilty man and to spare the innocent man, and then to give the man who has been arrested a fair trial. The trouble with crime and punishment as it concerns the press is that it is too interesting and too absorbing, and too convincing because it comes out of real life. Thus, the reporting of the news of crime and punishment often runs athwart the administration of justice.

This conflict is nowhere near to being resolved, and consequently, we should at least avoid the sin of complacency when we contemplate the real achievements of even the greatest of our newspapers.

As the function of a free press in a great society becomes more and more demanding, we are moving towards professionalisation. A few generations ago journalism was a minor craft which could be learned by serving an apprenticeship to a practising newspaper editor. Journalism is still far behind established professions like medicine and law in that there does not exist an organised body of knowledge and a discipline which must be learned and absorbed before the young journalist can practise. There are, moreover, only the first beginnings of the equivalent of bar associations and medical societies which set intellectual and ethical standards for the practice of the profession.

Journalism, we might say, is still an underdeveloped profession, and, accordingly, newspapermen are quite often regarded, as were surgeons and musicians a hundred years ago, as having the rank, roughly speaking, of barbers and riding masters. But the concept of a free press today has evolved far beyond the rather simple abstractions of the 18th century. We recognise to-day that the press as a whole must be capable of reporting and explaining, interpreting and criticising, all the activities of mankind. To be sure, not every reader of every newspaper cares to know about or could understand all the activities of mankind. But there are some readers, specialised in some subject, who have to be alerted to important new developments of even the most specialised activities, be it in the remote reaches of astrophysics, or microbiology or paleontology, or in the game of chess.

For this, the profession of journalism is becoming specialised, and the editor who presides over large staffs of local and national and international specialists, of political, commercial, financial, legal, medical, theatrical, musical, and cooking specialists, art critics and fashion writers, has to meet the specifications, which were current when I was at college, that an educated man should know everything about something and something about everything.

Just as the profession of journalism is the consequence of the organic need for it in a great society, so a direct consequence follows from this professionalisation. The ournalist is becoming subject to the compulsion to respect and observe the intellectual disciplines and the organised body of knowledge which the specialist in any field possesses.

This growing professionalism is, I believe, the most radical innovation since the press became free of government control and censorship. For it introduces into the conscience of the working journalist a commitment to seek the truth which is independent of and superior to all his other commitments—his commitment to publish newspapers that will sell, his commitment to his political party, his commitment even to promote the policies of his government.

As the press becomes securely free because it is increasingly indispensable in a great society, the crude forms of corruption which belonged to the infancy of journalism tend to give way to the temptations of maturity and power. It is with these temptations that the modern journalist has to wrestle, and the unending conflicts between his duty to seek the truth and his human desire to get on in the world are the inner drama of the modern journalist's experience.

The first and most evident of the conflicts is that between choosing, on the one hand, to publish whatever most easily interests the largest number of readers most quickly—that is to say, yellow journalism—and, on the other hand, to provide, even at a commercial loss, an adequate supply of what the public will in the longer run need to know. This is responsible journalism. It is journalism responsible in the last analysis to the editor's own conviction of what, whether interesting or only important, is in the public interest.

A second drama, in which contemporary journalists are involved, consists in the conflict between their pursuit of the truth and their need and their desire to be on good terms with the powerful. For the powerful are perhaps the chief source of the news. They are also the dispensers of many kinds of favour, privilege, honour and self-esteem. The most important forms of corruption in the modern journalist's world are the many guises and disguises of social-climbing on the pyramids of power. The temptations are many; some are simple, some are refined, and often they are yielded to without the consciousness of yielding. Only a constant awareness of them offers protection.

Another drama arises in foreign affairs from the conflict between the journalist's duty to seek the truth and his loyalty to his country's government—between his duty to report and explain the truth as he sees it and his natural and human desire to say "my country right or wrong." These conflicts are trying, and for the journalist striving to do his work there are two rules which can help him. One is to remember President Truman's advice that if you do not like the heat, stay out of the kitchen. It is always possible to retreat into less hotly contested subject matter. The other rule is that if you believe you must go into the kitchen, keep an eye on yourself, keep asking yourself: are you sure you are still seeking the truth and not merely trying to win the argument?

This brings me to my final point which is that as the free press develops, as the great society evolves, the paramount point is whether, like a scientist or a scholar, the journalist puts truth in the first place or in the second. If he puts it in the second place, he is a worshipper of the bitch goddess Success. Or he is a conceited man trying to win an argument.

In so far as he puts truth in the first place, he rises towards—I will not say into, but towards—the company of those who taste and enjoy the best things in life.

WHAT DO THE CENSORS FEAR?

ENID MARTELL OLSON

Secondary school teachers must wonder what academic freedom means to them. Generally, professional associations censure colleges and universities that brusquely reprimand or dismiss staff members for outspokenness. University administrators usually defend their own faculty's right of unrestricted assignment of reading lists and references. But what happens to junior and senior high school teachers when pressure groups attack classics as obscene, contemporary fiction of literary merit as corrupting, history texts as subversive, biology texts as irreligious? Who defends the English teacher's right to distribute required and suggested reading lists, the librarian's right to acquire both classical and contemporary works in the humanities, the economics teacher's right to present all theories of production and

FROM *Teachers College Record*, 66:565–573 (April 1965), Teachers College, Columbia University, N. Y. Reprinted by permission.

distribution, the science teacher's right to teach the history as well as the principles of physics or physiology? Who speaks for the teacher when a school board threatens his dismissal over a book?

An educational association or a teachers' union, when called upon, will often require a board to prove incompetence, rather than indiscretion, as a cause for dismissal. A subject-matter organization and a library association, when informed, will defend titles of books and the right of students to read. A civil liberties organization, when asked, will defend the teacher's right to teach. An able school administrator will support a teacher of his before parents and pressure groups and will enlist the board in behalf of the teacher.

But what does academic freedom mean when no one speaks for the teacher? When his texts are discarded and replaced? When his reading lists are edited and his library acquisitions screened by nonschool committees? When he is told to withdraw into silence and not make trouble? Or when he is encouraged to move to another school district?

BEYOND INCIDENTS

Censorship of the lower schools threatens the academic freedom of a large portion of the teaching profession. Too many school districts already know what censorship is for the teaching profession at large to ignore it. Enough procedures for coping with censorship are available for administrators and teachers to use when situations arise. To be especially effective, school personnel should be ready to move beyond an incident and be able to analyze the motivations of would-be censors.

Clear understanding of motives will help to furnish answers well matched to the questions which censors ask—whether prompted by simple inquiry, dogmatism, or veiled defiance. Understanding of motives will help provide resistance strong enough for either misguided or unreasoned attacks. It will help to educate critics by distinguishing the misinformed from the blindly or the deliberately prejudiced.

Are censors motivated by an overwhelming conviction in their own beliefs, a zeal to convert all other people to them? Are they driven by selfishness, a reluctance to share room with the ideas of others? Are they moved by a reactionary devotion to the status quo, a distrust of change? Are they stirred by hate or fear, and if so, fear of what?

And shall we just carelessly allow children to hear any casual tales which may be devised by casual persons, and receive into their minds ideas for the most part the very opposite of those which we should wish them to have when they are grown up?

We cannot.

Then the first thing will be to establish a censorship of writers of fiction . . . [1]

Plato,[2] in the fourth century BC, feared "the power which poetry has of harming even the good," and he feared for the purity of young minds.

[1] Plato, *The Republic* (New York: Oxford University Press, 1892).
[2] *Ibid.*

Thomas Hobbes[3] in 1651 feared discord and civil war from the mismanagement of opinions and doctrines:

... it is annexed to the sovereignty to be judge of what opinions and doctrines are averse and what conducting to peace; and consequently, on what occasions, how far, and what men are to be trusted withal, in speaking to multitudes of people, and who shall examine the doctrines of all books before they be published.

Plato and Hobbes both feared corruption of minds through unwise judgments of untrustworthy common people. They presumed the superior judgment of the intellectually elite or the politically sovereign.

DESCENT FROM PLATO

Is there a similar distrust of (politically) "nonprofessional" judgment in the mind of a South Dakota state representative who wanted to "... safeguard students from being subjected unawares to socialistic ideas"?[4] Or in this declaration from a Texas newspaper columnist (an exception to the generally widespread journalistic opposition to school and library censorship)?

Throughout this book [a high school text in economics], capitalism, private and competitive industry, is discredited. It promotes socialism and advocates the creation of a state of social equality, distribution of the wealth through income tax, inheritance tax, and other taxes. This would certainly lower the higher standards of living to the level of the lowest.[5]

Is there a similar skepticism about the trustworthiness of a school faculty in the offer of a Women's Christian Temperance Union chapter in Ohio to screen books for the schools, to protect them from such "blasphemous, filthy, communistic, and anti-white" books as *The Catcher in the Rye, 1984, Brave New World, To Kill a Mockingbird*, and the poetry of Langston Hughes?[6]

Is there the ring of superior authority in the urgent desire of the California State Superintendent of Public Instruction to protect schools and libraries from the *Dictionary of American Slang*, that "practicing [sic] handbook of sexual perversion"?[7]

Censors, it seems, fear differences of opinion and ideology, exchange of ideas, and nonconformity of thought. Robert H. Wyatt, when president-elect of the National Education Association, said,

Censors talk of freedom of thought, and freedom of assembly, but they believe that only those whose grasp of freedom coincides with theirs should enjoy the freedom they profess to embrace.[8]

Therefore, censors fear also the uninitiated mind: the one unlearned in the *right*

---

[3] T. Hobbes, *Leviathan* (London: Routledge and Sons, 1887).
[4] *Minneapolis Tribune*, January 27, 1963.
[5] *Borger News Herald*, March 14, 1962.
[6] *Ohio State Lantern*, October 23, 1963.
[7] *Los Angeles Times*, May 24, 1963.
[8] Quoted by Benjamin Fine, North American Newspaper Alliance staff writer, in papers nationally, July 11, 1963.

brand of patriotism, the one unschooled in the *right* theory of economics, the one unlettered in the *right* cult of social superstition.

NOBILITY OR PETTY FEARS?

Censors of books in classrooms and libraries often claim for themselves vantage points of prestige and knowledgeability, motives nobler than those of other people, and moral strength more stalwart than that of others:

Censors see themselves as capable of withstanding any book, lecture, or play, however dangerous, but insist that their weaker colleagues must be protected lest they fall prey.[9]

Often, as Plato did, they claim an educational superiority. But how does that idea explain the numerous instances of parents (whose educational levels can only be guessed at) who protest the presence of "controversial" books in English and social studies classes and in school libraries? What do they fear?

According to correspondence in the files of the National Council of Teachers of English, some parents fear profanity (in *The Grapes of Wrath* and *A Bell for Adano*), obscenity (in *1984*), and vulgarity (in *Death of a Salesman*). They object to chapters in *Only Yesterday* which deal with "public morals and the Harding scandals." They protest a folktale like *Wicked John and the Devil* because it sets a 'new low in moral standards with a hero too bad for hell" and because (even worse?) the grammar is "atrocious."[10]

These parents don't always presume moral daring:

We don't read this type of stuff ourselves nor permit our children to read it, and we resent it being forced on them at school. They learn all that filth soon enough without having it "spoon fed" to them in classes.[11]

But all too often they feel a moral smugness toward teachers and school administrators:

We do not want to pay taxes for rotten books. . . . These books are downright bad for kids, especially these days when teachers don't know the difference between Right and Wrong.[12]

Do parents really fear profanity, obscenity, and vulgarity in print when they must admit that "gutter filth" reaches their children from other sources? Do they feel threatened by subversion if they really believe, explicitly and simply as they say they do, in the Bill of Rights, the democratic process, and the pervasiveness of the Federal Bureau of Investigation? Do they actually fear realism and naturalism in contemporary literature when they must realize that these forces are illustrated in television films and motion pictures?

One objector admitted that her tenth grade daughter read *The Good Earth*, in which there is a fairly vivid description of childbirth, without suffering any noticeable damage.[13]

---

[9] North American Newspaper Alliance, National Papers, July 11, 1963.
[10] *New York World-Telegram and Sun*, May 29, 1963.
[11] *Detroit Free Press*, December 3, 1961.
[12] J. A. King, *Transcript* of a public hearing in Visalia, California, July 23, 1963.
[13] *Detroit Free Press*, November 23, 1961.

Rather, might it be an independence of thought and decision that parents fear in their maturing children? As Stanley B. Kegler of the University of Minnesota said when commenting on parental opposition to *The Catcher in the Rye*, "It is the perfect symbol of adolescent rebellion, the type of rebellion that parents fear."[14]

LONGING FOR CERTAINTY

An even deeper fear of parents and others who would be censors seems to be the fear of the change and the insecurity which jar people from comfortable grooves of living:

> Right has never changed, and our good old English language is all right the way it is. The kids aren't going to school to learn slang, but the right way.[15]

How complacent life would be for the censors if people could learn the right (and the only right) way once and for all, if they could teach it to their children once and it would be learned, if that way never had to be tested by new experiences, new crises, or changing public morality and personal sensitivity. Censors don't seem disturbed that most societies would revert to barbarism (if no progress in social order ever transpired), that most clans would collapse in chaos (because no generation would grant its predecessor the prerogative of its way), and that most cultures would degenerate to crudity (if no enlightenment in values occurred during the years). The very insecurity which censors fear in the strivings of the young would soon creep in through the stasis of a stagnant culture.

Junior and senior high schools are coping with censorship incidents now. Papers from the Sixth Annual Freedom of Information Conference present an unmistakable picture of the dimensions of the struggle.[16] Files of the American Civil Liberties Union, the American Library Association, the National Council of Teachers of English, and the National Education Association hold evidence of titles attacked, teachers and librarians intimidated. Surveys—regional like that of the Wisconsin Council of Teachers of English[17] and national like that of Nyla J. Ahrens of Teachers College, Columbia[18]—reveal the patterns of the problem and also the relative indifference of school administrators *until* censorship threatens in their own district.

As much as publishers and booksellers need to, textbook adoption committees, English and social studies (and science) teachers, and school librarians need to know what to do when the censors strike. In 1962, the National Council of Teachers of English urged personnel of school systems to formulate book selection policies

14 *Minneapolis Tribune*, January 27, 1963.
15 King, *op. cit.*
16 *Speeches, Sixth Annual Freedom of Information Conference* (Columbia, Mo.: School of Journalism, University of Missouri, 1964).
17 L. A. Burress, Jr., "How Censorship Affects the School," *Wisconsin English Journal* (October 1963), Special Bulletin No. 8.
18 Doctoral dissertation (in progress), Teachers College, Columbia University.

before problems arise to establish committees of teachers to select books and screen outside complaints, and to enlist community support for the freedom of school children to read.[19] Yet evidence being gathered begins to show a shockingly small percentage of schools adopting official book selection policies. The problem is national.[20] How can, or why do, schools remain indifferent?

In virtually every instance of school censorship, notes James R. Squire, executive secretary of the NCTE, schools which have met citizen complaints forthrightly have won, and books have remained in the school. But, Professor Squire has asked, how can school administrators ignore the hidden censorship in districts nearby in which books quietly disappear from classroom and library shelves ("to avoid any trouble here")? How can administrators condone the subtle ostrich trick of the superintendent who said, "So far as my experience goes, we have no censorship; we don't have trouble like other states," where *The Catcher in the Rye* was under fire? But further questioning revealed also that "there are no copies of the novel in the libraries" of his public schools, "nor is it included in the suggested reading list."[21] Or how do schoolmen react to the encroachment on the right to read of the librarian who said of *A Bell for Adano*, "I've put it in a special place and haven't told anyone about it. Isn't that a good way to handle it?"[22]

PARENTAL SELF-CONFIDENCE

As a parent, I repeat what I have said on other occasions: When community pressure groups consist of parents or claim to represent parents who wish to take from the schools the right of book selection, what little faith they must have in themselves or in their neighbors as parents. If they lack confidence in the training they have given their children, of course they will worry about the books those children read in school! If they have not taught their children how to meet an idea, how to weigh it and test it, how to accept or reject it rationally, naturally they will fear the new ideas their children face. If at home a family *has* learned how to discuss conflicting opinions, how to validate different values, how to live with changing cultures, the children will know how to read works of literature and history. If it hasn't, the family is in no position to criticize the schools for trying to turn its children into able citizens.

When censors fear samples of unsavory language and incidents in mature books of literary merit, they should remember what Ann Landers once said to a mother: "If the kids don't know the facts by the time they're 15 or 16 years old, you'd better get hopping."[23] They should listen to a young high school graduate in Wisconsin who, during the controversy over *1984, Crime and Punishment, Of Mice and Men,* and *The Catcher in the Rye*, commented on the 17 girls who had

---

[19] Committee on the Right to Read, *The Students' Right to Read* (Champaign, Ill.: National Council of Teachers of English, 1962).
[20] J. Nelson and G. Roberts, Jr., *The Censors and the Schools* (Boston: Little, Brown, 1963).
[21] *Wilmington Evening Journal,* April 30, 1963.
[22] *Atlanta Journal and Constitution,* May 12, 1963.
[23] *Detroit Free Press,* November 23, 1961.

dropped out of his senior class because of pregnancy and added, "If the girls had read these things, they might have known better." [24]

Katherine Kuh,[25] put it this way:

I have never understood why so many self-appointed moralists attack works of art they consider destructive. When they claim that the word "art" presupposes only exalted emotions, they restrict us to a Pollyanna world of good deeds and pure thoughts. But since life is not always sublime, inventive men will continue to find fresh ways to illuminate the truth. And it is the truth, not morality, we are after.

When censors fear divergent opinions and subversion of American political and economic principles, they should recall a wealth of guidance in the speeches and writings of public leaders who have distinguished themselves as guardians of freedom. From the Supreme Court, whose historic decisions have strengthened academic freedom, Justice William O. Douglas has spoken boldly and logically. He has underscored the schools and universities as the wellsprings of free inquiry and limitless search for knowledge.[26] Former President Eisenhower, in his inauguration as president of Columbia, in his Dartmouth address, and on other occasions, upheld the right of the new generation to learn and to know.[27] Ambassador Adlai Stevenson has clarified the *contradiction in terms* of irresponsibility in the name of rectitude and has deplored "striking the freedom of the mind with the fist of patriotism." [28]

SCHOOLMEN'S RESPONSIBILITY

If schoolmen are not familiar with the full discussions on censorship by public figures like these, they are ill prepared to answer censors who rationalize their fears in fallacious polemics. If they cannot select authority and evidence to match the political tenor of individual censors, they are inadequate debaters and diplomats. If schoolmen do not marshal to the cause of academic freedom the recorded thoughts and actions of great libertarians, they betray their own cultural and literary heritage. They also betray their students.

Schoolmen should keep their perspective on the kind of influence which books have on readers. Would-be censors invariably pose the "unanswerable" question when they ask, "If good books influence readers toward a wholesome life, don't bad books influence them toward evil?" Well, do they? Did the didacticism of the McGuffey Readers produce generations of ideal citizens? Are readers better for reading some books because the books have shaped behavior? Or do readers gain information which may or may not be translated into action by the conduct of the society around them?

I have known record-setting Bible readers who were neither Judaic nor Christian

[24] Quoted in editorial, *Columbus Citizen-Journal*, February 2, 1963.
[25] "Art's Voyage of Discovery," *Saturday Review* (August 29, 1964).
[26] W. O. Douglas, *Freedom of the Mind* (Chicago: American Library Association, 1962), and *The Right of the People* (New York: Pyramid Books, 1962).
[27] D. D. Eisenhower, *Inaugural Address* upon assuming the presidency of Columbia University, New York, October 12, 1948.
[28] *Speeches* (New York: Random House, 1952).

in theology nor particularly moral in deportment. I have known no teacher who ever hesitated to assign *Les Miserables* or who won't freely discuss Jean Valjean in class because he fears his students will become thieves—or who has feared his students will want to murder because of reading *Macbeth* or *Othello*. The behavior of family or peer group or community apparently reinforces or negates patterns of living portrayed in literature.

The late President Kennedy touched upon the idea at the close of *Profiles in Courage*: [29]

In whatever arena of life one must meet the challenge of courage, . . . each man must decide for himself the course he will follow. The stories of past courage can define that ingredient—they can teach, they can offer hope, they can provide inspiration. But they cannot supply courage itself. For this each man must look into his own soul.

Furthermore, as a parent and former teacher of teenagers, I doubt that modern teenagers merge their identity with the central characters created by Faulkner, Williams, or even Steinbeck as they do with the characters of such widely varied novelists as the Brontes, Dickens, Pearl Buck, Tolstoy, Wolfe, Wilder, or Cather. Hemingway and Farrell? Yes. Salinger? Perhaps. But Faulkner, Williams, O'Neill, and much of Steinbeck invite detachment from their readers—close scrutiny, keen observation, but hardly identification. It is easy even to overestimate youthful identification with Holden Caulfield. One perceptive adolescent said, "Of course he's right, but he goes at it all wrong." Huck Finn had a more magnetic appeal for the boys of his generation than Holden does for his.

WISDOM IN ASSIGNMENT

Always, school teachers and librarians must rely on common sense in assigning reading. The wonder is that so few seem to, if we can judge by the trouble that occurs.

By all means, teachers and librarians should use reading lists of recommended books. Such organizations as the National Council of Teachers of English, the American Library Association, and the Association for Childhood Education International publish helpful lists. Reading lists can be guides, but they should not be abused. The omission of a title may not necessarily mean condemnation of the book. Periodic revisions of reading lists often necessitate the omission of older classics to make room for worthy new titles. Flexibility in use is crucial to the value of a reading list.

By the sensible use of reading lists, a teacher can assure students, supervisors, and parents that he assigns some books for class instruction, some for library use and outside reading, some for group discussion, and some for individual reading and review. He can insure that he does not assign prurient books, but that at the same time he does not assign shoddily written trivia and thus waste his students' time with sleazy, though innocuous, stories.

[29] New York: Pocket Books, 1961.

Through guided reading for the students, the teacher helps them to appreciate vitality, animation, style, and originality in literature. But through wide and free reading, as through wide experience with other mass media, students can sometimes come to tell their teacher, as a ninth grader did, "I'm going to write a letter of complaint to our TV station downtown. All the late afternoon westerns are starting to sound alike. When you've seen one, you've seen them all."

Another common-sense precaution for a teacher is to remember (as my critic teacher told me when I was a student teacher) that some books students can read aloud together in class, others the teacher can read aloud to the class, but some the students should read silently to themselves. A teacher of high school sophomores who began reading *The Catcher in the Rye* aloud to them embarrassed them, not so much with the language of the book but with the wonder that she had no other way of spending class time.

Teachers must remember to work with human nature. The apocryphal anecdote of the publisher whose business was declining tells how he sought to have his new book banned in Boston because the stimulated sales would balance his accounts. Americans may have prolonged the life of many a book that would now be obscure or forgotten—simply by continuing to call attention to it.

Therefore, when a high school student asks, "May I read this book?" (or, more likely, "I'm going to read this one"), the proper answer is that of course he may read it. If it is very trivial or shoddy, the teacher may have to say he cannot give much if any credit for it because it is not challenging enough for the student's time and ability. If the book is mature for the youngster's age, the teacher may tell the student that he will get more out of it a year from now and perhaps would like to try another, more appropriate one at this time. But a good teacher, no more than a wise parent will, does not goad a student into reading by being secretive or embarrassed himself about books. Nor does the teacher stand between the student and his right to read a book. To prohibit the reading is surely to invite it.

Finally, when a student insists on finding out for himself what particular books are about, the wise teacher reserves the right to let that student discuss with him, in conference or in class, any books the student wishes to discuss. The teacher may help to interpret characterization, to explain motivation, to establish perspective, and to appraise values. Openness and frankness in book discussion forestall surreptitious distribution of books among students.

THE REAL EVILS

Schoolmen need to answer the fears of their censors. They also have another obligation to the censors and to their students: Education should strive for comprehension of ideas, not reprehension; for expression of thought, not suppression. They should help the censors to understand that there are more dangers to be feared than profanity, obscenity, vulgarity, and subversion—ignorance that prejudices people, naivete that entraps them, gullibility that victimizes them, and a lack of artistic discernment which blinds them to the splendor of life as well as its cheapness.

Few people are more tragic than teenagers growing up prejudice-bound and intolerant because they have not learned that the races of men have biologically equal chances for self-fulfillment. Few are more ridiculous than the youth who believe that economic status and financial resources determine a person's worth. Few people are more pathetic than adolescents who are socially unsophisticated and emotionally unsure because they have not been introduced to the amenities which bring poise and the knowledge which brings acuity and perceptiveness. Young adults who fall victim to bandwagon slogans, demagogic diatribes, and hate hysteria are more pitiable than their elders who are so afflicted. Young people who remain illiterate in the fine arts because they have not read, watched, or listened widely and deeply enough to develop standards of artistic judgment are handicapped indeed. The freedom to read—and to discuss what is read—can liberate people from those thralldoms of the mind. Though censors fear, let educators know what their duty is.

The educational profession at large should enlist itself in the cause of academic freedom in the lower schools. Many responsible classroom teachers and school librarians are courageous in using their academic rights to teach well and in defending those rights before censors. But individual teachers and staff members who must act without the support of their administrators are lonely and vulnerable. No one teacher should have to go it alone. Employed as a member of a faculty body, each teacher is entitled to the support of his colleagues, supervisors, and administrators—and his board of education. Hence the stress in this article on the role of schoolmen, who carry weight with school boards, who in turn speak to the community *for* the school and the cause of freedom to learn.

FREEDOM'S SEAMLESS ROBE

Some poorly prepared or inexperienced teachers fearfully or inadvertently shrink from using their rights to teach. They feed their students a bland diet of platitudes and send them on inadequately prepared for the next level of education and citizenship. Teacher education institutions must no longer avoid in their preparatory programs the reality of school censorship. To send young teachers into schools and communities, totally unprepared or meanly prepared to answer their critics (whether those of curricula, techniques, or materials) is an act of academic irresponsibility where it is least excusable or even explicable.

Censorship of the lower schools flings down a gauntlet also to college and university professors not engaged in teacher education. Successful censorship in a community becomes a habit, a way of mind that extends itself to larger areas. One unanswered censorship incident in the schools often leads to another; success is heady to censors. A college in such a community will soon find itself suspect and on the defensive before the same or newly aroused critics. Diminution of academic freedom in any segment of the teaching profession threatens all, just as it jeopardizes freedom of speech and freedom of the press in the entire community. As teachers themselves and as citizens who care, college and university faculty members should speak for a beleaguered teacher, defend a worthy book, and ally themselves with a cause which also is their own. Then the censors *would* have something to fear.

MUST SCHOOLS BE NEUTRAL?

RICHARD L. HART

Today, as perhaps never before in our history, sociological and political pressures are being exerted upon the public schools in most parts of our country. Solutions to all types of problems in which the school finds itself as the key social agency involved are reported daily in the local and national press; yet these solutions are almost invariably offered by persons who represent a company, corporation, bureau or agency other than the school. When the question is raised as to why the school, through its appointed leaders, does not assume a more active role in recommending solutions to the problem, the public is often given the answer that, "The schools must remain neutral."

This type of response poses at least two fundamental questions: "Is it really possible to be *neutral* in our schools?" and "Should educational leaders even attempt to remain as nearly neutral as possible in decisions which affect the educational development of students?"

It is my contention that it is not now possible to be neutral, nor has a policy of neutrality been followed in the past. Decisions which call for value judgments are made almost daily by most administrators and teachers:

Should "modern math" be offered in substitution for the more traditional method of teaching mathematics?

Should economics be included in the course of study as a separate subject, or should certain economic principles be included in an integrated social studies pattern?

Which textbooks should be used throughout the school?

What about the structural linguistics approach to the teaching of grammar?

How many basketball games should be included in the season's schedule?

The concept of absolute neutrality would seem to be destroyed each time a decision is made in regard to questions such as these.

It is true, of course, that these questions are concerned with problems relatively free from sociological implications. However, if we are willing to take positions on questions such as these, should we be less willing to assume the leadership necessary to solve political or sociological problems which probably have even greater educational implications for our students?

RESPONSIBILITY FOR INVOLVEMENT

If we can accept a point of view expressed by John Dewey over a quarter of a century ago, we cannot escape the responsibility for involvement: "... all social organizations get their significance from their promise to enhance the individual: to guarantee the sacredness of his person, to safeguard his rights, to extend his opportunities." [1]

It is interesting to speculate as to possible solutions Dewey might have suggested to today's critical educational problem of *de facto* segregation—an area in which many school people are suggesting neutrality as the proper position for the schools. This point of view obviously places the school in the position of doing only that which is *required* by law. How refreshing it would be to hear (emanating from the administrative offices of a school system) of a truly constructive and creative suggestion which would employ methods which are *permitted* by law; yet with this type of action we would lose our neutrality!

Thus far we have examined the concept of neutrality from a broad, system-wide point of view. There is an additional aspect of the educational picture which is critically affected by a position of neutrality within our schools, perhaps an even more vital aspect. It is difficult to imagine the type of material which could be presented or discussed in any classroom of the school if the teacher is required to accept the impossible role of intellectual neutral.

It should be pointed out that we are not speaking of objectivity but of neutrality. Objectivity in the classroom is difficult; neutrality is impossible. As John Childs explained in *Education and Morals*:

> The right to inquire and to analyze are basic rights, but candor demands that we point out that all inquiry into a culture has its standards of importance and relevance, and that all analysis necessarily involves emphasis. Indeed, ... *analysis* is *emphasis*.
> ... Parents must recognize that no educational discussion, either by textbook or teacher, can ever be free from historic and social presuppositions. Whatever objectivity in teaching may mean, it cannot mean the absence of values and a point of view. These are operative in each and every effort to introduce the young to our ways of living. [2]

WHICH HISTORY?

How can we deal with a subject such as United States history from a neutral point of view? Indeed, is it desirable for teachers to strain for neutrality in some

---

[1] John Dewey, "Education and Social Change," *The Social Frontier* (May 1937), p. 238.
[2] From: *Education and Morals* by John L. Childs. Copyright, 1950, Appleton-Century-Crofts, Inc. Reprinted by permission of Appleton-Century-Crofts.

areas? How do we deal with the contradictory points of view regarding most major events in American history? We are told to accept the word of the historian; yet which historian's account is the reliable, accurate, neutral account?

A recurring point in "A Conference on the American Heritage" which was held at the University of Wisconsin-Milwaukee in October 1963, was that even among reputable historians attempting to be objective, there is certain to be great diversity of interpretation. Even the choice of facts to be included in textbooks will vary from writer to writer. Is it not true, then, that a teacher's neutrality is in question when he makes the selection of a textbook or textbooks?

Again, we return to the point that neutrality within the schools is an impossibility; and there are, I hope, few classroom teachers who would see the neutral position as a virtue even if it were possible to attain. Most teachers would agree with Bertrand Russell that, "The kind of virtue that can be produced by guarded ignorance is frail and fails at the first touch of reality." [3]

Although it is probable that teachers in every generation have felt that their era represented the most crucial period in civilization, it cannot be disputed that our time is a perilous one and that our hope today is for a clear-thinking world citizenry which respects the rights of mankind. It seems apparent, then, that we should not do violence to the right and responsibility of individuals to examine points of view which are popular or unpopular, accepted by the majority or by only a minority.

Mankind can be rescued from the effects of closed-mindedness by training in open-mindedness. [4]

[3] Bertrand Russell, *Unpopular Essays* (New York: Simon and Schuster, 1950), p. 120.
[4] Ashley Montagu, *Education and Human Relations* (New York: Grove Press, Inc., 1958), p. 188.

A NEEDED DIALOGUE
Schools and Values

WILLIAM L. GRIFFEN

As modern industrial society has become more complex, our schools have become almost hopelessly submerged in the minutiae of providing services for their students and in training them for the variety of occupations we have developed. Such training is important, of course. But it is the school's unique

FROM *The Clearing House*, Fairleigh Dickinson University, Teaneck, N. J. (October 1964), pp. 67–71. Reprinted by permission.

function to help each new generation make some sense out of the complexity and diversity of society. Schools are therefore obliged, in addition to passing on our backlog of knowledge, skills, and attitudes, to ask the humanistic questions. We cannot act as if we believe the unexamined life *is* worth living.

A faith in the advantages of nurturing a variety of values or beliefs is crucial to the maintenance of a pluralistic society. Our schools, instead of using the variety of values to point toward a better life, elect or are forced to play it safe and honor competing values by pretending they don't exist. Why should a society that encourages many sets of values develop schools that are reluctant to examine critically the many different beliefs of its people?

Values and public morality change. A belief held sacrosanct by one generation becomes grist for satire by the next. I am thinking of morals and values, not in the sense of right and wrong, but in the wider sense of one measuring his own worth, his search for answers to the timeless questions, his pursuit of the beautiful, and his quest for justice. Historically, values and beliefs have been held if they could be footnoted to an acceptable authority—a tribal elder, a religion, a sovereign, a sacred work. As the population increased, the footnotes increased. However, in the era of scientific inquiry a number of footnotes were challenged and dropped. In our society some applied the pragmatist's knife to the existing values. They were quite willing to forego the eternal verities for a later model they claimed "really works." And so appeared all kinds of double standards, morality determined by social norms, and a variety of qualified value codes. The cry was raised by many that some were operating without any moral code and making a religion out of negating everyone else's values. However, values were considered by some not to have a timeless quality but to be subject to change, and the consequence of man's acts were said to form the standard of values and morals. But it was never as simple as the relativists versus the absolutists, or the secularists versus the non-secularists. When you examined your own and others' values, you discovered a goodly amount of jumping across the "versus" and a weakening of the good/bad polarization. This was interpreted by some as moral confusion.

The quasi-split between the believers in man-made values and the believers in religiously rooted values (with the eclectics anchored in neither) has erupted in a series of court cases to interpret the principle of separation of church and state in our public schools. The effect of the court cases and the notoriety surrounding the cases may drive the wedge deeper between the two groups and create a polarization that didn't previously exist. The separation of church and state debate delivers most schools to the position, "The devil with values and moral education. It's the job of the church and the family, and if we wanted to discuss morals and values someone in the community would be sure to protest." The teachers realize they must be extremely careful in footnoting values dispensed (and in many instances it is that mechanical). In a school thus sensitized, a value, belief, or statement on public morality is likely to have a warmer, unchallenged reception in the classroom if it appeared in *Life*'s series on our national purposes than if it appeared in the Bible. The community, locked in combat over whose beliefs get school time and whose beliefs ought to be barred, is sidetracked from a more fundamental task—examining the belief itself, regardless of origin. If the school were to allow time for discussion of beliefs and values regardless of origin, it might vitalize its now morally bland diet.

Current interpretation of the separation of church and state implies that neutralism is the proper role of the public school. This neutralist position on values does not have to, but usually does, tend to render the public school nonreflective. We have worked ourselves into the position that in order to offend no religious, agnostic, local, racial, or nationality group we play down discussion of values and moral choices. This would be like a psychiatrist telling a disturbed client, "If you are confused about what you believe in or what decisions to make, just don't think about it or discuss it." This head-in-the-sand approach is exemplified by the insistence that school is some kind of a grab-bag of knowledge, with different students on different tracks using differentiated bags. That wisdom will accrue from this sampling is doubtful. The objective stuff of the curriculum has to be played with, rearranged, challenged, and, if need be, rejected, if values are ever to mean more to the student than something you get at a discount center.

The fault lies in the fact that the school treats our most serious concerns like something on a laundry list—note it and check it off. In what course in the secondary schools do they talk about "the good life," the great threat of the annihilation of humanity, the dehumanization of work, a better society, the world's "have and have not" problem, utopias, loss of individualism, utilization of advances in science and technology, or man's alienation from man? We have operated on the premise that courses in the social studies will give the student a sense of man's historical development and hence a foundation for building a better future. But with a few exceptions the "building a better future" part remains frozen in a cliché. The school maintains its slavish devotion to the past and to what has been codified, classified, and mummified.

The school's apparent need to departmentalize information and skills does not necessarily force the school to a nonreflective attitude. The teacher of the specialty may still ruminate about his specialty (provided he "covers the ground"), but provision is lacking for the student to take a step backward and view the many specialities—the natural sciences, the physical sciences, the social studies, language and literature, the arts, mathematics, vocational subjects, physical education and health—and how they relate to himself and his society. Well, why not add another course to the secondary curriculum—"General Rumination"? This is education's reflex arc: when a need is demonstrated, add a course. In fairness to the school people, it is frequently the community which wields the reflex hammer. In this case an appeal to rationality should block the hammer's blow.

Examine the case against General Rumination as a course. First, we would have trouble pigeonholing it by department; it's more than citizenship education, sociology, literature, the arts, or philosophy, for it would borrow from each. Secondly, most states now issue dozens of certificates to teach based on a specialty, but no state is currently certifying general ruminators. And finally, the most serious objection is that as a course it suffers, as other courses do, from a finality stigma. A course in the mind of the student has a birth, a middle age, and a finish (assuming a passing grade). It seems a gross injustice to take the tremendous question "What does the individual *do* with the knowledge and skills he and his society have acquired?" and boil it down to a single terminating course.

There ought to be something added to the secondary school—not a course, but a format—to allow a subjective value dialogue to move parallel with and complement the primarily factual and objective course offerings. Every teacher worth his fringe benefits is now involved in something like this on a bootlegging basis. Teachers are always being paid the compliment by an inquiring student, "What do you think about so and so?" The trouble with this arrangement is that the teacher always feels he is stealing time from covering the course to elaborate on these questions. And then these "value asides" suffer from a disjointed quality because even the most articulate teacher has trouble dishing up values in parentheses.

I would answer affirmatively the question, "Should the school be concerned with the quality of living as well as how to make a living?" However, it is possible to pass through high school and never talk about self-realization beyond the occupational chats and inventory devices initiated by the guidance counselor or the clichés ("meet your civic responsibilities") and defense of the status quo of the social studies offerings. The dialogue ought to be much more intense.

The mechanics of the dialogue would best be left to the school faculty. Think of the useful byproducts. In a cooperative effort teachers would have an opportunity to converse with their colleagues on a level higher than "presenting the new salary schedule to the Board of Education" or "working out the details of the senior trip to Washington, D.C." Each teacher could play the role of philosopher during the time set aside for the dialogue and could sound his ideas and values against other faculty members and, when the spirit is caught, against the students. Books and articles that do not seem to fit a particular course could be read by the students and faculty and reacted to in a free give and take of ideas. There could evolve a wholesome candor in which the young's purpose to shock and our role of aggrievement could be replaced by a kind of intellectual "togetherness."

One can hear the objections already—"Most of my kids don't know or care enough beyond sports cars or the leaders of the personality cult to carry on a discussion that would fill a station break." Failure of the school to nudge the younger generation beyond this intellectual stage has already demonstrated some effects. The apathetic kid with the vacuous stare echoing Marty's query, "I don't know, what do you wanta do tonight?"; the teen-ager whose notion of the good life fits easily between the covers of *Life* magazine; the pretty seventeen-year-old whose ultimate question is, "Do blondes really get more fun out of life?"; the boy who doesn't know what he wants but has a solid list of what he hates and is willing to rebel against. Some psychologists have initiated an experiment at Harvard University that takes some of these no-motive youngsters (those classified as juvenile delinquents) and pays them to talk about themselves, their lives, and their daily routines, in an attempt to have the students gain insights into themselves. Doesn't this have implications for all children growing up? If the school had provided the opportunity and encouraged these young people to study themselves as well as their subjects, the school might have assumed a preventive rather than a remedial role.

But the value dialogue involves more than examining one's personal life and aspirations. In fact, a case may be made that the school is sometimes too successful in helping the young discover *just* themselves and "how to succeed without looking beyond your double-pane, thermal picture window." The success/failure point in the program I describe hinges on the ability of the school to help the student see beyond personal aims. This is not asking the school to turn out missionaries, but it is asking that the student develop a social conscience that goes beyond the ability to list social problems. There are signs that a few of the younger generation can move beyond the academic dimension of values: work in the Peace Corps, students demonstrating to protest racial injustices, and those who maneuver in society with their own gyroscopes.

Other objectors would challenge the right of the school to play doctor to society, to burden the young with the older generation's problems or to raise questions you are only supposed to ask in a philosophy course. These objections could be answered at two levels: viewing the individual and viewing society.

No individual should be denied the excitement of asking big questions, the chance for cathartic quarreling with "seasoned" minds, or the opportunity to be in the presence of elders who not only recite but reflect. The student should have a crack at building a utopia, if for no other reason than to take refuge in it from time to time. Everyone ought to have two worlds to inhabit—the immediate physical one and the do-it-yourself ideal world which someday may be partially realized if his teachers allow him his dream stuff along with reality. The young ought to discuss freely the many loyalties competing for their allegiance: home, church, community, school, state, and nation. Who knows, some foolhardy kid may someday suggest a loyalty beyond the nation-state; a loyalty to mankind. The dialogue might uncover a need for an expanded notion of success, where one relies more on internal cues than on the mass media for direction.

In our society no organization or group exists that is potentially as dispassionate as the school in discussing values. Neutrality, in the sense of the school's not aligning with a set of beliefs, can be maintained with the dialogue going on. Betterment for self and society will have different meanings in different times and settings and with different thinkers. If one thinks of the school as a medley of all groups and individuals having ideas of a better life, the school becomes the concert master instead of a public relations agent bent on staving off all controversy. Different authorities—or absence of authority—may be stressed in answering the questions in the dialogue, but no authority should be interposed to silence the dialogue.

The way to keep man a free agent is to involve him early in practicing how to decide his fate. If self-fulfillment implies a genuine choice and is not just a cliché, the possibilities for self-fulfillment ought to be studied as certainly as arithmetic, history, English, and science. Otherwise, one is at the mercy of knowledge. History is filled with illustrations of man's using advanced knowledge only to plunder fellow men or to ornament lives still devoid of the human potential. Knowledge and progress in science should be viewed as means for achieving a good life, not as ends in themselves.

When a society loses the ambition to identify values and pursue them, its members are likely to have their destiny fixed by an impersonal determinism. Events unfold and decisions are reached with only a vague questioning as to which choice is better for man. Philosophically, we operate *ex post facto*, rationalizing the values we live by simply because "they're there." The alternative is appealing and perhaps realizable: man determining his own fate with the aid of a moral dialogue in which student and teacher examine the range of possible sanctions for making moral choices—the individual, society, and/or transcendent authority.

CAN THE PUBLIC SCHOOL FOSTER CREATIVITY?

RICHARD J. MUELLER

Current educational research is focusing on various student types—the gifted child, the dropout, the low achiever. One type, however, the *creative* child, is emerging today as the most highly sought-after product of the educative process. Although potentially capable of making a unique contribution to society, he is also quite likely to be a gifted and troublesome *enfant terrible*.

This fact points up a formidable paradox in current research on creativity in the classroom: studies of the creative process stress the view that truly creative minds are invariably free minds—free to make choices and hold convictions in the face of society's restraints. Yet the public schools are a myriad of controls and forces that necessarily restrict the learner to culturally prescribed and approved learning tasks. Research on creativity in the classroom has not yet confronted this issue. What emerges instead is an interesting piece of educational doublethink.

Traditionally, creativity has been the distinguishing characteristic of artists, writers, poets, musicians, and occasionally a particular gifted embezzler or safecracker. By classical standards the artist was considered to be endowed with the "divine spark"—a highly unique, almost mystical quality that set him apart from

FROM the *Saturday Review*, XLVII, 51 (December 19, 1964), pp. 48–49, 64. Reprinted by permission.

the common man. More often than not, this attribute has landed him in a lot of trouble. Accounts of artists, writers, and scientists indicate their willingness to "make the great leap" into the nether region of profound insight and awareness, a region perceived by the common man with uncertainty and fear. For that willingness to depart from the conventional wisdom and give free rein to the intuitive powers, the creative man has often had to pay the price of loneliness, obscurity, and sometimes a life shortened by persecution and want.

This perception of the creative process is generally consistent with contemporary descriptions made by educational psychologists. One writer states that "the creative-intellectual students reveal a growing trust in the reality of their own perceptions and an unwillingness to accept authority and authoritarian statements without critical examination. Furthermore, these creative students often disagree with classmates and teachers and are willing to agree with those who hold unpopular ideas—if those ideas make sense." In a recent review of current research, another authority points out that "creativity is sometimes contrasted to conformity and is defined as the contribution of original ideas, a different point of view, or a new way of looking at problems; whereas conformity is defined as doing what is expected without disturbing or causing trouble for others." Undoubtedly the dominant theme here is the close relationship of the creative process with freedom.

Educational psychologists are apparently ecstatic over the potential outcomes of increased creativity in the classroom. One rather rhapsodic utterance admonishes teachers to "never forget that the very life and function of creativity is to go courageously into the darkness of the unknown.... [Furthermore] being a minority of one is tremendously uncomfortable and more than most people can tolerate. ... Thus, creativity takes great courage."

If courage is rated highly by psychologists as fundamental to creative behavior, it is not so viewed by teachers themselves. According to a recent study made by the National Education Association, 1,000 teachers were asked to indicate the degree to which they believed certain characteristics in students were to be encouraged or discouraged. In the list of sixty-two characteristics, courage ranked thirtieth. At the top of the list was "consideration for others." Although a commendable trait in itself, a concern for others is not a necessary part of the creative process.

Descriptions of creativity in students point out the likelihood of a "sponsor" who provides understanding and support. This is usually a teacher. According to one study, "regardless of his own views, the sponsor encourages and supports the other in expressing and testing his ideas and in thinking through things for himself." In contrast, however, research findings characterize the typical public school teacher as having strong needs for succorance and abasement, as well as wanting to "nurture" students. (This is especially true of elementary teachers.)

These qualities are useful in fostering wholesome learning in the classroom, but it is difficult to see how a teacher who does not have a strong characteristic of independence and "courage of convictions" can wholeheartedly accept—and stimulate—this behavior in children.

From this welter of conflicting conditions for creativity in the classroom we might draw one of the following conclusions: Possibly without consciously intending to do so, educational psychologists are attaching the label of "creativity" to what has always been the kind of high-level, divergent learning process that good teachers strive to bring about but that may not necessarily be creative thinking. Or, putting it another way, perhaps the behavior hasn't changed—only its description. Less facetiously, the only other conclusion to be drawn is that any real enhancement of creativity in young people must by its very nature be directly related to the degree of intellectual and emotional freedom that teachers, administrators, and the public are willing to extend to the classroom. Considering the realities of public schools today, there is little evidence of, and possibly some valid objection to, this free environment for creativity.

In fact, the discouraging aspect of this whole business of creativity in the public school classroom is its inevitable conflict with the ways by which young minds are guided to intellectual maturity. Certainly the ultimate goal of the educative process is the release of whatever potential creativity an individual possesses. This means greater and greater increments of free expression of thought and behavior through the early, formative years. In a sense, the learner must relinquish his freedom in order to gain the ultimate freedom—escape from the limitations of his previously fettered and superstitious mind.

Yet the natural limitations of today's classrooms cause these aims to be implemented in ways that are conventional, bounded, harmless, and quite often artificial. Students are allowed to perform "creatively," *i.e.*, act as individuals as long as this is clearly within the discernible and socially acceptable guidelines of the teacher's syllabus. In a sense, this means creativity in clay forms that can be displayed in any school trophy case without offending, suggesting, disrupting, or disturbing.

Real creativity, however, is independent, original thinking, and this could result in such things as strikes or boycotts against teachers or administrators; embarrassing questions concerning sex, the free enterprise system, race, and other controversial issues; or any number of creative questions or explorations that might disrupt the security and complacency of adults. (Significantly, creative students in high school often score rather high on a number of traits classified by most psychologists as "abnormal." How this is to be reconciled with the rather euphoric claims of authorities on creativity is not very clear.) Creativity in its fullest and richest sense has negative as well as positive overtones. The creative process by itself is unimportant; its resultant effects are what give it worth. Any judgment of the value of a creative process must necessarily be made on the outcomes, and this is a judgment made by society. If the outcomes are judged *prior* to the creative act, we are no longer encouraging meaningful creativity in the classroom, but rather a form of prescribed, structured learning activity.

It is interesting to note the close similarity of many of the current studies on creativity when compared with the enthusiastic outpourings of educational writers during the 1930's, the heyday of the so-called progressive education movement. Then, the dominant cry was for greater freedom in the classroom and away with the rigid, college-preparatory curriculum for all students. Undoubtedly the progressive educators provided a fresh and vitalizing influence on education, but this movement has long since been interred. If educators today reveal a reluctance to talk about greater freedom in the classroom, the reason may be that this is too likely to evoke painful reminders of the era of the progressive education movement on the part of the public. Whereas many educators have a private fondness for much of what progressive education stood for, any public allusion to such views is subject to immediate denunciation. In fact, a greater degree of freedom in the classroom is perhaps what educators would like to see; the current interest in the behavior called "creativity" may be a way of getting in by the back door.

But whether or not educators will succeed in fostering meaningful creativity in the classroom, their strong interest in this issue will remain indicative of a similar development in the world outside the classroom. Madison Avenue writers and others have been quick to note the public's positive reaction to the word "creative." The term is used again and again by the image-builders in the advertising world. Women's magazines discuss "creative cookery" and ways to raise children "creatively." Business circles acclaim the "creative salesman." Even politics has tapped the vote-getting possibilities of creativity. A Republican Congressman from Wisconsin calls himself a "creative conservative"—whatever that means. (I have a rather wistful memory of my old minister, who firmly believed that only God can create.) Apparently the release of each individual's creativity is perceived as the answer to our era's inexorable, creeping automation of the human personality. If the schools do in fact reflect the anxieties as well as the highest aspirations of society, then we can expect to see a lot more—not less—concern for creativity and individuality in the classroom.

Considering the nebulous state of current research on creativity, it might be profitable if the problem were approached more empirically, within the context of the public schools. Today's strong pressures toward conformity make it necessary, I believe, that we begin with the assumption that the best "sponsor" of creativity is the person who has himself demonstrated this talent—*whether or not he is a fully-accredited teacher.* One who has himself published, painted, or conducted some form of independent research might add more validity to the creativity search than is characteristic of recent theoretical approaches. He should function in two ways: as a "sponsor" for small, experimental groups of students, and as a resource person for teachers and curriculum directors. In this latter role, he would in fact be a staff specialist, much like the art or reading consultant. Of course, the long-range goal of any experimentation along these lines can only be the possibility that regular teachers can generate their own means of fostering creativity within the regular instructional program. And there is no guarantee that a really creative individual could be helpful to teachers, administrators, or even students. He may be totally ineffective in a public school setting, perhaps volatile. But certainly something can be learned through interaction with one who is accepted by both staff personnel and students as being creative. In any case, he must be allowed to function nondirectively.

Finally, on the assumption that truly creative youth are intrinsically motivated, conventional forms of goals, measurement, and rewards for creative effort should be abandoned. Goals will be generated by the students themselves, perhaps as a by-product of regular classroom study; measurement will also be a self-regulating process; and the rewards should come in the form of public recognition—science fairs, art exhibits, forums, or literary publications. Ideally, these should occur as often as report cards.

The chief implication of this direct approach is, I believe, readily apparent. For example, in providing experimental classrooms in creative writing, school authorities must face the almost inevitable certainty that at least one student—sooner or later—will produce a paper that will raise community eyebrows. Furthermore, youth who are given the opportunity to explore the frontiers of knowledge in their field (as they see them) can hardly avoid exposure to the creativity that is functioning in the field itself—the "theatre of the absurd," current issues in biology and human reproduction, contemporary right- and left-wing debate, or the eternal controversies in modern art. Understandably, these alert youth will be quick to identify with the men who have fostered this intellectual ferment, the creative idols who are themselves the centers of controversy. Rather than fear these possibilities, school authorities must consider them as part of the price to be paid. If a program of creativity is adequately interpreted to parents and the general public, it seems reasonable to expect their support. But for administrators to inform the public that real creative thinking can take place in classrooms without paying the price of increased intellectual freedom is, in my view, a policy of appeasement.

At the present, it is implied that creativity may easily be fitted into the school curriculum without many classroom changes. Teachers apparently need only to teach "creatively," allow children to think "creatively," and wait for the "creative" outcomes. This will largely be lip service until school authorities are willing to consider other approaches to the problem. This is not meant to decry the sincerity of recent efforts by educational psychologists and professional educators, but to point out the need for an alternative, albeit an administratively complicated one. Perhaps the experience gained through interaction with creative adults from the communities at large may contribute to a clearer definition of creativity within the context of the public school classroom.

Unquestionably, those children who possess the "divine spark" deserve to be identified and encouraged, as well as tolerated. This will entail considerable risk on the part of teachers, administrators, and the public. The same "divine spark" that can create a moving, poetic expression, artistic vision, or scientific hypothesis is also quite capable of setting fire to the complacent, staid world of the adult.

THE PRICE OF COMPETITION

CARL WEINBERG

In a paper in which students were asked to comment on their experience with competition in school and college, one student wrote,

> I had an A average in high school and pretty close to that since I've been in college. Last month I spent a week in the infirmary suffering from nervous exhaustion, and I told myself that it wasn't worth it, that I'd stop worrying about getting the best grades when I got out. Well, I haven't stopped worrying. I'm still competing for the top grades. I wish I could relax and enjoy my education. Maybe it would make a difference if I were learning a lot, but I'm not; I'm just getting good grades on tests. It's been like that all my life.

This student is not alone in her sentiments. More than half the 110 students reacting to this assignment expressed comparable feelings. Less than a dozen were not aware that they had been and still were in a battle for success, and very few were free of memories of pain, frustration, and strain in their struggles to compete successfully with their peers.

The areas of competition that had bothered these students, in order of those most frequently mentioned, were these:

1. Grades
2. Sports
3. Honors (academic awards, scholarships, etc.)
4. Student offices
5. Clothes
6. Popularity (number of dates)
7. Social awards (prom and homecoming queen)
8. Courses (being in the college prep course)

Competition in school may have begun on the first day the student made the childish supposition that teacher was like mother and that classmates were brothers and sisters in a fight for parental attention and affection. It is not uncommon to observe extensive "tattling," boasting to teacher, hand raising when one doesn't know the answer, and tears and tantrums upon perceived rejection or failure in the early elementary grades. Perhaps everything thereafter is simply a variation on the same theme.

There is no reason to expect that in the near future children will begin to surrender the need to seek personal gratifications from the teacher. It is more likely

FROM *Teachers College Record*, 67:106–114 (November 1965), Teachers College, Columbia University, N. Y. Reprinted by permission.

that it will grow worse because current educational philosophy, at the practitioner's level, dictates that the affectively oriented primary teacher be preferred
over the affectively neutral one.

SCHOOL AND HOME

The school and the home are distinctly different contexts and should stimulate
distinctly different responses. The school is not an institution that confers security
and love, yet school children operate in these familial terms. It is precisely because
they do that the school finds it is possible to control behavior by exercising
familial sanctions. Anna Freud[1] has expressed her concern over this problem. It is
her contention, based upon controlled observation in an experimental nursery
school, that the teacher-mother relationship causes children who have shown themselves to be adaptable and accommodating under group conditions to "become
insufferably demanding and unreasonable." This is produced by affect inappropriately introduced into the teacher-pupil relationship. She goes on to suggest that
too frequently the spontaneous attachments of children to teacher arise in response
to feelings emanating from the adult. The motherly qualities which we frequently
look for in our primary grade teachers would appear to be detrimental to both the
emotional and educational development of the child. They set the stage for sibling
rivalry, the first form of competition, in the classroom.

As the areas of competition mentioned by students suggest, there is little in
their academic life that is truly free from competition. There is no opportunity to
call a moratorium on the struggle in order to enjoy learning and follow the dictates of curiosity. These students feel that too much will pass them by if they get
off the treadmill, that they'll never be able to catch up. They never consider the
possibility that catching up has no particular advantage.

WHAT MEANS OF MOTIVATION?

If a mechanism or a technique appears to be producing desirable results, decisions
are quickly made to instill it into an educational curriculum. The fact that such an
implementation may be solving one problem and creating others is seldom considered unless negative consequences are so obvious that they cannot be ignored.

In attempting to handle the problem of motivation to achieve, many techniques
are employed, some creatively, others artificially. In one case, something in the
structure of American society itself appears to be working for the school—the
phenomenon of competition. To date we have not invented an artificial technique
with the power of competition to motivate school children to attain goals set for
them by the school. Competition is, then, functional to the accomplishment of some
educational goals and is emphasized intensively in every educational setting.
However, there should be some awareness by educators that for every item we

[1] Freud, Anna, and Dorothy Burlingham, *Infants Without Families* (New York: International University Press, 1944), pp. 53–64.

treat as functional there is the possibility of dysfunctional consequences—dysfunctional in the sense that agreed-upon educational goals may be more undermined by such an item than implemented. It is the argument of this paper that competition is more dysfunctional than functional.

DYSFUNCTIONAL CONSEQUENCES

Five major dysfunctional consequences of competition in the schools will be considered briefly.

GENERAL ANXIETY

A little bit of anxiety is natural and useful; too much interferes with problem-solving ability. Where failure to achieve is equated with losing out in a competitive struggle with peers for the affection of the educational system, the stakes are high and take their toll of all, particularly those who have doubts about their ability to achieve.

Anxiety is painful. We typically employ defensive techniques to protect ourselves from it. The most frequently employed defensive technique used by school children who are afraid that they cannot compete successfully is "reaction formation." They retreat to the opposite of their original feelings. They decide they don't care about school, don't want to do well, because if school isn't important, their failure isn't important. Such children represent the increasing legion of "under-achievers." We know they have the ability but we cannot accept their hesitancy to enter the battle for high achievement.

CULTURAL DEPLETION

The distinction between affect for persons and affect for materials or process is crucial. Affect for persons in a school setting may be the major source of dysfunction. Affect for materials may be the most critical goal we can attain. The feeling of joy or pleasure that accompanies one's involvement with educational materials is a goal worthy of attainment. But enjoyment, in a competitive society, does not "pay off" in the same way that performance does. The ultimate cues for motivation in an other-directed society such as ours come from without. The evaluation of one's own performance in terms of the amount of satisfaction reaped from the experience does not appear to be sufficient. No major institution acts upon the fact that somebody does not enjoy or appreciate what it has to offer. This is deemed a purely personal option, to be exercised at the discretion of the individual. Students are never required to *enjoy* learning, art, beauty, aesthetic principles or the like; they are asked only to understand to the extent of performing on tests and papers. This kind of orientation is not self-motivating in the way that enjoyment is.

An important work by James Coleman [2] has demonstrated the final victory of the peer culture. Adolescents are influenced in their goals and performance

---

[2] Clark, B., *The Open Door College* (New York: McGraw-Hill, 1960).

primarily by the values of their peers. Teachers no longer serve as role models; and attempts to recruit students to their way of thinking about learning, about cultural and spiritual experiences, seem destined to fail. Perhaps because the teacher represents a negative role model, any plea she may make for the acceptance of her perspective and values is by definition rejected. Because of this kind of social interaction between the adult members of the schools and the society of peers, the problems of the school are compounded. If the goal of the school is to instill in children the capacity for enjoying a wide range of cultural and intellectual phenomena, it will have to seek a way to make this capacity acceptable and desirable from the standpoint of both the peer group and the classroom. If students find that they are not pressured to attain grades by regurgitating facts, they may take the time to seek other advantages of being in an educational setting. If the teacher is not seen as the judge of their academic status, then she will not be viewed as a negative role model. As long as competition is the mode, someone has to decide the winners. If competition should disappear, and with it the judging teacher, it is likely that students will react more positively to attempts to help them discover their capacities for enjoying the worlds that education can open for them.

OCCUPATIONAL DISSATISFACTION

The individual is forced to surrender the capacity for enjoyment in order to attain other ends. Success in the eyes of others is instrumental to the goal of educational and occupational rewards. Even if wholly desirable occupational designations were attained, we would still want to question the process. But there is considerable evidence that many people are unhappy in their work, that if given a second choice they would turn to another career. Robinson and Conners' [3] review of the job dissatisfaction research published in one year (1962) suggests a growing concern with this topic. The review reports percentages of job dissatisfaction ranging from 1 to 92 per cent. One area where occupational mobility appears to be extensive is in teaching. Although the flow of personnel seems to be running against the profession, there are still indications that many hundreds of persons from other careers are willing to expend time and effort and eventually to sacrifice salary to occupy the teacher role. Persons who have received non-educational degrees and who are working in non-educational settings are constantly being converted to teachers. In a recent survey of 462 institutions,[4] 183 such conversion programs were discovered. At the writer's own institution 250 students are working toward teacher certification, even though they have degrees in other fields. Those who are leaving teaching may be doing so for money; those who are coming the other way must certainly have other motives. They may have discovered that competing successfully in a materialistic society is not intrinsically fulfilling.

---

[3] H. A. Robinson and R. P. Conners, "Job Satisfaction Researches of 1962," *Personnel Guidance Journal* (October 1963), pp. 136–142.

[4] H. Harap, "Fifth Year Programs of Classroom Teacher Education: A Digest of the Survey Report," *Teacher Education Series* (Washington, D. C.: United States Office of Education, July 1962).

In an accelerated scientific age the danger is even greater that we will produce a generation of discontents. Science and industry have guaranteed that the ultimate question guidance counselors may be forced to introduce into their career guidance sessions is not "What would you like to do?" but "With what kind of a machine would you like to do it?" The kind of machine may eventually designate the income and status of occupational groups, and while this would simplify things for those engaged in research on social class, the consequence for the individual would not seem salutary, if our concern as educators is to avoid an alienated and dissatisfied labor force.

THE "COOLED OUT" GENERATION

If competition is to continue to provide the basis for motivating students, it is necessary to do something about the losers. Society has shown itself to be at least that concerned. What about those who compete for the rarified air of "professionalism" but are unable to make it? Burton Clark,[5] describing the Junior College system, employed the concept "cooling out" to refer to that process whereby individuals are given the illusion of going somewhere without much possibility of attaining the reality. These students,[6] primarily of working class or minority backgrounds, are given the opportunity to become engineer aides instead of engineers, with the same flair and seriousness that accompanies the training of engineers.

Americans, regardless of social status, have faith in the value of an education. Hyman's[7] analysis indicates that 40 per cent of the lower classes interviewed in 1947 recommended a college education. In 1959 a Roper[8] survey showed that 44 per cent of those in the four lowest socio-economic groups expected that their children would go to college. Percentages of higher socio-economic status groups recommending education were considerably higher. In contemporary society the avenues to high status positions through individual initiative, without education, are closed. Access to the upper reaches of bureaucratic society can begin only with higher education. This knowledge is not kept secret from any segment of our social structure. Simply living reveals it. For most of those already experiencing closed paths to occupational mobility, the choice of higher education may be superfluous. These people may hold their aspirations low but, like Chinoy's automobile workers,[9] higher aspirations are transferred to the children. If Chinoy's data is generalizable to comparable occupations, then the children of members of these groups will have been infused early with the desire for higher education.

This general acceptance of the value of education dictates that we must reward more than a select few. The importance of keeping the avenues of social mobility open necessitates that we provide at least a token reward for all who have

[5] B. Clark, *The Open Door College.*

[6] E. Chinoy, *Automobile Workers and the American Dream* (Garden City, N. Y.: Doubleday, 1955).

[7] H. Hyman, "The Value Systems of Different Classes: A Social Psychological Contribution to the Analysis of Stratifications," in R. Bendix and S. M. Sipset (eds.), *Class, Status, and Power* (Glencoe, Ill.: The Free Press, 1953), p. 427.

[8] E. Roper, "College Ambitions and Parental Planning," *The Public Opinion Quarterly* (Summer 1961), pp. 1959–1966.

[9] E. Chinoy.

demonstrated that they were willing to play the game according to the rules. Higher education is currently distributed differentially based on student standing at the end of the high school stage of competition. The advantages to those who do not achieve an accredited degree are dubious. If Clark's analysis is correct the only advantage is to certain segments of society whose desire it is to maintain the illusion of a highly mobile social structure. If interest or enjoyment rather than performance are the criterion, the "cooled out" generation may find more acceptable outlets.

STRATIFICATION, SEGREGATION, DROP-OUT

The notion of competition assumes that individuals become involved, "ego-involved," in their success. It assumes further that to know where one stands in a competitive order, one must first discover where others stand in order to know what must be done to pass them. For those at the top, it is important to maintain the value of what it was that got them there—successful competition. That certain segments of the social structure, lower classes and minorities, are inadequately endowed with experience to compete on an equal basis with the more fortunate is known, but is only of concern to some educators and social workers. To the majority of society it is only important to improve one's own status, not to worry about improving someone else's.

Status may be the most important single variable in driving students to one or another adaptation to the school. When it is unavailable in one system, persons shift to systems that will confer it. If competition for status in the school is too stiff for those who are disadvantaged by virtue of home motivation and lower-class manners, they usually find another institution that will reward them. They drop out of school, disavowing the value of education, and invest themselves completely in the values of the deviant peer group. They attempt to find status by their fists, by fast cars, or by sexual exploits. Status is necessary. If the competition system of the school confers status unidimensionally in ways for which some are not equipped, then other dimensions will be found outside of the school.

COMPETITION AS ROADBLOCK

If it is desirable to eliminate or at least reduce competition as we find it operating in the schools, then we are faced with what seem at first to be insurmountable obstacles.

The first obstacle rests in the attitude that, since American society is highly competitive, and the school's job is to prepare students to function successfully in the world outside the school, we would be doing our students a disservice not to ready them for such a highly competitive society.

The second barrier goes even deeper; it lies in the grain of what we would call the culture of the school, evolved through decades of inculcation into values intrinsic to the maintenance of that culture. What we are calling the culture of the school is the end product of decades of interaction between people and their ideas.

It is that set of values and operational beliefs that transcend the actors in the situation. It controls their behavior in almost every category. Competition constitutes a substantial element in this value system.

A third barrier lies in the notion that when we take something out of a system that is crucial to the functioning of that system, we must replace it with an alternative that does the job equally as well but without the dysfunctional consequences. Without such a replacement the individual or society faces either chaos, social or personal disorganization, or an apathetic demise. Such may be the case with individuals or whole societies who lose or have taken from them their religion, their work, even their rituals. The American Indian, Soviet Russia after the Revolution, the American man of the Depression of the early thirties are examples. Soviet society was finally given the State, American man of the Depression, a New Deal and a wartime economy, the American Indian nothing. Our historical and sociological knowledge warns us of the seriousness of our proposal but also dictates that a solution must be found. We must find something else and be sure that it does the job before we remove competition from the school.

How might we approach the first two barriers? The first possibility is to suggest that we do not equip students to survive in a competitive society as much as we infuse the value of competition into them. Our motivation to do this stems simply from our institutionalized commitment to perpetuate the system of values on which we were weaned. What compounds the improbability of seeking alternative values is that competition, for the educator, is more than a value; it is also an instrument by which his objectives are attained.

Students become infused with the value of competition as participants in the institution of the school. They may become engineers rather than teachers or artists because the choice corresponds to the value of success in a competitive society, not because they are invested with the spirit and joy of performing in this role.

ON VALUE ALTERNATIVES

These values begin with the culture of the school, not with the student. Competition resides in this culture and is transmitted to the student as one segment of a total cultural complex. This constitutes our second major barrier to the elimination of competition. We have suggested, however, that cultures do change when and if the alternative forms prove satisfactory, not only to the performance of institutional functions, but also to the motivational needs of individuals. World cultures are in transition everywhere today. Industry and ideology have transformed whole societies in Africa, Asia and Latin America. Tribal systems are being replaced by bureaucratic governments emerging charismatically and settling to formal organization and industrial order. Kinship systems have been exploded by broader communication, caste systems such as have been found in India and some places in America are being replaced. It is important to consider that they are replaced in the belief systems of people, since only then can social change of an enduring nature take place.

The final challenge rests in the discovery of a cultural value that can engender the positive functions of competition without concomitant dysfunctions. It may be that, without evidence that something else is currently succeeding in our terms, we shall have to operate arbitrarily and rely upon educated guesses.

It would seem that one important criterion for our selection requires that our choice should not allow the possibility of its being objectified in terms of a single standard against which all students can be judged, either by authority figures or each other. Any focus that allows the products of students to be assigned an arbitrary score or to be viewed in a better or worse than context is undesirable. It is the symbolic representation, the score or value of performance, that gives meaning to the task accomplished and not the intrinsic value of the performance. If amiability or cooperativeness were to become the operational theme of classroom procedure, and since individuals can easily be compared on both characteristics, students would certainly compete with each other for the honor of being most amiable or cooperative.

Education has been concerned for many years with problems of motivation and interest. Teaching techniques constantly rely upon some assessment of ways of creating interest, of motivating learners. Interest and/or motivation has held the center of the theoretical stage in current pedagogical literature as a means to some educational end. But these concepts never have been considered ends in themselves. As *ends* these concepts may provide the alternative to competition. The American Library Association is currently attempting to stimulate an interest in reading, to motivate young and old to read. The Association is not concerned with measuring what people have learned through their reading, only in interesting them in doing so. The typical educational situation is one in which we establish some criterion against which we can assess how interested or motivated the individual is. It is this standard that provides the basis for competition. Interest can be generally assessed but only artificially compared. Children do not have to worry about comparable products when the goal is interest since they can be as interested as they wish without worrying about proving it. Methodologically we would then have to rely upon techniques of stimulating curiosity, of familiarizing children with a whole range of phenomena in as interesting a way as we can and let their own inclination to learn satisfy itself.

If interest becomes the focus and we play down our social inclinations to stratify areas of interest—to place a higher value on an interest in reading than an interest in building, for example—it is not meaningful to say that Mary is more interested than Jane. We want only to function in terms of individual style, to encourage uniqueness of approach.

PROCESS NOT PRODUCT

The adult art class could easily represent the atmosphere we are seeking, where individuals are finding their unique approach to painting. To the observer these persons appear to be completely individualized, encapsulated in their own fascination over the revelation of their special capacities, and totally involved in the enjoyment of the learning experience. Legions of adults take courses for pleasure. Classes in art, music, Russian, comparative education, and the humanities attract students who have no instrumental purpose in taking courses other than to satisfy their curiosity or thirst for creative expression. The important motivation for these people lies in their feelings about the material to be studied. If the flavor disappears, like chewing gum, they are free to discard one interest and assume another. Competition in this form of voluntary education cannot have the misdirecting and detrimental power that it does in "instrumental" education; "instrumental" in the sense that the grades are usable rather than the understanding or appreciation. The difference between these two learning situations is the difference between process and product. Educational focus on product is dysfunctional since it necessitates relying upon group standards. Affect for process is exclusively the property of individuals, the only really independent and uncorruptible motivator.

We need to use the question "What can I get out of mathematics, or art, or literature considering the amount of interest I have in it?" as a rationale for the educative process. If we begin and end with the notion of universalistic goals for all we are asking for, possibly even guaranteeing, the dysfunctional consequences of competition.

If we were to reinforce the value of idiosyncratic approaches to individual goals, and extinguish the idea that product is of maximum importance, we would then eliminate the grounds on which invidious comparisons are made. External criteria for performance is oppressive, internal criteria realistic. If one sets his own goals, and works in his own style, gathering qualitatively different kinds of useful insights as he goes, opening doors to the next step in grasping the structure of disciplines, he is usually free to enter those doors. He does not set up or have set up for him the myriad threats to his ego that are associated with failure. If he is not in a race, he does not worry about losing.

The teacher's new role will then become one of assessing interest and its relation to skills. The teacher then becomes a predictor of the ability of each individual to attain his own goals, as well as a resource person who has the materials to ease the journey. This task has been set aside for the guidance counselor, perhaps because only he has the skills to measure abilities and interests. It should not be too difficult to train the teacher in these skills and with these skills he will advance his status as a professional person.

If we advance a convincing argument against institutional patterns that we consider to be dysfunctional and discover useful alternatives, these patterns can and will change. Institutions do change when the old order is no longer satisfactory. In some social situations the dysfunctions are obvious and gross. In schools, the dysfunctions are subtle and seldom understood, but the results are great. Yet, the causes are not so hidden that they can't be traced. It is our responsibility as educators not to superimpose new techniques upon defective structures, or even to root out these structures in any wholesale fashion, since parts of these structures may be usefully retained. We must instead take the time to analyze every item in our system and not to stop, as so often happens, when we discern some positive functions of these items. Let us take the scientific view that we are not looking for *a* solution to a problem, but the best solution.

MASS MEDIA AND
THE EDUCATOR

CHARLES S. STEINBERG

The development of such powerful mass media as the press, radio and television by which millions of persons can receive communications content simultaneously and over widely dispersed areas has resulted in a social and educational revolution as far-reaching as the Industrial Revolution of the Nineteenth Century. The reach and potential of mass media pose critical questions and alternatives for education from the elementary level through the graduate school and into broad areas of adult education.

The revolution created by mass media is not exclusively educational. It is economic in that it involves millions of dollars in advertising and consumer spending. It is political, since candidates for public office have largely by-passed the whistle-stop campaign in favor of mass press conferences and televised confrontations that bring issues before the voter with visual directness and immediacy.

But, since the ultimate effect of the media of mass communication is educational, cultural historians are likely to assess the significance of mass media in terms of their educational values. The historian, however, will encounter formidable difficulties in finding proper perspectives for such an assessment. Cultural historians seek information largely in the behavior and attitudes of the educated stratum of society, and the educators, in large measure, have tended to slough off the presence of such a mass medium as television in the hope that, by denigration or neglect, it will cease to be as popular as it is. The educated groups—particularly the growing number of holders of graduate degrees and the university teachers—have developed a curiously myopic and distorted view of the educational and social effects of the media of communication. Despite the fact that a major part of our society is virtually inundated by the flow of mass communication, far too many educators choose to demean and ignore it as unworthy of serious attention or thought. And this attitude persists, despite the fact that educational surveys indicate that students spend perhaps as much time watching television as they devote to their studies.

FROM *The Educational Forum*, 29:393–398 (May 1965). Copyright: Kappa Delta Pi, An Honor Society in Education. Reprinted by permission.

Mass media have been the subject of abysmal neglect or misunderstanding by the educator. Studies on the uses of television or radio in elementary and secondary education have not truly come to grips either with the potential or the limitations of these media, and have not gone beyond their superficial uses as audio-visual aids. There has been no genuinely comprehensive study, for example, of the effects of mass communication in the area of the social studies. Yet it is the social studies expert who is frequently called upon to render judgment about the social effect of mass media before this committee or that convention.

These judgments are curiously ambivalent. Too many educators feel constrained to discuss mass media without seeking an actual confrontation with them. Unfortunately, since mass media are not physical sciences but social phenomena, questions involving their meaning and influence cannot be discussed abstractly. Only by trial and error of exposure can one discover their assets and their liabilities. And, by trial and error, one can determine what useful purposes they may serve in a mass society. In order to appraise mass media, educators must "suffer" exposure to them, however outrageous their slings and arrows may be.

For some curiously perverse reason, the learned society—particularly sociologists, whose domain would seem to include a proprietary interest in mass communication—have chosen largely either to ignore mass media or to deliver uncritical judgments about them. Because of this neglect, critical evaluations of mass media by educators cannot be taken seriously, because there is too little evidence that such analysis stems from direct experience. A large percentage of educators attending a convention of the New Jersey State Federation of District Boards of Education were asked about their television viewing habits and choices. The vast majority of those who deplored the paucity of "good" programs admitted ignorance when asked whether they were aware of any of the following presentations: Leonard Bernstein and the New York Philharmonic, Hamlet, Robert Frost reading his poetry, the Boston Symphony, reports on integration, on the population explosion, on birth control and other programs with a social or cultural orientation.

This ignorance of the content of mass media is echoed at other educational conclaves. For the plain fact is that those who are most articulately critical of the effects of mass media are least exposed to these influences, or simply not exposed at all. Those educators who score the mass communicators for dereliction of responsibility either pay scant attention to the mass media, or do not behave as their public pronouncements indicate. Surveys have shown that people simply do not read what they say they would like to read, nor do they watch what they say they would like to watch. The difference in television viewing habits between those who have had a college education and those who have not gone beyond the high school is only about one percent! Even those who have gone to graduate schools devote more than 50% of their viewing time to entertainment programs, yet in response to surveys they indicate that television does not offer sufficient public affairs or news.

The pattern is much the same among teachers of courses in the mass media who devote more time to abstract research based on secondary sources than to direct exposure to the daily experience of mass communication over the airwaves or in the press or magazines.

The curiously inverted intellectual snobbery toward mass media is not only evident at the academic meeting. It is equally prevalent among teachers of the humanities who deliver devastating manifestos before the P.T.A. and other such similar organizations. Indeed, the National Parent Teacher publication has illustrated how slipshod this attitude can be by reviewing television programs which were either no longer on the air or by attributing them to the wrong channel. To educators who do not watch them, mass media are responsible for a variety of social ills from juvenile delinquency to lack of reading readiness.

If mass media are remote phenomena to educators, they are close to the people. The invention of the printing press, as far reaching as its consequences have been, did not exert immediate influence on its society, since few could read or write. But television and the movies are within arm's reach of the wise and the ignorant, the learned and the illiterate. The effects of the mass media are too far-reaching to be ignored. It is high time the learned society recognized this fact and undertook a realistic appraisal of the enormous significance of mass communication in the daily existence of almost everyone within reach of a radio, a television set, a theater magazine or a newspaper. This cannot be accomplished by reading someone else's research. It can only come from exposure.

Fortunately, there are stirrings of discontent with blanket pronouncements on the effects of mass media. Margaret Mead, the distinguished anthropologist, points out that "television, with the strongest immediate appeal to the child and adolescent viewer becomes—because more potent—more likely to be blamed for anything that is wrong in children's and adolescents' adjustment to contemporary society." And some other writers and researchers have concluded that there are other influences and other voices in society which have some relevance to people's behavior patterns—the family situation being a significant one. Mrs. Clifford M. Jenkins, former president of the National Congress of Parents and Teachers, told the United Press International that "parents have a strong responsibility in the control of what children are seeing on their home screens . . . television can't be a baby sitter." Further evidence that conclusions not based on exposure are meaningless is offered by a study of over four thousand British school children. The research by Hilde T. Himmelweit, A. N. Oppenheim, and Pamela Vince indicates that "television is used by different children in different ways." In other words, no conclusion on the effect of mass media is justified without paying heed to such determining factors as age, home, environment, and individual personality differences. Dr. Benjamin Spock, a medical authority widely accepted by parents, admonishes that parents need to keep track of what their children are viewing or reading. "They shouldn't be hesitant in forbidding programs or books which they consider definitely incompatible with the family's needs."

Mass media need the appraisal and criticism of educators. But criticism in the abstract cannot be taken seriously unless it is based on particular experience. The educator who refuses to expose himself to the infinite variety of mass media is like the scholar who refuses to read a best-seller because everyone is reading it. He is hard-pressed to reconcile popularity and mass approval with quality. Carried to its ultimate consequences, such an attitude would not only prove abortive to the developing potential of mass media, but would also restrict popular education to a select few. It would insist that the content of mass media meets only the needs of the minority, while depriving the vast majority of the broad spectrum of education, entertainment, and information which a mass medium like television offers the public.

In a society where scientific method has assumed a quasi-religious significance, even for humanists and social scientists, such an unscientific viewpoint is deplorable. In his failure to confront mass media with the same scientific curiosity as he brings to other disciplines, the educator provides a striking illustration of the other-directed man of David Riesman's "The Lonely Crowd." Riesman's other-directed individual was happier to accept the judgments and values of the peer group, rather than to wrestle with opinions of his own. By abdicating independence of thought and action, the other-directed man achieves acceptance by the peer group without struggle or tension. Hence, the educator finds it easier to fall into the trap of unsubstantiated criticism of the effects of mass media, without a genuine effort to document criticism by experience.

In academic life, too, approbation from the peer group frequently provides a more satisfactory adjustment to life's stresses and strains than the hard search for scientific evidence through the crucible of direct experience. As a result, educators tend to accept uncritically the assumption that the welter of words and pictures emitted by mass media accounts for a flat, inert, stereotyped mass society. The flaw in this hypothesis is that it is false. The truth is that mass media tend to reflect society far more than they influence it. John Dewey's conviction that there was a constant interaction between the organism and its environment is no better illustrated than in the interaction between mass media and mass society. Each counterbalances the other. The public influences media content at least as much, and probably more, than it is subject to the influence of mass media. And it is strikingly evident that other factors, particularly the school, make a formidable contribution to public preference and taste. Not a sociologist, but a physician and a psychologist have turned up evidence that "TV is no bogeyman after all." Doctors Frances Ilg and Louise Ames, of the famed Gesell Institute, confirm a study by Josette Frank, of the Child Study Association of America, indicating that "there was not the expected retardation of school work or reading, damage to eyesight, or serious interference with sleep." Indeed, TV gets many pre-schoolers off to a fast start.

Scholars are in a unique position to evaluate the effects of mass media. They have the training and the technique. What they must do is to devote to mass media the same quality of research which they devote to other disciplines. But the temptation to reject all popular mass entertainment as shoddy is irresistible to the scholar. It is easier to hold mass media culpable for juvenile delinquency than to weigh the effects of such media against the effects of such basic institutions as the home, the school, and the religious institution in the community.

The consequences of this studied disengagement from mass media adds up to a distinct loss to the rest of society. The vast majority is deprived of any serious body of opinion, thought out and arrived at on the basis of experiment, of the limitations and the true potential of mass communication. Teachers who refuse to recognize the influence of mass media in the lives of their students turn away from a confrontation with reality. How much wiser would the educator be if, like the Medieval scholar, he recognized that education is a community matter, not a private affair. By careful study of programs on the air and selection of those newspapers and magazines which have relevance both to school and to society, the educator can provide a criterion of value for students, for mass communicators, and for the whole of society. What is desperately needed is involvement, not neglect, of mass media by the educator and others of the intellectual minority. The great problem resulting from the invention of the printing press was not that it provided literacy for the majority, but that it reached only the very select few who could read and write. The situation is precisely different today. Mass media reach the many, but are neglected by the few.

A balanced appraisal of mass media, rendered by interested educators, would recognize that media content ranges in quality from excellent, to fair, to inferior. Like the publishers' booklists, there is a variety of choice. The newspaper and magazine offer similar gradations in quality, ranging from the pundit on the editorial page to the creator of the daily cartoon narrative. The magazine world ranges from relatively low circulation semi-scholarly publications, designed for the scholar, all the way down the scale to the tawdriest of action-sex-adventure publications. Yet, publishers of books and magazines recognize that audience tastes and needs vary.

For those educators who will evaluate them with taste and discrimination, the mass media have much to offer and leave much to be desired. Certainly, they serve a vital function in the educational process of a democracy. By bringing the world of reality into the home and the school, through exposure of vital social and political issues, mass communication becomes a stimulus to the development of intelligent opinions and attitudes on these very issues. Through the presentation of drama and music, television and radio contribute to the main stream of our contemporary culture. Through coverage of current events, newspapers, radio and television contribute significantly to the information of our citizenry.

What can the educator do to bring about a more discerning attitude toward mass media? It is clear that educators who are exposed to mass media are in a unique position to make valid value judgments. The most constructive step toward an improvement in mass communication content is encouragement based upon involvement. The educator must abandon the dual bandwagon of uncritical acceptance and critical ignorance and render praise for what in his own judgment and from his own experience is meritorious. Let him discover that, in the area of mass media, there is more demand for good books, great music and fine plays than at any other time in our history. There is also much that can stand improvement. And distinctions based on quality can result only from direct experience, not from secondary sources.

Let the educated man be less sensitized to the verdict of his peers and more courageous in his own opinions based on direct experience. And let the educated man act less in a climate of ignorance and more out of a knowledge of the many positive contributions which mass media make to a mass society.

Given proper encouragement, mass media can serve as sources of emancipation and liberation from both extremism and ignorance. They can become energizing sources toward the development of independent judgment and responsibility. And the educator can provide the dual stimulus of greater public discernment in the choice of communication content and greater responsibility for that content on the part of the communicator. In this way, the educator contributes significantly toward responsible mass communication which, in the long run, will provide a better press and a superior television service to the American people.

PART III
THE YOUTH
Demands and Challenges

Many labels have been used to characterize the present generation of American youth: "the tense generation," "the cool generation," "the fun-oriented"—and its opposite, "the violent-oriented generation"— "the conforming generation," "the new breed," "the alienated," "the uncommitted." As labels, they serve the same function as all such terms when used with any social group or subdivision of the population. They serve to stereotype whole segments of persons with characteristics attributable to only a portion of them; they serve to fragment and divide a large problem or central concern by showing it in a narrow context—so narrow, in fact, that the whole is obscured. Yet the real danger in the use of such labels is that they are not totally untrue; because they do express a partial truth, the acceptance of them without further examination of how or why they came about prevents any real understanding. In the case of youth, the labels inhibit their achieving a more positive orientation.

If they are the tense generation, can it not be said that the age itself is a tense one to live in, for youth and adults alike? Their "coolness" is one way of responding to baffling situations over which they may have little control. If they feel alienated from the rest of society, particularly the adult world, can this not be accepted as a response to the triviality of life that often characterizes adult society and creates in youth a desire for thrills, excitement and "kicks"? Or is it because certain youth see earlier, and more clearly, than others the "phoniness" of adults—the wide divergence that exists between their professed beliefs and values and their actions? Is this alienation not accentuated by the "cult of youth" developing rapidly in adult society itself? The adult members of this cult, who lack the ability or the willingness to provide direction, models, or guidance for the young, adopt in an indiscriminate, wholesale fashion the ideas and values (or the lack of them) of youth themselves. This adult worship at the shrine of youth is expressed in many patterns—in the commercial exploitation of the adolescent market for monetary gain, in a misunderstood "permissiveness" that caters to youthful desires, in attempts of adults to relive their youth or to realize their ambitions in the lives of their children, or in a simple belief that "if you can't beat them, join them."

This adult fawning is interpreted by youth as a sign of weakness (a feeling they themselves are experiencing) that breeds distrust of the adult society as a whole. Alienation is further increased. What most youth want, and what they want adult society to assist them in achieving, is not exploitation, but the development of some sense of their own worth; not worship, but the achievement of some measure of self-esteem; not to have adults join their society, but to have adult guidance in helping them create some conception of their own identity. Although it must be admitted that schools alone cannot be charged with the full responsibility for this task, they should not shrink from providing a large measure of assistance to youth in making a better transition into adulthood. Too often, however, the schools are guilty of perpetuating adolescence into adult life.

The schools are frequently guilty of providing no more guidance to the young than that of instilling a willingness to accept things as they are. The competition, the system of rewards and punishments, the preference given to the "well-adjusted" student forces a conformity that soon dulls the young person's feelings and intellect. The young become trained in accepting at face value whatever is said, and soon they are responding automatically to the world around them. Each new idea presented, each new fad to come along is accepted without real discrimination. Before long they are not engaged in any worthwhile endeavor, nor vitally concerned in anything. They are uncommitted, alienated, cool. In this state, youth not only reject adult values, but are not even concerned with adults' existence.

Real growth in children and youth comes about through struggles and conflicts. It comes about when realistic opportunities are provided to develop an awareness to alternatives, to examine, to analyze, to discuss, to refine, to discriminate, to evaluate all areas of life including their own. When these opportunities are made available by the adult society and when positive guidance is given, most youth respond eagerly. Such experiences among youth and adults would aid tremendously in establishing, or reestablishing, a needed rapport between the young and old based on mutual regard and respect.

These and other concerns are discussed by a distinguished group of authors represented in the first seven articles of this section. Their positions vary widely because they are approaching their task from different perspectives. They represent a spectrum of views ranging from the cautious to the radical, and each in his own manner presents challenging ideas and stimulating thoughts. The authors' positions regarding youth in contemporary society should be viewed against the background of material read in the first two parts of this anthology.

The remaining eight articles in Part Three deal with the special problems of a large portion of youth in America, referred to in one article as the "educationally difficult" students. By far the largest portion of these students are those who are generally regarded as the *socially disadvantaged* although the term *culturally different* has fewer negative connotations. These include all who are deprived of social and economic means, the poor, but primarily it refers to Negro youth, who comprise the greater numbers. All minorities, however, are represented in their deprivation by the example of the Negro. These include the Spanish-speaking Puerto Ricans of New York City, Cubans of Florida and Mexicans of the Southwest; the Indians on reservations throughout the land; the poor of urban areas and of Appalachia, as well as migrant farm workers. These are the rejected—shut off from society and shut out of it. These are the young people who have trouble in fitting into the routines and demands of the school, and who are further penalized in adult life in the occupations they are able to find. The extension of equal educational opportunity to all minority and deprived groups is perhaps one of the greatest, if not the most crucial, challenges that the public school system of the United States has ever faced. The following authors give their critical estimation of the schools' response to this challenge.

Dr. Robert Havighurst of the University of Chicago presents a rather thorough discussion of the various classifications of difficult students, as well as pointing out some dangers and cautions in reorganizing the educational system to meet the difficult students' special needs. An early advocate of special attention to cultural deprivation among youth, Dr. Frank Riessman, makes a plea to those who work with these students for more concern for their individual differences. The labels that are used to identify these youth, Riessman believes, makes it easier to assume that their talents, their abilities, their potentials are identical. What we need to emphasize with these students are differences, with a capital *D*. Robert J. Fisher explores other negative connotations of the labels we attach to the poor. Such terms prevent the full development of a valuable human resource. The youth about whom we are speaking are not only those who have the greatest difficulty with school, but also the ones who form the largest percentage of drop-outs, for precisely this reason. Professor Thomas Millard of Upsala College charges the schools with an almost total lack of understanding of those who leave school. Those who come back soon drop out again, "for what else is there to expect, re-exposing them to the same learning situation and frustration which caused the initial withdrawal." He calls for a "searching reappraisal of previously defined educational goals."

Joseph Roucek draws attention to a group that has suffered oppression longer than any other group in America—the Indian. The account of an almost endless period of vacillation by the Federal Government in providing educational facilities for them will prevent many readers from sharing Roucek's optimism when he concludes that "the Indian experience will produce some useful knowledge which can be applied to similar situations." Doubt of the same kind is expressed about the current efforts of the Federal Government in its attempts to provide educational opportunity for minority groups.

Dr. Maxine Greene, Editor of the *Teachers College Record* at Columbia University, examines the disturbing inability of white teachers to see the Negro child as a live human being instead of an object to be labeled. This "invisibility" is not necessarily overcome by an overly sympathetic attitude, which might gloss over the very distinctions that need to be recognized. In this area there is not much expert advice for a teacher to follow in over-coming this difficulty. Dr. Greene suggests that it is important to try to empathize through many encounters with Negro children, their parents, and their neighborhoods. The teacher must act *as if* understanding were possible. Professor Sol Elkin of Wayne State University continues the dis-cussion of discrimination in the treatment of Negroes and other minorities in textbooks. This discrimination cannot be dismissed, Elkin feels, by arguing that the teacher's manner in handling the material is more important than the text. He contends that definite discrimination exists and must be eradi-cated, a goal that can best be achieved by the constant effort of concerned groups, particularly at the local level.

This section closes with a charge to schools to take a more positive stand and to exercise more leadership in getting society desegregated. Many com-munities will not desegregate without this leadership. Dr. Benjamin Mays, President of Atlanta's Morehouse College, believes this leadership to be the role of the school in a social revolution, a revolution to achieve the American Dream.

QUESTIONS FOR DISCUSSION AND FURTHER STUDY

1. In *Compulsory Mis-Education* (see Selected References), Paul Goodman charges that the school has become a "universal trap" for all children and youth.

They provide a convenient, captive audience for the "school-monks" to flaunt their ignorance. He doubts that going to school is the best use of their time of life for the majority of youth, because the schools emphasize the worst features of society. The school "cons" students into thinking that what goes on in it is education. The students go through the paces mechanically. "They 'do' Bronx Science in order to 'make' M.I.T., and they 'do' M.I.T. in order to 'make' Westinghouse. . . ." Many youth, Goodman believes, both poor and middle class, might be better off if the system did not exist at all, "even if they had no formal schooling."

What are your reactions to Goodman's charges? If you are inclined to agree with him, what other alternatives to formal schooling would you propose? If you disagree, what questions would you want to ask him in an interview? Which of the authors in this section would be sympathetic to Goodman's analysis of the "universal trap"?

2. The following two additional references continue the discussion in the Introduction concerning the "cult of youth" in American society:

Goldberg, Arthur. "Juvenatrics: Study of Prolonged Adolescence," *Clearing House* (April 1964), pp. 488–492.

Hechinger, Grace and Fred M. *Teen-Age Tyranny*. New York: William Morrow and Company, 1963.

Goldberg believes that adolescence is a period of life itself, "not a transition to an ever-postponed adulthood." The Hechingers point out that "American civilization stands in such awe of its teen-age segment that it is in danger of becoming a teen-age society. . . ." If these authors' views are valid, what can, or should, the school do to reverse this trend?

3. An interesting contrast is presented in the view of Harold Taylor as opposed to that of Andrew M. Greeley. Both are essentially sympathetic with the youth of today, yet they disagree about youth's purposes and motivations. From your own experience, with which author are you more inclined to agree? Do you see your generation in the manner in which it has been characterized? What additional ideas need to be presented for a more adequate presentation?

4. This last suggestion is not one for discussion or further study. This can, and should, come later. Here is a call to action. It is the editor's belief that some of the most stirring actions in the past decade have come not from adults, but from students; not on the battlefield, but in the peaceful pursuits of helping others. In spite of all the negative remarks made by writers about this generation of youth, a sizable number have become, and still are, committed. They are engaged in worthy pursuits in the Peace Corps and in its domestic counterpart, VISTA. They are serving as volunteers in student help projects in countless neighborhoods, helping children to read, taking small groups to museums or plays or simply on long walks; they volunteer for service in schools, playgrounds, community agencies, and in churches and synagogues. Every neighborhood and community has "culturally different" youth who need help, who are waiting to be helped.

Other college students like yourself have found a rewarding satisfaction and fulfillment that can come only from involvement in such projects. What can *you* do in your community?

SELECTED REFERENCES

Alden, Vernon. "Planning for Education's Forgotten Men," *Saturday Review* (May 15, 1965), pp. 68–69, 85–86.

Association for Supervision and Curriculum Development. *Learning and Mental Health in the School.* Washington, D. C.: The Association, 1966.

Bauer, Francis C. "Fact and Folklore About Adolescents," *The Bulletin of the National Association of Secondary School Principals* (March 1965), pp. 172–182.

Bettelheim, Bruno. "Teaching the Disadvantaged," *NEA Journal* (September 1965), pp. 8, 10–12.

Coleman, James S. *The Adolescent Society: The Social Life of the Teenager and Its Impact on Education.* New York: The Free Press, 1962.

Coles, Robert. "What Migrant Farm Children Learn," *Saturday Review* (May 15, 1965), pp. 73–74, 88–89.

Crosby, Muriel. "Poverty and the School," *Educational Leadership* (May 1965), pp. 536–539.

Dentler, Robert A. "Dropouts, Automation, and the Cities," *Teachers College Record* (March 1964), pp. 475–483.

Deutsch, Martin. "Early Social Environment and School Adaptation," *Teachers College Record* (May 1965), pp. 699–706.

Eames, T. H. "Attitudes and Opinions of Adolescents," *Journal of Education* (April 1965), pp. 3–43.

Erikson, Erik H. (ed.). *Youth: Change and Challenge.* New York: Basic Books, 1963.

Friedenberg, Edgar Z. *Coming of Age in America: Growth and Acquiescence.* New York: Random House, 1965.

Gardner, John W. *Self-Renewal: The Individual and the Innovative Society.* New York: Harper and Row, 1963.

Goldberg, Arthur. "Juvenatrics: A Study of Prolonged Adolescence," *Clearing House* (April 1964), pp. 488–492.

Goodman, Paul. *Compulsory Mis-Education.* New York: Horizon Press, 1964.

Harris, Dale B. "Changing Values 1," *Young Children* (March 1965), pp. 230–248.

Hechinger, Grace and Fred M. *Teen-Age Tyranny.* New York: William Morrow, 1963.

Henderson, George. "Pupil Integration in the Schools: Some Reflections," *Teachers College Record* (January 1966), pp. 276–281.

Isaccs, William. "Dissenting Thoughts on School Integration," *High Points* (May 1965), pp. 17–29.

Jaffa, Neubert. "The Disadvantaged Child," *The Instructor* (May 1965), pp. 15–18.

Liddle, Elizabeth Ann. "Pressures on the Young Child," *Educational Leadership* (November 1965), pp. 113–116.

Matza, David. *Delinquency and Drift.* New York: John Wiley and Sons, 1965.

Musgrove, F. "Teen-Age Aristocracy," *The Nation* (April 26, 1965), pp. 439–442.

Olsen, James. "The Verbal Ability of the Culturally Different," *Educational Forum* (March 1965), pp. 280–284.

Parsons, Theodore H. "Attitudes and Values: Tools or Chains?" *Educational Leadership* (March 1964), pp. 343–346, 415.

Persky, Blanche. "Changing Values II," *Young Children* (March 1965), pp. 249–258.

Porter, Blaine. "American Teen-Agers of the 1960's—Our Despair or Hope?" *Journal of Marriage and the Family* (May 1965), pp. 139–147.

Riessman, Frank. "Overlooked Positives of Disadvantaged Groups," *Journal of Negro Education* (Spring 1965), pp. 160–166.

Ristow, Lester. "Much Ado About Dropouts," *Phi Delta Kappan* (May 1965), pp. 461–465.

Robb, Herbert E. "Youth, the Power Structure, and the Role of Education," *Clearing House* (April 1965), pp. 451–455.

Sacadat, Evelyn. "Helping Culturally Handicapped Children," *Educational Leadership* (April 1965), pp. 505–513.

Schrag, Peter. "The Schools of Appalachia," *Saturday Review* (May 15, 1965), pp. 70–71, 87.

Schueler, Herbert. "Education in the Modern Urban Setting," *Law and Contemporary Problems* (Winter 1965), pp. 162–175.

Schwebel, Milton. "Learning and the Socially Deprived," *Journal of Personnel and Guidance* (March 1965), pp. 646–653.

Seidman, Jerome (ed.). *The Adolescent: A Book of Readings.* New York: Holt, Rinehart, and Winston, 1965.

Shriver, Sargent. "Challenge with a Difference," *Saturday Review* (December 5, 1964), p. 30.

Silberman, Charles E. "What Hit the Teenagers?" *Fortune* (April 1965), pp. 130–133.

Smith, Ernest A. *American Youth Culture: Group Life in a Teen-Age Society.* New York: The Free Press of Glencoe, 1962.

"The Negro American—1," *Daedalus* (Fall 1965).

"The Negro American—2," *Daedalus* (Winter 1966).

VALUES AND OUR YOUTH

GORDON W. ALLPORT

One aim of education is to make available the wisdom of the past and present so that youth may be equipped to solve the problems of the future. If this is so, then we have good grounds for a feeling of consternation concerning the adequacy of our present educational procedures. The reason is that in the immediate future, the youth of today will have to live in a world very unlike the world of the past from which our store of wisdom has been drawn.

SOME PROSPECTS

Think of the vastly changed nature of life in the future, for which we have little relevant wisdom from the past to call upon:

1. The new generation of students will have to face an ever increasing domination of life by science, by technology, and by automation. (One thinks of the story of two cows grazing along the roadside. An immense milk truck passes with the painted legend: Pasteurized, Homogenized, Vitamin B Added. One cow turns to the other and says, "Makes you feel inadequate, doesn't it?")

2. The new generation will have to recognize the impossibility of living any longer in a state of condescension toward the colored peoples of the world (about three-quarters of the world's population). Centuries of comfortable caste discrimination and segregation are from here on impossible to maintain.

3. The coming generation will have to deal with a population explosion whose predicted magnitude staggers our imagination.

4. It will need a completer understanding of world societies and their marked differences in values. In the past, we could be politely ignorant of such places as Africa, Latin America, and Asia in a way that is no longer possible.

5. It will have to create a world government or, at least, an effective confederation to forestall the threat of thermonuclear war.

6. As if a planetary world view were not difficult enough to achieve, the coming generation may have to develop an interplanetary point of view. (I find this prospect especially alarming because we seem to be solving the problems of outer space before those of the inner space of mind, character, and values.)

FROM *Teachers College Record*, 63:211–219 (December 1961), Teachers College, Columbia University, N. Y. Reprinted by permission.

It is no wonder that this preview of problems confronting our youth throws us educators into a state of self-scrutiny bordering sometimes on panic. Where can youth find the needed equipment? Are they sound enough in mind and morale? Sometimes our dismay finds an outlet in gallows humor. They tell of the benevolent lady who saw a depressing specimen of the very young generation sprawled on the curb of a city street, swilling down cans of beer. Greatly shocked, she asked, "Little boy, why aren't you in school?" "Cripes, lady," he replied, "I'm only four years old."

And they tell the story of the London bobby. London police, we know, are well trained for social work, even for psychotherapy. This bobby's beat was Waterloo Bridge. He spotted a man about to jump over and intercepted him. "Come now," he said. "Tell me what is the matter. Is it money?" The man shook his head. "Your wife perhaps?" Another shake of the head. "Well, what is it then?" The would-be suicide replied, "I'm worried about the state of the world." "Oh, come now," said the bobby. "It can't be so bad. Let's walk up and down the bridge here and talk it over." Whereupon they strolled for about an hour discussing the state of the world, and then they *both* jumped over.

Humor helps us put our dilemma into sane perspective, but it does not solve the problem. The vague apprehension we feel has led to certain empirical studies of the values of today's youth, with results, alas, that are not reassuring.

ASSESSING VALUES

Not long ago, Professor Phillip Jacob undertook to survey [1] all available studies concerning the values held by college students. He found a marked uniformity among them. Fully three-quarters of the students were "gloriously contented, both in regard to their present day-to-day activity and their outlook for the future." Their aspirations were primarily for material gratifications for themselves and their families. They "fully accepted the conventions of the contemporary business society as the context within which they will realize their personal desires." While they will not crusade against segregation and racial injustice, they will accept non-discrimination when it comes as a "necessary convention in a homogenized culture." They subscribe to the traditional virtues of sincerity, honesty, and loyalty, but are indulgent concerning laxity in moral standards. They normally express a need for religion, but there is a hollow quality in their beliefs. They do not desire to have an influential voice in public policy or government. Their sense of civic duty stops at the elementary obligation of voting. They predict another major war within a dozen years, but they say that international problems give them little concern and that they spend no time on them. Only a minority value their college education primarily in terms of its intellectual gains. They regard it as good because it gives them vocational preparation, social status, and a good time. Such is the flabby value-fibre that Jacob discovers among college students of today.

[1] P. Jacob, *Changing Values in College* (New York: Harper, 1957).

The picture becomes more vivid when viewed in cross-national perspective. James Gillespie and I, in a comparative study[2] of the values of college youth in 10 nations, asked students to write their autobiographies of the future ("My life from now until the year 2000") and also gave them an extensive questionnaire. The instrument was translated into nine different languages.

In comparison with youth of other nations, young Americans are delightfully frank and open, unsuspicious and cooperative. Their documents had no literary affectation (and, I may add, little literary quality). But the most important finding was that within these 10 nations, American students were the most self-centered, the most "privatistic" in values. They desired above all else a rich, full life for themselves, and showed little concern for national welfare or for the fate of mankind at large. The context of their outlook was private rather than public, passive rather than pioneer. The essential point is made clear by two excerpts, the first drawn from the autobiography of a Mexican girl, 18 years of age, and the second from a Radcliffe student of the same age:

> Since I like psychology very much, I wish, on leaving this school, to study it, specializing in it and exercising it as a profession. I shouldn't like to get married right away, although like any woman I am desirous of getting married before realizing all my aspirations. In addition, I should like to do something for my country—as a teacher, as a psychologist, or as a mother. As a teacher, to guide my pupils in the best path, for at the present time they need solid basis in childhood in order in their future lives not to have so many frustrations as the youth of the present. As a psychologist, to make studies which in some way will serve humanity and my beloved country. As a mother, to make my children creatures who are useful to both their country and all humanity.

Now follows the Radcliffe document. Its flavor of privatism is unmistakable:

> Our summers will be spent lobster fishing on the Cape. Later we'll take a look at the rest of the country—California, the Southwest, and the Chicago Stockyards. I want the children, when they get past the age of ten, to spend part of the summer away from home, either at camp or as apprentices to whatever profession they may show an interest in. Finally, I hope we will be able to take a trip to Europe, especially to Russia, to see what can be done about Communism.

Many critics have called attention to the same American value predicament. Our current social pattern, they say, is almost completely geared to one objective alone, namely a profitable, expanding production. To insure expanding production, there must be more and more consumption. Hence comes the expensive glamor of our advertising and its control of our mass media. The sole objective seems to be to stimulate the accretion of goods. Self-respect and status, as well as comfort, are acquired in this way. Someone has called our national disease "galloping consumption." Half a century ago, William James saw the peril and was much worried by what he called "the American terror of poverty." He saw there was truth in the jibes that other countries direct at our "materialism."

[2] J. Gillespie and G. Allport, *Youth's Outlook on the Future* (New York: Random House, 1955).

HOPE IN UNEASINESS

Now a high standard of living is not in itself an evil thing. All the world wants what we already have. But the single-minded pursuit of production and consumption has brought a dulling of other values. One consequence is symbolized by the scandal of rigged quiz programs. These were in the service of advertising, which in turn was in the service of a profitable expanding economy. Another consequence is the accumulated froth of our TV, radio, and movies. Another is the widely discussed conformity of the organization man, as well as the futile rebellion of the beats. An especially peppery critic, Paul Goodman,[3] has shown that the starved lives of juvenile delinquents and of young people caught in the organizational grind are at bottom much alike. Both are attracted to the cult of easiness and aspire to nothing more than amiable mediocrity. Both styles of living fail to prepare youth for the problems that lie ahead for themselves and for the nation.

All this familiar criticism is irritating; yet the fact that it flourishes is a hopeful sign. We suspect it may be too harsh. I am inclined to think so. It is rash indeed to indict a whole generation. At worst, Jacob's gloomy picture held for three-quarters of the college students studied, but not at all for a vital and far from negligible minority. And even though the gloomy generalizations have some truth in them, are the assets given fair attention? I myself have some favorable impressions, although one man's view is not reliable. But youth today appears to enjoy a certain freedom and flexibility that was not common in the more rigid days of our parents and grandparents. I even have the impression that there is less neuroticism among students now than among those of a generation ago. What is more, young people, I find, are not blind to the world changes that are occurring. Their apparent repression of the challenge is due largely to their bewilderment concerning proper paths to take. (And one has the feeling that our own statesmen in Washington are no less bewildered.) All in all, these are hopeful signs that should not be overlooked.

VALUES AND THE SCHOOL

Another hopeful sign is the fact that many teachers are asking, "What can we do to be helpful?" They know, and we all know, that the ability of the school to give training in values is limited. For one thing, the home is vastly more important. A home that infects the child with galloping consumption, that encourages only canned recreation and has no creative outlets, can only with difficulty be offset by the school. Another limitation lies in the fact that the school is ordinarily expected to mirror current social values and to prepare the child to live within the existing frame. It is an unusual school system and an unusual teacher who even *wish* to transcend the current fashions of value.

[3] P. Goodman, *Growing Up Absurd* (New York: Random House, 1960).

But assuming that we have an unusual school system and an unusual teacher, what values shall they elect to teach ? If they do not choose to follow the prevailing fashions, what standards shall they follow ? The ancient Romans were fond of asking, "Who will judge the judges ?" and "Who will guard the guardians ?" Can the guardians turn perhaps to standard discussions of "the aims of education" ? Such discussions are numerous, abstract, and often dull. Their weakness, I feel, is their effort to formulate absolute goals, vistas of abstract perfection. The result is often a series of platitudes or generalizations so broad as to be unhelpful. Of course we want to develop "good citizenship"; we certainly want to "free the child's intellect." These and all other absolutes need to be reduced to concrete, stepwise processes before they can guide us in the strategy of teaching values.

The teacher must start with the situation as he or she finds it and in concrete instances sharpen the value-attributes of the lesson being taught. To a considerable extent, these value-attributes can be drawn from the códified wisdom of our nation. We cannot neglect the value of profitable production and high living standards, for all our vocational and professional education contribute to this end. But the codified wisdom of our unique society extends far beyond the obsession of today. Our values include also such matters as respect for civil liberties. Does the school accent this value ? They include approval for individual initiative, for philanthropy, for compassion. And they imply much concerning civic duties that are the reciprocal of civic rights. What must we do to deserve our precious cornucopia of freedom ? Vote ? Yes. But voting does no good unless the voter is informed above the stereotyped level of the mass media. He must also pay taxes willingly. Do schools and colleges teach the young to pay a glad tax ? I wonder. To me the most disturbing finding in *Youth's Outlook on the Future* lay in the elaborate talk about one's right to a rich, full life and in the almost total silence regarding one's duties.

I am saying that in the first instance teachers should choose the values they teach from the whole (not from a part) of our American ethos. Deep in our hearts we know, and most of the world knows, that our national values, derived, of course, from Judeo-Christian ethics, are about the finest mankind has yet formulated. In no sense are these values out of date, nor will they go out of date in the world of tomorrow. Yet many of them are badly rusted. Unless they are revitalized, however, our youth may not have the personal fortitude and moral implements that the future will require.

THE LARGER ANCHOR

Excellent as the American Creed is as a fountainhead of values, it does not contain them all. It says nothing explicitly, for example, about intellectual curiosity. And yet surely schools exist to augment this value. The most severe indictment of our educational procedures I have ever encountered is the discovery that a sizeable percentage of graduates of our colleges after completing their formal education never afterward read a single book.

There are other important values that are not spelled out in our American Creed. I am thinking of those details of human relationships that make all the difference between boorishness and brotherhood in the human family. As our population increases, it becomes more and more important to teach the elements of the new science of human relations which go far toward smoothing the roughness of common life by leading us to respect effectively the integrity of the other fellow. I recall a teacher of English whose class was studying *The Merchant of Venice*. She turned a wave of incipient anti-Semitism in her class to a sound lesson in values. Shylock, she explained, was like the resentful, self-seeking portion of every person's nature. We are all potential Shylocks. But while self-love is prominent in all of us, we are so constructed that it need not be sovereign in our natures.

To return for a moment to the relation between home and school—the former, as I have said, is far more important. Recognizing this fact, some people say, "Well, let's leave the teaching of values to the home and to the church. Schools can't do much of anything about the matter."

This position is untenable. If the school does not teach values, it will have the effect of denying them. If the child at school never hears a mention of honesty, modesty, charity, or reverence, he will be persuaded that, like many of his parents' ideas, they are simply old hat. As they grow toward adolescence, children become critical of the teaching of both parents and the church. They are in a questioning stage. If the school, which to the child represents the larger outside world, is silent on values, the child will repudiate more quickly the lessons learned at home. He will also be thrown onto peer values more completely, with their emphasis on the hedonism of teen-age parties or on the destructiveness of gangs. He will also be more at the mercy of the sensate values peddled by movies, TV, and disk jockeys. What is more, some homes, as we have said, give no fundamental value training. In such a case, it is *only* in the school that the child has any chance at all of finding ethical anchorage.

This brings us to the hardest question: How does the teacher, the instructor, the professor, handle his assignment in the classroom? How is it possible to teach values, including the value of intellectual curiosity?

THE MEANING OF VALUE

Before tackling this question, we must pause to define what we mean by value. You will recognize that I am using the term psychologically, not in its objective philosophical sense. Values, as I use the term, are simply *meanings perceived as related to self*. The child experiences value whenever he knows that a meaning is warm and central to himself. Values, to borrow Whitehead's term, are "matters of importance" as distinct from mere matters of fact.

So much for definition. Now the hard-pressed teacher is given a solid substantive curriculum to teach. The curriculum in its original state consists of mere matters of fact. And on the number of facts absorbed the pupil's standing depends.

It takes virtually all of a teacher's time to convey factual information and grade the pupil on his achievement. There is little time left to transmute these matters of fact into matters of importance, let alone teach all of the moral and social values we have thus far been discussing.

The curriculum itself is not, and should not be, a direct aid. Prescribed instruction in values would be laughed out of court. We have recently been bumped by Sputnik headforemost into core subjects. Get on with science, mathematics, language! Away with courses in folk-dancing, personal adjustment, and fudge-making! I agree that value-study has no place in curriculum planning, but not because it is a frivolous subject—rather, because it is a subject too hard and too subtle for curriculum makers.

Education for values occurs only when teachers teach what they themselves stand for, no matter what their subject is. If I were to write a treatise on the teaching of values, I would give most of my emphasis to the moral pedagogy that lies in a teacher's incidental comments, to the *obiter dicta*. The hard core is central, but the hard core has a penumbra of moral significance. I mentioned the teacher of English who made a value-lesson out of Shylock. I recall also my college professor of geology who paused in his lecture on diatom ooze to say to us, "Others would not agree with me, but I confess that whenever I study diatoms, I don't see how anyone can doubt the existence of God because the design and behavior of these protozoa are so marvelous." Is it not interesting how we all recall the *obiter dicta* of our teachers, the penumbra of value they point out to us, surrounding the hard-core data? We remember them better than the subject matter itself.

Why does the student remember them so well? No current theory of learning seems able to tell us. I suspect it is because values, being matters of importance to the self, are always warm and central and ego-involved and therefore claim priority on our attention. The child, being value-ripe, cannot help being impressed when the teacher betrays excitement and enthusiasm for a mode of thought or for the content of the subject being studied. True, the youngster does not, and should not, adopt the teacher's values ready-made; but the teacher's self-disclosure leads the student to self-discovery.

What wouldn't we give if we could develop intellectual ardor in every child for hard core subjects? Why is it that for most pupils arithmetic, spelling, physics, remain forever full matters of fact and never become a meaning perceived as related to the self? One reason, I think, is that the weary teacher fails to convey his own sense of the importance of the subject to the student. If he did so, he would, as I have said, at least fix attention upon the value-potentiality of the subject.

Another reason perhaps is that not all of a teacher's *obiter dicta* are wholesome. Some, indeed, may be deeply damaging, though the teacher may be innocent of any such intent. Sometimes we hear incidental (but still attitude-forming) remarks like this one: "All right now, children. You have had a good time playing at recess; now settle down to your English lesson." Play is recognized as a matter of joyful importance. English, the teacher is saying in effect, is a mere routine matter of fact.

VALUES AND LEARNING

I think our educational psychology has been mostly wrong about the process of learning—or perhaps not so much wrong as woefully incomplete. At the beginning of his learning career, a young child cannot, of course, be expected to feel adult enthusiasm for the intellectual content of his studies. He does his work in the first instance to avoid a scolding or because he has a habit of obeying instructions. Soon he finds added incentive. The teacher—really in the role of mother—gives praise and love ("Susan, I am proud of you"). There is a great deal of such dependency in the learning situation. Love and social reward (as well as some fear of punishment) sustain the processes of attention and retention. When the child puts forth intellectual effort, he does so in order to obtain a gold star, commendation, or other symbols of love.

All these incentives are extraneous to the subject matter. The youngster does not learn it because it is a matter of importance. When he leaves school or college, he loses these extraneous supports. He finds his love relations directly; they are no longer a reward for intellectual effort. Hence, intellectual apathy sets in, and, distressing to say, no further books are read.

In such a case as this, intellectual curiosity was never tied to independence, only to extraneous supports. At some point in the schooling—and the earlier the better —intellectual activity should become not a second-hand but a first-hand fitting to the sense of self. At the beginning, all learning must be tied, perhaps, to specific reinforcements; but if the dependency is long continued, authentic curiosity fails to develop.

It would be going too far to put the blame for intellectual apathy onto our current teaching of educational psychology. Yet I am inclined to feel somewhat punitive about this matter. Psychology has not yet settled down to the problem of transforming matters of fact—whose acquisition current learning theories explain fairly well—into autonomous matters of importance—which they do not explain at all.

Our emphasis has been on learning by drill and by reinforcement. Such "habit acquisition" receives all the emphasis. But the learning theory involved postulates a continuing dependency relation (extraneous reinforcement). When the relation terminates, the habits of study simply extinguish themselves. I am surprised, therefore, that stimulus-response psychologists do not see this consequence of their own theory. Insofar as teachers employ an educational psychology of this order, they are not likely to break the dependency relation, which belongs properly only to the earlier stages of schooling.

Matters of importance, I strongly believe, are not acquired by drill or by reinforcement. They are transformations of habits and skills from the "opportunistic" layer of personality into the ego-system itself.[4] Once inside the ego-system, these habits and skills turn into true interests and utilize the basic energy, the basic spontaneity, that the organism itself possesses. They are no longer sustained as "operant conditionings" by outside rewards. The interest, now being the very stuff of life itself, needs no outer supports.

FUNCTIONAL AUTONOMY

I have called this process of transforming means into ends, of changing extrinsic values into intrinsic values, *functional autonomy*. Concerning this concept, I am often asked two questions: How do you define "functional autonomy, and how does functional autonomy come about"?

For a definition, I offer the following: Functional autonomy refers to any acquired system of motivation in which the tensions involved are no longer of the same kind as the antecedent tensions from which the acquired system developed.[5] To answer the question of how functional autonomy comes about requires a more extended and technical discussion. I can only hint at the direction of my answer. Neurologists are gradually discovering a basis for what I would call "perseverative functional autonomy." I refer to the "self-sustaining circuits," "feedback mechanisms," and "central motive states" that are now commonly recognized to exist in the nervous system. This line of discovery, I find, provides a partial answer to the question. But I believe we have to go further and call on the concept of self. Values, we have said, are meanings perceived as related to the self. Functional autonomy is not a mere perseverative phenomenon; it is, above all, an ego-involved phenomenon. Besides admitting an opportunistic layer to personality, which is the exclusive concern of most current theories of learning, we have no choice but to admit also a "propriate" layer. It is in this layer that all matters of importance reside.

The goal of the educator, then, is to shift the content of the subject he teaches from the opportunistic (matter of fact) layer to the propriate. But there is no sure-fire, mechanical strategy to use. The best general rule, one that John Dewey saw clearly, is to strive ceaselessly to integrate routine matters of fact into the growing experience system of the child himself. It would take a long treatise to specify various detailed strategies of teaching that help achieve this goal.

Let me focus on only one aspect of this topic, upon a common mistake that teachers make. I myself am a continual offender. It is to present students with our own carefully thought out conclusions when they themselves lack the raw experience from which these conclusions are fashioned.

This particular error is inherent, for example, in the lecture system. Instead of lecturing on comparative religion, for instance, it would be much better to require all students to attend services of worship that are unfamiliar to them. If raw ex-

---

[4] G. Allport, *Becoming* (New Haven: Yale University Press, 1955).
[5] If this definition seems too technical to be immediately helpful, see Ch. 10 of *Pattern and Growth in Personality* for a more extended treatment of functional autonomy.

perience is present, then perhaps a lecture may be effective. Much of the intellectual apathy we complain about is due to our fault of presenting conclusions in lieu of first-hand experience. To us, our well-chiseled conclusion, summing up a long intellectual struggle with a problem of knowledge or of value, seems like a beautiful sonnet. To the student, it may be gibberish.

The fallacy of giving conclusions holds both for subject matter and for values. A lad of 15 cannot profit from the fully fashioned philosophy of life of a man of 50. To register at all, a statement about values must fall precisely on his present growing edge.

Teaching, then, is not the art of offering conclusions, however hard won and valid they may be. No teacher can forcibly enter the students' proprium and plant a functionally autonomous motive. He can at best open channels of experience and, by his *obiter dicta*, sometimes lead the student to see the value-potential in the experience.

The theory of personality that we need to guide a more fully developed educational psychology will teach us something important about our basic verb "to educate." It will show us that only at the outset of learning is it a transitive verb. By drill, by reward, by reinforcement, the teacher does indeed educate the child —in matters of fact. But true maturity comes only when the verb is reflexive. For in matters of importance, where values lie, the growing individual alone can educate himself.

SOCIAL CHANGE
Impact on the Adolescent

JAMES S. COLEMAN

Adults have a special reason today to shake their heads and mutter, "the younger generation . . .," as adults are wont to do. For today's adults and today's teenagers have special problems of communication that make it more and more difficult for each to understand what the other is up to. These communication problems arise not because teenagers are in some strange new way different than ever before, but because of changes in the structure of our society. These changes have produced a number of special problems in education and in the whole process of growing up, of which the communication gap is only one. I would like to indicate what some of these structural changes are, and some of their consequences for adolescents.

Reprinted by permission from the *Bulletin of the National Association of Secondary-School Principals* (April 1965). Copyright: Washington, D. C.

SOCIETAL CHANGES AND FAMILY COHESION

A number of changes have combined to make the family a less cohesive, less effective agent within which to raise children than ever before. One of these changes is the entry of large numbers of women into the labor force. Prior to World War II, in March 1940, 16.7 per cent of married women held jobs outside the home. By March 1961, this had doubled to 34.0 per cent. (In 1890, it was 4.5 per cent.) This change need not, of course, make a given family less tightly knit, nor give adolescent children a less rich "psychological home," but it tends to do so, and the overall social impact must be in this direction.

Another change is the smaller and smaller number of families that have relatives—aunts, uncles, grandparents—living in the household. This means that the typical family of today in America is parents and children, with nothing more. Thus the family's strength depends far more on the parents than ever before. The relatives are not there to provide adults for the children to model themselves after, or adults in whom they can confide.

A third change, which reinforces the preceding one, is the greater geographic mobility of families, particularly since World War II. An urban or suburban family today does not have a homestead that passes from one generation to another; nor does it even have a stable place of residence for a single generation. More and more, the typical "life-cycle" of a family begins with a newly-married couple living in an apartment in the city; then with the first child comes a move to a suburb of families with young children; then later, as income and family grow, to a suburb of larger houses and older children; then finally, after the children are gone, back to an apartment in the city.

Such moves mean that the adult neighborhood, which was once an extension of the household itself, is hardly so now. Children make neighborhood friends quickly, but their parents do not; and perhaps most important, the children have few contacts and even fewer stable relationships with other adults in the neighborhood.

Finally, a change that has been going on for a long time is the shift of the father's work from the home or the neighborhood (e.g., the farmer or merchant) to a distant office or factory. Thus, the son knows only abstractly what his father does; and he can never enter into the father's work.

CONSEQUENCES OF CHANGE

The effects of these changes on the adolescent are many. One of the most interesting indicators is the recent large increase in "going steady" among adolescents. This phenomenon, virtually unknown in Europe, can be explained only in terms of overall changes that have taken place in the teenager's life. Looking closely at the practice of going steady indicates that it is not (as some adults fear) principally a license for sexual freedom. Instead, its basis is more nearly in the kind of psychological security it provides, a psychological closeness that today's adolescents seem to need. When we ask why they need it, the answer is clear: the family no longer provides the closeness and security it once did. Because of the structural changes indicated above, the family fails to provide the kind of close secure relationships that the adolescent had as a child and will once again have when he himself forms a family. His response comes by finding that close security in an attachment to another.

Going steady is only one of the consequences of these structural changes in society. Another is the greater and greater burden that falls on the school. The school was once a supplement to the activities of the family in making adults of its children. But the roles have reversed for today's adolescents: the home is more and more merely a supplement to the adolescent's life, which focuses more and more on the school. It may be, as some school administrators feel, that this places too great a responsibility on the school. Yet the condition exists, and many families, with their working parents, high mobility, and lack of other relatives in the household, are in no position to change the condition. The adolescents turn to one another, to the school, and to the entertainments of the larger society, for these are their only resources.

Another consequence of the family's weakness, one that stems from the same needs as does going steady, is the earlier age of dating and of interest in the opposite sex. The consequences of this for interest in schoolwork is particularly marked for girls. There is a sharp shift in early adolescence from a high evaluation of the bright girl to a much lower evaluation—for the girl who appears especially bright does not fare well in dates with boys. Among schools I studied a few years ago, this shift started slightly later in the rural schools than in the urban and suburban ones. In the former, the shift occurred during the ninth grade; in the latter, the shift had largely taken place before the ninth grade. In both sets of schools, the devaluation of brightness and the emphasis on good looks and popularity with boys was at its peak in middle adolescence. In the rural schools, it had sharply declined by the senior year in high school, while in the urban and suburban ones, the decline had already begun in the junior year. It appears that the most intense focus of adolescent girls on problems of popularity and dating, and the greatest devaluation of schoolwork occurs when the rating and dating system is still unsettled, and the uncertainty of who will ask whom for a date is at its height. These years, among modern adolescents, are earlier than ever before—in junior high school and early high school. The consequence for schools may be a peculiar one: to make the junior high school years more difficult ones than in the past, for adolescents and for teachers and school administrators, and to make the senior high school years (in three-year high schools) less difficult.

The earlier age of interest in the opposite sex, and the consequent earlier shift of adolescent values in this direction derives only in part from weakened family ties. It derives in part from all the changes in society that bring about early social sophistication among adolescents. Partly urban and suburban living, partly television and other mass media (for example, both popular music and movies have come to be more and more oriented to teenagers), partly the money they now have to spend, partly their better-educated parents, and partly the school itself, have made adolescents more wise in the ways of the world.

THE DESIRE FOR SOPHISTICATION

In the schools I studied recently, the sharpest difference I found in the adolescents of the most rural schools and those of the most middle-class urban and suburban ones, was in the sophistication of the latter. The rural 9th graders were still children, obedient to teachers, and the middle-class suburban pupils were already disdainful of the ways of childhood. Such sophistication, and desire for sophistication, is a double-edged sword. It means that adolescents are more ready for new ideas, new experiences, quicker to grasp things. But it also makes them far less easy to teach, less willing to remain in the role of a learner, impatient with teachers, less likely to look at the teacher as a model or an authority. It need not make them more interested in school, but perhaps even less so. For the world whose sophistication they are taking on is one outside the school. Schoolwork, with its daily assignments and homework, they associate with childhood. Many of these children learn only years later, in college or after, that hard work and carrying out of assignments, attention to the demands of the teacher, become more important, rather than less, the farther they go in school.

Of all the recent changes in adolescents, this early desire for sophistication poses perhaps the greatest problem and the greatest challenge for secondary schools. Teenagers are less willing to respond to the teacher just because he is a teacher; less willing to "be taught." But they are more responsive *if* their imagination is captured, more able and willing to respond to a real challenge. It makes the school's task more difficult, for it cannot take the adolescent's interest for granted; it must find new ways of capturing this interest and energy. It has no other alternative but to accept these more sophisticated adolescents, and turn their sophistication to the advantage of education.

Altogether, recent changes in society have had a sharp impact on our adolescents. They present now, and they will present even more in the future, both difficulty and opportunity to the schools.

EARLY ADOLESCENCE
IN THE UNITED STATES

MARGARET MEAD

When the behavior of young American adolescents is compared with the known behavior of adolescents in other modern industrialized societies and in developing countries, and with their own behavior in past decades, several things stand out.

American adolescents are expected to mimic the ways of adults, long before they are emotionally ready for them. The category *teenager*, inclusive from 13 through 19, has resulted in a public image which expects great precocity from the *young* teenager and irresponsibility from the *old* teenager. This category inappropriately lumps together immature children whose growth spurts have hardly begun and mature young people who are permitted to marry and produce children and expected to support themselves. By making "the teens" a category, within which a nineteen-year-old hoodlum's vicious destructiveness and a thirteen-year-old's mischief are bracketed together, we have endowed the younger teenager with a whole series of real and potential precocities that are not only inappropriate but also burdensome.

One of the striking features of the last two decades has been the steady spread downwards in age level of dating; going steady; pairing-off (rather than one-sex friendship); and in emphasis on vocational choice, criminal behavior, competitive athletics, religious affiliation, and permission to spend money on an increasingly lavish scale. The recent book, *Teen Age Tyranny*, which reifies the teenager into a kind of mass menace, documents this money-spending phase heavily, perhaps too heavily, relying on quantity—amount spent in the United States—to overwhelm the listener with numbers.[1]

This precocity, which exists in all fields of life, may be partly exaggerated by other trends in the society—the enormous dependence upon the automobile for transport; the dependence of this age-group on their parents' driving them wherever they go; the increased importance of the mass media, especially television (which means that individual homes and even individual schools have a hard struggle against a commercially supported and propagated national style); the expectation of many more years of schooling which is complemented by a

Reprinted by permission from the *Bulletin of the National Association of Secondary-School Principals* (April 1965). Copyright: Washington, D. C.

[1] Hechinger, Grace and Fred M., *Teen Age Tyranny* (New York: William Morrow and Company, 1963).

demand for some real life now. The student, who has entered school in kinder-garten or nursery school, and who has traveled laboriously through every grade of elementary school, with high school and post-high school education all to come, feels as if school would last forever. The fact that the schools have been geared to help the more poorly prepared students, have insisted on children staying within their age group, and have discouraged the participation of parents in their young children's education, all adds to the thirteen-year-old's feeling that school is an endless and wearisome process. It might as well be enlivened by as much simulation of adult life—which seems impossibly far off—as can be arranged.

This early reaching for the signs of adulthood, such as clothes, dates, spending money, alcohol—all the things to which age and work were once the tickets of admission—is undoubtedly accentuated by the orientation of older brothers and sisters. They, at sixteen and eighteen, are being forced to reach for adult status parenthood for which they are neither economically nor emotionally ready. The attempt of the older adolescent to become a parent before his time reflects the general uncertainty in American society today about the future of the world. Our apprehension that any change may be a change for the worse leading to economic depression, if not to nuclear catastrophe, makes for a restless drawing upon the possibilities of the present and a decline in the willingness to save, to postpone spending, or to defer marrying, buying a house, having children, or taking a trip. The pervasive fear that the future can only be worse than the present, is accom-panied by this clinging to and exploitation of the present, which parents in turn express in letting their children do everything earlier rather than later. The Ameri-can tendency of noting what other people are doing and attempting to do it a little bit better means, now that national mass media are so important, that every time some precocity is reported, other towns, other high schools, other junior high schools, other clubs will try to emulate it. And the direction of emulation since World War II has been toward precocity, marrying younger—and among juvenile delinquents, sensitive to the world stage on which the mass media place them, committing crimes younger.

This emphasis on earlier and earlier participation in adult activities is super-ficially incongruent with the junior high school movement designed as it was to protect the young adolescent by a separate pace of slower induction into the com-plexities of high school life. The whole movement began when thinking in chrono-logical age group terms had not been amplified by our knowledge of the great extremes of variation in the ages that boys and girls enter their growth spurt and enter puberty. Junior high schools were designed for children in three "grades" of school: 7th, 8th, and 9th. The grades were postulated on age and not on size, strength, or stage of puberty. They have resulted inadvertently in classifying together boys and girls at the age when they vary most, within each sex, and between the sexes, and are least suited to a segregated social existence. Also, they have divorced them from the reassurances of association with the children like their own recent past selves and older adolescents like whom they will someday become. When a type of school that was designed to cushion the shock of change in scholastic demands has become the focus of the social pressures which were once exerted in senior high school, problems have been multiplied.

KILLING THE ABILITY TO EXPERIENCE

Young adolescents today are bored. They have received too many slight and superficial communications about almost everything. They have "had" something about almost everything, and the tendency to give predigested easy previews of what will come later acts as a kind of deadening of the ability to experience. Bright children are bored with this repetition, and other children are not stimulated to more effort. During the early adolescent years children are now developing one strong definite purpose, to get it over with—school, or college, or living at home—and get the real autonomy and independence that is now only spuriously theirs, as mother drives a 14 year old boy and his "date" to the movies.

The appropriate experiences of the early teens are pair friendship with members of their own sex, a just-emerging recognition that the other sex can after all be interesting, admiration and emulation of adult models, heroes, and ideals (who reincarnate the early childhood sense that the parents and teachers were all-knowing and wise), and an enormous curiosity about the outside world, about their own changing bodily responses and shifting sense of identity. At present all of these are inhibited by the present cultural style of aping of a later stage.

Another set of pressures on this age comes from the present styles of education and social life of smaller children. The dull routine of schools, in which children learn a tenth of what they could, results in blunting the curiosity that might carry them through junior high school. More ambitious kindergarten and elementary school programs, entrance to school based on readiness and not on birthday date, might produce a group of early teenagers with more capacity to be interested in what the junior high school could offer them.

The delimitation of the teens has also produced a decrease in the sense of individual growth; where the onset of puberty for a boy or girl once marked a stage in the individual life cycle, emphasis is placed on grade and age alone. Just as we keep children born a day too late out of school for a year, doing an injustice comparable to some of our worst forms of ethnic discrimination, so the fine nuances of individual growth and change are obscured by the magic of the 13th birthday. Assurance that one will be a "teenager" for seven whole years is like being handed life on a silver platter at 13. It is an intolerable tyranny at 19 when—grown, subject to the draft, married, and a parent—the drinking laws and car insurance rules treat one as a child.

The crying out against conformity which has been such a prominent feature of the post World War II years is partly a response to this kind of stylization of a whole decade of life in which the most dramatic changes occur as if it were in fact, one single decade, the sections separated by junior high school, senior high school, and college, with the overall style still that of a teenager. "She's a typical teenager," says the older sister. "She might have come right out of television." And indeed she did.

There are further complications. The children of today mature earlier and grow taller than their parents. These coupled with clothes which thirteen-year-olds share with nineteen-year-olds, make them seem bigger, older, more able to handle adult activities. The parent compares his son with his own image of himself as a boy. His junior high school son looks like a college student to him; often without consciously recognizing his own feeling, he treats him as older than he is.

Furthermore, through the mass media, adolescents who knew about adolescence, consider themselves as *teenagers* and include in their self picture the research that is done on their age group. Just as adult educators have tended to take behavior that was found to be average, and transform the average into the norm, and therefore the desirable, so every bit of uproar over teenage characteristics helps form their self-image. By locating most of the behavior which is appropriate to the late teens in the early teens, we have increased this quality of acting out a kind of behavior which has no emotional or intellectual basis.

It is true that the greatest tragedy of our present day adolescents are the million that are condemned by social circumstances to learn very little at school, and to live a life in which their potentialities are practically unrealized. This great wasting of youth is due to the present inability to manage cities, deploy resources, and deal with economic and ethnic minorities. The specific smaller tragedies of our present cultural style for the junior high school age are dropouts in high school, after high school and college, too early marriage, too early parenthood, under-achievement for a third of our young people.

WHAT ABOUT THE FUTURE?

Corrective measures are on the horizon: far better early childhood education, including the permission to parents to teach their own children what they know; school admissions as a result of readiness not birthday month; more differentiation by special interests within junior high schools; more association of junior high school students with younger and older students; consciously diversified summer experiences; and not least important but with possibilities for great good and great harm, the increasing strength of the organizations for junior high school teachers, principals, and curriculum specialists. If this increasing organizational strength of a field that has always been treated as somehow transitional and with very little sense of special status and identity is used to increase sensitivity to the problems of the junior high school students, great changes for good may be expected. But it might work the other way. We have imprisoned our adolescents within a category, *teenager*, and our early adolescents with all the striking differences and discrepancies within a category—*junior high school student*. To date the junior high school teacher has been less categorized, more transitional, just out of elementary school or just moving in to senior high school styles of teaching. If the organizing of junior high school administrators, teachers, curricular specialists, is spelled with a capital, and results in their being frozen in a single style, this may intensify the way in which all junior high school students are treated alike, regardless of their levels of physical, emotional, and intellectual maturity. This would be a loss rather than a gain. Junior high school students are more unlike each other than they have ever been before or ever will be again in the course of their lives. If a lively sum of these differences can be maintained and strengthened among those who plan for them and teach them—the whole school system, and the adolescents of the coming generation will be the gainers.

PRESSURES ON MIDDLE-CLASS TEEN-AGERS

SIDNEY BERMAN

The demands on youth are much greater today than they used to be, and on the basis of my relationship with teen-agers, I would say that many of them are not as adequately equipped to meet these stresses as we would hope they would be.

Many of today's pressures stem from the fact that the values of our social system are so nebulous. Expressions like the *new frontier* and the *good day of tomorrow* are vague cliches. As our teen-agers look ahead to the future, there is nothing that specifically spells out for them the goals and objectives of our society.

Parents can't help their sons and daughters very much because they too are uncertain of what should be expected of children and of what kind of preparation young people need to ready them to take their places in the social system. Parents aren't able to lay down good guide lines because our society doesn't have good guide lines.

The schools are not particularly helpful either, because they are also victims of the social system. Despite a host of technological and educational advances, I doubt that many educators are clear about what they want to achieve in terms of educating a child to become a member of our society. What are their goals in teaching him mathematics, for example? Is their only consideration the child's present and future needs to know a specific body of data as required to graduate or do they also weigh the needs of the social system for such training?

Educators have a big task to do. They do it to the best of their ability, but they are just as much influenced by the culture in which we live as are the parents. Furthermore, I think that today parents expect the schools to bear too much of the burden of rearing children. But this is really another topic, so let's get back to the matter of pressures.

FROM the *NEA Journal* (February 1965), pp. 17, 20, 60. Copyright: National Education Association. Reprinted by permission.

In some instances, homework assignments have become so heavy that they put young people under unreasonable pressure.

A teacher, for example, may load so much work on bright children that he creates depression and discouragement in these youngsters. I suspect such a teacher of being more interested in puffing up his own reputation as a producer of champions than he is in encouraging delicate, pliable human beings to perform well within reasonable boundaries.

On the whole, however, I think the problem is not so much that of overwork as it is of the inevitable clash of values in an affluent society: What should come first when there are so many conflicting demands on one's time and interest?

Parents who go out on the town three or four evenings a week are unrealistic to expect their children to dedicate themselves to work, to deliberate training, to a concentrated effort in terms of their studies. I don't suggest that parents should stay home to help do the homework, but I think that the physical presence of the parents in the home during the evening indicates their acceptance of the parental role. This, in turn, conveys to the child the responsibility of a young person to learn how to be a good scholar and a good citizen.

Of course, parents make a drastic mistake when they bear down mercilessly on their children in an effort to get them into a prestige college. A son at Harvard or a daughter at Smith has become a great prestige symbol these days, and yet it's ridiculous to think that any particular institution is the sine qua non of all education. It's the basic dedication of the student that determines what he takes from school.

Our social system asks too much of young people by demanding that all of them go to college. Goals should be set in a more realistic fashion. Good counseling would be valuable here, but unfortunately counselors are influenced strongly by pressures brought to bear by parents and teachers. As a result, they oftentimes act more as arbiters than as counselors.

The fact that so many students are going to college merely to meet the expectations of their parents is probably a major cause of the high rate of college dropouts —about 50 percent do not graduate, I've been told.

Another dropout factor is that our society makes it extremely difficult for young people to have any kind of meaningful work experience before they get to college. As a consequence, they often don't know what they want to specialize in when they reach the third and fourth years of college.

On the one hand, our social system infantilizes the youngster, keeps him parasitic; on the other hand, when he graduates from high school, he's suddenly expected to be a man. This is extremely hard on our young people: They cannot learn how to become adults overnight. Because they have been raised in an affluent society in which everything has been done for them, even very talented youngsters lack the psychological drive and the know-how to do for themselves.

Another type of pressure results from pushing youngsters into sophisticated experiences for which they are not ready. Seventh grade girls wear lipstick, high-heeled shoes, and evening dresses, for instance, and their seventh grade escorts present them with corsages.

These young people can't direct their energies to spurious pleasure and dedicate themselves to the learning experience at the same time. This doesn't mean that learning has to be a drab, monastic type of experience; the pursuit of knowledge can be a rich shared experience, supplemented by the coordinated wholesome type of social activity that a school can provide.

Eighth grade Susie isn't likely to eat her heart out about not going to a dance unless her mother and father feel she is a failure because she hasn't been invited. Parents who have that attitude can destroy a child's feeling of worth; furthermore, by focusing attention on a material and pleasurable existence, they are diverting energies that should be directed to the tasks of maturing.

Parents who mobilize sexual stimuli in girls eleven or twelve should not be surprised if their youngsters get sexually involved in their teens.

Speaking of youngsters, this age brings to mind the junior high school, which, I think, unwittingly exerts great pressure and stress on preadolescent and early adolescent youngsters. Why? Because, in my opinion, the whole idea of the junior high school goes counter to what we know of child growth and development.

The boys and girls that we put in junior high school are going through a major disorganization: Their bodies are undergoing the massive changes associated with the metamorphosis from childhood to adolescence. Naturally they are preoccupied with this transformation, and as a result, their thinking processes are fragmented and their behavior is disorganized so that they are less disciplined than they have been in the past or will be in the future.

In the face of all this, they are taken out of their familiar setting and placed in a different school with different teachers, different routine—different everything. That's the last thing in the world these children need. What they need is stability.

In my opinion, during the highly volatile years of eleven through thirteen or fourteen, youngsters should have a familiar, secure background in which to operate. In the midst of deciding who they are, they shouldn't have to waste any energy in finding out where they are.

To recapitulate: Pressures on young people may arise in relationship to the expectations of the school; they may arise in terms of the expectations of the family; or they may develop out of the internal disorganization of the youngster during the upheaval of adolescence.

Teachers can generally recognize when a child has been under too much pressure: He may strike out against his fellows, he may withdraw, or his marks may go down.

When the teacher recognizes by one or more of these symptoms that a youngster is overwhelmed by pressures, he should talk with the child, try to find out what the problems are, and do what he can to lessen stress. Whenever possible, he should also confer with the child's parents as well as review the pupil's past record to see what his performance has been, to see what level of potential he has.

Of course, these suggestions are predicated on the theory that the teacher is skilled in human relationships and is not overburdened with an unreasonable work load. Nothing in our social system is more precious than our children, and this means that those to whom we entrust their care should be the finest teachers obtainable.

One final word—I don't want to leave the impression that teachers should try to eliminate competition, because some youngsters seem to need this stimulus and because competition is an inherent part of our culture. Whenever possible, however, I would emphasize the importance of achieving excellence as a means of being better able to share with others and to participate with the group rather than of making others feel inadequate by comparison.

ADOLESCENCE IN AN
OPEN SOCIETY

EDGAR Z. FRIEDENBERG

What is most extraordinary about youth today is that adults everywhere should be so worried about it. I do not mean to suggest that this concern is groundless; on the contrary. A great many young people are in very serious trouble throughout the technically developed and especially the Western world. Their trouble, moreover, follows certain familiar common patterns; they get into much the same kind of difficulty in very different societies. But it is nevertheless strange that they should. Human life is a continuous thread which each of us spins to his own pattern, rich and complex in meaning. There are no natural knots in it. Yet knots form, nearly always in adolescence. In American, British, European, Japanese, Australasian, and at least the more privileged Soviet youth, puberty releases emotions that tend toward crisis. Every major industrial society believes that it has a serious youth problem.

Adolescence is both a stage and a process of growth. As such it should proceed by doing what comes naturally. Instead, there is a widespread feeling that it cannot be allowed to proceed without massive intervention. The young disturb and anger their elders, and are themselves angered and disturbed, or repelled and depressed, at the thought of becoming what they see their elders to be. Adults observe and condemn the "teen-age tyranny" of "the adolescent society," over which they seek to establish and maintain hegemony by techniques of infiltration and control.

Adolescents are among the last social groups in the world to be given the full nineteenth-century colonial treatment. Our colonial administrators, at least at the higher policy-making levels, are usually of the enlightened sort who decry the punitive expedition except as an instrument of last resort, though they are inclined to tolerate a shade more brutality in the actual school or police station than the law allows. They prefer, however, to study the young with a view to understanding them, not for their own sake but in order to learn how to induce them to abandon their barbarism and assimilate the folkways of normal adult life. The model emissary to the world of youth is no longer the tough disciplinarian but the trained youth worker, who works like a psychoanalytically oriented anthropologist. Like the best of missionaries, he is sympathetic and understanding toward the people he is sent to work with, and aware and critical of the larger society he represents. But fundamentally he accepts it, and often does not really question its basic values or its right to send him to wean the young from savagery.

Like the missionary among his natives, the youth worker finds the young in no virgin state. By the time he gets there it is too late for that. "Youth cultures" vary from the more flamboyant forms of delinquency to the conservative eroticism of the college fraternity. But all of them have been altered by continuous interaction with the adult world; the youngsters, unlike natives of a primitive tribe, have never known anything else and have no traditions wholly their own. The idols of the "teen-age" culture are the entertainers who use their "teen-age" clientele to make it as disk jockeys, on TV, or within the residually "teen-age" enclave of the B-movie. The explicit values of the juvenile gang are taken from the adult world; they, too, covet status and success, and do not imagine that these could be conceived in terms more compelling than those they find familiar. The worst off, perhaps, are the traders and interpreters: the big men on campus, the boys who wear the sports jackets clothing manufacturers are trying to introduce to the "teen-age" market, the occasional gang leader who, at seventeen, is already working up the memoirs of his reformation, as told to the youth worker or his parish priest. In any society, marginal individuals have especially severe problems.

The economic position of "the adolescent society," like that of other colonies, is highly ambiguous. It is simultaneously a costly drain on the commonwealth and a vested interest of those members of the commonwealth who earn their living and their social role by exploiting it. Juvenile delinquency is destructive and wasteful, and efforts to control and combat it are expensive. Schooling is even more expensive. Both undertakings are justified on the assumption that youth must be drawn into the social order if the social order is to continue, and this is self-evident. But both act as agents of society as it now is, propagating its values and assumptions among a youth often cynical and distrustful but ignorant of the language or the moral judgments in terms of which its complaints might be couched. Neither the youth agency nor the school is usually competent or sufficiently independent to help adolescents examine the sources of their pain and conflict and think its meaning through, using their continuing experience of life to help them build better social arrangements in their turn. This, in a democracy, ought clearly to be among the most fundamental functions of citizenship education; in a public school system geared and responsive to local political demands and interests it may well be impossible. Official agencies dealing with youth vary enormously in the pretexts and technics with which they approach their clientele, from those of the young worker attached to a conflict gang to those of the Cit Ed teacher in the academic track of a suburban high school. But they all begin, like a Colonial Office, with the assumption that the long-term interests of their clientele are consistent with the present interests of their sponsor.

Like other colonial peoples, adolescents are economically dependent on the dominant society, and appear in its accounts as the beneficiaries of its philanthropy. Like them also, adolescents are partly dependent because of their immature stage of development, but even more because of restrictions placed upon them by the dominant society. In the United States at present, one of the most serious sources of difficulty for adolescents is that few can find jobs. There are not many jobs for "boys" any more: delivery, elevator, messenger, and house have all largely disappeared in the wake of automation and the decline of small business and the Sahib. Even when these jobs were not worth doing they provided the adolescent with some money and a valid social role. Their disappearance has left him with no legitimate role except that of high school student, which provides no income and no independence. If he leaves school before graduation he is almost certain to be unemployed for months before getting one of the few dead-end unskilled or semi-skilled jobs available to him; he faces a lifetime of substandard living and sporadic unemployment. Wide recognition of this fact has led to stepped-up efforts to keep adolescents from dropping out of school; we are less willing to recognize that they may, quite literally, have no business there. In any case, until they are old enough for the Army, they have none, and are permitted none, anywhere else.

Nevertheless, "teen-agers" do have money, about ten billion dollars a year of it, though this comes to only about ten dollars a week as an average. They scrounge it from home or earn it at odd times, and this, too, contributes to their colonial status. The "teen-age" market is big business. We all share an economic interest in the dependency of the "teen-ager." The school is interested in keeping him off the streets and in its custody. Labor is interested in keeping him off the labor market. Business and industry are interested in seeing that his tastes become fads and in selling him specialized junk that a more mature taste would reject. Like a dependent native, the "teen-ager" is encouraged to be economically irresponsible because his sources of income are undependable and do not derive from his personal qualities. He can be very responsible in buying things that are closely related to his real skills and interests and his evolving sense of himself: sporting equipment, used cars, the things that mean something to him. But he cannot easily work out an entirely personal and responsible pattern of economic behavior because he has no serious economic status; he is treated like a plantation worker whose benevolent master allows him a few dollars to take into town on Saturday afternoon, though they both know he will only spend it foolishly.

Other forms of colonialism are dead or dying. A technically developed society has no use for a pool of unskilled labor which at its cheapest is far costlier than machinery and which nevertheless cannot afford to buy machine products. By one of these strokes of precious insight that the sociology of knowledge has led us rather to expect, the Western world began to perceive colonialism as immoral almost as soon as it became patently unprofitable. The missionary spirit and the White Man's Burden have yielded to the anthropologist's relativism and the Common Market. Why has the "teen-ager" then remained, so stubbornly, the object of colonial solicitude?

Primarily because we are dependent on him, too. Disorderly as it is, our house needs an heir. The colonial analogy is defective at a crucial point. The essence of the "teen-ager's" status is that he is in transition; the essence of the native's status is that he is not supposed to be. The maintenance of a colonial system requires that the native accept enough of the dominant culture to meet its schedules, work for payment in its smaller currency, desire and consume its goods, and fight in its armies; and so far the analogy holds for the "teen-ager." But the native is not expected—indeed, not usually permitted—to actually "pass"; he is never granted full membership in the dominant culture, and the dominant culture does not depend for its survival on his ultimate willingness to accept it.

But every society depends on the succession of generations, and adults usually assume that this means that their values and life style should be transmitted to the young. Youth cannot be allowed to "go native" permanently; some writers and artists may be allowed to live as beachcombers and to go on negotiating with other adults in beat and jive as if it were pidgin, but the rest have to grow up to be like their elders. When adults observe that a large proportion of youth is becoming threateningly unfamiliar and uncongenial, there is said to be a youth problem, and deliberate efforts are made to induce or compel the young to accept and participate in the dominant culture.

At this point, therefore, the position of youth is less that of a colonized native than it is that of a minority group that is gaining status and being assimilated. The plight of the adolescent is basically similar to that of an emigrant in that he can neither stay what he was nor become what he started out to be. Minority-group status occurs, and is recognized as such, only in societies that are abandoning a colonial stance and accepting the position that the lesser breeds over whose destinies they have assumed control are to be brought *within* the law and ultimately to be treated as equals. In the United States, this position has been part of our ideology from the beginning; our true colonial subjects have been the Negroes, who have actually been native Americans for a century but who are only now being taken really seriously as citizens.

The "Negro problem" and the "youth problem" have many features in common. In one fundamental way, however, they are in sharp contrast. The "Negro problem" is exacerbated by the urgency with which Negroes seek the integration to which they are legally and morally entitled. But only those youth who resist integration into the ordinary folkways of our life are regarded by adults as a problem; those who accept the world in which they live and work or scheme to make it within the prevailing framework of values and practices are thought to be doing fine; they are taken as a model. Apart from the Black Muslims, who have made up a version of Islam suited to their present emotional needs as insulted

Americans, most Negroes seek equal status in the larger society. So do most young people, ultimately. But, meanwhile, many behave in such a way as to frighten adults into fearing that they will never accept or qualify themselves for what American life has to offer.

As Paul Goodman points out in the last chapter of *Growing Up Absurd*,[1] we rarely finish our revolutions; we manage to avoid the moral issues that occasion them by devising technical solutions to the immediate problems they present. This is what we are trying to do with our youth and Negro "problems"; we may succeed. But our habitual evasion of moral issues by turning them into empirical problems is more likely to make things a little worse for youth. The absence of ethical clarity, the overriding commitment of our culture to working compromises, even when they weaken the whole fabric of individual experience, create the situation youth protest against, surrender to, or seek to escape by finding a personally meaningful style of life even if it be destructive or nihilistic.

Erik Erikson—in my judgment the most astute and perceptive living student of human growth and development—in an article entitled "Youth: Fidelity and Diversity,"[2] stresses that adolescents must experience both these in order to become themselves. Fidelity, he defines as "the strength of disciplined devotion. It is gained in the involvement of youth in such experiences as reveal the essence of the era they are to join—as the beneficiaries of its tradition, as the practitioners and innovators of its technology, as renewers of its ethical strength, as rebels bent on the destruction of the outlived, and as deviants with deviant commitments."

It would seem, then, that societies that are passing from colonialism to a period in which they recognize and accept as constituents a variety of minority groups ought to provide specially good opportunities for growing up. At such a time, there are many different ways to express fidelity in action. There is, or should be, opportunity for real social action and political commitment; for trying out roles and experimenting with new causes and foci for loyalty. Indeed, in one instance, it has turned out so. The Freedom Riders' buses, I believe, are carrying their Negro passengers to suburbia; but they are certainly carrying both them and their white fellow travelers a long way toward self-realization as well. The issue seems almost ideally suited to the needs of the better sort of American youth today; it is fundamental to human dignity, involves real sacrifice and personal danger freely undertaken in comradeship. Yet it is legitimate, and does not alienate youth from the expressed values of the larger society as a continued struggle for "Fair Play for Cuba," for example, would. Few revolutionaries in history have enjoyed the comfort, as the cudgels of the police descend, of knowing that the Supreme Court was behind them and moving along with all deliberate speed.

Few other American youngsters seem to have found so relevant a focus for fidelity. "The strength of disciplined devotion" that innovators, renewers, and committed deviants need is gained only through "involvement of youth in such experiences as reveal the essence of the era they are to join" if such strength already

---

[1] New York: Random House, 1960.
[2] In *Daedalus*, Winter 1962: an entire issue devoted to the topic *Youth: Change and Challenge*.

colors those experiences. In our era it doesn't, not predominantly anyway. Examples of individual integrity can still be uncovered, but they hardly set the prevailing tone of our life. The essence of our era is a kind of infidelity, a disciplined expediency.

This expediency is not a breach of our tradition, but its very core. And it keeps the young from getting much out of the diversity that our heterogeneous culture might otherwise provide them. This kind of expediency is built into the value structure of every technically developed open society; and it becomes most prevalent when the rewards of achievement in that society appear most tempting and the possibilities of decent and expressive survival at a low or intermediate position in it least reliable. Being different, notoriously, does not get you to the top. If individuals must believe that they are on their way there in order to preserve their self-esteem they will be under constant pressure, initially from anxious adults and later from their own aspirations, to repudiate the divergent elements of their character in order to make it under the terms common to mass culture. They choose the path most traveled by, and that makes all the difference.

To anyone who is concerned about what his life means, this pressure is repugnant. "Every human being is of supreme value," writes Rebecca West in *Black Lamb and Grey Falcon*, "because his experience, which must be in some measure unique, gives him a unique view of reality; and the sum of such views is needed if mankind is ever to comprehend its destiny." [3] The abandonment of this quest is what really appalls us; this is what we mean when we deplore that we live in an age of conformity. But this is too simple. Conformity is a very useful economy when what the individual conforms to grows out of and expresses the meaning of his own experience. If we are to make sense of ourselves and the world we live in, most of our behavior must express the pattern of our growth in the symbols and through the roles available in our culture. Patterns, however original, are partly composed of repetitive and traditional elements; and symbols, to be intelligible, must be held in common. The proverbial Englishman, by dressing for dinner in the jungle, expressed his conviction that he was still an Englishman who knew where his home was and that it was far away. On ceremonial occasions, officials of the new African nations array themselves in the magnificent costumes of their culture; while conducting the daily business of the state they assert, by wearing a conventional business suit, their membership in the dowdy bureaucracy of contemporary statecraft. Both modes of dress are, in a sense, conforming, but neither is a form of self-denial; each is appropriate to, and expressive of, the actual meaning of the occasion for which it is worn.

What is immeasurably destructive is rather the kind of conformity that abandons the experience of the individual in order to usurp a tradition to which he does not belong and to express a view of life foreign to his experience and, on his lips, phony. For an adult this is self-destructive; for an adolescent it is the more pitiful and tragic, because the self that is abandoned is still immanent and further growth

[3] New York: The Viking Press, 1940.

requires that it be nurtured and continuously clarified and redefined. A pregnant woman may recover, more or less, from abortion; the foetus never does.

For nearly a decade, sympathetic adults have been complaining that contemporary youth is apathetic and conforming, until new cults of nonconformity have arisen to give us what we now want and to exploit the new opportunities created by our wanting it. Many a bright young man has concealed himself strategically behind a beard and a uniform "beat" costume ill suited to his nature; and who can deny that the managers of the Hiltons of tomorrow may gain useful experience in the coffee houses of today. But actual autonomy, when it can be found, looks and sounds different.

AMERICAN IDEALISM, 1965

HAROLD TAYLOR

> "If we're going to stay in the Movement, we've got to watch ourselves, we've got to control ourselves all the time. It's like a war."—Mississippi civil rights demonstrator, 1962.

In the 1930s, the war that university students cared about was the Spanish Civil War. In the 1960s it is Vietnam and Mississippi, the moral equivalent of war, where the nature of a bigger world can be seen on a personal scale and public events can be directly known and acted upon.

The Spanish war was ideologically close and physically distant. Mississippi and Alabama are physically close, emotionally real, and have little to do with abstractions. Political action there is personal. The names are known, and ideology has given way to the politics of personal commitment. And that of course, is exactly what today's students are seeking—a sense of involvement with history.

Between Spain and Mississippi lies a stretch of time that has changed the response of the West to the occasions demanding moral sympathy. Few would now volunteer for an ideological war. The idealist's protest is against war itself, as in Vietnam, and ideological reasons are insufficient to condone the possibility of enormous disasters. The context of moral decision has shifted. The situation of the American Negro and the American poor in the 1920s and 1930s was worse than it is now, yet the strongest rallying point for liberal thought and action was not at home in

FROM the *Saturday Review*, XLVIII, 26 (June 26, 1965), pp. 14–16. Reprinted by permission.

the South but in Spain, where the abstract forces of history each had their public representatives in the field—fascists, Communists, anti-Communists, militarists, capitalists, clericalists, anti-clericalists, progressives, reactionaries.

In the 1920s and 1930s, those among the young who were alienated from middle-class white America went to Europe to write, to paint, to compose, to study, to fight, to be free from an America they had come to condemn for its cultural and social impurities. In the 1960s the young go to Africa, Asia, or Latin America for the Peace Corps, they teach in Mississippi, demonstrate in Alabama, tutor in Chicago slums. They do the work they are doing, not in support of an abstract idea, but for the sake of the people they are able to help.

The liberal ideology of the 1930s, which linked together students, trade union-ists, Negroes, the poor, the unemployed, the teachers, anti-Fascists, and political radicals, no longer exists. Teachers are nonpolitical members of guilds and associa-tions, the unions are conservative in social philosophy, some are anti-liberal. The tension between labor and capital that gave an ideological flavor and a moral content to political and social action has disappeared into a dialectic of bargaining strategies supported by economic and social ambitions on both sides.

The leadership has accordingly shifted away from the older generation, into the hands of the young, whose style is that of the Peace Corps volunteer, the SNCC worker, the CORE activist, the Berkeley Free Speech student whose slogan is "You can't trust anyone over thirty." The term "white liberal" becomes in these quarters a label for middle-class compromisers—the faculty member who calls for orderly discussion instead of demonstrations, the social worker who plans poverty programs for the poor instead of joining rent strikes, the Democrat who supports American foreign policy while expressing doubts about it.

The younger generation has inherited the tougher traditions of the Depression years and of those who then fought the battles of the sharecroppers, the Negro, and the poor. The problems of the Depression were never solved. They were absorbed into the mobilization for war. After the war they were hidden from view in a society almost totally concerned with achieving political and military security against Communism and obtaining material prosperity for an expanding middle class.

That the Depression issues have now broken the surface of the public mind in an explosion of consciousness is due, in the area of its beginning, to the courage, initiative, and steady moral sense of young Southern Negroes in the late 1950s. Against the warnings of their parents, their teachers, and the Negro leaders in their own communities, the boys and girls quietly began their lunch-counter demonstra-tions to achieve a limited objective of almost unlimited symbolic value—the right to be served at a lunch counter, the peoples' eating place. Lacking in political inhibition, knowing little of political strategy, strong in comradeship, they formed their own small band of witnesses and suffered reprisals with a dignity plain for all to see.

Through the mass media, the youth of the country, white and black, saw at that time the members of their generation beaten, jailed, molested, bombed, shot at, set upon by dogs, jabbed by cattle prods, threatened by bullies, and denied the simple rights and forms of justice that Americans have come to take for granted. The quickening of conscience from that experience has set in motion a stream of ideas and acts among the young which almost no one foresaw.

Until then, the youth of America had known little of the problems of the Thirties, or even of the Fifties. Depressions, Fascists, poverty, social justice were seldom mentioned. In R. H. Tawney's words, ". . . the agonies of peoples [had] become the exercise in the schools." The young had been taught, not the reality of their age, but the simple notions of cold war politics in which friends were those who would fight Communists and enemies were those who thought otherwise.

Colleges had in fact become a refuge into which the young could escape, by the possession of sufficient funds and sufficient grades, to find a shelter from the immediacy of finding a job, serving in the military, finding a place in society. College already was a place in society, one in which rewards were assigned to the educated; education was defined as academic skill, and the college student was both a symbol and a hostage of the organized establishment.

Then the message of the Negro broke through. The drama of his struggle was publicly enacted, often on the campuses themselves, as in the Meredith case, and the moral issue for members of the younger generation was sharply raised in the context of their personal lives. Students began to see, in ways they had never seen before, that the situation of the Negro was the situation of the victim everywhere and that it was linked to poverty, unemployment, inequality, and injustice in a society they had been told was affluent and just.

Out of that awakening a new leadership has formed among the young, resulting in a movement with a character of its own and a new coalition of social forces. During the 1950s a class division had begun consciously to develop within the society and among the young. It was not the European class-consciousness of workers and owners, or even rich and poor, but a class division between the young ineducables—dropouts, delinquents, draftees, wage-earners and hot-rodders—those who did not or could not go to college, and those who could and did—the Merit Scholars, fraternity men, straight-A students, pre-medical, pre-law, pre-professionals of all kinds, and the rest who went to Fort Lauderdale. In one dimension the division was between the middle-class whites and the poor whites and Negroes. In another it was between the political sophisticates and the non-committed. In another, it was between affluent, white, middle-class America and the poverty-stricken colored races of the world.

The new liberal coalition finds a common base among the young by rejecting the idea of a half-affluent society, that is to say the idea of a class society composed of two classes, the white well-to-do and the others. The coalition of young Negroes and whites is founded on the commitment to an equalitarian ethic that can act on a world scale. There is the same sense of alienation from white middle-class society that marked the liberal movement of the 1930s, but a new sense of identity by the liberal with the poor, the uneducated, and the unemployed. The white youth in the movement find in the character of the Negro people the qualities basic to a new democratic culture. The music, the songs, the humor, the wit, and the style of the Negro community have an authenticity they find lacking in their own lives.

These are the young who wish to get out of the middle class if they are in it, and to move, not into a hierarchy above or below, but into the classless society of those to whom the acquisition of money, property, or social position does not matter. In becoming social activists they draw their parents and the members of the older generation into the swirl of social consequence. They go first to the South from the North, to be followed, months later, by clergymen, doctors, lawyers, and older-generation liberals who then march in Alabama with the established Negro leaders. The transaction between the generations has shifted the moral authority to the young who act first and explain later.

Their explanations are precise and far-reaching. They are against war because it is literally a dead end and solves nothing. They are for international cooperation, disarmament, international peace controls, and negotiation of conflict since these constitute the alternative to war. They are for equality in education and in economic and social opportunity, and they take practical steps to bring it about. They have few slogans, few ringing statements about democratic values. It is as if, having seen hypocrisy in the proclamations of politics and having examined the nature of the political process, they have decided to proceed by individual acts bearing witness to beliefs, rather than by public statements about belief.

Political action by the idealist of the 1930s was marked by the prevalence of liberal propaganda and public statement, an emphasis on mass movements organized around political strategies and tactics set by the leadership. The young activists of that time were in rebellion against an older generation and its conservative values, against a generation which had failed to stop war, cure poverty, prevent the rise of fascism. But the young joined political movements organized by their elders.

The activists of the present generation have not rebelled. They have simply bypassed the older generation and its political apparatus and have acted on their own, calling upon certain of their elders to help them if they cared to. They are skeptical of heroes; they owe allegiance to those with whom they work and to the people they are trying to help. In voter-registration projects, Freedom Schools, community organization, tutoring programs, they are acting outside the organized institutions of society, inventing their own curricula as teachers, often withdrawing from school and college to work in the field of education and social change.

They have also developed new forms of organization for themselves, in which the older patterns of the liberal movements have been replaced by loose membership arrangements and a casual kind of leadership marked by an easy interchange of members and leaders. The character of the leadership depends on the nature of the job to be done.

The new generation does its own research in foreign policy, economic reform, disarmament, education. When volunteers return from Peace Corps service abroad, they bring with them bodies of knowledge derived from direct experience; they have knowledge unavailable to any except those who have served in the field. They are impatient with a society that takes its knowledge and values at second hand. As a result, they are often misunderstood by those of the older generation, especially among the educators, who have not themselves had the experience of direct involvement with the situation of the world and who have not entered, either directly or in imagination, into the lives of the younger generation. Were they to enter into them, they would discover how far behind they have fallen in understanding the nature of contemporary social change and the role of youth in bringing it about.

They would understand that the demand of youth for a share in the reform of the universities is part of a larger demand for the achievement of democratic rights and the reconstruction of society through education. They would also understand that the reason so many of the young reformers seem radical in social philosophy and intransigent in social action is that there are almost no radicals in the older generation to compare them with, and that the complacency, conservatism, and paternalism of the educators give them a reference point too distant from the reality of the student to make informed judgment of student thought and action even remotely possible.

The universities of the United States are not only the center of the knowledge industry. They are certainly that. But they must also be centers of creative thought on matters having to do with public policy. The leaders of the liberal movement among students know this. They have learned through experience in Mississippi and the slums that the secret of social power lies in possessing the right to make decisions about matters affecting one's own situation. They claim that right to decision in the context of their own education and their own place in the society, and they claim the right not only for themselves but for everyone else.

It is a sign of the failure of higher education in America that it has had in the past so little to do with the needs of the Negro, the poor, the deprived, and the socially depressed, and so much to do with the success of the money-making classes. It is another sign of failure that, rather than taking leadership in the political and social education of the student, the university has done everything possible to insulate him from direct confrontation with the reality of his society by hedging him around with prohibitions on political and educational action, by treating the educational process as if it were simply a matter of academic busy-work.

The time has come for a change in all this. The younger generation has won, in the field, the right to represent the forces of intellectual and liberal reform. It is entitled, in this gallant endeavor, to the respect and support of those who control the universities.

THE TEMPTATION
OF THE NEW BREED

ANDREW M. GREELEY

A year ago in America, May 23, 1964, I tried to tie together some impressions about modern youth under the label of the "New Breed." I must confess I was overwhelmed by the reaction. All sorts of people announced—some of them validly—that they were members of this New Breed and happily proclaimed that at long last there was someone who understood them. (Alas, it is not true; I do not understand them.) On the other hand, many of those who had identified in the New Breed a dangerous enemy blamed me for the New Breed phenomenon—on the same principle, I suppose, that ancient kings invoked in executing messengers who brought bad news: he who announces bad news is the one responsible for its coming to be.

Not having learned my lesson from this experience, I am now venturing back into the land where the New Breed dwell, with some new impressions. I have not changed my mind about the New Breed. I still like them; I am still sympathetic, puzzled and hopeful. But I think now I understand more clearly what their problems are and what is the crucial temptation they face. My friends in the New Breed must excuse me for sounding more critical in this article than in the previous one; but a year ago I was talking *about* the New Breed, and at this point I am talking *to* them. If I may borrow a tactic from their own approach to life, I would say that honesty compels me to write the things that I am writing here.

First of all, I feel that the New Breed are increasingly handicapped by a lack of ideology. What I mean by ideology is something rather different from what the New Breed mean by it. I mean a coherent and specific set of goals, a consistent series of norms according to which society is to be remade.

We ask the New Breed what they want of us, or what they want of society, and they say: "We want you to love us, we want you to permit us to make something of the world where you have failed." But then if we ask: "How have we failed, and how do you want us to love you?" their words become vague. They tell us simply that we have failed because there is not enough love or freedom in the world.

"Freedom," "self-fulfillment" and "love" are for them the only ideology necessary. These are ends sufficient in themselves, and they need not be specified

FROM *America* (May 22, 1965), pp. 750–752. Reprinted with permission from *America*, The National Catholic Weekly Review, 106 W. 56th Street, New York, N. Y. 10019.

any further. When you ask them: "Freedom for what?" "Self-fulfillment toward what goals?" "Love in what systematic fashion?" they look at you as though you were a relic of another era.

Secondly, the lack of ideology interferes in many instances with the critical social analysis and the systematic commitment to work that is necessary to accomplish a change. The "radicalism" of the New Breed is too often a kind of free-floating social concern. There are all sorts of things wrong with society, and the New Breed are going to do something about these things; but they are not very specific about what is wrong with society—or what must be done about it—aside from saying that they do not feel free in it to be themselves. As one very honest member of the New Breed put it: "It's not just that we don't know the answers to what is wrong with the world; we don't even know the proper words to phrase the question."

It is relatively easy to throw up a picket line, or to tutor a culturally deprived child in the inner city, or even to join the Peace Corps or go to Mississippi. But these actions, while they demonstrate concern and, in some instances even heroism, deal generally with the symptoms of social problems and not with the roots. All the picket lines in the world will not resolve the difficulties of segregated education in the large urban centers unless the tax structures and the revenue codes under which these giant cities must operate are drastically reformed.

Young people ask me what organization they should join if they wish to accomplish social change in the Chicago metropolitan area. They wonder if it ought to be CORE, or SNCC, or the Catholic Interracial Council. When I reply that they ought to consider becoming precinct captains or assistant precinct captains in the Cook County Regular Democratic Organization, they look at me as though I were insane. The New Breed seem to have little taste for acquiring the knowledge and skills necessary to deal with the causes of social problems. They have no taste at all for the complicated details of revenue codes or the grubby day-to-day work of a political organization.

Thirdly, the New Breed, for all the skill they can display when they finally commit themselves to organizational work, are basically suspicious and distrustful of organization of any kind. They just want to love, and they think that love and interpersonal relationship more or less by themselves are enough to solve the problems of society. Organizations cramp the style of the human spirit: they restrict the spontaneity and creative love of the individual person. The New Breed want no part of this. They find it hard to believe there was a time in the not too distant past when young people could enthusiastically dedicate themselves to an organization—whether the Young Peoples' Socialist League in the 1930's or the Young Christian Students immediately after World War II.

It seems to me, however, that in the absence of carefully planned organizations, human love will, in the final analysis, become weak and ineffective. Even the most elemental kind of human love only becomes really effective when it is put into the organized structure we call the family. To be able to love at all effectively, the New Breed will have to overcome their distrust of organizations. They must learn to distinguish between those organizations that stifle the human spirit and those that create a situation where the human personality can flower much more fully than it could if left to itself. Unless they do so, they will pass from the scene without having accomplished much besides stirring up quite a bit of noise and excitement.

Here, then, is the crucial temptation facing the New Breed: either they acquire at least a provisional and concrete ideology and the ability to commit themselves to organizational work, or they expose themselves to becoming disenchanted and disillusioned idealists.

One hears that some of the young people coming back from the Peace Corps, or from PAVLA, or from Mississippi, are disappointed in their experience. They have left the comfort of their homes to help others, to love them, and they have found that many people don't seem to want their love, won't co-operate with them, won't accept the values that these young Americans bring. Those who were to be helped will not "relate" in a satisfactory fashion and will not behave like upper-middle-class white Americans. Love is just not enough; to re-evaluate everything that has been done in the past does not furnish automatic answers as to what must be done in the future. Our social problems are more complicated than they thought.

Feeling rejected, discouraged, disillusioned, the member of the New Breed is strongly tempted to give up, to retreat, to find some comfortable ivory tower where he can "relate" to a small group of like-minded people. Thus, the disillusioned New Breeder often thinks he will find in the academic life the love and freedom he is seeking. (Yet, in a year or two, he will undergo the even worse disillusionment of discovering that the academic life is the last sanctuary of the inner-directed man—the last of the "jungles" to be found in the Western world.)

The alternative for the New Breeder is to drastically change his style—to become concerned with the technical, the political, the organizational; to acquire the competencies and the skills necessary for the complicated grubby work that must be done if the social structure of the world is to be even slightly modified. For whether the problems are in South America, or Mississippi, or the inner city of Chicago, solutions cannot be discovered without profound understanding of law, government methods and the economics and social organization of modern life. The New Breeder, too, must fashion for himself a highly specific set of goals and norms; without these, any human effort is likely to flounder in the sea of well-meaning but ineffective good intentions. If he is to manage to keep alive the bright enthusiasm of his early days in the New Breed, he must abandon the cheap clichés and slogans of the books of existentialist philosophy and become hard-nosed and practical. As yet few have attempted this.

The problem of disillusionment is aggravated by the fact that the New Breed seem to have their own built-in variety of mental disturbance in the "identity crisis" syndrome. There isn't much doubt to any of us who have tried to work with the New Breed that they go through tremendous mental anguish in the process of growing up. The basic problem is that the very best young people we have simply are not sure *who* they are, *where* they are going, or *what* they want out of life. Erik Erikson's phrase "identity crisis" serves only to give a name to an experience that especially torments the members of the New Breed.

As Erikson has pointed out, it is essential to the weathering of this phase in the struggle for maturity that the young person be able to fashion an ideology that will guide the rest of his life. Part of the New Breed's problem arises because they do not know what they want, because they have no ideology. But part of the problem, too, comes from the "honesty" and self-consciousness of the New Breed. Young people today have discovered, to a greater extent than any of their predecessors, that they have an unconscious. They feel compelled to question and examine constantly their motives and their emotional states. As one fairly cynical New Breeder put it: "The trouble with us is that we must make a great big hairy deal out of all our problems." The difficulties that previous generations might have dismissed as minor take on major importance with the New Breed. This is especially true of "problems of faith." Religious doubts are not new, but the seriousness with which they are pondered seems to be much more intense with the New Breed.

The result of this intense emotionalism is that psychological ups and downs are greatly magnified. New Breeders seem to be manic-depressives. This is why it is so difficult to work with them. For all their organizational skills, one can never be quite sure that, when the chips are down, the young person may not find himself in a paralyzing emotional crisis. One finds oneself in the position of saying: "Follow me. We are going to storm the barricades!" and then looking around and finding one's followers sitting down and pondering the latest phase of their identity crisis. Again, their moods force them into taking extreme positions. Many of them leave college or seminary because, as they say, "I will be destroyed if I stay here any longer." Perhaps, indeed, they *will* be destroyed, though one wonders if the problem may be, more simply, that they lack the emotional fortitude to stick out a difficult situation.

I cannot help feeling that, for all their rejection of "phoniness," the New Breed's emotionalism has just a bit of the phony about it, too. The problems they have can be solved with intelligent effort; it is possible for the New Breed to take counsel, to put their life in order. What I find almost inexcusable is the tendency of so many of them to drift. It seems to me that in their lives there are, indeed, just too many "great big hairy deals."

Surely I am too harsh in judging the moods and identity crises of the New Breed. For New Breeders have grown up in a very different world, a world that I do not know and cannot really understand. No doubt I have permitted myself to become embittered because I have seen so many of their efforts collapse under strain. I know such a great number of young people going through these intense emotional crises. I wish there was something I could do to assist them, but having failed so many times, I fear there is nothing I can do. Sometimes I am tempted to believe that all that any of us from the older generation can do is leave them alone and let them work things out by themselves.

Thus, the final element in the temptation of the New Breed is the almost total misunderstanding between them and their predecessors, a misunderstanding perhaps more acute than has ever before separated an older and a younger generation. The older generation interprets the constant questioning of established traditions, the incessant demand for explanation, the persistent and often apparently unreasonable criticism as being signs of revolt. But this revolt is one that can neither describe what it opposes nor make clear what it wants to substitute for the present order of the Church and of society. Superiors, parents, teachers, advisors—all of us find it exceedingly difficult to communicate with these young people. The New Breed will have to excuse us of the older generation if, in the absence of a more articulate description of their goals, we say that we simply do not understand them. We would like to enter into dialogue, but there seems to exist an almost insuperable barrier to communication. Even those of us who admire them, who are sympathetic to them, who want to help them, find the languages we speak, the cultures from which we come, discouragingly different.

And so the New Breed feel, in the words of one member of the Free Speech Movement, that "you really can't trust anyone who is over thirty." The New Breed want to start all over again; they want to remake the world into a place of love and freedom. This desire of theirs to remake the world is a laudable one, indeed, but it seems to me that they will never accomplish their goal unless they can re-establish communication with those who have gone before them. In the absence of communication, we cannot help them and they cannot help us—and I think that they're going to need our help if the temptation to disillusionment and discouragement is not to overwhelm them. Nor do I think they can resolve their problems of identity unless they find at least some of the older generation who can, in some vague fashion, understand what they are trying to say.

These are dark days for the New Breed. They are going through a particularly unpleasant form of hell—a hell that they have made for themselves but that results also from the misunderstanding of those who are older. For the New Breed, the future still looks bright. They shall overcome—someday. The older generation, we Old Breeds and Half-Breeds, are no problem in the long run. But the crucial question is: can the New Breed overcome themselves, their own inarticulateness, their own confusion, their own uncertainty? At times, I confess, I have my doubts. But I am certainly not prepared to bet against the New Breed. Everything is still on their side.

THE EDUCATIONALLY DIFFICULT STUDENT
What the Schools Can Do

ROBERT J. HAVIGHURST

When we are confronted by a baffling phenomenon, our first impulse is to name it. During the past five years, educators have been baffled by a substantial number of pupils who do not learn in spite of instruction by reasonably well-trained teachers in well-equipped schools.

We suppose that these pupils come to school under some kind of handicap that makes it difficult to teach them. We have given them a variety of names—"culturally deprived," "intellectually deprived," or "socially disadvantaged." These names imply our belief that these children are not innately dull, but that they have been denied some experiences that other "normal" children have had. If the schools can discover what these mind-building experiences are, perhaps the schools can compensate for the handicaps which the pupils have suffered. Hence we speak of "compensatory" education.

The title of this paper—the difficult student—gives a different name to the phenomenon and suggests a deeper perspective which can include other types of pupils as well as those with social handicaps.

There are three visible and bothersome groups of "difficult" students which are especially important today. They are: The Socially Disadvantaged; The Mentally Handicapped; and The Privatist Non-Conformer.

THE SOCIALLY DISADVANTAGED

The socially disadvantaged pupils may be defined and described in three ways: in terms of certain family characteristics relating directly to the child; in terms of their personal characteristics; or in terms of the social group characteristics of their families.

Family Characteristics. Compared with other children whose families give them average or better advantages for getting started in modern urban life, the socially disadvantaged child lacks several of the following:

Reprinted by permission from the *Bulletin of the National Association of Secondary-School Principals* (March 1965). Copyright: Washington, D. C.

A family conversation which: answers his questions and encourages him to ask questions; extends his vocabulary with new words and with adjectives and adverbs; gives him a right and a need to stand up for and to explain his point of view on the world.

A family environment which: sets an example of reading; provides a variety of toys and play materials with colors, sizes, and objects that challenge his ingenuity with his hands and his mind.

Two parents who: read a good deal; read to him; show him that they believe in the value of education; reward him for good school achievement.

Bernstein[1] has studied the language behavior of families that relate to the intellectual development of their children. He distinguishes between two *forms* or *types* of language. (These language types are statistically related to social class, as will be pointed out later.) One form of language is called *restricted* and the other form is called *elaborated*. A family which employs restricted language gives a child a language environment characterized by:

1. Short, grammatically simple, often unfinished sentences with a poor syntactical form stressing the active voice.

2. Simple and repetitive use of conjunctions (so, then, because).

3. Little use of subordinate clauses to break down the initial categories of the dominant subject.

4. Inability to hold a formal subject through a speech sequence; thus a dislocated informational content is facilitated.

5. Rigid and limited use of adjectives and adverbs.

6. Constraint on the self-reference pronoun; frequent use of personal pronoun.

7. Frequent use of statements where the reason and conclusion are confounded to produce a categoric statement.

8. A large number of statements/phrases which signal a requirement for the previous speech sequence to be reinforced: "Wouldn't it? You see? You know?" etc. This process is termed 'sympathetic circularity.'

9. Individual selection from a group of idiomatic phrases or sequences will frequently occur.

10. The individual qualification is implicit in the sentence organization; it is a language of implicit meaning.

On the other hand, a family which employs an *elaborated* language gives the child a language environment characterized by:

1. Accurate grammatical order and syntax regulate what is said.

2. Logical modifications and stress are mediated through a grammatically

---

[1] Basil Bernstein, "Language and Social Class," *British Journal of Sociology* (1960), 11:271–276; "Social Class and Linguistic Development: A Theory of Learning," in A. H. Halsey, J. Floud, and C. A. Anderson (eds.), *Economy, Education and Society* (New York: The Free Press of Glencoe, 1961), pp. 288ff.; "Social Class, Linguistic Codes and Grammatical Elements," *Language and Speech* (October–December 1962), 5:221–240; and "Elaborated and Restricted Codes: Their Origins and Some Consequences," (mimeographed) (Committee on Human Development, The University of Chicago, 1964).

complex sentence construction, especially through the use of a range of conjunctions and subordinate clauses.

3. Frequent use of prepositions which indicate logical relationships as well as prepositions which indicate temporal and spatial contiguity.

4. Frequent use of the personal pronoun 'I'.

5. A discriminative selection from a range of adjectives and adverbs.

6. Individual qualification is verbally mediated through the structure and relationships within and between sentences.

7. Expressive symbolism discriminates between meanings within speech sequences rather than reinforcing dominant words or phrases, or accompanying the sequence in a diffuse, generalised manner.

8. A language use which points to the possibilities inherent in a complex conceptual hierarchy for the organising of experience.

A child who has learned a restricted language at home is likely to have difficulty in school, where an *elaborate* language is used and taught by the teacher; and the difficulty of the child is likely to increase as he goes further in school, unless he learns the elaborate language that is expected in the school. On the other hand, the child who had had experience with an elaborate language from his earliest years has a relatively easy time in school, because he must simply go on developing the kind of language and related thinking which he has already started.

Personal Characteristics. The family environment with the characteristics just cited tends to produce children with certain personal deficits. Martin Deutsch[2] has studied such children with techniques of the experimental psychologists, and he finds them to have inferior auditory discrimination, inferior visual discrimination, inferior judgment concerning time, number and other basic concepts. He finds that this inferiority is not due to physical defects of eyes and ears and brain, but is due to inferior *habits* of hearing and seeing and thinking. Presumably, the family environment of these children did not teach them to "pay attention" to what was being said around them, or to the visual scene. Then, when they came to school, their school performance suffered because they had not learned to "listen" to the teacher and other important people or to "see" the things they are shown in the school.

Social Group Characteristics. We introduce the social group characteristics of socially disadvantaged children last so as to avoid giving the impression that there is a hard-and-fast relation between socio-economic status, or some other group characteristic, and social disadvantage for the child. While there are statistical relations and very important ones between socio-economic status and social disadvantages of children, there are so many individual exceptions to the statistical generalizations that any educational policy aimed at identifying socially disadvantaged children should avoid reliance upon general socio-economic characteristics as the decisive criteria.

---

[2] "The Disadvantaged Child and the Learning Process," in Harry A. Passow (ed.), *Education in Depressed Areas* (New York: Bureau of Publications, Teachers College, Columbia University, 1963).

Above all, it is important to avoid the error of saying that all children of working-class families are socially disadvantaged. Approximately 65 per cent of the children of this country are living in working-class homes. That is, their fathers or mothers do manual work for a living. The great majority of these families give their children a fairly good start for life in an urban industrial democratic society. Their children are adequately fed and clothed. They are loved and protected by their parents. They learn to respect teachers and to like school. They do fairly well or better than that in school.

While working-class children as a group are somewhat different from the children of white-collar workers, it would not be reasonable to say that the working-class children are socially disadvantaged or culturally deprived. Working-class children as a group score slightly below children of white-collar families in intelligence tests; they fall slightly below on tests of school achievement; they attain somewhat less formal education. But the differences are relatively small, and become even smaller when the socially disadvantaged children are removed and the majority of working-class youth who remain are compared with white-collar children.

Most working-class families participate fully in the American mass or core culture. This is certainly not a culture of deprivation. While the differences between the upper working class and the lower middle class are real and they are interesting, these differences should not be described in terms of social advantage or social disadvantage. The great amount of movement of people across the boundary between these two classes as they grow up is evidence that the differences between these two classes are not fundamental ones.

Who, then, are the socially disadvantaged when we attempt to describe them in terms of observable social groups? They are groups with the following characteristics:

1. They are at the bottom of the American society in terms of income.
2. They have a rural background.
3. They suffer from social and economic discrimination at the hands of the majority of the society.
4. They are widely distributed in the United States. While they are most visible in the big cities, they are present in all except the very high income communities. There are many of them in rural areas, especially in the southern and southwestern states.

In racial and ethnic terms, these groups are about evenly divided between whites and non-whites. They consist mainly of the following: Negroes from the rural south many of whom have migrated recently to the northern industrial cities; Whites from the rural south and the southern mountains many of whom have migrated recently to the northern industrial cities; Puerto Ricans who have migrated to a few northern industrial cities; Mexicans with a rural background who have migrated into the west and middle west, also rural Spanish-Americans in the southwestern states; European immigrants with a rural background, from east and southern Europe.

Altogether, these groups make up about 15 per cent of the United States population. Since they tend to have large families, their children make up as much as 20 per cent of the child population. Not all socially disadvantaged children come from these groups, but the great majority do. Not all children in these groups are socially disadvantaged, but the great majority are.

How Many Are Socially Disadvantaged?   There is an infinite gradation of social advantage-disadvantage, and therefore any quantitative estimate of the number of socially disadvantaged children and youth must be a personal rather than a scientific statement.

The writer would place the number of socially disadvantaged children at about 15 per cent of the child population. One basis for this estimate is the proportion of unemployed, out of school youth between the ages of 16 and 20. These young people have been relatively unsuccessful in school and in the labor market. The great majority of them come from the social groups listed above. There are about 11 per cent of boys and 17 per cent of girls in this group. The boys are clearly maladjusted to society. Some of the girls are not; they are simply doing what girls have done for a long time, helping out at home while waiting to get married. But these figures place a minimum on the numbers of socially disadvantaged youth. There are a few others who have jobs which are below their capacity or are disadvantaged in other ways—enough to bring the total up to about 15 per cent.

Since these children and their families tend to concentrate in the large cities, while upper-income people tend to move out from the cities to the suburbs, the socially disadvantaged children are in big cities in larger proportions than 15 per cent. Probably *30 per cent of the children* in such cities as New York, Chicago, Philadelphia, Washington, Detroit, Cleveland, and Baltimore fall into the socially disadvantaged category.

THE MENTALLY HANDICAPPED

The truly mentally handicapped child is one with inborn mental deficiency, indicated by an IQ below 75 or 80, depending on the definition adopted by the state or the school system. Some of these children have clearly marked physical signs of mental deficiency, but others do not. The number of mentally handicapped children is estimated by various authorities to be about two per cent of the age group.

However, it is not an easy matter to distinguish a true mentally handicapped from a socially disadvantaged child. Mental retardation is no longer regarded as a condition easily diagnosed. It appears that a considerable fraction, perhaps as many as half, of the school age children now treated as mentally retarded could have developed normal intelligence if they had had expert treatment in their pre-school years.

Thus we may expect to see school programs designed for young children who appear to be mentally retarded with the aim of bringing some of them into the range of normal intelligence.

THE PRIVATIST NON-CONFORMER

An entirely different kind of "educationally difficult student" is found mainly in the economically favored communities and schools. This is a youth of average or superior intelligence, who has done well in school until he reaches high school age, and then seems to lose his drive and direction. Some observers would identify this kind of youth as a "beatnik," but this is not a thoroughly satisfactory name for the youth of high school age whom we shall call the *privatist non-conformer*.

This kind of boy or girl has such doubts about the quality of his society that he refuses to commit himself to supporting the political and business and educational institutions around him, but prefers to lead a life of private or asocial activity.

At the coming of adolescence a person must commence to achieve his own self-esteem and his social fidelity. This is a part of his achievement of his *identity* as a person in his own right. It comes about normally as a part of his adolescent experience in school, work, play with his age-mates, and association with adult citizens and workers. The youth as he achieves identity narrows and focuses his personal, occupational, sexual, and ideological commitments by getting started in one occupation, getting married and starting a family, and beginning to take part in community civic life.

Apparently this process of growth toward identity is more difficult today than it was a generation or more ago. The evidence for this statement comes from the testimony of high school counselors and teachers, from parents of intelligent and sensitive children, and from psychologists and sociologists who have studied youth culture. A discussion of this form of deviancy is given by Erikson, Keniston, Parsons, and others in a special issue of the journal, *Daedalus*.[3]

Privatism has always been present, but has not been so noticeable formerly as in the most recent years. The tendency in former years has been to attribute youth problems to poverty. Therefore it is a shock to discover a problem group who are not poverty-stricken. Parsons and Keniston, especially, concern themselves with middle-class youth.

Talcott Parsons sees young people generally learning the dominant American value pattern of *instrumental activism*, in which responsibility, autonomy, and individualism are motives and achievement is best demonstrated through work. The American youth is oriented toward control or mastery of the human condition by working at the task. But as work opportunities for youth have decreased, the demands on youth have become more complex. A young person must learn more than ever before in order to become an effective citizen, worker, and husband or wife in a society where many marriages break up. There is a rising general level of expectation of performance by youth in comparison to previous decades or generations. Also, youth have the opportunity and the responsibility of making more choices—such as the increasing range of vocational choices for boys and especially for girls.

[3] "Youth: Change and Challenge," *Daedalus* (Winter 1962), pp. 158–166.

Inevitably there is some strain for many young people in this complex situation, and some lose their nerve. Youth has some right to complain that he has been brought into "a world I never made." But Parsons takes an optimistic view.

Kenneth Keniston is less optimistic about the situation of youth. He sees the "youth culture" as a culture which is *non-adult*, if not *anti-adult*. He says it has roles, values, and ways of behaving all its own; it emphasizes disengagement from adult values, sexual attractiveness, daring, immediate pleasure, and comradeship in a way that is true neither of childhood nor of adulthood. Eventually a young person must leave this youth culture and enter adult life, but Keniston believes that in this process few young people are becoming deeply involved as citizens and workers. Instead, they tend to be alienated, refusing to accept the adult world with positive feeling, and retreating to a world of private and personal satisfactions. He calls this attitude *privatism*. Such a person declines to become involved with political and social problems, and prefers to spend his time with music and art. He feels powerless to affect the great society, and turns to the things closer home that he feels able to control. He may value family closeness above meaningful work because he can control things within his family, but not in his occupation. Leisure activities may be more important to him than work because he can control what he does in his free time. "Many young people expect to find in leisure a measure of stability, enjoyment, and control which they would otherwise lack. Hence their emphasis on assuring leisure time, or spending their leisure to good advantage, or getting jobs with long vacations, and on living in areas where leisure can be well enjoyed. Indeed, some anticipate working at their leisure with a dedication that will be totally lacking in their work itself." But Keniston does not believe this will be satisfactory. He thinks this will cause a fatal split in a person's life. "The man who spends his working day at a job whose primary meaning is merely to earn enough money to enable him to enjoy the rest of his time can seldom really enjoy his leisure, his family, or his avocations. Life is of a piece, and if work is empty or routine, the rest will inevitably become contaminated as well, becoming a compulsive escape or a driven effort to compensate for the absent satisfactions that should inhere in work. Similarly, to try to avoid social and political problems by cultivating one's garden can at best be only partly successful. . . . Putting work, society, and politics into one pigeon-hole, and family, leisure and enjoyment into another creates a compartmentalization which is in continual danger of collapsing."

The mood of our society includes frankness in formerly taboo areas, self-criticism, and skepticism. Youth are exposed to this mood very directly through the mass media (television, cinema, paper-back literature, etc.). They read such books as Salinger's *Catcher in the Rye* and Golding's *Lord of the Flies*, and they are encouraged to read such literature by high school teachers of literature who represent the mood of society. These books are true portrayals of a part of human nature—an unpleasant part, and not the whole truth, by any means. Perhaps these are more accurate than the literature adolescents read a generation or more ago—*Rebecca of Sunnybrook Farm*, *Strive and Succeed* (Horatio Alger). Furthermore, the sober and realistic writing about the dangers of nuclear war and the difficulties of international control of armaments give young people an ample picture of the immorality of national policies.

Boys and girls are shown the seamy side of personal and political life and then asked to commit themselves to social loyalty.

At the same time boys and girls are confronted with the tasks of making good in school, of choosing an occupation, of establishing themselves with the opposite sex, and these tasks are set for them a year or two earlier than they were a generation or two ago, due to the social forces making for social precocity in the middle-class part of society.

Under the circumstances it is not surprising that contemporary middle-class youth show a considerable degree of self-doubt and lack of confidence in the political and economic structure of modern society. It is not surprising that a *privatistic* life is preferred to one of greater social commitment. Boys find it difficult to make up their minds what occupation they will prepare for. Some of them engage in a kind of sit-down strike against the academic demands made on them by school or college. Their fathers wonder why sons are so in-grown and uncertain, as compared with the greater assurance and task-orientation they remember as normal for their generation. There is not so much concern about girls, since they are not expected to show the degree of *instrumental activism* expected of boys. With them there is more concern about their sex-role, and about the place of sexual activity in the life of a teen-age girl.

The number of privatistic non-conformers is hard to estimate because we know no measure of this quality and because a great many youth show this quality only to a limited extent. But the number who show it in such an acute form that they are recognized by their teachers and age-mates to be in a special category is probably no more than two or three per cent of an age-group.

EDUCATIONAL PROGRAMS FOR DIFFICULT STUDENTS

The first two groups of students have been observed and studied with enough research to serve as a basis for educational programs. The third group is only just beginning to receive special educational attention.

For the socially disadvantaged and for the mentally handicapped there is emerging a program of "compensatory" education with something for every age level from pre-school to the end of the teens.

Pre-school Classes. There are strong indications, based both on scientific data and experimental programs, that the earlier the child can be reached, the more effective the program will be. J. McVicker Hunt of the University of Illinois and Martin Deutsch[4] of the New York Medical College are among the scholars who have marshalled impressive evidence for the thesis that the nature and extent of experiences in the years from 1 to 5 have much to do with school achievement.

[4] Martin P. Deutsch, J. McVicker Hunt, *et al.*, "Selected Papers from the Arden House Conference on Pre-School Enrichment of Socially Disadvantaged Children," *Merrill–Palmer Quarterly* (July 1964).

Bloom has published a study[5] supporting the proposition that variations in the environment can produce changes in human characteristics and that such variations have the greatest effect at the period when the particular characteristic is changing most rapidly. This bears out Hunt's thesis (which was also that of Mme. Montessori) that different age levels are crucial for different kinds of learnings, and that children go through various phases of learning, with each phase lending support to those which follow.

Bloom has also assembled the results of research indicating the extent of educational growth experienced by children at various age levels. Results indicate that at least one-third of the learnings which will determine later levels of school achievement have already taken place by age 6, and at least 75 per cent by age 13. These findings point to the most important periods for school programs directed to raising achievement levels of children. Based on the estimate that 33 per cent of educational growth takes place before age 6, Bloom suggests that "nursery schools and kindergartens could have far-reaching consequences on the child's general learning pattern." The approximately 17 per cent of growth which takes place between ages 6 and 9 suggests that elementary Grades 1 to 3 are also crucial. Tending to support this suggestion in another way are the rather disappointing results now being reported of the Higher Horizons program in New York, which has not attempted to reach any children below the third grade. On the other hand, experimental programs at the prekindergarten level in Baltimore, New York, and elsewhere have already shown gratifying results in better performance on IQ tests and other measures of readiness and achievement.

A final quotation from Bloom sums up the situation:

A conservative estimate of the effect of extreme environments on intelligence is about 20 IQ points. This could mean the difference between a life in an institution for the feebleminded or a productive life in society. It could mean the difference between a professional career and an occupation which is at the semi-skilled or unskilled level. . . . The implications for public education and social policy are fairly clear. Where significantly lower intelligence can be clearly attributed to the effects of environmental deprivations, steps must be taken to ameliorate these conditions as early in the individual's development as education and other social forces can be utilized.[6]

Primary Grades. The effect of successful compensatory education at the preschool level is to get children ready for reading in the first grade. In 1963, 45 per cent of Chicago first-graders scored "below average" in the Metropolitan Reading Readiness Test. This meant that they would have difficulty in first-grade work and would not learn to read unless they were given a good deal of individualized help. In two of the city's 21 districts, two-thirds of the first graders were in the "difficult" category. For these children, an expert on the teaching of reading comments,

Tried and true traditional approaches are not working. In Chicago, in those districts with the largest percentage of culturally disadvantaged families, standardized reading tests indicate

---

[5] Benjamin Bloom, *Stability and Change in Human Characteristics* (New York: John Wiley and Sons, 1964).
[6] *Ibid.*, p. 89.

one and a half to two years' retardation. A highly visual and tactile approach to words growing from students' experiences should be explored in the early grades. These students should not meet typical basal readers and other books until they have more familiarity with the concepts attached to the printed symbols. This early approach might capitalize on audio-visual approaches, manipulative materials, and very brief booklets.[7]

In the primary grades the "non-graded" form of organization is now being widely used. If this method is used skillfully, it may be good for disadvantaged children. Skillful use with disadvantaged children means, among other things, that they should have materials adapted to them, that teachers should be trained to work with them in small groups, and that their reading and arithmetic work groups should be organized separately.

Intermediate Grades. In the intermediate grades the difficult pupils are just beginning to emerge as behavior problems. A few become aggressive and hostile to school and to authority. Others become apathetic. This is the period in which least is now being done for such pupils. Sometimes they are given remedial instruction; sometimes they are put in low ability classes. Nobody seems to know how to help them, and they are not yet big enough to be a threat to order in the school and community, thereby forcing the schools to pay special attention to them.

Junior High School Level. By the 7th or 8th grade these boys and girls are a clear threat to the smooth running of the school. In slum schools they may constitute 50 per cent of the enrollment. The hostile aggressive ones make it difficult for the teacher to really teach because he is so busy merely controlling behavior. The apathetic ones become a dead weight on the class. These pupils have given up on school, and come to class merely because they have to or because their friends are there.

There is a good deal of experimentation with educational programs for this group. One kind of program is a remedial academic one. They are given extra drill in reading and/or arithmetic, with a variety of remedial methods. Sometimes they are set aside in special classes or special "upper grade centers." Some improvement has been claimed for such programs. Even as much as a two or three-year gain of reading level has been claimed for a six-month remedial program. However, the writer does not know of any carefully designed research with a control group which substantiates these claims.

It is reasonable to suppose that, with sympathetic and realistic counseling and direction, some of these boys and girls would make a serious effort to overcome their academic deficiencies at this age. The basic question is whether their earlier disadvantages and deficiencies are so deep and damaging that they can no longer learn the mental skills they would have learned at a much earlier age if they had been taught more effectively in earlier years.

The only alternative program which has been extensively tried is a work-experience program. This has generally been used with boys, though girls have been

---

[7] Robert J. Havighurst, *The Public Schools of Chicago* (Chicago: Board of Education, 1964), p. 119.

included in some projects. Work-study programs fall into three general groups:

(a) Those which are part of a regular vocational high school program, and for which alienated or marginal youth cannot qualify.

(b) Those which are for youth aged 16 or 17, who are about to drop out or have dropped out of school.

(c) Those which are for junior high school youth, aged 13 or 14 and up.

Experience to date with work experience programs for difficult youth has given equivocal results. Some youth profit from this kind of program, while others drop out or are expelled after they have proven to themselves and their teachers that they are not meeting the requirements or getting satisfaction from the program.

The best estimate the writer can make now is that about half of the boys who are identified as socially disadvantaged are likely to learn the habits and attitudes and skills of a work-study program well enough to get and hold steady work at the age of 18.

Since there are as many girls as boys, if not more, in the marginal group, it is important to note that very little has been done of an experimental nature for girls. They do not show as much delinquency, and consequently tend to be ignored by society, though their performance as mothers of the next generation is perhaps more dangerous, potentially, to society than the actual delinquency of their sociological brothers.

Programs for Youth After 16.   Nearly all of the socially disadvantaged youth drop out of school at age 16 or 17. Most of the girls get married within a year or two. Most of the boys have a period of three to five years in which they are idle most of the time, employed fitfully but unable to keep a steady job, and a few of them have a brief and unsatisfactory experience in the armed services. The numbers of this group will increase during the next five years, due to increased birthrates after World War II combined with the disappearance of juvenile jobs from the labor force.

Schools have begun to serve these young people in the most recent years, under programs supported by the federal government through the Manpower Development Training Act, and under the Economic Opportunities Act of 1964. There are also some possibilities for experimental vocational programs under the Vocational Education Act of 1963.

We may look ahead to a substantial program under public school auspices of work experience for youth aged 16–21. This will tax the ingenuity of secondary school personnel, both in the vocational education and the general education fields. An important part of the program will be work-related schooling. Some of the young people in the program will want to get credits toward a high school diploma, and the high schools will be under pressure to offer some basic English and mathematics courses for these boys and girls.

Another element in such a program will be the placement of youth in jobs and the counseling necessary for helping youth who are marginal to the labor force to adapt themselves to the requirements of a steady job.

The secondary schools are just at the beginning of a tough and challenging experience of providing personally and socially useful educational experience to young people over 16 who have consistently failed in their earlier school work. It will require imagination, ingenuity, and perseverance on the part of secondary school administrators and staff to measure up to this new kind of responsibility.

Differentiation Between Socially Disadvantaged and Mentally Retarded. It has been noted that the true "mentally retarded" cannot be readily distinguished from those who are learning poorly because of social disadvantages, especially in the early years. This seems to argue for similar forms of compensatory education in preschool classes, except for the children for whom a diagnosis of true mental retardation has been made. These exceptional children will generally show certain physical characteristics and they will come from homes where the emotional and intellectual environment is average or better.

By the age of eight or nine, however, the child who is clearly retarded in the judgment of a clinical psychologist will generally be placed in a special class of "educable mentally handicapped" or "trainable mentally handicapped," with a specially trained teacher. This teacher can generally do more for such a child than an ordinary teacher in a regular classroom. But provision should be made for transfer of some of these children to regular classes as they improve.

At the high school level there is need for classes for retarded children—that is, for children who read at the fourth grade level or below. Such classes should have work-experience programs, since a large number of retarded pupils can become self-supporting workers if trained suitably.

EDUCATIONAL PROGRAMS FOR THE PRIVATIST NON-CONFORMIST

What can the schools do about the difficult student who is a privatist non-conformist? If the analysis of the preceding pages is reasonably correct, boys and girls of average or superior intelligence need an educational program during the high school period that is designed to build self-esteem and social fidelity. The characteristics of the youth who tend toward the privatist position are the following: lack of self-esteem based on their own achievement in school and society, uncertainty about vocational choice, cognitive development more advanced than personal autonomy, lack of naive faith in society, and discontent with school.

The educational program should be designed to build social fidelity as well as self-confidence. It might contain the following elements:

1. Opportunity for service to society. A variety of projects during the school year and during the summer for improvement of the school, the local community, and the wider community. This will lead to a commitment to social welfare and a faith in the improvability of society.

2. Positively oriented study of society. Stress in courses in social studies on the achievement of modern society in solving problems of public health, poverty,

educational and economic opportunity, and the building of an interdependent world.

3. Use of adult models who demonstrate both self-esteem and social fidelity. Choice of teachers who are socially optimistic, active, and oriented toward the improvement of society. There is a greater chance in the future for the selection of teachers with appropriate personalities for certain age groups, as the teacher shortage decreases and opportunity increases to select the better ones. The use of biography in literature and the social studies could stress heroes with these positive qualities. A new set of biographical films produced by Elizabeth Drews of Michigan State University centers on the lives of contemporary people who are making positive contributions to the life of society, who have faith in the improvability of this society, and who lead personal lives that can serve as models of youth.

Good education strikes a balance between analysis and affirmation. Perhaps the education of middle-class children in recent years has been too strong on analysis and too weak on affirmation.

DANGERS AND CAUTIONS

So much attention is being paid to the socially disadvantaged pupil that we are in danger of organizing a large section of our educational program around his problems, especially in the big cities. While certainly it is necessary to give major attention to this type of pupil, he only represents some 12 to 15 per cent of youth, and secondary education cannot be structured primarily around him.

A major problem in connection with this type of youth is found in some of the high schools in low income areas of the big cities. Table 1 illustrates this problem, by comparing the students of such a high school with those in a high achievement suburban-type high school in Chicago.

School A differs from School B in being about twice as large, and containing many more low achieving, socially disadvantaged pupils. Note that the ratio of 9th to 12th grade students is 4 to 1 for School A and 1.5 to 1 for School B. The "basic courses" in Chicago high schools are for pupils who are three years or more retarded, while the "essential courses" are for pupils who are between one and three years retarded. School A has two-thirds of its 9th graders in these two categories, while School B has one-eighth in the "essential courses" and none in the "basic" level. On the other hand, School B has many more pupils in "honors courses," which are for students at least one year advanced.

School A is in a position to specialize in the adaptation of curricula and methods to socially disadvantaged pupils. School B might specialize in gifted pupils. But this might be bad for the goodly number of above average pupils in School A.

There is much to be said for the "mixed school"—that is, mixed in socioeconomic status and mixed in achievement of its students. Ideally, this kind of school can challenge its best students and also use their performance as a model for other students while at the same time being realistic about their lesser ability. But

Table 1
Comparison of Two Contrasting High Schools
(Schools A and B)

AGE	Grade 9 A	Grade 9 B	Grade 10 A	Grade 10 B	Grade 11 A	Grade 11 B	Grade 12 A	Grade 12 B
			PERCENTAGE DISTRIBUTION OF AGES					
11-9 to 12-8	2	0						
12-9 to 13-8	6	16	0	0				
13-9 to 14-8	31	53	2	10	0	0		
14-9 to 15-8	39	23	25	58	4	14	0	0
15-9 to 16-8	18	7	43	23	35	56	10	14
16-9 to 17-8	3	1	24	7	38	28	35	69
17-9 to 18-8	1	0	5	2	18	2	38	16
18-9 to 19-8			1	0	4	0	15	1
19-9 and over								
Number	2,039	668	1,246	549	676	524	503	443
			PERCENTAGE ENROLLMENTS IN BASIC, ESSENTIAL, AND HONORS COURSES					
Basic course								
English	35	0	23	0	—	—	—	—
Mathematics	19	0	0	0	—	—	—	—
Essential course								
English	30	12	36	0	42	0	31	0
Mathematics	56	14	44	0	—	—	—	—
Honors course								
English	1	12	2	5	4	5	7	6
Mathematics	2	12	0	23	0	10	0	18

Source: Havighurst, Robert J. *The Public Schools of Chicago* (Chicago: Board of Education, 1964), p. 42.

there are major problems of discipline, of school climate, and of curriculum adaptation in School A.

One way to get around these problems and others as well is to adopt the Educational Plaza or Educational Park plan, which is now being discussed widely. Essentially, this is a plan which brings a mixed group of pupils in terms of ability and vocational interest and socio-economic status together on a particular school campus, but organizes their work so that a part of it is done in common and a part in sub-groups of similar ability and life-expectation. Additionally, the Educational Park idea may include a wide age range of students, certainly from grades 7 to 14, and possibly from the 1st–5th grade on through junior college.

Such a program is especially desirable in a self-contained or cross-sectional community of 50 to 150 thousand population. However, it can also be adapted to a section of a big city with 100 to 400 thousand population.

The American ideal of a comprehensive high school may only be realizable under urban conditions by the Educational Park.

The Privatist Non-Conformist Needs Leeway.   Another danger lies in too naïve and didactic an approach to the complexity of the privatist non-conformist. This kind of person has much to contribute to the social welfare if he acquires a social conscience and a social commitment while retaining his faculty for criticism and non-conformity. There is a danger of "brain-washing" him with over-simple and over-optimistic and over-patriotic teaching during his high school years. Perhaps he needs these years to grow in his powers of analysis and social criticism, even though he may be somewhat unhappy and he may make his family uncomfortable.

The art of teaching this kind of boy or girl is to combine experiences of basic affirmation of democratic social values with experiences of analysis and criticism of social reality, so that the youth discovers and works out for himself his identity both as a conformer to some social values and a non-conformer to some social practices.

LOW INCOME CULTURE, THE ADOLESCENT, AND THE SCHOOL

FRANK RIESSMAN

The major question I want to confront in this article is, "How can we provide an appropriate curriculum for the detected potential dropouts?" I think implicit in a good deal of thinking in this area is that the dropout is inferior mentally. I think that this is not true at all. Schreiber pointed out that the Maryland study showed that about *half of the dropouts were average or above average in their ability.* This statement is a bare minimum because the criteria used are typical intelligence tests which do not adequately measure students from lower socio-economic backgrounds. What I will try to show is that a large number of dropouts from a lower socio-economic background have a different style of thinking, a different way of learning, and that the school is not attuned to this. In order to do this, I want to discuss two simple concepts.

First is the concept of "school culture" and second is the concept of "learning style." The school organizes learning in certain ways. It is often presumed that this is the only way you can learn. If you stop to think about it a minute, you will

Reprinted by permission from the *Bulletin of the National Association of Secondary-School Principals* (April 1965). Copyright: Washington, D. C.

realize very quickly that this isn't the case. For example, schools use tests very heavily, and test-taking techniques are implicit skills that the student must learn in the school.

The school emphasizes speed a great deal. It emphasizes being able to answer questions in class very quickly. It emphasizes certain styles of learning and de-emphasizes other styles of learning. For example, it de-emphasizes and typically penalizes slow learners. In fact, we very often believe that slow learners are poor learners or that they are dull. This isn't necessarily true. There are some slow learners who are dull. But people may be slow for a great variety of reasons. They may be slow because they are painstaking, because they are very careful, because they are very concerned about doing things with great pride, because they are distractable, or because of many other causes.

We should start to think anew about slow learning. There are many positive qualities in it, and we should not think of the slow learner as somebody you should put on a separate track or imply that he is negative intellectually. I think extremely good work can be done in a slow fashion. If you are going to be a great mathematician, it makes little difference whether it takes you five times as long to learn long division as it takes me to learn it. The point is that after we both learn it, you, who were deeply involved and interested in it, may go on to do significant mathematics work while I, the fast learner, might not do this. I might jump to something else, skip around, do a variety of things. The point I am trying to make is that the school culture rewards the fast learner, builds his ego, pushes him on in the school, and encourages him, while the slow learner is pushed out of the school's mainstream. His ego is depleted and he comes to feel that he is dull. He doesn't develop involvement in the work and he becomes in many cases a dropout.

THE PHYSICAL STYLE

In addition, the school does not emphasize the physical style. I think that low socio-economic youngsters very often learn in what I call a physical style. They have to do something physically in order to learn about it. They can't simply talk about it. They are quite able to verbalize and quite able to conceptualize. But essentially they learn through physical things—through touching, through moving, through gestures—and the school doesn't particularly reward this pattern. The school emphasizes two other dimensions of learning—reading and writing. I am not suggesting there is anything wrong with learning through reading and writing or learning through hearing and speaking. I happen to learn best through hearing and speaking, particularly, speaking.

I am suggesting that methods attuned to physical styles would bring out the latent ability of the disadvantaged far more. I strongly believe that we are not in any way coming near tapping the latent ability of large numbers of low socio-economic youngsters in school. It is true that the school today has started to use some physicalistic techniques and, of course, they have used visual techniques for a long period of time. However, you cannot use them with the implicit notion that the students are inferior intellectually and that you have to approach them visually and physically because they are inferior. I am suggesting instead that these are perfectly valid styles. The school should be more pluralistic, and different ways of learning should be accepted and developed.

I am merely touching the surface, but what I am trying to say is that the school culture itself is very narrow. It has organized learning in certain kinds of ways which have operated negatively for the lower socio-economic dropouts.

SPECIAL TALENTS AND THINKING

Large numbers of children from lower socio-economic groups have great potential talent. Goodwin Watson, for example, in the introduction to my book [1] states that there is more talent in the lower socio-economic group because there are more people there. But I mean much more than this. I mean there are special kinds of talent and thinking there. Dr. Irving Taylor in his studies of creative people observed that certain types of creative persons in the United States have a style that very much resembles the intellectual style of this lower socio-economic group. This style is characterized by the following attributes: it is physicalistic, it is visual, it is concretistic, it verbalizes in relation to things it can see and act upon and do. It is not what Taylor calls word-bound, over-verbal, where the person cannot think without words, where the semantic structure of the language determines the whole nature of thinking. Creative people have broken out of this. There are large numbers of people in lower socio-economic groups who might be called slow-gifted or physically-gifted—a different kind of giftedness, a different kind of creativity.

In essence, we need to reflect in the school system much more of the unorthodox learner. This is needed not only for the lower socio-economic groups. For example, large numbers of people learn in unorthodox ways. Some learn only if they are thinking through the problem in their own way. They don't follow other people well. I call this a "one-track learner." These people, by the way, are not rewarded in the school system until they get to graduate school—and they typically don't get there. If you get to graduate school, you are expected to be creative and think along your own lines. But before you get there, you have to be much more conformistic in your learning. There is a great need to develop the unorthodox, the different styles of learning in all of us.

The point is that we don't accept different styles. We are sure that the youngsters that come from so-called deprived homes have only negative qualities in relation to the school. I don't accept this. They have many positive qualities which we have to build into the school culture. We have to have a place for their slowness, for their physical style, not deprecatingly or because we want to be democratic—or because we want to be nice to them, or because we want to patronize them, or

---

[1] *The Culturally Deprived Child* (New York: Harper and Row, 1962).

condescend to them. We must do it essentially because they have a positive style which will enrich the school as it interacts with the other styles in the school.

A NEW APPROACH TO GUIDANCE

I want to mention a new approach to guidance which flows from the idea of learning styles. Much guidance and counseling in the United States today is psychologically oriented. I should like to suggest by contrast that what we should try to do is to study the learning style of the child and to try to develop it. In other words, to find out the way that he learns. Young children in most cases and a large number of adult people as well do not know their own learning styles. They do not know how they learn and they do not know how to change and develop their styles. A student tells you, "I can't concentrate." What he means is that when he sits down to work with the material, he can't get into it; he walks around, looks out of the window, plays the radio, does a whole series of things. While he is doing this, struggling to get into the work, his whole ego is being smashed. He thinks, "I can't concentrate—I'm stupid—I'm not going to learn this." He develops a great deal of anxiety. He must recognize the fact that this is the way he gets into work and that there is nothing wrong with it. There is no need to be anxious. A large number of people take a half hour to get into work, require a long warm up, and they have to do something physically in warming-up. There are a great variety of things that can be done in organizing the warm-up period. But the student should know or be guided to know that there is nothing peculiar about him or inferior about him because he has this long warm up. He should recognize it and plan his work accordingly. In other words, you can't plan work for an hour if it takes you a half hour to warm-up! I can plan work for 25 minutes because it takes me 20 seconds to warm-up, but I can't work very long. I can't sit down and work for hours at a stretch. I don't work that way. There are weaknesses in my style and strengths in my style and weaknesses in other people's styles and strength in their styles. This is what we have to recognize.

I want to train guidance personnel to work with the child's style—not to give him the standard study habits that everybody knows about, but to develop particularly his specific style of learning and working. You can use some of the classic work on learning and study habits, but this is not enough. You have to find out much more about the way the child learns and then experiment with a series of schedules for him. I would like to see guidance and teaching people give more attention to this. I think they can be trained to do it quite easily; I don't think it takes four years of graduate study to acquire these skills.

Let me close by repeating that there needs to be more recognition of differences. In essence, I would like to put the D back in Democracy—the D for differences!

CAN WE CATEGORIZE
THE CHILDREN OF
THE URBAN POOR?

ROBERT J. FISHER

One of the curious by-products of the awakening interest in the educational fate of the children of the urban poor is the inappropriateness of vocabulary in current usage. Every few years a new term is coined, but none of the terms is quite satisfactory. Who are these children and how shall we describe them? How can we counteract stereotypes, avoid a patronizing point of view, and keep from offending the people themselves? If these children are *culturally-deprived*, who deprived them of their culture? If they are *underprivileged*, what privileges have been taken away? If they are *educationally-handicapped*, what evidence do we have to support this? If they are *lower-class*, why won't they admit it?

If we cannot find a word or a concept to encompass adequately what we want to say, could it be that we really are not clear about what we are trying to describe? We are trying to reduce a complicated convergence of forces, problems, conflicts, and social dislocation involving a multitude of people into simplified descriptive terms. We are currently seeking answers to failures we have long recognized: our inability to provide adequate educational opportunities for the children of the urban poor. Within the older sections of our larger cities the most pressing problems of our nation converge and baffle us. As usual, our society looks to education for long-range social solutions. But we have difficulty even trying to describe the people who live in our cities. Sometimes, we assume that if we give them a name we will create a reality with which we can then deal as if it were something tangible and capable of descriptive analysis.

Taking five of the current terms in common usage, we can ask: How adequately do they really describe reality?

(1) *Culturally-Deprived Children.* Anyone who is deprived of a culture must certainly be in a bad way. We get visions of illiterate children grunting incomprehensibly at each other, living in barren rooms, stricken by the debilitating influences of poverty, neglect, and cultural disorganization. In actuality, no children can exist deprived of a culture. Children who grow up in the inner city have an

FROM *The Educational Forum*, 29:285–290 (March 1965). Copyright: Kappa Delta Pi, An Honor Society in Education. Reprinted by permission.

influential, meaningful, even rich and varied culture which often teaches them more quickly and forcefully how to cope with the demands of the environment than the culture of suburbia teaches suburban children.

The cultural demands of the big city may be neither pleasant nor enhancing. There is nothing romantic about poverty. But children learn to cope with demands, meet crises, and survive challenges. They just do not learn much of this in school rooms; they learn more on the streets and in overcrowded living quarters. Some facets of the subculture stimulate the fears, angers, and disapproval of many middle-class educators, but in some respects this is because educators themselves are "deprived" of an understanding and appreciation of the culture in which these children function.

What people really mean to say when they use the term "culturally-deprived" is that these children do not have the advantages of a culturally-rich environment with a capital "C." These children do not have books and magazines in the home, stereophonic records, well-furnished rooms, green grass, and frame houses. Their parents do not use a rich and varied vocabulary, buy their offspring educational toys or children's books or records, nor indoctrinate them with the niceties of acceptable manners and morals.

Instead, culturally-deprived children are viewed as functionally illiterate for school achievement, unable to communicate, with limited experience, flattened by an impoverished environment. Pre-school programs which attempt to foster communication skills, build experiential backgrounds, and release potentials of creativity are noteworthy attempts to enrich the "impoverished culture." Such programs may improve falsely-depressed intelligence test scores and stimulate initial success in reading, that over-riding criterion of school adequacy.

But what is overlooked in any assessment of cultural deprivation are the cultural opportunities and cultural challenges which the neighborhood environment does provide. After all, have not people been living in cities for hundreds of years and learning much that is significant from the streets and alleys, store fronts and city playgrounds, schools and churches, and crowded living quarters?

(2) *Underprivileged Children.* What privileges have poor children in the city been denied? Do we assume that to be denied the opportunity to grow up in the suburbs to the hum of power lawnmowers, the smell of backyard barbecues, and the ting-a-ling of the Good Humor man's truck is debilitating? We dislike the hustling traffic of the city streets. We reject the noises, smells, dangers, and disorganization of crowded living conditions. We flee, if we are able, to the suburbs and create family patterns, recreational patterns, and housing facilities that symbolically serve to ward off the unpleasant reminders of our harried existence.

We assume that city children are denied the good life by not partaking of the joys which relative economic security and relatively stable family patterns provide. This may be true enough, but there are still large numbers of tense and anxious children living in suburbia. On the other hand, even though the children of the urban poor lack many economic and cultural privileges and may even have to endure hunger and neglect, they may not be suffering as much from lack of privilege as is sometimes assumed. The handicaps of the underprivileged are relative. How hurtful is the lack of privacy? What is the consequence of a diet which lacks food from the Basic Seven? The absence of a father figure is a more serious deprivation, but are there not other male models in the neighborhood who are available to the children of a fatherless home? Often overlooked in descriptions of the instability of the urban family are the available sources of love and support and even encouragement from parents, siblings, neighbors, and members of the extended family.

No useful purpose is served by either deploring, on the one hand, or disregarding, on the other, the difficulties of overcrowded urban living. It is tough to grow up without the privileges which a stable family life and relative economic security can provide. But it is a mistake to categorize the central city and the suburb as two opposing poles on the happiness-misery continuum. The city and the suburb are simply different locales where people struggle, with not much more success in one place than another, to meet a host of challenging demands. There are "underprivileged" children trying under serious handicaps to mature in both kinds of settings. There are "privileged" children who are being given help and support in both settings as well. Needless to say, the significant privileges may well be the more intangible factors involved in loving relationships than those resulting from material surroundings.

(3) *Educationally-Handicapped Children.* A large number of children in the central cities suffer educational handicaps. They may be receiving an inappropriate education at an inadequately supported school in an out-dated building staffed by personnel who have considerable difficulty identifying with their culture, motivation, behavior, and moral code. But this term is not used, as a rule, to describe the handicaps encountered by these children in their attempt to make sense out of the education provided for them. Instead it usually is used to *describe the children* who do not seem to succeed in large enough numbers in meeting the extrinsic demands of the school system.

Existence of educational handicaps is simple to document. When compared to children in more favored sections of the city or in the suburbs, the mean scores of central-city children on standardized achievement tests is lower. The children start out with lower mean achievement scores in the first grade, and, as the children progress through the grades, the mean achievement scores become somewhat lower yet than those of their counterparts in more well-to-do neighborhoods. Later the young people drop out of school in larger numbers, attend college in smaller numbers, get into trouble in larger numbers, and are a credit to their teachers in smaller numbers.

Various explanations are given. Seldom do we now hear that this lower educational achievement is the result of biological or cultural inferiority. Instead the surroundings are blamed. The parents, the neighborhoods, the peer groups, the crowded conditions, and all the results of cultural deprivation and poverty are deplored. Programs to modify the culture and to enrich the environment in order to stimulate higher achievement test results have been given considerable publicity.

And yet just what do standardized test results reveal? What do they measure? How does the reporting of mean scores obscure differences? What kinds of comparisons are being made between groups and how valid are such comparisons?

In the first place, standardized achievement tests are ill suited to measure even the present achievement and certainly not the potential achievement of children whose culture deviates from the norm. The educational profession has already accepted this limitation of standardized intelligence tests. But achievement test scores with their seemingly self-evident grade-level norms need to be as rigorously challenged.

In the second place, standardized achievement tests in wide use today measure only a small segment of the curriculum. They may not even measure the important objectives in the skill subjects; they usually pay scant attention to the content fields in science and social studies; and they certainly do little to measure such objectives as problem-solving, creative thinking, artistic expression, skills of group living, independent judgment, and physical strength or dexterity.

In the third place, it is likely that achievement tests ignore the motivation, the thinking patterns, and even the environment and vocabulary of children in the central cities. If this is true of standardized intelligence tests, why would it not be equally true of standardized achievement tests? What if children lack understanding about what they are asked to do? What if children are not challenged to "do their best" on a seemingly meaningless task with no rewards that make any sense to them?

But with all the weaknesses of achievement tests—and there are many others—the startling surprise is that a large number of poor children do "pass" the tests. To report test results in terms of mean scores always obscures the great variability within any given sample. Many children in the most impoverished neighborhoods score at or above grade level on even the most inappropriate instruments.

The term "educationally handicapped" when based upon test results has the weakness of reducing that which is used to judge adequacy of performance to that which is currently being measured. One of the greatest educational handicaps many children suffer results from the attempt to assess achievement and potential by inappropriate instruments and the unwarranted generalizations made on the basis of such inadequate evidence.

(4) *Lower-Class Children*. So far in this discussion, the term "lower-class" has been deliberately avoided. It is a useful term, a sociological construct, commonly employed to describe behavior and conditions which can be contrasted with another sociological construct, the middle-class. In using these constructs we need to recognize that they are abstractions which obscure or ignore more differences than they describe.

Of course, the term "lower-class" or that more precise descriptive category the "lower-lower class" tends to be offensive to the people described. Educators have shied away from these terms and have been searching for a euphemism which seems less offensive. At times the terms "working-class" or "blue-collar class" have been used, but these two concepts are not interchangeable with the "lower-lower class" category.

None of the class-associated terms has been successful in communicating with teachers. They tend to create stereotyped images which block effective communication. They also make people who are not sociologists uncomfortable. Indeed, much of the effort to find a term to describe poor people and their children is the search for an inoffensive, non-judgmental term which will communicate accurately. None of the terms thus far discussed seems adequate.

(5) *Children of the Urban Poor.* This is a concept which is seldom applied in the current literature, perhaps because it is largely an economic rather than a cultural or a sociological term. In one sense, it may well be that which most of the people discussed do have (or lack) in common. Poor people do not have enough money. With few exceptions they exist at a standard of living which is inadequate. The children of the poor are very different from each other, but the children and their parents have poverty in common.

As a profession we have recently become more concerned about the education of children in congested urban areas. We are concerned about poor children. We are talking about large numbers of fairly recent migrants to the city as well as the long-term urban poor who have been trapped in deteriorating sections while others have escaped to the outer rings of the city or the suburbs. We are talking about the Negro poor, the Puerto Rican poor, the Appalachian white poor, and the second and third generation poor of earlier immigrant families. We are talking about poor people, but we have difficulty understanding that most poor people retain a sense of dignity and purpose in life and that they subscribe to positive cultural values.

There are sub-cultural differences among ethnic segments of the poor, and there are cultural differences between the poor and those with adequate incomes in our society. There is plenty of evidence of cultural disorganization in the so-called "slums." But in popularized articles, at least, this cultural disorganization is often overdramatized. Conditions in the congested urban areas are bad enough, but there are patterns of life available which can and do provide children with psychologically healthy means for learning to accommodate to cultural demands.

The trouble is that once we have agreed that poor people have poverty in common, we have not said very much. Poor people have many children, and these children are very different from each other. They grow up in an environment which confronts them with untold hazards but which also offers a larger degree of release from parental pressures, more freedom to move about and explore, and more ready access to immediate sources of pleasure and satisfaction than the more supervised play of more economically favored neighborhoods. Schools just do not happen to be one of the sources of pleasure and satisfaction for many of the children of the urban poor.

The schools which these children attend will need to build upon the sounds and smells, the voices and vocabulary, the motives and the problems which the city culture provides. One move in this direction will be a readiness on the part of educators to accept cultural differences in the infinite variety in which they are found on the big city streets and to stop trying to reduce this variety by use of terms that tend to obscure reality.

In summary, each of the terms in current usage has unfortunate connotations, since each encourages stereotypes, is based on faulty conceptualization, and detracts from the potential of the surrounding environment for learning. The most accurate and the least offensive concept is poverty, particularly if poverty is conceived as an objective economic condition. Current federal poverty legislation is designed to improve economic opportunities. This is probably what the poor need most of all—the opportunity to take their place within the mainstream of American culture through better available economic opportunities. Educational opportunity is increasingly the door to economic opportunity. The poor need not always be with us. With adequate educational provisions, the children of the poor are still our greatest untapped resource.

DROPOUTS AND THE SCHOOL

THOMAS L. MILLARD

When a youngster elects to quit school before formal completion, he is in effect removing himself from a potential lifetime income officially estimated at $165,000 for the high school graduate. A 16- or 17-year-old youngster simply may not comprehend the enormity of such a decision, or he may not possess the maturity of judgment to understand fully his own life situation, enabling him to arrive at such a decision intelligently. Such a youngster needs intensive guidance and counseling. The dropout may be a person with serious personality and environmental conflicts rather than an immature person who simply decides to walk away from his responsibilities.

We live in a fast-tempo, ever-changing, ever-demanding society characterized by a high success-value orientation. With this in mind, educators must not simply write off as failures the young people who follow sudden whims to "go it alone" in a job market, which, unknown to them, is rapidly closing its doors to individuals like themselves. Such youngsters need adult attention, understanding, sympathy and expert guidance that enable them to appreciate fully the serious

FROM *Educational Leadership*, 22:247–250, 261 (January 1965). Reprinted with permission of the Association for Supervision and Curriculum Development and Thomas L. Millard. Copyright © 1965 by the Association for Supervision and Curriculum Development.

consequences of their "decision" which, in all probability, guarantees them permanent retirement from work, before they even begin.

Even a cursory review of the statistics bears this out: The unemployment rate among dropouts is double that of the general population; they are also out of work for longer periods; dropouts are identified as that hard core of uneducated young people who perform the most menial and routine work tasks.

Taking this further, in terms of upward strivings, some writers have suggested that social mobility is becoming less and less possible in America. When one considers the growing unemployment rate, especially among youthful workers, in the ranks of a diminishing unskilled labor class, it almost suggests that as class affiliation goes, we are probably witnessing the emergence of an "economically disaffiliated class" in the economic structure of a super-scientific America.

Reversing this possibility must begin in adequate school programs. Such programs incorporate the best that we know in educational principles and practices, including experimentally tested concepts and procedures in learning, resulting from present-day technological requirements and social demands found in an automated society.

A CHALLENGE TO THE SCHOOLS

To be sure, there is no easy solution toward arresting these statistics. However, enough is known about the social, emotional and educational syndrome for dropouts and the myriad problems facing the dropout to permit parents, employment counselors, social agencies, business and industry and, more especially, the public schools to do something meaningful and lasting about the situation.

But present-day school programs dealing with the dropout crises are, but for a few exceptions, grossly unrealistic, inadequate, unimaginative and unsympathetic.[1] Too often, interested and willing teachers are frustrated by indifferent school administrators, jerry-built curricula that favor the "middle class child" and a superfluity of hurried and aimless "crash programs" that collide with each other with incredible clumsiness. One example: The nationwide campaign in the summer of 1963 to induce dropouts to return to school, which to date has met with indifferent success.

An alarming percentage of those who came back are dropping out again—and rightly so—for what else was there to expect, reexposing them to the same learning situation and frustration which caused the initial withdrawal.

The concern is that this is taking place within the school. Historically, the school has been the major social institution capable of influencing the child.

As an agent representative of the larger, more comprehensive and more complex organization we call "society," the school fittingly may provide that specialized assistance and all that socializes the individual into a useful and productive citizen.

[1] For a capsule review of some of the projects now being conducted in various school districts, see Monica Bayley, "A Renewed Effort to Solve the Problem of Dropouts," *School Life*, Vol. 46, No. 3 (December 1963), pp. 11–16.

Education is one of the two major influences in the life-preparatory experience of the child in terms of meaningful training for lifetime labor productivity. Thus, education can be an effective agency in developing the child's life goals and adequacy in meeting the labor requirements of an expanding, technological society.

Even such eminent investigators as Jersild,[2] Sullivan,[3] and Warner[4] view the school as second only to the home in its influence to shape the self-concept and self-esteem of the child. Yet in dealing with the dropout problem, it is a waste of time to point our fingers toward the home. The modern nuclear-age home simply does not have the preventive or "holding power" in regard to dropouts. If one must look for an institution that is big enough, with power and resources, the public schools are the answer. Within this framework, the central problem for public education is one of developing an imaginative and far-reaching curriculum with bold new concepts in teaching and with new techniques and devices for the prevention and/or holding of dropouts. Such an instructional program promises the highest potential for modifying the reactions of those students who find school an unrelated life experience in terms of the meaning which they invest in school.

For the almost one million youths who yearly quit the classroom, leaving school is nearly always a symptom indicative of overwhelming academic and social frustrations. To a great extent, they see themselves as "misfits" in the currently prescribed curricula in social and life-preparatory experiences. They mask their feelings of insecurity, inadequacy and loneliness by withdrawing from basic social learning.[5] That there is a significant relationship between the way a person views himself and the way he looks upon others has been shown by Berger,[6] Sheerer,[7] and Raskin.[8]

Thus there appears to be general agreement that how a child views himself is his most important belief. This is actually the psychic foundation for his very being. Snygg and Combs[9] suggest that the child not only values his self identity, but that he will engage in certain activities designed to protect and/or enhance it. Thus, the person derives meaning from his social situation only as he brings meaning to it.

This, in effect, means that the individual comes into a social situation prepared to learn certain things and also ready to resist or ignore those social situations which

---

[2] Arthur T. Jersild, *In Search of Self* (New York: Bureau of Publications, Teachers College, Columbia University, 1952).

[3] Harry Stack Sullivan, *Conceptions of Modern Psychiatry* (New York: W. W. Norton and Co., 1953).

[4] W. Lloyd Warner, Robert J. Havighurst and Martin B. Loeb, *Who Shall Be Educated?* (New York: Harper and Brothers, 1944).

[5] The reader's attention is directed to *School Failures and Dropouts*, a new Public Affairs pamphlet in which Edith G. Neisser summarizes what is known about the course and treatment of this serious personal and social problem. Also see Edgar Friedenberg, "An Ideology of School Withdrawal," a chapter in the NEA publication, *School Dropouts*, Daniel Schreiber, editor, 1963.

[6] E. M. Berger, "The Relation Between Expressed Acceptance of Self and Expressed Acceptance of Others," *Journal of Abnormal Social Psychology* (1953), 47:778–82.

[7] Elizabeth T. Sheerer, "An Analysis of the Relationship Between Acceptance of Self and Acceptance and Respect for Others in Ten Counseling Cases," *Journal of Consulting Psychology* (1949), 13:169–75.

[8] Nathanial Raskin, "An Analysis of Six Parallel Studies of the Therapeutic Process," *Journal of Consulting Psychology* (1949), 13:206–20.

[9] Donald Snygg and Arthur W. Combs, *Individualized Behavior* (New York: Harper and Brothers, 1949).

seem unrelated to his needs. Each individual has formulated these goals from his own unique life experience, no matter how enriched or deficient this may be.

In terms of the learning situation, Robert Bills[10] suggests that learning is a self-actualizing process and that the self-concept of the child influences his ability to function effectively.

EDUCATION MUST COMMIT ITSELF

Study of the available data suggests we will not be able to eliminate the dropout problem at any time in the foreseeable future. Nevertheless, some inroads on the problem are possible, though only when public education realizes the commitment it must make and is aware of its own cumulative impact potential.

The focal point of any commitment must insure for the individual maximum learning opportunity to grasp the interlocking nature of social institutions that comprise our social and economic system,[11] to understand the emerging requirements for economic participation and to think in a more meaningful way about his productive talents and their ultimate contribution to the economic system. Above and beyond this, what we really need is a sweeping and exacting program of self-criticism and analysis that will enable us to understand the "whole person" in the total context of his sociocultural life; but to date, no one has thought through just how this ought to be done. Apparently this is only a sociologist's pipe dream, for there is little evidence such a possibility is forthcoming to deal with the dropout problem.

Lacking this approach, the socio-pathological conditions that spawn dropouts will continue to be a blight upon a nation whose chief characteristic is human betterment and social improvement. It is precisely this aspect of an affluent society, the impossibility of achieving material well-being and adequate comfort, that is proving to be a cultural eyesore in an age of plenty and in a still expanding economy.

The need for such a program is clear enough, but the lack of interest is at least matched by the widespread and glaring deficiencies in imagination concerning it. This much, however, is true: It will only be through the long-term labor of genuine collective action of school, community and social agency, with the resourceful help of government and industry, that the roots of the dropout problem will be unearthed and the disease destroyed.

THE NEGRO DROPOUT PROBLEM

The dropout problem is particularly severe among Negro youngsters, who comprise a large percentage of today's unemployed youths. Negro youths, even

[10] Robert Bills, "Believing and Behaving: Perception and Learning," *Learning More About Learning* (Washington, D. C.: Association for Supervision and Curriculum Development, 1959), pp. 55–73.

[11] This is a vital point, for the school is the only tax-supported institution devoted exclusively to the training of the young. Commenting on American education, Hofstadter suggests that our society has been "passionately intent upon education" but the results of our educational system have been "a constant disappointment." For more on this, see Richard Hofstadter, *Anti-Intellectualism in American Life* (New York: Alfred A. Knopf, 1963).

when they are high school graduates, may experience even greater frustration in job finding than do their white contemporaries. In 1962, for example, about one out of every four Negro youngsters in the labor force was out of work, compared with about one out of every eight white youngsters. Since 1955, the jobless rate among Negro youngsters, according to official reports, has risen faster than among white boys and girls—up about 60 percent among Negroes compared with 30 percent among whites.[12]

From the Negro point of view, the greatest domestic challenge facing American society is making manifest and real equal opportunity for all so that we may live constructively and independently in modern society. As the Educational Policies Commission has pointed out:[13] "If the problems of the disadvantaged are to be solved, the society as a whole must give evidence of its undifferentiated respect for all persons."

UNDERSTANDING THE DROPOUT

A random sampling of the life histories of most dropouts would seem to suggest the etiology of the dropout syndrome as falling into two groups:

(a) Those syndromes which develop slowly out of social and academic failures on the part of the individual to incorporate in his life-scheme orientation those attitudes and values which are in harmony with the larger society.

(b) Those syndromes which develop relatively rapidly, due to sudden deleterious influences in the person's social or academic milieu, precipitated either by the socio-physical difficulties of marginal living or the inadequacy of mutually reinforcing social interaction.

The influence on human personality of these social and psychological agents lies in the fact that it stirs up easily aroused feelings of envy towards the self-adjusted, goal-directed school child, contempt for the adult figure and distrust and/or perhaps hostility toward everyone in comfortable identity with the cultural values and their expectant goals.

In consequence, all the satisfaction and experiential background which the school experience can offer the individual meets with only limited success and subsequent failure as the individual becomes more or less socially and emotionally isolated from the mainstream of socialization.

To the disinterested, unattached school child (as with most dropouts) the school experience becomes an abstraction in which he plays an uncreative role in the discovery of ideas and meaning (whatever they are). While he does not know it, his unresponsiveness or anti-learning behavior, is, in part, external dramatization of powerful instinctual urges, unhampered by self-regulating experiences.

[12] *Welfare in Review, 1963.* Vol. 1, No. 4 (Washington, D. C.: U.S. Department of Health, Education, and Welfare), p. 19.
[13] *Education and the Disadvantaged American* (Washington, D. C.: Educational Policies Commission, NEA, 1962).

Obviously, it is the school's responsibility to ascertain the cause or causes for the child's unproductivity and, once the reason is found, the school program must be adjusted to meet the child's needs, or the child must be helped to adjust to the program. This must bring into play the full resources of the school—the psychologist, vocational counselor, the classroom teacher, the guidance personnel, the psychiatrist and the social worker in one collective and concerted act.

To find the root cause for disinterest in learning is a critical point, for learning to find satisfaction and pleasure in the immediate personal-social situation of school is the basis of the maintenance of educational interest.

In terms of the individual's need to acquire an understanding of the harmony and workings of his social environment and its varied parts, one looks to education, for it is education that bestows comprehension.

This must lead us to a searching reappraisal of previously defined educational goals, of methods and content and of our present ability to impart the message to children in the earliest grades.

Only so can they understand that school is the place where they belong and that taking advantage of its preparatory experiences is prerequisite for any meaningful relationship in an automated, nuclear society which calls for abilities of the mind as contrasted with previous needs of brute strength.

Seldom, if ever, has education been the instigator of important social change. It has, in fact, reflected more closely the basic social, political and economic changes going on around it and, in this sense, it lends itself beautifully to the requirements of pedagogical change.

THE MOST OPPRESSED RACE
IN THE UNITED STATES
The Indian

JOSEPH S. ROUCEK

The 400,000 American Indians living today on reservations constitute "the most oppressed minority group in the United States," according to the then Senator Hubert Humphrey, who pointed this out at the beginning of May, 1964, at a national conference in Washington on improvements in education, housing, and

FROM The Educational Forum, 29:477–485 (May 1965). Copyright: Kappa Delta Pi, An Honor Society in Education. Reprinted by permission.

health for the underprivileged citizens. He stressed also that the average family income is low, and that their unemployment rate was "seven or eight times" the national average. "Poverty is the everyday life of the American Indian. No other group in American Life is so victimized," he said.

Another example of the fate of the Indians is provided by the current treatment of the Seneca Indians. They are being driven from their homes by the rising waters of the Kinzua Dam in Western Pennsylvania, although in 1794 the United States signed a treaty with the Seneca Indian nation granting it a reservation along the banks of the Allegheny River in Western New York which the Senecas were to enjoy undisturbed "forever" or, at least, "as long as the grass grew green."

Obviously, government, like young suitors, should not be taken seriously when they use words like "forever," for the Indians are being dispossessed, because most of their land will be submerged under water when the Kinzua Dam flood control project 27 miles downstream will have been completed.

The Indians may, in their wisdom, understand that the living cannot always be bound by the promises of the dead. In 1794, the America west of the Atlantic coast was a great wilderness that Thomas Jefferson thought would take a thousand years to settle, and no one could foresee that the United States population would multiply 45 times in 170 years. No man dreamed of the mechanization, the rapid transportation, and all the other things that created a larger human gap between 1964 and 1794 than existed between the infant United States and the Roman Empire.

One thing, however, the Indians cannot understand is why it should take so long for them to be paid for their land. A twenty million dollar reparations and rehabilitation bill, passed by the House (and cut down to $9.1 million by a Senate sub-Committee), lay in limbo sidetracked by apparently more pressing business, although some 140 Indian families had to find new homes by October 1. They no longer referred to the President as "the Great White Father," and as far as they can tell, the white man still speaks with a forked tongue.

JOHNSON'S WAR ON POVERTY

Yet, the problems of the Indian have not been entirely forgotten in Washington. With the accession of Johnson to the Presidency, the administration's war on poverty has been focusing attention on the American Indian such as he has probably not enjoyed since the end of the Indian Wars in the late 19th century. The Indian has been singled out in talks by President Johnson, Secretary of the Interior Stewart L. Udall, and, of course, by United States Indian Commissioner Philleo Nash, as a special target of the anti-poverty campaign. The emphasis on Indian poverty has been, in turn, focusing attention on the great confusion that sometimes results when people start trying to find practical means of fighting poverty. For, ironically, the Indian in the United States has been the subject of such concern by the federal government for a longer time than any other group in the nation. In fact, the special character of the Indian problem is attested by the foundation of the Indian service as a branch of the federal government with no counterpart in all the other American minority situations—although the problem of the American Red Man concerns directly less than one-half of one percent of the total American population.

Mr. Udall says that he agrees with Senator Humphrey that the logical opening battle against poverty would be pilot projects on Indian reservations. Both men agree that a major problem involved in fighting Indian poverty—and no one denies it is some of the worst poverty in the nation—centers on the reservations. Should the aim be to end the reservation system and force the Indian abruptly to enter the "mainstream" of American life? Or should it be to strengthen the reservation, to cause the Indian to turn more toward his own culture and its ways of solving problems?

These two approaches represent the two extremes. The former was the policy of the New Deal under which Indian Commissioner John Collier sometimes set up schools to teach Indians their own language. The latter was the policy of the Eisenhower administration which sought to "terminate" Indian tribes, to bring to an end the special relationships they had had with the federal government.[1]

Nevertheless, neither approach appears to have brought the Indian very far up from poverty. All evidence shows that the "terminated" or otherwise "landless" Indians have frequently ended up in Indian slums, such as can be found in Rapid City, S. D., or in Billings and Great Falls, Montana. The responsibility for the care of them has been simply shifted from the federal to local governments. On the other hand, the Indian living on a reservation has realized a strong sense of identification with it, often becoming completely dependent on a paternalistic federal government, refusing to be budged into any movement toward self-sufficiency.

Using as a guide a report prepared by a task force headed by Commissioner Nash, the Kennedy and Johnson administrations tried to find a middle way and, at the same time, have stressed less a "way" than a pragmatic approach to each problem, an approach geared to the general belief that self-sufficiency is needed.

"There are many encouraging signs of success," claim some Indian leaders.[2] But these leaders also emphasize that these programs have been scratching only the surface, and that they must be greatly expanded before they make a significant and permanent dent in Indian problems.

THE ROLE OF EDUCATION

Most of the Indian leaders agree that training or educating young Indians so that a large percentage can live away from the reservation is an important goal. They add, however, that many Indians will remain on the reservation, and that general welfare programs, housing sanitation, and education there must be improved.

[1] John Collier, "A New Deal for the Red Men," in W. E. Washburn, *The Indian and the White Man* (New York: Doubleday, Anchor Books, 1964), pp. 392–396.

[2] Dick Gilluly, "War on Poverty Fixed on Indians," *Christian Science Monitor* (June 8, 1964).

The whole history of the efforts of the federal government to "educate" the Indians is rather sordid, since the Federal Bureau of Indian Affairs has often failed to interest the Indians in education and self-improvement and has come to be looked upon as a "father figure" which would solve the Indians' problems. Thus, the Indians have declined in a "welfare culture" basically alien to them. In fact, this is one of the most pitiful stories of the misguided educational efforts in American educational history in regard to America's original "minority."

The historical background is quite interesting in this respect. The original colonies were little interested in Indian education, although several colleges, including Dartmouth and Harvard, made provisions for tuition-free admissions of the Red Man, and the Continental Congress employed, in 1775, a schoolmaster for the Delawares.[3] The Revolution stopped educational efforts on behalf of the Indian, and until 1819 Indian education was left entirely to a few missionary societies; from that year to 1873 ten thousand dollars was appropriated annually for the work, and most of it was turned over to the missions.[4]

In 1871, Congress decreed that no Indian tribe shall be acknowledged or recognized as an independent nation, tribe or power, with whom the United States may contract by treaty,[5] thus marking the beginning of a definitely new phase in Indian-white relations. The Indians became wards of the federal government, a unique status for any minority group in the United States. The policy of the Indian Office from that time on aimed at weakening the tribal organization of the Indians, destroying their culture, and forcing their assimilation as individuals into the normative American way of life.

One phase of forced assimilation concerned the educational program. Indian children of school age were taken out of their tribal homes and placed in boarding schools, where the use of Indian languages and the practice of Indian folkways and mores, such as dress and hair styles, were prohibited. The curricula there were largely those of the white schools, without any consideration as to the particular needs of the Indians. Whatever practical training the Indian children secured either for making a living or making better homes was gained from the labor they performed to help to support the schools; thus a mediocre school system tried to prepare Indian children to live like white people, when in fact most of them would return home to live as Indians.[6]

It is true that the appropriations by the federal government were increased regularly after 1873; but until 1929 Indian education had been a hodge-podge. Most Indians attended public schools—and this is still true—while large numbers went to mission schools. Many attended boarding schools, both on and off the reservations, established late in the last century on the theory that Indian education

[3] Alden Stevens, "White American Indian," *Survey Graphic*, XXIX (March 1940), pp. 168–174.
[4] For details, cf. Clifton E. Olmstead, *History of Religion in the United States* (Englewood Cliffs, N. J.: Prentice-Hall, 1960), pp. 179–182, 415–418.
[5] Ray A. Billington, *Westward Expansion* (New York: The Macmillan Co., 1949), p. 668; pp. 651–680 covers Indian-white relations from 1860 to 1887.
[6] Gordon Macgregor, *The Changing Indian Warriors Without Weapons* (Chicago: University of Chicago Press, 1944), pp. 116–127.

needed the removal of the children from their parents and home life, so that they could be "civilized." Force was often used to take them from their homes, and the schools were characterized by a rigid discipline and a standardized, outmoded course of study. Half of the time was devoted to school work, the other half to doing routine institutional tasks such as laundering, cleaning, wood-chopping and food preparation. Since the work was hard, physically, and required many hours a day, this often affected the health of the pupils. Conditions were worsened by insufficient operating funds, resulting in dangerously low standards of living. Forbidden to speak their own language in school, out of touch with family and tribal life, denied the normal experience and education needed to prepare them for life as Indians, the children would return home from school dissatisfied misfits, unable to readapt themselves to reservation life and equally unable to find a place in a white community. They had learned to read and write, but they were unfamiliar with the customs and language of their own people, and found their schooling of little use in making a living. . . . [7]

The New Deal policy replaced this first phase of the Indian reservation policy in 1934. Yet, even the new ideology has hardly made any dent in the over-all problem of Indian education. Economically, the American Indian was pauperized, and the education of the younger Indians had made them marginal individuals *par excellence*, not ready to take their place in the white American world, and unsettled for Indian life. This policy of "acculturation" had failed simply because the forms of Indian culture patterns still were more divergent from the dominant WASP (White-Anglo-Saxon-Protestant) culture pattern than that of any other American minority. A complicating element was introduced by the record of low standards of personnel of the Indian service.[8]

THE INDIAN PROGRAM SINCE WORLD WAR II

It is true that World War II did much to have the American Indian accepted into the American stream of life, yet, in September 1951, John R. Ride, Winnebago Indian killed in action in Korea, could not be buried in a cemetery in Sioux City, Iowa, because he was not of the "Caucasian race." It was only because of the direct intervention by President Truman that he was buried with military honors in the Arlington National Cemetery.[9]

Furthermore, in spite of the hopes to liquidate the government's responsibility to the Indians by the policy of "relocation" and "termination," the United States has been unable to convert the American original natives to the "American way of life."

[7] Stevens, *op. cit.*

[8] Clark Wissler, "American Indian Tribal Groups," in Frances J. Brown and Joseph S. Roucek (eds.), *Our Racial and National Minorities* (New York: Prentice-Hall, 1937), pp. 37–55. Also Robert F. Heizer, "The American Indian," in Brown and Roucek (eds.), *One America* (New York: Prentice-Hall, 1952), pp. 27–31, and R. A. Schermerhorn, *These Our People: Minorities in American Culture* (Boston: D. C. Heath, 1949), pp. 57–82.

[9] Joseph S. Roucek, "The American Indian in Literature and Politics," *Il Politico*, XXVII (1962), pp. 569–585.

In 1952 the Bureau of Indian Affairs scheduled the Voluntary Relocation Program under which reservation Indians, as individuals or as families, were granted financial and other help to move to industrial centers for permanent employment and settlement. The Bureau put the proportion of relocated Indians who by 1955 had returned at about 24 per cent. This program hardly influenced the more basic problem of helping the reservation Indians to develop viable economies, working out their own problems, and being able to decide how much of the traditional Indian heritage they might want to retain.

On August 1, 1953, Congress passed the "termination" program, aiming to have tribes request termination of their relations to the federal government. But this meant also in many cases dissolution of tribal organizations and the division of tribal assets among the members, with the resulting demoralization and pauperization of many tribes.

PERENNIAL EDUCATIONAL PROBLEMS

Noteworthy in the present situation are the difficulties faced by the Indians of school age.

The Indian youngster, even today, lives in a continuous state of conflict. This is especially true in regions where the color line is not sharply drawn, and where there are no absolute prescriptions marking off the role shared by all other citizens and the role of Americans shared only by those with colored skin. Under such circumstances, the Indian can never be certain of his status or sure of his welcome. While restricting casteways are undoubtedly detrimental under any conditions, they are bound to be more traumatic to the individual when they are not an integral, inevitable, and therefore impersonal part of the social structure. School segregation in former days also had a most unfavorable effect on the Indian pupils, seriously interfering, in extreme cases, with both their work and play. Confused by the failure of the authorities to offer a rational explanation for it, such children sometimes reached the conclusion that it must be a form of punishment for being "red." Many, therefore, on the basis of surface impressions, developed defenses against their anxiety by repressions, substitutions, overcompensations, and antisocial behavior.

This, therefore, presents the perennial problem of American education when confronted by the existence of "minorities:" how to relate the concepts of cultural pluralism to total assimilation. Should young Indians be integrated into American society as Indians, or should they be encouraged to acculturate as rapidly as possible to the typical "American way of life," although this might lead to complete estrangement of their families' background?

Obviously, the integration of Indian children into schools off their reservation has been a mixed blessing. The Indian child's clothes, language, and social customs set him apart psychologically, and the situation was complicated by his inability to participate financially in most extracurricular and social activities on equal terms with his white classmates. This feeling of being different accounts in large measure for the 60 per cent drop-out rate among Indian high school children.[10]

Then there are the conflicts in the educational goals. While the typical American educational system favors individualism and competition, the Indians are group-minded. For the Navaho Indian, for instance, to take initiative in any obvious manner has the psychological effect of separating him from his own social group. By training and experience he works best as a "member of a familial group where authority is diffuse, informal, and shared, and where adequate performance is enforced by the subtle action of 'shaming.'"[11] In fact, most American Indians see no value in competition. To strive to excel in games or compete in school work is to them quite impolite, to say the least. For instance, some Hopi school children evidenced embarrassment and resisted the injunction to turn around from the blackboard just as soon as they had finished a problem. Distinction of this sort was not a part of their culture.[12]

The "deculturalization" of the Indian child has, in turn, produced quite an abyss between the world of their families and of the school, reaching the point where the federal government once withdrew rations on an Indian reservation to force Indian parents to send their children to school.[13]

Underlying all these factors has been the persistent race consciousness of dominant-status Americans, evaluating often Indians as "colored" peoples and hence, as inferior.

The contemporary goal of governmental policy toward the American Indian is that he should attain economic self-sufficiency and develop skills in retaining his lands and natural resources. The assumption is that this will make them no more vulnerable than other Americans and enable them to compete with the rest of the world. The goal is also to have the Indian assume full responsibilities for citizenship, including payment of taxes on land now held in trust for him by the government. (In the opinion of most specialists this is not likely to be reached any earlier than the year 2,000.) In fact, some critics stress that there is still no firm, definite program to reach such goals, and no rigorous timetable to achieve it. Nor, they claim, is there even a real trend of policy or a vigorous drive among officials to head for it. Indeed, the Bureau of Indian Affairs has been accused of arbitrary methods that inadvertently reverse the advance of the Indians toward "complete self-reliance and delay the end of their paternalistic supervision by the government."[14]

THE VIEWS OF THE INDIANS

So far, we have been viewing the problem of the American Indian from the "American" point of view. Little is actually known about the social attitudes of

---

[10] "U.S. Indians," *New York Times* (May 31, 1964).

[11] Dorothea Leighton and Clyde Kluckhohn, *Children of the People* (Cambridge: Harvard University Press, 1947), p. 107.

[12] Franklin J. Shaw and Robert S. Ort, *Personal Adjustment in the American Culture* (New York: Harper & Row, 1953), p. 33.

[13] E. E. Dale, *The Indians of the Southwest* (Norman: University of Oklahoma Press, 1949), p. 182.

[14] Milton L. Barron, *American Minorities* (New York: Alfred Knopf, 1962), p. 154.

the Indians, especially of the youngsters. In this respect, two pieces of research on Indian attitudes—from a relatively small sample—by Spindler using the Rorschach technique lead to some interesting conclusions.

The Spindlers describe a rather remarkable group of Indians "who had attained occupational and social positions equivalent to those of high status in the nearby white towns," and had undergone a psychological transformation toward the middle-class American value system; in the other case, the Indians who have appeared acculturated, gave evidence of a corroded psychological structure, in which such shifts as had taken place were "regressive and disintegrative." [15]

The conclusion of the Spindlers is that there are some older Indians still holding to the ancient values of their people with conviction, but that the great majority of adults stand between the old and the new in various degrees of confusion and society. But all are "insecure." [16]

About half of the American Indians are under the age of 20, and we can only guess how much regression and disintegration found by the Spindlers among older Indians exists among them. We do know, however, that the young Indians tend to leave school earlier than white children. While the average number of years of schooling for adults over 25 in the general population is over 10 years, for Indians on reservations it is between 5 and 6.[17] The proportion of Indian children who graduate from high school is less than two-thirds of whites.[18]

An analysis of the hopes of the young Indians is offered by Hoyt who studied 582 essays on "My Hopes for My Life in Leaving School" from Indian children 15 to 17 years of age in all types of schools (boarding and day, federal public integrated and public exclusively, Indian, missionary, vocational and nonvocational institutions) in the Southwest. He then secured 207 essays from white children of the same ages for purposes of comparison.[19]

Hoyt's report is that reference to the old values of Indian "was entirely negative. This is the more striking since the essays were from the Southwest. There was incidental reference to values learned in school, values some children wanted to carry back to their people." But nearly one third of all these children featured love or concern for their parents, family or tribe, "references to family being about twice as common as references to tribe, and especially common among the children of the least sophisticated of the schools. No white child of native parentage spoke of love for parents or family, but a few white children spoke of love for humanity or desire to serve it." [20]

Regarding the material aspects of the standard of living, one-third of the Indian

[15] G. D. and L. S. Spindler, "The American Indian Personality Types and Their Socio-Cultural Roots," *The Annals of the American Academy of Political and Social Science*, CCCXI (May 1957), p. 152. Also, A. T. Hallowell, *Culture and Experience* (Philadelphia: Univ. of Pennsylvania Press, 1957), Chaps. 5, 19, 20.

[16] Spindler, *op. cit.*, pp. 154–167.

[17] *Educational Cutdown* (Washington, D. C.: Bureau of Indian Affairs, 1959), p. 9.

[18] *Today's Dropouts, Tomorrow's Problems* (Washington, D. C.: Bureau of Indian Affairs, 1960), p. 2.

[19] Elizabeth E. Hoyt, "Young Indians: Some Problems and Issue of Mental Hygiene," *Mental Health*, XXXXVI, 1 (January 1962), pp. 41–47.

[20] *Ibid.*, p. 44.

children wanted to own something of their own, "car" being most frequently noted. But white children favored cars, too, although "less frequently, no doubt taking them for granted." Thus "in general the frequency of expression of interest in material things to be owned was similar among Indian children and white children."

Most interest was shown in a job by the Indian children: 91 per cent wanted a regular job, and most wanted it off the reservation. Nearly the same percentage of white children wanted a job, but mentioned nothing steady or regular about it "which was no doubt taken for granted."

"The concentration of interests in jobs and the remarks relating to achievement—and possible frustration"—were the most striking thing about these essays. The mention of "steady" and "regular" was particularly interesting in view of the fact that Indians have the reputation for being interested primarily in casual or seasonable labor, tasks which require a major but temporary concentration of effort.

But these children knew hardly anything about the jobs available to them or what was needed as preparation for them. The uncertainty of Indian children seemed primarily to be uncertainty as to what possible jobs there might be; the uncertainty of white children seemed to rise from knowledge of too many jobs, from which they could not choose.

In general, "Indian children in integrated schools knew somewhat more about jobs than the other Indians; these schools were in urban communities and the Indian children were rubbing shoulders with other children whose fathers had a variety of jobs." And the second "most striking thing about the essays was the psychological insecurity some children expressed. They had much more humility of ambition and much more lack of confidence than the white children." In fact they had "various fears that they might not 'make the grade,' even for low-level jobs. Many were concerned for their family and tribe should they have to leave them for jobs. While the older and embittered Indians ascribe Indian failures to the prejudices of whites, these children felt no bitterness about this."

It is obvious that formulating an approach to the war on poverty among Indians is immensely complex, and that much confusion exists. Undoubtedly this is true of the war on poverty in general, and Indian leaders and federal officials hope that the Indian experience will produce some useful knowledge which can be applied to similar situations.

THE TEACHER AND THE NEGRO CHILD
"Invisibility" in the School

MAXINE GREENE

In a fundamental sense, the civil rights struggle is a struggle for dignity, for what Martin Luther King calls "somebodiness." The goal may not be so defined by the rank and file of activists; nor may the mass of Negro people articulate it in such terms. But this is the note sounded most often in literature by and about the Negro since the Civil War. It is one of the aspects of the Negro Revolt with which teachers must be concerned.

The acknowledged purpose of the public school today is to teach all children to think as intelligently as they can, to conceptualize, to form their worlds. No classroom teacher, however, can ignore the difficulties due to the "degenerating sense of 'nobodiness'" which, we are told by Dr. King,[1] afflicts every Negro, adult as well as child. To feel, in James Baldwin's language, "faceless" is often to feel indifferent to the demands made by the world. In the classroom, this may result in failure to master elementary skills; it may affect an individual's attitude towards any sort of work and make him "play it cool" when asked to feel responsible for what he does or does not do. If this happens, the effects of early impoverishment are confirmed. The disabilities most obvious to employers— unreliability, poor work habits, lack of skills[2]—are built into character and style. And the vicious circle that supports so much discrimination is tightened once again.

This is not, of course, to say that the predicament of the Negro is the "fault" of those who have taught him in the school. It is to suggest that one of the contributing factors may be dealt with in the school if teachers can be brought to see the meaning and somehow feel the pain of "facelessness." As the widow of Willy Loman says in *Death of a Salesman*, "Attention must be paid."

One way to see and to feel is through imaginative engagement in presentations like Ralph Ellison's exemplary novel entitled—all too relevantly—*Invisible Man*.

FROM *The Educational Forum*, 29:275–280 (March 1965). Copyright: Kappa Delta Pi, An Honor Society in Education. Reprinted by permission.

[1] "Letter from a Birmingham Jail," in *Why We Can't Wait* (New York: Harper and Row), p. 84.
[2] Abraham L. Harris, "Education and the Economic Status of the Negro," in Robert A. Goldwin, (ed.), *100 Years of Emancipation* (Chicago: Rand McNally & Co., 1964), pp. 152–153.

The nameless hero of that work suffers from what he calls "invisibility," a condition not of his own making but due to a "peculiar disposition in the eyes"[3] of others. Those others are white people; and it makes little difference if they are benevolent or malign. The disposition in their eyes enables them *not* to see the Negro as a living human being, a creature of "substance, of flesh and bone, fibre and liquids,"—of mind. They see him, rather, as an object, an abstraction: "Negro," "member of a subculture," "culturally deprived."

Ironically, it is the humanitarian concern for the poor and underprivileged that has led to teaching teachers terms and categories like these. They are obviously useful if linked to understanding of special circumstances influencing learning in the school. But they are also potentially dangerous. They may lead some teachers to regard their pupils as "cases," even "causes,"—to forget that they are individuals, to impose on them (with the best of intentions) a new invisibility.

This is important because of the duality of the work the classroom teacher is asked to perform. The teaching act is, on the one hand, a behavioral affair, rationally conducted, and guided (hopefully) by theory. On the other hand, it is an affair of face-to-face encounters, dependent for their validity on the teacher's own authenticity, on his ability to identify imaginatively.

If he has been recently educated in the art of teaching, he is likely to be familiar with the structure of his subject matter. He is probably equipped to organize the materials of his teaching in accord with the logic of the subject and, at once, with the conceptual level of the learners concerned. There is no question but that he *knows* more and communicates more effectively than some of those who were taught to teach "not the subject, but the child."

If the teacher is a fairly recent graduate, he is also likely to be committed to a subject matter specialty which he finds exciting, complex, "real." He may be exposed, therefore, to a frustration unknown to some of his older colleagues; and this may make it even harder for him to engage in encounters with youngsters innocent of the joys of learning, pupils who "couldn't care less."

When we link such frustration and estrangement to the increasing professionalism and precision of instruction in the schools, we can easily envisage the consequences for the nurture of identity. Yet neutrality and, perhaps, impersonality may be a function of the cognitive orientation becoming characteristic of the schools.

This orientation has been accounted for by Sputnik I and the subsequent panic over "mediocrity." More significant, however, is the general acknowledgement that it is the only appropriate educational response to a society growing more organized, automated, and intricate each day. The person adequately prepared for the jobs to be done requires more than rudimentary literacy. The citizen equipped to make a choice in an election or in a local controversy must be able to conceptualize, to *form* the world about him in a variety of cognitive ways. We have only to recall some of the recent battles over school desegregation or housing exclusion

---

[3] Ellison, *Invisible Man* (Signet edition), p. 7.

laws, or the issues raised in the Presidential campaign. Far more than factual information is needed in each case. The individual asked to take a stand must know how to reason, how to visualize alternatives, how to evaluate—how to think. The recent innovations in the fields of curriculum construction and subject matter organization have been responses to these necessities.

Further research, further experience in programming teaching machines, for instance, may increase our understanding of the slow learner and his requirements; but the special problem of the Negro child in the slum school may still remain. This is in part because of the ineradicable effects of deprivation in early life. It is also because of the larger problem of the Negro in America, and the uncertainty regarding his identity. Although—theoretically—every child can be taught any subject, the actuality of the Negro child's expectations is not yet fully understood.

There is a growing consensus that severe impoverishment in early childhood makes "normal" concept development impossible.[4] If a child is deprived of a range of sensory stimulations, of linguistic experiences, individualized care, security, and continuities, he is likely to be doomed to perpetual "underachievement" when measured against the cultural norms. The only hope is said to be compensatory prekindergarten education, as in the experimental programs developed by Martin Deutsch and his associates at the Institute for Development Studies in New York. The focus there is on pre-school enrichment, "to reduce the attenuating influence of the socially marginal environment."[5] Because the pupils are three- and four-year olds, the teachers can devote themselves to cultivating the sense of individual personhood, enriching sensory experiences, cultivating curiosity, teaching the children to know their names. The work done already gives evidence of releasing some children from the limitations of impoverishment, of enabling them to learn to learn.

But there are thousands of equally impoverished youngsters moving through the grades and into high schools. If not helped before the age of six, we are told, the influence of the early environment cannot be reduced. In any case, the Deutsch program—*qua* program—can scarcely be adapted to grades where skills and subject matter must be taught. It holds clues, nonetheless. Something must be done to nurture child identity, even if it is too late for him to be "saved."

The teacher, then, confronts ambiguities and perplexities of all sorts when he takes the responsibility for a Negro child. He realizes that he will be hard put to motivate and teach if there is little feeling of self-regard or worth. He may realize, too, that there is little hope of the child's becoming cognitively excellent if he has not been helped when very young. To complicate his task, he may find that his own view of worth—because of his commitment to subject matter and to learning in general—is linked to his prime regard for capacity to learn.

---

[4] See, for example, Bruno Bettelheim's review of Benjamin Bloom, *Stability and Change in Human Characteristics* in *The New York Review of Books* (September 10, 1964).
 [5] Martin Deutsch, "The Disadvantaged Child and the Learning Process," in A. Harry Passow (ed.), *Education in Depressed Areas* (New York: Teachers College, 1962), pp. 163–179.

The very terminology of his trade, "cultural deprivation" and the rest, may intensify this difficulty. A majority or middle-class bias is implied; and, although it may be pragmatically warranted, it is potentially hurtful as far as certain patterns of individuality are concerned. The bias may be reinforced by the teacher's own middle-class values, which often interact with commitment to his discipline to form a kind of screen in front of him. And the screen, once again, obscures his vision of the Negro child as creature "of substance, of flesh and bone. . . ."

He no longer is made to feel guilty about being middle class, as he might have been ten or fifteen years ago. With the exception of those public school people who romanticize the working class and the values they ascribe to it (lack of hypocrisy, delinquent "chivalry"), most teachers tend now to acknowledge at least the expediency of middle-class restraints, aspirations, codes.

Even if he has no feeling of guilt or shame at being middle class and intellectual too, the teacher must still break through the barrier his loyalties tend to raise. If he does not, he will not succeed in "fascinating" children, as Frank Riessman puts it,[6] with what there is to be known. If he cannot reach his pupils, he will be unable to discern the variety of "learning styles" that may be used. If he is unable to individualize the members of his class, he will be unable to adapt the strategies at hand, the techniques that might involve them, as individuals, in the struggle to learn. Clearly, he must do all he can to promote the cause of rationality—using flexible time schemes, allowing for alternative ways of framing material and responding to it, being permissive with some children and structured with others. But as he attempts to promote the cause in diverse ways, he must also try to enlarge his own conception of worth. He cannot exclude the life styles which seem to him to be non-rational, frivolous, shallow, "low"; because, if he does, he excludes individuals from his category of the worthy—and, perhaps, from his category of the human. And he cannot teach those he excludes.

If he succeeds in diversifying, in enlarging his conception of worth, if he succeeds in distinguishing among individual youngsters—his task has only begun. He cannot be "color-blind" when he considers his pupils; since this is often to become unintentionally discriminatory. He cannot treat his Negro pupils and his middle-class white pupils equally; since that would lead to thrusting the children of the poor into fixed positions of inequality. He needs to make distinctions and to be non-discriminatory as well. He needs to find a way of permitting every child to express his own uniqueness visibly, to "become" in his own authentic way.

What is authenticity for a Negro child? And how is the white teacher to know? If he cannot know, if he cannot empathize, it will be difficult to move a child to trust—to trust in a way that builds what Erik Erikson calls "fidelity," one of the building stones of personal identity. How can the white teacher find out how it is with his Negro pupils, what it is like to yearn (as a Single One who is deprived and Negro) to become someone—to *be*?

He is told by some articulate Negroes that he can never know, not if he is the

---

[6] *The Culturally Deprived Child* (New York: Harper and Row, 1962), p. 94.

Man, "Mister Charlie," white. Le Roi Jones, in his play called *Dutchman*, suggests that no white man can conceivably know, that no white man can even comprehend Negro jazz or Negro blues. When Robert Kennedy met with Dr. Kenneth Clark and James Baldwin, the estrangement between Negro and well-meaning white was dramatized in the public eye. Kennedy, taken unaware, was told that he could not possibly understand. John Oliver Killens, the novelist, explains this with talk of a difference in "psyche"[7] and in emotional chemistries. Yet all stress the importance of respect and regard; all speak of integration; all give voice to the need for a recognition of identity.

The teacher, with his unique responsibility, cannot expect clear directives from the side of his profession or from the Negro people themselves. Day after day— unless he chooses to remain "scientific" and impersonal—he will find himself asked to make particular choices, urgent choices; and no one, in or outside his school, will be able to tell him with certainty that his choices are right or wrong. If he is fortunate, he will have contact with the parents or with other people from his students' neighborhood. It may be that some of them will be equipped to mediate, somehow, between his professional function and the particularities of life on the streets and in tenement rooms. It may be that he will come in touch with the fabric of puzzlements on which his Negro pupils are trying to work with their few cognitive skills. Or he may become acquainted with the jobs that are open— and the jobs that are not. He may learn to help them develop a conception of work for work's own sake, for the sake of meanings in their lives.

It is important for him to try. It is important for his professional effectiveness to consider the significance of encounters, of what Martin Buber (and Martin Luther King) call the "I-Thou." His own humanity may deepen if he reaches out and tries to see; since he could not even begin to reach without becoming open to himself.

Again, literature may play a part. There is not only the possibility of vicarious participation when he reads; there is also engagement on his own terms, engagement in a fundamental human quest for meaning, identity, "somebodiness." He will find no final answers, certainly not to questions about the crippled and the illiterate and the poor; but he will, among all the ambiguities in what he reads, experience the power of possibility.

In *Invisible Man*, there is the question: "Yes, but what *is* the next phase?" There is the perception of diversity and oneness in America; there is the fruitful decision "to put it down," to refuse to "file and forget." And there is, just before the end:

I denounce because though implicated and partially responsible, I have been hurt to the point of absymal pain, hurt to the point of invisibility. And I defend because in spite of all I find that I love. In order to get some of it down I *have* to love. I sell you no phony forgiveness, I'm a desperate man—but too much of your life will be lost, its meaning lost, unless you approach it as much through love as through hate.

[7] Killens, "Explanation of the 'Black Psyche'," *The New York Times Magazine* (June 7, 1964).

Through encounter, through the search for meaning—the forms can be imposed and the children can be taught to make sense of it too, to try to learn in their own terms, "to put it down."

The teacher can do no more than explore and pay heed and try to see. He can act *as if* understanding were possible, *as if* youngsters will become visible once he chooses to open his eyes. And he is likely, after a time, to discover that nothing is lost where mastery is concerned—that he has it in him to be a Teacher when he becomes a man.

MINORITIES IN TEXTBOOKS

The Latest Chapter

SOL M. ELKIN

There is an aspect of school desegregation—practically buried in the avalanche of protests, picketing, and lawsuits—that is of particular professional interest to educators: the treatment of Negroes in American history textbooks.

The image of the Negro projected by these books is being criticized with increasing frequency by representatives of the Negro community, and this criticism is having an impact on all texts that touch upon the subject. In fact, responses to protests thus far portend extensive changes in the treatment of all minority groups in school textbooks.

It is worthwhile to consider the experience of Detroit. Following a protest there, materials on American Negro history were placed in the public schools; a recently adopted textbook was dropped, and a major textbook publisher changed its editorial policy with regard to Negroes.

The object of the attack was the American history text[1] adopted one year previously for use in the 7A and 8B grades. In the fall of 1962, the local branch of the National Association for the Advancement of Colored People asked the Detroit Board of Education to withdraw immediately *Our United States* as a required text, alleging that it is "an insult to every Negro in Detroit and promotes an image of the Negro in the remainder of the community that is not only false, but helps to lay the foundations for future community problems."

FROM *Teachers College Record*, 66:502–508 (March 1965), Teachers College, Columbia University, N. Y. Reprinted by permission.

[1] H. H. Eibling, F. M. King, and J. Harlow, *Our United States* (River Forest, Ill.: Laidlaw Brothers, 1962).

The request was documented by a lengthy critique,[2] detailing "distortions and omissions."

Superintendent Samuel Brownell appointed a committee of school personnel to review the problem and to make recommendations for a solution. In the months that followed, a lively debate took place in the schools and community and was fully reported in the local press.

THE CHARGES

The critique cites seven major categories of objections to the treatment of the Negro in the American history textbook. Most relate to the period from the beginning of the North-South dispute to the Reconstruction Period following the Civil War:

(1) The book's casual approach to the introduction of slavery in colonial America.

(2) The presumed lack of interest of the Negro in freeing himself from slavery.

(3) The thesis of the positive, paternalistic role of the slave owner.

(4) A biased description and discussion of the Reconstruction Period.

(5) An image of the Negro as a dependent, servile creature who, with the exception of his ability to sing and make music, has contributed minimally to the development of his country and is incapable of functioning as a responsible person.

(6) Failure to discuss the historic and current struggle of the Negro to achieve equitable civil rights.

(7) Failure to mention the emergence of a single black African nation, although the book does discuss the UN and the evolution of governments in Europe, Asia, and Africa.

These general objections are spelled out in considerable detail in the NAACP protest. Allegedly, the book gives the impression of the Negro as one who did not particularly suffer from the institution of slavery, who has passively acquiesced in his servile condition since 1865, and whose progress to date is due largely to the efforts of others. This is the major basis for the charge that the book is "an insult to every Negro in Detroit." As the critique puts it,

. . . This book gives little justification to the Negro child to consider himself or his heritage as worthy and significant. Rather, he is forced by this book to look to other sources to refute the negative image of himself as presented by this alleged history of his native land. Unfortunately, such material is not always made easily available to him and he is forced to adjust to a self-image which he instinctively rejects but cannot easily invalidate.

Despite the consequences of this negative self-image of the Negro child, the result of its impact on the white student is even more alarming. All too frequently, there is no opportunity to expose the white child to information which might effectively correct or condition the impressions that result from a description of the Negro as presented in this book. The many distorted and erroneous impressions of the Negro that are shared by a significant

[2] See the unpublished critique of *Our United States*, prepared by the Detroit branch of the National Association for the Advancement of Colored People.

portion of the remainder of the community are inappropriately validated by such material as that presented in *Our United States*. Such impressions are reflected in their adult fears regarding integrated schools and other aspects of community life.

QUESTION AND RESPONSE

There is thus raised, for the first time, the question of how the story of the Negroes' role in American history affects the Negro child who reads it. How does it affect his feelings about himself to learn not only of the lowly position of his forebears, but that they apparently had nothing to do with achieving their present state in life? Or that the current struggle of his people for full citizenship, in which he must have a strong emotional investment and of which he cannot help but be aware, is not of sufficient importance to the community at large to be included in his school curriculum? (By the same token, what effect is exercised upon the white student by repetition of the traditional stereotype of the Negro which is fast losing whatever validity it may once have had?)

For some weeks, while the committee sat, Detroiters discussed whether the protest should be considered seriously or ignored as an over-strenuous effort by one pressure group to advance its own interests. Some felt that this was an instance of a newly militant and oversensitive minority wishing to idealize their past and that, understandable as this might be, it would be straining at the limits of historical accuracy to revise the textbooks. Further, to submit to this kind of pressure opens the door to still further revisions at the behest of such other minorities as the Puerto Ricans in New York, the Orientals in the West, and the Mexican-Americans in the Southwest. Obviously, what holds true for the Negro student must be equally valid for the children of all minority groups.

An editorial in a Detroit neighborhood newspaper[3] spoke of bowing to the demands of "political pressure groups" and "textbook censorship":

The American Indian . . . so far has had no advocate for rewriting United States history to suit the Indians. Nor have nationality groups such as Polish, German, French, Dutch, etc., put in their requests for altered historical treatises in teaching history.

Others felt just as strongly that there was nothing wrong with political pressure exerted openly and through legitimate channels—that this in fact is part of the democratic process. Thus, the NAACP protest should be examined on its merits.

The decision of the review committee of the Detroit schools was that the complaints were justified and that corrective steps should be taken. Two things were done: The Board issued a statement reaffirming its commitment "to a policy of having the schools contribute in maximum degree to understanding and good will among different racial, religious, and nationality groups." It also advised publishers and school personnel that teaching materials must "contribute significantly to understanding and good will among different racial, religious and minority groups."

[3] Redford (Mich.) *Record*, 9 May 1963.

More concretely, the Board ordered written a supplementary booklet to be used as a basic text along with *Our United States*. Although that was held to be the best general textbook available, the supplementary booklet was to correct its deficiencies in Negro history. Entitled *The Struggle for Freedom and Rights* and subtitled "Basic Facts about the Negro in American History," the booklet was written by school personnel and published by the Detroit Public Schools.[4] A guide for social studies teachers was also prepared to overcome inadequacies of the text.

FREEDOM AND RIGHTS

The purpose of the supplemental text is affirmed in the first sentence of the foreword:

United States history textbooks generally do not include adequate treatment of the Negro in American history and culture. *The Struggle for Freedom and Rights* was written to partially overcome this deficiency and to give pupils a fuller and more factual statement on the role of the Negro in the study of our country.

Divided into three major sections, the booklet devotes Part I to the history of slavery from prehistoric times to the Civil War. Full treatment is given to the slave's own feelings as well as to how he expressed his rebellion; the slave is regarded as a *person* throughout. On the question of the morality of the institution, no doubt is left in the readers' minds as to the writers' position. Prominent mention of Negro as well as white abolitionists avoids the impression that Negroes did little to gain their own freedom.

The history of slavery and the Negro continues in Part II, "The Civil War Period." The contributions of the pre–Civil War free Negro, participation of the Negro in the Union Army, and the positive achievements of the freedmen during Reconstruction are fully treated.

Part III, "Since the Civil War," again deals with the contributions of outstanding Negroes in all fields of endeavor and concludes by recounting the Negro movement for equality right down to the present day.

The supplement satisfied the critics' substantive objections to the textbook and accordingly was introduced into the schools. But many regarded this solution as a stopgap. Information on Negroes would appear to the children as supplementary, and therefore as peripheral, to their study of "real" American history.

In November of 1963, the Detroit Board of Education voted to discontinue use of *Our United States*, and the process of selection of a replacement was set in motion. Meanwhile, a revised edition of the same book was issued and was considered together with the competing texts.[5] It was this new edition of the rejected book that was adopted for use, beginning in September, 1964.

The revised edition omits the objectionable features of the earlier one and

[4] Detroit Public Schools, *The Struggle for Freedom and Rights* (Detroit: Board of Education, 1963).
[5] H. H. Eibling, F. M. King, and J. Harlow, *History of Our United States* (River Forest, Ill.: Laidlaw Brothers, 1964).

incorporates much of the material found in *The Struggle for Freedom and Rights*. It is sure to meet the approval of the critics of the original edition.

POTENCY OF PROTEST

The Detroit dispute and its resolution, however, have ramifications that extend beyond a particular book and a particular school system. The 1962 edition of the text broke no new ground in its retelling the history of the Negro in America. Rather, it adhered to a traditional approach, essentially the kind that previously had been widely acceptable.

As in many school systems, the Detroit Public Schools employ a procedure for textbook adoption designed to assure selection of the best textbook available for its needs. A committee of classroom teachers, administrators, and supervisors carefully reviews every publisher's offering before making a final choice. This decision thus represents the combined judgment of many professional educators. Detroit's educators were not alone in their choice. Hundreds of cities all over the nation selected this same text, including both New York City and Birmingham, Alabama. Why, despite the effort to ensure a wise choice, and despite the selection of a book that is substantially similar to previously acceptable books, did *Our United States* become a target of this unprecedented barrage of criticism?

The explanation lies in the increasing pace and intensity of the Negro's assault on the barriers that block his full participation in the life of "our United States." Pressure to revise this text can be viewed as a part of the greater protest. The disputed textbook, like other alleged discriminations, is not really new; neither is its unacceptability to Negroes. Only now, however, resentment at the negative image of the Negro in school textbooks has found organized expression.

The apparently sudden demand by spokesmen for the Negro community for immediate removal of the offensive book should not have taken unawares those familiar with the movement to evaluate school materials in the light of the increased interest in intergroup relations. Secondary school social studies texts were subjected to rigorous scrutiny for minority-group bias in a study by the American Council on Education in 1949.[6] The report's conclusions are not dissimilar from those filed 13 years later by the NAACP.

In 1960, another study for the purpose of measuring progress toward eliminating bias from textbooks found little improvement.[7] The treatment of American Negroes, when contrasted with the 1949 findings, showed these characteristics:

A. The Negroes' position in contemporary American society continues to be very largely ignored. There is a tendency to treat racial inequality and attempts at its eradication with complacent generalizations, not hard facts. In most cases, the

---

[6] American Council on Education, *Intergroup Relations in Teaching Materials* (Washington, D. C.: The Council, 1949).

[7] L. Marcus, *The Treatment of Minorities in Secondary School Textbooks* (New York: Anti–Defamation League, 1961).

presentation of the 1954 Supreme Court decision on public school desegregation by-passes any consideration of the underlying principles and of the subsequent, ongoing attempts at both compliance and evasion. The achievements of living Negro Americans are mentioned in only a small minority of books. Residential segregation by race is seldom discussed.

B. Historically, American Negroes continue to be portrayed primarily as simple, childlike slaves and as uneducated, bewildered freedmen. Most textbooks do not chronicle the achievements of this people in the years from 1876 to the present. Where attention is given to outstanding Negroes in American history, the presentation is insufficient to counterbalance the previously created stereotype of a racially inferior group.

C. The scientific knowledge underlying sound understanding of the basic similarity and equality of the races of mankind is absent from the great majority of the textbooks.

D. With few exceptions, photographs and other illustrations in textbooks continue to portray America as an all-white nation, not as an interracial and increasingly integrated one.

"With some exceptions," the report notes, "the main criticisms of the American Council on Education report of 1949, as they relate to textbook treatment of the Negro, are equally valid for the year 1960." And so, it seems, are they equally valid today.

FEAR OF CONTROVERSY

Apparently, analyses of texts by educators and civil rights organizations had failed to produce a shift in attitudes on the part of the people who write and edit the books. Here then was an area clearly demarcated for action by civil rights organizations.

Interestingly, none of the major analyses here quoted suggest actual falsehoods in traditional textbook treatment of the Negro, but generally allege misleading implications, distortions, and—most frequently—omissions.

Omission has long been a favored device by which the textbook makers seek to avoid controversy; educators have for just as long a time objected to the resultant dull, lackluster texts. This circumstance is known and surprises no one. But the protest by the Detroit NAACP goes further. It contends that wholesale omission has the more serious effect of distorting history, that distortion builds up an unfavorable and untrue image of the Negro, and that this in turn creates deleterious psychological effects upon Negro and white children alike. In other words, the offensive stereotype noted in scholarly studies (the Negro as a passive, music-loving slave who is grateful for help extended to him by the whites) is broadened. We are on notice to educate our youth to the Negroes' active participation in his own emancipation, from the early beginnings of slavery on down to the latest mass demonstration.

It might be comforting to think that controversial issues in textbooks could be handled in a "balanced" fashion—*i.e.*, include all points of view and placate them all. In this dispute, as in others, this now appears to be impossible. Presenting the pros and cons of slavery or of the right of Negroes to equality is just not acceptable any longer.

The difficulty of "balancing" is compounded when dealing with children. Teachers are acutely conscious of the need for an appropriate vocabulary level and the presentation of concepts commensurate with the maturity of the student. Examining the past from diverse points of view may give the impression of ambiguity and confuse rather than clarify.

Some may wonder why we do not simply present "objective" history, dealing only with facts untainted by the point of view of the writer. Most historians would reply that this is impossible. One does not have to hold a completely relativistic view of history in order to suggest that the definitive history of the world has not been written, if indeed it ever will be. Each generation undertakes to reexamine the past—asking new questions, using new tools, and seeking new answers to the pressing social problems of the day. In short, we cannot regard the traditional interpretation of the Civil War and Reconstruction Period as an immutable body of knowledge that we tamper with only at the cost of falsifying history.

If this problem is a technical one in historiography whose full treatment is beyond the scope of this article, it was nevertheless crucial in the Detroit textbook dispute. No one accused *Our United States* of outright falsehoods; of not containing "facts." Neither, to our knowledge, has anyone pointed to untruths in the supplement which was published by the Detroit schools. Both, we can be sure, contain only the truth. Yet they differ substantially from one another. The difference lies in the interpretation of the same historical events, in selection of facts, in relative space allotments, and in emphasis. The result is two disparate accounts of the same history—both equally true.

TEACHERS AND TEXTS

In discussions of any controversial aspect of textbooks, attempts are often made to depreciate the importance of the issue by arguing that the teacher, after all, is the crucial element in the learning process. It is the way he handles the material rather than what is written in the textbook that makes the difference. Hence, it follows that there is no urgent need to revise the book.

Without doubt, the teacher is the crux of the teaching situation. But that does not detract from the importance of the text. As much as we may wish it were otherwise, the textbook is the *de facto* course of study for most classrooms and sometimes even the major source of information for the teacher. The printed word, particularly in a school textbook, has great authority for most of us.

Perhaps continued controversy over textbooks, on this and other issues, will hasten the day when the single textbook will lose its present predominant position in the educational enterprise. Some observers see a solution in the use of general texts together with supplementary books, perhaps paperbacks, designed to accompany the basic text. One major publisher has a text on American politics with 25 separate case-study pamphlets from which each school system can make selections for particular purposes.

But diverse texts encourage sectionalism. And whatever their advantages, they sacrifice the value of the single textbook as a unifying element in American education. There is surely something to be said in favor of a text that is able to transmit a common body of information to all children. How to evolve a single text that is historically accurate, that reflects present-day realities, and that is appropriate for adoption by thousands of school boards across the country is the problem broached here.

While these issues are debated, a widespread departure from the traditional treatment of Negroes in American history textbooks seems imminent. Textbook publishers obviously follow such developments closely, and more are certain to provide the kind of books that large school systems like Detroit (and New York City) have declared they want. All indications are that other school systems across the nation will reappraise their books and that many will find them deficient in their treatment of American minorities.

The Detroit experience has initiated in earnest the search for solutions. Perhaps new and wiser approaches will evolve as the problem is recognized and honestly wrestled with in countless communities across the land.

THE ROLE OF THE SCHOOLS IN A SOCIAL REVOLUTION

BENJAMIN E. MAYS

I take it for granted that the role of the schools in a democracy differs from that of schools in a fascist or communist country. I also take it for granted that the social revolution means the struggle for civil rights in which Negroes are deeply involved. In asking about the role the schools *should* play, I imply that our schools are not functioning as they should to insure the peaceful success of the present social revolution.

To begin on a negative note, the schools, including colleges and universities, have done very little to advance the humane revolution now underway. The major battle for a change in the Negro's status in American life was fought in federal courts between 1935 and 1955. Although schooled men waged the legal

FROM *Teachers College Record*, 65:684–688 (May 1964), Teachers College, Columbia University, N. Y. Reprinted by permission.

battle, university officials for the most part resisted every inch of the way the Negro's effort to enter state universities. For example, the Universities of Maryland, North Carolina, Missouri, Georgia, Texas, Oklahoma, Louisiana, Alabama, Mississippi, and Clemson in South Carolina were forced only through court action to admit Negroes. The universities contributed to the tension by opposing social change. The University of Mississippi and Governor Barnett are responsible for the bloodshed and death that resulted when James Meredith was enrolled with the aid of federal troops. The University of Alabama hardly showed its mettle when Autherine Lucy was admitted or more recently when Governor Wallace stood in the door to prohibit its integration.

There are noticeable exceptions. When a near riot forced Hamilton Holmes and Charlayne Hunter to flee by night from the campus of the University of Georgia, the faculty of the University stood up almost 100 per cent for their return. Officials at Clemson similarly took a heroic stand in paving the way for their first Negro student. There have been other examples of wisdom and courage.

FEAR VS. FREEDOM

But if what I gather from many sources is reliable, in the year or two immediately following the May, 1954, decision of the United States Supreme Court, professors in the universities of the deep south were afraid to say in their classes that the Court's decision was the law of the land and should be obeyed. There is no doubt that many of them would have lost their jobs if they had openly supported the Court. There certainly was no open debate on the subject. If students and faculties spoke, it was to denounce the decision.

Academic freedom just did not exist. It could hardly have been worse in a totalitarian country. With this kind of resistance, the universities cannot be given credit for contributing to the peaceful success of the social revolution in education. It is the essence of freedom to permit free discussion and debate. This was not the case in the period immediately following the order in the historic *Brown* case.

The same situation obtained in the public schools. Most public schools opened only under court orders. Few did it voluntarily. During the court battle, school officials and both Negro and white teachers were, for the most part, conspicuously silent on the subject of integration. They feared social ostracism, violence, loss of jobs, or all three. Although school people were not basically responsible for the disgraceful situations in Little Rock, New Orleans, and Nashville, they can hardly go scot free of blame. If teachers are afraid to discuss the issues of integration, their silence says to students that desegregating society is something essentially undesirable.

Among the public schools, as among the universities, there were notable exceptions: Washington, D.C., St. Louis, Louisville, and later, Atlanta, for example. In these cities, school officials did not abdicate their responsibilities, but in shouldering them bravely were largely responsible for the peaceful integration of the schools in their communities.

It is clear that all too many schools provide no leadership to insure peaceful desegregation, either educationally or in the larger society. The proper role of the schools, up to now, should have been what it was not—the provision of a more positive and constructive leadership to insure peaceful change and acceptance of change.

A CONSTRUCTIVE ROLE

The question is, What should this constructive role be? It is obvious that Negro Americans will never again accept complacently second class citizenship based solely on color and race. That day has gone with the wind. How can the schools most productively react to this new spirit of democracy?

The schools, especially the colleges and universities, should provide objective understanding and truth, especially with respect to racial differences. Although there are many people who believe that certain races are inferior to others, the colleges and universities must make it clear that science has reached no final conclusion as to the validity of this assertion. It is clearly established that differences within a so-called racial group are just as wide as the differences between the races and that very superior people are found in all groups.

I think too the time has come for schools to examine the concept of superiority. Superior in what? Persons are superior in only one or a few areas. The most brilliant person is inferior to somebody in something. Is superiority merely mental? Should superiority include morals? If it does, what race on earth or in history can claim moral superiority? Economic exploitation, war, and sexual immorality are rife among all groups. Superior in what?

Similarly, schools should help people to understand the causes of the current social revolution as a part of our history. Social revolutions do not spring full grown from the head of Zeus, nor do they develop overnight. Western man embraced the most revolutionary doctrine ever expounded to man. It is not communism but the Judaeo-Christian religion, with its emphasis on one God and the worth and value of every person, that provides the basic dynamic of today's revolution. Even during slavery, the Christian gospel upset men so much that they had somehow to justify slavery to their own souls as being God's will.

When Thomas Jefferson and others prepared the Declaration of Independence, they declared that life, liberty, and the pursuit of happiness are gifts of God. We fought two world wars, one to make the world safe for democracy and the other for the four freedoms. In both wars, we used Negroes who had never experienced the principles for which they fought.

While these things were going on, the countries of Asia and Africa were struggling to throw off the yoke of colonialism, and Negroes in the United States, having become skilled in the law, started the present social revolution in the courts and continued them in sit-ins, picketing, and boycotts. Expounding the principles of an ideal democracy, clinging to an all-embracing religion, and fighting abroad for a democracy denied the Negro at home, they produced the social revolution now going on. To know the causes of the revolution promotes an understanding of why it comes at this particular period in history and softens the resistance to it. Instead of being afraid to discuss the revolution and its causes, the schools should provide the platform and the forum for debate and the free airing of ideas.

If denied this freedom of discussion and debate, the schools should fight for this right. The freedom to discuss, to debate, and to seek truth and understanding are the ingredients that make a school or a college great. As the church should be free and unafraid to expound and implement a universal Gospel, the schools should be unshackled in their pursuit of truth and understanding. Teachers in the humanities and social sciences should fight for freedom to search without fear for truths about human relations, just as the men in the natural sciences battle to be free to explore the world of matter.

REVOLUTIONARY MEANING

As one who lives in the south by choice after being trained in the south, east, and west, I think I know the south pretty well. I get the impression that the south and, for that matter, the nation have a narrow conception of the meaning of the social revolution. I sense the feeling that white students in the U.S. are not deeply concerned about what is going on. A white student said to me a few years ago that if the Negro can gain a larger foothold in the American economy, more power to him; but it is the Negro's fight, not his. The idea seems to exist that the social revolution is something isolated from the rest of our culture, affecting only Negroes.

Here the schools have a definite part to play. The struggle to make democratic principles applicable to all people alike is not a one-sided proposition. Every American is involved. Either the American Dream applies to all, or it applies to none. The Negro is not on trial; American democracy is. More people look to the United States for guidance, financial assistance, and leadership than to any other nation. No nation has espoused the cause of freedom as sincerely or as vigorously as has the United States. No nation has fought for democracy abroad, quite without any motive of conquest, as has the United States. But the test of this democracy is not what we do abroad but what we do at home. If the democratic torch is put out here, or if it always dims and gutters before the problem of white versus black, I fear for its survival in the world.

It is clear that it is the responsibility of every school to become a citadel of democracy. Trustees and board members, administrators, and faculty should make it plain to the students and the public that no color barriers exist on its campus. All facilities on a given campus or in a given school should be open to all students who are properly enrolled. The policy of the institution on this point should be made quite definite. Where violence has erupted on university campuses, the administrative policies were not known that students of all races and creed were welcomed. When the key leadership is clear about policies, things usually work out reasonably well. Schools have influence in the community, and what happens on the campus of an important institution is bound to have some affect in its community. Attitudes are moulded in the classroom and in college activities, and the attitudes formed in a responsible academic setting will feed back into the various locales from which students come.

Because the aims that Negroes seek in the push for full desegregation of society in every aspect of American life are simply those already achieved by the majority in our population, and because the fight to eliminate racial discrimination is all America's not just the battle of Negroes alone, white students should become deeply involved in the struggle. In the centers where Negro students have sacrificed for freedom, it is regrettable that white students have typically done little to help their Negro confreres to achieve full-fledged citizenship in the United States. I know the problem. I know students have parents and that they must abide by rules and regulations handed down from above. And yet much more sympathy should have been shown Negro students than has been the case up to now. Understanding on the part of white students would have served to ease tension and possibly to avert violence. Even in the effort to register voters, Negro students have enjoyed little support from their white counterparts.

In all fairness it must be said that once public schools were desegregated and Negroes enrolled in state universities, administrators, professors, and students accepted the fact and things moved along smoothly except in places where political leaders misled the people—as was the case at the University of Mississippi.

DEMONSTRATIONS AS METHOD

It is unfortunate that Negroes had to demonstrate in order to bring the power structures in communities to the point where negotiation was possible. But it is equally unfortunate that Negro students got little help from the white students in the south who live in the cities where demonstrations took place. If white students and white faculty people had taken a more sympathetic attitude and had themselves become involved, then progress would not have been so slow, and the white community would have understood the problem more quickly.

I know all this is easier said than done because schools all too often merely reflect the attitude of the community, and because administrators and professors are understandably anxious to keep their jobs. But violence has erupted because white elements have bitterly and ignorantly opposed the Negro's goals and objectives.

For this reason, Negro schools and Negro leaders are due great credit for preaching a nonviolent doctrine to Negro adults and Negro students. Throughout the south, Negro students have conducted themselves in an orderly and intelligent manner. Had this not been so, violence would have broken out all over the place, and we would have had race riots. Thousands of Negro students were arrested in Atlanta, Nashville, Augusta, Savannah, Albany, Birmingham, Orangeburg, Greensboro, Salisbury, and other places. At no time did they become violent and thereby precipitate a riot. The attitude of nonviolent leaders like M. L. King, Jr., and Roy Wilkins was supported in the Negro public schools and on the campuses of Negro colleges.

THE POSITIVE STAND

Now that desegregation is being generally accepted, the schools should take a more positive stand and exercise more positive leadership in getting society desegregated. It will be easier and safer for administrators and teachers to guide students along the line of accepting the inevitable—a nonsegregated America.

I wish I could believe that from now on the communities in the south and certain areas in the north would voluntarily desegregate all aspects of society so that the revolution as it continues to roll will be essentially peaceful. But there is all too much truth in what the demonstrators say. They argue that there must be demonstrations before the power structure in a given community will agree to negotiate. They say further that all too often there must be still more demonstrations before those in power will negotiate in good faith. The schools can help to interpret the situation by making studies of the communities where progress has been made in desegregating certain facilities. They will probably find, unhappily, that communities as a rule are not ready to negotiate until the normal life of the community has been interrupted.

Finally, schools should encourage a direct and informed response to legislators when relevant bills are before them. If there is a filibuster in Congress, the schools should help students to write their Senators or Representatives, urging them to vote to invoke cloture and to deal with the substantive issues. When civil rights laws are enacted, schools should urge community acceptance. If the churches and schools had taken a moral stand immediately after 17 May, 1954, calling on men to accept the *Brown* decision as the law, we might have been spared the turmoil and strife through which the nation has been passing. When civil rights bills are defeated, then schools should interpret for the community the nonviolent protesters who demonstrate but who are sworn to the nonviolent way of life and they should permit all students to join in such nonviolent protests.

The sooner all walls of separation are torn down and all discrimination based on race is abolished, the sooner we will have peace and calm in the south and in America. There will be no permanent peace if these things are not done. Can the schools do other than work for peace?

PART IV
THE PROFESSION
Authority and Autonomy

The articles in this section fall basically into four major areas of conflict and controversy:

1. The changing relations of the Federal Government to state governments and local school districts.
2. The changing relationship of religion to public education.
3. The issues centered in the changing conditions of professional autonomy.
4. The conflicting opinions about education as a discipline.

The first two of these areas—Federal authority and religion—have long histories of conflicting views and spirited disputes, though the issues and problems in these areas today are quite different from those of the past. The last two—professional autonomy and the discipline of education—have come into real prominence only recently, yet they show promise of becoming the center of significant changes.

The Federal Government's role in education has become increasingly prominent in the immediate years past. There are two major aspects of Federal participation. The first is in financial aid to the schools. The passage of the Smith-Hughes Act in 1916 marked the first time that Federal funds were used for schools below the college level. This aid was specified for vocational education and has been enlarged and extended in this field by subsequent legislation. Yet at the time of this writing there has been no general Federal aid to education; what has been voted by the Congress in the past has been financial assistance to special areas of the curriculum. The nearest thing to general over-all aid to schools came with the passage of the 1965 Elementary and Secondary Education Act, which provides funds in five specific categories. Since this act is discussed in greater detail in the

271

272   THE PROFESSION: AUTHORITY AND AUTONOMY

articles that follow, no detailed account will be given here. It is important to note, however, regarding this act that for the first time below the college level, Federal monies will be used to aid private as well as public schools—private schools including sectarian and non-sectarian institutions.

The second important aspect of Federal participation in education is the role of the Office of Education, located in the Department of Health, Education and Welfare. Traditionally, the Office of Education has had little authority, serving only in an advisory capacity. It provides services to local districts and state departments of education; it collects and publishes voluminous material on almost every phase of education in America; and it conducts research on its own, and grants funds to colleges and universities to conduct educational research. With few exceptions, the men who have served as United States Commissioner of Education, the active head of the office, have not been a distinguished lot. Since 1960, however, under Presidents Kennedy and Johnson, the Office of Education has enjoyed considerably more prestige for two reasons. First, these two presidents have appointed distinguished educators to serve as Commissioner of Education, men who saw their role as one of active leadership in the field. Further, there has been created within the Department of Health, Education, and Welfare a new post, that of Assistant Secretary for Education. The second major reason for a strengthened Office of Education stems, primarily, from the 1965 Education Act, which gives the office wide power in dispensing huge amounts of money.

Underlying all this increased interest in education at the Federal level is the belief by a growing number of educators and laymen that education is too important a matter in today's world to be left to states and local districts. They argue that, ultimately, our national welfare is at stake because education is the means of developing the potential of our greatest resource, the youth of the nation. This argument runs counter to the traditional view, which supports decentralization in all educational concerns. There exists the fear that greater Federal participation will bring greater Federal control, but the proponents for an enlarged Federal role have been making serious inroads in the traditional position. Almost every recent session of Congress has produced, but never passed, legislation creating several different forms of greater Federal involvement, ranging from permanent advisory groups of distinguished citizens to advise the President on educational matters to bills providing the Office of Education with broad control over education as it affects the national welfare.

The issues in newly changing relationships in education between the Federal and state governments on the one hand and the state and local governments on the other are discussed by Dr. Wayne O. Reed, Deputy Commissioner of Education, Office of Education; Dr. Galen Saylor of the University of Nebraska; and Dr. Donald Nugent, Executive Director of the Texas Association of School Boards. Another article in this group is by John W. Gardner, written before he became the Secretary of Health, Education, and Welfare. His view regarding leadership has been widely discussed and is another indication that under his leadership the Federal Government will become increasingly concerned in educational matters.

Much controversy has been aroused in recent years over the United States Supreme Court's decisions regarding prayers and Bible readings in public schools. Churchmen as well as laymen are divided in their reactions to these decisions, and even the Court itself has not made its stand absolutely clear, although its decisions point to the outlawing of all official participation in religious acts and functions. The article by Dr. Robert Ulich, former Professor in Harvard's Graduate School of Education, provides excellent material on the historical role of religion in the schools, useful as a background for observing today's conflicts. Clarence Hall's article looks at alternatives open to the school in the light of those recent Supreme Court decisions.

What promises to be a growing area of shared concern between public and parochial schools is the practice known as "dual enrollment" or "shared time." By this arrangement, students from parochial schools, predominantly Roman Catholic schools, spend a portion of their school day in public schools and the rest in the religious schools. Currently, there are thirty-five states in which local communities have provisions of this kind, some programs having been in existence for fifty years. Sam Duker's article points to the potential growth of the shared time arrangement. Although any sizeable increase in the program must await legal decisions, Mr. Duker feels that the plan would meet any test of constitutionality. Another aspect of religion and education is centered in the public school–private school debate. For the past thirty or forty years enrollment in private schools was maintained at nearly 10 per cent of all youth in school. In recent years the percentage has increased to nearly 18 per cent. This growth in private education is the concern of Dr. Edgar Fuller, Executive Secretary for the Council of Chief State School Officers. He fears the time when Federal, state and local funds will be available on an equal basis to public and private schools. The 1965 Federal legislation, he feels, paves the way for such an event.

The public's image of the teacher, developed in a rural America, as a shy retiring individual who attends dutifully to his classroom, but seldom ventures into public life, and who meekly submits to rules, regulations and decisions regarding salaries and working conditions, is dying a slow death. The picture has been changed radically in the past five years by the militant action of teachers in many sections of the country—boycotting schools; waging strong, well-organized campaigns in state legislatures; blacklisting whole state systems of schools where desirable conditions were not maintained; and using labor's effective weapon, the strike. An evaluation of this newly developing image of the teacher and an analysis of the issues underlying this changed role are presented by Dr. Michael H. Moskow of the Drexel Institute of Technology. The conflict he examines is basically that between the National Education Association and the American Federation of Teachers, who are both waging a strong battle for the loyalty of American teachers.

While it does not provide the excitement and drama of the conflict between the NEA and AFT, the issue, "Is Teaching A Profession?" may have more long-term effect on teachers. Louise L. Tyler throughtfully examines current conflicting views and presents several answers to the question, but she leaves the final decision with her readers. Two other vital concerns of teachers are merit rating and teachers' social mobility. Teachers have traditionally opposed merit rating, yet the author of this article, Francis R. Link, sees attitudes changing as successful programs of rating are initiated in a growing number of local districts. Also, newer conceptions of teaching are helping to overcome conventional resistance. Professor N. R. Dixon of Southern University calls for a "virtual revolution" among teachers in American society in order to effect the upward social mobility of teachers. He comes to his position after a brief survey of mobility in a historical setting, and he concludes with seven recommendations for vigorous action.

The last two articles in this section center on an issue that gives every indication of becoming one of the most important in the history of education. Is education a discipline? Does it have an identifiable content? A methodology? What is its unique function? In what respects is it related to other existing disciplines? In what respects is it different? These questions and others are raised by Dr. William K. Frankena of the University of Michigan and by Dr. Marc Belth of Queens College of the City University of New York.

QUESTIONS FOR DISCUSSION AND FURTHER STUDY

1. Certainly the editor can suggest no question that will start a greater intellectual adventure than the one asked at the close of the Introduction—Is education a discipline? Both articles bear rereading, but the effort should not end there. Dr. Belth's rationale should be examined more fully in his book *Education As a Discipline*. Another valuable reference is *The Discipline of Education*. Both books are listed in Selected References.

2. As a follow-up study on teacher's organizations, two articles referred to in Dr. Moskow's essay from *Teachers College Record*—one by Carl Megel, represent-

ing the American Federation of Teachers, and the one by Marion Steet, presenting the view of the National Education Association—should be examined. In what respects do these two organizations share a common concern? In what respects do their views differ? Are these views mutually exclusive? In what desirable directions do you expect both organizations to move in the future?

3. The issues of great Federal participation in education and those surrounding the general area of religion and public education enjoy great popularity. In both of these areas, students can find more published material than can be read. Care should be taken to select intelligently from the wealth of resources. A particularly fine guide to periodicals is the *Social Science and Humanities Index* (called *The International Index* before June 1965) in which excellent scholarly material may be located from fields other than education. It is important with topics such as these, where so many points of view are represented, to identify carefully what you regard as the major issues, and then to concentrate on the varying shades of opinion surrounding each issue.

SELECTED REFERENCES

Belth, Marc. *Education As a Discipline*. Boston: Allyn and Bacon, 1965.

Biddle, Bruce J., and William J. Ellena (eds.). *Contemporary Research on Teacher Effectiveness*. New York: Holt, Rinehart, and Winston, 1964.

Binzen, Peter. "How to Pick a School Board," *Saturday Review* (April 17, 1965), pp. 72–73, 83–84.

Callahan, Raymond E. *Education and the Cult of Efficiency: The Study of the Social Forces that Have Shaped Administration in the Public Schools*. Chicago: University of Chicago Press, 1962.

Canavan, F. "Changing Jewish Attitudes," *America* (February 13, 1965), pp. 214–215.

Chase, Francis S. "Educational Policy at the Federal Level," *Wisconsin Journal of Education* (February 1965), pp. 25–26.

Conant, James Bryant. *The Education of American Teachers*. New York: McGraw-Hill, 1963.

Cremin, Lawrence A. "The Education of the Public," *Harvard Graduate School of Education Bulletin* (Fall 1964), pp. 2–6.

Davis, E. W. "Extremists, Critics, and Schools," *Educational Leadership* (October 1965), pp. 53–75.

"Dual Enrollment," *American Education* (March 1965), pp. 24–26.

Exton, E. "Will the New Federal Aids Strengthen or Weaken the Public Schools?" *American School Board Journal* (February 1965), pp. 75–76.

"Federal Aid and Judicial Review," *Christian Century* (April 14, 1965), pp. 451–453.

Frankena, William K. *Three Historical Philosophies of Education*. Fairlawn, N. J.: Scott, Foresman and Company, 1965.

Freund, Paul A., and Robert Ulich. *Religion and the Public Schools*. Cambridge, Mass.: Harvard University Press, 1965.

Fulbright, J. W. "Education and Public Policy," *The Bulletin of the National Association of Secondary School Principals* (March 1965), pp. 151–157.

Garber, Lee O. "Where Church-State Feelings Now Put the Schools," *Nation's Schools* (June 1965), pp. 42–44.

Greely, Andrew M. "Catholic Education," *America* (April 17, 1965), pp. 22–28.

Green, Edith, and Walter P. Reuther. *Education and the Public Good.* Cambridge, Mass.: Harvard University Press, 1964.

Lieberman, Myron. "Teachers' Strikes: Acceptable Strategy?" *Phi Delta Kappan* (January 1965), pp. 237–240.

———. "Who Speaks for Teachers?" *Saturday Review* (June 19, 1965), pp. 64–66, 74–75.

Macdonald, James B. "Myths About Instruction," *Educational Leadership* (May 1965), pp. 571–576, 609, 611, 613, 614–617.

Mackenzie, Gordon N. "The School in a Political Setting," *Educational Leadership* (November 1964), pp. 75–77.

Megel, Carl J. "Teacher Conscription—Basis of Association Membership?" *Teachers College Record* (October 1964), pp. 7–17.

Metcalf, Lawrence E. "Poverty, Government and the Schools," *Educational Leadership* (May 1965), pp. 543–546.

National Society for the Study of Education. *Education for the Professions.* 61st Yearbook, Part II. Chicago: University of Chicago Press, 1962.

"Religion and Public Education" (Special Issue), *Theory into Practice* (February 1965).

Robinson, Donald W. "How Sinister Is the Education Establishment?" *Saturday Review* (January 16, 1965), pp. 56–57, 75.

Shedd, Mark R. "The Federal Colossus in Education—Curriculum Planning," *Educational Leadership* (October 1965), pp. 15–19.

"Special Report: The Elementary and Secondary Education Act of 1965," *American Education* (April 1965).

Stanley, William. "Freedom of Conscience, Religion, and the Public Schools," *The Educational Forum* (May 1965), pp. 407–415.

Steet, Marion L. "Professional Associations—More Than Unions," *Teachers College Record* (December 1964), pp. 204–218.

Stimbert, E. C., and A. R. Dykes. "Decentralization of Administration," *Phi Delta Kappan* (December 1964), pp. 174–177.

Stinnett, T. M., and Albert J. Huggett. *Professional Problems of Teachers.* New York: The Macmillan Company, 1963.

———, Jack H. Kleinmann, and Martha L. Ware. *Professional Negotiation in Public Education.* New York: The Macmillan Company, 1966.

Van Dorn, Harold A. "Efforts to Keep Schools Out of Politics," *Educational Leadership* (November 1964), pp. 93–95, 138.

Walton, John, and James L. Kuethe (eds.). *The Discipline of Education.* Madison: University of Wisconsin Press, 1963.

THE FEDERAL
GOVERNMENT AND
EDUCATION

WAYNE O. REED

The practical needs of the days ahead, together with the aspirations of our people, call perhaps more compellingly than ever in our history for leadership that is boldly creative.

We cannot afford to listen to those who would settle for standing still, for that in itself would mean a disastrous loss of ground. We must have leadership that is on the march . . . leadership that looks beyond the horizon. For it is beyond the horizon set by poverty and ignorance and inequality that we are now moving and must continue to move.

In no aspect of our life is this kind of creative leadership more necessary than in education. The inescapable fact is that young people today must know more. And there is a great deal more to know. Much of what is taught in high school today would have been beyond the depth of yesterday's college student. Equally remarkable advances are taking place in a wide range of technologies. Today's skilled craftsman speaks a different language than his father knew—a complex language that is translated for the rest of us into tools and machines and gadgets that help make ours the most abundant life man has ever known.

The prospects for education 10 years ahead can be wondrous to behold. We are faced with the opportunity to create a truly democratic system of education, a system of quality education, at every level, for every youth throughout the land.

Let us look at a recent projection by the U.S. Office of Education. Today 46 million youngsters are enrolled in public and private elementary and secondary schools. By 1974 the total is expected to soar to 54 million. This year two million young people received high school diplomas. By 1974 the number is expected to climb to three million, and continue to increase by one million per year. By 1974 we shall need more than two million teachers for these schools. By 1974 the

Reprinted by permission from the *Bulletin of the National Association of Secondary-School Principals* (March 1965). Copyright: Washington, D. C.

number of students seeking degrees in our colleges and universities will have increased 100 percent—climbing to about eight million.

As enrollments increase, as the costs of facilities and teachers' salaries move upward, the expenditure for education must also increase. This fact does not portend calamity. It portends wider horizons, if we have creative leadership.

For more than a century there has been a growing awareness, a consistent policy on the part of the federal government, that the job of increasing the supply of trained manpower is a national responsibility. The threads of federal aid have been woven into the pattern of education. Even before this country had its first President, the Northwest Ordinance of 1787 provided that each new state apportion public land for education.

The Morrill Act of 1862 was a continuation of the policy of granting public lands for education, but introduced a new approach. It specified the type of education which was to be provided: ". . . to teach such branches as are related to agriculture and the mechanic arts." The Act can be considered the first example of matching requirements in federal legislation to support education—concern with increasing the supply of trained manpower.

The passage of the Smith-Hughes Act in 1917 was the beginning of a new policy of federal partnership with the public schools. The purpose was to provide the skills needed in business, agriculture, and commerce.

Federal aid to education through the GI Bill was another major step in reflecting nationwide need for manpower development.

When the Russians successfully launched Sputnik I, the failure of the United States to be first in space dramatically focused the attention of the American people on our schools.

When the nation woke up to the realization that it was short of well-trained scientists, translators, and foreign language scholars, of mathematicians, and of specialists in a number of other critical subjects, Congress set about to close the gap with the National Defense Education Act.

NDEA represented a new congressional approach: It was a broadly conceived Act touching for the first time on the entire American education system—representing the consistent federal interest in trained manpower.

The purpose of the Act spelled out in no uncertain terms that improvement of quality education was vital to the defense of the country. "The Congress hereby finds and declares that the security of the Nation requires the fullest development of the mental resources and technical skills of its young men and women." The continuing concern of the federal government to invest more of America's resources in people led to the historic enactments of the 88th Congress—sometimes referred to as the Education Congress.

Congress passed legislation for vocational and technical training, manpower development and retraining, higher education, medical education and graduate schools, teaching the handicapped, a broadly expanded NDEA and, most recently, civil rights and equal economic opportunities, encompassing nationally important education objectives.

I know you are well aware of President Johnson's emphasis on the importance of education. In the education message, "Toward Full Educational Opportunity," sent to Congress January 12, 1965, he said:

... during the periods when the country has been most astir with creative activity, when it most keenly sensed the sturdiness of the old reaching out for the vigor of the new, it has given special attention to its educational system. ... Once again we must start where men who would improve their society have always known they must begin—with an educational system restudied, reinforced, and revitalized.

We have reached the point in time when the needs of education and the needs of the whole nation are considered inseparable. But this concern of the American people places heavy obligations on the teaching profession.

Merely to provide schooling for all, helpful and essential though it is, is not the fulfillment of our national ideal. We are beginning to sense that something more is required. We need to emphasize quality in all our education.

To be sure, we see this new goal as in a mirror, darkly. In the words of St. Paul, we see it only in part, and we prophesy in part. Some people see the need for excellence as requiring more emphasis on education for children and youth of superior capacity. This work is essential. But, to quote John W. Gardner:

We cannot have islands of excellence in a sea of slovenly indifference to standards. In an era when the masses of people were mute and powerless it may have been possible for a tiny minority to maintain high standards regardless of their surroundings. But today the masses of people are neither mute nor powerless. I am not saying that we can expect every man to be excellent. ... All too many lack the qualities of mind or spirit which would allow them to conceive excellence as a goal, or to achieve it if they conceived it.

But many more can achieve it than now do. Many, many more can *try* to achieve it than now do. *And the society is bettered not only by those who achieve it but by those who are trying.*

We are making some progress. We are, for example, learning how to provide schooling for many children whose modest talents or handicaps would once have ruled them out of any school. We are making strides in the vocational rehabilitation of handicapped youth and adults. We provide college preparation and college education for thousands upon thousands of youth who could never have such opportunity in any other country. We are at least trying to lower the bars of economics and prejudice which have hindered many from getting the education which they sought and which our national well-being requires. There is a growing public awareness of what we have doubtless known in our conscience for a long time—that poor education and poverty are closely linked. This fact has stimulated educators to action on behalf of those in our society who are known as the culturally deprived.

But these efforts do not yet adequately provide truly suitable education for everyone. Anyone who thinks they do should ponder the thousands of immature boys and girls who drop out of our schools each year with all too little attention from us. He should ponder the lot of scores of thousands of migrant children whose educational opportunities are at best very limited. He should ponder the conditions and the consequences of our having such an increase of violence on the streets, and a disturbing number of delinquents—young delinquents and old delinquents—in our society. It is very, very questionable whether most of the individuals in these groups have had quality education. If we are going to commit ourselves boldly to the future of this nation, we must find new ways to reach these children. This will call for creative leadership, particularly at the state level.

Commissioner Keppel made the statement recently that "through state educational leadership with local autonomy, the American public school has been a prime contributor to our personal, social, and national well-being. It has kept education close to the people. It has been a moderator of conflicting issues, a harmonizer of special interests. It has provided a training ground for leaders and responsible citizens in our free and open society. It has long been a guarantee that no central agency could control the minds of our young, and a built-in safeguard that if mistakes are made at the state and local level, they can usually be corrected before becoming national mistakes."

I am convinced that a well-organized, adequately staffed and sufficiently financed state department of education will be the key factor in maintaining an effective decentralized public school system. The state department of education must be the major force to carry out the state's constitutional provisions and legislative enactments for the organization, management, evaluation, and coordination of the public schools. It should have the strength to administer mandated programs and establish adequate standards for local schools. It should provide leadership in planning and policy making, and disseminate necessary information on the condition of education. It should become a center for research and development activities, and assume major responsibility for the continuous up-grading of personnel in service.

In brief, the goal is to make education more rewarding in all subjects, at all levels, and for all students. This is a job for state and local school authorities. The appropriate federal role is to help identify the nationwide needs in education and to assist state and local authorities in meeting these needs.

The Office of Education is concerned with contributing appropriately to this relationship. Since I am sure you are generally familiar with the various grant programs, I shall briefly comment on research and development activities. The Cooperative Research Program has been an area of significant progress.

We are supporting a number of curriculum improvement projects, such as English and Reading, Social Studies, and Talent, through three types of programs: basic and applied research projects, curriculum study centers, and conferences and seminars.

In order to concentrate extensive human and financial resources on particular problem areas over an extended period, a number of Research and Development Centers are being established. The first of several new proving grounds are now located at the University of Pittsburgh, the University of Oregon, the University of Wisconsin, and Harvard University under an annual grant of $500,000 for each center. Here we hope to develop a healthy dialogue on new theories rather than defensive monologues on entrenched ideas.

A natural follow-up of this activity has been the expansion of the Demonstration Program for the purpose of displaying to the profession the new materials, methods, and programs proven effective through research. One of the important roles the federal government can play here is in funding efforts to produce a variety of tested new elements, so that the principal has a pharmacopoeia to help him to build a dynamic curriculum. The future looks bright indeed in this direction, but the process itself is unending, and the full growth potential is yet to be realized.

The vital link in the improvement of our great decentralized educational enterprise rests in the teacher-student contact, in other words, the learning situation. It is the major role of the school principal to set the tone for the optimum learning situation. If he fails to show concern for quality education, nothing very much happens.

As the principal is, so is the school. He is the instructional leader. He is the social engineer. He is the educational statesman. It is his responsibility to be aware not only of the objectives of education, but of the new sources available in curricular development, training of staff, new methodologies, and evaluative techniques.

He must be aware of the pupils' need for independent study and the development of skills. The objective being not solely the acquisition of knowledge but also of inquiry, since it is almost naïve to expect that information learned today will be the information needed tomorrow.

The principal must be concerned with the quality of the educational experience. Because quality is related specifically to the capacities of the individual student, he must be able to harness the teaching talent for children with many differences.

He must be willing to experiment with new administrative patterns. What is the promise for the ungraded high school where pupils progress at their own rate rather than in lockstep with those who are their chronological peers?

Teaching will become more differentiated, more demanding, as the curriculum is broadened and individualized for the bright, the handicapped, the deprived, and the emotionally different. This will call for master teachers and for flexible educational planning.

The principal and his staff must budget both time and money in order to keep up with the new knowledge—as individuals and as professional team members.

Education in the coming decade will be used increasingly as an instrument to serve the public interest. It has already become an integral part of the national effort to combat unemployment, discrimination, poverty, and delinquency. Education can no longer be considered solely the responsibility of the local unit. It will be used deliberately as a nationwide movement to expand individual opportunity.

The principal may well ask: In our zeal for excellence, our concentration on mass education, are we in danger of depersonalizing education, of allowing the student to become the forgotten man?

The basic concern in the school of high quality has always been, and must always be, *the individual pupil*.

There are some people who act on the premise that centralization of educational authority is necessary to solve our problems and to handle our difficulties.

I submit that decentralized educational control and management with shared responsibility and cooperation among local, state, and federal educational agencies is more than a tradition. This system is the best arrangement we could have to stimulate creativity as we face the challenges of the next decade. But creative leadership does not flourish easily, even under favorable circumstances. Creativity, like freedom and other priceless human attributes, comes only from resolute dedication and vigorous exercise.

THE FEDERAL COLOSSUS IN EDUCATION—THREAT OR PROMISE?

GALEN SAYLOR

That the federal government is contributing in a colossal manner to the support of education from the nursery school level through the graduate college is, of course, a fact. A mere listing of some of the important acts that provide federal funds for the support of education reveals the tremendous scope of federal participation in the educational endeavors of this country:

GI Rights Act (education for veterans), 1944; Aid to Federally Impacted Areas, 1950; Library Services Act, 1956; National Defense Education Act, 1958; Juvenile Delinquency and Youth Offenses Control Act, 1961; Manpower Training and Development Act, 1962; Health Professions Educational Assistance Act, 1963; Mental Retardation Facilities and Community Health Centers Act, 1963; Higher Education Facilities Act, 1963; Vocational Education Act, 1963; National Defense Education Act—Extension and Amendments, 1963–64; Library Services and Construction Act and Amendments, 1964; Civil Rights Act—Titles IV and VI, 1964; Amendments to Juvenile Delinquency Act of 1961, 1964; Economic Opportunity Act, 1964; Elementary and Secondary Education Act, 1965; and the Higher Education Act, 1965.

There are many other federal assistance programs, such as the school lunch program, the educational phases of the National Science Foundation Act, and a multitude of other forms of federal aid for education, broadly conceived.

FROM Educational Leadership, 23:7–14 (October 1965). Reprinted with permission of the Association for Supervision and Curriculum Development and Galen Saylor. Copyright © 1965 by the Association for Supervision and Curriculum Development.

The increase in appropriations of federal funds for education is even more revealing of the extent to which the federal government is making a gigantic effort in the support of education. The comparative report prepared each year by the U. S. Office of Education entitled, "Federal Funds for Education," shows that in 1945 $291,500,000 was appropriated by the Congress for the direct support of education and related activities; in 1955, this sum had increased to $1,523,700,000; in 1960, the amount was $2,324,100,000; in 1965, it was $6,328,907,000; and the estimate for the fiscal year 1966 is $8,711,131,000. This is to say that in two decades federal appropriations for the support of educational programs and activities have increased thirty-fold.

A further revealing fact is the increase in the amount of direct appropriations to the United States Office of Education for support of that office and the aid programs directly administered by it; the office received $34,336,483 in 1950; in 1960, it was granted $474,280,893; and it is estimated that in 1966 the comparable amount will be $3,905,708,000. This constitutes more than a hundred-fold increase in the direct appropriations to the U. S. Office of Education.

The best estimates made available to the House Appropriations Committee indicate that federal support for education, nursery school level through graduate college, this year constitutes one-sixth of all funds spent for education in this country, and that in 1965–66 it will constitute one-fifth of all such expenditures. The federal government is indeed a major source of support for education and the programs and activities which it subsidizes are widespread and far-flung.

THREAT OR PROMISE?

This stupendous amount of federal support for education is indeed both a threat and a promise to good education for children, youth and young adults in America. Let us explore both possibilities more fully.

THE PROMISE

Federal programs for the support of education in the United States show great promise for the development and advancement of the total opportunities for the education of children, youth and adults in this country for these reasons:

1. *Much greater sums of money become available for the support of the educational effort of this nation.* Obviously, the appropriation of more than 6 billion dollars directly for the support of education in this country is a huge sum of money and it represents a major contribution to our effort. If such sums of money were not available, the total program would of course be curtailed, or the citizens through local or state units of government would have to raise these large sums of money to maintain even our present effort.

2. *Extensive national effort of this size provides programs and services not possible or not feasible through local and state efforts.* Generally speaking, the program of elementary, secondary and collegiate education as it exists in this country is inadequately supported now by local and state agencies. The pressure everywhere on these units of government is to appropriate ever expanding sums of money for the support of

our regular program of education. Little, if any, of their revenues can be used for new services, new programs, and new ventures of an educational nature even if it is generally agreed that such an expansion is desirable.

Moreover, some aspects of educational development, by their very nature, should be undertaken on a larger base than is possible by local or state authorities. Many of the existing programs of federal support are of this nature, such as the programs and services provided by the mental retardation act, the cooperative research program, the research and development centers, the various curriculum projects and commissions that are extensively engaged in the formulation of new instructional materials and plans for various areas of the curriculum, the establishment of educational service centers, and many other endeavors of this kind.

3. *The federal government is able to support and foster the development of new programs and new types of educational undertakings that generally would not be undertaken by local educational authorities.* Generally local boards of education, state departments of education, and the power structure of local communities would not countenance or approve the undertaking of the types of new educational programs that the federal government frequently fosters and supports. Examples are the entire program being developed under the Economic Opportunity Act and most of the activities that will be possible under the Elementary and Secondary Education Act of 1965.

4. *Federal support for the existing educational enterprise frequently stimulates local and state agencies to increased effort in support of the regular and traditionally accepted program of education.* Good examples of such nudging are the Higher Education Facilities Act, which provides a portion of the cost of new facilities for higher education, Title III of the National Defense Education Act, which provided partial federal subsidy for the improvement of facilities and teaching resources in science, mathematics, and foreign languages, and the Vocational Education Act of 1963. Similarly, Title II of the Elementary and Secondary Education Act will induce many school districts throughout the United States to expand and improve library service and to develop much more rapidly than they would be inclined to do otherwise their library resources for elementary and secondary schools.

5. *The federal government has clearly demonstrated that it can rapidly initiate the development and support of new programs in areas of urgent need that become evident because of new economic, social and cultural conditions.* In my belief, the Congress of the United States and the educational agencies established by it have shown dexterity and willingness to move rapidly when great need for new kinds of programs is evident. Examples of this, of course, are the Manpower Training and Development Act, the National Defense Education Act, and the redesigning and expansion of the vocational education programs.

6. *Federal efforts in education serve to prod the pedantic, nudge the lethargic, and inspire the imaginative school officials and boards of education of local educational agencies throughout the nation.* Of course, we do have highly imaginative, creative, and aggressive educators and members of local boards of education throughout the nation, for it is such professional educators and scholars that advise the Congress

of the United States and our national leaders on new developments and new programs that should be undertaken. Nevertheless it is evident that far too many of our local educational officials simply lack the professional qualifications to invent new programs needed to serve adequately all of the educational needs of their localities. But once the federal government provides support for new types of educational endeavors, a political climate is created in which the pedantic are prodded, although sometimes reluctantly, into action.

7. *Federal efforts in support of education clearly demonstrate a desire on the part of the Congress to develop a total program for the education of all Americans regardless of any economic, social, cultural, or racial factors that may under existing local programs deny or curtail the equality of access to educational opportunity.* The widespread nature of the federal programs clearly indicates that the Congress is insistent that every American have the privilege of participating in the types of schooling and in educational programs that will enable him personally and individually to realize the maximum of his full potentialities regardless of any factors that in the past have restricted or curtailed these opportunities.

8. *The total federal effort in behalf of schools, colleges, and all educational agencies has fostered a new national interest in education and has made education a matter of great national concern.*

Everyone is well aware of the fact that the presidents of the United States in recent administrations, with the support of Congress, have been responsible for a reawakening and a revival of the American interest and concern for the education of its people.

THE THREAT

Yet there are also some threats evident in our present national efforts in support of education. Chief among these I detect the following:

1. *The stifling of the creativeness, inventiveness, and skill of discovery of local educational leaders and officials.* It is not, in my opinion, an inevitable corollary of federal participation in education that creativeness and inventiveness of individual practitioners, researchers, and scholars is stifled. Such an outcome, however, certainly is always a threat and such a possibility should be clearly recognized not only by the Congress of the United States and federal officials, but by the educators and citizens themselves so that conditions will be maintained that encourage stimulation of such inventiveness by everyone concerned with the educational enterprise.

The very nature of federal support itself makes possible if not encourages a situation in which those who administer the federal programs approve and support only those things that appeal to them or that carry out their ideas and desires. For example, in the cooperative research program decisions obviously must be made about what proposals to approve.

Similarly, in the establishment of research and development centers now under way in this country, someone must make a decision as to which proposal for a center shall receive federal support and which proposal shall be rejected. Whose philosophy of education, whose concept of what is good and what is not good, whose concept of what should receive the blessing of the federal government, and what should be denied its support are to prevail? Although these types of programs are at present only one small aspect of the federal participation, the possibilities here are very serious and indicate the nature of the problems that face us.

2. *Invidious control over the program of education itself.* Here I point to direct federal control of education through the acts that provide support for these programs. I believe that the actual curriculum and other types of educational programs provided children in the classrooms and schools of this nation must be determined by the teachers and their fellow staff members who guide and direct the development of learning opportunities and plan the total program of education for the children of a particular school and school system. Lessening the responsibility for such decisions by the staff of the individual school system reduces the possibilities for adaptability, flexibility, experimentation, innovation, and, most seriously of all, administration to the educational needs of each child enrolled in school.

The threat that such decisions will be curtailed as a result of federal support is a serious one. I see no threat in the national curriculum projects that have been substantially subsidized by the National Science Foundation and the U.S. Office of Education. The local school authorities and teachers still have complete freedom insofar as those programs are concerned to decide whether they want to use the instructional materials, plans, and the recommendations formulated by these commissions and curriculum development centers, modify them, use some aspects and reject others, or completely reject the whole project itself. These projects represent one of the very rich resources being made available through federal support for the upgrading of various aspects of the educational programs of the schools and are indeed to be lauded and encouraged.

The real threat, I believe, comes from control by federal officials over the educational aspects of the plans developed for carrying out some of these acts, particularly the Elementary and Secondary Education Act. *This act gives the United States Commissioner of Education authority to approve plans for carrying out the act and hence the conditions within provisions of the law under which grants will be made.* The Economic Opportunity Act, Title II, prescribes the nature of community action plans and further states that "The Director is authorized to prescribe such additional criteria for programs carried on under this part as he shall deem appropriate." This is the title under which many of the educational activities can be established for children.

Now being proposed to carry out provisions of the Elementary and Secondary Education Act are testing programs and programs for the assessment of educational outcomes that indeed, in my opinion, constitute a serious threat to the prerogatives of the teachers and local school officials in each school district, and hence to sound educational planning and administration. It is a very alarming development in the history of federal support for education that for the first time in its history the federal government is demanding that evidence be submitted by local school systems on the effectiveness of these programs.

Title II of the Elementary and Secondary Education Act requires that the local educational agency include in its plans, "effective procedures, including provision for proper objective measurements of educational achievement, will be adopted for evaluating at least annually the effectiveness of the programs in meeting the special education needs of educationally deprived children." Further, the Act requires that the local education agency report annually to the state educational agency "information relating to the educational achievement of students participating in programs carried out under this title." In turn, the state educational agency must "make to the commissioner periodic reports (including the results of the objective measurements required by Section 205[A] [5]) evaluating the effectiveness of payments under this title and of particular programs assisted under it in improving the educational attainments of educationally deprived children."

If this is not direct federal control over the curriculum of the schools, I do not know what federal control is. When you require a school system to report on the effectiveness of the program, you are requiring that school to report on its curriculum. Pure and simple. If the purpose of such a report is not to control the program, then why make it? It is presumed by the very wording of the Act that the Congress of the United States will use these reports on the measurement of educational attainment to determine what the nature of the programs shall be in subsequent legislation by Congress. And it should be pointed out that this Title of the Act is only authorized for one year and hence will be subject to scrutiny by Congress next year, at which time Congress will determine whether it wants to extend this program, modify it, or terminate it. Presumably, then, if the schools want to continue to receive such aid, they will have to establish programs that within even the next few months would demonstrate to Congress that they are "effective" with "effectiveness" in no way being defined or described.

As I state, it is to me a terrifying development that such provisions were written into the most recent federal program for the support of education. I remind the reader that *no such provisions requiring objective evidence of effectiveness were ever written into any other acts for the federal support of education in the entire history of the United States.* The land grant universities were not required under the Morrill Act to report to the Commissioner of Education and hence to the Congress of the United States on their effectiveness in carrying out the provisions of that Act; the Smith-Hughes law in 1917 made no such requirements of any kind on the secondary schools of the United States that accepted federal support for vocational education and neither does the new Vocational Education Act of 1963. No one, local schools, colleges who administer institutes, or any agency that receives grants for research projects or other types of money under the National Defense Education Act is required to report to the United States Commissioner of Education on the effectiveness of these programs.

Any one who has had such grants or worked with such programs knows that the federal government in the past had relied on the imagination, creativeness, and integrity of the local agencies to provide outstanding programs under the provisions of these acts. Why has the Congress of the United States suddenly written into its most recent federal subsidy bill provisions that require the local school to gather evidence on the effectiveness of the program and then to submit this evidence directly to the United States Commissioner of Education through the state educational agency?

Title IV of the Civil Rights Act, moreover, requires the U.S. Commissioner of Education to gather evidence on the lack of availability of educational opportunities because of race, color, religion or national origin—a provision that gives the Commissioner authority to study schools at the local level.

3. *Development of attitudes and modes of operation of dependency and indifference, of kowtowing to entrenched bureaucrats.* A third threat of federal support correlative to the other two is the possibility of the gradual evolvement on the part of local citizens, boards of education, and school officials of an attitude of indifference to educational matters in the local communities and lethargy in doing anything to improve the quality of the program. There is a serious possibility of a decline in local interest and concern for education as support and control from sources beyond the local community increase. Anyone who has studied closely schools and educational programs in European countries, most of which have highly centralized and nationalized systems of education, is well aware of the almost total apathy and indifference of the citizens of the local community about the state and conditions of the educational programs of the community. Certainly, there is a gross lack of any effort to introduce change, to experiment, and to innovate.

Although such a threat, obviously, is one of long-term development, I nevertheless fear a gradual weakening of the concern local citizens in many communities now have about their schools as federal involvement increases.

THE FUTURE

For the future, I believe the following things should be done:

1. Much greater support for the total program of education should be provided by the federal government. Federal support for education should double and then triple and then continue to increase in the years immediately ahead.

2. Federal support should be provided for a great variety of programs, projects and other educational undertakings of all kinds. The total effort of the federal government should reach out into all aspects of education and the funds should in large part be used to stimulate and support more comprehensive and extensive educational efforts than are carried out as a part of our traditional program of schooling in local districts.

3. A large part of the program of the federal government should constitute research and development activities of broad scope, such as would not be feasible for local educational systems or even state departments of education to undertake. A part of these research efforts should consist of broadly conceived and widespread efforts to assess educational outcomes and evaluation of the effectiveness of educational programs, but only on a basis that ensures integrity of local control over the curriculum provided pupils.

4. In providing categorical aid, the federal government should be certain that it supports only those aspects of the total educational program that represent a wise investment of funds. Philosophically and educationally, programs supported by the federal government should offer great promise for major advances in the education of this country.

5. All educational efforts should be correlated and unified through a common administrative agency at all levels, federal, state, and local. This is not to say that the school district or the school system itself must carry out and administer all programs, but rather that all programs whether receiving federal support or not should be part of a comprehensive and planned program of total education for all children, youth and young adults.

6. The administration of and carrying out of federally-supported educational programs should under no circumstances be placed in the hands of persons who lack extensive and adequate professional preparation for such positions. There should be no place in such federal programs for politicians not fully qualified by training and experience to administer such programs.

ADDENDUM

A serious intrusion by the federal government into the local administration of public school systems is now occurring under the general provisions of Title IV, Section 402 of the Civil Rights Act. On June 10, 1965, U. S. Commissioner of Education Francis Keppel, wrote the state commissioners of education about the plans being formulated for carrying out this Section. His letter states that "Congress has instructed the Commissioner of Education . . . to conduct a survey of inequality of educational opportunity in public educational institutions by reason of race, color, religion, or national origin. . . . It will attempt to deal with the problem of inequality by developing comprehensive statistical information and evaluation for items that educators agree are relevant to quality. . . . In my judgment, it is necessary to assess the relative importance of these by means of aptitude and achievement results if the survey is to serve its purpose. This part of the survey will be voluntary; that is, substitutes will be found for those local school systems which do not wish to participate in the program. In the schools which agree to cooperate, pupils in the 1st, 3rd, 6th, 9th, and 12th grades will be tested. . . . This survey will be done entirely at U. S. Government expense."

The U. S. Office of Education, a federal agency, therefore, has now contracted with a testing agency to carry out directly tests of achievement in American public schools. In further explanation of the program, the Project Coordinator of the U. S. Office, in a letter to state representatives in July, stated that "basically, the survey will examine characteristics of schools . . . that affect educational success." Although local schools may refuse to participate, the federal agency is selecting the school systems, merely asking the state departments to approve their selections.

Inasmuch as Congress required that the survey be made, presumably the results are to be used by the Congress to determine what further steps it should take to control the nature and character of educational opportunities in the local school systems of this nation. However laudatory legislation to ensure equality of educational opportunity may be, this legislation, and the steps taken by the Commissioner, part of which are based on "my judgment," to carry out the act, move us rapidly down the road of federal dictation of the curriculum and programs of public schools in this country.

ARE LOCAL CONTROL AND LAY BOARDS OBSOLETE?

DONALD G. NUGENT

A vocal critic of the schools recently wrote, ". . . the greatest single obstacle to a revamping of education in this country lies in the fact that the control and financing of schools is in the hands of thousands of local boards." This is a mild condemnation when compared with Mark Twain's earlier observation, "In the first place God made idiots. This was for practice. Then he made school boards."

Contrasting with these views was the opinion of the late John F. Kennedy, who said, ". . . . service on a school board is one of the most responsible and important tasks entrusted to the public-spirited citizen. Today when schools fill the most complex demands in history, the selection of the school board member is more vital than ever before not only to each community but also to the entire nation."

School boards are seldom ignored when public education is discussed. This indicates that school boards occupy a key position in our structure of public education and government. As Texas' State Commissioner of Education J. W. Edgar says, "In Texas, the floor for local school operation is established by law and state aid; the ceiling is established by local school authorities and their communities." This is true in most states.

Recent developments—such as teacher strikes and sanctions, state legislation in regard to course content and graduation requirements, federal legislation to encourage pupil testing programs and improve instruction in specific subjects, and foundation-sponsored experiments in educational television, teaching machines, and ungraded schools—demonstrate the growing importance of influences and controls from other than local sources. These developments also demonstrate that vacuums in local leadership are usually filled from other than local sources.

FROM *Educational Leadership*, 22:85–87 (November 1964). Reprinted with permission of the Association for Supervision and Curriculum Development and Donald G. Nugent. Copyright © 1964 by the Association for Supervision and Curriculum Development.

These developments, however, do not necessarily imply that local control is obsolete. Rather they imply that those responsible for local control have been naive. Teachers and their organizations, state legislature and Congress, and foundations planning programs for local schools should have the advice and counsel of local school leaders—both lay and professional. The fact that these leaders have not exerted leadership beyond their school district lines indicates a lack of understanding and acceptance that public education is indeed a political issue deserving political activity. The fact that outside agencies have found vacuums in local school programs indicates that local control has not been as aggressive and progressive as our public has wished.

THE PUBLIC INTEREST

Public education, being public business, must be political. Public funds are raised and allocated through political processes. Public education is a subject of intense public interest—and public interest is the business of politics or government.

If a substantial number of school boards are naive enough to believe that public education and politics do not mix, they are not alone. A substantial number of professional educators are equally naive. Four recent studies offer ample evidence of professional educators' attempts to divorce schools from politics.[1] Thus, the public schools, which strive to train the leaders and the electorate for our political system, would play no part in the political system.

On the other hand, there is evidence that school boards are not uniformly either politically naive or obsolete. In Texas, which I know better than other states, school boards have an unusually good record of public acceptance of school bond issues; they have had public support for increased local property taxes; and they have encouraged the state to increase its contribution to education substantially during the postwar period. It is in the realm of finance for public education that school boards—and other school authorities—are most politically astute and active. On the state level, school boards generally have a good record in this regard; on the federal level, they have had noticeably less success.

In some other states, notably New York and Illinois, school boards through their state associations have been extremely active and quite successful in state politics for the public schools. In Texas, a young and growing state school boards association, working with state educational groups, has helped influence state legislation for educational improvements on several occasions. Local boards in the state have expressed growing interest in the association's providing a more frequent

[1] Jesse Burkhead, *Public School Finance: Economics and Politics* (Syracuse, N. Y.: Syracuse University Press, 1964).

Masters, Salisbury, and T. H. Eliot, *State Politics and Public Schools: An Exploratory Analysis* (New York: Alfred A. Knopf, 1964).

James A. Maxwell, *Tax Credits and Intergovernmental Fiscal Relations* (Washington, D. C.: Brookings Institution, 1962).

Gary S. Becker, "Investment in Human Capital" (Washington, D. C.: National Bureau of Economic Research).

and comprehensive legislative reporting service. This is obvious evidence of increased awareness of the state politics involved in public education.

INFLUENCE OF POLITICAL DECISIONS

The relationships between local, municipal and county governments and public school boards are as spotty as the local board-state government picture. In Texas, an ever-growing number of local boards are working more and more closely with these governments, particularly in the fields of taxation, recreation, health and planning. In those instances in which these local governmental units cooperate, better plans and programs are achieved at less cost to the taxpayers.

It is my belief that if there is an area in which local boards are nearing political obsolescence, it is in their relations and effectiveness with the federal government. They have not had the success in Washington which they have enjoyed in their state capitols and their city halls. Oversimplified, there are probably two reasons for this. First, local boards are less regimented in their attitudes toward federal involvement in public education than are professional educators. Second, local boards have no organized voice which can be heard in the halls of Congress or the White House. As a result, most local boards' major contribution to federal politics revolves around their decisions to accept or reject voluntary programs of federal assistance. Here, of course, the local voters hold the ultimate veto power.

RESPONSIBILITY FOR LEADERSHIP

If I cannot now agree that school boards are politically obsolete, this does not preclude the possibility that they may become so one day soon. Unless school boards find ways to be informed about political decisions which will influence the public schools and about ways to express informed opinions regarding these decisions before they are made, both local control and the school boards which are supposed to exercise such local control will be as necessary as the human appendix appears to be. Hope for the future improvement of school boards in exercising political leadership lies in school boards associations. Cooperative effect among school boards associations, professional educators associations, and other interested groups can be politically very successful for education. New York State's Educational Conference Board proves this.

Who are the people who serve on these lay school boards about which we are concerned? Over 90 percent of them are elected officials. Over 80 percent of them serve without pay. Educationally, they are well above the average population (nearly one-half are college graduates, while only 7.7 per cent are not high school graduates). In occupational classification over one-third are business owners, officials and managers; over one-fourth are professional and technical service personnel; only 1.8 percent are semi- or unskilled workers. A vast majority of school board members are also active members of civic, professional, business, and/or social groups which have both political and educational interests. It would be hard to imagine people such as these being politically obsolete. If they are naive about the politics of public education, it is because professional educators and school boards associations have not informed them of the potential political power which school boards wield.

Although I may not have convinced anyone else, I believe I have demonstrated my conviction that local control and lay boards are not yet politically obsolete. I am convinced, however, that unless local boards awake to their responsibilities of political leadership both within and beyond their school district lines, the answer may be different within a relatively short time. It has been demonstrated that school board members can be a powerful and constructive influence on education and on local and state governments. More communities, more influential organizations and foundations, and more state governments need to feel this influence. And, somehow, this influence must be extended to Washington if lay boards of education, local control, and our American public school systems are to survive.

INNOVATION AND LEADERSHIP IN AMERICAN EDUCATION

JOHN W. GARDNER

I suppose most American presidents have believed deeply in education. A number of them have spoken eloquently in its behalf. And some, of whom John F. Kennedy was one, made vital contributions to its advancement. But for a president to describe education as the cornerstone of his administration's program, as President Johnson has done, is unprecedented. That intention of President Johnson constitutes the most significant development in our recent educational history.

This is an exhilarating moment for those concerned with our schools and colleges. Their needs have been brought emphatically to the nation's attention. But it is not a moment for complacency. What it means for those of us who spend our lives on the problems of education is intensive renewal of our efforts.

That, indeed, is the President's intention. He has issued a stirring challenge to us.

Reprinted by permission from the *Bulletin of the National Association of Secondary-School Principals* (March 1965). Copyright: Washington, D. C.

He has proposed that the federal government put some much-needed dollars on the line. And then he proposes to hand the ball back to us, as a President must.

In his message, he touched on something that you and I know very well, but sometimes choose to forget—that education needs more than dollars. It needs to be better than it is—not just somewhat better but a great deal better. We are not going to succeed in making it that much better, nor succeed in solving the major problems facing us without substantial innovation. Without such innovation, the new billions that are going to be poured into the system will simply strengthen and confirm outworn practices.

In thinking about the kinds of innovation our system needs, we have to hold in mind two aims that must guide all our efforts. They aren't the only important aims, but they are so fundamental that they bear repeating.

First, the final justification of all the billion dollar programs, all the lofty educational policy, all the organizational efforts is that somewhere an individual child learns something that he might not have learned, or grows in understanding, or gains in skill or capacity or insight. The hope of every true teacher is to find ways to awaken that young mind, to set it going under the natural propulsion of its own curiosity, eagerness to learn and enjoyment of competence. Every great teacher knows that the awakening is possible. Every true teacher cares whether it happens or not. When you find teachers who care and who have the capacity to evoke that awakening, bind them to you. No ingenuities of automated education will ever make them out of date.

I mention that obvious central aim only because we all find ourselves so busy with the complexities of educational organization that we are in danger of forgetting it. It is so easy to fool ourselves with numbers—of total school population, of dollars spent, of grades completed. It is so easy to imagine that when we are processing millions of children through school we are actually educating them. We may be, or we may not be.

The other aim that must guide our efforts is the goal of opportunity for all— and that doesn't mean equal exposure to identical environments, it means meeting each child on his own ground, providing the learning opportunities that are right for him. Our gravest problem in providing suitable opportunities for all is to achieve school desegregation, and we must keep it at the top of our list. But it is not our only problem. Economically disadvantaged children of any race may be inadequately served by the school system. And so, to lesser degrees, may all who deviate from the great middle range for whom most large-scale education has been designed; and among those who so deviate we can list the academically talented *and* the academically retarded, the artistically gifted, the physically handicapped, and others.

But large-scale education doesn't have to be designed that way. In fact, the notion that large-scale education must necessarily be designed for the average student stems from an archaic conception of large-scale organization. Properly conceived and designed, large-scale education can serve individual differences in a way that smaller-scale efforts could not afford to. The one-room schoolhouse offered much individual attention, but its capacity to serve the individual student was in reality very limited indeed. So is the capacity of a very small school district.

What are some of the high priority areas in which innovations are needed?

One is the whole area of teacher education and re-education. In my judgment it is at the top of the list. Let us not allow disagreements over this or that specific solution to divert us from the fact that we are *not* doing a good job. Or that we ought to be in full agreement. We are going to have to find or invent new ways of getting the job done. Anyone in the field of teacher education today who is not impatient with the *status quo* and eagerly seeking new solutions is more insulated from reality than he has any right to be.

Obviously another high priority area for innovation is the curriculum. It is a controversial subject today. If you ask seven mathematics teachers about the new math, you'll get seven different answers. And you don't need to be an expert on set theory to know that that's a lot of disagreement. But the moral is simply that it isn't the function of innovation to make you happy. And you must not imagine that what is at stake is in any significant sense a choice between the old curriculum and the new. We'll never go back to the old. The real choice is between the new curriculum and some alternative revision of the old, or some further revision of the new.

Curriculum improvement must and will spread to all fields. English is about to have its turn, as is social studies—and occupational, vocational and technical education—and every other subject at every level. Curriculum improvement today is hampered by the fact that we have very inadequate institutional arrangements for innovation. Science, industry, and the military services have magnificent facilities for basic research, excellent arrangements for testing new ideas, and sound procedures for putting proven ideas into practice. In the field of education we have almost literally none of these advantages. The Regional Educational Laboratories which the President mentioned in his message are an attempt to solve that problem. They will create fruitful alliances between the subject matter specialist and the experienced teacher, between university and school system, between innovation and teacher training, and among all of the various innovators concerned with education today.

There are a number of other high priority areas for innovation, but you know the list as well as I do. I'm going to mention just one more. We need some major *organizational* innovations in education. The supplementary educational centers described in the President's message represent such an innovation in organization. In fact, in the long run that may prove to be the most important thing about them.

We need substantial improvement in the functioning of our boards of education. I yield to no one in my admiration for the tens of thousands of Americans who do faithful service as school board members. But they are often defeated by the system of which they are a part. Some boards have no arrangements that will ensure the selection of outstanding members. Some boards have far too little insulation from politics. Some are under the tyranny of self-appointed community watchdog groups. Some are simply badly organized, so that they soak up the time of busy board members without commensurate results.

Mr. Conant has made it clear that at the state level, organizational innovation is badly needed. I am well aware that big-city school people are apt to be extremely skeptical of any move that would strengthen educational machinery in the state capital. Many of them believe that they have been treated shabbily by the state capital in the past. They consider that the most attractive feature of state educational machinery today is that it is too weak to do them much harm.

Weak it certainly is. But it is folly to imagine that such weakness is a virtue. The state has a role that *cannot* be played by the local district and *must* not be played by the federal government. If it isn't strong enough to play that role well, it will play it badly. If it cannot contribute to progress, it can often block progress.

In the American educational pattern federal, state, and local leadership must *all* be vigorous and effective. No one of the three should assume that it will be stronger if the other two are incompetent.

Turning to the federal level, there are many who believe that we also need organizational innovation there. The Office of Education has in my judgment had superb leadership from the present Commissioner of Education. I don't think that the educational community has even begun to understand what an extraordinary job Francis Keppel has done in behalf of American education.

Thanks to recent large congressional appropriations, the Office has been strengthened in ways that may enhance its effectiveness. But it is no secret to you that despite recent gains, the Office is still handicapped in a variety of ways. At this point I don't intend to discuss possible kinds of re-organization, but this is sure to be a lively topic in the immediate future.

So much for just a few of the kinds of innovation we are going to have to accomplish. Now what is the appropriate role of the members of this Association in the process of innovation? You do not have to be experts on all of the varieties of innovation that are occurring. But you *do*—and I say this with all the emphasis I can summon—you do have to create in your schools an atmosphere friendly to innovation.

Innovation is usually controversial. Attempts to accomplish it are often clumsy, and they are easily criticized by those who are not participating in it. But a system that isn't innovating is a system that is dying. In the long run, the innovators are the ones who rescue all human ventures from death by decay. So value them. You don't have to be one yourself, but you should be a friend of the innovators around you. And if you don't have any around you, you had better import some.

So now if I may return to the theme I had originally planned to discuss today, the theme of leadership, here is one vitally important leadership function for the years ahead: to create the environment in which innovation can flourish.

But let me discuss briefly your broader leadership role. Let me begin with a few comments on the nature of leadership in our society generally. I have been much amused by those people who believe that this country is run by a tightly knit power group. A sociologist, the late C. Wright Mills, was a leading preponent of that view. He spoke of the Power Elite. Many European intellectuals share the belief that this nation is run by a relatively small and coherent leadership group that operates behind the scenes. Perhaps they believe that no society could be as lacking in coherent leadership as ours appears to be on the surface. They imagine that there must be some hidden leadership that keeps the society from flying apart. But I think I have had a fairly thorough exposure to the leadership levels of American life, and I can tell you that there is no tightly knit leadership group in this country—not behind the scenes, not in front of the scenes.

The President of the United States is, as he has said on more than one occasion, concerned with all the people, all the regions, and all the factions in our national life. But he is just about the only one whose concerns are that broad. All other leadership in our society is segmental. We have leaders in business and leaders in government, leaders in labor and leaders in agriculture, leaders in education and leaders in the world of art. And as a rule, leaders in any one of these fields do not recognize the authority of leaders from a neighboring field. Often they don't even know one another, nor do they particularly want to. Mutual suspicion is just about as common as mutual respect.

I need not add that in the matter of leadership, American education mirrors the condition of the whole society. It is not tightly knit. At its best it is loosely knit, and at its worst completely unravelled. It's a mystery that it works at all. But that's how we want it, and that's how it is going to remain.

But the fragmentation places a heavy responsibility on all the scattered elements of educational leadership. The system permits great freedom of action. But if American education is to cope with the problems facing it, the scattered leadership elements must *occasionally* pull together to accomplish vital gains for the system as a whole. Not always, not even most of the time, but occasionally. And now is such an occasion.

This Association is an important element in American educational leadership. You can play a crucial role in enabling both the educational community and the society as a whole to respond to the challenge the President has placed before us.

Like all leaders in this society, educational leaders must be willing to operate in terms of the fluid and dynamic alliances between leadership groups that characterize our society. And educational leaders must live with and contribute to the balance between federal, state, and local levels in education. They must work in terms of the traditional American balance between governmental and non-governmental worlds. And they must establish a working alliance between their own professional community and lay leadership in the surrounding community.

It all sounds terribly complicated; and it is. But members of your group are superbly fitted to provide precisely that kind of leadership. Leaders in many other areas of our national life are relatively insulated from the realities of the American community. No one ever accused you of such insulation. If anyone should have a first-hand knowledge of the complex and untidy nature of American social organization, you should.

You live and work at a strategic level of the system. You are at the grass roots of American education yet your administrative responsibilities give you a perspective that reaches far beyond the grass roots. No group is in a better position than you to knit together the sprawling world of American education.

My final comment has to do with the task of leadership that we all must face with respect to the community at large. Just as the President cannot bring about a new era in education without our help, so we cannot do without the help of the rest of the community. In the long run, education will flourish only if the society as a whole believes in it—believes in it enough to try to understand it, enough to support it in discriminating ways, enough to protect it from those who would warp it to their own uses.

That is a message that you and I have to carry to the American people generally. *They* create the climate in which our schools will flourish or stagnate. *They* create the environment in which our children will either value learning or hold it in contempt.

In closing, let me say again that the history of American education cannot have offered many moments more exhilarating than this. The prospects never looked brighter and the problems never looked tougher. Anyone who isn't stirred by *both* of those statements is too tired to be of much use to us in the days ahead.

PRIVATE SCHOOL— PUBLIC SCHOOL

What Are the Issues?

EDGAR FULLER

American public education is by design one of the most sensitive and daring of our institutional innovations. It is necessarily fragile because its unity depends on continuous public support and operation of schools by the people of each state, adapted to maintain the flexibility and diversity in education required to permit effective local autonomy in local school communities. Impacts from national insecurity, desegregation and technological change have in recent years placed public education under exceptional political, economic and social tensions. The

FROM *Educational Leadership*, 22:88–92, 133 (November 1964). Reprinted with permission of the Association for Supervision and Curriculum Development and Edgar Fuller. Copyright © 1964 by the Association for Supervision and Curriculum Development.

result has been an unusual amount of discord over such topics as content and methods of instruction, pupil services, district organization, and especially local and intergovernmental financing. Public education has become more vulnerable than for many decades, and those among us who would curtail or eliminate it have become more active.

A contest over national policy involving both public and private educational institutions currently centers on federal legislation to authorize tax support of education. A secondary phase is developing which involves judicial definitions of constitutional limitations on private and sectarian school aid as authorized by some federal laws and as may further be authorized.

There are several reasons why the federal government is the principal arena for this fundamental controversy. In the first place, it collects two-thirds of all taxes, and spends in billions rather than in millions. The large, zealous, and well-organized groups that lead the movement for tax support of private education are a dominating political influence in Washington, with their strength conveniently concentrated where public school influence is weakest. They do less well in the state legislatures because state constitutions and laws unambiguously prohibit state or local tax support of sectarian institutions of education. At the national level, however, the ambiguous Federal Constitution tends to encourage efforts to obtain federal tax funds for private schools because federal taxpayers have been denied jurisdiction in court to ascertain the constitutionality of a federal expenditure.[1]

Under these circumstances there should be no surprise that private education is receiving increased tax support in the Congress. Public and private colleges and universities are tax supported alike. Federal funds for private elementary and secondary schools are increasing. Proponents hope for a breakthrough comparable to that in higher education. Leadership in these directions has been assumed by authorized agencies of the Roman Catholic Church, which operates parochial schools enrolling a large majority of all private school pupils in the country. These agencies oppose federal funds for public schools if for any reason their own schools cannot share them.

The principal proponents of tax support for church schools work zealously to implement religious doctrines and civil policies that require the Church, rather than all of the people acting through government, to assume primary responsibility for organized education beyond the home.[2] Public schools are authoritatively

---

[1] See the stimulating article by the late Edmond Cahn, "How to Destroy the Churches," in *Harper's Magazine* for November 1961. Here it is argued that if the principle of separation of church and state gets tangled up with legalities in courts, and self-pity among church members at the burden of financing their own sectarian institutions brings the churches to seek and use tax funds, the result will be secularized churches supported on the state's terms and stripped of independence to assert moral issues involving the state. Since 1962 Congress has rushed ahead of the courts, expediting what Cahn says will destroy the churches, so that now the courts may be the best recourse of the people to slow or prevent such destruction.

[2] Explained in detail in the Encyclical "Christian Education of Youth" of Pope Pius XI. Title XXII of the Canon Law deals with schools. Canon 1381 provides that the religious instruction of children in *all* schools is subject to the inspection and authority of the Church. Of course this is not implemented in the United States.

regarded as unsatisfactory for its members.[3] The combination of religious doctrine, church policy and strong political action supported from sanctuaries of organized religion poses a crisis for the public schools more fundamental than mere competition for tax funds. The real issue is the religious claim of primary responsibility for all of education both religious and secular, on the ground that the religious and secular aspects cannot satisfactorily be separated. Such an authoritative position is quite as difficult to reconcile with the idea of cooperative pluralism in American society as it is with the idea of public responsibility for the education of all the people.

Private and parochial schools operated for church members and others who may be admitted are constitutionally protected within American standards of religious freedom.[4] When financed by their supporters, such schools supplement without substituting for systems of tax-supported education available to all. The current difficulty is caused by hardships among users of nonpublic schools in financing as many schools as they desire, their persistent political demand for tax assistance for their own schools that teach their own religion, and more specifically their direct opposition to tax support for public schools unless their own schools also receive tax funds.

THE DRIVE FOR TAX SUPPORT OF PRIVATE SCHOOL SYSTEMS

There is a drive in Congress to provide federal tax funds equally to public and private schools for general purposes. This is the purpose of a bill introduced by Congressman James J. Delaney of New York[5] that would authorize general federal payments to parents of private school children and equal payments to public school districts for public school children. Bidding for constitutional approval, the payments would theoretically be for the individual educational benefit of each child in elementary and secondary schools in all states. The bill's sponsor calls it the "G.I. bill for children." Along with other proposals, it is supported by the forces seeking federal aid for denominational schools.

The Delaney bill differs only slightly in factual details, and not at all in legal theory, from the Virginia Assessment Bill which led to the adoption of the First Amendment. The Virginia legislation would have authorized tax funds to be paid directly to the taxpayers, who in turn would pay them to the churches of their

---

[3] Canon 1374 requires permission of the bishop of the diocese before Catholics may attend public schools, and has been extended by some diocesan authorities to include attendance at non-Catholic colleges. See references to St. Louis and Cleveland in *St. Louis Post Dispatch* (June 7, 1960); *New York Times* (June 19, 1960); *Lorain* (Ohio) *Journal* (June 8, 1958); *Washington Post* (January 26, 1963).

[4] *Pierce* v. *Society of Sisters*, 268 U.S. 510 (1925). Such protection applies to religious and private secular schools alike, but both must meet state standards for secular education. For reasons that go beyond our scope here, most states seldom define or enforce any substantial educational standards for these schools, although the minimum secular education program of the state can be legally enforced even over religious objections. The constitutional protection of religious liberty to operate religious schools involves no obligation of the government to finance them. On the contrary, the Supreme Court has repeatedly held that tax financing of sectarian institutions of education violates the "establishment" clause of the First Amendment, which protects religious freedom through separation of church and state.

[5] H. R. 320, introduced January 9, 1963.

choice or to general education. Madison and Jefferson defeated this proposal in Virginia in 1785, and wrote the First Amendment precisely to prevent such legislation as the Delaney bill from using religion "as an engine of civil policy."

The Delaney approach is a logical first step toward dividing all school tax funds from all levels of government among public and private schools on a per capital basis. Msgr. Francis T. Hurley, a representative of the National Catholic Welfare Conference, supported such legislation at a meeting called jointly by the American Council on Education and the National Education Association in Washington on February 8, 1963. He also promised church-wide opposition to every new proposal for federal aid for public elementary and secondary schools not including parochial schools, saying that this decision of policy is "irrevocable," and that it "will be implemented to the full." He said his organization was examining all present federal public school aids, considering whether to oppose them when they come up for extension or amendment in Congress unless they include parochial schools. This attitude is faithfully reflected by some Congressmen today.

Congressman Hugh L. Carey of New York has recited the great gains in the drive for federal aid for denominational schools and colleges in a recent report to his constituents. He began by saying, "The Higher Education Facilities Act is the first general college aid program ever enacted. It provides for loans and grants for both public and private colleges on a fair and equal basis." Up to the time of final decision in the House-Senate joint conference committee compromise on this Act (P.L. 204 of 1963), its sponsors claimed that it did not provide for *general* aid. Perhaps this view was assumed because the legal brief released in March 1961 by the Department of Health, Education, and Welfare, and approved by the Department of Justice, cast doubt on the constitutionality of *general* federal aid to sectarian colleges.

Congressman Carey feels no need for such fiction, however, and honestly calls the Higher Education Facilities Act one of general aid. It is the type of legislative precedent he seeks to establish at all levels of education. The Congressman concluded his report as follows:

This entire report could be devoted to our gains in education but to do so would be to slight our progress in many other fields. But before leaving the subject of education, I wish to emphasize that every bill we passed made adequate provision for fair and equal treatment for all students and all interests in education—public and private—without discrimination. In considering every bill that comes before my committee I will continue to urge that the basic American principle of equality in educational assistance at every level of government must prevail. In general education, our G.I. bill for junior is earning support steadily.

More recently, Msgr. Frederick H. Hochwalt and others from the National Catholic Educational Association have encouraged experimentation with shared time. However, Msgr. Hochwalt has informed a Congressional committee that even general adoption of shared time would not change the policy of his organization on federal aid to education. Much more substantive steps than shared time have been and are being taken to obtain federal funds for private schools.

LEGISLATIVE TACTICS

Pending action on more comprehensive legislation, proponents of federal aid for private schools have taken preliminary steps through a series of tactical legislative devices. These can be illustrated by the legislative history and the text of the Vocational Education Act of 1963 (P.L. 210), and by the so-called "anti-poverty" legislation signed into law August 20, 1964 (P.L. 452).

The new vocational education law marks the first use of federal tax-raised funds for vocational education below the college level in other than tax-supported and publicly controlled schools. One provision authorizes *direct* federal tax funds for private schools, higher institutions and other agencies to pay part of the cost of research and training programs or experimental, developmental, or pilot programs of vocational education below the college level. These project grants are to be made at federal discretion.

Another provision of this new law suggests an *indirect* approach by defining the term "vocational education" to include *contracts* for vocational education between eligible public school agencies and private agencies "to utilize existing facilities of private schools as a normal procedure." Private business schools and technical institutes were referred to specifically in statements on legislative intent involved in such contracts in a colloquy between two House Subcommittee Chairmen on December 12, 1963, but both their language and the language of the statute may be broad enough to include parochial schools. Said one of the chairmen ". . . it is the intent of this measure to grant as a normal administrative procedure the right of the States to conduct these programs in public schools *or under contract* in a manner which can most efficiently and economically respond to local needs and situations."[6] Thus the proponents of private school tax support are inviting local private school pressure on public school boards to divide federal funds between public and private schools by contract. A similar colloquy between two Senators was also made part of the legislative record.[7]

The "anti-poverty" law illustrates both the power of the proponents of federal aid for denominational schools in the House of Representatives and their resourcefulness in avoiding probable constitutional limitations. By whatever name they may be called, many of the activities to be undertaken under this legislation are formal education.

As introduced in the House, the anti-poverty bill recognized education as such. To illustrate, Title II authorized federal grants or contracts to pay for community action programs in ". . . such fields as education, employment, job training and counseling, health, vocational rehabilitation, housing, home management, and welfare." It provided that educational funds must be administered by local public school authorities, but that all children and youth would be eligible for the classes irrespective of their school connections. This would have been the rule whether the program was administered through a general community agency or directly

---

[6] Emphasis supplied. See *Congressional Record* (December 12, 1963), pp. 23112–23113.
[7] See *Congressional Record* (December 13, 1963), p. 23307.

from the federal director of the program to the local school in cases where such was authorized.

The private school forces fought against this arrangement vigorously in the House Education and Labor Committee, and succeeded in eliminating it. The category of "education" was eliminated entirely, along with any specific reference to public schools. Trying to make "welfare" out of "education" for obvious reasons, "education" was reworded to become "special remedial and other noncurricular educational assistance." Then the provision for public school management of federal funds for education was replaced by the following prohibition: "No grant or contract authorized under this part may provide for general aid to elementary or secondary education in any school or school system."

Under P.L. 452 as enacted, the federal director is fully authorized to pay part or all of the costs of anti-poverty programs approved by him and administered by public or private nonprofit agencies, or combination thereof also approved by him.[8] Private agencies, including schools, may conduct the only "anti-poverty" program in a community, if named by the federal director to do so. This is the policy of all parts of the legislation. Except for work by trainees on ". . . projects involving the construction, operation, or maintenance of so much of any facility used or to be used for sectarian instruction or as a place for religious worship,"[9] or sponsorship of a project by a political party,[10] the personal restraint of the federal director will be the measure of a federal restraint on tax support of nonprofit private institutions on any project under Titles I and II of the Act not vetoed by the governor of the state where it is located.[11]

WHY SHOULD AMERICANS BE CONCERNED?

It is fair to ask how the public schools would be damaged if private and sectarian schools should share tax funds with them. The dividing of tax funds would mean the splintering of elementary and secondary education into denominational and other private schools and school systems. Four decades after Holland adopted a similar program, enrollment in its public schools declined from 75 percent to 30 percent of the total student population, with only the Protestant and Roman Catholic systems growing rapidly. A larger number of denominational and private school systems and special interest schools operated by nonprofit tax-exempt organizations could be anticipated in this country. The rate of decline of public education would depend on the amount of tax funds for private schools and necessary reduction of services in the public schools.

Our elementary and secondary public schools would be left to educate children from denominations too small to operate their own schools, the unchurched, the culturally deprived, and the rejects and problem students from the private schools which can choose their own pupils. Adding tax funds and private funds for schools

[8] P. L. 452, Title II, Sec. 205. Compare with H. R. 10440, Title II, Sec. 204 (a).
[9] *Ibid.*, Title I, Sec. 124.
[10] *Ibid.*, Sec. III.
[11] P. L. 452, Title II, Sec. 209.

segregated on the basis of religion, race, social status, wealth and special interests would seriously affect the public school as an effective educational agency in thousands of American communities. Its educational programs would necessarily be lean, its students and teachers could scarcely be expected to achieve high standards, and its community support for facilities and funds would be on a charity basis from the community power structures whose members would ordinarily be patrons of their own private schools.

Most serious would be the religious, social, political and economic divisiveness that would follow. In Holland almost the total of society is organized along the lines established in the three school systems. It is divided into Catholic, Protestant and neutral clubs, civic associations, political parties, merchants' groups, labor unions and trade associations. In this country the splintering of society would probably be even more serious because of the great size and diversity of our country and its people. The minority public school with its underprivileged clientele could no longer be an effective force for unity. It could itself become as divisive in many ways as the denominational and other private schools at a time when its great unifying function would be needed as much as at any previous time in our national history.

THE FEDERAL DANGER

The federal government is today moving into a position from which it could undermine the fiscal base of the public schools within a few years. This might be done through categorical as well as through general laws to lessen the constitutional risks. Once large federal funds have been made available to the states to match and distribute, with both private schools and public schools eligible under federal law, federal financial incentives and internal political pressures on the states promise to become irresistible in making private schools eligible for full tax support along with public schools. Thereafter, as soon as a number of states have been led to amend their state constitutions to permit state matching of federal funds for private schools, the next step could be the short one of a requirement in the federal law that private schools must be included as eligible under state law before any state can qualify to receive the federal matching funds for either public or private schools.

THE ISSUE OF SHARED TIME

SAM DUKER

Of the many current issues in education in the United States today one of the most important potentially is the issue of shared time. At a time when many private and parochial schools are finding great difficulty in meeting financial obligations, this plan offers a possible solution which would not involve the elimination of grades and even of schools. The entire question of federal aid to education, which has so long been stymied by conflicting views concerning the propriety of including religious schools as partakers of its benefits, might perhaps be solved by the general acceptance of the shared time concept. There are many advocates of both public and religious schools who see shared time programs as a solution of the dilemma existing as a result of hitherto irreconcilable differences in educational philosophy and views concerning the wisest policies to be followed in education.

Any plan which even presents the slightest potential for these solutions is important and worthy of consideration for that reason alone. This is not in any way to imply that there is a unanimity of views concerning either the desirability or the administrative practicality of this plan. There is still further conflict in the views presented concerning the legality of the proposal.

Shared time or, as some prefer to call it, "dual enrollment," is not a new concept but it has only recently been put into practice in a large number of school systems. The discussion of the pro's and con's of this proposal has taken place largely during the past two or three years. The widespread interest in this plan is, therefore, quite recent.

The concept is not a complicated one. Children who are enrolled in a private school (actually, in a Catholic parochial school in all instances I personally know of) enroll in public school classes on a part-time basis. While they are in the public school they are under its jurisdiction and follow the set curriculum in the subjects taken by them. These subjects are usually selected for their "neutral" nature in the sense that they do not primarily involve philosophy, ethics, or religious values. Subjects that have been taught in public schools to non-public school pupils under the shared time plan have included industrial arts, vocational education, home economics, music, physical education, science, foreign language, and mathematics.

Late in 1963, the Research Division of the National Education Association found that 280 school systems enrolling over 300 pupils reported shared time programs. On a follow-up, 183 of these schools reported in some detail on their programs.

FROM *The Educational Forum*, 29:235–241 (January 1965). Copyright: Kappa Delta Pi, An Honor Society in Education. Reprinted by permission.

Unfortunately, only a breakdown by states is given, showing one or more programs in each of 25 states, and no information is made available as to the particular school systems involved. The number of schools engaging in shared time programs is increasing by leaps and bounds and statistics for the 1964–65 school year should show a considerable rise. Among larger cities, the shared time experiment in Chicago commencing in September 1964 has attracted widespread attention and interest.

Certain benefits of shared time seem almost incontrovertible while others are less generally agreed upon. Some benefits often mentioned from the standpoint of the public school are:

1. A broader base of popular support for the public school is built up. This is sometimes reflected in votes on bond issues and tax increases.

2. Training in important subjects is given to children from non-public schools which might otherwise have been omitted. This helps fulfill the obligation of the public school to educate *all* children.

3. In the many communities where all children attend the public high school, shared time programs in the upper elementary grades help the transition of non-public school pupils into the public high school.

4. Added enrollment often results in the offering of a broader curriculum to public school children than would otherwise have been possible.

5. The tradition that public schools are open to all is supported.

6. The democratic tradition of the public school is implemented by the joint attendance of members of diverse religious faiths.

From the standpoint of the religious school the benefits often cited include:

1. The financial strain which has recently forced the abandonment of some grade levels and the closing of some schools is relieved to some extent.

2. Parents of non-public school pupils who have paid tuition in addition to sharing in the tax support of the public school obtain a direct benefit in return for this support.

3. The lightening of the burden of the religious schools enables them to enroll additional children. This is of particular importance to parents who have been concerned about the recent decisions of the Supreme Court barring religious observances such as prayer and Bible reading in the public school classroom.

4. Pupils are given training in subjects which it would be difficult, if not impossible, to include in the private school curriculum.

5. Religious training, which is the primary *raison d'être* of parochial schools, is expanded because of the pressure relieved by part-time attendance of pupils at public schools.

6. Relations between public and nonpublic personnel are improved, and the public image of the private school is enhanced.

An additional benefit claimed by proponents of shared time has to do with the matter of federal aid for education. It is common knowledge that one of the principal reasons for the failure of Congress to pass legislation for general federal aid for education has been the controversy about the inclusion of non-public schools sponsored by religious organizations among those eligible for sharing in such assistance. One view is that the Establishment clause of the First Amendment would prohibit such inclusion, while the other view is that the exclusion of such schools would be the grossest type of injustice. The result has been an impasse resulting in the failure to pass any federal aid bill. It is now suggested that shared time might serve to create a compromise acceptable to all. This is, no doubt, a rather optimistic viewpoint as there are numerous organizations as well as individuals who would oppose the very concept of shared time entirely apart from any question of federal aid. During the previous Congress, hearings were held on a proposed amendment to the federal aid to education bill which provides for federal aid to public schools operating shared time programs. The very fact that this is seriously proposed and has considerable support, both in and out of Congress, gives the whole subject of shared time additional importance.

Entirely aside from constitutional questions, which I will discuss a little later on, there are certain practical administrative difficulties involved in shared time programs. Among those most frequently cited are:

1. The obvious difficulties involved in scheduling
2. Transportation problems
3. Possible attempts to interfere with public school teaching on the part of non-public school personnel
4. The necessary adjustment of state aid formulas
5. The problem of finding space and teachers in already overcrowded and under-staffed schools
6. Record keeping and credit allotments
7. Differing marking policies of the two schools involved
8. Discipline
9. Meeting the financial cost

Two groups find the idea of shared time obnoxious for different reasons. First, there are those who contend that, apart from any legal limitations, the operation of this plan would be an objectionable and unwise breach of the wall of separation that should stand between Church and State. Second, there are those who contend that shared time would thwart the purposes parents have in sending their children to religious schools. It is argued that it is a fundamental assumption in religiously oriented education that religious values are intimately connected with each curricular area. Therefore, to teach any subject on a secular basis defeats the fundamental purpose of a religiously oriented education.

Most difficult to resolve is the question of the constitutionality of the practice of shared time. Opinions differ on the matter. No one is in a position to give a conclusive answer to this question until the matter is ruled on by the Supreme Court of the United States. It should be borne in mind that the subject of discussion here is confined to the question of constitutionality under the Federal Constitution.

The possible invalidity of the concept of shared time under state constitutions' provisions is not within the scope of the present treatment. Fifty differing state constitutional provisions would be involved as well as the opinions of state courts interpreting these constitutions.

The First Amendment of the Constitution of the United States provides in part that: "Congress shall make no law respecting an establishment of religion." It should first be noted that this is a prohibition on the Federal Congress, not on the individual States. It is only because of the interpretation given by the Supreme Court to the "due process" clause of the Fourteenth Amendment that this prohibition applies to the States as well as to the Federal Government.

Just what constitutes state action "respecting an establishment of religion"? Curiously enough, the first Supreme Court decision giving us a clue to the answer was one in which the First Amendment was mentioned neither in the briefs nor in the opinion of the Court. Nevertheless, in *Cochran* v. *Louisiana*, 281 U. S. 370, decided in 1930, the doctrine was laid down that when a State furnished textbooks to public and nonpublic school pupils alike, no aid was given to the private school since the benefit was given to the child. Thus was born the "child benefit" theory under which many forms of state, as well as federal aid have been given to individual children whether they were pupils of public schools or not.

This theory was confirmed in terms of the Establishment clause in the famous case of *Everson* v. *Board of Education*, 330 U. S. 1, decided in 1947. In this case the point at issue was the constitutionality of the reimbursement by a school board of a district which had no high school for transportation costs incurred by parents in sending their children to a Catholic parochial school in another school district. This practice was held to be unobjectionable in terms of the Establishment clause since the benefit of this policy of reimbursement accrued to the children and not to the religious school they attended. It is interesting to note that this decision is best remembered and most often cited *not* for what was decided, but because of the statements made concerning the necessity of maintaining a sharp separation between Church and State. Technically, such statements were *obiter dicta* (a legal term for matter included in a court's opinion which is not strictly germane to the issue involved and thus not binding on the court in future decisions in the same sense that relevant statements are) but it is these statements that are most often cited.

Justice Black, who wrote the opinion for the 5 to 4 majority, stated with reference to the Establishment clause:

The "establishment of religion" clause of the First Amendment means at least this: Neither a state nor the Federal Government can set up a church. Neither can pass laws which aid one religion, aid all religions, or prefer one religion over another. Neither can force nor influence a person to go to or remain away from church against his will or force him to profess a belief or disbelief in any religion. No person can be punished for entertaining or professing religious beliefs or disbeliefs, for church attendance or non-attendance. No tax in any amount, large or small, can be levied to support any religious activities or institutions, whatever they may be called, or whatever form they may adopt to teach or practice religion. Neither a state nor the Federal government can, openly or secretly, participate in the affairs of any religious organizations or groups or *vice versa*. In the words of Jefferson, the clause against establishment of religion by law was intended to erect "a wall of separation between church and State."

Justice Black continued by stating:

Measured by these standards, we cannot say that the First Amendment prohibits New Jersey from spending tax-raised funds to pay the bus fares of parochial school pupils as a part of a general program under which it pays the fares of pupils attending public and other schools. It is undoubtedly true that children are helped to get to church schools. There is even a possibility that some of the children might not be sent to the church schools if the parents were compelled to pay their children's bus fares out of their own pockets when transportation to a public school would have been paid for by the state. The same possibility exists where the state requires a local transit company to provide reduced fares to school children including those attending parochial schools, or where municipally owned transportation systems undertake to carry all school children free of charge. Moreover, state-paid policemen detailed to protect children going to and from church schools from the very real hazards of traffic, would serve much the same purpose and accomplish much the same result as state provisions intended to guarantee free transportation of a kind which the state deems to be best for the school children's welfare. And parents might refuse to risk their children to the serious danger of traffic accidents going to and from parochial schools, the approaches to which were not protected by policemen. Similarly, parents might be reluctant to permit their children to attend schools which the state had cut off from such general government services as ordinary police and fire protection, connections for sewage disposal, public highways and sidewalks. Of course, cutting off church schools from these services, so separate and so indisputably marked off from religious function, would make it far more difficult for the schools to operate. But such is obviously not the purpose of the First Amendment. The amendment requires the state to be neutral in its relations with groups of religious believers and non-believers; it does not require the state to be their adversary. State power is no more to be used so as to handicap religions than it is to favor them.

This Court has said that parents may, in the discharge of their duty under state compulsory education laws, send their children to a religious rather than a public school if the school meets the secular educational requirements which the state has the power to impose. See *Pierce* v. *Society of Sisters*. It appears that these parochial schools meet New Jersey's requirements. The State contributes no money to the schools. It does not support them. Its legislation, as applied, does no more than provide a general program to help parents get their children, regardless of their religion, safely and expeditiously to and from accredited schools.

The First Amendment has erected a wall between church and state. That wall must be kept high and impregnable. We could not approve the slightest breach. New Jersey has not breached it here.

The decision on the legality of the shared time proposal must rest on the above language. Nevertheless, it is well to bear in mind that the Supreme Court can and sometimes has changed its previous rulings instead of following them. The reversal of the *Plessey* v. *Ferguson* ruling in *Brown* v. *Board of Education*, dealing with school desegregation, is probably the most familiar instance. It is interesting to note in this connection that Justice Douglas, who had joined in the majority opinion in the *Everson* case, stated in his concurring opinion concerning the New York State Regents' prayer, *Engel* v. *Vitale*, 370 U. S. 421, that "The *Everson* case seems in retrospect to be out of line with the First Amendment." It is also worth noting that the child benefit theory has not fared well in State Courts. It is true that State constitutions were being interpreted, but the language involved was not very different from that used in the First Amendment as interpreted in the above quotation from Justice Black's opinion. Nevertheless, since the *Cochran* case only the Mississippi courts have upheld the validity of furnishing textbooks to non-public school children while the courts of New York, South Dakota, and New Mexico reached contrary decisions. Since *Everson*, the highest courts of Iowa, Washington, New Mexico, Missouri, Alaska, and Wisconsin have ruled against tax paid bus transportation for non-public school pupils while in only one state, Connecticut, was this practice sustained as a valid one.

George R. La Noue, who has written widely in the area of school law, has stated three principles that can be "translated into concrete administrative practices which do distinguish aid to the child from aid to the school." They are:

1. *No religious institution acquired new property through the state action.* The aid went directly to the child or to the parent. No public funds went to the parochial schools directly or indirectly. In *Everson*, the state had no contract or relationship with any church or church school. Separation was maintained.

2. *The state kept complete control of the administration and spending of all public funds.* In *Cochran*, the state chose the books and lent them to the children, making no special arrangements for those books used by children attending parochial schools. In *Everson*, the local public authority made the rules and contracts for transportation and the children rode on "regular buses operated by the public transportation system."

3. *No religious use was made of what the state provided.* The textbooks could not be adapted for religious instruction, and Black noted that the permissible state-provided services for church schools were "so separate and so indisputably marked off from any religious function."

Under these standards it appears to me that the institution of shared time programs would clearly meet the test of constitutionality. No appropriation of public funds would go to the parochial school directly and only a strained interpretation could lead to the conclusion that such a plan would constitute an indirect grant of funds. Certainly it would be essential to the constitutional acceptability of the plan that the public school have and retain complete control over the shared time instruction taking place in the public school. The religious use made by the parochial school of the instruction given in the public school would be no more and no less than the religious use made of any out of school experiences of the pupils.

The argument made by opponents of the legality of shared time is that the "child benefit" theory of *Cochran* and *Everson* is unsound because aid given to a pupil is in fact aid given to the school he attends. It is obvious, so it is argued, that the parochial schools will benefit financially from shared time practices. This being so, it is said, the aid given parochial school pupils by a shared time program is an unconstitutional procedure barred by the terms of the First Amendment.

To my knowledge no decision has been rendered by any high court on the legality of shared time. Several legal opinions issued by State Attorney Generals have sustained the validity of the plan. If the practice of shared time grows at the rate it now seems to appear that it will, it seems not at all unlikely that before many years pass this matter may well be placed before the Supreme Court of the United States for its decision. It is, of course, possible that some state courts may in the meantime rule the plan invalid under the provisions of the particular state constitution involved. Such decisions would not be affected by a subsequent decision of the United States Supreme Court.

Since the legality of the plan will, of necessity, remain an open question for the immediate future, decisions on whether or not to participate in shared time programs will have to be based on matters of policy rather than on legality. There can be no doubt that policy in this respect will vary. In the meantime the issue of shared time and the various actions taken concerning it will be watched with the greatest interest and the closest attention by alert educators who wish to remain cognizant of current developments in American education.

THE SCHOOLS
AND RELIGION
The Historical Present

ROBERT ULICH

In view of the centuries-old interpenetration between government, religion and education, the First Amendment (1791) represents an astonishing act of legislation. Its far-reaching character has never before been so evident and at the same time so confusing as today, certainly much more confusing than the founding fathers ever anticipated. The Amendment says that "Congress shall make no law respecting an establishment of religion, or prohibiting the free exercise thereof."

To be sure, the First Amendment was never intended to drive religion and prayer out of the school. Rather it wanted to guarantee the right of the states to regulate their religious affairs independent of federal control. And, as Professor William H. Marnell has shown in his book *The First Amendment*, the advocates of disestablishment did not act out of personal animosity against religion as such,

FROM the *Harvard Graduate School of Education Association Bulletin*, X, 2 (Summer 1965), pp. 2–6. Reprinted by permission. For more extended remarks by Dr. Ulich on this topic see: Paul A. Freund and Robert Ulich, *Religion and the Public Schools* (Cambridge, Mass.: Harvard University Press, 1965).

whatever their personal opinions in this matter. They simply saw themselves confronted with the growth of rival sects, the Presbyterians against the Anglicans in the South, and the Baptists, Methodists, Unitarians, Catholics and other denominations against the Calvinists in the North. As a matter of fact, at several places disestablishment existed before the Bill of Rights, either out of convenience or out of respect for religious liberty or out of both.

It is also certain that our early legislators did not consciously aim at founding a "Christian nation," as so often has been said. Rather they considered the Constitution a political document to be kept free from the strife of religionists as much as possible. Nor is it correct to assume that the people of North America of the eighteenth century were altogether church-devoted folks. In his book *From State Church to Pluralism*, Franklin H. Littell, Professor of Church History at Chicago Theological Seminary, has proved the contrary. If the statistics (which I have to take on faith) reflect reality, not more than five percent of the population belonged to any church in 1776. The fact that at the present the majority of the American citizens are church-affiliated is largely due to later immigration and the changes in the cultural climate during the second half of the nineteenth and during the twentieth century.

However, whether the population of the early United States was more or less religious or secular (and we all know that church membership is no clear indication), the curricula and the textbooks of the time prove that religion was taught wherever there was a formally established public school. State establishments, according to Professor Paul A. Freund, continued in New England until the 1830's. Even Horace Mann, a liberal who so valiantly fought the educational backwardness of the Boston ministers and teachers, nevertheless wanted to save religion in school by reading the Bible without note and comment.

Nor did the majority of the teachers of the time of Horace Mann and even later object to religious instruction. Rather it was the intolerance of the clergy in regard to different interpretations of the Gospel that made it difficult and wellnigh impossible for the schools to transmit the religious heritage to their pupils without creating denominational protests. At the same time the growing number of immigrants of different faiths, some of them not Christian, aggravated the situation, while the growth of humanism, of atheism, of relativistic philosophies and of new scientific theories such as Darwinism created a widespread indifference, erosion and even hostility in regard to the Christian tradition of this country. Now nothing I believe, besides communism could more persuade the average American citizen that, whatever the past, he belongs to a "Christian nation"—so-called—than the belligerent attitude of Mrs. Murray who forced upon the Supreme Court its decision concerning religious ceremonies in the public schools.

THE PRESENT SITUATION

As is well known, legal decisions do not easily change the minds of people who believe in their defending a rightful cause. So it is also with the just-mentioned interpretation of the First Amendment by the Supreme Court. Thus one cannot be surprised that there is now a movement to secure a constitutional amendment that would permit voluntary prayers in public schools. According to my information, nearly one hundred and fifty proposed amendments have been submitted to the House Committee on the Judiciary. There is certainly a profound irony in the fact that a part of the Constitution, originally designed to allow the States the necessary freedom in matters religious, has now become not only a restriction upon their autonomy, but also on the religious freedom of local school boards and parents. Was it, so many people ask, logically cogent and historically wise on the part of the highest judges to go all the way they went? Indeed, the formal logic of law is not always the logic of history, especially when the experts disagree about the first.

Naturally, educators as well as parents are confused by the ambiguous language of the Supreme Court. Judging from my own inquiries from the East to the West of this country, prayers are still offered in a number of schools, and grace is said before luncheon. The argument that as a consequence of the pluralistic composition of the school population some pupils might be offended or at least embarrassed by religious exercises, did convince some, but not others who pointed at the chance given to dissidents to abstain from prayer or to leave the school room. Nor were these teachers impressed by the possible uneasiness of a child who has to display his nonconformism (or better, that of his parents) before his critical coevals. However, the school principals who attended a seminar I conducted at a Western university felt no desire for becoming religious martyrs themselves. They just continued the custom of prayer because they hesitated to offend the majority of the parents in their community. They would have preferred not to be bothered.

Interestingly enough, those who unequivocally supported the Supreme Court came from two opposite camps: the strict secularists on the one side, and the honestly religious believers on the other, the latter protesting that school prayers had often degenerated into a mere formality skirting on blasphemy. On the whole, it seemed the teachers were less excited about "the great debate" than certain parent groups to which the prayer decision offers a welcome change for righteous indignation and for quarreling with neighbors and schools.

But let us talk about the serious among the opponents. They are aroused by the fear of taxation of religious institutions and by the threat of an unhistorical disruption of national customs and symbols (which today have more of a patriotic and aesthetic appeal, anyway, than a deeply-felt religious one). But there are even profounder, though sometimes unconscious, reasons for the anxiety of many people. These reasons became clear to me when I read the book by the novelist Herman Wouk, *This is My God*. The author rightly believes that the Jewish people could not have survived the long era of persecutions without their faithful adherence to its rituals, festivals and prayers. May then the loss of the Christian past not jeopardize the future of *this* nation, just as the desertion from the Covenant would have jeopardized the survival of the Jews? Nations as well as men, though living on bread, do not live on bread alone.

Indeed, such concerns about the conditions of deeper cultural survival cannot simply be brushed aside as superstitious. For every historian knows that rituals, religious as well as secular, help men, families and whole communities to preserve their identity. Even a superficially understood ceremony may keep warm the ember so that it bursts into flames when survival is threatened. Many a German Jew who had rarely been in a synagogue became proud and spiritually supported by his awakening faith under Hitler's persecutions. The same happened, *mutatis mutandis*, with many Christians. And if rituals were merely a sort of decorative superstructure over the life of a body politic, why then would all revolutionary leaders of the past and the present have been so eager to replace the old symbols of allegiance by new ones to which they would like to attach a strongly emotional, almost religious, appeal?

Nor is the problem solved by the remark of the late President Kennedy that the home should take care of the child's religious education. How many do? And if they do, should home and school be divided?

Finally, the proponents of religious education are afraid that with the banishment of prayer (a merely negative act that they consider indicative of the abandonment of religion as a whole) the public school will devote itself entirely to instructional drill devoid of deeper meaning, to sport and other surface activities. Thus, as its enemies already assert, it will become more and more a "godless" institution. Patriotism, symbolized by the daily salute of the flag and the oath of allegiance, will then be the only gesture that points toward trans-individual values. But all forms of national incorporation of the individual (even those under democratic auspices) need, besides the horizontal line of collectivization, the vertical line that makes man conscious of his obligation to universal human values. No nation can decently survive unless it develops, together with the sense of national self-preservation, the moral urge to help the whole of mankind in its struggle for ever higher achievements. Only that political education which reminds youth of this fact is good education. Without this transcendent urge every institution will sooner or later become totalitarian.

As an answer to these predicaments, more and more parents will send their children to private and denominational schools. Indeed, several articles have already appeared in public and scholarly journals that predict that the growth of nonpublic schools, enhanced by the religious issue, may sooner or later force the public schools into the role of a minority.

I personally do not in the least deny that a comprehensive understanding of the sciences may help a person to transcend his ego and the boundaries of national interest just as much as religion, and that a deep understanding of idealistic, humanistic and existentialist philosophies can achieve the same result—certainly a better one than mere religious conventions. And so much have the established churches connived at, and enhanced, divisive and aggressive tendencies among men and nations that one may sometimes ask, "How much have they really contributed to the progress of mankind?" However, the modern national states have not behaved better. Humility and a mighty bad conscience are needed with regard to both the ecclesiastical and the secular powers.

THE MORALITY ISSUE

Then the question arises whether the future of the public school in the United States will be completely separated from the nation's religious heritage. The answer will be "yes," and Jefferson's famous metaphor about the wall of separation between church and state will apply to our public schools, if by religion is meant allegiance to a particular creed. But the answer will be "no," if the term "religion" connotes an attitude or a sentiment that expresses a person's reverential feeling concerning the cosmic powers that surround him, that nourish and sustain him and on which he depends in birth, life and death. Under this aspect, how can any sensitive person avoid religion, and how can any good form of education remain completely aloof from it? And let us assume that, as a consequence of a radically secular education, such aloofness be achieved, would not that also be a kind of indoctrination in regard to the metaphysical aspects of humanity?

Therefore, the Court's legal decisions concerning prayer ceremonies in no way relieve the American public school from its responsibilities for the whole and wholesome development of the student's personality. And no legal decision should be or can be a complete answer to the question concerning the inner relation between education and religion. Rather, after the liberation of the public school from denominational pressure, the conscientious educator should feel like a strategist who after a serious battle has moved his army into an advanced position, but knows that he will not be able to hold it unless he prepares his troops with a new spirit of initiative. Or, in order to phrase it differently, I personally regard the end of interference of political or ecclesiastical powers with religious convictions as one of the greatest, though not yet fully accomplished, achievements of the modern mind. For, among other similar events, I cannot easily forget that as late as in 1732—less than two decades before the birth of Goethe—the archbishop Firmian of Salzburg, a graduate from the Jesuit college of Rome, dared expel more than twenty-two thousand Protestants from his realm. But I would also be afraid of an atmosphere in our schools where freedom from religious indoctrination becomes an excuse for comfortable laziness with respect to the spiritual tradition of humanity. If education fails in this realistic appraisal of the situation, the victory over sectarianism will be a Pyrrhic victory, an impending defeat rather than a success.

However, so many people will argue, in raising the issue of religion in our schools, we raise at the same time the issue of moral education. For schools are not merely centers of learning. They should also be moral institutions as, so many parents will contend, true morality needs the support of religious convictions, just as the philosophical discipline of ethics, according to their opinion, requires the assumption of a metaphysical order. I have no intention to discuss this problem which is as old as systematic philosophy. However, in this context we cannot avoid the question of whether the school can discharge its moral obligations unless it moors its teaching to a religious ground.

Now, we all know that nonreligious or even anti-religious persons have been virtuous people and have educated their children accordingly, whereas many saints have arrived at sainthood after a rather wild youth, being as it were, disgusted with themselves. To confess it frankly, sometimes the suspicion has crept on me that some people might be so concerned with religion because they suffered from such severe conflicts of self-alienation that they lost the courage necessary for a normal and natural life as, e.g., that most influential modern theologian Soeren Kierkegaard. Subjectively, of course, these people are right and just as justified in defending and systematizing their inner experiences as their opponents. No doubt they have contributed decidedly to the deepening of man's self-understanding. But are they right objectively?

Furthermore, when I read about the moral conduct of certain pious folks, confessedly unable to imagine a school without prayer, against the atheist fighter Mrs. Murray (resembling the conduct of other pious whites against Negroes), then I have difficulty in discovering any positive interrelation between the public display of religion on the one hand, and moral behavior on the other. Or can anyone prove that French morals have suffered after the introduction of "morale laïque" in their public schools?

Finally, modern anthropological and psychological investigations concur increasingly with the old human experience that the only sound basis of personal development is provided not by ideological factors but by the example of the parents, the right mixture of love and discipline on their parts (especially that of the mother), and the natural relation of the child to his playmates.

Thus, rather than get violently aroused about religion inside or outside the school, should a nation not be grateful if it has a public school that teaches honesty, cooperativeness, truthfulness and the other virtues in the code of civilized societies? Why then add the religious issue to its many difficulties? And if the public school, as we hope, conveys to our youth a sound moral conscience, does it then not also provide a firm underpinning for a productive religious life? For even though religion transcends morality, what else is it but an aesthetic and vacuous sentiment unless it expresses itself also in moral action and commitment?

Nevertheless, religious people will always remain convinced that there is no first and second. Either religion and morality are jointly interwoven by early forms of education and indoctrination, or neither one will yield the full human harvest. And about this proposition one can and will argue endlessly. Neither party will convince the other.

THE FUTURE

Must we then leave the educational scene of the United States with a feeling of unresolved and insoluble conflict? No doubt the rivalry between secularism and transcendentalism will persist with all its intellectual ferment, but also with its dangers for the spiritual unity of this nation and of other nations too, for our whole modern culture reflects a split mentality.

However, are the defenders of the so-called "secular" public school entirely defenseless against the reproaches of the religious critic? In answering this question,

I may refer here to an earlier statement where I said that whatever the decision of the Supreme Court, it will never be able to divorce the religious from the educational spheres in our educational system. Somehow, the two will always encroach upon each other, simply because a good life refuses to squeeze the imminent and the transcendent into watertight compartments. The human soul is a whole; it cannot be bisected.

It will, then, depend on our teachers whether they want to be paid merely as "instructors" of a number of skills and knowledges, go home and leave the inner life of their charges to the chances of the environment, or whether they think that their pupils, while learning the so-called subjects of the curriculum, should at the same time learn about the meaning of these subjects within the larger meaning of human existence. There is a world of difference between the gladly forgotten drillmaster, on the one hand, and the teacher whom his pupils will later remember as a source of personal enrichment because he has shown them that the special areas of knowledge are not merely isolated islands on the *globus intellectualis*, but appear to the searching mind as integral parts of a "cosmos" or a "universe," instead of a "chaos" or "multiverse." If our teachers conceive of their mission in such a comprehensive way, they will educate free minds who, on the one hand, appreciate the depth in man's religious tradition, but to whom, on the other hand, the old denominational and dualistic conflicts appear secondary, if not inhibitive to, the formation of a unifying world outlook, or a Weltanschauung.

If a teacher who possesses such an understanding of human existence and would like to convey it also to his pupils, if such a teacher is in charge of mathematics, he will make it clear to his pupils that mathematics is not merely a series of tricks, but the language of measure. He will show them that it was the discovery of measures and proportions existing in the world as we see it that made curious astronomers out of the Babylonian and Mexican priests and caused a Pythagoras to marvel at the relation between numerical ratios and certain regularities in the physical world. Most great mathematicians were philosophers of a kind, sometimes very great ones, and many, if not most, of the great philosophers were mathematicians. Also music and mathematics have always been akin. Johann Sebastian Bach, so I have been told, wrote mathematical formulae on the margins of his compositions. And if you study the minds of the great mathematicians who originated the scientific revolution in the seventeenth century, you will see that they did not merely wish to produce new empirical data, but that they were inspired by the desire to discover the deep inner harmony in the multifarious events of the universe. Constantly, their search bordered on both, the religious and the aesthetic.

And if mathematics and the sciences, imaginatively taught, can help the student to see the world in a mood of philosophical curiosity, how could it be possible for a teacher of literature to conceal from his students the intimate kinship between a country's poetry and its religion? Similarly, a teacher of history must be mentally blind who fails to explain to his students the interrelation between religion and the great landmarks of culture—between the rise of Christianity and the decay of the spiritual and social foundations of the Roman Empire, between the disintegration of medieval Christianity and the emergence of the Renaissance and the Reformation, between the corruption of churches and the growth of liberalism during the eighteenth century, or between the retardedness of Russian orthodoxy and the victories of communism in our time. No doubt, such a historical perspective would create exciting discussions about our present when our old national states are confronted with the idea of mankind, and our old religious denominations with the idea of a world religion.

TO THE TEACHER

But will we have the teachers who can combine the sincere desire for objectivity (more we cannot demand) with the capacity for creative inspiration?

The answer will depend on the spirit of the institutions entrusted with the professional preparation of our teachers. There is now a tendency even among schools of education to relegate the teaching of the broad cultural subjects to departments in the university at large. Indeed, that is necessary. For what, after all, does the liberal arts college exist? The first pamphlet that I published in this country, with the title "On the Reform of Educational Research," resulted more or less from my disappointment in the lack of cooperation between the schools of education and the university as a whole. If the latter does not feel the obligation to widen the cultural horizon of the future teacher, the departments of education will work against insurmountable odds.

But I also know that mere scholarly knowledge of a subject does not yet make a good teacher. Necessary as it is, it is not enough. Just as important is the teacher's capacity for getting intellectual materials out of the academic storehouses where they have accumulated in the course of centuries of specialization, and rendering them vital and meaningful to the young learner. Only in very rare cases can this process of transformation be taught by the typical academic courses in the sciences and the humanities. It is even not their purpose. Nor can it be their purpose to relate their instruction to the functions and responsibilities that the teacher will have to discharge in his community. Our society expects from him more than the instructing of children; rather, it wants his advice concerning the guidance of the young, the resolutions of parent councils and the educational policy of the town. If a community considers the teacher merely a person hired for cramming and giving grades, then it is the fault of the teaching profession itself. It has submitted too willingly to the American prejudice that the teacher should not mingle in public affairs and should leave the "pioneer spirit" to other citizens.

For these and other reasons the task of the schools of education, especially those on the graduate level, will become greater and greater every year.

There has now emerged an increasing number of people I may call "efficiency experts," concerned with the improvement of teaching and teacher education. We should be grateful for their advice as far as it can help the schools of education and the public schools to achieve better results in the various subjects of the curriculum. But in their aversion to the discussion of the broader human goals of education, these experts seem to forget that efficiency in learning, just as anywhere else, can be used for evil as well as for good purposes. It is used for the good only if it helps the maturing person to understanding the truth in Socrates' famous statement that the morally unexamined life is not worth living.

This continued self-examination that should be required from every educated person will confront our teachers with problems that reach far beyond the immediate utility of this or that subject of learning. What, after all, is the purpose of learning? Merely to provide a "union card" for this or that vocation or profession, now generally called a "job," or also for the formation of a full and meaningful life? Sometimes it seems to me that the confessed atheist and the agnostic are more interested in these eternal problems of humanity than the conventional Christian and the satisfied and well-paid specialist.

If our departments of education fail to understand their task of providing the competent, and at the same time searching, teacher, they will increase the dangers of modern mechanization, conformism and other depersonalizing trends in our modern civilization. If, on the other hand, they succeed in making the teacher conscious of his broad cultural mission, they will help our nation to survive both physically and spiritually and raise even the religious life of modern man to that stage of maturity where at the present, despite millennia of history, it is not, but where, for mankind's sake, it should be.

IS RELIGION BANNED FROM OUR SCHOOLS?

CLARENCE W. HALL

The United States Supreme Court in June 1962 declared unconstitutional the use of a brief, voluntary, nonsectarian prayer by children in public schools. A year later, another decision outlawed Bible-reading and recitation of the Lord's Prayer in classrooms. These two decisions aroused a storm of protest that still shows no signs of abating. Perhaps no controversy in the long history of America's public schools has evoked such an emotional backlash of anger and frustration, or so divided public opinion.

Basically at issue is the question: To what extent will Americans stand for their public schools' being denuded of all emphasis on America's unique religious heritage and on religious values generally? That question remains unanswered.

Religious leaders were split in their reaction to a proposal to upset the Court's rulings. Most Roman Catholics were for it, most Jewish leaders against it; Protestants were about equally divided. However, the laity of *all* faiths heavily favored religious observances in public schools. A Gallup poll in August 1962 disclosed that 80 percent of American parents approved such observances.

To Pray or Not to Pray? School people reacted variously. While representative bodies such as the National Education Association accepted the Court decisions without official protest, many state and local boards of education either openly defied the rulings or quietly pursued their former practices.

Some school boards used dodges to keep within the letter of the law. The school board at Manchester, N.H., for instance, substituted for prayer the daily recitation of the first and fourth stanzas of "The Star-Spangled Banner." Others used the fourth stanza of "America." Pennsylvania's superintendent of public instruction proposed "an inspirational period, silent meditation, and readings on religion's role in literature and history." In New York, the American Legion distributed book covers imprinted with a 60-word nonsectarian prayer, and urged schoolchildren to read it quietly at the start of the school day.

Elsewhere, school officials leaned over backwards to play it safe. Many teachers dropped all activities about which there was the slightest chance of controversy. Some school administrators even ruled out religious-holiday observances (such as Christmas, Thanksgiving, Easter), canceled invitations to clergymen to offer invocations at commencement exercises, banned Christmas crèches from school grounds. At least one school librarian removed all Bibles from the shelves.

Error in the Court? Behind all the agitation lies a deep public concern over the Court's decrees. Testimony taken at last year's Congressional hearings on a proposed amendment to the Constitution disclosed a conviction on the part of many Americans, including experts on constitutional law, that the Supreme Court had erred.

By reading into the First Amendment's prohibition of "any law respecting an establishment of religion" much more than its authors intended, the Court had in effect "amended the amendment"—not only usurping powers belonging to law-making bodies but arrogating to itself decisions traditionally left to local and state school authorities. By forbidding Bible-reading and prayer, as well as any and all "religious exercises," the Court had, in the words of Princeton's Prof. Edward S. Corwin, a leading authority on constitutional law, "itself promulgated a law prohibiting the free exercise of religion."

By pronouncing, for the first time in American history, the absolutist dogma that as between religion and irreligion "the state is firmly committed to a position of neutrality," the Court was, in the words of Episcopal Bishop James A. Pike, "establishing by judicial fiat a religion of secularism." This is surely a doctrine foreign to a land whose founders regarded religion as the bulwark of the state, who saw themselves accountable to "the Supreme Judge of the world," and whose citizens' rights to freedom and self-rule were "endowed by their Creator."

Criticizing the Court's decree, Erwin N. Griswold, dean of the Harvard Law

School, said, "This is a Christian country, in origin, history, tradition and culture. It was out of Christian doctrine and ethics that it developed its notion of toleration. The Muslim who comes here may worship as he pleases, and may hold public office without discrimination. But why should it follow that he can require others to give up their Christian tradition merely because he is a tolerated and welcome member of the community?"

In God We Do Trust. Americans, going to their history books, found little support for the notion that "separation of church and state" meant separation of religion from government. Thomas Jefferson believed that not only a nation's moral base rested on religion, but its civil liberties, too. "Can the liberties of a nation be thought secure," he demanded, "when we have removed their only firm basis: a conviction in the minds of the people that these liberties are the gifts of God?"

America's founders not only recognized the existence of God but wrote that recognition into their founding documents. Onto the new nation's coinage went words later adopted as the national motto: "In God We Trust." Into the Great Seal went Latin legends asserting that "God has favored the undertaking." Into the nation's patriotic songs went expressions of national dependence upon God; some of the stanzas are actually prayers in song.

Acknowledgment of America's strong religious base abounded in virtually every state constitution. Chaplains were officially appointed to all lawmaking bodies. Religious oaths were required for officeholders, religious exercises ordered for official ceremonies. To encourage the spirit and practice of religion, tax laws exempted church property and allowed deductions for gifts to religious cases; U.S. postal regulations granted special rates to religious magazines; draft exemptions were made for clergymen and divinity students. In contrast with Justice William J. Brennan Jr.'s dictum that "government may not support or directly aid religious activities," all the foregoing do precisely that.

"Metaphysical Handsprings." Against this background, many Americans questioned how the Court could possibly affirm that, as between religion and irreligion, this is a "state firmly committed to neutrality." Even some justices of the Court had misgivings about so sweeping a commitment, Justice Arthur J. Goldberg, joined by Justice John Marshall Harlan, wrote in his concurring opinion: "Untutored devotion to the concept of neutrality can lead to a pervasive devotion to the secular and to a passive or even active hostility to the religious. Such results are not only not compelled by the Constitution but are prohibited by it."

Newspaper comment was even more blunt. The Cincinnati *Enquirer* put its finger on the real reason for Americans' concern: "They don't like to be pushed around in religious matters; they don't like to be denied what they regard as historic rights. Most of all, they are disturbed by the receding role of religion in the nation's official life when immorality and corruption and apathy about waning standards of conduct seem almost rampant in the land."

Following the 1962 decision ruling out the New York State Regents' nonsectarian prayer, *The Wall Street Journal* editorialized, "Only a violent wrenching of language can produce the interpretation that the prayer establishes a religion. It does not augur well for the future to see our highest judges torture history and turn metaphysical handsprings to justify that which they wish to decide."

The New York *Herald Tribune* snapped, "Prayer in public schools should not be discussed as if it were some malignancy injurious to a child's well-being." Then it fell to worrying editorially whether the Court's "anti-prayer reasoning, if carried to its logical (or illogical) conclusion," would not lead to "the elimination of all prayers and religious comment from other public institutions and ceremonies."

Many Americans were persuaded that only a constitutional amendment would halt the anti-religious trend. Former President Herbert Hoover, who called the Court's ruling on school prayers an affront to "one of the most sacred of American heritages," said, "The Congress should at once submit an amendment to the Constitution which establishes the right of religious devotion in all government agencies—national, state or local."

Joining in the demand for an amendment were almost all of the 50 state governors, who at their 1962 annual conference resolved to "urge the Congress to make clear and beyond challenge the acknowledgment by our nation and people of their faith in God, and permit the free and voluntary participation in prayer in our public schools"—a resolution reaffirmed at their 1963 meeting.

Confusion in Congress. Congressional reaction was immediate. Into the legislative hopper went no fewer than 154 resolutions calling for amendment. Hearings on these resolutions before the House Judiciary Committee in mid-1964 lasted seven weeks, took 2774 pages of testimony from hundreds of individuals and groups, provoked endless headlines and editorials—and left most Americans as divided, confused and frustrated as ever.

The trouble was with the wording. Almost all the proposed resolutions were too narrow in scope, their aim limited to restoring the right of voluntary devotions in schools and other public places. The simplest and least-involved suggestion came from Bishop Pike who proposed that the amending be limited to a clarification of the establishment provision, making it read: "Congress shall make no law respecting the recognition as an established church of any denomination, sect or organized religious association."

In Congress, calls are already being made for additional hearings on this and other proposed amendments. However, it is doubtful that the battle to upset the Court decisions by constitutional amendment will be renewed in sufficient strength.

A Way Out? The question remains: How are we to restore to our schools—and to all public life—the recognition of religion's place in our society?

The answer lies in a scarcely noted paragraph by Associate Justice Tom C. Clark in the majority opinion: "It might well be said that one's education is not complete without a study of comparative religion or the history of religion and its relationship to the advancement of civilization. It certainly may be said that the Bible is worthy of study for its literary and historic qualities. Nothing we have said here indicates that such study of the Bible or of religion, when presented objectively as part of a secular program of education, may not be effected consistent with the First Amendment."

The challenge was plain: if teaching of religion in public schools was banned, teaching *about* religion was clearly encouraged. And in that challenge lay potential gains vital to both religion and education.

Vacuum at the Center. Over the years, teaching about religion has fallen to a low estate, and skittish school authorities have increasingly dropped all emphasis on the role of religion in civilization. The result, said Walter Lippmann, is "a moral and intellectual vacuum at the center of education."

Prominent religious figures such as Dr. George A. Buttrick, of Garrett Theological Seminary, have often deplored the vacuum. Finding in the schools "almost no room given to study about religion," said Buttrick, "we have by our silence indoctrinated children to believe that God does not exist. Or if He does exist, He doesn't matter—at least not enough to risk religious controversy. We teach the literature of Shakespeare: why not teach the literature of the Bible? We teach the life and sayings of Benjamin Franklin; why not the life and sayings of Jesus Christ?"

New Understanding. Education's higher echelons, too, have shown concern over the vacuum. Recently the American Association of School Administrators, which includes almost all superintendents of local and state school systems, appointed a special commission and charged it with producing a set of guidelines for those who establish school policy.

Meanwhile, many teachers and school boards are devising their own ways and means to do the job. Teaching the Bible as literature has perhaps won more practitioners than any other. In Indiana, almost two thirds of the public schools use the Bible in their literature classes, and a course in "Biblical literature" is an authorized elective for high-school students. Many secondary schools across the country have introduced courses in comparative religion. In Georgia, the state board of education asserts, most teachers are now including the Bible as a text in literature courses.

Teachers of history are making similar efforts. In California, public-school teachers are now required to include in their courses appropriate study of the role of religion in the story of mankind. In Texas, history teachers stress the relationship of church and state in the United States by discussing it in terms of specific cases reaching the courts.

Sociology offers another field wide-open to a study of religion's role in human affairs. One project tested successfully in New York schools divided sociology classes into small discussion groups, with Protestant, Catholic and Jewish students asked to explain their own faiths. Afterwards, students wanting more information on their own or others' faith framed questions which were then passed on to clergymen invited to lecture the class. In other schools, teachers of sociology take their students on visits to local churches and synagogues to learn of different religious practices. One reports: "This almost always promotes tolerance and respect for the different groups, without in any way weakening the student's own faith."

Though there is "a very fine line between advocating a specific point of view and teaching, impersonally and objectively, facts about religion," the AASA commission reported last June, "many teachers, exercising common sense and good manners, have proved they can handle this delicate task with propriety, fairness and objectivity."

Says one teacher whose school gave up its long tradition of classroom devotional exercises: "We had made just that polite little bow to religion, and assumed that was enough. I realize now how much more we can and must do."

Dr. Archibald B. Shaw, associate secretary of the AASA declared, "If we school people are up to its implied challenge, the Supreme Court's decisions may well turn out to have done more for both education and religion than all the legislative hearings and church pressures together. Now we can at last get to work at building a curriculum that will lead our young people to a steadily broadening understanding of the role religion plays in the affairs of mankind."

IS TEACHING
A PROFESSION?

LOUISE L. TYLER

This paper deals with the question, "Is teaching a profession?" There are two aspects to this question, both of which will be examined. First, does teaching require the attributes and characteristics of a profession? Second, do the practitioners in teaching positions possess these necessary attributes and characteristics?

Good, in the *Dictionary of Education*, defines a profession as:

... an occupation usually involving relatively long and specialized preparation on the level of higher education and governed by its own code of ethics.[1]

According to Everett Cherrington Hughes, who is one of our outstanding sociologists:

Many new and some old occupations have sought for themselves the envied status of *profession*; some of them succeed in gaining that esteem, that broad license to control their work and that social mandate over affairs pertaining to it that the term *profession* connotes.[2]

FROM *The Educational Forum*, 28:413–421 (May 1964). Copyright: Kappa Delta Pi, An Honor Society in Education. Reprinted by permission.

[1] Carter V. Good (ed.), *Dictionary of Education* (New York: McGraw-Hill, 1945), p. 415.
[2] Everett C. Hughes, *Men and Their Work* (Glencoe, Ill.: Free Press, 1958), p. 7.

However, there is no authoritative set of criteria that all students will acknowledge. One of the most insightful students of the professions, Abraham Flexner, in a paper entitled, "Is Social Work a Profession?"[3] gave six criteria that are widely quoted and are of value in the attempt to formulate a definition.

Flexner states: "Would it not be fair to mention as the first mark of a profession that the activities involved are essentially intellectual in character?" For example, medicine and law essentially involve the application of the thinking process to the solving of problems. Although physical skill may be involved in certain kinds of work, such as surgery, the skill is guided by intellectual activity. In addition, Flexner points out that where the use of intelligence operates so freely, there is much individual responsibility. The doctor, for example, must exercise great discretion in deciding what should be done for his patient. The doctor has taken on a risk—and he could fail.

The second criterion of a profession, according to Flexner, is that the profession resort to the laboratory and the seminar as continuous sources of new facts and ideas. Only by constantly utilizing the new knowledge developed in areas basic to the activity is it possible for an activity to continue its intellectual character.

The third criterion is that professions are practical:

No profession can be merely academic and theoretic; the professional must have an absolutely definite and practical object. . . . Physicians rely mainly on certain definite sciences—anatomy, physiology, pharmacology, etc., and apply these to the restoration of health.

The practical object is to preserve or to restore health.

The fourth criterion is that the objects of the profession be capable of "communication through an orderly and highly specialized educational discipline." This, of course, requires that the members of the given profession be agreed on the concepts, skills, and attitudes required for carrying out the objects of the profession. Once these are determined, the kind of educational program required for their development can be formulated.

The fifth criterion is that of "self-organization." Flexner comments:

Professional activities are so definite, so absorbing in interest, so rich in duties and responsibilities, that they completely engage their votaries. In addition a profession must be efficiently organized—standards of selection, of participation, of ethics, must all be formulated and adhered to by the members.

The sixth criterion postulated by Flexner, is that of motivation. Flexner suggested that, as a result of public opinion, professional groups concern themselves more and more about the achievement of social ends rather than about the rights or interests of the members. As professional development occurs, "the pecuniary interest of the individual practitioner . . . is apt to yield gradually before an increasing realization of responsibility to a larger end."

[3] Abraham Flexner, "Is Social Work a Profession?" *School and Society* (June 26, 1915), pp. 901–911.

I. Applying the Criteria of a Profession to the Teaching Act

Now, to answer the question, "Is teaching a profession?" we must *first* consider whether teaching requires the abilities, skills, and discipline implied by our criteria.

Intellectuality. The first criterion of a profession is that of intellectuality, applying the thinking process to the solution of problems. Does teaching require any intellectual analysis? Let us consider what a teacher must do in planning instruction for a group of students. There are three steps.

1. Formulate appropriate objectives.
2. Select and arrange learning opportunities.
3. Select and construct evaluation devices.

To repeat, is there any intellectual analysis required to accomplish these tasks? In considering the first task, it comes as no surprise that there is a good deal of controversy about the objectives of schools. Should the school be developing moral and spiritual values? Well-adjusted personalities? Is the basis for the decision about appropriate objectives entirely personal preference? Mutual compromise? What?

One procedure valuable in formulating objectives requires the analysis of data and information about the learner, about society, about subject matter as well as the utilization of a philosophy of education and a psychology of learning. Let us give a brief explanation of this way of formulating objectives for a high school class to show that a teacher's activity requires intellectuality.

The teacher assembles information about the abilities, interests, and needs of the individual learner. What needs do adolescents have? According to Robert Havighurst, there are nine needs or development tasks that adolescents ought to solve.

Let us suppose that adolescents in a particular high school are having difficulty in achieving one of these—the task of developing emotional independence of parents and other adults.[4] The students are unable to formulate desirable codes of conduct and they vacillate between being defensive to even minor suggestions from an adult, etc. A teacher looking at this kind of information about the class could infer several objectives:

1. Develop an understanding of the functions of family life and the responsibilities and roles of members of the family.
2. Develop an understanding of the developmental stages of human behavior.
3. Develop attitudes of acceptance of the stages of growth and development.

The teacher after inferring these objectives, must decide in the light of his philosophy and his knowledge of learning theory, whether they are desirable and attainable. A teacher who believes that the school's role is an intellectual one would consider objectives having to do with developing understanding appropriate.

---

[4] Robert Havighurst, *Developmental Tasks and Education* (Chicago: University of Chicago Press, 1948), pp. 30–55.

The teacher's psychology of learning also functions in the selection of objectives. Consider one of the objectives just inferred, to develop attitudes of acceptance for the stages of growth and development. A teacher with some background in psychology and a learning theory which holds that attitudes are learned would accept this objective as possible of attainment. Another teacher who holds that attitudes are dependent on basic personality structure and that they can be developed or changed only slightly, if at all, and generally only by therapeutic means, would reject this objective.

In addition, there are a number of other questions that pertain to this illustration, such as: What kind of community is this school a part of? What is the subject matter content of a good high school program? What is the intellectual level of the student's ability? All these factors must be considered if a teacher is to formulate a valid group of objectives for this class. The kind of thinking involved in planning instruction does require intellectuality.

Learned. The second criterion of a profession is that it be learned, that it be dependent on the laboratory and seminar for a continuous source of new facts and ideas. How does teaching draw upon them for new facts and ideas? Let us return to our previous illustration of planning instruction for a high school class. The procedure suggested for formulating objectives was to analyze data and information about the learner, about society, and about subject matter in order to formulate some tentative objectives and then to apply philosophy to determine whether the objectives are desirable and then psychology to determine whether the objectives are feasible.

At present, much knowledge about the learner is being accumulated from such areas as psychology, psychoanalysis, sociology, anthropology, etc. For example, for the teacher working with adolescents, material from Anna Freud is useful:

. . . We know that the character structure of a child at the end of the latency period represents the outcome of long drawn out conflicts between id and ego forces. The inner balance achieved, although characteristic for each individual and precious to him, is preliminary only and precarious. It does not allow for the quantitative increase in drive activity, nor for the changes of drive quality which are both inseparable from puberty. Consequently, it has to be abandoned to allow adult sexuality to be integrated into the individual's personality. The so-called adolescent upheavals are no more than the external indications that such internal adjustments are in progress.[5]

This information about the learner sets some limits on what teachers can hope to achieve with adolescents. Therefore, it is extremely helpful as a background for the formulation of aims. The upsetting of the inner balance results in swings of mood and behavior. The adolescent behaves inconsistently and unpredictably. However, even though the adolescent behaves inconsistently, the school can have as its aim the development of the intellect. It is not possible for the adolescent to master his pressing biological, cultural, and emotional problems directly, and the alternative is mastery through thought. Thinking strengthens the adolescent's ego,

[5] Anna Freud, "Adolescence," *The Psychoanalytic Study of the Child*, Vol. 13 (New York: International Universities Press, 1958), p. 264.

and consequently the school can make a contribution by emphasizing the development of the intellect.

Practical Object. The third criterion is that a profession have an absolutely definite and practical object. What might it be for education, or more limitedly and accurately for schooling? The practical and definite object of schooling is to develop the inquiring mind. This conception of the inquiring mind includes more than merely the outcomes of inquiry but also an understanding of the data which support them and the conceptual framework in which they are defined as well as inquiry into phenomenon for which problem, method, solution are unstated.

This choice of object possibly needs some substantiation, first on its general desirability and second, on its desirability for all participants. Its general desirability rests ultimately on the belief that the inquiring mind is essential if knowledge about ourselves and our universe is to be acquired. Its desirability for all participants rests ultimately on the belief that the object of schooling is identical for all students.

Communicability. The fourth criterion requires agreement on the knowledge and skills necessary for carrying out the object of a profession as well as their communication through an orderly discipline. Certainly, we can say that the teacher must possess some knowledge of the material which he is to teach and must also know about the various instructional materials and be able to use them adequately. Teachers must have skills for working with individuals and with groups. And teachers must have inquiring minds about the teaching process. Some of these knowledges and skills can be learned in courses established for his training.

Organization. The fifth criterion, that of organization with emphasis on standards of selection and participation and a code of ethics, is essential for education.

It would appear obvious that if the teaching act as described earlier is to be adequately carried out, prospective teachers must be selected in the light of their ability to do intellectual analysis, to acquire understanding and skills in various fields, and to develop the inquiring mind in their students, as well as to be inquirers into education. Selection to make certain that all who become teachers possess these characteristics is extremely important, for it is highly unlikely that only individuals possessing these traits will choose teaching as a career.

Codes of ethics are developed basically to guide a practitioner's behavior in carrying out his practical object so that humanity is served in the best way possible. Other functions of codes may be to discipline members of the group, to protect group members, and to educate the lay public. However, all these minor functions are important only as they contribute to the major one of advancing human welfare. Clergymen, doctors, lawyers, architects, accountants, engineers, and educators all have codes of ethics.

The significant question here is, does education need a code of ethics? As a basis for analysis, the act of teaching will again be used. The first step, that of formulating objectives, requires an understanding of the learner, society, subject matter, philosophy, and psychology. We found that the teacher needs to use intellectual ability as well as his knowledge. A teacher who fails to utilize his rational powers in formulating objectives but determines them in the basis of dogma, or as a result of public pressure groups, is unethical. Because there are many dogmas and pressure groups (well intentioned as they may be) in our culture, the student (and consequently the public) can only be protected by a teacher firmly committed to the use of rational powers in determining objectives. But, at the same time, the public is in no position to evaluate the teacher's method of making decisions. It is interesting to note the American Medical Association statement of Principles of Medical Ethics, on a similar point:

Duties of Physicians to Their Patients, Standards, Usefulness, Nonsectarianism

Section 1. In order that a physician may best serve his patients . . . he should not base his practice on an exclusive dogma or a sectarian system, for "sects are implacable despots; to accept their thralldom is to take away all liberty from one's action and thought." [6]

Another example from the field of education, a teacher might not have either the requisite knowledge or skills necessary to instruct in an area of the curriculum and the public needs to be protected from incompetence.

The medical Code in general, appears to assume capability or competence on a doctor's part. However, the code recognizes the possibility of incompetence but indicates its unacceptability as is clear from the following:

(Exposure of Unethical Conduct)

Section 4. A physician should expose, without fear or favor, incompetent or corrupt, dishonest or unethical conduct on the part of members of the profession. [7]

Because the public is unable to determine competence, adequate working conditions, etc., it is clear that education requires a code of ethics.

Motivation. The last criterion is that of motivation, or being concerned about social ends rather than personal rights or interests. Certainly, this is the goal we expect clergymen, lawyers, and doctors to subscribe to, but why? Probably, we make this demand because these disciplines deal with human beings in vital and essential aspects of their lives: medicine, the body; the church, the soul; law, the ascertainment of justice and mercy between two human beings. Frequently these vital problems occur at inconvenient times, and to the indigent, but they are so important, we expect them to be promptly and adequately cared for. And because for the majority of individuals intellectual growth and development is vital if they are to become mature men, and because this growth and development depends on what happens to individuals in schools as a result of their contact with teachers, teaching must also be more concerned with social ends than with the rights or interests of the members.

II. Applying the Criteria of a Profession to Teachers

The task of evaluating whether teaching, as practiced by teachers, is a profession is not simple. Unfortunately, teaching and the teaching act have not been studied

---

[6] Thorsten Sellin (ed.), "Ethical Standards and Professional Conduct," *The Annals* (The American Academy of Political and Social Science, 1955), p. 31.

[7] *Op. cit.*, p. 32.

carefully enough to build up a body of reliable knowledge. As a result, the evaluation of teaching as a profession is necessarily loose. (According to Flexner's fourth criterion, this looseness might automatically relegate teaching to the rank of an occupation.)

Intellectuality. Are teachers intellectual in their activity? There is no study which bears directly on this question. On the basis of personal observation and experience the majority of teachers do not meet this criterion. The majority of teachers function either by accepting the objectives and the instructional procedures and materials set forth by their schools, or by developing their objectives and instructional methods from textbooks which have been widely advertised by publishing organizations.

Learnedness. In our training of teachers, do we assume that teachers must be learned? There is some data available on teacher certification which may be of value here. The purpose of certification is to guarantee that the person holding the certificate is qualified to perform his duties. What can we infer from certification requirements?

According to Stinnett:

By September 1, 1960, a total of 42 states and territories (hereafter "state" will be used to designate the 50 states, the District of Columbia, and Puerto Rico) will be enforcing the minimum requirement of the bachelor's degree for the lowest regular certificate for beginning elementary teachers; and all states will be enforcing this minimum for high-school teachers.[8]

These data would certainly permit us to infer that some requirements of learning are essential.

However, since the number of teaching positions is greater than the number of qualified teachers available, the practice of issuing emergency certificates has been resorted to. LaBue points out that:

The issuance of current emergency certificates . . . continues in all but two or three states. . . . In recent years, the minimum requirements in years of preparation for emergency certificates have been advancing about as rapidly as those for regular certificates. Little gain, however, has been made in recent years in decreasing the proportion of emergency teachers employed. In 1958–59, the ratio of emergency teachers was 1 to 13; in 1949–50, it was 1 to 10.[9]

Data of this kind suggests less favorable ideas about the competence of many teachers on the basis of certification.

To determine how learned the teachers are who meet state certification, degree requirements may be of value, but we must also know what constitutes the degree program. It is well known that generally, the required median semester hours for

[8] T. M. Stinnett, "Certification Requirements and Procedures Among the States in 1960," *Journal of Teacher Education*, II, 2 (June 1960), p. 173.

[9] Anthony C. LaBue, "Teacher Certification in the United States: A Brief History," *Journal of Teacher Education*, II, 2 (June 1960), p. 166.

teaching fields are greater than for education courses. However, in many states, requirements for major teaching subjects are lower than in education and minors are even lower. Certainly, we must conclude that the certification requirements in some states make it possible to hire teachers who would be considered incompentent to carry out their duties in other states.

To further complicate the issue of whether teachers are learned or not, is the fact of assignment. A teacher may have a certificate, but is she teaching what she is competent to teach? Studies of how teachers are assigned would give more information about learnedness.

Practical Object. The third criterion is that of having a practical object, which for teaching, is to develop the inquiring mind. Few studies have any direct bearing on the inquiring mind, and no studies have been done to determine whether teachers have this conception of education.

However, studies that have been made of student achievement demonstrate well that students possess more information and greater intellectual skills (ability to attack cognitive problems) at the end of a course of study than before.

Other types of evidence which might be drawn upon are such as creativity in the various areas of knowledge—science, mathematics, art, music, literature.

Communicability. The fourth criterion is that the objects of the profession be capable of being taught. Our reply to criterion three seems appropriate here. Inasmuch as higher education is effective in passing on information and developing intellectual skills, the part of a teacher training program that includes these objectives can certainly be taught.

Unfortunately, however, there is considerable disagreement in the field of teacher education about what knowledge, skills, and abilities are required by teachers. In addition, even when there is agreement on the objectives of teacher education, the educational programs devised vary from one institution to another. This disagreement with regard to ends and means of teacher education could suggest that teaching does not meet the fourth criterion.

But, perhaps, Dr. Flexner's fourth criterion is in contradiction to his first two. That is, Flexner's first criterion of intellectuality, the application of reasoning to solving problems, certainly admits of the possibility of differences of opinion, for no two people ever reason exactly the same. If differences of opinion are admitted in this first criterion, logically there must also then be admitted disagreements about the objectives of a field of knowledge because they are arrived at by a reasoning process.

Flexner's second criterion of the learned nature of a profession, that is, the dependence on new knowledge from basic disciplines, can place an occupation at a disadvantage. If it is constantly attempting to integrate this new knowledge into its discipline, there is bound to be disagreement among the participants.

The very existence of these questions and the methods to be used in solving them confirm the opinion that teaching is a profession according to the first and second criteria.

Organization. The organization and ethics of teaching have been most thoroughly discussed by Lieberman in *Education as a Profession*[10] and *The Future of Public Education.*[11]

Lieberman in *The Future of Public Education*, concludes that the educational power structure has been largely ineffective and proposes a single powerful professional organization that will have full responsibility for educational policy on a nation-wide scale. Lieberman documents well, the lack of an organization in education to establish and enforce entrance and training standards. He criticizes the National Education Association, as a professional organization, stating:

> The NEA deplores low standards for teaching. In fact, the standards are low because teachers have no control over them, and they have no control over these standards because the NEA does not believe in it. Since 1921, at least, the NEA has advocated non-professional control of the state boards which set the standards for teacher certification.[12]

The existence of the National Education Association Code of Ethics is unknown to many teachers. That there is no enforcement of the Code is understandable according to Lieberman, because:

> It is a confused ragbag of platitudes and contradictions which would be quite dangerous if its enforcement were taken seriously. For instance, Section 1, Principle II, of the Code asserts that 'a teacher will adhere to any reasonable pattern of behavior accepted by the community for professional persons.' This presumably means that it is unethical for a teacher in Mississippi to condemn racial segregation.[13]

On the basis of Lieberman's analysis, we would have to conclude that teaching is not a profession by Flexner's fifth criterion.

Motivation. The sixth criterion, concern with the welfare of society, has certainly been emphasized in teacher-training curricula. However, whether this is the inner motivation of individuals who choose to become teachers is another matter. Of course, there have been many studies done to determine the reasons for selecting teaching as an occupation, using the questionnaire method, but these are so open to criticism on the basis of research design that the findings are of little value. A series of studies is needed to obtain evidence on whether teachers are altruistic and why individuals select teaching. It would be interesting to compare motivations for entering law, medicine, and teaching to determine similarities and differences.

Whether teaching meets this criterion or not, it is impossible to answer. The author would like to say, however, that from personal experience, she is very impressed with the devotion to children and to education that thousands of teachers show.

CONCLUSION

The teaching act *requires* professional status because it is basic to providing a quality education for all who attend our schools and colleges. If the teaching act

[10] Myron Lieberman, *Education As a Profession* (Englewood Cliffs, N. J.: Prentice-Hall, 1956).
[11] Myron Lieberman, *The Future of Public Education* (Chicago: The University of Chicago Press, 1960).
[12] Lieberman, *op. cit.*, pp. 184–185.
[13] *Ibid.*, p. 186.

is to be excellently executed, the teacher must be intellectual, learned, and altruistically motivated. And the teacher must have been adequately educated and carefully selected by professional peers.

However, if we evaluate teachers and the teaching act as it is now being executed, we can only conclude that teaching does not completely meet the criteria set forth by Flexner.

If teaching is to become a profession, educators must be able to explain and defend their professional positions on the important questions of ends and means in education. This can be accomplished only by systematically studying the problems of ends and means by appropriate techniques, which in turn, can be done only by able personnel.

TEACHER ORGANIZATIONS: AN ANALYSIS OF THE ISSUES

MICHAEL H. MOSKOW

The recent development of negotiation procedures between school boards and teacher organizations has had a strong impact on the teaching profession and on teacher organizations. Both the American Federation of Teachers and the National Education Association have developed their own concepts of negotiations, and they have made strong efforts to persuade school boards to conduct representational elections and to negotiate with the designated teacher organizations. To say that competition has been spirited here is to illustrate dramatic understatement.

Although the two organizations have been competing since 1919, the struggle gained new impetus in December, 1961, when the United Federation of Teachers, a local affiliate of the AFT, was elected bargaining agent for 44,000 New York City public school teachers. The UFT received nearly three times as many votes as the NEA's hastily formed contender, the Teachers Bargaining Organization. More important, though, was the fact that for the first time the labor movement gave active support, in the form of personnel and financial resources, to a local of the AFT. Shortly after the victory, the AFT joined the Industrial Union Department of the AFL-CIO, the major contributor to the UFT.

FROM *Teachers College Record*, 66:453–463 (February 1965), Teachers College, Columbia University, N. Y. Reprinted by permission.

Since that time, the IUD, headed by Walter Reuther, has been deeply involved in organizing public school teachers and conducting campaigns for collective bargaining. In response to this challenge, the NEA formed a department called the Urban Project to direct its fight against unionization. In the ensuing struggle, large sums of money have been poured into the campaign by both contenders.

NEA BACKGROUND

The NEA has a membership of over 900,000 consisting of "classroom teachers, school administrators, college professors, college administrators, and specialists in schools, colleges, and educational agencies which are both public and private." Classroom teachers in public schools constitute over 85 per cent of the total membership. One of the major beliefs of the NEA, however, is that since education is a profession unique unto itself, membership in associations should not be limited to classroom teachers. Therefore, *all* state affiliates and most local associations accept both teachers and administrators as members.

In line with its concept of professionalism, the NEA uses the term "professional negotiations" to distinguish its efforts at bargaining from the traditional collective bargaining procedures of the labor movement.When an impasse arises, it advocates various forms of third-party intervention, most of which consist of modified types of mediation and fact finding, requiring the bargainers to accept a decision of an impartial arbiter. At no time, however, does it advocate using state labor relation agencies or state mediation agencies since, in their opinion, disputes should always be settled through "educational channels." In extreme cases, when agreement cannot be reached, the Association may resort to sanctions ranging from publicizing unfavorable teaching conditions in a particular school district to a mass refusal to sign contracts by all teachers employed in the district.

In reality, "professional negotiations" is a generic term which the NEA uses to refer to a wide variety of different relationships between school boards and local teacher associations. For example, a local affiliate is considered to have a Level I professional negotiations agreement if the school board has made a written statement, which may be in the minutes of the board meeting, that it recognizes the association as the representative of all teachers in the district or even merely as the representative of its own members. Level II agreements consist of recognition and establishment of a negotiations procedure. If a means for settling impasses is added, the agreement is then considered Level III.

It is interesting to note that the Association classifies as professional negotiations a general school board policy statement which establishes a procedure for recognizing employee organizations, but names no specific representative of the teachers. In addition, dual and proportional systems of representation are considered professional negotiations. On the basis of this inclusive definition, it is not surprising that the NEA can claim over 346 local affiliates that engage in professional negotiations. It does not mention, however, that most of these local groups are merely recognized by the school board as the representative of their members or of all teachers in a district—often a far different thing from the actuality of meaningful negotiations in practice.

UNION'S RISE

Nationally, the AFT has over 100,000 members, the majority concentrated in large cities. The constitution grants locals the right to determine on an individual basis whether or not administrators shall be admitted as members; but few administrators join, and they are often prohibited from holding office or even voting on motions. Thus, the Federation emphasizes that it is the only organization specifically devoted to the interests of classroom teachers.

As expected, the AFT makes no effort to distinguish its approach to teacher-board relations from traditional collective bargaining. Although it does not advocate strikes as a means of settling impasses, the 1963 national convention passed a resolution (No. 79) which recognized the right of locals to strike under certain circumstances and urged ".... the AFL-CIO and affiliated international unions to support such strikes when they occur." This resolution is of special importance because previously there had been no official strike policy even though locals had been supported when they went on strike.

Although the AFT has been advocating collective bargaining for over 20 years, it has displayed no clear understanding of exactly what collective bargaining for teachers distinctively entails. In fact, the confusion over the AFT's definition of collective bargaining is quite similar to that exhibited by the NEA on professional negotiations. For example, although the AFT claims to have approximately 12 written agreements between school boards and teachers' unions, only four of them include terms and conditions of employment, while the others are merely recognition agreements. In addition, several agreements do not provide for exclusive recognition; and in two cases, the school boards have signed written agreements with both the NEA affiliate and the AFT local.

It is clear then, that in reality, many of the local affiliates of both organizations, while supposedly negotiating, are doing little more than making statements at open meetings of their school boards. It appears, however, that both the NEA and the AFT are aiming for a procedure whereby the school board and the teachers' organization would jointly determine the salaries and conditions of employment of the teachers. Only when this is achieved will true negotiations take place.

In terms of the effect upon school administration, no significant difference between the approaches of the NEA and the AFT seems discernible. Although there are broad ideological differences between the two organizations, the practical impact of their policies is almost identical. The school superintendent finds great difficulty in distinguishing between the NEA's "professional holiday" and the AFT's "strike." If it is often claimed that the AFT is more militant than the NEA, many local instances have been found to the contrary. When negotiations are conducted by either of the two organizations, essentially the same problems arise, and the participants assume essentially the same roles. And even the general tenor of negotiating sessions seems very similar.

Meanwhile, the battle ranges between the NEA and the AFT for the power and prestige that teachers' loyalties will bring and for the dominance of one broad ideology over the other. That battle is well reflected in the recent debate in the *Record* between Carl Megel,[1] representing the union, and Mrs. Marion Steet,[2] spokesman for the Association.

WHO COERCES WHOM?

Megel pictures the AFT as a strong defender of teacher rights and liberties. After labeling the NEA a "company union," he then attempts to document his argument that administrator coercion is responsible for most of the NEA membership. He presents examples of teacher contracts and salary schedules which contain clauses requiring membership in educational associations. He quotes from administrator bulletins to teachers, urging them to join educational associations, and he then questions the mystique of a voluntary membership of 100 per cent. After giving several other examples, he restates the AFT's position on the freedom of teachers to join organizations of their own choosing.

In explaining his criticism of administrator coercion to join educational associations, he claims that, "it keeps teachers weak; it denies them an opportunity for real leadership in an educational democracy." At another point, he claims that "an intimidated teacher is a frightened teacher. A frightened teacher becomes a poor teacher, unable to teach democracy properly to sons and daughters of free Americans."

Mrs. Steet takes up this challenge and, in her usual eloquent manner, makes the best of a bad case.[3] Her central claim is "*not* to justify any coercive or conscriptory membership practices of teacher associations or teacher unions, nor to attempt to prove that there is no coercion of membership in teacher organizations anywhere in the United States." Yet she later asserts that a careful study of Mr. Megel's documents ".... causes one to doubt seriously whether Megel has uncovered even a small coercion conspiracy against teachers." She does admit, however, that four of the bulletins which Megel presented "do say crassly that teachers are either required or expected to join specific professional organizations."

She then very cleverly puts Megel on the defensive by presenting a well documented case that the AFT engages in coercive practices. Mrs. Steet concludes that,

It should be noted that in all his efforts to round up documentary evidence of membership coercion in professional associations, the author has not submitted a single teacher *contract* within the decade of the 1960s containing a clause requiring membership or "service fees" to any professional association.

[1] "Teacher Conscription—Basis of Association Membership?" *Teachers College Record* (October 1964), 66:7–17.

[2] "Professional Associations—More Than Unions," *Teachers College Record* (December 1964), 66:203–218.

[3] Mrs. Steet has debated with AFT representatives before my education classes at Temple University on three different occasions.—MHM

APPEARANCE AND REALITY

Thus, although she claims that she does not try to prove that "there is no coercion of membership in teacher organizations anywhere in the United States," what she ends up doing is first, to criticize coercion of any kind to join teacher organizations; second, to attack Megel's evidence that there is coercion to join NEA affiliates; and third, to attack the AFT for engaging in coercive practices. She leaves the reader with the impression that there is no evidence to support Megel's contention that coercion is applied to teachers to join education associations, and that if there is any coercion (which she admits is wrong), then it occurs in such a small number of cases that it is of no great concern.

Unfortunately, this approach by Mrs. Steet is somewhat misleading. She would have been on much safer ground if she had said that the NEA realized that there was administrative pressure on teachers to join educational associations in some school districts, but that they were attempting to eliminate this practice. She could have documented this contention by showing that teachers are more active in the Association than they had been in previous years.

My own opinion is that anyone who claims that administrator coercion does not exist simply has not come in contact with classroom teachers. It is quite common for a teacher to be told by his principal or superintendent that he is expected to join the Association. Obviously, pressures of this type will rarely be overt or in written form because the practice of forcing a public employee to join an organization as a condition of employment is almost always considered illegal. This does not mean that informal pressures are any less formidable to the teacher.

Pressures will usually be similar to the type described by the Wisconsin Employment Relation Board in the following case:

It was found that the superintendent had unlawfully assisted the local education association in obtaining recognition on the basis of signed authorization cards checked by the school auditor, while at the same time, the superintendent told the local union affiliated with the Wisconsin Federation of Teachers to petition the WERB for an election if they wished to secure representation rights.

In a later case the Board held that

a school district, by the action of its principal in soliciting membership applications and dues and by selling tickets for the convention of the Wisconsin Education Association to the teachers employed by the school district, unlawfully assisted such organization and interfered with the rights of its employees to join or refrain from joining a labor organization.

Even though most pressures will be informal, a surprisingly large number of documented cases exist. For example, if Mrs. Steet doubted Megel's contention, all she had to do was to read a letter in the November, 1964, issue of the *Journal* of the NEA. Addressed to the Educational Policies Commission under the date of 10 September, 1964, it said,

I am a new teacher beginning my teaching career. As a part of my orientation, I was told that I *must join* my professional organization—the NEA. I have done so. However, I have been unable to find out just what I will receive in return for my membership dues and loyalty (italics supplied).

The 1955 report of the Committee on Government Employee Organization Relations of the American Bar Association contains the report of a study conducted by the NEA in 1952. In a survey of 1,516 superintendents, over 16 per cent reported that teachers were required to join education associations.

Further evidence of teacher conscription is supplied in my own survey of 150 public school teachers from three different sections of Pennsylvania. Forty-eight per cent of the respondents said there was administrative pressure placed on them to join a teacher association.

When presented with evidence that an administrator is forcing teachers to join, Mrs. Steet's response, typical of the NEA's attitude, is that "professional teachers should and do rebel against such practices. Moreover, the NEA and its affiliates encourage and support teachers in throwing off any such tyranny."

COERCION AND UNION SHOP

Things, however, are not quite so simple. It is unreasonable to expect a teacher to rebel against his supervisor when it may mean his job; it is equally unreasonable to expect the NEA to be with him at the barricades. A bit of analysis may help.

First, for example, it is necessary to separate the problem of *administrative* pressure to join teacher organizations from *organizational* pressure to join teacher organizations. The latter refers, of course, to the union shop issue, a controversy all its own that must be separated from the former problem.

Under the union shop, the majority of employees force a minority of employees to join their organization. Instead of being unilaterally decreed by the administrator, it is a right which an organization of employees has obtained through negotiations. If the majority of employees are opposed to the organization security provision, they then have the right to vote out the organization in a secret ballot election.

The union shop issue is basically one of "majority rights" versus "individual rights." It is often terms the "right to work" issue, but a much more accurate statement is "the right to work at terms that have been rejected by the majority of employees." Although this is a question on which reasonable men disagree, Mrs. Steet assumes that the union shop can never be educationally sanctioned.

Forced membership, however, is not necessarily an evil if it is controlled by teachers. Actually, it can be argued that if teaching is ever to be truly a profession, it will be necessary for teachers themselves to control entrance to the profession. Under these circumstances, forced membership into the teachers' organization becomes only an integral aspect of professionhood. A requirement of this type is far different from coercion by administrators, which usually interferes with the effectiveness of a teachers' organization.

Failing to recognize this distinction, Mrs. Steet lumps together the union shop and administrator coercion and then argues against both as if they were the same thing. Ironically, Megel agrees with Mrs. Steet on this point. His opening sentence is, "The American Federation of Teachers maintains that teachers have the right to join professional organizations of their own choice without coercion or intimidation." In a later section of the article he restates that, "The American Federation of Teachers has historically supported the right of teachers to join the organizations of their own choosing."

SISTERS UNDER THE SKIN?

Megel's views and those of the AFT are completely opposed to the attitude of the AFL-CIO. In fact, Megel's arguments are quite similar to those used by the Chamber of Commerce and the National Association of Manufacturers in their fight against the union shop. In arguing for a right-to-work law, the Chamber of Commerce states that, "A right to work law guarantees that an employee will have the right to work at his job without being *forced* by anyone—the government, an employer, or a union—to join a particular union."

As the AFT grows in size and wins exclusive representational rights in other school districts, their present position on teachers' freedom to join organizations will become less tenable. Local affiliates which have won exclusive representational rights will want to strengthen their position and thus eventually obtain union shops. A step in this direction has already been taken in New York City, where the UFT has negotiated a provision that prevents an officer of any other teacher organization from representing a teacher who has a grievance. In the near future, pressure from locals will force a change in the position of the AFT on this issue.

The NEA will find itself in the same situation. In fact, leaders of their local affiliates who were victorious in elections with the AFT have already felt the need to strengthen their position as the dominant organization. The Milwaukee Teacher Association, which won a representational election last spring, has petitioned the Wisconsin Employment Relations Board to deny the Milwaukee Teachers Union the right to a dues check-off and to prohibit the MTU from representing teachers when they have grievances. This type of local pressure will produce a change in the NEA's national policy, and eventually the NEA will have to find some euphemism for the "union shop" and begin to advocate it for "professional" reasons.

ADMINISTRATOR DOMINATION

Unfortunately, the arguments of both Megel and Mrs. Steet are somewhat misplaced. With the advent of collective negotiations, one of the most important issues facing any group of teachers is administrator domination of teacher organizations. In order for negotiations to be effective, teachers must be represented by an organization that is primarily concerned with their own interests. If an administrator controls a teacher organization, there is no guarantee that the best interests of the teachers will be represented at the negotiating table.

The NEA is correct in saying that teachers have a great deal in common with other educators (*i.e.*, administrators and supervisory personnel) because they are working in the same field. They do not recognize, however, that a teacher organization controlled by administrators will not be as effective in meeting the distinctive needs of teachers as will be an organization that is controlled by teachers themselves.

Whenever the subject is mentioned, administrators frequently assume that a personal attack is being made, and an objective discussion of the problem becomes exceedingly difficult. On the contrary, most administrators would never think of attempting to dominate their local organizations. But the fact remains that there are instances where this practice occurs, and where the threat exists at all, the classroom teacher clearly needs protection.

Since the supervisor has the authority to act in the interest of the employer, there is no assurance, of course, that he will act entirely in the interest of the employees. In addition, because of the great difference between the job of the supervisor and those of his subordinates, their separate interests may not be served best by the same decisions. Maximum benefit for the teacher can only be obtained when leadership of his organization is devoted exclusively to his interest. Thus, when a teacher organization is controlled by administrators, the conflict of interests is most likely to produce an unjust situation for the teacher.

This conflict is illustrated vividly in the not unusual circumstances exemplified in Missouri:

> MSTA [Missouri State Teachers Association] leaders take great care to avoid actions that would result in divisions in the educational lobby. As we shall see later, in 1961, MSTA shied away from taking stands that might alienate school boards or county superintendents. Indeed it seems fair to say that a major reason Missouri has no teacher tenure or minimum salary laws is that the MSTA has not wished to alienate its school board supporters in behalf of its classroom teacher constituency by recommending such proposals to the legislature. Unity strengthens MSTA's bargaining position, but also imposes limits on its objectives.[4]

There are many other cases in which the interests of the administrator and those of the teachers will conflict. Suppose, for example, that the teachers decide it is necessary to invoke sanctions against their school district. If a principal or superintendent were leading the teacher organization, it is inconceivable that he could take such an action against himself; an administrator understandably has too great a vested interest in seeing that the schools remain open and that a large number of prospective teachers apply for jobs in his jurisdiction. Comparable trouble arises when a teacher organization urges the reinstatement of a teacher fired for reasons unacceptable to his peers, but must do its urging through the same superintendent responsible for the contested dismissal.

These examples only appear far-fetched. One result of collective negotiations

4 N. A. Masters, R. H. Salisbury, and T. H. Eliot, *State Politics and the Public Schools* (New York: Alfred A. Knopf, 1964).

of all types is that teacher organizations will become much more active, and under these circumstances, it is essential that the organization be controlled by the teachers. If control rests anywhere else, the negotiating power of the organization will be diluted.

A VOICE WHOLLY LOST?

Documented cases of administrator domination of teacher organizations are numerous. For example, in the 1952 yearbook of the American Association of School Administrators, results were reported of a survey on the role of the superintendent in the comprehensive local education association in his community. Out of 3,135 replies, 50 per cent of the rural superintendents and 56 per cent of the city superintendents reported that they were regular members and participated on a par with other individual members. Over 32 per cent of the rural superintendents and more than 20 per cent of the city superintendents stated that they were influential members and were consulted on the selection of officers and determination of policies.

Further evidence is supplied in the survey I conducted of 150 Pennsylvania teachers. Sixty per cent of the respondents said that their teacher associations were dominated by administrators.

Even if it is not admitted that the NEA is dominated by administrators, it must be recognized that the organization does not speak for the classroom teacher. At its 1963 convention, the Department of Classroom Teachers, which "represents" 85 per cent of the membership, voted to invoke sanctions against the state of Utah. It also voted for a resolution that would have forced segregated local and state affiliates of the NEA to admit Negro members or drop their affiliation. On the next day, the delegate assembly voted against both of these resolutions; consequently, they were not put into practice. In effect, even though the classroom teachers were in favor of these two resolutions, the NEA took an opposite stand.

Too, the AFT claims that although 85 per cent of the NEA's membership is classroom teachers, their executive committee of 11 members has only two classroom teachers; their board of trustees of six members has only one classroom teacher; and the 75-member board of directors involves only 22 classroom teachers. To the best of my knowledge, the NEA has never denied these allegations. When questioned about the subject, NEA representatives claimed that they have no figures on the subject. Thus, there is no reason to think that the AFT's charges are inaccurate. The crucial problem, then—with which neither Mrs. Steet nor Mr. Megel really come to grips—is one of how to prevent administrators from dominating teacher organizations. An outright ban on administrator membership in teacher organizations would be one possible solution to the problem. Given present conditions, however, a more feasible solution would be to permit supervisors to join teacher organizations but with certain safeguards to prevent basic conflicts of interest. Such safeguards would exclude administrators from elective office, from important committee chairmanships, and from voting; they might even entail a provision for having administrators leave the meeting room when a controversial topic is discussed.

Some of these procedures are followed by public employees' unions recognized under President Kennedy's executive order No. 10988. In addition, some private employee unions have provisions to accept supervisors into membership but without eligibility to serve on the executive board or on the negotiating committee.

NEA'S MAJOR FAILURE

Mrs. Steet refers to the "substantial contribution of the professional teacher association to public education and teacher welfare." In one place, she points to the "impressive accomplishment" of the NEA, and later she even refers to the "phenomenal success" of the NEA. In talking about the rate of increase in teachers' pay, she considers the 65 per cent increase in salaries and the fact that teacher salaries are now about "16 per cent above those in industry" to be "impressive."

It is difficult for me to see how Mrs. Steet can claim such sweeping success for the NEA in improving teacher welfare when the average salary of all teachers in 1963–1964 was $5,963. Teacher salaries were only 1.7 per cent above earnings for all employees in manufacturing industries, and average earnings of federal civilian employees in 1962 were 12.6 per cent above those of teachers. In 1959, earnings of all teachers ranked 14th among average earnings for 18 professions. Only social and welfare workers, librarians, clergymen, and dieticians earned less on the average than all classroom teachers in the public schools. In Mrs. Steet's own school district in Philadelphia, the *maximum* a teacher can earn with a master's degree plus 30 credit hours is $8,750.

Another indication of the NEA's failure is the success of the AFT in winning nine of the 20 representational elections held since 1961. On close examination, the victories prove to be remarkable accomplishments: Not only is the AFT generally lacking as a professional organization, but its affiliation with the labor movement is anathema to many teachers. There seems little doubt that that affiliation has seriously hampered its organizing efforts, yet many AFT leaders still view their labor connection as something close to holy and, consequently, refuse to examine its actual benefits and costs. In any case, the AFT victories can only mean that teachers are dissatisfied with the NEA.

THE UNION IMPACT?

At the 1964 NEA convention, many of the speakers discussed the challenge created by the labor movement's active interest in organizing teachers. Had the NEA been successful, it would not today be facing this particular challenge.

This challenge of the AFT has apparently produced many drastic changes in the organizational structure of the NEA. For example, the funds allocated to the NEA's Urban Project, which is responsible for teacher negotiations, have increased remarkably since 1961–1962, when only $28,000 was spent. In succeeding years, expenditures increased to $215,000, then to $389,000, and finally this year to over $440,000. In addition, the Board of Directors ". . . authorized expenditure of an additional $500,000 to be expended this year through national, state, and local action to strengthen the local affiliates."[5] Consequently, over 10 per cent of the NEA's budget is now being spent on teacher negotiations—which indicates that at least financially the Association is becoming more of a teachers' organization.

On the local level, collective negotiations have caused a similar trend. For example, in the districts where representational elections were held and eligibility to vote was determined by an impartial person, principals and other administrators have always been excluded from the unit of representation. This trend can only result in administrators' being forced into a secondary role in the NEA. In fact, it could easily result in administrators' withdrawing from the NEA.

As it is now organized, however, the NEA can never be an effective organization for representing teachers in negotiations with school boards. The average teacher currently pays $10 national dues, $10 state association dues, and approximately $2 local dues. This dues structure is top heavy. Because the bulk of the funds must be expended at the local level, if the school district is too small for sufficient money to be accumulated, then possibly county or even state associations will have to direct negotiations. At present, the Urban Project has approximately 25 staff persons who have been attempting to service from Washington the local and state associations. After two years of traveling the country, the Urban Project staff is finally beginning to realize that its task is impossible. Unable to serve effectively in this way the thousands of school districts in the United States, the NEA has begun to allocate funds directly to state and local associations.

Traditionally, local education associations have been inept in improving teacher welfare. For example, in a 1959 NEA survey of the activities of local education associations, 80 per cent of the local associations reported that they sent two or fewer communications to their school board during the past year. Ninety per cent of the local associations said they received two or fewer communications from the school authorities. As expected, 75 per cent of the associations reported that they spent the majority of their time participating in social activities.

ORGANIZING FOR THE FUTURE

From all indications, it appears that this image of the local association is changing and that teachers are finally realizing that it is essential for them to form effective organizations. Obtaining funds for education involves a sophisticated power struggle, and teachers are rather late in accepting this fact.

Since teachers have no power to bargain individually similar to some college professors, the role of the teacher organization in this struggle will be crucial. Because teachers can only be protected by an effective organization, it seems

[5] National Education Association, *Addresses and Proceedings*, Vol. 102 (Washington, D. C.: The Association, 1964).

probable that the teacher organization of tomorrow will be quite different from either the AFT or the NEA.

First, it will be structured to function effectively in collective negotiations. Most likely, negotiations will be conducted at the local level, but if they move upward to a county or regional level, then the county organization will control the majority of revenues and full-time personnel. State and national organizations will provide support in the form of consultants and research services; but in large school districts, the local organization will retain full control. In smaller districts, the state organization will play a more important role, and in some states, negotiations will move rapidly to the state level.

Second, the primary function of the organization will be to serve the needs of the teachers. As collective negotiations become more widespread, administrators will be pushed out of any decision-making positions in the teacher organization unless they are completely dedicated to the welfare of the teachers. A very loose affiliation will be retained with organizations of principals and superintendents.

Third, negotiated compulsory membership provisions will be widespread. Not only will teachers be required to join organizations after they have been hired, but in some cases school boards will only be able to hire teachers who are organization members.

Fourth, subject-matter organizations, like the National Council for Social Studies, will continue to be organized on a national basis, and most original contributions in curriculum and study materials will come from national committees specifically organized for the purpose.

Fifth, each local organization that is negotiating will have at least one full-time person, and dues will have to be sufficient to pay for assistance from various specialists such as attorneys and consultants. The rapid increase in the number of full-time executive secretaries working for local teacher organizations indicates that a trend in this direction has already begun.

Finally, as the negotiating organization obtains higher salaries for teachers, its concern will begin to shift toward professional issues on which teachers can act effectively. Such problems as the management of dropouts, the preparation of students for college, and the improvement of guidance systems are illustrations. This shift to a dual orientation has already begun in New York, where the United Federation of Teachers, the exclusive bargaining agent, has expended enormous energies on the "effective schools plan" for long-range improvement of the city's public schools.

MERIT RATING: HAVE THE ISSUES CHANGED?

FRANCES R. LINK

It is possible to point to school districts, including my own, in which merit rating works. We can devise rating scales and use them. We can devise a team approach to supervise the evaluation of teachers. Within this system we can select our "superior" and our "inferior" teachers with some degree of accuracy; and we can feel reasonably comfortable that careful supervision and the independent judgments of principal and supervisor concur. This is what we mean when we say—"it works."

However, there is an accompanying phenomenon. Teachers begin to perceive themselves, each other, and their supervisors in new ways. As a supervisor, I hear teachers developing a classification system somewhat as follows:

One type says, "Why should I lose money because of a limiting factor?[1] I received 'merit,' so I'm not eligible for three more years—that doesn't make sense. Why can't I get a merit raise every year?" This is the "I want merit every year" teacher. "If I'm good this year," she says, "I'll be the same, next year. Why should I lose money because of a limitation factor?"

Another type says, "I did not receive merit; perhaps I should leave the profession." He may add, "I received 'good' supervisory reports. I felt certain I was a merit teacher. Why didn't I get a merit rating? I don't care about the money; I feel I'm a failure." He asks the supervisor, "Do you think I should stay in teaching?" He is not asking how to improve his professional competence; rather, he is feeling failure to the point of considering leaving his chosen career. He asks for advice but he wants ego restoration.

Still another type says, "You don't have to visit my classes, I'm not interested in merit." This teacher has adopted a limited concept of the purposes of supervision. This creates a chain reaction. The supervisor visits his classes feeling unwanted and struggling to know how to help the teacher grow professionally. The teacher, the supervisor feels, has equated improvement of instruction with merit rating. The supervisor wonders whether the teacher really wants to grow professionally and a chain of negative feelings interfere with the supervisory act.

In 1950, the Commission on Teacher Education of the Association for Supervision and Curriculum Development conducted a study that resulted in a pamphlet

FROM *Educational Leadership*, 22:322–326 (February 1965). Reprinted with permission of the Association for Supervision and Curriculum Development and Frances R. Link. Copyright © 1965 by the Association for Supervision and Curriculum Development.

[1] The Cheltenham plan makes a teacher eligible for a merit increment, once every three years. Four hundred dollars is added to the normal increment.

entitled, *Better Than Rating*.[2] In this most provocative work, written for the Commission by Robert R. Leeper, new approaches to the appraisal of teaching services are presented. In the section concerned with "How Rating Affects the School Program," the following statement appears.

The teacher, knowing he has been rated, usually says, "But I can't find any trace of myself or of my work in these results!" He feels his work has been compared, almost always unfavorably, with the ideal practices of a teacher who never existed in reality.[3]

THE "ELUSIVE IDEAL TEACHER"

Most school rating schemes have evolved as descriptions of so-called ideal practices which have little or no basis in instructional theory or research. Most merit rating schemes would never have evolved in schools without the pressure from School Boards or some force outside the profession. It is not surprising that the teaching profession and school systems, not ready to develop merit rating, have selected models for rating schemes from outside the profession.

Merit rating models have come, in the main, from business and industry, and the pressure to institute them has come largely from School Board members associated with such merit programs in their own work.

Many school systems have abandoned merit rating programs after several years of trial. In systems where it continues, I am convinced that it "works" only because those who administer it admit to the limitations of the system and that the teachers involved basically trust their supervisors. I am also convinced that school morale is affected by merit rating to a lesser degree than we thought, but that the subtle and persistent pressure felt by some individual teachers serves to inhibit their personal development and their teaching performance.

Better Than Rating makes a strong case for the profession's concern for respect for the individual teacher.

School people in modern times have come more and more to base the educational program upon the premise of respect for the individual. In order to guide his development, they must start with the individual child, accept him where he is, as he is. Beginning with this acceptance and understanding, they can guide his development in accordance with his own rate of growth. The child is thus not always unfavorably compared with an ideal child who never really existed. His achievements and shortcomings are interpreted, for the most part, in the light of his own rate of growth and development.

This acceptance of the individual person where he is and as he is accords with the basic democratic principle of respect for individual personality. This applies to adults as well as to children.

Teacher-rating plans, whether they rank teachers in a certain arbitrary order, give an overall score or mark on performance, or judge teachers according to a listing of ideal

---

[2] Association for Supervision and Curriculum Development, *Better Than Rating: New Approaches to Appraisal of Teaching Services* (Washington, D. C.: The Association, 1950), p. 83.
[3] *Ibid.*, p. 55.

qualities, are administrative plans which do not basically respect individual personality. These plans do not provide for acceptance of the individual as a competent professional person, where he is and as he is. Neither do they encourage an attitude of acceptance on the part of the rater that would cause him to point out any change and growth which may have been achieved by the individual, or what the direction of change should be to further his professional growth.[4]

Much of what is quoted here is reflected in the feelings of teachers who attempt to exclude the supervisor from the classroom because they are not interested in merit rating. Many supervisors have tried to separate improvement of instruction programs from merit rating. This is possible and perhaps even desirable, for until we can more precisely describe the act of teaching, how can we really place a value judgment on it?

Better Than Rating makes an important statement on rating scales.

If teachers know that their teaching is going to be judged in certain predetermined ways, it is only natural that they will plan their teaching in such a way that they will show up well in the judging. Educators, for example, have long recognized that if teachers knew in advance that the growth and development of their pupils was to be measured by the use of standard achievement tests or regents or college board examinations, they would plan their teaching so that pupils would have as adequate as possible a mastery of the facts to be measured. In like manner, teachers who know that their efficiency as a teacher is to be judged in terms of predetermined items listed on a rating scale or in a personnel record, will plan their teaching so that they will make as good a showing as possible when the scale is applied to their work.[5]

In practice, this is indeed true. As a matter of experience, the inadequacy of the rating scale looms large as teachers work to fit the scale. We have experienced some difficulty in trying to guide a teacher out of the profession because she or he *can* be rated satisfactorily on most single items on the teacher rating scale. The ASCD Commission on Teacher Evaluation found very few teacher rating scales which provided for weighing the component traits to be rated, and they state that "the impossibility of assigning weights is obvious, since the matrix of factors that makes one teacher eminently successful may not be the same combination of qualities that account for the success of another."[6]

RETHINKING THE ISSUES

Firsthand experience with merit rating had led the writer to reexamine the literature and rethink with colleagues the issues involved in merit rating. Four significant issues were identified 14 years ago by the ASCD Commission on Teacher Evaluation in the pamphlet, *Better Than Rating.*

[4] *Ibid.*, pp. 55–56.
[5] *Ibid.*, p. 58.
[6] *Ibid.*, pp. 64–65.

The first of these issues has to do with motives which underlie efforts of individuals toward self-improvement. Does the reward-or-punishment provision implicit in most rating plans help the individual to make his greatest effort toward professional growth? Does fear of demotion or of reduction in pay cause the teacher to strive consciously and intelligently to "mend his ways"—even though he has to go in the direction prescribed by the rating plan or by the person who does the rating? Or has modern psychology not found sounder principles upon which to base a program for encouraging teachers' efforts to accomplish best results in working with children?

A second issue involved in teacher rating has to do more directly with the process of evaluation. What is the purpose of evaluation? If evaluation is part of the means by which people judge and guide the direction of their growth, then this process should be thoroughly understood and participated in by all concerned. The question involved is whether we, in a democracy, want a type of authoritarian evaluation which guides individuals into unquestioning obedience and submissiveness to persons superior in status. On the other hand, would it not be preferable to develop a type of democratic organization in which qualities of cooperative evaluation would be explored, understood, and used continuously, freely and creatively by all concerned in the process?

A third issue has to do with the effect of current teacher-rating practices upon professional growth. Just what are the characteristics of the main types of rating plans currently in use? Do these plans actually help the teacher see his "points of weakness," and thus automatically encourage him toward greater efforts to overcome these faults? Or do the plans, because of their very nature, cause greater tension and anxiety, and thus have an undesirable, and sometimes disastrous effect upon the professional development of the individual?

A fourth issue relates to the kind of organization which will best foster and encourage professional growth on the part of individuals and groups. Is the school, or the superintendent, alone concerned in evaluation of the school's program, of results of instruction? Or is evaluation the privilege and responsibility of every person affected by the school's program? An organization is shaped by people, and yet an organization also shapes people. The important thing in evolving an organization to foster professional growth in democratic schools is that it faithfully exemplify the soundest principles of democracy and thus make possible effective working of cooperative evaluation procedures.

These four issues, *fourteen years later*, are still crucial. An issue which becomes increasingly sensitive as one experiences merit rating is *how* an *organization is shaped by people* and how an *organization also shapes people*. A rating scale becomes a shaping device no matter how supportive the supervisor, the principal or the system may be. With "merit rating" the classroom visit is "different," no matter what the relationship has been with the supervisors. Staff relationships, which shape the school atmosphere, become difficult to assess—and often guarded. Parents inadvertently shape a new problem by saying to a teacher, "Of course you got a merit raise, didn't you?"

STYLES OF TEACHING

If we could effectively deal with the issues stated above, the issues to be proposed might not be forthcoming. One "new" issue relates to the research and knowledge being developed about the styles of teaching, theories of instruction, the nature of classroom interaction, and the relationship of personal mental health to professional growth. Some educators who have been doing research in the area of teaching and classroom interaction have stated that their work is not to be used to evaluate teachers. Perhaps this should be true in the initial stages of research. The issue seems to be, however, what will be the effect of current research on teacher education, instructional theory, and "styles of teaching" on the evaluation of teacher performance. There is a need to bring together new knowledge and research from a variety of disciplines in order to rethink the nature of teaching and the structure of better teacher evaluation procedures.

Rating or evaluation of one's work as a teacher is not an issue in most school systems today. Whether it be formal or informal, rating exists. Will we be able to resolve old issues and professionalize our task of rating teachers when we use what we know from both experience and research about the phenomena of teaching and learning? This leads to the related issue of the nature of teacher preparation. The work in curriculum development and even school building design for future needs has already surpassed efforts to study and improve teacher preparation. Teacher education has many dimensions, some of which will have a powerful influence on teacher education in the future. These are defined in *The Education of the American Teacher* by James B. Conant and *The Miseducation of American Teachers* by James D. Koerner.

The writings of these men will no doubt have an immediate influence, but whether or not their recommendations will improve the quality of teaching is central to the issue of teacher performance and ultimately teacher evaluation. My hunch is that we will find more effective guides for understanding teaching in the research on teacher education conducted at San Francisco State College by Fred Wilhelms and others and in the work of Ned Flanders, N. A. Fattu, Arno Bellack, B. O. Smith, Hilda Taba, Elizabeth S. Maccia and others who have been engaged in developing "models" of instructional theory and classroom interaction. Once we know *who* should teach and *what* teachers *do* that results in learning, then we will begin to know what to value and reward in teaching.

TEACHERS' SOCIAL
MOBILITY

N. R. DIXON

No one who has felt the recent jerks and starts in American society can seriously doubt the authenticity of the social revolution in which we are involved. Old gods are crumbling: a new iconoclasm is emerging.

History has turned a sharp corner. For instance, the Negro, who for decades meekly accepted a position of social inferiority, has decided that the United States Constitution was meant to include him too. He has become an activist—seeking better housing, education, jobs and recreation. The Negro has demanded equal opportunity to share in all that America offers. He has fought his battle in conference rooms, in the courts, and in the streets. Armed with successes achieved by these means, by the 1964 Civil Rights Act and by the zeitgeist, the Negro has shown that he will continue, accelerate and widen his fight to attain his rights.

The war on poverty which is designed to raise the standards of living for millions of Americans is an assault on want—an assault which will result in a rise in status. The onset of a cybernated age which is eliminating 40,000 jobs per week and dramatically creating new jobs has caused continuing crises in employment. Market-supported jobs are rapidly declining.

The increasing action of the federal government in matters of education and community uplift signals the opening of a new era in politics. In this age of social upheaval, teachers and teaching must assume a new posture. Institutionalized education must supply the intellectual resources with which American society delivers optimally on its long-awaited promise of equal opportunity for all.

AN OPEN SOCIETY: THE DEMOCRATIC IDEAL

The widely accepted ideology of an open society in America is becoming a suspect one. Social class status is conferred on individuals and groups. The indicators are "social power, wealth, and esteem."[1] Despite its commitment in theory to equality of opportunity for all, this country—for all its material riches—has never come close to making its ideal a reality. Lynd and Lynd have brilliantly

FROM *Educational Leadership*, 22:564–566, 603 (May 1965). Reprinted with permission of the Association for Supervision and Curriculum Development and N. R. Dixon. Copyright © 1965 by the Association for Supervision and Curriculum Development.

[1] Don Martindale, *American Social Structure* (New York: Appleton-Century-Crofts, Inc., 1960), p. 442.

shown how basic American beliefs are eroded by juxtaposed contradictory values.[2] These conflicting ideas, which are found pulling against each other, tend to make vertical social mobility extremely difficult—often impossible!

For classroom teachers, the matter of vertical social mobility is complicated by the fact that there is social stratification within the education establishment and in the community. Classroom teachers usually have lower status than guidance counselors. Elementary teachers usually have lower status than high school teachers. Teachers of science and mathematics have higher status than social studies teachers. Athletic coaches have higher status than classroom teachers or guidance counselors. Principals and supervisors have higher status than classroom teachers, guidance counselors, or coaches.

Without a doubt, the superintendent has the spot of number one hen in the educational pecking order. Administrators and supervisors who man the controls in education exert power throughout education. Despite the fact that educators professedly work equally with their peers, those lower on the totem pole often fear to express honest doubts and sharp disagreement with the holders of the controls lest they be charged with everything from "fighting my program" to insubordination.

The value of the respective roles and role occupants in education is not only reflected in power, but also in the salaries paid. Stratification in organized education is dangerously divisive—especially so since it often subverts energy into searching for ways to attain "higher" positions with the accompanying increased power and money. The danger comes from the *reasons* for the seeking and the diverting of energy and effort from the main business of education. To liquidate stratification within organized education requires a new astuteness in schoolmanship.

In the community there are categorical limitations on the upward social mobility of teachers. For instance, laws in some states forbid teachers to engage in activities which are open to those in other professions. In many instances, teachers cannot seek and hold political office while teaching. In other instances, community tradition and expectancy limit the extent to which teachers may seek to gain upward social mobility.

Teachers today teach children against the backdrop of democratic ideals. They teach freedom, independence and responsibility as the bedrock of the democratic ethic. Yet, the community denies them the very rights and privileges for which it professedly stands. In such instances, teachers may come to feel that achieving vertical social mobility is difficult—if not impossible—in a society devoid of vibrant moral commitment.

SOCIETY'S VALUATION OF TEACHERS AND TEACHING

"One who chooses to become a teacher must be willing to join a profession which receives little recognition or position in the occupational structure of his

[2] Robert S. Lynd and Helen Lynd, *Middletown in Transition* (New York: Harcourt, Brace and Co., 1937), Ch. XII.

community."[3] Furthermore, he must content himself with modest public esteem despite the fact that Plato felt that esteem was of primary importance.[4]

In most cases, he must realize that he will receive poor pay and will be insecure in his job. Worse yet, he will be enmeshed in a web of restrictions manufactured and labeled "For teachers only." One joining the teaching profession should readily discern that teachers are almost powerless to change public policy as it relates to schools. Also, teachers are not in the social class which sits at the controls of society; consequently, they occupy an impotent position in the community power structure.

Paradoxically, society values the results of teaching (education) far more highly than it values teachers. With the increased need for scientists and technicians, however, a higher status has been conferred upon teachers of science and mathematics. Along with higher public esteem has gone the correlative—higher pay. Teachers of science and mathematics have also had more social power bestowed upon them—because of the functional importance of their work and the scarcity of personnel.

Low public esteem for teachers may be traced, to some extent, to the quarrel—even among educators—as to whether teaching is a profession. This argument often shows up in conflicts between protagonists for the NEA and the American Federation of Teachers. It is easy enough to define the term "profession" and to plaster it on teaching. But, operationally, is teaching a profession? For lack of a categorical answer of "yes," large sectors of the American population still feel that "anyone can teach." Such an attitude toward teaching does nothing at all to reflect a shining image of teachers or to foster the upward social mobility of teachers.

When it comes to upward social mobility, the case of Negro teachers is a study of entrapment. Most of them, living and working in the South, have little hope of vertical social mobility either in the profession or in the Southern community. They have little or no chance of becoming a school board member or a school superintendent. Negro teachers have been an unusually docile group—especially so since they often feel that they may be the victims of illegitimate power. Only now are they beginning to seize the opportunity to overcome more than three centuries of enforced mediocrity.

Since American democracy and the teaching profession are sensitive to race, Negro teachers, North or South, are hopelessly trapped in a caste system. In general, Negro teachers are highly valued by Americans—but only "in their place," where they are, in "Negro society." This view is easily verified by the paucity of qualified Negroes serving in prestigious national educational positions: e.g., on editorial boards of national journals and as major participants on national programs. What is worse is the fact that neither the teaching profession nor the public has strained its voice, to call for a change in this policy which bespeaks low esteem.

[3] Joseph J. Cangemi, "Raising the Status and Esteem of Public School Teachers," *Clearing House* (May 1964), 38:540–42.
[4] Don Martindale, *op. cit.*, p. 448.

TOWARD GREATER SOCIAL MOBILITY

In order to increase the tempo and amount of upward social mobility for teachers, a virtual revolution must be effected among teachers and in American society. The job is not insuperable for knowledge-bearers and for those whose mission is to refine the democratic way of life. To secure greater esteem, wealth, and social power, teachers should launch the following actions:

1. Work to strengthen teaching as a profession. Roles, role occupants, and role performance must all be upgraded. Professional associations should strive to gain control over admission to and retention in the profession. They should seek to license teachers and retain only role occupants of decided competence.

2. Work to secure adequate salaries for teachers. Many teachers are required to attend summer school periodically to hold their jobs. Also, they must buy the trappings of class status which the community requires. Often through no fault of their own, many teachers are victims of loan sharks. Others, especially men teachers, turn to moonlighting to supplement their inadequate salaries.

3. Work to attain job security for teachers. Teachers should not have to bow before school boards and the public to maintain their jobs. Teacher tenure laws should be sought. Teachers should be protected from scurrilous attack by laymen and the caprice of administrators.

4. Work to develop a national system of award for outstanding teacher performance. Such awards should be as significant as the Pulitzer prizes and should be based upon clearly defined criteria.

5. Work to develop a strong, positive image of teachers. Mass media should be carefully studied to determine the image cast about teachers. Ways should be devised to prevent an Ichabod Crane image of teachers from being disseminated. Professional associations on all levels must themselves develop a strong, effective system of public relations which adequately portrays the profession to the public.

6. Work for full and complete involvement of Negroes in all aspects of professional endeavor. Professional associations need to purge themselves of the guilt of moral bankruptcy caused by decades of silence and lethargy in this matter.

7. Work to exert greater influence in local, state, and national politics.

Vigorous and intelligent action can foster greater social mobility for teachers. With the war on poverty already joined, teachers and teaching assume a new importance. This, coupled with a greater need for lifelong education, forecasts teachers as more important role occupants. A country which rests upon an informed citizenry must commit itself to increased wealth, esteem, and social power for teachers.

THE PHILOSOPHY
OF EDUCATION AND
ITS PROBLEMS

WILLIAM K. FRANKENA

THE HUMAN PROBLEM

A crucial part of the human problem, for both individuals and societies, is the acquisition and transmission of excellences of body, mind, and character. This is a problem for human beings because such excellences are neither innate nor automatically acquired in the course of their natural experiences. Knowledge of one's language is almost automatically acquired in the course of social experience, and so are moral habits in a tradition-bound society, but only because social life has an educational aspect built into it. The cultivation of excellences is only part of the human problem because more is needed for the life and well-being of an individual or society than the mere possession of certain abilities and traits. Needed also, as Aristotle pointed out, are adequate native endowment, favorable physical conditions, and a not too brief span of life.

In saying this, I am assuming, of course, that the goal or task of human beings is not simply to acquire a certain group of excellences, moral or otherwise—as Kant and others sometimes seem to imply. It seems to me Aristotle is right when he says that our goal or task cannot be merely to *have* excellences or to *be* excellent, since a man may be excellent or have all the excellences and yet be asleep or unconscious. In short, I believe that the point of having an excellence is that it is necessary for engaging in worthwhile activities of a waking and conscious sort, just as the point of being able to play chess is to play it on occasion. Excellences, like the Sabbath, are made for man, not vice versa. Even if I am wrong about this, however, the formation of the required excellences remains a problem for human beings.

It may be asked at this point, Why should we worry at all about the acquisition or transmission of such things as abilities and traits? Why are any such things necessary or desirable? Why should we not simply go ahead and engage in the worthwhile activities that constitute the good or happy life? One might reply shortly by remarking that this would be like playing chess without learning how.

FROM *Three Historical Philosophies of Education* by William K. Frankena. Copyright © 1965 by Scott, Foresman and Company.

This answer is, in fact, correct, but it needs to be spelled out. We must try to see what kind of a thing an excellence is and why it is necessary and desirable for us to acquire such things, since we are not born with them.

(1) When a man is said to know geometry or to be just, he is being said to have an excellence (if we assume that knowing geometry and being just are in fact desirable). But it is not being said that he is engaged in doing geometry or in doing just actions; it is not being said that he is engaged in any activities or having any experiences or feelings at all. He may, as Aristotle remarked, be asleep or unconscious and yet be correctly said to know geometry or to be just. What is being said, rather, is that *if* he is awake, *then* he *can* do things like proving the Pythagorean theorem if he is asked or decides to, or that, *when* he is awake, he *tends* to act justly in situations where this is called for. That is, an excellence is not an activity, action, experience, or feeling; it is what Aristotle calls a *hexis* and Dewey a "habit." A *hexis* is a disposition or dispositional property of a mind or person, something that need not be activated at a given time and yet may correctly be said to be present. One may know how to play chess when one is not playing it or even thinking about it. All such things as abilities, habits, skills, and traits of character or personality are dispositions in this wide sense. All excellences, then, are dispositions of this sort, though, of course, not all such dispositions are excellences, since some of them are bad or undesirable—like being unjust or ignorant, or indifferent—like the habit of tying the left shoestring first.

A word about my terminology is needed here. It is convenient in thinking about education to have one word for all of the desirable abilities, skills, states, traits, etc., to be produced or fostered, and works like "character" and "virtue" are too purely moral in connotation to include such things as an ability to speak French or a knowledge of geography. Some writers use the term "values" to refer to such desirable abilities, etc.—for example, in discussing "moral and spiritual values" in education. But the term "values" is much too vague and much too broad. For one thing, it covers not only desirable abilities, traits, etc., but also what I have called worthwhile *activities* (i.e., not only what Aristotle called *hexis* but what he called *energeiai*). I have therefore decided to use the term "excellences" as I have. It has the incidental advantage of fitting in with the concern about excellence in education today.

It is also convenient to have a word to cover both desirable and undesirable abilities, traits, etc., of all kinds, and I have elected to use the term "dispositions" for this purpose. Ordinarily we use "disposition" in a narrower sense, as in saying that Jones has a sunny disposition and Smith a disposition to be bashful or to waste time. We should not ordinarily say that being able to skate and having a knowledge of mathematics were dispositions. But philosophers do sometimes use terms like "disposition" and "dispositional property" in a wider sense, and since we need a term to use in this wide way and have no ordinary one to do the job. I shall do likewise. That "dispositions" is being used in this way must, however, be constantly remembered in what follows.

What I am calling dispositions and excellences may be of various sorts. Sunniness and bashfulness are dispositions, and the former is also an excellence. Qualities of personality like charm, traits of character like benevolence, skills like knowing how to dance, and states like having a knowledge of the kings of Britain—different as these are, they are all dispositions in my sense and presumably excellences as well. Their opposites, of course are also dispositions but presumably not excellences.

(2) Now, why is it desirable or necessary that we have any dispositions at all other than those we may be born with? In a way, this is an academic question, because, as many writers have pointed out, including those we shall be studying, the formation of habits and other kinds of dispositions is inevitable in the course of our lives. As William James puts it:

> Could the young but realize how soon they will become mere walking bundles of habits, they would give more heed to their conduct while in the plastic state. . . . Every smallest stroke of virtue or of vice leaves its never so little scar. . . . Nothing we ever do is, in strict scientific literalness, wiped out.[1]

Such is our nature (or, according to James, our nervous system) that we form dispositions of one sort or another willy-nilly; the question really is not whether we shall have dispositions but which ones we shall have.

There is, however, something more to be said than merely that, since we must have dispositions, we might as well cultivate desirable ones. This is that we cannot, in any case, simply go ahead and enjoy or engage in the worthwhile activities and experiences that make up the good or happy life. Except possibly for purely passive perceptions and pleasures, if these exist, we cannot enjoy or engage in these valuable activities and experiences unless we first develop certain abilities, habits, or traits rather than others. To play chess or prove the Pythagorean theorem, I must first develop a number of abilities. I must also learn self-control so as not to be diverted by other attractions. Moreover, being finite and unable to do everything I wish to do or ought to do at the same time, I must have the capacity, as it were, to store one thing away while I do something else, and to control its return when I want it again. God, at least in one view, is pure act and is infinite; He can have no dispositions and has no need of them. He enages eternally in all worthwhile activities all at once, and has no problem of learning or control or storing away. We human beings, however, are not so blessed, and hence must regard certain dispositions as not only necessary but desirable because they are the condition and underpinning of the good life. We must acquire them in order to put ourselves in the position of engaging in worthwhile activities if and when we choose to.

The matter also has a social side. If any given individual is to be able to enjoy and engage in desirable experiences and activities, then not only must he have certain dispositions, but so must others. They must be disposed to treat him in certain ways, for example, with some tolerance, and they must have abilities and habits which maintain and provide the best possible environment for him to live in. He himself, on his part, must acquire corresponding dispositions that bear on

[1] William James, *The Principles of Psychology* (New York: Henry Holt & Co., 1890), Ch. I, p. 127.

the goodness of their lives. Hence, as Dewey says, society must be concerned to transmit

. . . habits of doing, thinking, and feeling from the older to the younger. Without this communication of ideals, hopes, expectations, standards, opinions, from those members of society who are passing out of the group life to those who are coming into it, social life could not survive.[2]

Society could not even maintain life, let alone promote worthwhile activities and experiences for its members.

THE ROLE OF EDUCATION

If both individuals and societies must be thus concerned about the acquisition and transmission of certain dispositions rather than others, or of what we have termed excellences, then the next question is: How are excellences acquired? Can they be transmitted from the older to the younger at all, and, if so, how? This question was nicely posed by the Greeks, who were the first to really see how crucial it is. Plato's *Meno* begins with Meno asking Socrates,

Can you tell me whether [excellence] can be taught or is acquired by practice, not teaching; or, if neither by practice nor by learning, whether it comes to men by nature or in some other way [such as luck or divine gift]?[3]

Here four possibilities are recognized:

(a) Excellences are transmitted by being taught and acquired by being learned.
(b) They are transmitted and acquired by practice.
(c) They are natural or innate.
(d) They are gifts of fortune or of the gods (or God).

Socrates, who holds that excellence is knowledge, would like to say (a), but in the *Meno* at any rate he settles for (d). He neglects (b), which is taken seriously by Aristotle. Christianity holds to (d) for all or at least some of the excellences. Kant's position is rather difficult to make out, as we shall see, but his mentor, Rousseau, roughly speaking, was betting on (c). Dewey, like Plato (in the `Republic*) and Aristotle, is betting on a combination of (a) and (b).

To me, as to Socrates, Plato, and Aristotle, it seems clear that such excellences as we need are not innate, except in potentiality, or even automatically acquired. To say, however, that these excellences depend entirely on fortune and luck is to say that the solution of the human problem is entirely beyond the scope of our endeavor—and this simply is not true, though it is true that its solution is not wholly in our hands. We must allow that the achievement of the good life, whether on earth or in heaven, does depend, in part at least, on fortune or on something besides ourselves, and perhaps even that the acquisition and possession of at least

---

[2] John Dewey, *Democracy and Education* (New York: The Macmillan Company, 1916), pp. 3ff.
[3] *Laches, Protagoras, Meno, Enthydemus*, trans. W. R. M. Lamb (New York: G. P. Putnam's Sons, 1924), p. 265.

some excellences, possibly of all of them, depends in some degree on something not ourselves that makes for excellence. But our hope may and must still lie, in large part, in (a) and (b)—that is, in education. Even if one believes, as Christians do, that something in the way of a divine gift or regeneration is required for certain excellences like faith and perhaps also for the perfecting of any excellence, it does not follow that the human effort of education is unnecessary as a condition of other excellences or of the divine gift itself. Certainly Christianity has in general not drawn this conclusion about education, though Christians have often held rather strict views of the kinds of excellence that are necessary or desirable. In fact, Christianity has usually regarded "the propagation of the gospel in foreign parts" and Christian education at home as duties and even as normal preconditions of the action of divine grace. For civilized man, at any rate, Christian or not, the question is not whether education is necessary and effective in the acquisition of excellences, but which excellences are to be cultivated or prepared for by education (teaching or practice), and how, when, and why.

THE NATURE AND AIM OF EDUCATION

We come, thus, to the subject of education. What is it? Actually the term "education" is ambiguous and may mean any one of four things:

(1) The *activity of educating* carried on by teachers, schools, and parents (or by oneself),
(2) The *process of being educated* (or learning) which goes on in the pupil or child,
(3) The *result*, actual or intended, of (1) and (2),
(4) The *discipline* or field of enquiry that studies or reflects on (1), (2), and (3) and is taught in schools of education.

We may begin to define education in sense (1) by saying that it is the activity of fostering or transmitting excellences. It is true that we sometimes use "education" in a wider sense to mean any shaping of a mind or character; in this sense Rousseau said that education comes to us from nature, from men, and from things. But in this wider sense, we are being educated no matter what dispositions are being fostered in us. In a narrower and more usual sense, however, we decline to call anything education unless it fosters or is intended to foster desirable dispositions and not undesirable ones, and this is the usage which is important for the philosophy of education and which we must try to define. One addition must be made to this definition. If the desired excellences could be produced by giving drugs, we probably would not call this way of producing them education (though we might then resort to the drugstore instead of the schoolhouse). To complete our definition we must say that education in sense (1) is the use of certain kinds of methods to foster excellences or desirable dispositions—namely, those belonging to the family which includes teaching, instruction, training, learning, practice, and the like. For a really careful definition all of these methods would, of course, have to be defined further, but this statement will suffice for present purposes.

Bertrand Russell once wrote,

> Education in the sense in which I mean it, may be defined as the *formation, by means of instruction, of certain mental habits and a certain outlook on life and the world.*[4]

If we take "instruction" to cover the whole family of methods mentioned before and read "desirable" for "certain," this will serve very well as a definition of education in sense (1). Then education in sense (2) is the *acquisition by learning* of desirable dispositions or excellences, and education in sense (3) is the *possession* of excellent dispositions. Education in sense (4) is different; it is not an activity of teaching or a process of learning, it is a *field of study* like history or physics—namely, the field of study and thought *about* education in the other three senses. Many other definitions of education have, of course, been given, but I think it can be shown that they are either inadequate, unclear, mistaken, or compatible with those just stated. Ours certainly fit the views of Aristotle, Kant, and Dewey, as we shall see.

If all this is so, then whatever we may think about the *ultimate* aim or aims of education, we must take as its *proximate* aim the formation or fostering of excellent dispositions. As Aristotle put the matter, though the *end* of political science (which for him includes the art or science of education) is the highest good,

> ... the principal care of this science is to produce a certain [disposition] in the citizens, namely, to make them [excellent] and capable of performing noble actions.[5]

Or, if we say that the *immediate* aim of education is to do the things that will form or foster excellences of disposition, as Dewey's follower W. H. Kilpatrick does, then we may prefer his way of stating it:

> The *remoter* and inclusive guiding aim of education is to rear the young *to live the full good life*, both individual and social. The *intermediate* aim is to build such character in the young as will guarantee, so far as this is possible, that they *can* and *will* live the desirable good life.[6]

My only objection to this statement is that it uses the term "character" for the intermediate aim of education—just as Kant, Ruskin, Mill, and many others, including Dewey sometimes, do. This suggests that the *moral* excellences constitute the whole intermediate aim of education, unless it is carefully explained that "character" is being used to cover all of what I am calling excellences, which is not usually done by those who use it in talking about education. Now, it may be true that education should concern itself only to promote the moral virtues. But this must be shown and cannot be taken for granted at this point in the discussion. I think, in fact, that it is false, but here, at any rate, we must leave open the question which dispositions are to be cultivated. I should, therefore, amend Kilpatrick's statement by substituting "dispositions" for "character," thus allowing for the cultivation of a knowledge of physics or an ability to paint or do geometry, as well as of courage, integrity, and the like.

---

[4] Bertrand Russell, *Mysticism and Logic* (London: George Allen and Unwin, 1917), p. 37.

[5] Aristotle, *Nicomachean Ethics*, Book I, Ch. 9, 1099B (trans. H. Rackham) (Cambridge, Mass.: Harvard University Press, 1934), p. 47.

[6] W. H. Kilpatrick, *Philosophy of Education* (New York: The Macmillan Company, 1951), p. 427; cf. p. 301.

PHILOSOPHY OF EDUCATION

The philosophy of education is part of the discipline of education as defined earlier. It may be either *analytical* or *normative*. It is normative insofar as it is concerned to propose ends or values for education to promote, principles for it to follow, excellences for it to foster, or methods, contents, programs, etc., for it to adopt or employ, in general or in specific situations. It is analytical insofar as it is concerned merely to analyze, clarify, or elucidate, or to criticize and evaluate, our thinking about education—the concepts or terms we employ, the arguments we use, the assumptions we make, the slogans we proclaim, the theories we formulate. In this introduction I am doing mainly analytical philosophy of education. Aristotle, Kant and Dewey, however, did normative philosophy of education primarily, though in the course of doing so they included a good deal of analytical discussion. Some recent philosophers—for example, C. D. Hardie and D. J. O'Connor— believe that philosophy should be confined to logical analysis and so have been advocating a purely analytical approach to the philosophy of education. Since we mean to study the educational philosophies of Aristotle, Kant, and Dewey, however, we must take seriously the notion of a normative philosophy of education.

From what was said in the previous section it follows that there are three questions for any normative philosophy of education:

(1) *What* dispositions are to be cultivated? *Which* dispositions are excellences?

(2) *Why* are these dispositions to be regarded as excellences and cultivated? What are the aims or principles of education that require their cultivation?

(3) *How* or by what methods or processes are they to be cultivated?

The first two questions clearly go together. For to tell which dispositions are to be fostered, we need a criterion or rationale, and in order to have such a criterion or rationale, we must have an answer to the second question. I should like now to exhibit the general logic of such a rationale—one by which an answer to the first question is justified via an answer to the second. First, however, we must observe that some theories of education seem to rest simply on the premise that an educational system should promote the dispositions regarded as excellent by its supporting society—by Catholics if it is a Catholic system, by Americans if it is a public system in the United States. But if this answer to our question is to have the status of a *philosophy* of education, its proponent must explain why we should promote whatever dispositions are considered excellent in our society, and then his rationale will have much the same logic that I shall describe. In general, if one's culture has passed the stage of being purely tradition-bound and directed, as ours has, one cannot escape doing at least a minimum of philosophy. At any rate, even if an actual system of education must in a sense take as its business the implementation and transmission of the ideals of its supporting church, state, or class, the task of a normative philosopher of education is still to say what ought to be done and why, even if in doing so he only expresses the ethos of his group.

For the logic involved in a normative theory of education I shall adapt what John Stuart Mill says in his *System of Logic* (1843), Book VI, Chapters V and XII. According to this conception, one must begin one's educational thinking with one or more premises stating what the basic ends or principles of human action are. For Mill the basic principle is that of utility: do what will promote the greatest balance of pleasure over pain in the universe as a whole. For Kant (in one formulation) it is to do what you can will to be done by all rational beings in the kind of situation you are in. Whatever one's basic premises, it follows that certain dispositions are to be cultivated. First, we must cultivate the dispositions to act for the ends or on the principles affirmed; for instance, in Mill's view, we must promote the disposition to act for the greatest general happiness. Second, we must cultivate whatever dispositions are required for promoting the end or carrying out the principles in question. Both Mill and Kant think, for example, that it follows from their premises, different as they are, that we should develop our intellectual abilities and a will to be honest.

In general, one's thinking here will take the form of a kind of "practical syllogism," as Aristotle called it.

(a) The major premise will consist of a normative statement of basic ends or principles.

(b) The minor premise will consist of factual beliefs about life, human beings, and the world, taken from psychology, sociology, history, or from metaphysics, epistemology, or theology.

(c) The conclusion will be a normative judgment about the dispositions to be fostered by education.

In the case of Mill, for example, the reasoning will be as follows:

(a) We ought to do what is conducive to the greatest general happiness.

(b) The development of our intellects, honesty, etc., are conducive to the greatest general happiness.

(c) Therefore we should develop our intellects, be honest, etc.

The other question for a normative philosophy of education is *how* to foster the dispositions or excellences thus decided on—what practically is to be done or not done, when, in what way, with what means, in what order, by whom, and so on. Here enter all of the rules of teaching, learning, educational policy, curriculum and school administration, from fairly general ones like Aristotle's "Use practice to realize the moral excellences" or Dewey's "Always relate what is done to the interests of the child" to rather specific ones like Kant's "If a child tells a lie, a look of contempt is punishment enough," but not including completely particular instructions like "Do . . . now." Such particular conclusions about what to do are, of course, the final outcome and application of the whole process of educational reasoning, but they are not part of the philosophy involved. Philosophy, as I once overheard a student remark, is always "in general."

For thinking about this second, practical question the logic is again that of a kind of practical syllogism. This time the major premise is usually a normative statement about an excellence or set of excellences to be fostered. The major premise will, in fact, normally be a conclusion (c) from a piece of reasoning of the sort just described. The minor premise (d) consists again of one or more factual propositions taken from psychology, history, or some natural or social science (including educational science and experimentation), or perhaps from metaphysics, epistemology, or theology. And (e) the conclusion is what Mill calls a "practical precept" for the guidance of the teacher, parent, child, or administrator. Thus Kant's reasoning in connection with the precept just quoted might be:

(c) We ought to cultivate a disposition of honesty.
(d) Looks of contempt help to cultivate such dispositions.
(e) Therefore, if a child tells a lie, we should give him a look of contempt.

The two stages of reasoning we have been analyzing may, of course, be combined as follows:

(a) We ought to promote the greatest general happiness.
(b) Dispositions of honesty, etc., promote the greatest general happiness.
(c) Therefore we ought to cultivate honesty, etc.
(d) Looks of contempt help to cultivate honesty.
(e) Therefore, if a child lies, we should give him a look of contempt.

Kant would not accept the opening utilitarian line of argument here given for (c), as we shall see, but Mill, if he is willing to agree to (d), could accept this entire chain of thought from first principle to practical precept.

In practice, educational thinking cannot be quite so simple and straightforward as this. Whether we should actually give a lying child a look of contempt does not depend merely on (a), (b), (c), and (d); it depends also on further considerations. It may be, for instance, that giving looks of contempt is ruled out by some basic ethical principle other than (a); or it may be that it would have such undesirable concomitant effects that it should be avoided even on utilitarian grounds. That is, its total effect on the child's dispositions may be so undesirable that it is better to use some other way of fostering honesty. Such possible complications must always be kept in mind, but the model of reasoning presented remains instructive nevertheless.

The model at least makes it clear that a normative philosophy of education, if it is completely worked out, must include:

1. A list of dispositions or excellences to be cultivated, with definitions.
2. A statement of the basic ends or principles taken as normative *premises*.
   a. for showing why these dispositions should be cultivated (or that they are excellences),
   b. for showing what is to be done or not done in cultivating them,
3. Factual *premises*, empirical, philosophical, or theological,
   a. for showing what dispositions are excellent and to be cultivated,
   b. for showing what is to be done, and how, in order to cultivate these excellences,

4. Normative *conclusions* about what to do, and how and when, in cultivating them.

Thus the schema we borrowed from Mill can be used in the analysis of any given normative philosophy of education, as well as in the development and exposition of one's own. It is also useful in comparing philosophies of education, in seeing the issues between them and in judging the merits of one as against another; for it exhibits the points at which different normative philosophies of education may disagree. (1) They may differ in the lists of dispositions they regard as desirable—i.e. in their lists of excellences. Or even if they agree in their verbal lists, they may still define their terms differently; they may both hold integrity to be an excellence but mean different things by "integrity." (2) They may differ in the ends or principles they take to be the basic in moral, social, and educational thinking, as Mill and Kant do. If so, they will give different rationales for their lists of excellences to be cultivated, even if their lists are the same. (3) They may differ in their factual premises—that is, their authors may have different views as to the relevant facts about the universe, human nature, child psychology, learning, motivation, the effects of corporal punishment, etc. Then, even if their basic ends or principles are the same, they will advocate different lists of excellences and/or different concrete precepts about how to foster them. Here we must notice that different philosophers have different views about the *kinds* of factual premises that may be used. Confident metaphysicians and speculative philosophers like Aristotle will regard metaphysical premises as admissible, but positivists and agnostics will not. Kant holds metaphysics to be impossible, and Dewey rules out all metaphysical premises that cannot be interpreted pragmatically. Mill admits only empirically verifiable premises. A religious thinker may be willing to use premises based on authority, revelation, or faith—as Christian philosophers of education do —but Aristotle and Dewey are against doing so, though Kant, in a sense, is not.

(4) And, of course, philosophers of education may differ in their practical conclusions about teaching methods, curriculum, school administration, and so on. However, unless they are simply illogical, they should not differ in their conclusions about such matters unless they also differ somewhere in their normative or factual premises (they might differ in their definitions of terms, but if they differ *only* in this way they are disagreeing only verbally, not in substance). On the other hand, they may agree completely or at least to a very considerable extent in their working conclusions, even though they differ fundamentally in their normative and/or factual premises; then they will agree in practice but differ in their rationales. In short, different normative philosophies of education must disagree in at least one of the categories, (1) to (4), and may disagree in more than one; if they disagree in (4), they must disagree in one of the others, but they may agree in any one of them and yet disagree in all the others.

THE LOGIC OF A
DISCIPLINE OF EDUCATION

MARC BELTH

THE DILEMMA OF EDUCATION

Education assuredly has many dilemmas. But more than any other arena of concern, more even than philosophy, education begins with the dilemma of establishing its own identity. Many are urged into the field, but what is to be studied is so indeterminate that a course is determined by its instructor, not its content. The need for definition is never answered. All there is is a kind of generalized area. Education is something that takes place in a school—but not always, and certainly not exclusively. Even the study of schooling practices, is no assurance that we are in the arena of education and not psychology, or sociology or the physiology and economy of growth. What criteria do we have to enable us to separate these? Can they never be separated? The schools, after all, are built by societies for such social purposes as will shape newer generations. Everything that happens in the school which influences the growth of the child is surely to be studied. Those who come to learn and to be shaped for effective conduct in a desirable future are being educated, are they not?

Assume for a moment that we accept this very familiar view. Education is the process of influence which societal institutions exercise on the young. It transmits to them the most desirable beliefs, the most demonstrable truths, the most approved modes of conduct. As such, education molds the young to become members of the very society which has erected the institution of the school. Now, precisely what shall we study in order to equip ourselves as the educators of the new world?

The answer is quite simple. Study all of the subject areas whose truths are to be transmitted; become sensitive to the values and the behavior patterns which are held to be desirable; and become technically efficient in the modes of communication within which these truths, values, and the conduct desired are to be transmitted to the young. Study the ways of making knowledge and value part of the habits of thinking and acting of each group of youngsters in school.

Certainly there is enough matter for a study of great depth, of very long duration, of much subtlety. If there is a dilemma over the terms of the definition that

The editor is deeply grateful for the privilege of publishing this original paper for the first time in this anthology. All rights are retained by the author.

is implied, it is a dilemma of shortness of time against the size of the obligation.

And yet this dilemma, when considered seriously, may well reveal itself to be specious, hiding a much more curious and difficult problem. The fact is that as long as there is no actual definition can we be sure of the time needed or the obligation to be met? When an area which is urged as a study reveals itself to be so very broad, and to that extent indefinable, the need to identify just what can be studied which is not already being studied in other disciplines becomes absolutely necessary.

There is a clearly defined discipline of communication, and there are developing theories to accompany its study. There are disciplines of sociology, and history, psychology and philosophy. Does this mean that in order to teach, to be an educator, to study the learning processes that occur, one must first study each of these already defined disciplines? Is it obligatory to become competent in them, and enter into this other educational arena, armed with equipment derived elsewhere? So it would seem. But if we do just this, *are* we studying education? Is there anything left to study? Is it anything more than a name which identifies nothing that does not already belong somewhere else?

What is the dilemma then? Quite simply, it is the obligation to study something which cannot be defined, explore something which cannot be distinguished, theorize upon actions which are explained already by the theories of well-established disciplines.

It is also the dilemma created by a presupposition that the instruments of one discipline can be used to transmit the findings of a second, third, fourth, and fifth discipline, and thereby produce a field unique unto itself.

But in spite of this imponderable state of affairs, the derivative approach to education goes almost unchallenged. The result is that at least two additional dilemmas are to be noted. One is rather minor yet needs to be mentioned. The other is much more interesting because of what might be done when a correction is offered.

On occasion education is given the honorary title of "discipline." It is honorary because it is given credit for having established theories of its own when in fact it has derived those theories from established disciplines by simple adoption. The concept "implicit in" is used as the courtesy term to account for that adoption. It is said, for example, that the fact that children learn readily what interests them implies that the classroom should be made informal in order to permit that interest to make its appearance. So a psychological theory becomes an educational principle, by untroubled adoption.

However, when discipline is defined meaningfully it has determinate reference. A discipline is bounded by a set of rules for inquiry and criteria for the evaluation of the applicability of those rules. A theory which serves as the explanatory system for the acceptability of those rules must be available. Finally, the action that occurs under these strictures produces newer rules, newer modes of developing cumulative inquiry, newer models for analysis of experience.

None of these can be truly pointed out as occurring in educational inquiry as such. The disciplinary characteristics described above are all borrowed from the surrounding or the parent disciplines. But like all offspring, it all too often claims as its own accomplishments the achievements of the parents. Yet as with all children, it takes more than such claims to establish these as belonging to the offspring because it belongs to the parents. We may be free to borrow from the accomplishments of our elders but we must be sure that these accomplishments are converted into a form which becomes distinctively ours. Either that, or the hat and the shoes never really do fit.

The easy borrowing, however, produces some fascinating linguistic confusions as we go deeper into our investigation. It is recognized that at best education must be an applied discipline, or an applied science. When we become alert to the rather doubtful character of "applied" anything, we seek a little better identity.

When we recognize that under the circumstances described there is truly nothing of its own that can be studied as education, we sometimes produce the much more interesting idea that everything we do study has educational implications. Thus, we come to consider education as the common denominator of all studies. Whatever we study, whether it be history, or physics, or art or philosophy, biology or psychology, produces educational implications. When all these implications are brought together and formed into a common, harmonizing denominator we are embarked on an educational career.

Now, "common denominator" is a common enough metaphor, though in this case it will be noted as a misplaced one. For in a case where the denominator does not in any way alter the value of the numerator, the metaphor is probably only another courtesy title and provides us with no genuine denominating function. To call education the common denominator of all other studies because it is an integrative act is to misconstrue the concept of a denominator and actually leave those studies untouched. To know all that one knows in one or another of those disciplines, and to assume that this is all that is required to teach or to educate in those disciplines, is to employ a metaphor without using it at all.

But take this notion seriously for a moment. What could possibly be meant by a denominator common to all of the distinctive disciplines? Is it possible to make it identifiable, in a larger sense, on its own terms? Conclusions in the various fields differ, since they are about different things. Methods of arriving at those conclusions differ since they are conclusions about different facets of experience. Modes of inquiry will also differ since matter, objectives and methods, interplaying with one another, will demand development of modes of thinking that are unique to the disciplines they represent.

What is left? The generic act of thinking. That is, a theoretical, conceptual approach to thinking at a level more abstract than the modes of thinking that distinguish the special disciplines from one another. As such, the generic act of thinking would have much to say about the character and the transmittability of the specific modes of thinking and the conclusions they have produced. This does indeed take advantage of a metaphor in a fruitful way.

THE SUBJECT MATTER OF EDUCATION

Consider in greater detail what is involved in the notion of a common denominator. Properly identified, the metaphoric use may well provide opportunity for an analysis of unexpected force. Necessarily, this consideration will be very brief since it is intended not as an analysis in its own terms but as a model for analysis of the education to which the analogue will be applied.

Denominators suggest the presence of fractions. They also suggest the presence of a numerator. When denominators differ nothing is to be inferred about the value of the numerator. When denominators are the same again nothing is to be inferred about the value of the numerator. But what is made possible is the performance of some operation upon the fractions as a whole in which the numerators will change values because of the existence of the common denominator and the operating rules brought into play

It is also to be noted that nothing in the numerator necessarily indicates the value of the denominator. When alteration in the denominator is to be achieved, it is achieved in light of two conditions. First, there must be a clear purpose in the mind of the individual considering the various fractions. Second, the conversion is determined by the rules that identify number systems and the operations those rules make possible among the numbers of that system. Nothing in any numerator, or set of numerators, indicates what shall be established as the common denominator among 2, 3, 4, 6. The rules of operation between these numbers themselves indicate that the lowest (most parsimonious) denominator would be 12 if within a prevailing system operations of computation are to be performed.

When the denominator is established the operation indicates the necessary compensating operation to be performed upon the numerators in order to maintain the relationships between the fractions in balance.

The use of this computing concept, this series of operations, as an analogy for the character of education is probably evident and quite simple. Yet for all its simplicity it is quite significant.

The fraction itself is analogous to the notion that every discipline is but a fraction of what goes into the whole of the educative process. The knowledge that is treated is a fraction of all knowledge attained or possible. The values are a fraction of all values held. The behavior patterns are no less fractional of all the possibilities of behaviors that could be nurtured.

The numerator is the segment of knowledge, value, or behavior patterns we have been able to encompass to any given moment. And the denominator is what each fractional discipline shares as an operating rule with every other fractional discipline. (It is important to note that in dealing with disciplines no claim is made that at some time a fractional discipline will be complete. Reality seems not to allow for such a development. But this is no part of the concern here though it is important to mention. In the Platonic sense, the experiential world is always partial or, in terms of our metaphor, fractional.)

Pursuing the analogy, we can expect that when the denominator is seen as common, the effects on the numerator are such as to require them to be converted to maintain the proper relationships to the converted denominators.

Consider the way in which this would now appear. The physiologist, the artist, the psychologist, all direct their studied attention to the human organism. Each then is a fraction of a much larger concern. Even if there were only these three disciplines each would be concerned with a fraction of the concerns of all three. Since there are many more disciplines also concerned with the human organism the fractional character of each should be obvious.

At first glance, however, each fraction is identified by the specific aspect of its concern. (The artist with the structure and the features of the body; the physiologist with the functions of the various elements of the organism; the psychologist with the relationships between functions and behavioral patterns of the organism.) In each case the denominator is in some way bound up with each specific concern reflecting in its methodological limits the focus of that numeratorial concern. In fact, each denominator refers to the full method of which the numerator uses only a part. The methods of inquiry which each uses is directed and limited by the goals sought and by the particular facet of the organism being examined. The mode of thinking that is employed by each fraction (or discipline) is determined in a like manner, though no two modes being identical with one another, conditions being determined as they are.

But now consider an entirely different objective introduced into this situation. Instead of the specific concerns of knowledge of the artist, the physiologist, and the psychologist, there is developed a concern with the common aspect of all of these modes of inquiry. What would occur?

Clearly, although the three inquirers share a common subject matter, it is not quite so common as first appears. What each is specifically concerned with is unique to the objectives and to the methods or means by which the objectives are attained. Psychological thinking is very clearly different from physiological thinking. Just how they differ will be of great interest and importance to use, noticeable only when we move toward the more defensible identification of what would appear to be a common denominator.

Assume the objective of the physiologist is an understanding of the organic operations of the body in its internal transactions. Assume the objectives of the psychological inquiry is an understanding of the effects of inner organic functioning on overt behavior. What is common to these? Add that the concern of the artist is the understanding of the anatomical features of the organism under certain conditions so as to be able to understand its structural appearance. What is common to all three? Only this: that each is a mode of thinking. As such, though it may differ in its methods and in its objectives, it must be characterized by a set of generic traits which, few though they may be, appear in all acts of thinking.

When we identify the objective of a study that is the common denominator of all inquiry it can only be the understanding of the functioning of the thinking act which all of the particular disciplines share. But it can only be those acts or traits which they all do in fact share. Thus, the common denominator will be less detailed, more abstract, less inclusive of the specific determinants that enter into thinking. They will be noted not as physical description but rather description as such; not scientific or aesthetic explanation, but explanation as such; not psychological, or historical, or sociological interpretation, but the conception of interpretation in itself.

The common denominator of all of the disciplines is the variety of elements that enter into each, transformed into the most inclusive state (yet most parsimonious so as not to overextend the arena of study) by means of which the specific disciplines are seen to be the specific acts of thinking that they are.

Now the list of common traits which thinking in all disciplines employ has no well-ordained existence. They can be listed almost arbitrarily, in terms of the purposes desired. In this case, since the purpose is to distinguish the pursuit of knowledge in specific arenas of experience from the pursuit of the knowledge of knowledge making, the list will be organized to include those which seem necessary for the act of thinking. These would include exploration, or observation, depending upon what is examined, description, definition, explanation, interpretation, invention (or introduction of novelty by means of alternative organizations of materials), and evaluation. Each discipline uses each of these to some degree, the whole, weighted uniquely in the terms of the objectives sought, making for the distinctive character of the thinking of each discipline. But generically, the concern is not to *use* these elements of thinking, but to study, to confront, to explore and analyze, to discover the range possibilities the various combinations make available to those who come to learn.

Thus, while the subject matter of the physiologist is the functioning of the human organism and that of the psychologist the relationship between those functions and the overt behaviors (and soon, for all of the other specific disciplines), *the subject matter of education being common to all disciplines is the very thinking which each uses in the pursuit of its objectives.*

All thinking involves the series of acts listed above. But these, of course, are not random acts. They occur systematically, each element having influence on the others and taking leads from those others. Each specific discipline follows rules of thinking. The rules employed derive from the organization of the discipline itself and this organization can best be identified as the set of models that each discipline uses in pursuit of its objectives. To say that psychological thinking differs from philosophical thinking is to say that psychological models will be discovered to be quite distinct from philosophical models of inquiry and explanation. It will also be noted that teaching the use of each set of models requires yet another, more inclusive set.

What education studies are the characteristics of models as the determinants of thinking as they appear distinctively in each of the prevailing specific disciplines.

If there is some concern that both philosophy and psychology are already identified as disciplines whose focus is on thinking, it must be remembered that the former is concerned to clarify what the concept itself is held to include and to exclude, what can and cannot be validly said in light of prevailing or accepted definitions.

And psychology is concerned with discovering the effects of organic conditions on such matters as motives, aspirations, perceptions, responses. But not even together do the fractional disciplines constitute all that can be studied as *thinking*. Neither separately nor together are they concerned with the study of the actual range and limitations which the employment of definitive models makes possible as modes of explaining, ways of describing, forms of interpretation, methods and tactics of exploration.

Only education finds itself concerned with this. For education the subject matter turns out to be the processes of inquiry of each of the specific disciplines. But these must (as the analogue shows the role that numerators play) be first converted into some larger, more generic, less specific but more inclusive value. Thinking, in this generic sense, is the subject matter of education and its illustrative arenas are the specific modes of use which can be observed in the separate disciplines.

THINKING AS THE COMMON DENOMINATOR

If this were all that could be set forth about thinking and about the differences in the levels of abstraction that distinguish education from other so-called parent disciplines, the difficulties would hardly be resolved. The act of thinking must be open to description in some set of elemental terms or we have nothing to evaluate. If we can describe the specific procedures undertaken in the various disciplines we encounter and if we need to generate a greater level of abstraction, we shall have to be able to extract from the specific acts statements that identify the traits held in common by all of them. In this way we will be able to distinguish the *types* of models used by a psychologist, or a chemist, for example, and the *forms* of models that all disciplines use, regardless of the particular type employed, and the particular goal sought.

Following the most widely accepted notion of thinking as problem solving, the psychologist addresses his observations and explorations to what he sees to be a problem. He sets about describing that particular problem so that in the description he will have data for the construction of some explanation of the difficulty and a recommendation for its resolution. Undertaking an active experiment, overt or intellectual, he observes the consequences of his exploration and evaluates them in the light of the problem-explanation he has envisioned and the actual outcomes. The sequence of steps taken here, it has long been argued, are, in general, the steps taken in any inquiry.

At the philosophical level of inquiry much the same could be held, except that problem is a purely cognitive one, in which the clarification of the meanings of various aspects of the procedure is sought. Psychology, then, addresses itself to empirical problems we confront, and philosophy to cognitive ones.

But education is concerned not simply to perform the same operations as psychology and philosophy, but to analyze both cognitive and empirical operations in the terms of the elements that comprise the whole. Psychology will use the powers of thought, and philosophy will seek to clarify the meanings of " powers of thought." But education attempts to analyze those "powers" in order to be able to see the variety of characteristics they take on, the variety of roles they play in different settings and different pursuits, and to evaluate the ways the clustering of the elements affect the range of thinking made possible.

The very act of thinking here set down can be converted into a more general form and made a condition for the examination of the particular modes of thinking represented by any particular discipline.

It is in that movement that the act of thinking comes to be identified as the integrated activities of observing, exploring, describing, defining, explaining, inventing or hypothesizing, reasoning, evaluating. But in the larger sense, what is said about each of these elements will not be descriptive of any specific act which actually occurs. It will be a description of description, of explanation, and the rest. It will be an explanation of description, of explanation, of exploration, and the others. It will be a purely intellectual exploration of the limiting role played by each of the elements on the entire act of thinking as this is determined by the interplay of the elements in some form of a model.

In this way we come to the point of recognizing that description, for instance, has many faces not all of which contribute to the improving act of thinking. Even explanation, when uninfluenced by active operations of the other elements, is a dredging up of the language of models which hold us in thrall and a repeating of what old and remembered convictions oblige us to repeat.

It is, in fact, in the analysis of each of these elements that we can identify the limits of the act of thinking, and those occurrences which appear to be thinking, but which can now be identified as alternatives to the very act that education is concerned with studying and fostering.

Most significantly, a consideration of the elements of thinking at this level of abstraction is a purely theoretical operation. We are not simply theorizing. We are exploring and describing, explaining and inventing, interpreting and evaluating the *act* of theorizing at a non-empirical level to begin with and at an experimental level on later classroom occasions. We are seeking to learn the range of thinking and valuing that becomes possible in the various models for thinking, but we are doing so in the strictest of theoretical methods.

In such a study the basic character of each of the disciplines stands revealed in the types of models it makes available to its practitioners, and the additional models each discipline builds to alter and improve its own functioning.

MODELS AND EDUCATION

Consider that a theory, when fully coherent, is a model of some frankly imagined state of affairs. We accept it not in the hope of proving it someday to be just what we imagined it to be. Rather, we accept it because with it we can account for and describe what otherwise is unaccountable and indescribable. Theory, then, becomes for us an archetype model which enables us to understand what functions all other forms of models perform.

For theories are not the only forms that models take. In order to perform the explanatory, descriptive functions earlier noted, we sometimes develop scale models, or analogue models (analogies), or mathematical models, or linguistic models. This does not exhaust the list, of course, but however many we may add, each model will be limited in the kind of explanation it can make, the kind of descriptions it permits, the explorations it makes available, and the modes of reasoning that are acceptable. These models, each in their own forms, provide the forms for the thinking they make possible. A brief series of distinctions will demonstrate this idea.

Scale models are re-presentations of selected features of real events into an event of another quality. A model train, for example, is an illustration of the selected re-presenting of the observable event that is the real train, and it makes possible a kind of exploration that no other model makes possible.

Analogue models are models in which features and relationships from a familiar realm of existence are used as a means of looking at another realm which may or may not be familiar. It makes possible an imagining of the operations of some event in ways not usually imagined. An analogy produces an image, a "mental" picture reflected by something quite familiar. When we analogize the effects of persistent television viewing with the addiction produced by certain mind-expanding or mind-limiting drugs, a description of the effects of the drug are translatable into a description of the effects of the persistent watching of television's present programs upon the mental powers of its users.

Theoretical models are models in which *conceptual* features are the focus of concern. Such features cannot be treated as descriptions of existential events, though they can be described as mental operations. To accept such conceptual features makes possible an explanation and an interpretation of the behavior of real events, by a logical deduction of the relationship postulated as existing between the elements of that model. What we say deductively about possible further relationships we now can say about actual events. As Max Black says, theory is "an imaginary analogy." Since it is not constructed in the empirical sense that a scale model is, it presents us uniquely with a way of *talking* about experienced events.

Mathematical models are akin to the theoretical. In their form they set forth the rules of deduction used and the limits of the reasoning permitted between the symbols connected by given operating indicators. Such models make it possible to evaluate the consistency between the terms and inferences made in theoretical models. But mathematical models provide no possibility for developing hypotheses about the events of nature, nor of predicting what can or might occur. The very form and concern of a mathematical model directs thinking to concern itself with deductive inferences that are permissible in the formal connections that statements are held to have with one another. Thus, mathematical models provide us with ways (rules) for thinking about the tenable and valid relationships that concepts have with one another. We create in these models rules for performing certain mental operations (addition, commutation, transformation, disjunction, and the like) for applying certain qualitative and quantitative forms to events, and for following this application with the rules which enable us to establish validity in later conclusions about the relationships created.

It is important to note that each discipline uses each of these model forms in its own ways. But as it refines its capacities to explore and explain the common materials of experience, each discipline produces models of a type unique to itself. Each discipline increases in its capacity to give broader and more discriminating accounts of the dimensions of experience it seeks to explain as it develops a whole family of model types. When, within an otherwise integrated discipline, we find that the types begin to include different *kinds* (as when, for example, some historians use mechanical models while others use organic models to explain the events examined), the discipline itself begins to break apart, sometimes to its advantage in growth, sometimes to its disadvantage in the loss of community among the scholars who are its membership. An examination of history as written by Toynbee demonstrates incisively the same theoretical *forms* taking different types and producing different explanations as compared with Trevor-Roper, for example.

Since every discipline is a precise model-using art, we must assume that if education is to be a discipline, it must have no less an identifiable cluster of models. By means of them it performs its distinctive functions and by means of them makes possible thinking which is uniquely educational. If models do not yet exist, they can certainly be invented, even if, to begin with, they are borrowed from successful disciplines. The borrowing, however, must be accompanied by transformation (or conversion, to say with the metaphor) to permit the fulfillment of educational objectives for the nurturing of distinctive ways of thinking. For, just as history is not psychology, however much the historian may wish to borrow the insights of psychology by borrowing some of his models, so education is not any other discipline, however much it may avail itself of the models of those other disciplines.

We have more educational models available to us than we might have been aware of. Dialogics, didactics, scholastics, experimentalisms, among still others, all have been employed to lay bare the characteristics, limitations, and functions that the different discipline-models possess for developing each their distinctive knowledge. Even further, educational models as the common denominator for the study and nurture of the models of each numerator-discipline make possible the study not only of the sources, conditions and status of the knowledge produced, but of the values that are developed and the desirable behavior differently espoused.

A CONCLUDING ILLUSTRATION

In place of a recapitulation of the analysis of the role of models as the subject matter of the discipline of education perhaps it would be of greater value to illustrate, however briefly, how a model, in this case an analogue model, is employed to direct thinking about a particular problem and how such a model is analyzed in educational thinking.

One of the recurrent areas of study in courses in education is that of the relationship between the community and the teaching profession. We know from much of the evidence that has been produced by sociological and psychological studies that the teacher occupies a position of a relatively low status in community activities. In spite of this, he is expected to bear extensive obligations in the matter of caring for and helping to develop children attending school. The low status is measured by the relative low earning power, by the small amount of community responsibilities permitted him, by the conception of the little competence he is regarded as having, and by the rather simple requirements a community or state establishes for becoming a teacher.

Now, the conclusions produced by inquiry vary, according to the particular discipline. In the explanation of these facts and the ways in which they are described, the profession itself is evaluated in the social or psychological models used. The results are quite familiar in the sterilizing they have on the teachers themselves.

In considering the profession as a possible choice for herself, one student sought a more fruitful model to explain in more penetrating clarity, and more luminous descriptive terms, just how the relationship between a teacher and the community might be thought about and understood. Deliberately mixing her metaphors, she chose to analogize education as a profession with a very familiar literary construction, and produced an interesting and original exposition. She recommended that the community was collectively Sancho Panza, and that the teacher individually was Don Quixote.

From the model which Cervantes created, she recast the characters of that school-community relationship. The teacher was the noble, foolish quester after purity and perfection in the world, derided by the realists he encountered, yet in some unexpected way, admired and revered for the integrity of his pursuit of a vision which could not possibly be attained.

Merely to recommend Don Quixote as the model is to enable anyone who knows the character and the story to describe the teacher in such metaphoric terms as adds new meaning to his efforts. It also provides explanation for his conduct, for the conduct of the community (Sancho was crude, earthy, concerned with staying alive, enjoying himself at the levels available to him, yet in such awe of the mournful knight that he half believed what in fact he knew to be delusion) and for the relationship between them.

Is all this literally true, this analogy? Of course not. Does it invalidate the prevailing models? Of course not. But it adds dimension to understanding and variety to thinking. Analogues are not scale models. In their uses we grasp deeper significances in both familiar or unfamiliar relationships. And once established, what a world of further consideration, exploration, alteration, evaluation suddenly becomes available. Imagine, too, the experiments or the dialogues (to suggest but two educational models) that can be employed to further lay bare and nurture expanding use of this literary mode of thinking about education and schooling, and you begin to have an insight both of how thinking occurs in the presence of deliberately used models, and how education by use of its own models, makes such models available to those who learn.

PART V
EUROPEAN SCHOOLS
Issues and Innovations

The specific reasons for including a section on European schools in an anthology entitled *Controversy in American Education* are three: Students, educators and laymen have always evinced a great deal of interest in European education, yet the present interest seems to be in becoming more informed about foreign schools in contrast to the sophomoric comparing of American schools with educational systems of other nations that fascinated Americans a few years ago; secondly, rapid changes are affecting all countries in Europe and with these changes have come important educational reforms, reforms basically designed to provide greater educational opportunities for more youth and for longer periods of time; in the third place, accompanying these changes have been an intensity of criticism and conflicting opinions that rival those found in the United States. Implicit in these reasons is a desire to have the reader take a closer look at American education from a different perspective, where the issues may be viewed in a new context.

This section is intended to be nothing more than a brief introduction to some of the current concerns of schools found in Europe, with particular emphasis on three countries: France, England and the Soviet Union. It is hoped, however, that, brief as this section is, an enthusiastic interest will be developed that will lead to further study in the field of comparative education. The reading of any of the general books listed in Selected References would be an appropriate place to begin.

SELECTED REFERENCES

Cramer, John F., and George S. Browne. *Comparative Education: A Comparative Study of National Systems* (2nd ed.). New York: Harcourt, Brace and World, 1965.

Eckstein, M. A. "Present Trends in Public Secondary Education in Western Europe," *High School Journal* (October 1960), pp. 8–19.

Hanson, John W., and Cole S. Brembeck. *Education and the Development of Nations.* New York: Holt, Rinehart, and Winston, 1966.

Hennessy, Maurice N. "New Directions for British Education," *Saturday Review* (August 21, 1965), pp. 58–59, 65–66.

Kazamias, Andreas M., and Byron G. Massialas. *Tradition and Change in Education: A Comparative Study.* Englewood Cliffs, N. J.: Prentice-Hall, Inc., 1965.

King, Edmund J. *Communist Education.* Indianapolis: Bobbs-Merrill Co., 1963.

————. *Other Schools and Ours* (Rev. ed.). New York: Holt, Rinehart, and Winston, 1963.

————. *World Perspectives in Education.* Indianapolis: Bobbs-Merrill Co., 1962.

Mallison, V. *An Introduction to the Study of Comparative Education.* New York: The Macmillan Company, 1957.

Noah, Harold J., "Soviet Education's Unsolved Problems," *Saturday Review* (August 21, 1965), pp. 54–56, 64–65.

Reller, Theodore L., and Edgar L. Morphet. *Comparative Educational Administration.* Englewood Cliffs, N. J.: Prentice-Hall, Inc., 1962.

Shafer, Susanne M. "Germany's European Children," *Teachers College Record* (January 1964), pp. 361–371.

Thut, I. N., and Don Adams. *Educational Patterns in Contemporary Societies.* New York: McGraw-Hill, 1964.

Ulich, Robert. *The Education of Nations.* Cambridge, Mass.: Harvard University Press, 1961.

Vredevoe, Lawrence E. "School Discipline—Third Report on a Study of Students and School Discipline in the United States and Other Countries," *The Bulletin of the National Association of Secondary School Principals* (March 1965), pp. 215–226.

THE CHANGING
EDUCATIONAL SCENE ON
BOTH SIDES OF THE
ATLANTIC

JAMES B. CONANT

One again I have the privilege of addressing the annual meeting of the National Association of Secondary-School Principals. Once again I thank the officers of the Association for their hospitality which I have enjoyed so often in the past, and once again I should like to acknowledge my indebtedness to many members of this Association for their help when I undertook to study the American high school in 1957. It was to a meeting of this Association that I made my preliminary report in 1958. The comments which I received in informal conversations after my address resulted in worthwhile changes before the report was published in January 1959.

In those days, you will recall, not a few Americans were questioning the ideas of the comprehensive high school. The suggestion was made more than once that we would do well to reverse the trend in American education, we should give up the comprehensive high school; instead, we should establish academic selective high schools for those with more than usual scholastic ability. The European system was held out as a model. Indeed even today I run into people who say, "You have been in Berlin a year and a half; of course, you've found the German system of education to be far superior to ours." To which I can only reply some Germans don't think so. Indeed, there are many who are extremely dissatisfied with the current situation, indeed alarmed for the future of free Germany unless drastic changes are quickly made. And the basic question is just the question which has been raised in recent years in the United States, namely, should the more intellectually able youth be separated from the others at an early age and provided with special opportunities for the study of strictly academic subjects? The European pattern has been one in which after four years of schooling those who are judged

Reprinted by permission from the *Bulletin of the National Association of Secondary-School Principals* (March 1965). Copyright: Washington, D. C.

EUROPEAN SCHOOLS: ISSUES AND INNOVATIONS

to be academically talented are enrolled in what might be called university preparatory schools (the German gymnasia, the French lycées, and the British grammar schools). A rigorous eight or nine years course heavily weighted with the study of ancient or modern languages then culminates in a diploma or certificate admitting to a university—a university in the European sense of the word, essentially a collection of professional schools; for there is no equivalent of the four-year American undergraduate college anywhere in Europe or Great Britain.

The system I have just described is being seriously challenged today in all or almost all the free nations of Europe. In some countries the challenge has not gone much beyond the state of a vigorous discussion. In one nation, however, namely Sweden, the old system has been abandoned and a new one introduced after ten years of debate. The change is interesting and important. But the reasons given for the change are more important still, for they reflect a basic unrest among the leaders of European thought, a deep concern for the consequences, if the old pattern of selective schools is retained. The economist has entered the educational scene, and his arguments are listened to by governments with more attention than has been paid to pedagogues in the past. One leading German industrialist said to me just a few years ago that if the Germans don't overhaul their schools and universities quickly, they will soon be an underdeveloped nation.

But I am getting ahead of my story. Let me sketch in briefly what has happened in Sweden and what is about to happen. Selection at age 10 + for entry into a pre-university school has largely disappeared and will soon disappear completely. A nine-year comprehensive school provides education for all the children and youth from age seven to sixteen inclusive. Attendance for all within this age span is compulsory. For those who so desire, education is provided beyond the ninth grade in three types of higher schools, one of which is a pre-university school corresponding somewhat to the last three years of the German gymnasium. At present about 20 per cent of the relevant age group are thus preparing to enter the universities; thirty years ago the corresponding figure was over 9 per cent; by 1970 it is expected to rise to 35 per cent and at least 80 per cent of this group are expected to enter a university or a corresponding technical institute.

In the Federal Republic of Germany taken as a whole, only about 6 per cent of an age group complete the pre-university work, and in some of the German states the figure is as low as 4. (In Free Berlin it is about 9.) When one keeps these figures in mind and compares them with the Swedish projection for 1970, 35 per cent, one can imagine what an impact the Swedish example is having on the thinking of forward-looking Europeans, and I might add Britishers as well. But who cares what fraction of an age group prepare for a university, one may ask. Indeed, the standpatters are now asking just that question in the Federal Republic of Germany. And they are adding the comment that unless you lower the standards you can't increase the numbers who enter the universities, for already every young person who has the ability can obtain free education through the pre-university period of schooling. It is just these statements which have been questioned in Sweden since the close of World War II.

The Swedish approach to the question of school reform is illuminating as it illustrates how in a small nation of about 8 million something approaching a rational answer to complex problems may be arrived at as a result of a careful scholarly inquiry! The proponents of the traditional European system have long maintained that one could spot the intellectually able as readily at age 10 or 11 as at 16. Studies by Swedish psychologists made in the 1940s tended to support this claim. But it is a long jump from such a conclusion to a further claim that an educational system based on selection at an early age uncovers all the potential talent of a nation. What have been omitted in such reasoning are the consequences of parental desires and the tendencies of a society to perpetuate class differences. These realities were studied in the 1950s by Professor Torsten Husen of the University of Stockholm, and his results were largely instrumental in bringing about the reform of Swedish education.

Professor Husen has estimated that in many European countries the proportion of the country's potential academic talent that is left undeveloped when selections for secondary school are made at the age of 10 was between 40 and 70 per cent. Professor Husen writes, and I quote, "The selective school, *i.e.*, the school which seeks to separate the book learners from the rest as soon as possible, inflicts a fearful wastage of talent; in my opinion, the wastage is much greater than would result from allowing pupils of different gifts to stay together in the same classes as long as possible." And Professor Husen concludes that a modern industrialized society, if it is to be competitive with other nations (note the economic argument), requires "an *elective* school, not a selective school." By elective school he means a school in which the pupils, by being permitted a "phased choice of electives" can gradually focus their studies "in a direction to which they are drawn by their abilities and interests."

An American reading about what is happening in Sweden might jump to the conclusion that the Swedes had adopted the comprehensive high school. Such a conclusion would be false. The comprehensive Swedish school is a 9-grade school though the leaving age is 16+ because in Sweden the children enter grade 1 at about 7 instead of with us at about 6. The elective principle which Professor Husen emphasizes and which takes place within a single school, begins in grades 7 and 8 but only reaches its full extent in grade 9 which is not unlike grades 11 and 12 with us insofar as the differentiation is concerned. But the Swedish pupils in grades 10, 11, and 12 are separated into at least three types of schools with quite different offerings.

The social argument which to us is so compelling for the American comprehensive high school—the importance of mixing up all type of youth—this idea seems to have been of secondary importance in the Swedish thinking. The clinching argument has been economic. What seems to be demonstrated in Sweden is that unless a school system postpones the separation of the university bound from the others until age 16 a great deal of potential academic talent is lost and the nation suffers. Furthermore, by continuing full-time compulsory education through age 16 a considerable portion of the youth is ready to enter two-year courses in business and technical areas and thus be prepared for many essential activities in a highly industrialized society.

I should point out, perhaps, that the Swedish reforms start from some assumptions about the importance of a knowledge of foreign languages and mathematics which until very recently most Americans would repudiate. The 35 per cent of the age group which in 1970 will finish the three-year course in the pre-university school in Sweden will have a command of one modern foreign language (English), a considerable knowledge of a second foreign language and a knowledge of mathematics through the calculus. Such accomplishments are as high as those demanded by the German gymnasia.

I have spoken of the entry of the economist into the discussion of education on the other side of the Atlantic. I should have said, perhaps, the economist and the educational planner. What I have in mind are the activities of the Organization for Economic Cooperation and Development composed of 17 European nations, Great Britain, and the United States. The convention which established this organization in 1960 provided that it should promote policies designed "to achieve the highest sustainable economic growth and employment and a rising standard of living in member countries, while maintaining financial stability and thus contribute to the world economy. . . ." A Study Group on the Economics of Education has been established. It has just issued a voluminous report on Economic Aspects of Higher Education. The Directorate for Scientific Affairs of the OECD is in the process of reviewing the policies for science and education in the member countries. The reviews thus far issued include those of Denmark, Sweden, and the United States. The reviews are carried out periodically, we are told, and I quote, "as a means of assessing the progress and problems of the individual members of the organization in educating and effectively using a sufficient number of scientists, engineers, and technicians to meet their present and future economic needs." This quotation will show you what I mean when I say the economist has moved into the educational picture. More striking evidence is provided by an 11 page brochure on the Mediterranean Regional Project. The needs of Greece, Italy, Portugal, Spain, Turkey, and Yugoslavia are surveyed, forecasts are made, and educational recommendations laid down in specific terms. Whether these recommendations will be followed is very much of an open question. Actions by governments involving education are slow both for financial and ideological reasons. They have been talking vigorously about changing education in Italy for at least 10 years to my personal knowledge, but little or nothing has as yet happened.

To some of you, what I have been reporting about the changing educational scene may be highly distasteful, not because you do not welcome the expansion of educational opportunities in other countries, but because of the arguments which are used to support the change. To say that they were permeated with utilitarianism and nationalism would be an understatement—not a competitive military nationalism I must hasten to add, but a highly competitive industrial nationalism. Yet when we look at the situation in the Federal Republic of Germany in a little detail, it is hard to separate the economic factors from the cultural. The cultural life of a nation is closely bound to the welfare of its schools. To find enough teachers and professors to keep their present system going may be very difficult for the Germans in the next ten years. The Nazi regime, the War, the reconstruction of their industry and their cities, and the strict federalism of their educational system all have led to an alarming state of affairs which has only just come to light. A great many teachers are reaching the retirement age; there have been far too few new teachers trained since 1945. As a consequence, by 1970 it is estimated that out of 500,000 who will have completed the pre-university schools 300,000 should be recruited as teachers—a most unlikely result. The impending "catastrophe"— that is the word used by many German writers—highlights the question of what per cent of an age group should receive advanced education. Certainly 6 per cent is far too small a figure; some say the percentage should become at least 16 and very soon. But how, without greatly lowering standards? That is the question. A similar question is being asked in England and in France.

Does the Swedish experience point the way toward the answer for other nations? In Germany the fact that the proportion of youth ready for university work varies enormously from state to state and from place to place within a state certainly seems to bear out Professor Husen's hypothesis that parental decisions are often determining. A story I heard in Berlin illustrates this point. One mason said to another as they started work together one morning, "Hans, why are you so depressed today?" "Oh," replied the other, "I have bad news. My son has just passed his examinations and will soon enter the university. It will be years before he can earn any money." "I am lucky," said the other, "my son flunked out of school three years ago and is now at work." To understand the significance of this little story one must remember there is full employment in Germany and a flourishing apprentice system with a place ready for almost any youth who applies after leaving school at age 15.

The educational authorities of free Berlin are experimenting with comprehensive schools more nearly in the American than in the Swedish sense of these words. The fact that in the one school of this type which has been functioning for some years, about 16 per cent of the age group pass the school-leaving examination as compared with less than 8 per cent in a comparable Berlin neighborhood seems to me significant. Further, schools are in the planning stage but outside of Berlin there is little enthusiasm for the idea of substituting an elective system for a selective system (to use Husen's terminology). The voice of the economist and educational planner is drowned out by those who shout for retaining the traditional pattern and these arguments are cultural and pedagogic. I underline this point lest what I have said so far has given the false impression that utilitarianism has come to dominate educational discussions on the continent of Europe. Such is far from being the case. More often than not the discussion centers on the question, what should constitute a liberal education for a professional man or woman. It is an article of faith among the traditionalists that a truly educated person must have studied Latin for nine years, because it is claimed that the difficulties of the language cannot be mastered in lesser time. From this premise it follows that the separation of the pre-university students from the others must take place after four years of elementary education, and a mixing of students with different programs is regarded with pedagogic horror. Against such arguments, those who are advocating a comprehensive school, even for only 8 years, make little headway. The needs of a modern industrialized society seem to be on a collision course with the German concept of "Bildung"—a sacred word which one might translate as liberal or classical education.

If I am to discuss the educational scene on both sides of the Atlantic, however, it is more than time that I left the continent of Europe. I cross the channel with just a fleeting glance at France where there is much ferment. Economic and technological considerations seem to be winning the battle against conservative forces. At all events the plans call for an expansion of the proportions of those completing a pre-university type of secondary education from the present figure of 11 per cent to 19 by 1970. These developments are pointed to by the German reformers as proof of the backwardness of German educational planning. The projected figure for free Germany as a whole is only 8 per cent for 1970.

In Great Britain at present the selective pattern prevails. At the age of 11 + pupils are chosen for the grammar schools which prepare for entrance to a university. Something like 7 per cent of an age group finish pre-university secondary education. The projected figure for 1970 is only 9 per cent. Not a few are dissatisfied with the present system. The reform movement, if I may call it that, has been centered on developing two other types of schools parallel to the grammar school —the Secondary Technical School and the Secondary Modern School of which there are several modifications. The trend in the development of the Secondary Modern School is in the direction of approximating the American Comprehensive High School. An increasing number of pupils in these modern schools which are not selective, elect courses in academic subjects. Such preparations enable the pupils to compete with grammar school graduates in those examinations which control entrance to the universities. Though these modern schools were originally intended for the "non-academic child" it looks as if they would more and more become a recognized road to the university. What the new Labor Government will do about these schools and about the selective grammar schools with the 11 + examination, is one of the most interesting questions of the moment.

What about the educational scene on this side of the Atlantic? One can prove almost anything about American education if one is permitted to generalize on the basis of a small sample. But no informed person will challenge one fact—namely, that the scene is in rapid movement. Indeed I have found to my chagrin that writing about American education is almost as breathtaking as writing about international politics. Before a book is in print, parts of it are already out of date! Therefore, change and talk of change are characteristic of the educational scene on both sides of the Atlantic. But the focal points are quite different. What I have been recounting about the European concern for increasing the fraction of an age group finishing an academic secondary education and raising the school leaving age for all, sounds strange to American ears. As far as attending school full-time is at issue, we went far beyond any European goals a long time ago. One is tempted to say that we in the United States accepted the comprehensive high school as a permanent fixture of our system before World War II. I am tempted to make such a sweeping generalization particularly when talking to my friends in Berlin. But now I raise the question of whether we are not witnessing a drift away from the widely comprehensive high school. Not that I see much danger of a growth in the number of selective academic high schools which exist in a few areas, but I wonder if there may not be a trend towards increasing the number of vocational high schools. For example, in the recent *NASSP Spotlight* there is a paragraph on area vocational schools. In Pennsylvania last week I heard an interesting discussion on area vocational schools. I think I understand the difficulties and the expense in providing modern up-to-date vocational programs in a comprehensive high school. I realize further that in a number of the larger cities the separate vocational high schools are so well established that it is not practical to think of giving them up. But it could be that the point of view of those who are active in the large cities has tended to make us forget the real arguments in favor of the comprehensive high school.

What are these arguments? I hardly need remind you that they are based on some fundamental ideas about the kind of society we have and want to have in the United States—a society that is different from that of European nations. Perhaps we have taken these arguments so much for granted that we have forgotten their importance. At least one does not hear nowadays much about the comprehensive high school as an instrument for forwarding democratic ideals, about its promotion of the cohesiveness of our society. The increasing homogeneity of the suburban communities makes the problem difficult. Yet in many suburban schools there is still a group who do not want to go to college. I still think the concept of skills marketable on graduation from high school is useful for counseling certain types of students. I wonder how many of you agree. I am sure the vast majority of secondary school principals do not have to be reminded of their responsibilities for providing opportunities for students of varying backgrounds and ambitions to understand one another. But perhaps in some appropriate way NASSP could reaffirm its belief in the widely comprehensive high school and be prepared to look with favor on any district reorganization which would insure that the high school involved would be widely comprehensive.

Now granted the elective pattern for secondary education as compared with the selective, two problems immediately arise. First, what should be the content of the many elective courses; second, how shall one proceed so that the students make wise elections? These problems have not yet been fully faced by the Europeans who look with favor on our system. They do not understand the role of the counselor or the necessity for standardized achievement tests. Indeed we ourselves are baffled by many problems which arise when we talk about helping students make a wise choice among electives. Now some would say that within the comprehensive high school the changes made in the last half dozen years have been chiefly changes in content of the courses. But I would disagree.

I would list eight significant changes, all of which would readily come to mind. These are:

1. The disappearance of the 6-period day and the emergence of new organizational patterns evolved under the leadership of this organization;
2. The wide acceptance of ability grouping together with new schemes for grouping;
3. The multiplication of summer schools for other than remedial purposes;
4. The increasing emphasis on improving writing skills (and again the NASSP has shown the way);
5. The revolution in the teaching of foreign languages.

And on this point I must dwell a moment. Ten years ago the accepted pattern was to start the study not earlier than grade 9 and then offer two years of Latin and two years of French or Spanish. And only a small fraction of even the ablest students selected such a program, which was, perhaps, just as well, as such a fragmentary exposure was essentially worthless. The idea of learning to speak a foreign language was alien to both pupils and teachers in most of the schools I visited in 1957 and 1958. Now language laboratories are to be found on every hand and instruction is by the direct method often started in the lower grades. An acceptance of the idea that the purpose of studying a foreign language is to master it, is now spreading throughout the land. But there is no need to tell this audience about the revolutionary changes in the foreign language field which are under way. Only yesterday I was talking to a principal of a high school who told me that formerly in his language department students were taking two years of French and two years of Spanish, etc., but now the emphasis is on four years of one language.

6. The sixth significant change is the introduction of new curricula: new mathematics of several kinds, three kinds of new biology; two kinds of new chemistry. The new physics was first developed by Professor Zacharias who deserves credit for starting the movement for curriculum reform in our high schools.
7. Television, programed instruction, and team teaching are innovations which may be listed as the 7th change which is affecting the educational scene, though opinions differ on the effectiveness of all three.
8. Perhaps the most significant change is the 8th I shall list. That is the changed relationship between school and college.

I know the situation is different in different parts of the nation and from school to school. But the competition for places in a relatively few colleges has had a profound effect on what goes on in many schools. For better or worse there has been a great shift in emphasis. The old fashioned academic subjects once only tolerated by the educational reformers are now back in fashion. I have already referred to foreign languages and the revolutions in instruction methods in this field and the new mathematics, new physics, chemistry, and biology. Indeed one might say the old fashioned subjects were now back in favor but so modernized as to be quite reformed. In talking about the relation of school to college one must emphasize the importance of the advanced placement program on the one hand, and the growth of the two year college on the other. The old line separating school from college has become very fuzzy. Which fact has many implications for the planning of education state by state.

Before long in many states nearly a half of an age group will enter a two or four year college. We are on our way towards universal education for those 19 to 21 years of age. Yet I defy anyone to come up with anything like an accurate estimate even within a single state of the fraction of an age group which has completed a high school course of study appropriate for the academically talented youth. We don't know and frankly few of us seem to care. There are no statistics, no standards, no definitions. When I speak of a high school course appropriate for an academically talented youth, I mean at least four years of one modern foreign language, and the study each year of mathematics, a natural science, English and social studies—5 solids—such a program begins to be comparable with the pre-university education obtained by the students in the English grammar schools, or the German or Swedish gymnasia, at the end of the 12th grade. These schools include a 13th grade and with the heavy emphasis on foreign languages are hard to compare with the American high school.

Unlike those on the other side of the Atlantic, we have no deeply rooted traditions of what a well educated person should have studied. The land grant college movement introduced the idea of parity of esteem between practical and academic subjects a century ago. The classical tradition was disappearing even in our older private colleges before the turn of the century. After sixty years and more a discussion of what constitutes liberal or general education we have no agreement except in the vaguest terms.

Within limits I think such educational anarchy has much to commend it. But I believe there are limits which can be defined in terms of the national welfare. I still think the concept of the "academically talented" is a useful one even if inexact. These youths constitute one of our great national resources. We ought to know state by state what sort of education the academically talented are being offered and what in fact they are electing.

If one reads the volumes of the report of the NEA project on the Instructional Program of the Public Schools summed up in *Schools for the 60s*, one sees how different are the concerns on this side of the ocean from those on the continent of Europe. Such words as research, experimental innovation, pilot projects, individual differences occur time and time again in American publications. The idea of developing the potentialities of the individual is recurrent, which idea assumes some methods of measuring both these potentialities and the degree of development attained—in short a sophisticated use of tools developed by psychologists. We in the U. S. A. emphasize many aspects of school life besides intellectual skills, curiosity, and powers of abstract thinking. Above all we talk in terms of the individual and attempt to give reality to the talk. The elective system in school and college expresses this outlook. In recent years, the advanced placement program has made concrete our realization that even among able students some can reach certain academic goals sooner than others. The ungraded primary at the other end of the learning spectrum is another manifestation of the same basic principle. And if I were venturing to be a prophet I would hazard the opinion that along these lines will come the most significant changes in the next ten years.

At times in the recent past it has seemed as if some of the older leaders of education were in opposition to those who were talking about the national needs of the 1960s and 1970s. But I doubt if there is today any real conflict. As a nation in which science and technology must flourish if we are to survive, we cannot think in terms which emerged before World War II. We cannot afford the rampant individualism of those days in any field, least of all in education. No matter who pays for the schooling, the education of each individual must today be a concern of all of us. Without retreating a step from our belief in judging education, individual by individual, we recognize that the United States has specific needs for trained manpower in many fields. We realize that to provide adequately for the oncoming generation requires the cooperation of the federal government, the state governments, and the local boards set up by each state. And this brings me to what many would say was the most dramatic shift in the educational scene in the United States in the last decade, namely, the entry in force of the federal government. NDEA may be considered the first step in this process; the next was the series of acts passed in 1963 by the Congress of the United States. And now we have the magnificent message of President Johnson of January 12—a message which John Gardner has characterized as "the most significant development in our recent educational history." And he added "This is an exhilarating moment for those concerned with our schools and colleges." All the many far reaching implications of what President Johnson has proposed none of us can foresee. But as more and more federal money flows to the public schools, it is evident it must flow through the state educational machinery. This means that the state departments of education must be immediately strengthened—it is impossible to administer from Washington alone what is proposed. To me it is highly significant that a whole section of the President's message is concerned with strengthening state educational agencies and he proposes grants to this end.

It is evident that the dramatically changed scene in the U. S. demands an increased emphasis on the role of the state boards of education. Without departing from our historic emphasis on the local control of education, I believe in most states the state educational officials can be asked to exercise far more leadership than they have in the past. But over and above that, I believe we should try to develop a new mechanism for formulating not a national educational policy but a nationwide educational policy. To that end I have suggested an Interstate Commission for Planning a nationwide educational policy by means of an interstate compact— such a commission to do its work through a series of subcommittees.

In the first place I hope I have made it clear that those who say European education is far superior to American are talking utter nonsense. Some reformers are trying to move the European system towards the American, but no one of them has the idea of copying our system in its entirety.

The changing scene on this side of the Atlantic has on the whole represented an adjustment between two distinct goals of formal schooling—education of an individual for the good life, and education of future citizens for a significant role in a modern highly industrialized society. The adjustment has been made because the proponents of the two points of view have come to understand that their ideas are not antithetical but complementary. That the same spirit will prevail as the educational scene shifts even more rapidly, I have not the slightest doubt. That is why I am optimistic about both the future of our schools and colleges and the strength of this nation in the days that lie ahead.

THE JUNIOR HIGH YEARS TAKE OVER IN EUROPE

ROBERT E. BELDING

Today four out of every five American children are involved in a school system which contains a junior high school. While our transitional school designed for the early teens was established near the turn of the century, the idea of such a block of school years has taken decades and wars to penetrate to some of the tradition-bound countries of Western Europe. Indeed, pursuit of secondary education in West European schools has long been a sudden decision, based as much on an early, sink-or-swim test score as in tradition and noble genes. So schools there have been slow to move into a block of adjustment years designed for youngsters reaching an age when important academic and vocational decisions must be made.

It is since the Second World War that European school systems have focussed much of their attention on the appropriate sorting of such youths into proper secondary school channels. It continues to be a shock to most Americans that the initial step in this process has necessitated creating a secondary education for *all* youths. Some of their ideas have been based in our own maturing experiences with the junior high; others are plans and implementations less familiar to us, and might well hold lessons for us. For each European country it has proven a more traumatic break from the usual pattern of schooling than the insertion of such a separate school level has made on the more flexible and pioneering Stateside. But this difference in itself makes it difficult to compare the academic, transitional years on both sides of the Atlantic.

FROM *Journal of Secondary Education* (November 1964), pp. 304–310. California Association of Secondary School Administrators. Reprinted by permission.

Yet the European experience, country by country, shows clear progress toward adjustment of the child into the appropriate type of secondary education, and should cement our confidence in the junior high as a successful institution which serves as a model for European school improvements.

The impact of the American junior high is not always clear, for not all European nations will readily admit such borrowings from the neophyte country to their West. For the purposes of this report, four European countries have been chosen to demonstrate varying degrees and methods of adoption of the junior high concept. By no means are these the only countries which have concerned themselves with the proper channeling of youths. France and Sweden are treated as countries which have done sufficient experimentation to stand ready for adoption, with confidence, of a set of determining years; Germany and England are treated as countries which have suggested patterns but which have lacked both concerted experimentation and legislation to implement their changes. In common, all four countries show a move in the right direction from too much confidence in noble genes or an early sink-or-swim test as determiners of future education, vocation and status. In its own way each shows how it plans to expose each child to the variety of available possibilities, appraising his developable skills and interests over a reasonable period of time.

Uniquely among the countries selected, Sweden has given overt credit to the United States for its introduction of a classless comprehensive school.[1] It has also done more experimenting than other nations, so that it legislates and progresses with full confidence in its own plan to smooth the adjustment of children between primary and later years. In fact more than half the children in Swedish schools between 1950 and 1962 were involved in systems experimenting with the new comprehensive school, so that for many such a plan will be no shocking novelty.

In 1962 the Swedish Parliament legislated that the nine-year comprehensive school should replace the traditional parallel-track system which had abruptly separated those headed for the university from the "lesser" adolescents. By stages the unitary school will develop until, in the academic year 1972, all children between the ages of seven and sixteen will be attending the same type of comprehensive school. New schools are being realistically built around research findings which have disclosed that children's interests, and occasionally their aptitudes, do not crystallize until about age fifteen. This nine-year school will comprise three distinct levels, with children between seven and nine in the lower department, between ten and twelve in the middle department, and from thirteen through fifteen in the upper department. The novel part will be at the last of these levels, for the traditional plan had already involved pupils in a more-or-less common *Folkskola* which had embraced the first six years of education.

When a child enters his teens he will remain with his age-mates as, together, they enter the upper department of the comprehensive school. This seventh grade, corresponding roughly with our first junior high year, will comprise thirty-five

---

[1] Torsten Husen, "A Liberal Democracy Adopts the Comprehensive School System," *Phi Delta Kappan* (November 1961), p. 86.

periods a week, of which only five will be devoted to optional courses. Elective areas will be German, French, maths, typing, handicrafts and Swedish in specified combinations, while the remaining thirty class periods will comprise a prescribed block of nine subjects. Decision for electives will be made by parents and pupils in the spring before entry to the seventh grade, and the school nominally will furnish information for guidance of family decisions.

By the same vernal process, parents and children will decide on electives for the eighth grade, and at that level electives will spread into seven out of thirty-five periods per week. A feature of this year is the exposure of all students to "practical vocational guidance" through actual participation in a variety of working experiences.

Although children remain under the same school roof, the ninth year sees them separated into five distinct channels or courses. Here preparation for the *Gymnasium* which leads to the university becomes a distinct channel, while other single-year grooves lead toward the Humanistic school, or toward further schooling and careers in nursing, home economics, in technical or business fields.

The new school will be characterized by no testing between departmental levels, and a real effort will be made to keep classmates together, because "there exists a comradeship between individuals who may be quite differently gifted and who may come from different classes of society." [2]

Distinctions can be made between features which constitute radical changes to the Swedish system and ideas which seem worthy of our further scrutiny. For example the inclusion of all early teenagers behind one school wall, rather than separating the college potentials from the less promising by age eleven, is a startling and at times uncomfortable transition to the natives. The fanning out of electives as the students progress, the parent-pupil decisions based on information provided by the school, and the middle-year feature of "practical vocational guidance" might well be worthy of our examination. Furthermore any inquisitive American educator would certainly wish to see how great are discrepancies between the theory of the new school idea and its practice, for the idea of the schoolmasters leaving decisions to parents, for example, is still most unusual in the public schools of Europe.

In the past, Germany served as the respected educational model for kinder-gartens, for vocational and teacher training as well as for university institutions. Despite its flourishing economy today, its present education is marked by its static nature. Of the four European countries treated here, Germany has proposed sound plans which in particular would improve the junior high years, but it has been unable to implement features of the plans. In themselves the plans are worthy of inspection, for they would seem not only to hold the key to jogging German schools into meshing with the country's economic and cultural demands, but the proposals for adolescents in particular are comparable to projects and implementations in other West European countries.

---

[2] National Board of Education, *Den Nya Skolan* (Stockholm, 1962), p. 30.

Both the proposed *Rahmenplan* and the *Bremerplan*[3] possess built-in changes for fifth and sixth grades (ages eleven and twelve). In some West German states the four primary years would be extended into the first two of secondary, and all students of eleven and twelve would thus be together; in other states these same grades would be made into a general secondary school (like our junior high) for all youths to attend. Whatever the state, children in such newly created common grades would be involved in two realistic years for ascertaining what stream to pursue at age thirteen rather than letting middle or upper class status, or a single examination at age ten, determine a student's entire future life.

Both plans would only slightly disturb the *Gymnasium* content and structure, yet that traditional school for university prep has consistently resisted changes which would affect its sequence of nine solid secondary years. Teachers themselves in the *Gymnasium* have, through their formidable union, been responsible for blocking certain mutations.

In particular the *Rahmen* (skeleton) *plan* was proposed in 1959, after five years of careful study by a group of twenty German citizens thoroughly interested in retuning levels and types of education to be in accord with the modern demands of a thoroughly industrialized country.[4] Children between eleven and thirteen years of age would continue together in a common program, but memorization would be replaced by what John Dewey once called "opening the classroom window to let in the world."

In this plan all would have a taste of secondary education, a level heretofore reserved mainly for potential university material. While this proposed *Forderstufe* (further step) would keep age mates together in a common school extension, the *Gymnasium* would, without benefit of anaesthetic, see its two lower grades amputated. Elementary teachers were in accord with the plan, but the classical *Gymnasium* teachers raised powerful and concerted objection. Also *Lander*, or states, in Germany have been proud of their school differences and resisted any effort which might pour them into a common plan.[5]

Less disturbing to the tradition-bound *Gymnasium* would have been the *Bremerplan*. It would make delayed shifts to the *Gymnasium* possible, or to the university from traditionally "lesser" schools by a reform in the middle elementary years (grades five and six) into an intensive determination cycle. As the Teachers Union which devised the *Bremerplan* says, two years of contemplated selection is better than eight days of rigid examination at the age of ten.

Not so pertinent to the junior high level is the intent to retain upper-primary students (up to age fourteen) in one additional year of school so their pre-apprenticeship will be strengthened and citizenship instruction injected. The eleven-twelve

---

[3] Herbert Enderwitz, "Two German Education Reform Schemes: The Rahmenplan and the Bremerplan," *Comparative Education Review* (June 1963), pp. 47–50.
[4] Theodore Huebener, "Proposed Reforms in German Schools," *Comparative Education Review* (June 1962), pp. 44–47.
[5] Any too common a plan has already been discouraged, or forbidden, by the Potsdam Agreement, for a centralized education during Hitler's hey-day had proven altogether too effective in pulling the country together in a bellicose cause.

age aspect as well as the extension on school-leaving age would, according to the plan, facilitate belated transfer into a university pattern.

The *Bremerplan* was worked out by the Teachers Association from 1960 to 1962 and because of its internal professional sponsorship and because it would prove less traumatic to the *Gymnasium*, it would appear to enjoy better chances than its older brother *Rahmen* for eventual adoption. However, lack of legal recognition of either plan at this point places Germany considerably behind schedule in implementing the equivalent, in either content or physical structure, to the American junior high school.

In many ways English schools are as autonomously run as our own. Although the country has a central educational ministry, local counties and communities hold out for running their individual school shows. In such a condition it would be difficult to identify in Britain any concerted effort to establish a recognizable set of junior high years. This does not mean, however, that nothing has been done on the local level to get away from the instant determination of secondary schooling and to create an atmosphere of exploration and guidance in early adolescent years.

There was a time when British youths of less-than-university-prep qualification never saw the inside of a secondary school. The traditional university prep establishment there has been known as the grammar or the equally time-honored boarding school. However, following the Second World War the Labor Government in power placed its brawny muscle behind the building of secondary modern, technical and comprehensive high schools, with intent to accommodate all youths.[6]

Although children are already sorted into the various types of secondary schools at age eleven, they take a program more or less in common to all schools during the first two years in whatever secondary school they attend. This brings the child up to the third year of secondary school, a year which has been an acceptable one for entrance to private schools preparing students for the university. For this common feature as well as for other reasons, all types of secondary schools have borrowed both academic and vocational courses from each other, and in doing so have become more alike at earlier levels than they are different. Because of the more-or-less common program for all in these lower secondary years, it is possible, although not usual, for students to transfer from one school type to another.

Beyond this single evidence of agreement in junior-high practice, the story of the junior high ethos on the compact island is culled from editorials as to what early teenagers need, as well as from what isolated efforts communities or counties have made to establish a fair plan for appraising students over a period of time to sort them into the proper type of education at the secondary level.

Newspaper headlines culled only within the past year in England have screamed "Maturity Comes at Varying Ages," "More Guidance Needed," "Eleven Years Too Early," or "Early Examination Challenged." Mainly the articles or editorials have questioned the use of a single test, administered to children at age eleven (or

[6] See A. Harry Passow's *Secondary Education for All—The English Approach*, Kappa Delta Pi monograph #3 (Ohio State University Press, 1961).

earlier) to determine which type of secondary school each shall attend. Despite the proverbial British coolness and climate, parents perspire at least as much as do their offsprings as this sink-or-swim examination of academic aptitude threatens downward through the primary years.

Some counties and communities have not been content to read headlines and articles, but have taken action. Within the past year the cities of London and Manchester as well as several counties have eliminated the Eleven-Plus as a further school shuttle.

An alternative action to the elimination of this early pass-or-fail exam has been proposed in the recently published Newsom Report, the result of the Minister of Education's Central Advisory Committee's efforts to up-grade education. This late 1963 report recommends lifting the school-leaving age to sixteen and delaying the eleven-year test to the twelfth year. This would mean students would enjoy an additional pre-segregation year together in the common, primary school, and would undergo the school determining test when slightly more mature. Whatever the solution, the evidence accumulates that the Eleven-Plus examination is thought by many to be too sharp a determiner and/or administered at too early an age.

While many education councils continue to yawn, the county of Leicester has gone ahead with full exercise of its democratic privilege to implement its own junior high school.[7] This Leicestershire Plan has placed children living within certain county areas into a single comprehensive junior high. There is no Eleven-Plus entrance exam, for children within the area enter the school together. It embraces children between ages eleven and fourteen, but contains an additional year for those who choose to remain in school only until school-leaving age (fifteen). Programming within the schools under this plan includes a number of electives, and children do remain together while their special academic talents are being identified. The plan has by no means engulfed the county's schools, but it has attracted wide and critical attention, and boosters of it have been quick to produce evidence of its success.

Like Sweden, France has a highly centralized system of education, and when changes are finally legislated there is a confidence that they will be implemented. Also like Sweden, sound experimentation has backed up France's new school laws, so they are progressing into what should be, by 1967, a school system with a clearly defined junior-high organization in action.

As in other countries considered here, France has recently become conscious of the necessity to deliberate over the correct distribution of children into secondary schools. It has a plan, however, which differs considerably from those of other countries, and because of the research years behind it, there seems considerable assurance it will work.[8]

Presently all French children attend the common primary school for five years. At eleven they are sorted either into a type of secondary school or remain, as in Germany, in extended years of primary until the school-leaving age of fourteen.

---

[7] Stewart C. Mason, *The Leicestershire Experiment and Plan* (rev. ed.) (London, 1963).
[8] Ministry of National Education, *Que Ferez-Vous de Vos Enfants?* (Paris, 1963).

The January 1959 Education Law indicates, however, that the school-leaving age will be raised to sixteen, and it is anticipated that by 1967 the children born before 1953 will be fulfilling the new regulation.

At the same time the extended elementary years will be abolished, every adolescent to age sixteen will be attending a secondary school, and the special sorting process to assure that each child gets the proper secondary education will be in operation.

Mainly there are four types of secondary school, the classical *lycée*, comparable to the *Gymnasium* or grammar school, the modern secondary, the professional secondary and the terminal secondary. Henceforth children will be sorted into one of these school types, but whatever the school name, all children will commence their two years in a common program known as the *cycle d'observation*, or determination block. At the end of the initial term of three months an orientation committee will decide the gross shunting of each child into either a classical or a modern stream.

The orientation committee here should be introduced, for it will presently be met again. It comprises the teachers who have taught the child in his first term, plus a psychologist, plus an M.D. This committee makes a recommendation to the child's parents, and if at any step the parents object to the professional decision, the child is entitled to a reappraisal through testing.

Just half way through the *cycle* (at the end of the first year) the orientation committee reviews the student's progress and fitness for the stream he is in. A change to the alternate channel is possible here, again subject to the challenge of parents.

Finally, after the end of the two-year *cycle* and when the child is thirteen years old, the orientation committee reviews each child's case on the basis of achievement records. It recommends assignment to the most appropriate type of secondary school. This may mean a shift in school building for the child, or it may mean he continues his secondary education in the building where he has undergone the *cycle d'observation*. Even after this final assignment the parents are entitled to challenge the committee's judgment, but again the student must pass a test to permit him to shift streams.

The Plan conforms to the familiar pattern of Continental respect for the judgment of the school, and it perpetuates the parental privilege of asking for retrial, yet the main lesson for American consideration would seem to be in the several levels of reappraisal which are built into the two-year progression of the *cycle*.

Only the most superficial aspects of the junior high invasion in four sample European countries have been reviewed here. Obviously the chief concern is for academic rather than all-around adjustment. Yet each nation's exposure to these restricted phases of the middle school should indicate its problems are strangely different from our own. Centralized educational systems, such as France and Sweden possess, would seem to hold an advantage over others in that they are able to legalize and to implement an extended period of time for determining which academic stream pupils should pursue.

In reviewing some of the Continental implementations and projects at this school level questions arise which, if answerable, might shed light on some of our own problems centering on the early adolescent. For example, do our junior highs smooth the transition as we would like, or should there be more appraisal, from more directions, along the line, with an increased injection of electives so that children can discover their aptitudes and interests? Should the school take more responsibility than it does in assigning students to their future academic channels? What is the nature of the devices utilized to replace the pass-or-fail examinations, or proper birth, earlier used as determiners of further school attendance? Do European schools share the same tribulations we do in staffing schools at this level, and in managing and understanding children of this separate age group? Finally, who has his bag packed to wing Eastward and investigate the junior high systems treated here only in suggestive and skeletal form?

THE FRENCH EDUCATION
SYSTEM

LEONARD A. OSTLUND

One of the most unique contributions of France has been the worldwide dissemination of a high standard, classically oriented education system—a mental, international medium of exchange in which culture, language and education are fused.

An understanding of French education requires a perspective. It requires journeying back over two thousand years to the Greek settlement of Massilia (now Marseilles), which was founded in the 6th Century B. C. and continued to flourish even after Rome conquered Gaul.

The Greek influence was notable in the teaching of the arts, science, and philosophy. In addition, Druids imparted knowledge and skills in nature and science. Roman education was installed in Gaul after Caesar's conquest. Imperial policy favored the spread of state-controlled education, because it furnished civil servants and propagated Roman culture.

The subject matter was the classics, Roman and Greek. The goal was to form an orator, since mass media for communication were lacking. Hence, Roman education was a discipline which served the State.

Reprinted from the October 1963, issue of *Education*. Copyright, 1963, by the Bobbs–Merrill Company, Inc., Indianapolis, Indiana.

Thus, classical tradition and professional orientation were indigenous. Likewise, the following methodology, described in the Gallo-Roman era, is prevalent today: the teacher read a passage aloud, followed by an exposition, grammatical, historical, philosophical, scientific, artistic, or literary, in which the teacher displayed his erudition in an analysis of all the fine points. This was followed by dictation. Moreover, rote learning and practice in writing were important activities.[1]

The interrelationships between politics and education were apparent in the decline and fall of the Roman educational system, since the government was in sole control of education. Masters of rhetoric became versed in parrot-like repetitions, empty postures, process without content, imagination without soul. Rather than concern themselves with current problems, they dealt in a mythical world of happenings and impossible events. The epitome of their abasement was the panegyric, in which they praised the Emperor, who, if sufficiently impressed, rewarded them with titles and riches.[2]

As the power of Rome waned, however, that of the Church increased in education. After the Dark Ages, Charlemagne emerged as Holy Roman Emperor. He chose Alcuin, master and librarian of the Cathedral School of York, to become Master of the Palace School in 782 A. D. at Aachen. He gained fame at the court and established a nationwide education system.[3]

The next great revival of learning took place towards the end of the 11th Century in Paris, which had become the center of European learning. This accounts for the emphasis upon philosophy and the classical tradition.

Though there was friction between Church and State for control of education, the Kings permitted the Church monopoly in education because the Church paid the bill and indoctrinated their pupils to be submissive to the "divine right of kings." For these reasons the French Revolution insisted that the State control education.

It was Napoleon Bonaparte who actualized the ideas of the French National Convention of 1792 by creating a public corporation, entitled the Imperial University, to control education.[4]

During the 19th Century, the struggle between Church and State for the control of French education and the rationalizations of social Darwinism seriously hampered educational reforms.[5]

Not many changes took place during the first half of the 20th Century because of the advent and aftermath of World War I, which was followed by a depression that saw the rise of Fascism in Europe and which culminated in World War II.

---

[1] Theodore Haarhoff, *Schools of Gaul* (London: Oxford University Press, 1920), pp. 46–50; and Daniel Behrman, "Progressive Education—The French Way," *Réalités* (July 1961), 128:17–21.

[2] Theodore Haarhoff, *Schools of Gaul* (London: Oxford University Press, 1920), pp. 46–50; and Jerome Carcopino, *Daily Life in Ancient Rome* (New Haven, Conn.: Yale University Press, 1941), Ch. V.

[3] Frederick Farrington, *French Secondary Schools* (New York: Longmans, Green and Co., 1919), pp. 1–6.

[4] A. Rambaud, *Histoire de la Civilisation Française*, II (Paris: Armand Colin, 1921), p. 260.

[5] André Siegfried, *L'Âme des Peuples* (Paris: Hachette, 1950).

NATIONALIZATION AND CENTRALIZATION

French education is nationalized in that the government through the Minister of Education, who is a member of the Cabinet, controls every aspect of education, from kindergarten through the university. All school personnel from the custodian to the professor are on civil service. The system, originated by Napoleon Bonaparte, is centralized in that its headquarters is at Paris, and decisions made there are implemented throughout the country.

Thus, the curriculum for students at all levels, including teachers in training, is the same throughout the country. The result is uniformity at a high level of performance. Education is free and compulsory to the age of sixteen.

STUDENTS, TEACHERS, CURRICULUM

One of the most salutary aspects of French education is the fact that all French teachers have been selected and trained rigorously. All must take the same curricula and examinations which serve to maintain high standards. Communication is a one-way street in that the teacher tells the pupils and parents, and they listen respectfully.

All through school, pupil-teacher relationships are formal and impersonal. The pupil-teacher relationship is that of subordinate to superior, since pupils are taught to respect authority. This is probably a cultural value dating from the days of the authoritative clergy, kings, and military rulers.

Many children go to pre-primary schools because entrance to primary schools is dependent upon preparation given in the pre-primary years. The child anticipates school with a favorable attitude since he has been impressed with its general importance as well as the fact that it marks a milestone of maturity. He has been briefed, clothed, and armed with a dragging briefcase full of supplies.

The child learns quickly that he must do as he is told and work by himself. The teacher transmits the cultural norm that "school means business—no tears or nonsense will be tolerated." The child adjusts quickly as he has no alternative. He knows that his parents will unequivocally take sides with the school and the teacher.

Primary schools are divided as follows: elementary course, middle course, higher course, and final section. Next, the child enters a collège or lycée. These comprise the equivalent of a United States junior high, senior high, and junior college. Education at the secondary level is divided into two sections: a period of orientation and general studies, and a phase of specialization.

There are sixteen universities in France. Only a select few students are admitted. Children are examined at the age of twelve to determine whether they have college possibilities. Only those who pass are allowed to take preparatory studies for the next six years. They still must pass an entrance examination—the famous Baccalauréate—which in 1958 was so difficult that two-thirds of the candidates failed.[6] In

---

[6] *La Croix* (Paris, August 11, 1958), p. 8.

recent years the failures have been reduced to 40 per cent.[7] For these reasons a degree from a French university is recognized internationally as an outstanding achievement.

The astronomic rate of attrition may be attributed to many socio-economic factors and, in the writer's opinion, to the fundamentally low cultural value placed upon psychology, guidance, and counseling.[8]

INTERNATIONAL INFLUENCE

France occupies a strategic position astride the crossroads of Europe. For this reason French for centuries has been considered an international language. It was recognized as such in the Treaty of Rastatt in 1714 and is similarly recognized by the United Nations today. Moreover, French is taught universally.

French is one of the official languages of Canada, Switzerland, and Belgium; and the total population of all countries where French is an official language is well over 100 million.

France subsidizes the proliferation of her culture, language, and education more than most other countries. The official agency is the Musée Pédagogique, which functions as an internal clearing house.

French institutions, staffed by French personnel who follow the traditional system, exist in 75 countries. On the university level, there are exchanges with 35 countries. One source lists hundreds of French organizations throughout the world.[9]

In time and space, the extent and importance of past and present educational influences has been truly global. During the Roman Empire, Bordeaux and Marseilles were lights of learning.[10] The Middle Ages witnessed students from many lands studying in Paris and returning to their native lands to propagate French culture, language, and education, as they do today.

Later, French priests accompanied French and Spanish explorers to the ends of the earth, teaching and converting. Their activities in religion and education abroad continued despite political changes at home.

The French Court at Versailles dictated not only taste and manners, but education as well. During this period the Encyclopedists focused world attention on knowledge and education.[11] The educational goals of the French Revolution engendered admiration and emulation abroad. In Sweden early in the 19th Century, Napoleon's General, Bernadotte, was chosen as King. This resulted in a further cultural diffusion.

---

[7] *Education in France* (New York: Cultural Services of the French Embassy), XX, p. 18.

[8] H. Danon-Boileau, "Problèmes Posés par l'Hygiène Mental des Étudiants," *Évolution Psychiatrique* (October–December 1956), XXI, No. IV, pp. 809–824. (A translation by the writer appeared in *Psychological Abstracts*, XXX, No. 2, p. 210.) Also, Leonard A. Ostlund, "Contemporary European 'Type' Theories," *Psychological Newsletter* (1958) 9:81–84.

[9] *L'Enseignement Français à l'Étranger* (Paris: Service d'Éditions et de Vente des Publications, January 1959).

[10] Louis Desgraves, *Bordeaux* (Paris: B. Arthaud, 1957), pp. 15–17.

[11] Diderot (ed.), *Encyclopédie*, II (Geneva: Pellet, 1777), pp. 914–940.

The remainder of the 19th Century witnessed the global establishment of French colonies and spheres of influence. Wherever Frenchmen settled, they established their culture, language, and education, for it is important to note that almost everywhere the French assimilate.[12]

FRENCH INFLUENCES IN QUEBEC

Nowhere in the world, except in France itself, is there such a concentration of people of French descent as in the Province of Quebec, Canada, where there are five million people in a land two and one-half times larger than France. French Canadians constitute one-fourth of the Canadian population and, in keeping with a well known sociological phenomenon, uphold their ancient culture more rigidly than does the Motherland. During the writer's travels in Quebec, he has been struck with the similarities to France—small farms, wayside shrines, tiny villages dominated by large churches.

French education in Quebec was established by the Catholic Church in order to teach and convert the Indians. A Jesuit Brother, Pacifique Duplessis, is acknowledged as the first teacher, for he established a school at Trois Rivieres in 1616, where he taught Indian boys.[13] Though Quebec was subsequently lost to England, the people changed little.

In education, the traditional French curriculum forms the basis. Unlike France, however, in Quebec there are more varied curricula of a practical nature—in business, agriculture, and technology—which serve a wider segment of the population. Further, religious education is universal.[14]

FRENCH INFLUENCES IN AFRICA

In North Africa, the Maghreb, which has a total population of twenty-seven million and is composed of Algeria, Tunisia, and Morocco, though newly and fiercely independent, remains tied to France, educationally and financially. Ethnically, the Berber stock predominates, the dominant language is Arabic, and the culture is Islamic. Tunisia, the size of Louisiana; Morocco, two-thirds the size of Texas; and Algeria, four times larger than France, were formerly exclusively in the French sphere of influence. Today, though nationalism is rampant, French language, culture, and education remain strong.

The French Communauté (Community) was established in 1958 as a result of the referendum that brought De Gaulle to power and which the writer was privileged to witness in Paris. The Community comprises France and some of her former African colonies that had just achieved independence, but voted to remain tied to France.

---

[12] Siegfried.

[13] Louis-Philippe Audet, *Le Système Scolaire de la Province de Quebec* (Quebec: Les Editions de l'Erable, 1951), pp. 28–31.

[14] Omer-Jules Desaulniers, *Report of the Superintendent of Education* (Quebec: Redémpti Paradis, 1962); and *L'annuaire Statistique—Le Province de Quebec* (Quebec: Redémpti Paradis, 1962).

At present, African members of the Community are: the Central African Republic, the Republic of Chad, the Republic of the Congo, the Gabon Republic, the Malagasy Republic, and the Republic of the Senegal. Their combined population is approximately 14 million.

The members have chosen French as their official language. Though English, Arabic, and Pidgin are current, French predominates. There are many native languages and many dialects. In French East Africa, for example, the ethnologist Maurice Delafosse has distinguished 126 different languages, many of which are not written. There are an estimated 600 dialects in the former French colonies.

With the French educational system as the basis, native teachers are being trained by France. Though the average school attendance is 30 per cent, progress is being made because the nations of the Community expend from 11 per cent to 24 per cent of their budget for education. The rate of progress will be difficult to predict because of many aspects—some cultural, some geographical, and some financial.[15]

In a sense, the future of the Community will provide an important test of the democratic form of government, since all are republics. Democracy must be learned—a process which takes time and education—whereas autocracy is imposed.

The following members of the French Community were not included in the foregoing list because their political status is different, but they still augment France's international dimension: Africa—The Comoro Islands, Réunion, French Somaliland, the Saharan Departments; North America—St. Pierre and Miquelon; South America—French Guiana; West Indies—Guadeloupe and Martinique; Pacific Ocean—French Polynesia, New Caledonia, Wallis and Futuna Isles[16]; and the Southern and Antarctic lands.

To paraphrase a famous slogan: "The sun never sets on French language, culture and education."

REFORMS—ACCOMPLISHED OR PLANNED

The post World War II years have seen more legislation aimed at changing French education than all the previous centuries. Only a few examples may be cited:

1. Extending the school-leaving age from 14 to 16

2. Creating the integrated or combined school, which encompasses a wide variety of subject matter fields

3. Providing centers for adult education

4. Providing scholarships—in 1962, approximately 795,700 were awarded, worth $132 million

5. Relaxing classroom discipline and providing group projects and student discussion

[15] *African Affairs Pamphlet*, No. 20 (New York: The French Embassy, May 1958); *French Economic Assistance in West and Equatorial Africa—1948–1958* (New York: The French Embassy, November 1958); *The New York Times* (October 30, 1960), Section 11; and *Time* (August 3, 1962) LXXX.

[16] The New Hebrides is not a member of the French Community, since it is under a condominium with Great Britain.

6. Increasing subsidies for physical education, including summer and winter educational-recreational camps

7. Extending guidance and counseling services

8. Increasing the salaries, opportunities, and facilities for teachers and professors

9. Establishing the "cycle d'observation" under the Law of January 6, 1959, giving guidance upon entrance into secondary school.[17]

FRENCH CRITICISMS OF THE REFORMS

Generally, post World War II French critics claim that the reforms have not gone far enough. Specifically, they say that:

1. Administratively, excessive centralization and bureaucracy make changes difficult and hamper adaptation to the tremendous variety of local conditions.

2. Education must become more democratic and embrace a wider population, regardless of age, sex, socio-economic factors, etc. An educational system geared to the scholarly life is an anachronism—a luxury France can no longer afford.

3. Methodology must change from emphasis upon literary and abstract reasoning. Teachers have been too active, students too passive.

4. The severely competitive examination system creates too much psychological strain on pupils and parents.

5. The curricular emphasis has been on intellectual skills and has ignored personal and social needs.[18]

SUMMARY

The most important French contributions to education may be summarized as:

1. Centralization and standardization.

2. State support and control.

3. Separation, yet integration of all levels of learning.

4. Education free of charge and free from bias.

5. Perhaps most important, a traditional system of rigorous standards which embodies the highest humanistic values of scholarship, learning, and education.

Though France has relinquished territory and military power, the international prestige of her culture, language, and education has not diminished. Perhaps, here lies the true measure of the "gloire et grandeur" of traditional France.

---

[17] *Education in France*, I–XX (New York: Cultural Services of the French Embassy); Marcel Leherpeux, *La Réforme de l'Enseignement* (Paris: Institut Pédagogique National, April 1960); and *Les Principaux Projets de Réforme de l'Enseignement depuis le Premier Guerre Mondiale* (Paris: Ministère de l'Éducation Nationale, 1960).

[18] Behrman, *Education in France*; and *Le Monde* (Paris, September 9, 1960), p. 2.

THE SECONDARY MODERN
SCHOOL IN ENGLAND

ROBERT M. MARSH

Twenty years ago, Parliament in the United Kingdom passed an Education Act which had been planned as an act of faith during some of the grimmest years of our country's history. The task set to education authorities was the extension and modernization of a system which had proved sound but which needed to be adapted and enlarged to meet the requirements of a post-war world.

Primary education is defined as covering the age-range from 2–11 or 12, although attendance at school is not compulsory before the age of 5. This stage of education did not present the problems of organization which arise from doubts about differences of aim and content which are faced at the secondary stage. In the school year after their eleventh birthday children transfer from the primary stage of education to the secondary stage where they are required by law to remain until they reach the age of 15; the age of compulsory school attendance is to be raised to 16 in 1970.

In 1944 the only secondary education provided was in the grammar schools where an academic course leading to the universities and to professional training was provided for a selected twenty per cent of the children. The remaining children, some eighty per cent, were then attending elementary schools where the leaving age was 14; for many children this meant a separate school from 11–14 where education had already begun to develop beyond the elementary stage; for some children, particularly in the more sparsely populated areas, this meant a continuation of education in a school with an age from 5–14. The vital task, therefore, which faced those responsible for education was the planning and evolution of a system which would provide secondary education for every child "in accordance with his age, ability, and aptitude."

The responsibility for preparing and implementing a scheme to provide secondary education rested with the local education authorities which comprise the larger areas of local government—the county councils and the larger cities. Education powers had been taken away from the smaller towns as it was clear that they would not have the financial resources to tackle the problem successfully nor would they be large enough to provide a sufficient number of schools to offer an adequate variety of courses to satisfy the differing abilities and aptitudes of the children.

Reprinted by permission from the *Bulletin of the National Association of Secondary-School Principals* (March 1965). Copyright: Washington, D. C.

In the primary stage the education provided is broadly the same for all children, but in the secondary stage there is a natural demand for an adjustment of course and curriculum to the varying abilities, wishes, and future requirements of the pupils. There is, of course, a common aim and some common elements—certain basic subjects will be common to all students although, in the upper classes, even these should be handled and presented differently in different cases. As children grow up they begin to differ more widely in aptitude and interest and schools must therefore offer a sufficient choice of course, a variety both in curriculum subjects and indeed in the methods of teaching.

Our education authorities enjoy a considerable amount of independence in the organization of their educational systems and there is a variety of forms of secondary education. This may appear untidy and certainly makes a clear understanding of our educational system very difficult, but great advances have been made by the pioneer and experimental work undertaken in different areas. In some parts of England there is a growing number of comprehensive schools which serve the whole of a neighborhood unit and provide for children of every ability and aptitude from the age of 11 to 18. In other parts there is a tripartite system preserving the well-established grammar schools and providing in addition technical schools with a specifically scientific bias, and modern schools providing a wide and general education. Technical schools have been established more particularly in industrial areas, but my experience leads me to think that they do not provide anything which cannot be provided equally well in the grammar school for the technologist and in the modern school for the technician. In my own authority we have accordingly retained the grammar schools for about twenty per cent of the children who can work quickly and independently on academic subjects, and we have established secondary modern schools for the remaining eighty per cent. This is a pattern of secondary education which has been adopted in many areas, and it is about this type of school, the secondary modern school, that I want to speak.

Grammar schools were established in considerable numbers at the beginning of the century to provide academic courses for the ablest fifteen per cent of the age-group. Some are of older foundation and much of their organization and curriculum was inevitably based on what had proved successful over many years in the independent schools—which for some reason we call public schools and you more aptly call private schools. Entry to these schools is by an examination of ability and attainment with due account taken of a child's record in the earlier stages of education. The new secondary modern schools were set a considerable task in their endeavor to establish themselves in the public mind as capable of providing a full secondary education in which opportunity existed for every boy and girl to develop to the fullest possible extent. It was vital that they should not become the establishment for those who had failed to qualify for a grammar education and that parents and pupils should see their aims and should appreciate that a very wide variety of opportunity was open to those who were considered more suited to a modern school course. They have met with a varying degree of success—many have, after quite a short life, been accepted and are making an invaluable contribution to the welfare of our young people and the future of our country; a few have, through poor buildings and uninspired staff, advanced little from the old conception of elementary education, but it is mainly a success story and that is the side which I shall endeavor to describe to you.

The new schools quickly adopted some of the traditional features of the older established grammar schools. The school assembly, the house-system, the prefect-system, the Speech Day, and other features were adopted and assisted in providing a public image of secondary education. A great amount of care and thought, of test and trial, had to be given, however, to the curriculum content and teaching method necessary for a very wide range of aptitude and ability. The upper range of ability consisted of children who had quite narrowly missed selection for the grammar school course; this course culminates in an external examination which is a necessary requirement for entry to the university and to many professions. The selection procedure had never met with popular approval, certainly not amongst parents whose children had failed to secure a grammar school place, and no selection procedure is so good that mistakes are not made. The age for transfer from the primary to the secondary school is at present fixed at 11, which many regard as too young, and certainly there are a number of children who develop late and do not show an academic bent at the age of eleven. If the new schools were to win popular approval, they had to demonstrate clearly that no career was closed to any pupil selected for admission. As a result, at the top end of the school, an overlap of course has been provided with the grammar school and the more academic children are able to take a course leading to the same external examination as is taken by the grammar school children. These children may enjoy rather more 'teaching' and less 'study' than their colleagues in the grammar school, but this part of the experiment has proved an undoubted success. The number of children successfully taking this external examination is increasing rapidly and successes are being achieved by some most unexpected pupils. As a general observation, it would be true to say that the children in the top stream of the modern schools, in my own authority, are now securing better results in this public examination than the children in the bottom stream of the grammar schools. I do not think that this is primarily due to bad selection, but we are finding that a different and more practical teaching approach is bringing dividends. We are also finding that there are many children who produce better results through the confidence which they gain from being amongst the best pupils in the modern school and who would have abandoned hope if they had been struggling not to be bottom of the class in the grammar school. Probably the biggest academic award which a school boy or girl can gain in the United Kingdom is an open scholarship at Oxford or Cambridge University. Cases are now arising where these awards have been won by pupils who have attended the secondary modern school from the age of 11 to 16. It has therefore become apparent to the public generally that the selection decision reached at eleven leaves open every opportunity for future education and career, and this has done much to establish the new schools in the public esteem.

At the other end of the school, we have the problem of educating children, some of whom are bordering on the mentally deficient. Certainly we have our special schools for handicapped pupils, including those who are educationally subnormal and those who are maladjusted, but it is the aim of my authority to return as many as possible to the normal stream of education at the age of 12. If they are to become happy, useful, and self-supporting citizens in adult life they must learn to live, before they leave school, as members of a normal community. We therefore have to make provision for these children whose capacity both verbally and numerically is very limited. Children are placed in forms in the school but, in many subjects, they are placed in sets or groups according to their ability. Some of these children who are mentally slow show quite a good aptitude in some practical subjects and in sport and physical education. The weakest sets are always kept small so that individual attention can more easily be given by the teacher where it is necessary. The problem of teacher shortage is incidentally a serious one but it is probably worth mentioning that, in my authority, we provide a pupil/teacher ratio in grammar schools of 1 to 17 and in modern schools of 1 to 21—the preferential ratio in grammar schools being necessary to staff the wide range of smaller classes at sixth form level. I think that I can reasonably say that a good job is being done in our schools for the ablest and for the weakest pupils; the real problems have been in making the right provision for the average child. These constitute half the pupils of our secondary schools—young people who will eventually become half the citizens of our country, half the workers, half the mothers and fathers and half the consumers. Disraeli once said that on the education of the people of this country its future depended: in this context the education of the average child is of vital importance and a national committee has recently reviewed the problem in England and has issued a report entitled "Half Our Future" which tells the story of the progress made and sets out aims and suggestions for the future.

Two of the factors which have to be taken into account in contrasting our educational situation with yours is the size of the school and the availability of employment. There is a strong body of public opinion and of professional opinion opposed to the large school. Traditionally we have favored schools of such a size that the Head Master or Head Mistress can know every pupil; we have tended to avoid the large educational establishment because of the difficulty of maintaining an understanding personal contact between teacher and pupil. We have found, however, that a small secondary modern school cannot provide the variety of courses and training necessary to develop the varied aptitudes and interests of the pupils. Our better secondary modern schools have therefore a school roll of some 750–1000 children. In country areas this can mean quite a long journey to school if this sized school is to be provided; but, under our system, free travel is provided for pupils who live more than three miles from school. The second factor is the availability of employment: as I understand the position there is, in many parts of the United States, a high unemployment rate amongst school leavers, i.e., the 16–19 age groups. In the United Kingdom, on the other hand, many employers are short of labor and the financial inducements to leave school are considerable. It is therefore essential that it should be abundantly clear to the pupil and parent that the education which is provided is of real value and that it is indeed a good investment for a pupil to continue at school after reaching the statutory school leaving age in order to develop his ability and to become eligible for a wider range of better and more interesting employment. The temptation of immediate cash is a considerable one.

We are endeavoring to provide educational courses which make sense to the boys and girls and which can clearly be seen to bear some relationship to the lives which they will lead as adults. Whilst, therefore, the first two or three years of the secondary course will be of a wide and general nature, the latter period will bear a relationship to the type of career which the young person may follow when he leaves school. At this stage some will elect for the academic course, but the majority will be more successful in a course with a practical bias leading more obviously towards a particular type of employment. These courses for the average children will naturally vary in accordance with the interests and the employment prospects of the area which the school is serving; in the main, however, courses are developing for girls in commercial subjects, retail distribution, nursing, and catering, and for boys in engineering, building, and agriculture. These courses are not narrowly vocational, but all subjects are built around the special interest which the vocation arouses. For the average and below average child needs an education which is both practical and realistic; if he is given this, with a choice of courses with different vocational biases, secondary education begins to have life and meaning.

Practical subjects cover a wide field; in addition to wood or metalwork, rural studies, housecraft, and needlework they include art, music, and physical education. Through practical subjects and the vocational interest, an interest and an incentive can be provided to inspire even quite backward children to tackle the vital basic subjects of reading, writing, and numbers. English has a relevance to most jobs; in employment these young people will have to understand and later give oral and written instructions and clear expression in speech can be seen to be important in many situations which boys and girls realize they will have to face. Numbers will have more meaning to the practical boy when he has to appreciate the importance of accuracy of measurement and design in woodwork and metalwork, or to the girl when she is working out a budget for running a home or weighing the ingredients of a recipe in a cookery class. It is for the skilled teacher to contrive the right, practical situation to interest the children and by so doing make education realistic and meaningful to children who may be resistant and unaware of its relevance to the lives which they will lead.

The secondary modern school had no tradition or history—no set pattern—but they attracted to them many men and women with a desire to experiment and to pioneer. None of these schools was established until 1945 and they have not had a sufficiently long life to form any final judgment, but much interesting work is going on and the genius of individual teachers and groups of teachers has ensured that they are very varied in character. They have been helped by the fact that local education authorities, in collaboration with the state, have carried out a massive building program over the last ten to fifteen years. In the period 1954–61, more than 1800 new secondary schools were completed and by 1967 nearly two thirds of all secondary pupils will be either in new schools or in enlarged and modernized older buildings. The cost of education is shared between the state and the local education authority, roughly in the proportion of 60 per cent to 40 per cent, the salaries of teachers are fixed at national level and so the salary rate is the same whether a teacher works in London or in a remote village. The government has laid down minimum standards for school buildings and school playing fields and this ensures a uniformity of opportunity and a standard throughout the country. Good design and construction, gay color in decorations and attractively laid out grounds show to parents and pupils that the new schools have vigor and opportunity. New subjects have appeared on the curriculum and a great variety of new textbooks, library books, and teaching aids are visible in the classrooms. These physical improvements and the introduction of a variety of realistic courses are having their effect and are convincing boys and girls and parents that a longer education is worthwhile. In 1962, rather more than one pupil in six was staying at school beyond the statutory school leaving age. In some schools the proportion was very much higher and it is increasing steadily.

School has changed remarkably in the postwar period and, markedly, in the easier atmosphere and less formal relations between teachers and pupils. The school day is expanding into what is virtually a third session in the evenings when teachers and pupils develop and share in a wide range of interests. This is the time when many voluntary clubs and societies meet and practice, and these activities not only give an early training in responsibility and leadership for the pupils but also provide the good teacher with an opportunity to get to know his pupils better and to have an important influence on them both socially and morally.

These activities outside the limit of lesson times are a valuable and distinctive feature of school life in the United Kingdom, not least, perhaps, in the way they are literally widening the pupils' horizons. One outstanding, but by no means unique school, quoted in the report "Half Our Future," has undertaken in six years sixteen educational visits abroad and twenty-six in England: the program has included visits to Stratford on Avon, Edinburgh, and York; geographical surveys in the Isle of Man, Yorkshire, and the Lake District; historical surveys in Lancashire; cycling and Youth Hostelling trips in many parts of the country; crossing the Norwegian ice-cap above Hardanger, traversing mountain ranges in Austria, making a two hundred mile high-level walking tour in Switzerland, and climbing in the Dolomites in Northern Italy. Means of helping pupils who could not otherwise afford the journeys have been found and pupils of every grade of ability have taken part. My own authority charters a liner each year and takes a party of a thousand children to foreign parts: places we have already visited include Stockholm, Helsinki, Leningrad, Copenhagen, Athens, Delphi, Crete, Rhodes, and Venice—and in March we fly the whole party to Venice and sail through the Aegean Sea to Istanbul. The preparation for and the follow-up after these journeys is vital; school lessons and international understanding carry more meaning and gain realism when they refer to countries which have actually been visited and peoples whose representatives have been met personally. These varied activities and the new approach to teaching means a great amount of devoted work by teachers with a real love of young people and a complete sense of vocation. The work of a teacher is harder today than it was thirty years ago and we are fortunate that so many good people are still entering the profession. We are glad too that an additional year has been added recently to the period of teacher training; in addition to the acquisition by study of factual knowledge of a subject, a teacher today has to be conversant with an increasing range of visual and aural aids which can provide enrichment to a subject and inspiration to a lesson.

We must note that, since 1944, the record of secondary education in our country is one of progress—but we are still experimenting and we are not satisfied that a good deal more cannot be done. Education becomes dull if it settles into a routine; it remains alive and progressive only if teachers continue to experiment in an endeavor to find a fresh approach and a real contact with the child who still appears to be bored and apathetic in school. Recent years have shown that many pupils are educable beyond all previous expectations and the suspicion grows stronger that the rest may have been under-estimated also. Further means have to be discovered to make it possible for those who still don't see the point of school and who make little progress to secure an understanding and an enjoyment that breed self-respect and a reason for wanting to work well. Successes are being achieved and will be achieved; they will come more speedily if we can improve teacher-supply and reduce the size of classes. Anyone who has had the good fortune to be taught in a small class by a devoted and inspiring teacher knows how fortunate he is—and no amount of television or other forms of teaching aids, important as they are, will replace the influence which a mature and responsible teacher will bring to bear on the mental, moral, and spiritual development of a young student.

Our young people today are maturing and becoming young adults far more rapidly than in the past. In some ways this is good, in some ways it is bad; but it is a situation which has to be faced and which inevitably has an effect on the school situation. The older pupil needs to be given an experience of responsibility and an opportunity to learn the enjoyment that can be gained by service to others. Many schools engage in some form of community service, particularly to the handicapped, the sick, and the aged—and this is good.

For the older pupils the school program in the final year ought to be deliberately outgoing to the world in which they are to live. Just as the school curriculum can be directed towards the type of situation which young people will encounter in adult life, so interesting people from the community may be persuaded to enter into the life of the school. Men and women who have worked overseas, a local councillor, former pupils, parents, members of the Rotary Club can be invited into the school to take part in informal discussion groups and share their direct experience with the pupils. One of the virtues of such contacts can be simply in providing opportunities for ordinary adult conversations which are so often surprisingly lacking in the ordinary home.

I believe that you, in the United States, have been experimenting in providing limited experience of different kinds of employment, on a release from school basis, inside the educational program. In the United Kingdom local initiative has resulted in some areas in children having an organized experience of opportunities for employment in such varied places as an office, a library, a factory, a hospital, or a garage. This experience has been designed as part of a wider program of general preparation for school-leavers. The schools have been in close contact with the offices, works, and firms concerned and members of the staff have visited the pupils. But the intention has been to give the pupils a closer view of the world at work and some sense of being out on their own. Those who have experienced this kind of facility have come back with some useful matters for discussion and evaluation and a greater realization of the importance of school subjects in a future career. They give another example of ways in which teachers are endeavoring to bring a realistic approach to the final year at school.

One of the things boys and girls ought to know, and be encouraged to want to know, is how to continue their education after they leave school. Each school will have a careers master or mistress who will be in constant touch with the further education organizer and the youth employment officer. It is worthy of mention that the youth employment service which is responsible for advising on all career opportunities for young people between the ages of 15 and 18 is normally a part of the education service; this certainly provides the opportunity for the closest liaison between the school, with its intimate knowledge of the pupil, and the employment office, with its intimate knowledge of employment opportunities and prospects. Young people entering employment today will, we hope, have been provided with a good general education culminating in some form of vocational bias. When they enter employment they will, in the vast majority of cases, need further education specifically in the skills and techniques of the career which they have chosen. Indeed, they need to have been educated to be flexible and adaptable as modern industry is changing and developing so rapidly that they are likely to require retraining in some new skill or technology during the period of their working life. The knowledge of this need is bringing our schools and technical colleges closer in contact one with another. Open days are held in technical colleges when an opportunity is given to school parties to meet some of the staff and students and to see some of the opportunities which exist. A great deal more of this could be done and it would be of considerable benefit to all concerned if more reciprocal visits could take place, when technical college staff could visit schools and discuss with school teachers their aims and how they can more closely dovetail with one another. This has a direct relevance to the attempts that are being made to develop 'end-on' courses between the secondary schools and the technical colleges. The vocational impulse which the school has provided, the facility in the use of tools and the understanding of and the feeling for material—be it wood, metal, cloth, or clay—all provide something on which the technical college can build. Whilst the school's prime aim is education for citizenship—a training in body, mind, and spirit—the prime object of the technical college is training for a vocation. I am glad to say that there are signs that teachers in secondary modern schools and lecturers in technical colleges are getting closer together and planning their work in such a way that the school course with its vocational tinge or bias leads clearly on to a well-defined course at a technical college or train the school leaver to become a technician or a craftsman. It is good too that the technical college in planning its program is deliberately including in its more narrowly vocational courses a liberal content which may make the technician more articulate and will help to break down that "false dichotomy between vocational and liberal education."

In forging a closer link between schools and further education, a means has to be found of assessing a student's capacity to pass on to a particular stage of further education. Ambition is such that young people are inclined to aspire to a course which leads to a career that is beyond their capacities. The failure rate of students in colleges of further education is a testimony to this. The external examination which is set by the universities and taken by pupils in the grammar schools and the top stream of the secondary modern schools is a reasonable gauge of the capacity of a youngster to proceed to higher academic education. Initially we have avoided introducing in the secondary modern school another examination, because we have been fearful of the restricting effect which this might have on the curriculum. These examinations, however, do something to ensure the maintenance of a standard, and the quality of education in a school tends to be judged by the success of its pupils in these examinations. Employers, parents, and pupils in the new type of secondary school have been pressing for some means of assessing the standard achieved by pupils who are leaving those schools—some piece of paper which can form a school leaving certificate and can guide a future employer in assessing the type of work which his future employee can reasonably be expected to undertake. It has been argued too that some such form of assessment of the average pupil can provide both an incentive to work in school and an encouragement to complete an extended course at school. The outcome is the introduction this year of a new examination, the Certificate of Secondary Education. Great care is being taken to ensure that this examination will not put a brake on the development of the schools and will not impose restrictions on the exciting and eminently worthwhile work that so many of them are doing. The new examination will be controlled by examination boards on which the teachers in the schools concerned are in a majority. The people who devise the syllabuses and who set the papers will be teachers who are directly in touch with the schools concerned and many individual papers will be aimed directly at the type of study which is being followed in a particular school. It will be interesting to see how this new examination develops, but I have hopes that it will not in any way restrict the schools in their development and that it will provide an incentive and an encouragement to the average and below average child in providing him with a proof of standard and attainment reached in the secondary modern school. This can raise the status of the school, can be of value to the leaver in his application for an appointment, and can assist the technical college in guiding a student to a course of study suited to his ability and attainment.

In 1965 we have, each of us in our countries, the great responsibility of educating young minds and training young citizens in a world in which they will be responsible; their careers will carry them into the twenty-first century. Machinery and industry are becoming more complicated and, if we are to survive, we must educate young people to the utmost of their capacity and teach them to be adaptable and flexible to meet the challenges and the problems which they will confront. In the years ahead they are likely to have a great amount more leisure than you or I have enjoyed. We must, during their formative years, give them experiences and opportunities to develop talents and interests which they will enjoy pursuing much more than they will enjoy being entertained by some canned or boxed diversion. But, above all, we must, by example and precept, set them standards both moral and ethical which may enable them to raise a future generation whose standards we would wish to see higher than those which exist in the world today.

I have endeavored to tell you of an educational development in the United Kingdom which is designed to prepare boys and girls for their future as parents and citizens. It is, as yet, premature to form a judgment on the success of the secondary modern schools. Their life has been a short one but there are encouraging indications of progress made in certain fields. I hope that we shall continue to build on the foundations which were established in 1944. The future is, however, a little difficult to foresee. Public opinion is hardening against selection into different types of school at the age of eleven and, in a number of areas, experiments are being conducted with changes in organization. If there is more than one kind of school, then selection in some form is necessary. The most obvious answer is the comprehensive school, but many people are hesitant to do away with the well-established grammar school with its high and acknowledged academic standards. The grammar school does, however, carry with it a certain social status and the modern school is still having difficulty in securing recognition in its own right and on an equal footing. Some parents would still prefer their children to be educated in a grammar school without realizing that they are unsuited to the academic course and unable to benefit from it.

Furthermore, education has become a matter of political moment—the Labour Party's election program envisaged the abandonment of the examination at eleven and the general availability of secondary education on comprehensive lines. Local education authorities have always taken a considerable pride in their independence in matters of educational organization, and it remains to be seen whether the government will force through such a radical change in policy. In many ways the secondary modern school is comprehensive in its organization, catering as it does for the whole range of ability, apart from a minority who are considered capable of working at a faster pace. Stronger than any political pressure may, indeed, be public opinion demanding the removal of examination and segregation at 11 and, out of this, may come a compromise built on the foundations which have been established in the grammar schools over 60 years and in the modern schools over 20 years.

One interesting experiment is the high school to which all children proceed when they reach the age to transfer from primary education. This school provides an education leading to an external examination at the age of 16, but parents who are prepared to guarantee that their children will complete a secondary education up to the age of 18 can opt for their children to transfer after two years to the grammar school. The transfer is approved if the high school considers that he can benefit from the academic course. This is one of a number of experiments which are being made to secure a reorganization within the existing framework and in the buildings which are available.

I can only repeat that so long as teachers are prepared to experiment in the interest of their pupils, education will remain alive and will flourish. Our future progress and survival depends on the success of our educational system and we cannot afford to do other than go forward to provide more and better opportunities for our children and for future generations.

PROBLEMS IN EVALUATING SOVIET EDUCATION

SEYMOUR M. ROSEN

Analysis of education data requires valid criteria for selection and evaluation. The present may be compared with the past within the Soviet education system to trace growth, shifts of emphasis, and new developments in education. The pitfalls of relying on published statistics have already been alluded to, but it is possible to work with them in combination with whatever qualitative and definitional evidence that can be gathered, to formulate hypotheses assumed to be reasonably valid.

The problem of definition is recurrent. One can derive over-all pupil/teacher ratios easily, for example, by dividing the number of pupils by the number of teachers, both figures being published annually in the statistical handbooks. But of the "teachers", how many are full-time teachers and how many are part-time teachers and school service personnel? There is no clear answer since the definitions are not clear.[1]

FROM the *Comparative Education Review* (October 1964), pp. 156–163. Reprinted by permission.

[1] Using Soviet sources, the over-all statistical ratio for schools of general education in 1962–1963 was 42.4 million pupils to 2.2 million teachers, or about 19 to 1. A breakdown of numbers of teachers for grades 1–11, who are not administrators or supervisors, gives a total of only 1.75 million teachers. The ratio in the latter case, which appears a more accurate ratio is about 24 to 1. A variable which might considerably increase the ratio would be inclusion by Soviet statisticians of part-time teachers in the category of teachers for grades 1–11. The formula which would give a precise ratio, using full-time teacher equivalents (2 or 3 part-time teachers equals 1 full-time teacher) is not used in Soviet sources.

Another valid approach to analysis of education data, besides comparing the present with the past, is to compare the present with national goals, if the goals are formulated with sufficient precision to chart the current degree of success in meeting them. For example, a new system of boarding schools for pupils in elementary-secondary grades was announced by Premier Khrushchev at the 20th C.P.S.U. Congress in February 1956. The goal was to have 2.5 million pupils enrolled in them by 1965. By 1962 there were perhaps 500,000 pupils enrolled in the new schools, and it appeared that the goal would be difficult to meet, probably because of problems in constructing boarding school facilities.

One symptom of difficulty and at the same time the apparent solution to meeting the announced goal has been the lumping in Soviet statistics of enrollments in the new boarding schools with boarding and "extended-day" enrollments in regular schools. Extended-day pupils are those who stay at school for several hours after the regular classroom schedule each day, but go home to their working parents every evening. Possibly by this rather broad definition of "boarding school" students the original goal will be reached, but to be meaningful the categories of enrollments included will require specification.

The most difficult kind of evaluation to make with any validity is the one most commonly made: comparison of some aspect of Soviet education with a similar aspect of U.S. education, or blanket statements about the relative merits of the two systems.

Each system has its own basic, general goals which do not coincide, making most comparisons miss the point that the education plant in each country is a reflection of different value systems. Soviet education is primarily concerned with producing well-indoctrinated specialists, responsive to the economic and social needs of the country as defined by the state's leaders. The focus is on meeting manpower needs and producing the malleable Communist man, through centrally prescribed textbooks, syllabi and curricula, and through teachers who aim for pupil mastery of subject fields and of prescribed dogma.

Education in the United States has no centrally-prescribed goals though there are broad areas of agreement among educators. It may be said to have the open-ended goals of helping youth to develop their capacities to the limits of their abilities, exposing youth to a broad range of histories, cultures and ideas, stimulating them to develop their rational thought processes, and encouraging their respect for the individual and for responsible citizenship in a democracy. The U.S. classroom ideal is successful discussion, the Soviet is successful memorization.

Both systems fall short of their stated and unstated goals, and it seems of greater validity to chart the degree to which they meet their own goals than to compare them with each other.

Education in the U.S. and U.S.S.R. is not only a reflection of different value systems but of different histories, economies, and political and social systems. Countries at different stages of development have different needs in education. Determining the degree to which a system meets those needs has more validity than comparing enrollments of a given number of X specialists in one country with enrollments of a given number of X specialists in another.

If, despite inherent difficulties, comparisons are made between aspects of U.S. and Soviet education, it is the responsibility of the evaluator to elaborate major components comprising each factor in the education equation. In much of the reporting on the two systems analyses have suffered from superficial and misleading comparisons, most commonly involving critical errors of omission. For example, for elementary reading courses, one analyst has compared the number of different words in Russian and American readers on a grade by grade basis.[2] Mentioned by the analyst but neglected in the analysis, among other factors, is that the comparison is between readers for Russian 7-year-olds and American 6-year-olds (each in first grade in his own system), Russian 8-year-olds with American 7-year-olds (each in second grade in his own system), and so forth. Not elaborated or even mentioned by the analyst is his methodology for the word totals he cites in comparisons. A critical omission, which can be certified by examination of official syllabi, is that only a small part of the Soviet reader for each grade is used in either classroom or outside reading.

SPECIFIC PROBLEM AREAS IN EVALUATION

A few problem areas will be discussed next which have received considerable attention in reporting on Soviet education and which have been the focus of misleading statements.

Budget Expenditures. Soviet expenditures on education have been substantial each year, and the U.S.S.R. has made investments in education sufficient to build a broadly based education plant which places it among the leading countries of the world in this field. Having made that statement, however, it is important to add that in both Soviet and U.S. reporting, the Soviet education budget has been overstated and that the U.S.S.R. is not well ahead or even ahead of the United States in expenditures on education or in what has been popularly termed its "commitment to education."

The most generally quoted "education" figure or percentage in the Soviet budget is a catch-all, more properly termed "enlightenment," about a third of which is not education expenditure in the American sense of the term.

This education or enlightenment total includes expenditures for nurseries and kindergartens, general education, elementary and secondary schools, boarding schools and schools for the handicapped, adult education facilities, technical and trade schools of all types, and higher educational institutions. But it also includes expenditures for construction and operation of youth centers, club houses, recreation facilities, summer camps, public libraries and reading rooms, art exhibits, theaters and cinemas, and radio stations and newspapers.

It is obviously a questionable practice to compare this Soviet "enlightenment"

---

[2] Arther S. Trace, Jr., *What Ivan Knows that Johnny Doesn't* (New York: Random House, 1961).

total to U.S. education expenditures. It seems unlikely that those who make such comparisons would wish to add similar cultural and communications activities to U.S. education totals.

The error is compounded by confusion of Soviet state budget expenditures with its gross national product. The "enlightenment" total is about 15 per cent, and "education" in the more usual sense of the term about 10 per cent of Soviet state budget expenditures.[3] One or the other of these figures has been compared erroneously with the 5–5½ per cent that education consumes of the U.S. gross national product (GNP). Granted that the Soviet GNP is not reported but is an estimated figure, it can at least be said that it is considerably larger than state budget expenditures. Education, therefore, becomes a considerably smaller percentage of the estimated GNP.

A fair estimate of Soviet education expenditures in relation to Soviet GNP, allowing for some unlisted education expenditures, would place it in about the same percentage range as U.S. education expenditures are to its GNP, somewhat over 5 per cent. The relative "commitments to education," therefore, appear to be comparable, while absolute expenditures are higher in the United States.[4]

Literacy. The Soviets have made broad strides in development of a literate population, primarily through provision of compulsory elementary education to children. In discussions about literacy, however, Soviet sources do not take this position, but primarily credit their work with adult illiterates with having liquidated illiteracy. This becomes an important difference not only in terms of transferability of educational techniques in this international problem area but also in analysis of the repeated assertion that the Soviet system has abolished illiteracy.

In the 1920's and 1930's the Soviet government launched a series of literacy campaigns. Those who were literate in the population, not only teachers but also students, doctors, engineers, technicians, and others, were mobilized to teach illiterates to read and write. In urban areas, where most of the literate population resided, this task would appear to have been more manageable than in rural areas, where unfortunately most of the population resided. But assuming initial exposure of the peasantry to the elements of reading and writing because of the devotion and zeal of the literates, two elements would inevitably have limited the success of the campaigns.

The first is that most of those teaching literacy had no general teaching experience and certainly not specialized experience in the problems of teaching illiterates. The second is that there was no follow-up at periodic intervals to ascertain what number or percentage of those adjudged "literate," having initially mastered some

[3] Seymour N. Rosen, *Higher Education in the USSR* (Washington, D. C.: Government Printing Office, 1963), pp. 71–75. The appropriate statistics appear annually in *Narodnoe Khozaistvo* (National Economy), a statistical yearbook published by the Central Statistical Administration of the USSR Council of Ministers.

[4] Nicholas DeWitt, *Education and Professional Employment in the USSR* (Washington, D. C.: National Science Foundation, 1961) and *Costs and Returns in Education in the USSR* (Cambridge, Mass.: unpublished doctoral dissertation, Harvard University, 1962). See also Ingvar Svennilson *et al.*, *Policy Conference on Economic Growth and Investment in Education II, Targets for Education in Europe in 1970* (Paris: O.E.C.D., January 1962).

basic elements of reading and writing, had retained their literacy. Without constant use of these newly-acquired skills, the retention rate drops rapidly.

Much of the literacy problem has been eliminated in the long run by compulsory elementary education for children. An adult who achieved literacy at the age of 30 in 1934 is now 60. Even if he is in fact now illiterate, he no longer is counted in Soviet statistics on literacy. For when the Soviets make the statement that illiteracy has been abolished in the Soviet Union, they mean statistically that they are only considering the 9 to 49 age group. Anyone 50 years of age or over is not counted.

Engineering Graduates. Probably no one statement comparing Soviet with U.S. education has been repeated as often as, "the U.S.S.R. has 2½ to 3 times as many engineers graduating each year as the United States." Soviet statistical handbooks regularly make a special box-chart citing specific figures to prove this statement. While not attempting to dispute the bare total given (although Soviet sources slightly lower U.S. engineering graduations), there are a few comments which might be made to make the statistics more meaningful.

The first is one of proportion. Engineering graduates each year are about 10 per cent of total U.S. college graduates, while they are over 30 per cent of Soviet graduates. There is a much more even spread, or diversity, in the U.S. pattern of graduations, and much more emphasis on technical and agricultural fields in the U.S.S.R. That mere numbers have no special virtue is evident from the fact that the U.S.S.R. also has 2½ to 3 times as many agricultural specialists graduating as the United States. The problem is not one of quantity but of quality, the needs of each society, and the uses to which graduates are put in the economy.

To take these elements in reverse order, in the Soviet system diploma engineers are used as engineers, but they are also used in very large numbers in positions which should be held by technicians with less training and to some extent in administrative posts which could be held by persons with other kinds of training.[5]

As a highly advanced industrial society, the United States needs diversity in college graduates to serve not only heavy and light industries, but also business and commerce. Diversity is necessary to serve a sophisticated level of consumer needs as well as producer needs. The U.S. needs large numbers of social and physical scientists, English majors, philosophers, administrators, lawyers and others to provide for a well-rounded, dynamic, thoughtful and responsible citizenry. Soviet State

---

[5] The following quotation is from Oleg Hoeffding's article, "Planning of Manpower Requirements and Placement of Graduates," in *The Training, Placement and Utilization of Engineers in the Soviet Union* (The Report of an Engineers' Joint Council delegation to the USSR in July 1960 under an exchange agreement between the USA and the USSR), p. 50:

A finding of a general "shortage" of engineers would also be incompatible with our observations on the rather lavish use made of graduate engineers—and notably young men and women recently out of school—in relatively lowly functions; and also on the salary and wage structure, which provides no incentive for Soviet plant managers to economize in employing junior engineers and technicians by substituting personnel of lower qualifications.

We raised the question of the apparent inconsistency between this free use of highly qualified manpower in subordinate positions and the assertions of "shortage" of engineers with Mr. Sonin, a research economist in the Academy of Sciences' Institute of Economics in Moscow. His comment was that the USSR may tend to use more engineers in less highly-qualified positions than the United States because it was training many more engineers, and also because of "peculiarities of the production organization in Soviet industry," upon which he did not elaborate.

planners, on the other hand, have consistently set quotas in higher schools placing heavy priority on those fields which would primarily support industrial growth.[6]

The final question is one of quality. Competent observers have concluded that engineers emerging from higher schools in both systems are comparable in quality. Their focus, however, in these comparisons has been on the programs and graduates of regular higher schools. A large percentage of Soviet engineering graduates, perhaps as high as 40 per cent, are graduates of Soviet correspondence schools and correspondence divisions of regular schools. While these programs involve consultations and laboratory work, as well as other elements of regular school programs, and while students may even have higher levels of technical competence in narrow areas in which they have already worked than regular students, it is probable that the over-all quality of these programs is not comparable to the quality of regular engineering school programs.

Teachers Status and Salaries. The status of teachers is difficult to gauge as the elements are largely subjective or intangible or require sophisticated public opinion sampling techniques. Status involves attitudes of the society toward its teachers and attitudes of teachers toward their place in society. Foreign observers have generally concluded that the status of Soviet teachers is high, some have said higher than the status of teachers in the United States. They point to such factors as the deference paid teachers by children in Soviet classrooms, the large numbers of teachers who receive legislative posts or medals, and the comparability of their salaries to those of other Soviet professionals. The comments which follow do not pursue the point that American teachers have many times the salary and real income, and a much higher standard of living than Soviet teachers, but focus on the Soviet teacher within his own system.

The deference of pupils in class is a European tradition which encourages the orderly transmission of cultural values, information, and ideas from the teacher to the pupil. If status is defined as maintenance and overt display of authority, then the conclusion of observers is generally correct. A teacher-dominated classroom, however, in which pupils jump to attention, recite by rote memory, and sit quickly at the teacher's bidding is not necessarily a sign of teacher status. Conversely, a teacher-stimulated classroom in which pupils do not stand to recite, who mill around on occasion, and who debate with each other and with the teacher is not necessarily a sign of lack of status.

The best Soviet teachers encourage the implicit respect of pupils, having adopted elements of a system where the object is to stimulate expression and exchange of ideas with and by pupils and where there is less apparent deference to the teacher's authority.[7]

---

[6] These priorities are evident in the Soviet official compilations of higher education specialties, the number of higher schools devoted to various fields of specialization, and the number of students enrolled and graduating in various specialties. For details see Rosen, pp. 91–92.

[7] The author has visited, during three brief trips to the USSR (1960, 1961, 1963), about 40 classes in session, most of which were teacher-dominated in the manner described, but several of which, in various republics, could be described as teacher-stimulated. In nearly all cases the teacher appeared to be competent.

The political positions teachers receive, which are most frequently named by Soviet publications, are membership in local legislative bodies. These posts are honorary rather than functional in the Western legislative sense, and are intended by the Soviet government to represent status symbols. Serving the same purpose are awards and medals to teachers for outstanding service and national teachers' conferences addressed by top government and Party officials. These events are prominently published in *Pravda* and *Izvestia*. This writer is prepared to argue that these posts and honors and accompanying publicity are authentic status symbols, but an effective rebuttal could be made that they may not signify status but the lack of it, or are compensatory devices by the State in lieu of status.

The most commonly accepted, most tangible index of status is personal income, and here the primary error of some reporters has been failure to distinguish the range of teachers' salaries. An indication of this range would qualify statements on the comparability of teachers' salaries with those of other Soviet professionals.

The extreme range is between elementary school teachers and university professors, the latter averaging about 7 or 8 times the salary of the former. Elementary school teachers with 10 years' experience earn four-fifths the salary of secondary school teachers with similar experience, who earn only one-third to one-fourth the salary of docents, or associate professors.

From available data, the salary of doctors (Soviet doctors are involved in public health, not private practice) falls somewhere between experienced secondary school teachers and university instructors. It might be argued from this that the salaries of physicians and secondary school teachers are depressed, rather than viewing this as evidence of the high status of teachers, since the salaries of these groups of professionals are comparable to those of factory workers of average skill.

Engineers generally receive higher wages than elementary-secondary school teachers, falling in the range of university instructors, so that public school teachers are not comparable in monetary status to engineers. University professors and associate professors, on the other hand, average a higher income than engineers.

ACCOMPLISHMENTS IN MEETING GOALS

The Soviet system has been successful in a number of areas in the field of education, several of which will be discussed briefly.

Mass Education. The Soviet Union has made substantial advances in providing education for virtually all its youth in elementary school ages and in providing the majority of its youth beyond that age with at least some form of secondary education.

Inheriting an elite system of education, the Soviet Union has gradually increased the requirement of national, free, and compulsory education. A minimum general education was 4 years in 1928, 7 years in 1949, and 8 years in 1959. Opportunities for additional education beyond compulsory education are substantial; 15 or

16-year-olds may go on to complete secondary education in either general or technical schools or part-time while working. The more talented may continue, after completing any type of secondary education, to higher education.

The goal of 10-year compulsory education, announced at the 20th CPSU Congress in 1956, was temporarily abandoned under the education reform of 1958. A more modest goal of the reform, compulsory 8-year education, has been announced as largely completed. The program of the 22nd CPSU Congress in 1961 revived the goal of compulsory complete secondary education for all children of school age, now 11 years of schooling, to be introduced in 1970.

Education at all levels, from primary school through graduate training, is free of tuition. At the secondary specialized and higher education levels, the system binds the students to a 3-year job assignment following graduation. This may be viewed either as onerous or as a guarantee of a job after graduation, or as a combination of both.

"Education Linked with Life." A major aspect of the education reform of 1958, transforming 7-year and 10-year schools of general education into 8-year and 11-year " general education labor-polytechnical schools with production training," has been largely completed. This represents a considerable achievement toward meeting the state's declared goals for "education linked with life."

Of the various facets of polytechnical education for regular school pupils, the increase of practical training courses in schools, involving training of each pupil in one vocational specialty while continuing regular academic studies, appears to be more successful than the practical training that pupils receive in factories as part of the regular school program. Factory managers concerned with meeting production quotas are primarily concerned with avoiding disruption of their operations. Pupils are frequently given menial tasks to perform rather than work which will give them insight into over-all processes and the fundamentals of factory production.[8]

The considerable development of vocational and technical schools at the secondary level is also an accomplishment in providing youth, who generally will not go

[8] References to factory personnel indifference to student production training is fairly frequent in the Soviet press. To quote two Soviet references, one in which the situation has improved and one in which it has not:

It is clear to anyone that the significance of labor training is great but not everyone knows how to correctly realize it in practice. Formerly, in the Sverdlovsk Metal Machine Building Plant, pupils who arrived for production training were divided into small groups and scattered throughout the sections. On the days of practice, they were allotted tools and training was charged to the shop foremen. It appeared that everything was in order, but actually it was far from so. Coming to the plant twice a week, the children often found their tools being used. If some kind of work fell their way, then as a rule, it was accidental, not intended for the pupils. The foremen and workers paid little attention to them. This bitter experience was studied and production is now being organized differently. (Moscow, *Uchitel'skaia Gazeta,* February 23, 1963).

In Armavir, Krasnodarskiy Krai, there are 9 schools with production training. Their training base is 17 industrial enterprises. Only four of the enterprises have student production sections and those few are only trying to satisfy the present-day requirements. In addition, working places for students have been allotted in various shops of two plants. In the remaining enterprises, conditions are far worse. Production training there is of a "contemplative" nature. . . . It is impossible to say that the directors of those plants in which there are no production sections do not understand the state significance of the school reorganization. They understand, but do not consider it a part of their own production and party activity. (Moscow, *Izvestia,* February 14, 1963).

on to higher education, with the kind of training that prepares them for successful entry into the labor market.

Production of Specialists. The Soviet higher education system has achieved considerable success in its goal of producing specialists, many of them highly qualified, particularly in certain science fields.

Soviet higher education has no equivalent to liberal arts education. About 85 to 90 per cent of students in higher schools are studying in some 700 specialized institutes, primarily in narrow aspects of engineering, agricultural sciences, and economics, and in medicine, pedagogy, and other fields. The remainder are in 40 universities, training intensively in a somewhat broader field of natural sciences, social sciences, or humanities.

Graduates emerge from the system with the theoretical background of the general field of specialization and intensive study and training in such institute specialties as:

0207 Planning and exploitation of gas and petroleum pipelines, gas storage tanks, and petroleum bases

0505 Mechanical equipment of ferrous and nonferrous metallurgical plants

0811 Technology of varnishes, paints, and nonmetallic coatings

1710 Economics and organization of shipbuilding industry

2229 Interior decoration of buildings and production of decoration materials

The numbers preceding each specialty are official government classifications by which higher education admission quotas are made, students are enrolled, and graduates are assigned work.

Capacity for Innovation. Another area of accomplishment in meeting goals has been the Soviet capacity for innovation in specific directions which will support the objectives of the State.

Graduate research projects, for example, are intended to fit into the over-all programs assigned to each department of a university or institute. Graduate studies frequently are not carried out in a regular higher education institution; about half the graduate students are trained, essentially as assistants, in research institutes of the U.S.S.R. or republic academies of sciences or of various government ministries.

There are many recent innovations and experiments in the education system. Higher technical schools. are being established within major Soviet industrial plants. The Peoples Friendship University, or Lumumba University, is a well-publicized attempt at operating a university primarily for students from foreign, underdeveloped areas. The possibilities of teaching machines and television are being explored for potential large-scale use; cybernetics and its application to education has been the subject of discussion and experimentation.

The establishment of science cities in areas of the Soviet Union suffering deficits of science personnel is being explored. The first of these cities, founded at Novosibirsk in 1959, consists of a cluster of scientific research institutes and an allied university and will serve as a model for others.

The primary vehicle for research and development for the public school system is the Russian S.F.S.R. Academy of Pedagogical Sciences. This Academy, located in Moscow, is in effect a unified educational research establishment for the whole country.

The Academy contains separate research institutes for the theory and history of pedagogy, educational methodology, psychology, art education, training of handicapped children, physical education and school hygiene, national schools, and evening and correspondence education. Two of its institutes, for production training and for general and polytechnical education, are experimenting with differentiated instruction in the upper grades of secondary schools.

Each of the institutes has a staff of researchers and institute-allied experimental schools throughout the Russian republic. The other Soviet republics have pedagogical research institutes which also cooperate with the R.S.F.S.R. Academy of Pedagogical Sciences.

A direct connection is maintained between educational researchers and experimental schools on the one hand, and researchers and the ministries capable of transforming research into general school practice on the other. This system has the ability to translate recent research findings into education practice. The weakness is that of national directives automatically transmitted to the entire country's school system, accompanied by inflexibility in local school systems and their timidity in originating change.[9]

Indoctrination. The system seems to be generally successful in meeting its indoctrination goals. That is, obtaining general acceptance of Communist goals, institutions and stereotypes from those receiving their education in the Soviet school system.[10]

Currently the Party is calling for what may be considered a two-phased ideological operation. Textbooks are being revised to remove "personality cult" or "Stalin cult" elements. At the same time, general ideological requirements are being raised in both secondary and higher education.

A new required ideological course was introduced into secondary schools in 1963. Originally entitled "Fundamentals of Political Knowledge," it is now called simple "Social Studies" or "Social Science" (*Obshchestvovedenie*). Its purpose is to provide students, at a key point in their lives, just prior to graduation from secondary school, with a systematic and comprehensive survey of Marxism-

[9] For example, the same curricula, syllabi, and textbooks developed in the Russian S.F.S.R. Academy of Pedagogical Sciences and approved by the Russian S.F.S.R. Ministry of Education are sent to all 14 minority republics and used in all their schools. When minority republic education ministries translate the Russian education materials into Georgian, Armenian, Lithuanian, Kazakh, and so on, modest inserts are allowed on local culture elements. These slight changes of what are overwhelmingly Russian school materials, distributed nationally, must be approved by the Russian S.F.S.R. Academy of Pedagogical Sciences. As one Armenian educator put it to me when I asked about local initiative, "We use the materials that come from Moscow."

There must, of course, be some adaptations of materials in practice to various linguistic, cultural, rural-urban, intelligentsia-worker background and other differences. But adaptations (local) and initiative (central) are substantially different. Factors limiting adaptations, aside from the system of republic government-directed school inspectors, are the series of national examinations at terminal grades 8 and 11 and for admission and graduation from higher schools.

[10] Raymond A. Bauer, Alex Inkeles, and Clyde Kluckhohn, *How the Soviet System Works, Cultural, Psychological and Social Themes* (New York: Vintage Books, 1960), pp. 194–196.

Leninism and Communist domestic and international attitudes. This task had previously been performed only piecemeal in regular courses in history, the Soviet Constitution, and other subjects.

Probably in the 1964–1965 school year, a new course called "Scientific Communism" will be added to the higher education curriculum. Students at Soviet higher schools are already heavily loaded with the three required ideology courses, "History of the Communist Party of the Soviet Union," "Political Economy," and "Dialectical and Historical Materialism." Possibly slightly pared down, these three will be retained in the higher school curriculum.

Successes in terms of Soviet education goals, such as the primary focus on production of specialists and research under State plans and control, and indoctrination of students for propagation of authoritarian dogma and acceptance of rule by the few, are not models to be emulated by societies with democratic goals. Other criteria within the framework of their own goals must be applied to evaluate accomplishments of other societies.